World Map: Physical

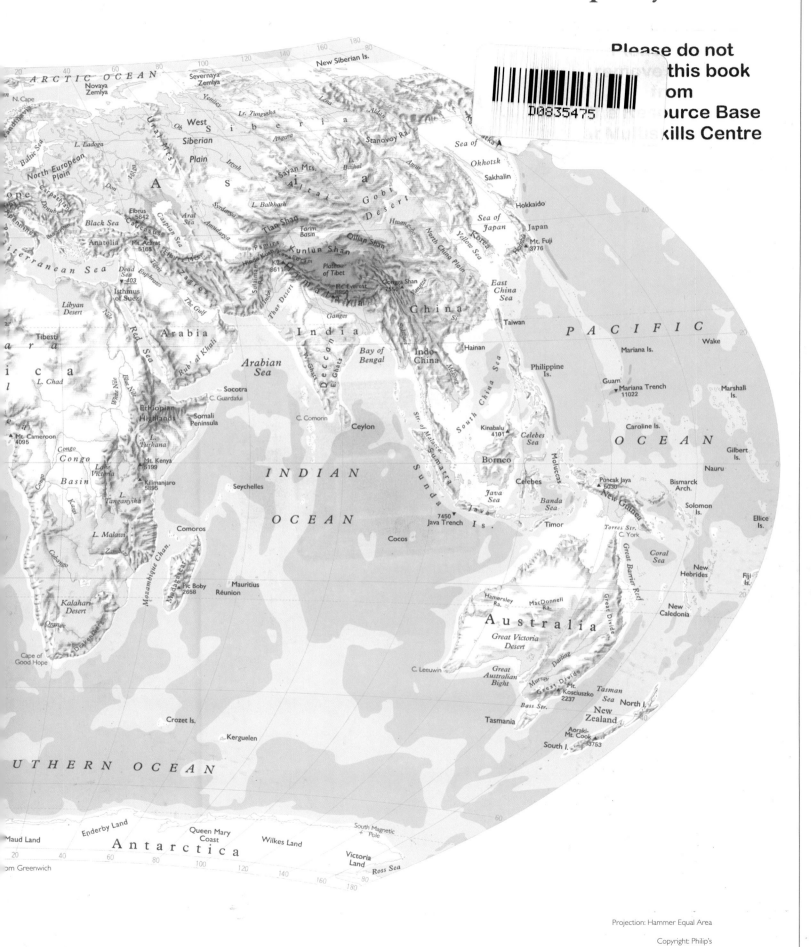

Projection: Hammer Equal Area

Copyright: Philip's

ENCYCLOPEDIC
WORLD
ATLAS

A–Z COUNTRY BY COUNTRY

A–Z COUNTRY BY COUNTRY TEXT
KEITH LYE

NAME FORMS

For ease of reference, both English and local name forms appear in the atlas. Oceans, seas and countries are shown in English throughout the atlas; country names may be abbreviated to their commonly accepted form (e.g. Germany, not The Federal Republic of Germany). Conventional English forms are also used for place names on the smaller-scale maps of the continents. However, local name forms are used on all the larger-scale country-by-country maps. For countries which do not use a Roman script, place names have been transcribed according to the systems adopted by the British and US Geographic Names Authorities. For China, the Pin Yin system has been used, with some more widely known forms appearing in brackets, as with Beijing (Peking). For major place names, both English and local forms appear in the index, the English version being cross-referenced to the local form.

WORLD CITIES
Cartography by Philip's

Page 11, Dublin: The town plan of Dublin is based on Ordnance Survey Ireland by permission of the Government Permit Number 7516. © Ordnance Survey Ireland and Government of Ireland.

 Page 11, Edinburgh, and page 15, London:
This product includes mapping data licensed from Ordnance Survey®
with the permission of the Controller of Her Majesty's Stationery Office.
© Crown copyright 2002. All rights reserved. Licence number 100011710.

Vector data: Courtesy of Gräfe and Unser Verlag GmbH, München, Germany
(city centre maps of Bangkok, Beijing, Cape Town, Jerusalem, Mexico City, Moscow, Singapore, Sydney, Tokyo and Washington D.C.)

All satellite images in this section courtesy of NPA Group Limited, Edenbridge, Kent (www.satmaps.com)

Published in Great Britain in 2002
by Philip's,
a division of Octopus Publishing Group Limited,
2–4 Heron Quays, London E14 4JP

Copyright © 2002 Philip's

Cartography by Philip's

ISBN 0–540–08237–6

A CIP catalogue record for this book is available from the British Library.

Printed in Spain

Details of other Philip's titles and services can be found on our website at: www.philips-maps.co.uk

Philip's World Atlases are published in association with The Royal Geographical Society (with The Institute of British Geographers).

The Society was founded in 1830 and given a Royal Charter in 1859 for 'the advancement of geographical science'. It holds historical collections of national and international importance, many of which relate to the Society's association with and support for scientific exploration and research from the 19th century onwards. It was pivotal in establishing geography as a teaching and research discipline in British universities close to the turn of the century, and has played a key role in geographical and environmental education ever since.

Today the Society is a leading world centre for geographical learning – supporting education, teaching, research and expeditions, and promoting public understanding of the subject.

The Society welcomes those interested in geography as members. For further information, please visit the website at: www.rgs.org

PHILIP'S

ENCYCLOPEDIC WORLD ATLAS

A–Z COUNTRY BY COUNTRY

TEXT BY KEITH LYE

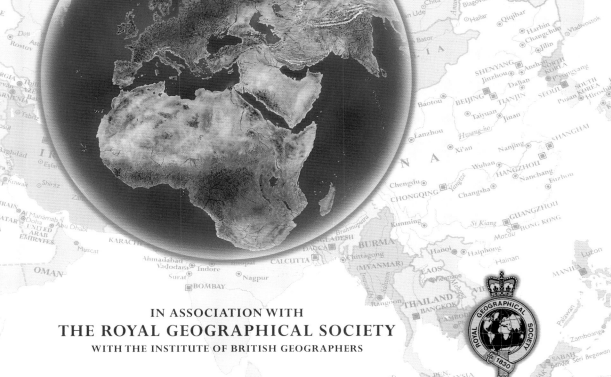

IN ASSOCIATION WITH
THE ROYAL GEOGRAPHICAL SOCIETY
WITH THE INSTITUTE OF BRITISH GEOGRAPHERS

CONTENTS

INDEX TO COUNTRY MAPS

WORLD STATISTICS: Countries

This alphabetical list includes all the countries and territories of the world. If a territory is not completely independent, the country it is associated with is named. The area figures give the total area of land, inland water and ice.

The population figures are 2001 estimates. The annual income is the Gross Domestic Product per capita† in US dollars. The figures are the latest available, usually 2000 estimates.

Country/Territory	Area km² Thousands	Area miles² Thousands	Population Thousands	Capital	Annual Income US $
Afghanistan	652	252	26,813	Kabul	800
Albania	28.8	11.1	3,510	Tirana	3,000
Algeria	2,382	920	31,736	Algiers	5,500
American Samoa (US)	0.2	0.08	67	Pago Pago	8,000
Andorra	0.45	0.17	68	Andorra La Vella	18,000
Angola	1,247	481	10,366	Luanda	1,000
Anguilla (UK)	0.1	0.04	12	The Valley	8,200
Antigua & Barbuda	0.44	0.17	67	St John's	8,200
Argentina	2,767	1,068	37,385	Buenos Aires	12,900
Armenia	29.8	11.5	3,336	Yerevan	3,000
Aruba (Netherlands)	0.19	0.07	70	Oranjestad	28,000
Australia	7,687	2,968	19,358	Canberra	23,200
Austria	83.9	32.4	8,151	Vienna	25,000
Azerbaijan	86.6	33.4	7,771	Baku	3,000
Azores (Portugal)	2.2	0.87	243	Ponta Delgada	11,040
Bahamas	13.9	5.4	298	Nassau	15,000
Bahrain	0.68	0.26	645	Manama	15,900
Bangladesh	144	56	131,270	Dhaka	1,570
Barbados	0.43	0.17	275	Bridgetown	14,500
Belarus	207.6	80.1	10,350	Minsk	7,500
Belgium	30.5	11.8	10,259	Brussels	25,300
Belize	23	8.9	256	Belmopan	3,200
Benin	113	43	6,591	Porto-Novo	1,030
Bermuda (UK)	0.05	0.02	64	Hamilton	33,000
Bhutan	47	18.1	2,049	Thimphu	1,100
Bolivia	1,099	424	8,300	La Paz/Sucre	2,600
Bosnia-Herzegovina	51	20	3,922	Sarajevo	1,700
Botswana	582	225	1,586	Gaborone	6,600
Brazil	8,512	3,286	174,469	Brasília	6,500
Brunei	5.8	2.2	344	Bandar Seri Begawan	17,600
Bulgaria	111	43	7,707	Sofia	6,200
Burkina Faso	274	106	12,272	Ouagadougou	1,000
Burma (= Myanmar)	677	261	41,995	Rangoon	1,500
Burundi	27.8	10.7	6,224	Bujumbura	720
Cambodia	181	70	12,492	Phnom Penh	1,300
Cameroon	475	184	15,803	Yaoundé	1,700
Canada	9,976	3,852	31,593	Ottawa	24,800
Canary Is. (Spain)	7.3	2.8	1,577	Las Palmas/Santa Cruz	17,100
Cape Verde Is.	4	1.6	405	Praia	1,700
Cayman Is. (UK)	0.26	0.1	36	George Town	24,500
Central African Republic	623	241	3,577	Bangui	1,700
Chad	1,284	496	8,707	Ndjaména	1,000
Chile	757	292	15,328	Santiago	10,100
China	9,597	3,705	1,273,111	Beijing	3,600
Colombia	1,139	440	40,349	Bogotá	6,200
Comoros	2.2	0.86	596	Moroni	720
Congo	342	132	2,894	Brazzaville	1,100
Congo (Dem. Rep. of the)	2,345	905	53,625	Kinshasa	600
Cook Is. (NZ)	0.24	0.09	21	Avarua	5,000
Costa Rica	51.1	19.7	3,773	San José	6,700
Croatia	56.5	21.8	4,334	Zagreb	5,800
Cuba	111	43	11,184	Havana	1,700
Cyprus	9.3	3.6	763	Nicosia	13,800
Czech Republic	78.9	30.4	10,264	Prague	12,900
Denmark	43.1	16.6	5,353	Copenhagen	25,500
Djibouti	23.2	9	461	Djibouti	1,300
Dominica	0.75	0.29	71	Roseau	4,000
Dominican Republic	48.7	18.8	8,581	Santo Domingo	5,700
East Timor	14.9	5.7	737	Dili	N/A
Ecuador	284	109	13,184	Quito	2,900
Egypt	1,001	387	69,537	Cairo	3,600
El Salvador	21	8.1	6,238	San Salvador	4,000
Equatorial Guinea	28.1	10.8	486	Malabo	2,000
Eritrea	94	36	4,298	Asmara	710
Estonia	44.7	17.3	1,423	Tallinn	10,000
Ethiopia	1,128	436	65,892	Addis Ababa	600
Faroe Is. (Denmark)	1.4	0.54	46	Tórshavn	20,000
Fiji	18.3	7.1	844	Suva	7,300
Finland	338	131	5,176	Helsinki	22,900
France	552	213	59,551	Paris	24,400
French Guiana (France)	90	34.7	178	Cayenne	6,000
French Polynesia (France)	4	1.5	254	Papeete	10,800
Gabon	268	103	1,221	Libreville	6,300
Gambia, The	11.3	4.4	1,411	Banjul	1,100
Gaza Strip (OPT)*	0.36	0.14	1,178	–	1,000
Georgia	69.7	26.9	4,989	Tbilisi	4,600
Germany	357	138	83,030	Berlin	23,400
Ghana	239	92	19,894	Accra	1,900
Gibraltar (UK)	0.007	0.003	28	Gibraltar Town	17,500
Greece	132	51	10,624	Athens	17,200
Greenland (Denmark)	2,176	840	56	Nuuk (Godthåb)	20,000
Grenada	0.34	0.13	89	St George's	4,400
Guadeloupe (France)	1.7	0.66	431	Basse-Terre	9,000
Guam (US)	0.55	0.21	158	Agana	21,000
Guatemala	109	42	12,974	Guatemala City	3,700
Guinea	246	95	7,614	Conakry	1,300
Guinea-Bissau	36.1	13.9	1,316	Bissau	850
Guyana	215	83	697	Georgetown	4,800
Haiti	27.8	10.7	6,965	Port-au-Prince	1,800
Honduras	112	43	6,406	Tegucigalpa	2,700
Hong Kong (China)	1.1	0.4	7,211	–	25,400
Hungary	93	35.9	10,106	Budapest	11,200
Iceland	103	40	278	Reykjavik	24,800
India	3,288	1,269	1,029,991	New Delhi	2,200
Indonesia	1,890	730	227,701	Jakarta	2,900
Iran	1,648	636	66,129	Tehran	6,300
Iraq	438	169	23,332	Baghdad	2,500
Ireland	70.3	27.1	3,841	Dublin	21,600
Israel	20.6	7.96	5,938	Jerusalem	18,900
Italy	301	116	57,680	Rome	22,100
Ivory Coast (= Côte d'Ivoire)	322	125	16,393	Yamoussoukro	1,600
Jamaica	11	4.2	2,666	Kingston	3,700
Japan	378	146	126,772	Tokyo	24,900
Jordan	89.2	34.4	5,153	Amman	3,500
Kazakstan	2,717	1,049	16,731	Astana	5,000
Kenya	580	224	30,766	Nairobi	1,500
Kiribati	0.72	0.28	94	Tarawa	850
Korea, North	121	47	21,968	Pyŏngyang	1,000
Korea, South	99	38.2	47,904	Seoul	16,100
Kuwait	17.8	6.9	2,042	Kuwait City	15,000
Kyrgyzstan	198.5	76.6	4,753	Bishkek	2,700
Laos	237	91	5,636	Vientiane	1,700
Latvia	65	25	2,385	Riga	7,200

Country/Territory	Area km² Thousands	Area miles² Thousands	Population Thousands	Capital	Annual Income US $
Lebanon	10.4	4	3,628	Beirut	5,000
Lesotho	30.4	11.7	2,177	Maseru	2,400
Liberia	111	43	3,226	Monrovia	1,100
Libya	1,760	679	5,241	Tripoli	8,900
Liechtenstein	0.16	0.06	33	Vaduz	23,000
Lithuania	65.2	25.2	3,611	Vilnius	7,300
Luxembourg	2.6	1	443	Luxembourg	36,400
Macau (China)	0.02	0.006	454	–	17,500
Macedonia (FYROM)	25.7	9.9	2,046	Skopje	4,400
Madagascar	587	227	15,983	Antananarivo	800
Madeira (Portugal)	0.81	0.31	259	Funchal	12,120
Malawi	118	46	10,548	Lilongwe	900
Malaysia	330	127	22,229	Kuala Lumpur	10,300
Maldives	0.3	0.12	311	Malé	2,000
Mali	1,240	479	11,009	Bamako	850
Malta	0.32	0.12	395	Valletta	14,300
Marshall Is.	0.18	0.07	71	Dalap-Uliga-Darrit	1,670
Martinique (France)	1.1	0.42	418	Fort-de-France	11,000
Mauritania	1,030	398	2,747	Nouakchott	2,000
Mauritius	2	0.72	1,190	Port Louis	10,400
Mayotte (France)	0.37	0.14	163	Mamoundzou	600
Mexico	1,958	756	101,879	Mexico City	9,100
Micronesia, Fed. States of	0.7	0.27	135	Palikir	2,000
Moldova	33.7	13	4,432	Chişinău	2,500
Monaco	0.002	0.001	32	Monaco	27,000
Mongolia	1,567	605	2,655	Ulan Bator	1,780
Montserrat (UK)	0.1	0.04	8	Plymouth	5,000
Morocco	447	172	30,645	Rabat	3,500
Mozambique	802	309	19,371	Maputo	1,000
Namibia	825	318	1,798	Windhoek	4,300
Nauru	0.02	0.008	12	Yaren District	5,000
Nepal	141	54	25,284	Katmandu	1,360
Netherlands	41.5	16	15,981	Amsterdam/The Hague	24,400
Netherlands Antilles (Neths)	0.99	0.38	212	Willemstad	11,400
New Caledonia (France)	18.6	7.2	205	Nouméa	15,000
New Zealand	269	104	3,864	Wellington	17,700
Nicaragua	130	50	4,918	Managua	2,700
Niger	1,267	489	10,355	Niamey	1,000
Nigeria	924	357	126,636	Abuja	950
Northern Mariana Is. (US)	0.48	0.18	75	Saipan	12,500
Norway	324	125	4,503	Oslo	27,700
Oman	212	82	2,622	Muscat	7,700
Pakistan	796	307	144,617	Islamabad	2,000
Palau	0.46	0.18	19	Koror	7,100
Panama	77.1	29.8	2,846	Panamá	6,000
Papua New Guinea	463	179	5,049	Port Moresby	2,500
Paraguay	407	157	5,734	Asunción	4,750
Peru	1,285	496	27,484	Lima	4,550
Philippines	300	116	82,842	Manila	3,800
Poland	313	121	38,634	Warsaw	8,500
Portugal	92.4	35.7	9,444	Lisbon	15,800
Puerto Rico (US)	9	3.5	3,939	San Juan	10,000
Qatar	11	4.2	769	Doha	20,300
Réunion (France)	2.5	0.97	733	St-Denis	4,800
Romania	238	92	22,364	Bucharest	5,900
Russia	17,075	6,592	145,470	Moscow	7,700
Rwanda	26.3	10.2	7,313	Kigali	900
St Kitts & Nevis	0.36	0.14	39	Basseterre	7,000
St Lucia	0.62	0.24	158	Castries	4,500
St Vincent & Grenadines	0.39	0.15	116	Kingstown	2,800
Samoa	2.8	1.1	179	Apia	3,200
San Marino	0.06	0.02	27	San Marino	32,000
São Tomé & Principe	0.96	0.37	165	São Tomé	1,100
Saudi Arabia	2,150	830	22,757	Riyadh	10,500
Senegal	197	76	10,285	Dakar	1,600
Seychelles	0.46	0.18	80	Victoria	7,700
Sierra Leone	71.7	27.7	5,427	Freetown	510
Singapore	0.62	0.24	4,300	Singapore	26,500
Slovak Republic	49	18.9	5,415	Bratislava	10,200
Slovenia	20.3	7.8	1,930	Ljubljana	12,000
Solomon Is.	28.9	11.2	480	Honiara	2,000
Somalia	638	246	7,489	Mogadishu	600
South Africa	1,220	471	43,586	C. Town/Pretoria/Bloem.	8,500
Spain	505	195	38,432	Madrid	18,000
Sri Lanka	65.6	25.3	19,409	Colombo	3,250
Sudan	2,506	967	36,080	Khartoum	1,000
Surinam	163	63	434	Paramaribo	3,400
Swaziland	17.4	6.7	1,104	Mbabane	4,000
Sweden	450	174	8,875	Stockholm	22,200
Switzerland	41.3	15.9	7,283	Bern	28,600
Syria	185	71	16,729	Damascus	3,100
Taiwan	36	13.9	22,370	Taipei	17,400
Tajikistan	143.1	55.2	6,579	Dushanbe	1,140
Tanzania	945	365	36,232	Dodoma	710
Thailand	513	198	61,798	Bangkok	6,700
Togo	56.8	21.9	5,153	Lomé	1,500
Tonga	0.75	0.29	104	Nuku'alofa	2,200
Trinidad & Tobago	5.1	2	1,170	Port of Spain	9,500
Tunisia	164	63	9,705	Tunis	6,500
Turkey	779	301	66,494	Ankara	6,800
Turkmenistan	488.1	188.5	4,603	Ashkhabad	4,300
Turks & Caicos Is. (UK)	0.43	0.17	18	Cockburn Town	7,300
Tuvalu	0.03	0.01	11	Fongafale	1,100
Uganda	236	91	23,986	Kampala	1,100
Ukraine	603.7	233.1	48,760	Kiev	3,850
United Arab Emirates	83.6	32.3	2,407	Abu Dhabi	22,800
United Kingdom	243.3	94	59,648	London	22,800
United States of America	9,373	3,619	278,059	Washington, DC	36,200
Uruguay	177	68	3,360	Montevideo	9,300
Uzbekistan	447.4	172.7	25,155	Tashkent	2,400
Vanuatu	12.2	4.7	193	Port-Vila	1,300
Vatican City	0.0004	0.0002	0.89	Vatican City	N/A
Venezuela	912	352	23,917	Caracas	6,200
Vietnam	332	127	79,939	Hanoi	1,950
Virgin Is. (UK)	0.15	0.06	21	Road Town	16,000
Virgin Is. (US)	0.34	0.13	122	Charlotte Amalie	15,000
Wallis & Futuna Is. (France)	0.2	0.08	15	Mata-Utu	2,000
West Bank (OPT)*	5.86	2.26	2,091	–	1,500
Western Sahara	266	103	251	El Aaiún	N/A
Yemen	528	204	18,078	Sana	820
Yugoslavia (Serbia & Montenegro)	102.3	39.5	10,677	Belgrade	2,300
Zambia	753	291	9,770	Lusaka	880
Zimbabwe	391	151	11,365	Harare	2,500

† Gross Domestic Product per capita has been measured using the purchasing power parity method. This enables comparisons to be made between countries through their purchasing power (in US dollars), showing real price levels of goods and services rather than using currency exchange rates.

*OPT = Occupied Palestinian Territory   N/A = Not Available

WORLD STATISTICS: Cities

This list shows the principal cities with more than 500,000 inhabitants (only cities with more than 1 million inhabitants are included for Brazil, China, Indonesia, Japan and Russia). The figures are taken from the most recent census or estimate available, and are the population of the metropolitan area as far as possible, e.g. greater New York, Mexico or Paris. Local name forms have been used for the smaller cities (e.g. Kraków). All figures are in thousands.

Population *Thousands*

Afghanistan
Kabul 1,565
Algeria
Algiers 1,722
Oran 664
Angola
Luanda 2,250
Argentina
Buenos Aires 10,990
Córdoba 1,198
Rosario 1,096
Mendoza 775
La Plata 640
San Miguel de Tucumán 622
Mar del Plata 520
Armenia
Yerevan 1,256
Australia
Sydney 4,041
Melbourne 3,417
Brisbane 1,601
Perth 1,364
Adelaide 1,093
Austria
Vienna 1,560
Azerbaijan
Baku 1,713
Bangladesh
Dhaka 7,832
Chittagong 2,041
Khulna 877
Rajshahi 517
Belarus
Minsk 1,717
Homyel 502
Belgium
Brussels 948
Benin
Cotonou 537
Bolivia
La Paz 1,126
Santa Cruz 767
Bosnia-Herzegovina
Sarajevo 526
Brazil
São Paulo 10,434
Rio de Janeiro 5,858
Salvador 2,443
Belo Horizonte 2,239
Fortaleza 2,141
Brasília 2,051
Curitiba 1,587
Recife 1,423
Manaus 1,406
Pôrto Alegre 1,361
Belém 1,281
Goiânia 1,093
Guarulhos 1,073
Bulgaria
Sofia 1,139
Burkina Faso
Ouagadougou 690
Burma (Myanmar)
Rangoon 2,513
Mandalay 533
Cambodia
Phnom Penh 570
Cameroon
Douala 1,200
Yaoundé 800
Canada
Toronto 4,881
Montréal 3,511
Vancouver 2,079
Ottawa–Hull 1,107
Calgary 972
Edmonton 957
Québec 693
Winnipeg 685
Hamilton 681
Central African Republic
Bangui 553
Chad
Ndjaména 530
Chile
Santiago 4,691
China
Shanghai 15,082
Beijing 12,362
Tianjin 10,687
Hong Kong (SAR)* 6,502
Chongqing 3,870
Shenyang 3,762
Wuhan 3,520
Guangzhou 3,114
Harbin 2,505

Nanjing 2,211
Xi'an 2,115
Chengdu 1,933
Dalian 1,855
Changchun 1,810
Jinan 1,660
Taiyuan 1,642
Qingdao 1,584
Zibo 1,346
Zhengzhou 1,324
Lanzhou 1,296
Anshan 1,252
Fushun 1,246
Kunming 1,242
Changsha 1,198
Hangzhou 1,185
Nanchang 1,169
Shijiazhuang 1,159
Guiyang 1,131
Ürümqi 1,130
Jilin 1,118
Tangshan 1,110
Qiqihar 1,104
Baotou 1,033
Colombia
Bogotá 6,005
Cali 1,986
Medellín 1,971
Barranquilla 1,158
Cartagena 813
Bucaramanga 508
Congo
Brazzaville 938
Pointe-Noire 576
Congo (Dem. Rep.)
Kinshasa 2,664
Lubumbashi 565
Croatia
Zagreb 868
Cuba
Havana 2,204
Czech Republic
Prague 1,203
Denmark
Copenhagen 1,362
Dominican Republic
Santo Domingo 2,135
Stgo. de los Caballeros 691
Ecuador
Guayaquil 2,070
Quito 1,574
Egypt
Cairo 6,800
Alexandria 3,339
El Gîza 2,222
Shubra el Kheima 871
El Salvador
San Salvador 1,522
Ethiopia
Addis Ababa 2,316
Finland
Helsinki 532
France
Paris 11,175
Lyons 1,648
Marseilles 1,516
Lille 1,143
Toulouse 965
Nice 933
Bordeaux 925
Nantes 711
Strasbourg 612
Toulon 565
Douai 553
Rennes 521
Rouen 518
Grenoble 515
Georgia
Tbilisi 1,253
Germany
Berlin 3,426
Hamburg 1,705
Munich 1,206
Cologne 964
Frankfurt 644
Essen 609
Dortmund 595
Stuttgart 585
Düsseldorf 571
Bremen 547
Duisburg 529
Hanover 521
Ghana
Accra 1,781
Greece
Athens 3,097

Guatemala
Guatemala 1,167
Guinea
Conakry 1,508
Haiti
Port-au-Prince 885
Honduras
Tegucigalpa 814
Hungary
Budapest 1,885
India
Mumbai (Bombay) 16,368
Kolkata (Calcutta) 13,217
Delhi 12,791
Chennai (Madras) 6,425
Bangalore 5,687
Hyderabad 5,534
Ahmadabad 4,519
Pune 3,756
Surat 2,811
Kanpur 2,690
Jaipur 2,324
Lucknow 2,267
Nagpur 2,123
Patna 1,707
Indore 1,639
Vadodara 1,492
Bhopal 1,455
Coimbatore 1,446
Ludhiana 1,395
Cochin 1,355
Vishakhapatnam 1,329
Agra 1,321
Varanasi 1,212
Madurai 1,195
Meerut 1,167
Nasik 1,152
Jabalpur 1,117
Jamshedpur 1,102
Asansol 1,090
Faridabad 1,055
Allahabad 1,050
Amritsar 1,011
Vijayawada 1,011
Rajkot 1,002
Indonesia
Jakarta 11,500
Surabaya 2,701
Bandung 2,368
Medan 1,910
Semarang 1,366
Palembang 1,352
Tangerang 1,198
Ujung Pandang 1,092
Iran
Tehran 6,759
Mashhad 1,887
Esfahan 1,266
Tabriz 1,191
Shiraz 1,053
Karaj 941
Ahvaz 805
Qom 778
Bakhtaran 693
Iraq
Baghdad 3,841
As Sulaymaniyah 952
Arbil 770
Al Mawsil 664
Al Kazimiyah 521
Ireland
Dublin 1,024
Israel
Tel Aviv-Yafo 1,880
Jerusalem 591
Italy
Rome 2,654
Milan 1,306
Naples 1,050
Turin 923
Palermo 689
Genoa 659
Ivory Coast
Abidjan 2,500
Jamaica
Kingston 644
Japan
Tokyo 17,950
Yokohama 3,427
Osaka 2,599
Nagoya 2,171
Sapporo 1,822
Kobe 1,494
Kyoto 1,468
Fukuoka 1,341
Kawasaki 1,250
Hiroshima 1,126

Kitakyushu 1,011
Sendai 1,008
Jordan
Amman 1,752
Kazakstan
Almaty 1,151
Qaraghandy 574
Kenya
Nairobi 2,000
Mombasa 600
Korea, North
Pyŏngyang 2,741
Hamhung 710
Chŏngjin 583
Korea, South
Seoul 10,231
Pusan 3,814
Taegu 2,449
Inch'on 2,308
Taejŏn 1,272
Kwangju 1,258
Ulsan 967
Sŏngnam 869
Puch'ŏn 779
Suwŏn 756
Anyang 590
Chŏnju 563
Chŏngju 531
Ansan 510
P'ohang 509
Kyrgyzstan
Bishkek 589
Laos
Vientiane 532
Latvia
Riga 811
Lebanon
Beirut 1,500
Tripoli 500
Liberia
Monrovia 962
Libya
Tripoli 960
Lithuania
Vilnius 580
Macedonia
Skopje 541
Madagascar
Antananarivo 1,053
Malaysia
Kuala Lumpur 1,145
Mali
Bamako 810
Mauritania
Nouakchott 735
Mexico
Mexico City 15,643
Guadalajara 2,847
Monterrey 2,522
Puebla 1,055
León 872
Ciudad Juárez 798
Tijuana 743
Culiacán 602
Mexicali 602
Acapulco 592
Mérida 557
Chihuahua 530
San Luis Potosí 526
Aguascaliéntes 506
Moldova
Chişinău 658
Mongolia
Ulan Bator 673
Morocco
Casablanca 2,943
Rabat-Salé 1,220
Marrakesh 602
Fès 564
Mozambique
Maputo 2,000
Nepal
Katmandu 535
Netherlands
Amsterdam 1,115
Rotterdam 1,086
The Hague 700
Utrecht 557
New Zealand
Auckland 1,090
Nicaragua
Managua 864
Nigeria
Lagos 10,287
Ibadan 1,432
Ogbomosho 730
Kano 674

Norway
Oslo 502
Pakistan
Karachi 9,269
Lahore 5,064
Faisalabad 1,977
Rawalpindi 1,406
Multan 1,182
Hyderabad 1,151
Gujranwala 1,125
Peshawar 988
Quetta 560
Islamabad 525
Paraguay
Asunción 945
Peru
Lima 6,601
Arequipa 620
Trujillo 509
Philippines
Manila 8,594
Quezon City 1,989
Caloocan 1,023
Davao 1,009
Cebu 662
Zamboanga 511
Poland
Warsaw 1,626
Lódz 815
Kraków 740
Wroclaw 641
Poznań 580
Portugal
Lisbon 2,561
Oporto 1,174
Romania
Bucharest 2,028
Russia
Moscow 8,405
St Petersburg 4,216
Nizhniy Novgorod 1,371
Novosibirsk 1,367
Yekaterinburg 1,275
Samara 1,170
Omsk 1,158
Kazan 1,085
Chelyabinsk 1,084
Ufa 1,082
Perm 1,025
Rostov 1,023
Volgograd 1,005
Saudi Arabia
Riyadh 1,800
Jedda 1,500
Mecca 630
Senegal
Dakar 1,905
Sierra Leone
Freetown 505
Singapore
Singapore 3,866
Somalia
Mogadishu 997
South Africa
Cape Town 2,350
Johannesburg 1,196
Durban 1,137
Pretoria 1,080
Port Elizabeth 853
Vanderbijlpark–Vereeniging 774
Soweto 597
Sasolburg 540
Spain
Madrid 3,030
Barcelona 1,615
Valencia 763
Sevilla 720
Zaragoza 608
Málaga 532
Sri Lanka
Colombo 1,863
Sudan
Omdurman 1,271
Khartoum 925
Khartoum North 701
Sweden
Stockholm 727
Switzerland
Zürich 733
Syria
Aleppo 1,813
Damascus 1,394
Homs 659
Taiwan
T'aipei 2,596
Kaohsiung 1,435

T'aichung 858
T'ainan 708
Panch'iao 539
Tajikistan
Dushanbe 524
Tanzania
Dar-es-Salaam 1,361
Thailand
Bangkok 7,507
Togo
Lomé 590
Tunisia
Tunis 1,827
Turkey
Istanbul 8,506
Ankara 3,294
Izmir 2,554
Bursa 1,485
Adana 1,273
Konya 1,140
Mersin (Içel) 956
Gaziantep 867
Antalya 867
Kayseri 862
Diyarbakir 833
Urfa 785
Manisa 696
Kocaeli 629
Antalya 591
Samsun 590
Kahramanmaras 551
Balikesir 538
Eskisehir 519
Erzurum 512
Malatya 510
Turkmenistan
Ashkhabad 536
Uganda
Kampala 954
Ukraine
Kiev 2,621
Kharkov 1,521
Dnepropetrovsk 1,122
Donetsk 1,065
Odessa 1,027
Zaporizhzhya 863
Lviv 794
Kryvyy Rih 720
Mykolayiv 518
Mariupol 500
United Arab Emirates
Abu Dhabi 928
Dubai 674
United Kingdom
London 8,089
Birmingham 2,373
Manchester 2,353
Liverpool 852
Glasgow 832
Sheffield 661
Nottingham 649
Newcastle 617
Bristol 552
Leeds 529
United States
New York 21,200
Los Angeles 16,374
Chicago–Gary 9,158
Washington–Baltimore 7,608
San Francisco–San Jose 7,039
Philadelphia–Atlantic City 6,188
Boston–Worcester 5,819
Detroit–Flint 5,456
Dallas–Fort Worth 5,222
Houston–Galveston 4,670
Atlanta 4,112
Miami–Fort Lauderdale 3,876
Seattle–Tacoma 3,554
Phoenix–Mesa 3,252
Minneapolis–St Paul 2,969
Cleveland–Akron 2,946
San Diego 2,814
St Louis 2,604
Denver–Boulder 2,582
San Juan 2,450
Tampa–Saint Petersburg 2,396
Pittsburgh 2,359
Portland–Salem 2,265
Cincinnati–Hamilton 1,979
Sacramento–Yolo 1,797
Kansas City 1,776
Milwaukee–Racine 1,690

Orlando 1,645
Indianapolis 1,607
San Antonio 1,592
Norfolk–Virginia Beach–Newport News 1,570
Las Vegas 1,563
Columbus, OH 1,540
Charlotte–Gastonia 1,499
New Orleans 1,338
Salt Lake City 1,334
Greensboro–Winston Salem–High Point 1,252
Austin–San Marcos 1,250
Nashville 1,231
Providence–Fall River 1,189
Raleigh–Durham 1,188
Hartford 1,183
Buffalo–Niagara Falls 1,170
Memphis 1,136
West Palm Beach 1,131
Jacksonville, FL 1,100
Rochester 1,098
Grand Rapids 1,089
Oklahoma City 1,083
Louisville 1,026
Richmond–Petersburg 997
Greenville 962
Dayton–Springfield 951
Fresno 923
Birmingham 921
Honolulu 876
Albany–Schenectady 876
Tucson 844
Tulsa 803
Syracuse 732
Omaha 717
Albuquerque 713
Knoxville 687
El Paso 680
Bakersfield 662
Allentown 638
Harrisburg 629
Scranton 625
Toledo 618
Baton Rouge 603
Youngstown–Warren 595
Springfield, MA 592
Sarasota 590
Little Rock 584
McAllen 569
Stockton–Lodi 564
Charleston 549
Wichita 545
Mobile 540
Columbia, SC 537
Colorado Springs 517
Fort Wayne 502
Uruguay
Montevideo 1,379
Uzbekistan
Tashkent 2,118
Venezuela
Caracas 1,975
Maracaibo 1,706
Valencia 1,263
Barquisimeto 811
Ciudad Guayana 642
Petare 176
Maracay 459
Vietnam
Ho Chi Minh City 4,322
Hanoi 3,056
Haiphong 783
Yemen
Sana' 972
Aden 562
Yugoslavia
Belgrade 1,598
Zambia
Lusaka 982
Zimbabwe
Harare 1,189
Bulawayo 622

* SAR = Special Administrative Region of China

WORLD STATISTICS: Physical Dimensions

Each topic list is divided into continents and within a continent the items are listed in order of size. The bottom part of many of the lists is selective in order to give examples from as many different countries as possible. The figures are rounded as appropriate.

World, Continents, Oceans

	km²	miles²	%
The World	509,450,000	196,672,000	–
Land	149,450,000	57,688,000	29.3
Water	360,000,000	138,984,000	70.7
Asia	44,500,000	17,177,000	29.8
Africa	30,302,000	11,697,000	20.3
North America	24,241,000	9,357,000	16.2
South America	17,793,000	6,868,000	11.9
Antarctica	14,100,000	5,443,000	9.4
Europe	9,957,000	3,843,000	6.7
Australia & Oceania	8,557,000	3,303,000	5.7
Pacific Ocean	179,679,000	69,356,000	49.9
Atlantic Ocean	92,373,000	35,657,000	25.7
Indian Ocean	73,917,000	28,532,000	20.5
Arctic Ocean	14,090,000	5,439,000	3.9

Ocean Depths

Atlantic Ocean	m	ft
Puerto Rico (Milwaukee) Deep	9,220	30,249
Cayman Trench	7,680	25,197
Gulf of Mexico	5,203	17,070
Mediterranean Sea	5,121	16,801
Black Sea	2,211	7,254
North Sea	660	2,165

Indian Ocean	m	ft
Java Trench	7,450	24,442
Red Sea	2,635	8,454

Pacific Ocean	m	ft
Mariana Trench	11,022	36,161
Tonga Trench	10,882	35,702
Japan Trench	10,554	34,626
Kuril Trench	10,542	34,587

Arctic Ocean	m	ft
Molloy Deep	5,608	18,399

Mountains

Europe		m	ft
Elbrus	Russia	5,642	18,510
Mont Blanc	France/Italy	4,807	15,771
Monte Rosa	Italy/Switzerland	4,634	15,203
Dom	Switzerland	4,545	14,911
Liskamm	Switzerland	4,527	14,852
Weisshorn	Switzerland	4,505	14,780
Taschorn	Switzerland	4,490	14,730
Matterhorn/Cervino	Italy/Switzerland	4,478	14,691
Mont Maudit	France/Italy	4,465	14,649
Dent Blanche	Switzerland	4,356	14,291
Nadelhorn	Switzerland	4,327	14,196
Grandes Jorasses	France/Italy	4,208	13,806
Jungfrau	Switzerland	4,158	13,642
Grossglockner	Austria	3,797	12,457
Mulhacén	Spain	3,478	11,411
Zugspitze	Germany	2,962	9,718
Olympus	Greece	2,917	9,570
Triglav	Slovenia	2,863	9,393
Gerlachovka	Slovak Republic	2,655	8,711
Galdhöpiggen	Norway	2,468	8,100
Kebnekaise	Sweden	2,117	6,946
Ben Nevis	UK	1,343	4,406

Asia		m	ft
Everest	China/Nepal	8,850	29,035
K2 (Godwin Austen)	China/Kashmir	8,611	28,251
Kanchenjunga	India/Nepal	8,598	28,208
Lhotse	China/Nepal	8,516	27,939
Makalu	China/Nepal	8,481	27,824
Cho Oyu	China/Nepal	8,201	26,906
Dhaulagiri	Nepal	8,172	26,811
Manaslu	Nepal	8,156	26,758
Nanga Parbat	Kashmir	8,126	26,660
Annapurna	Nepal	8,078	26,502
Gasherbrum	China/Kashmir	8,068	26,469
Broad Peak	China/Kashmir	8,051	26,414
Xixabangma	China	8,012	26,286
Kangbachen	India/Nepal	7,902	25,925
Trivor	Pakistan	7,720	25,328
Pik Kommunizma	Tajikistan	7,495	24,590
Demavend	Iran	5,604	18,386
Ararat	Turkey	5,165	16,945
Gunong Kinabalu	Malaysia (Borneo)	4,101	13,455
Fuji-San	Japan	3,776	12,388

Africa		m	ft
Kilimanjaro	Tanzania	5,895	19,340
Mt Kenya	Kenya	5,199	17,057
Ruwenzori	Uganda/Congo (D.R.)	5,109	16,762
Ras Dashan	Ethiopia	4,620	15,157
Meru	Tanzania	4,565	14,977
Karisimbi	Rwanda/Congo (D.R.)	4,507	14,787
Mt Elgon	Kenya/Uganda	4,321	14,176
Batu	Ethiopia	4,307	14,130
Toubkal	Morocco	4,165	13,665
Mt Cameroon	Cameroon	4,070	13,353

Oceania		m	ft
Puncak Jaya	Indonesia	5,030	16,503
Puncak Trikora	Indonesia	4,750	15,584
Puncak Mandala	Indonesia	4,702	15,427
Mt Wilhelm	Papua New Guinea	4,508	14,790
Mauna Kea	USA (Hawaii)	4,205	13,796
Mauna Loa	USA (Hawaii)	4,170	13,681
Mt Cook (Aoraki)	New Zealand	3,753	12,313
Mt Kosciuszko	Australia	2,237	7,339

North America		m	ft
Mt McKinley (Denali)	USA (Alaska)	6,194	20,321
Mt Logan	Canada	5,959	19,551
Citlaltepetl	Mexico	5,700	18,701
Mt St Elias	USA/Canada	5,489	18,008
Popocatepetl	Mexico	5,452	17,887
Mt Foraker	USA (Alaska)	5,304	17,401
Ixtaccihuatl	Mexico	5,286	17,342
Lucania	Canada	5,227	17,149
Mt Steele	Canada	5,073	16,644
Mt Bona	USA (Alaska)	5,005	16,420
Mt Whitney	USA	4,418	14,495
Tajumulco	Guatemala	4,220	13,845
Chirripó Grande	Costa Rica	3,837	12,589
Pico Duarte	Dominican Rep.	3,175	10,417

South America		m	ft
Aconcagua	Argentina	6,962	22,841
Bonete	Argentina	6,872	22,546
Ojos del Salado	Argentina/Chile	6,863	22,516
Pissis	Argentina	6,779	22,241
Mercedario	Argentina/Chile	6,770	22,211
Huascaran	Peru	6,768	22,204
Llullaillaco	Argentina/Chile	6,723	22,057
Nudo de Cachi	Argentina	6,720	22,047
Yerupaja	Peru	6,632	21,758
Sajama	Bolivia	6,542	21,463
Chimborazo	Ecuador	6,267	20,561
Pico Colon	Colombia	5,800	19,029
Pico Bolivar	Venezuela	5,007	16,427

Antarctica		m	ft
Vinson Massif		4,897	16,066
Mt Kirkpatrick		4,528	14,855

Rivers

Europe		km	miles
Volga	Caspian Sea	3,700	2,300
Danube	Black Sea	2,850	1,770
Ural	Caspian Sea	2,535	1,575
Dnepr (Dnipro)	Black Sea	2,285	1,420
Kama	Volga	2,030	1,260
Don	Volga	1,990	1,240
Petchora	Arctic Ocean	1,790	1,110
Oka	Volga	1,480	920
Dnister (Dniester)	Black Sea	1,400	870
Vyatka	Kama	1,370	850
Rhine	North Sea	1,320	820
N. Dvina	Arctic Ocean	1,290	800
Elbe	North Sea	1,145	710

Asia		km	miles
Yangtze	Pacific Ocean	6,380	3,960
Yenisey–Angara	Arctic Ocean	5,550	3,445
Huang He	Pacific Ocean	5,464	3,395
Ob–Irtysh	Arctic Ocean	5,410	3,360
Mekong	Pacific Ocean	4,500	2,795
Amur	Pacific Ocean	4,400	2,730
Lena	Arctic Ocean	4,400	2,730
Irtysh	Ob	4,250	2,640
Yenisey	Arctic Ocean	4,090	2,540
Ob	Arctic Ocean	3,680	2,285
Indus	Indian Ocean	3,100	1,925
Brahmaputra	Indian Ocean	2,900	1,800
Syrdarya	Aral Sea	2,860	1,775
Salween	Indian Ocean	2,800	1,740
Euphrates	Indian Ocean	2,700	1,675
Amudarya	Aral Sea	2,540	1,575

Africa		km	miles
Nile	Mediterranean	6,670	4,140
Congo	Atlantic Ocean	4,670	2,900
Niger	Atlantic Ocean	4,180	2,595
Zambezi	Indian Ocean	3,540	2,200
Oubangi/Uele	Congo (Dem. Rep.)	2,250	1,400
Kasai	Congo (Dem. Rep.)	1,950	1,210
Shaballe	Indian Ocean	1,930	1,200
Orange	Atlantic Ocean	1,860	1,155
Cubango	Okavango Swamps	1,800	1,120
Limpopo	Indian Ocean	1,600	995
Senegal	Atlantic Ocean	1,600	995

Australia		km	miles
Murray–Darling	Indian Ocean	3,750	2,330
Darling	Murray	3,070	1,905
Murray	Indian Ocean	2,575	1,600
Murrumbidgee	Murray	1,690	1,050

North America		km	miles
Mississippi–Missouri	Gulf of Mexico	6,020	3,740
Mackenzie	Arctic Ocean	4,240	2,630
Mississippi	Gulf of Mexico	3,780	2,350
Missouri	Mississippi	3,780	2,350
Yukon	Pacific Ocean	3,185	1,980
Rio Grande	Gulf of Mexico	3,030	1,880
Arkansas	Mississippi	2,340	1,450
Colorado	Pacific Ocean	2,330	1,445
Red	Mississippi	2,040	1,270
Columbia	Pacific Ocean	1,950	1,210
Saskatchewan	Lake Winnipeg	1,940	1,205

South America		km	miles
Amazon	Atlantic Ocean	6,450	4,010
Paraná–Plate	Atlantic Ocean	4,500	2,800
Purus	Amazon	3,350	2,080
Madeira	Amazon	3,200	1,990
São Francisco	Atlantic Ocean	2,900	1,800
Paraná	Plate	2,800	1,740
Tocantins	Atlantic Ocean	2,750	1,710
Paraguay	Paraná	2,550	1,580
Orinoco	Atlantic Ocean	2,500	1,550
Pilcomayo	Paraná	2,500	1,550
Araguaia	Tocantins	2,250	1,400

Lakes

Europe		km²	miles²
Lake Ladoga	Russia	17,700	6,800
Lake Onega	Russia	9,700	3,700
Saimaa system	Finland	8,000	3,100
Vänern	Sweden	5,500	2,100

Asia		km²	miles²
Caspian Sea	Asia	371,800	143,550
Lake Baykal	Russia	30,500	11,780
Aral Sea	Kazakstan/Uzbekistan	28,687	11,086
Tonlé Sap	Cambodia	20,000	7,700
Lake Balqash	Kazakstan	18,500	7,100

Africa		km²	miles²
Lake Victoria	East Africa	68,000	26,000
Lake Tanganyika	Central Africa	33,000	13,000
Lake Malawi/Nyasa	East Africa	29,600	11,430
Lake Chad	Central Africa	25,000	9,700
Lake Turkana	Ethiopia/Kenya	8,500	3,300
Lake Volta	Ghana	8,500	3,300

Australia		km²	miles²
Lake Eyre	Australia	8,900	3,400
Lake Torrens	Australia	5,800	2,200
Lake Gairdner	Australia	4,800	1,900

North America		km²	miles²
Lake Superior	Canada/USA	82,350	31,800
Lake Huron	Canada/USA	59,600	23,010
Lake Michigan	USA	58,000	22,400
Great Bear Lake	Canada	31,800	12,280
Great Slave Lake	Canada	28,500	11,000
Lake Erie	Canada/USA	25,700	9,900
Lake Winnipeg	Canada	24,400	9,400
Lake Ontario	Canada/USA	19,500	7,500
Lake Nicaragua	Nicaragua	8,200	3,200

South America		km²	miles²
Lake Titicaca	Bolivia/Peru	8,300	3,200
Lake Poopo	Peru	2,800	1,100

Islands

Europe		km²	miles²
Great Britain	UK	229,880	88,700
Iceland	Atlantic Ocean	103,000	39,800
Ireland	Ireland/UK	84,400	32,600
Novaya Zemlya (N.)	Russia	48,200	18,600
Sicily	Italy	25,500	9,800
Corsica	France	8,700	3,400

Asia		km²	miles²
Borneo	South-east Asia	744,360	287,400
Sumatra	Indonesia	473,600	182,860
Honshu	Japan	230,500	88,980
Celebes	Indonesia	189,000	73,000
Java	Indonesia	126,700	48,900
Luzon	Philippines	104,700	40,400
Hokkaido	Japan	78,400	30,300

Africa		km²	miles²
Madagascar	Indian Ocean	587,040	226,660
Socotra	Indian Ocean	3,600	1,400
Réunion	Indian Ocean	2,500	965

Oceania		km²	miles²
New Guinea	Indonesia/Papua NG	821,030	317,000
New Zealand (S.)	Pacific Ocean	150,500	58,100
New Zealand (N.)	Pacific Ocean	114,700	44,300
Tasmania	Australia	67,800	26,200
Hawaii	Pacific Ocean	10,450	4,000

North America		km²	miles²
Greenland	Atlantic Ocean	2,175,600	839,800
Baffin Is.	Canada	508,000	196,100
Victoria Is.	Canada	212,200	81,900
Ellesmere Is.	Canada	212,000	81,800
Cuba	Caribbean Sea	110,860	42,800
Hispaniola	Dominican Rep./Haiti	76,200	29,400
Jamaica	Caribbean Sea	11,400	4,400
Puerto Rico	Atlantic Ocean	8,900	3,400

South America		km²	miles²
Tierra del Fuego	Argentina/Chile	47,000	18,100
Falkland Is. (E.)	Atlantic Ocean	6,800	2,600

WORLD CITIES

CITY MAPS

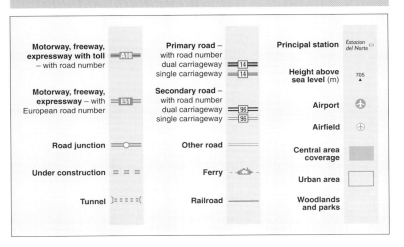

CENTRAL AREA MAPS

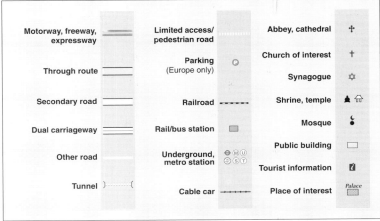

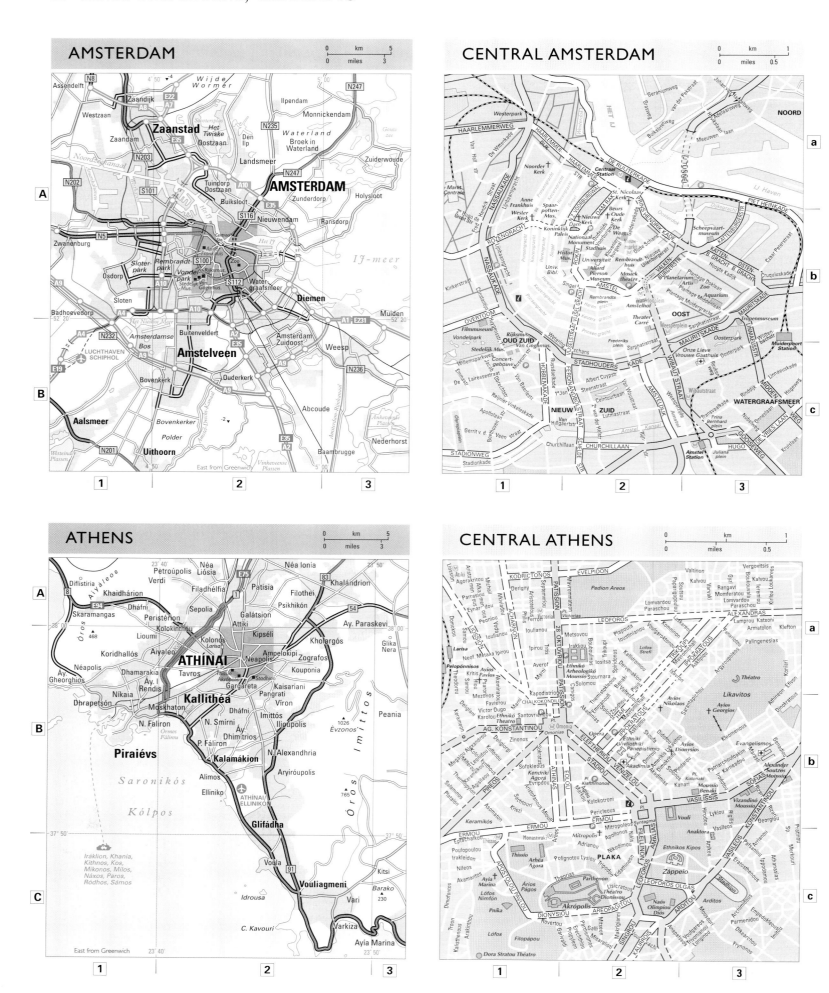

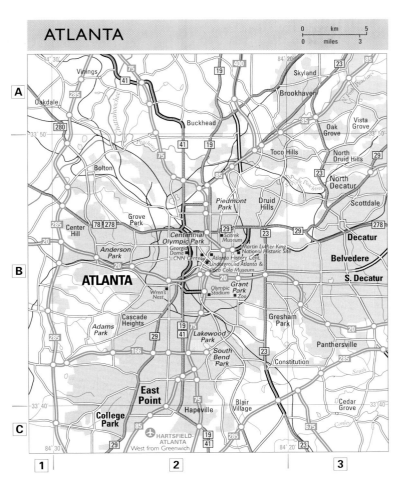

ATLANTA

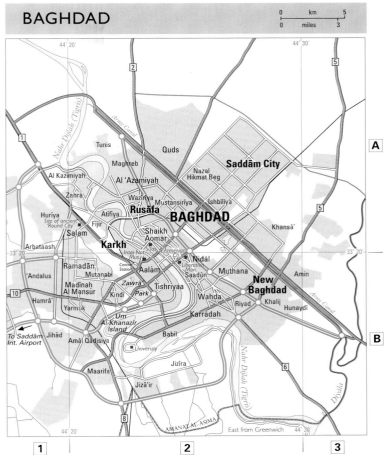

BAGHDAD

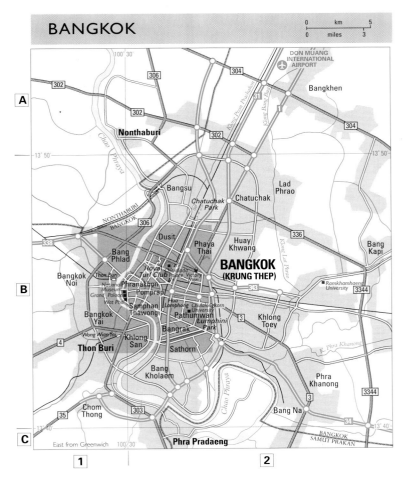

BANGKOK

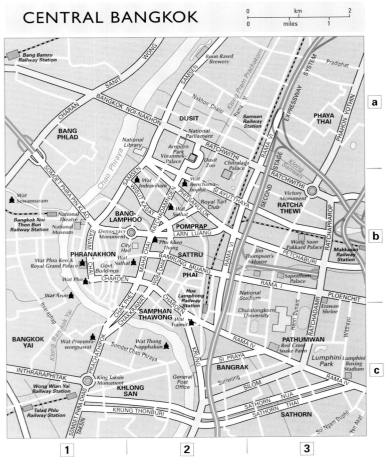

CENTRAL BANGKOK

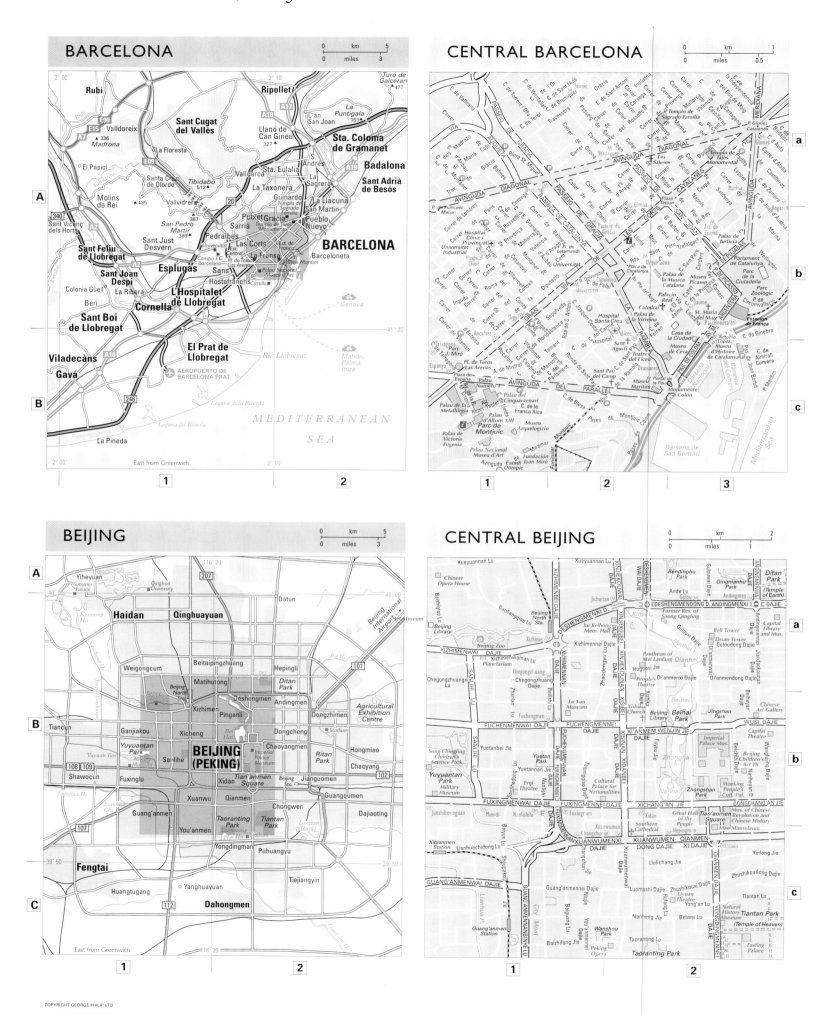

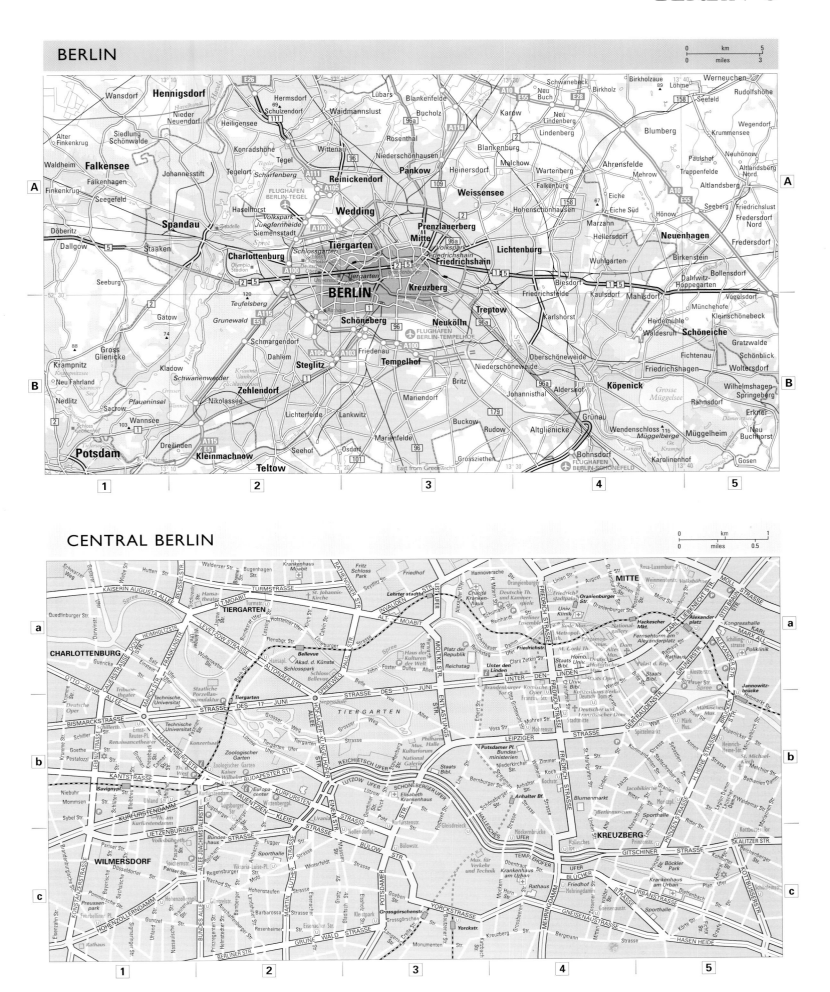

BERLIN

km 0 ——— 5
miles 0 ——— 3

CENTRAL BERLIN

km 0 ——— 1
miles 0 ——— 0.5

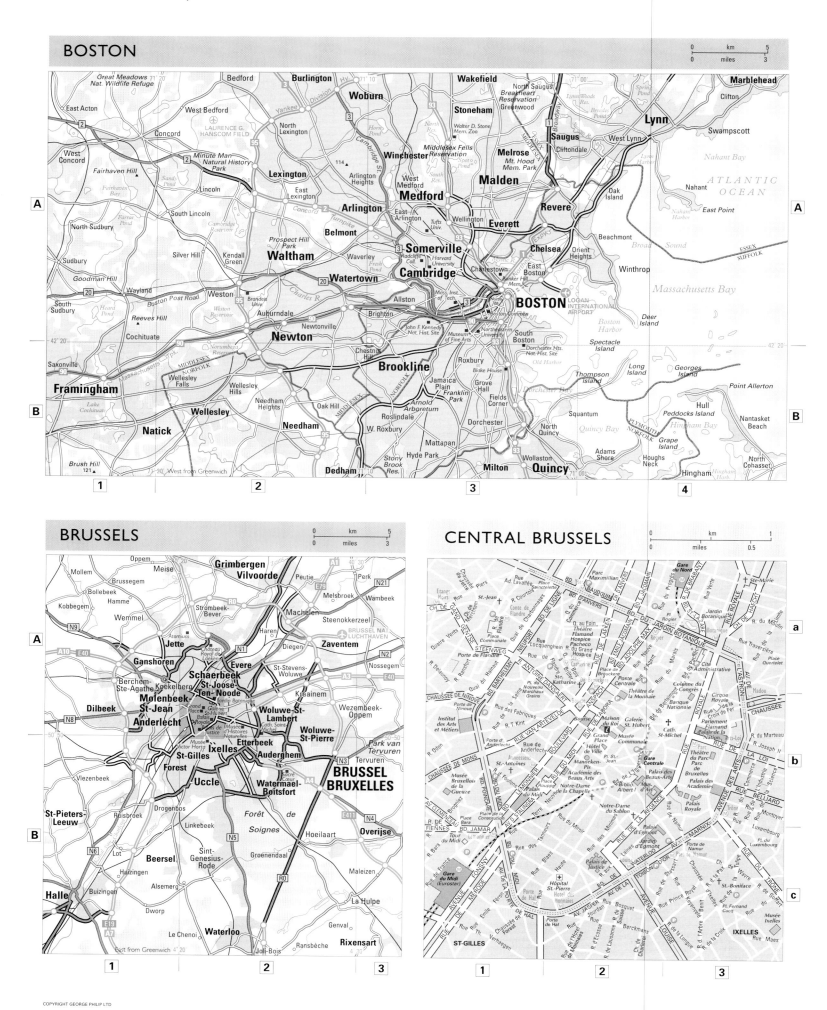

BOSTON

BRUSSELS

CENTRAL BRUSSELS

BUDAPEST

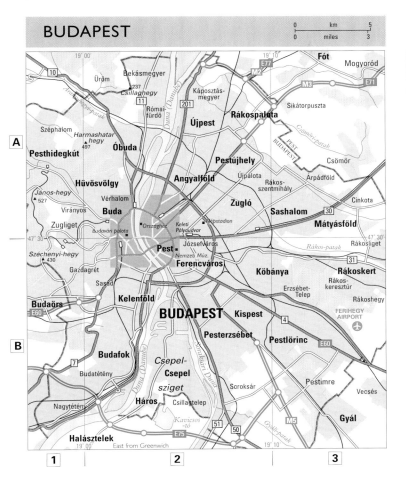

CENTRAL BUDAPEST

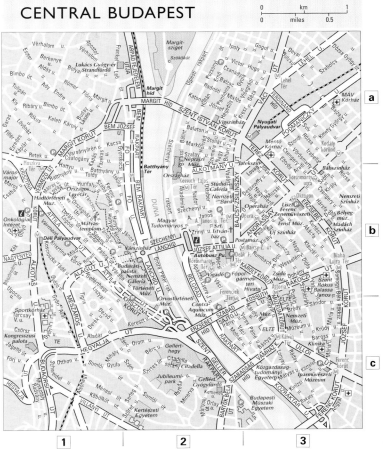

BUENOS AIRES

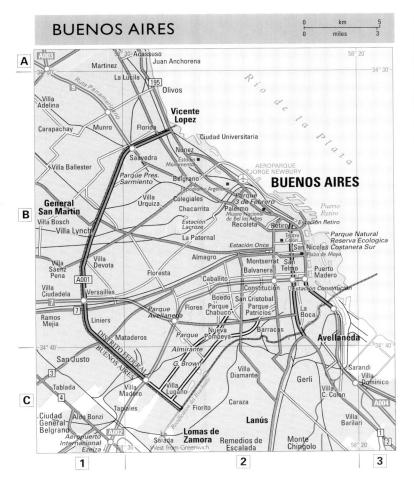

CAIRO

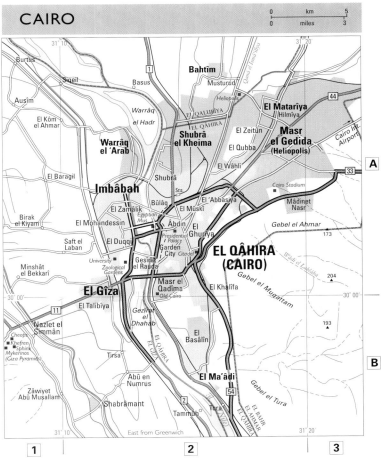

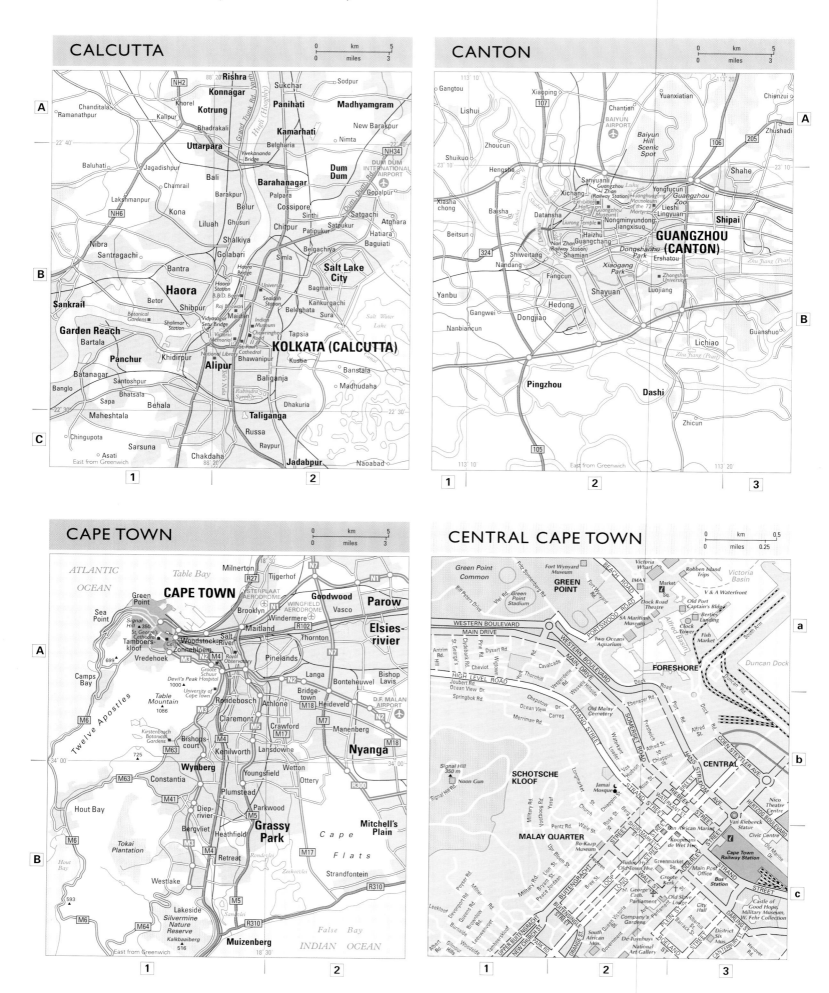

CALCUTTA

km 0 — 5
miles 0 — 3

Rishra
Konnagar
Chanditala
Ramanathpur
Khorel
Kalipur
Kotrung
Bhadrakali
Uttarpara
Baluhati
Jagadishpur
Vivekananda Bridge
Bali
Chamrail
Lakshmanpur
Barakpur
Kona
Liluah
Ghusuri
Nibra
Santragachi
Golabari
Bantra
Haora
Betor
Shibpur
Haora Station
B.B.D. Bag
Sankrail
Botanical Gardens
Raj Bhawan
Shalimar Station
Garden Reach
Bartala
Vidyasagar Setu Bridge
Panchur
Khidirpur
Alipur
Batanagar
Santoshpur
Banglo
Sapa
Bhatsala
Behala
Maheshtala
Chingupota
Sarsuna
Asati
East from Greenwich
Chakdaha
Sukchar
Sodpur
Panihati
Madhyamgram
Kamarhati
New Barakpur
Belgharia
Nimta
Dum Dum
Palpara
Cossipore
Satgachi
Atghara
Sinthi
Chitpur
Patipukur
Shalkiya
Simla
Bagmari
Salt Lake City
Beleghata
Kankurgachi
Sura
Tapsia
University
Sealdah Station
Indian Museum
Maidan
Chowringhee Road
Victoria Memorial
St. Paul's Cathedral
KOLKATA (CALCUTTA)
National Library
Bhawanipur
Kustia
Baliganja
Banstala
Madhudaha
Dhakuria
Taliganga
Russa
Raypur
Jadabpur
Naoabad
Rabindra Sarovar
NH2
NH34
NH6
Hugli (Hooghly)
Grand Trunk Rd (North)
Dum Dum Rd
DUM DUM INTERNATIONAL AIRPORT
Gopalpur
Hatiara
Baguiati
Salt Water Lake
Barahanagar
Belur

CANTON

km 0 — 5
miles 0 — 3

Gangtou
Lishui
Xiaoping
Yuanxiatian
Chientzui
107
BAIYUN AIRPORT
Baiyun Hill Scenic Spot
Zhoucun
Zhushadi
Shuikuo
106
205
Hengsha
Shahe
Xiasha chong
Xichang
Sanyuanli
Guangzhou Zhan (Railway Station)
Yongfucun
Guangzhou Zoo
Baisha
Exhibition Hall
Guangzhou Museum
Huanghuagang Mausoleum of the 72 Martyrs
Lieshi
Lingyuan
Shipai
Datansha
Nongminyundong Jiangxiuo
Beitsun
Liurong Temple
Nan Zhan (Railway Station)
Guangchang
Haizhu
Shamian
Dongshanhu Park
Ershatou
GUANGZHOU (CANTON)
Yanbu
Nandang
Shiweitang
Fangcun
Xiaogang Park
Zhongshan University
Zhu Jiang (Pearl)
Gangwei
Hedong
Shayuan
Luojiang
Guanshuo
Nanbiancun
Dongjiao
Lichiao
Pingzhou
Dashi
Zhu Jiang (Pearl)
105
Zhicun
East from Greenwich
324

CAPE TOWN

km 0 — 5
miles 0 — 3

ATLANTIC OCEAN
Table Bay
Milnerton
Tijgerhof
R27
CAPE TOWN
WESTERPLAAT AERODROME
Goodwood
Parow
Green Point
Sea Point
Brooklyn
WINGFIELD AERODROME
Vasco
Windermere
Elsies-rivier
Signal Hill 350
St. George's Cathedral
Tamboerskloof
Woodstock
Zonnebloem
Salt River
Maitland
Thornton
Vredehoek
699
Groote Schuur Hospital
Royal Observatory
Pinelands
Camps Bay
Devil's Peak 1000
University of Cape Town
Langa
Bonteheuwel
Bishop Lavis
D.F. MALAN AIRPORT
Table Mountain 1086
Rondebosch
Athlone
Bridge-town
Heideveld
Twelve Apostles
Claremont
Crawford
Manenberg
Kirstenbosch Botanical Gardens
Bishops-court
Kenilworth
Lansdowne
Nyanga
725
Wynberg
Youngsfield
Wetton
Ottery
Constantia
Plumstead
Parkwood
Hout Bay
Diep-rivier
Grassy Park
Mitchell's Plain
Bergvliet
Heathfield
Cape Flats
Tokai Plantation
Retreat
Strandfontein
Westlake
Lakeside
Silvermine Nature Reserve
593
Kalkbaaiberg 516
Muizenberg
False Bay
INDIAN OCEAN
East from Greenwich
Hout Bay
Zeekoelvei
Rondevlei
Sandvlei
M6
M3
M4
M5
M41
M63
M64
M7
M17
M18
N1
N2
N7
R102
R300
R310

CENTRAL CAPE TOWN

km 0 — 0.5
miles 0 — 0.25

Green Point Common
Fort Wynyard Museum
Victoria Wharf
Robben Island Trips
Victoria Basin
Bill Peters Drive
Green Point Stadium
GREEN POINT
IMAX
Market Sq.
Old Port Captain's Bldg
V & A Waterfront
WESTERN BOULEVARD
MAIN DRIVE
Two Oceans Aquarium
Dock Road Theatre
SA Maritime Museum
Berties Landing
Clock Tower
Fish Market
Antrim Rd.
St. George's Rd.
Clydebank Rd.
Pine Rd.
Dysart Rd.
Cheviot
Wigtown
HIGH LEVEL ROAD
Joubert Rd.
Ocean View Dr.
Springbok Rd.
Thornhill
Vesperdene Rd.
Cavalcade
Old Malay Cemetery
FORESHORE
Duncan Dock
Chepstow
Ocean View Dr.
Carreg
Merriman Rd.
Old Port Road
South Arm
Alfred Basin
Signal Hill 350 m
Noon Gun
SCHOTSCHE KLOOF
Jamai Mosque
Church
CENTRAL
Nico Theatre Centre
Van Riebeeck Statue
Civic Centre
MALAY QUARTER
Bo-Kaap Museum
Koopmans de Wet Hse
South African Market
Greenmarket Sq.
Main Post Office
Bus Station
Cape Town Railway Station
Old Slave Lodge
City Hall
Castle of Good Hope, Military Museum, W. Fehr Collection
St. George's Cath.
Parliament
Tudor Hse.
Grote Kerk
Company's Gardens
De Tuynhuys
South African Mus.
Government
National Art Gallery
District Six Mus.
STRAND STREET
BUITENGRACHT
UPPER BUITENGRACHT
NEW CHURCH ST
BUITENSINGLE STREET
ORANGE ST
LOOP STREET
LONG STREET
WALE STREET
ADDERLEY STREET
PLEIN ST
DARLING STREET
CANTERBURY STREET
HANS STRIJDOM AVE
COEN STEYLER AVE
HERTZOG BOULEVARD
BEACH ROAD
PORTSWOOD ROAD
WESTERN BOULEVARD
SOMERSET ROAD
STRAND STREET

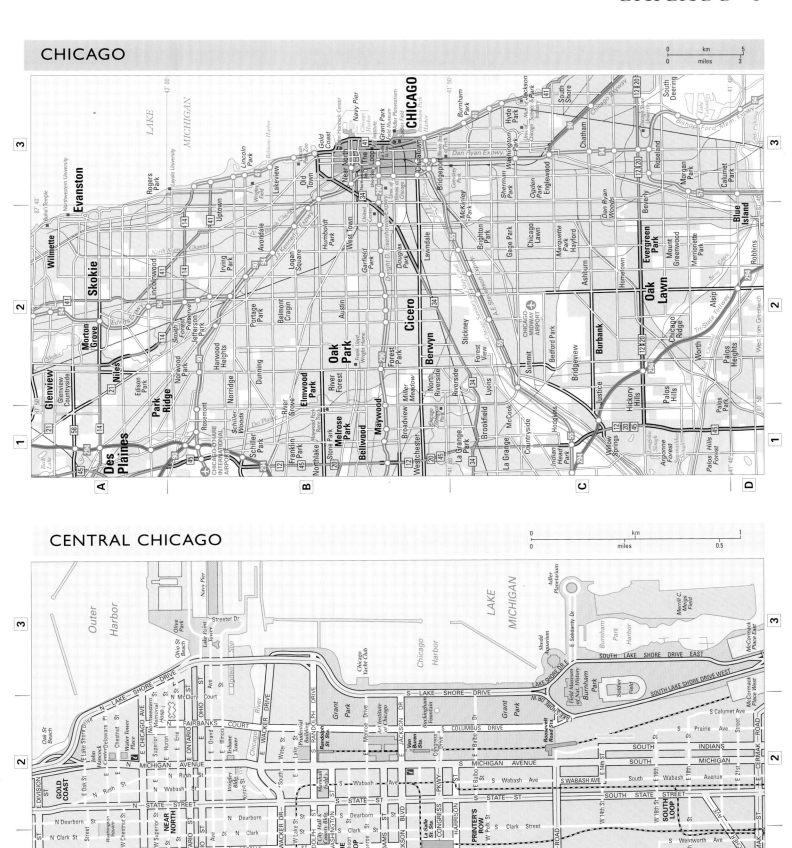

CHICAGO

CENTRAL CHICAGO

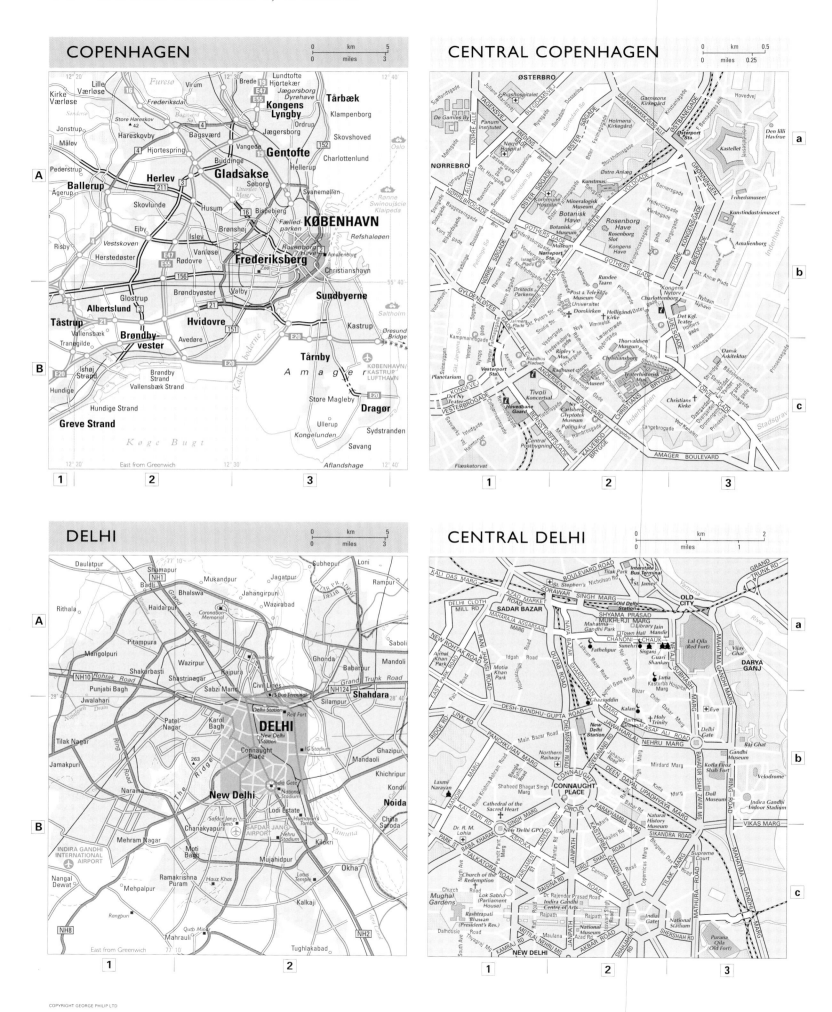

DUBLIN

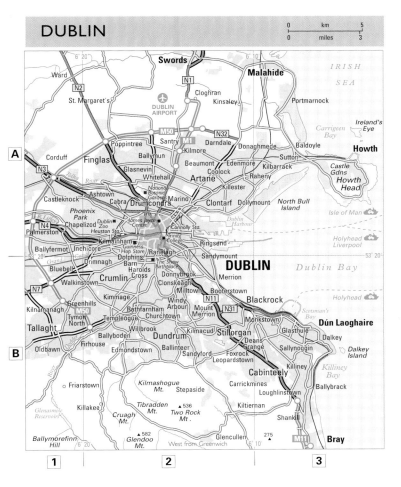

CENTRAL DUBLIN

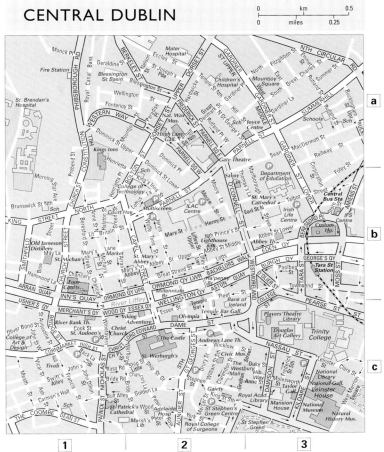

EDINBURGH

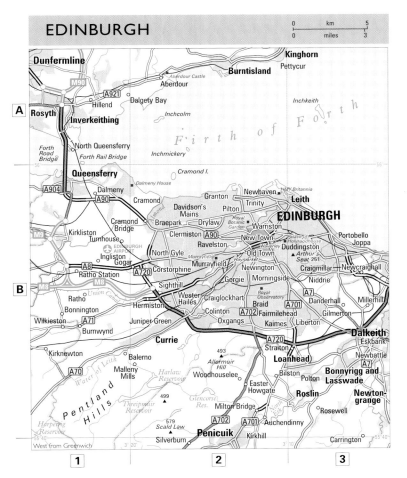

CENTRAL EDINBURGH

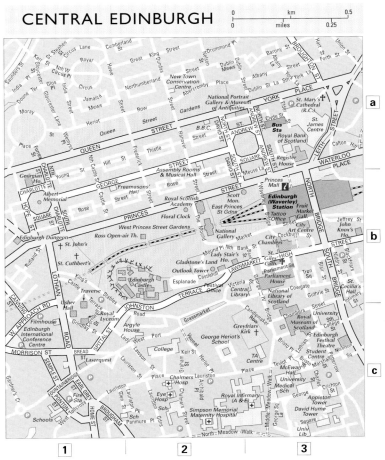

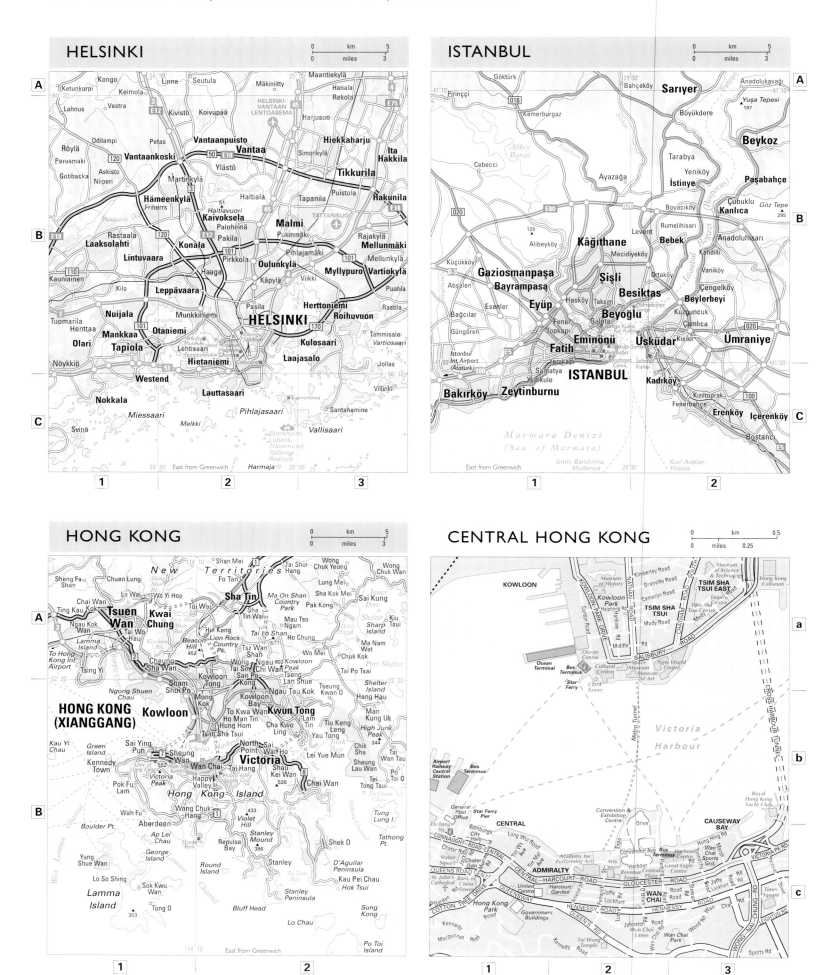

HELSINKI

km
miles

ISTANBUL

km
miles

HONG KONG

km
miles

CENTRAL HONG KONG

km
miles

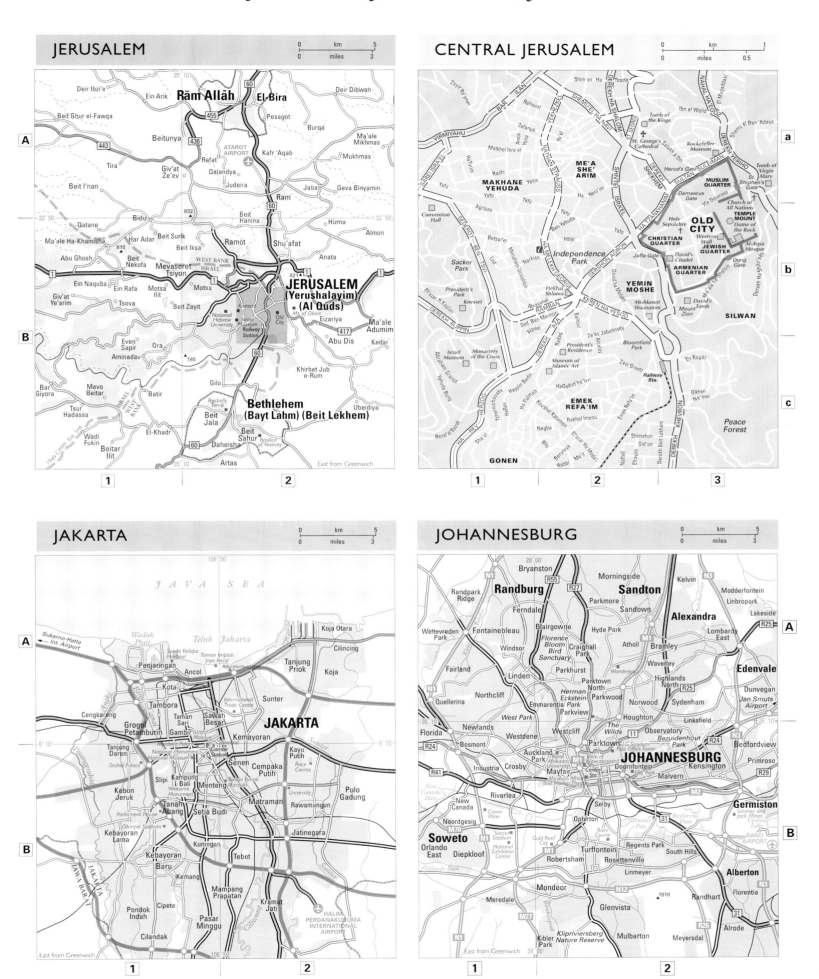

JERUSALEM

CENTRAL JERUSALEM

JAKARTA

JOHANNESBURG

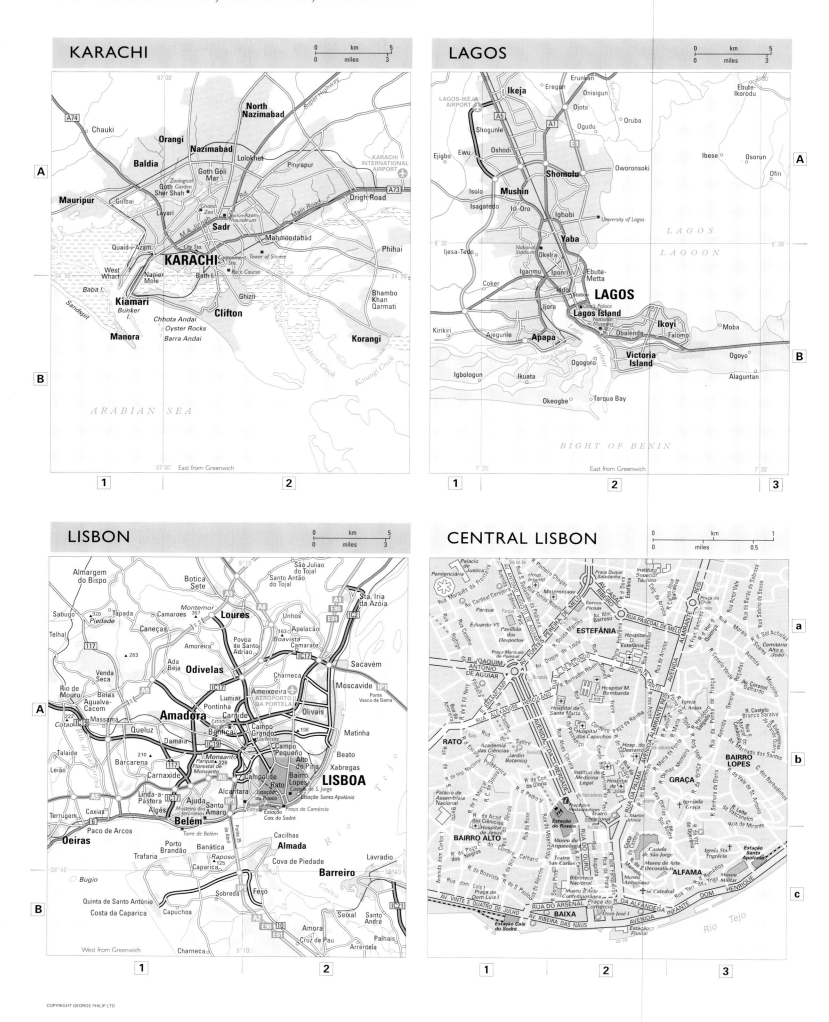

KARACHI

km 0 — 5
miles 0 — 3

67°00'

North Nazimabad
Orangi
Nazimabad
Baldia
Lolokhet
Goth Goli Mar
Pinjrapur
A74
Chauki
A
Mauripur
Zoological Garden
Goth Garden Sher Shah
Ghandi Zoo
Gulbai
Layari
Quaid-i-Azam Mausoleum
Sadr
Malir Road
A73
KARACHI INTERNATIONAL AIRPORT
Drigh Road
M.A.Jinnah Rd.
City Sta.
Mahmoodabad
Phihai
Quaid-i-Azam.
West Wharf
Napier Mole
Cantonment Sta.
Tower of Silence
Bath I.
Race Course
24°50'
Kiamari
Bunker I.
Clifton
Ghizri
Bhambo Khan Qarmati
B
Sandspit
Baba I.
Manora
Chhota Andai
Oyster Rocks
Barra Andai
Korangi
ARABIAN SEA
Korangi Creek
Ghizri Creek

67°00' East from Greenwich

1 **2**

LAGOS

km 0 — 5
miles 0 — 3

LAGOS-IKEJA AIRPORT
Ikeja
Erunkan
Eregun
Onisigun
Oruba
Ebute-Ikorodu
Shogunle
A5
A1
Ogudu
E1
Ejigbo
Ewu
Oshodi
Ibese
Osorun
Ofin
A
Isolo
Mushin
Idi-Oro
Igbobi
Oworonsoki
Shomolu
University of Lagos
Isagatedo
LAGOS LAGOON
Ijesa-Tedo
National Stadium
Yaba
Okelra
6°30'
Iganmu
Iponri
Ebute-Metta
Coker
Iddo
Station
LAGOS
Kirikiri
Oba's Palace
Lagos Island
National Museum
Ikoyi
Moba
Ajegunle
Ijora
Obalende
Falomo
B
Igbologun
Apapa
Lagos Harbour
Victoria Island
Ogoyo
Ikuata
Ogogoro
Alaguntan
Porto Novo Creek
Okeogbe
Tarqua Bay
BIGHT OF BENIN

7°20' East from Greenwich 7°30'

1 **2** **3**

LISBON

km 0 — 5
miles 0 — 3

9°10'
Almargem do Bispo
Botica Sete
São Julião do Tojal
Santo Antão do Tojal
Sabugo
Tapada Piedade
Montemor
Camaroes
A9
A8
Sta. Iria da Azóia
Telhal
Caneças
Loures
A1 E80 E01
IC2
Rio de Mouro
Venda Seca
Ada Beja
Povoa de Santo Adriao
Amoreira
Apelação
Boavista
Unhos
Camarate
Sacavém
Belas
Agualva-Cacem
Odivelas
IC17
Charneca
IC17
Moscavide
IP1
A
Massamá
Lumiar
Pontinha
Carnide
Olivais
Ponte Vasco da Gama
Cotao
IC19
Amadora
AEROPORTO DA PORTELA
Queluz
Benfica
Campo Grande
108
Matinha
Damaia
Monsanto
Campo Pequeno
Beato
117
Parque Florestal de Monsanto
Campolide
Alto do Pina
Xabregas
Barcarena
Rato
Bairro Lopes
LISBOA
Carnaxide
A5
Alcântara
Castelo de S. Jorge
Linda-a-Pastora
Ajuda
Santo Amaro
Estação Santa Apolónia
Terrugem
Algés
Mosteiro dos Jerónimos
Basílica da Estrela
Praça do Comércio
Caxias
Belém
Torre de Belém
Cacilhas
6
Paco de Arcos
Ponte 25 de Abril
Oeiras
Porto Brandão
Banática
Almada
Rio Tejo
Bugio
Trafaria
Raposo
Cova de Piedade
Lavradio
Caparica
Barreiro
38°40'
B
Quinta de Santo António
Costa da Caparica
Sobreda
Feijó
IC21
A2
E90 10
Amora
Seixal
Santo André
E01
Cruz de Pau
Arrentela
West from Greenwich
Charneca
Palhais

9°10'

1 **2**

CENTRAL LISBON

km 0 — 1
miles 0 — 0.5

Palacio de Justiça
Penitenciária
Praça Duque Saldanha
Instituto Superior Técnico
Rua Marquês da Fronteira
Hosp. Infantil
Maternidade
Praça do Chile
ESTEFÂNIA
Parque Eduardo VII
Pavilhão dos Desportos
a
Praça Marques de Pombal
Hospital D. Estefânia
Hospital M. Bombarda
RATO
Academia das Ciências
Jardim Botânico
Hospital de Santa Marta
Hospital dos Capuchos
BAIRRO LOPES
b
Instituto de Medicina Legal
Hospital de S. José
GRAÇA
Igreja Graça
Palácio de Assembleia Nacional
BAIRRO ALTO
Teatro Nacional
Estação do Rossio
Museu do Arqueologia
Castelo de São Jorge
Igreja Sta. Engrácia
Estação Santa Apolónia
Teatro San Carlos
Museu de Arte Decorativas
ALFAMA
Biblioteca Nacional
Museu de Arte Contemporânea
Sé Catedral
Museu Antoniano
Praça de Dom Luís I
Praça do Comércio
BAIXA
Estação Cais do Sodré
Estação Fluvial
Rio Tejo

1 **2** **3**

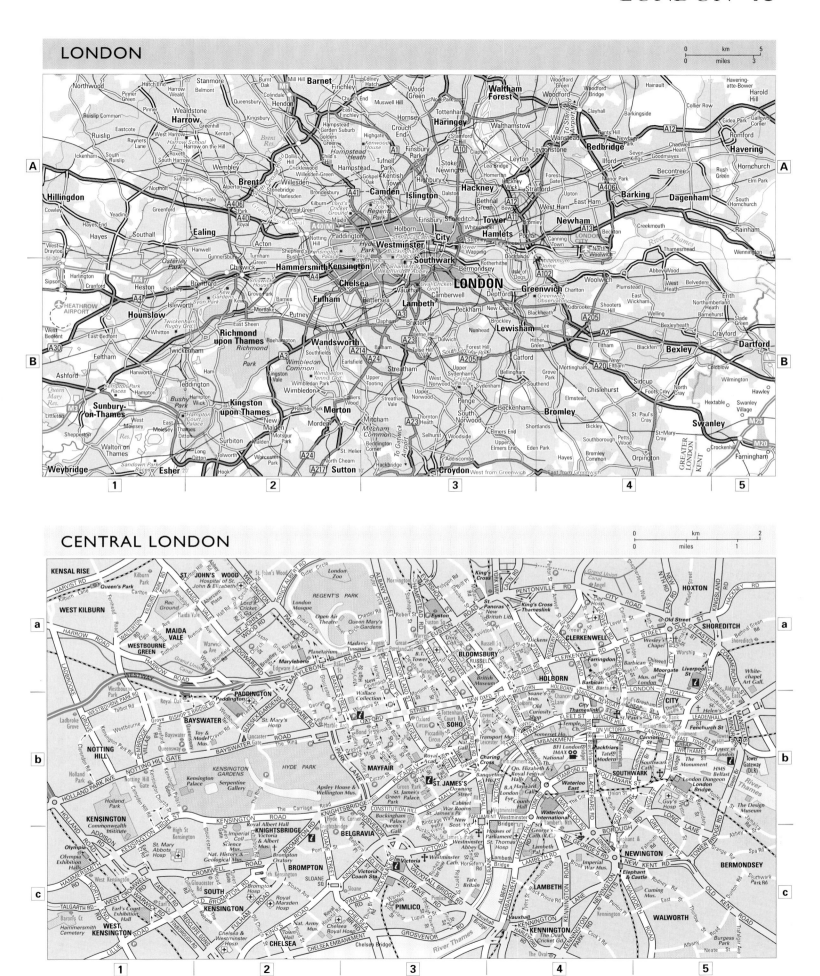

LONDON

0 — km — 5
0 — miles — 3

A · B

1 · 2 · 3 · 4 · 5

CENTRAL LONDON

0 — km — 2
0 — miles — 1

a · b · c

1 · 2 · 3 · 4 · 5

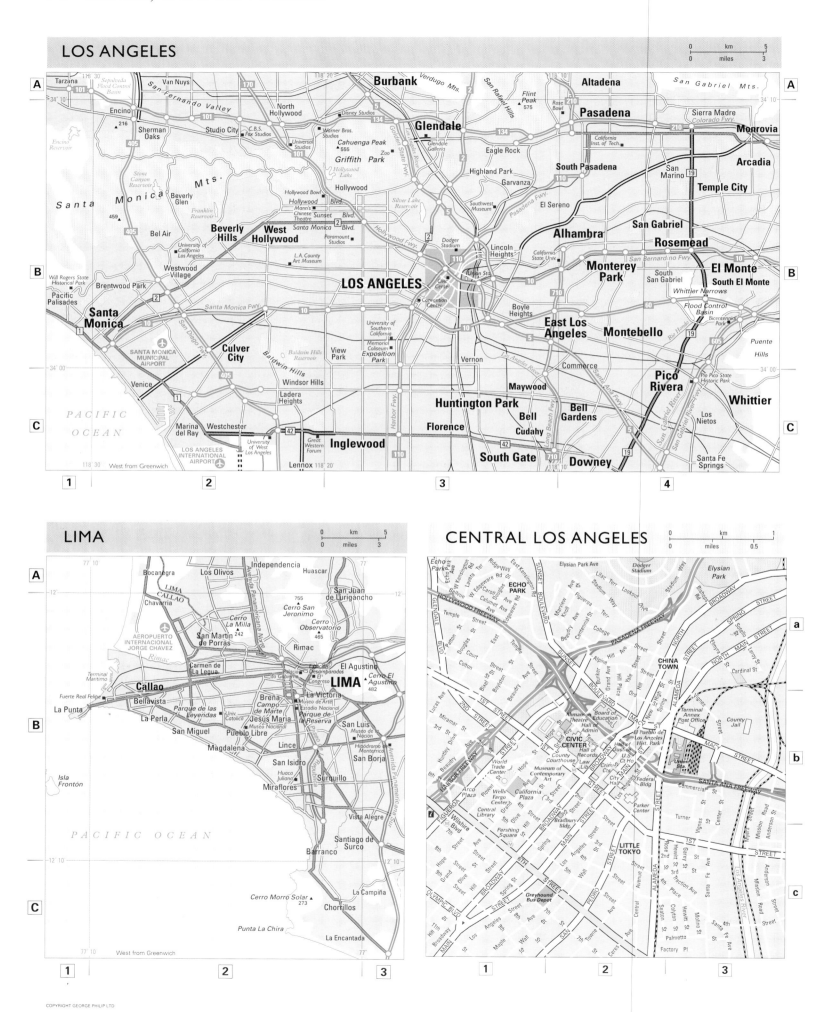

LOS ANGELES

LIMA

CENTRAL LOS ANGELES

MADRID

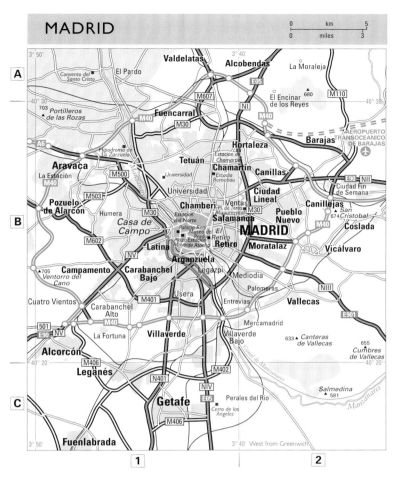

CENTRAL MADRID

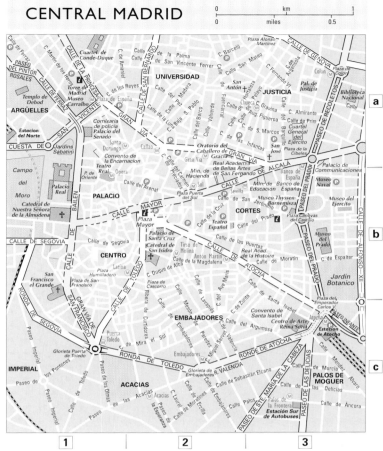

MANILA

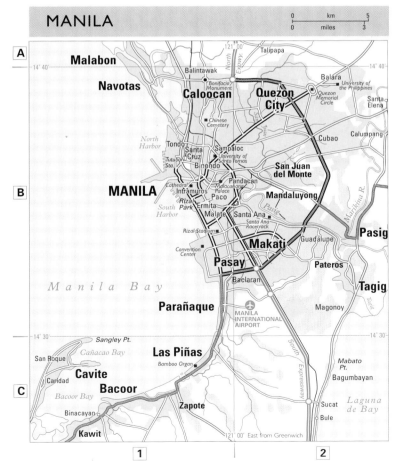

MELBOURNE

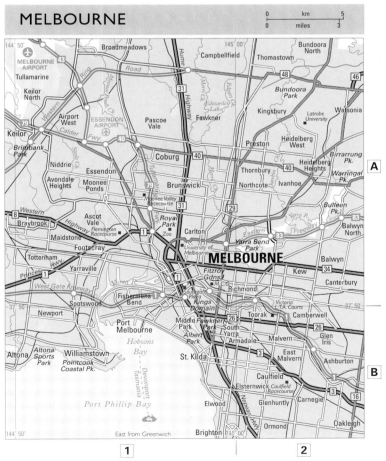

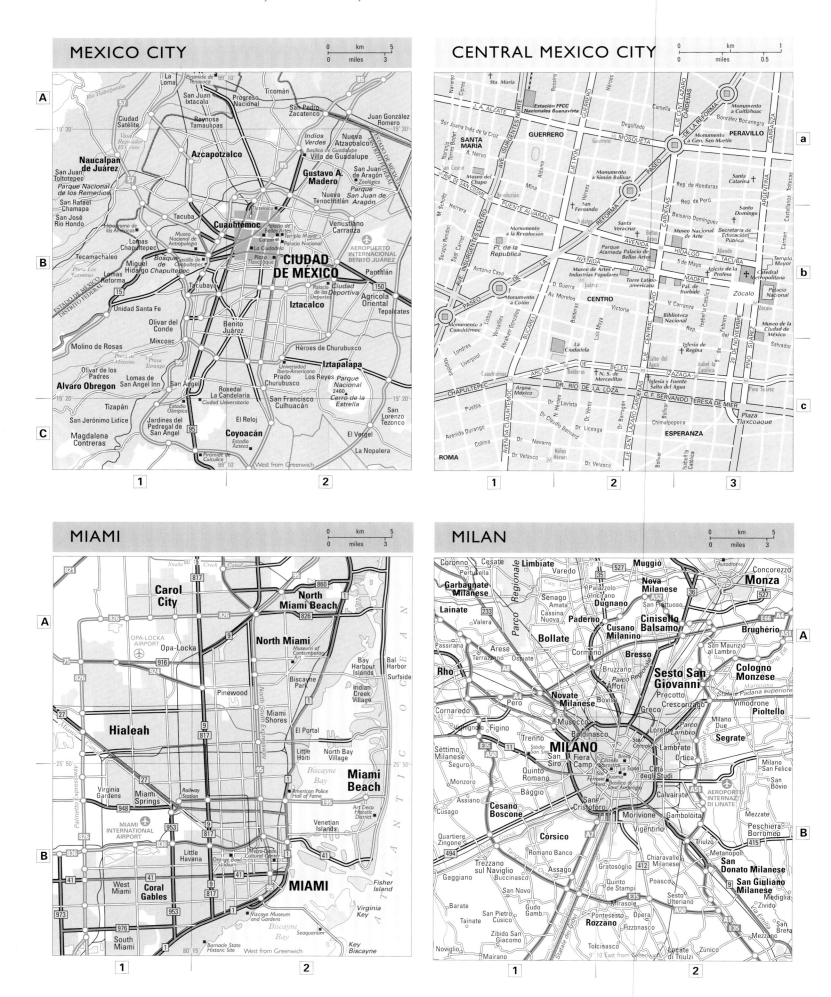

MOSCOW

km 0–5 / miles 0–3

A — Novonikolyskoye, Putilkovo, Mitino, Bratsevo, Sheremetyevo Airport, Degunino, Khimki-Khovrino, Vladykino, Babushkin 157▲, MOSKVA OBLAST, GOROD MOSKVA, Medvezhiy Ozyora, Medvezhiy Ozyora, Almazova

Chernyovo, Penyagino, Tushino, M10, Nikolskiy, Petrovsko-Razumovskoye, Timiryazev Park, Dzerzhinskiy Park, M8, Pekhra-Pokrovskoye

Krasnogorsk, Golyevo, Pavshino, Myakinino, Strogino, Pokrovsko-Sresnevo, Ostankino, Bogorodskoye, Galyanovo, Vostochnyy ▲140, Balashikha, Novaya

M9, Arkhangelyskoye, Troitse-Lykovo, Petrovskiy Posadok, Sokolniki Park, Sokolniki, Izmaylovo, Gorenki, M7, Pekhra-Yakovievskaya

B — Zakharkovo, Rublovo, Tatarovo, Cherepkovo, Khorosovo, Frunze, Dzerzhinskiy, Sverdlov, Leningrad Station, Ploshch, Kazan Station, Yaroslav Station, Izmayloskiy Park ▲150, Léportovo, Novogireyevo, Vishnyaki, Nikolyskoye, Saltykovka, Serbryanka

Razdory, Krylatskoye, Mnevniki, MOSKVA, Krasno-Presnenskaya, Bolshoy Theatre, Red Square, St Basil's Cath, Kremlin, Bauman Station, Kursk Station, Novogireyevo, Perovo, Reutov, Kuskovo, Serebryanka, Kutsino, Zheleznodorozhnyy

Barvikha, Romashkovo, Kuntsevo, Fili-Mazilovo, Kiev Station, Tretyakov Art Gallery, Zhdanov, Plyushchevo, Veshnyaki, Kuskovo, Fenino, Temnikovo

Poduskino, Nemchinovka, Davydkovo, Pavelet Station, Lenin, Gorky Park, Moskvoretskiy, Vykhino, Volgogradskiy Prospekt, Kuzyminki, Zhulebino, Kosino, Kozhukhovo, Mikhelysona, Chornaya

Novoivanovskoye, Lochino, Aminyevo, Luzhniki Sports Centre Lenin Stadium, Lomonosov University, Leninskiye-Gory, Moscow Circus, Oktyabrskiy, Tekstilyshchik, Kuzyminki, ▲94, Marusino

Mamonovo, Bakovka, Zarechye, Ochakovo, Ramenki ▲150, Nogatino, Lyublino, Lyubertsy, Nekrasovka, Korenevo

C — Odintsovo, M1, Meshcherskiy, Nikulino, Troparevo, Yugo-Zarad, Cheryomushki, Dyakovo, Maryino, Kuryanovo, Kotelniki, Tomilino, Kraskovo, Malakhovka

Choboty, Solntsevo, Belyayevo Bogorodskoye ▲250, Zyuzino, Volkhonka-Zil, Lenino, Brateyevo, Kapotnya, Tokarevo, Chkalova

Peredelkino, Orlovo, M3, Certanovka, M2, Certanovo, Lenino, M4 M6, Borisovo, M5, Dzerzhinskiy, Chaikovo

Vnukovo, Rasskazovka, Rumyantsevo, East from Greenwich 38

MONTRÉAL

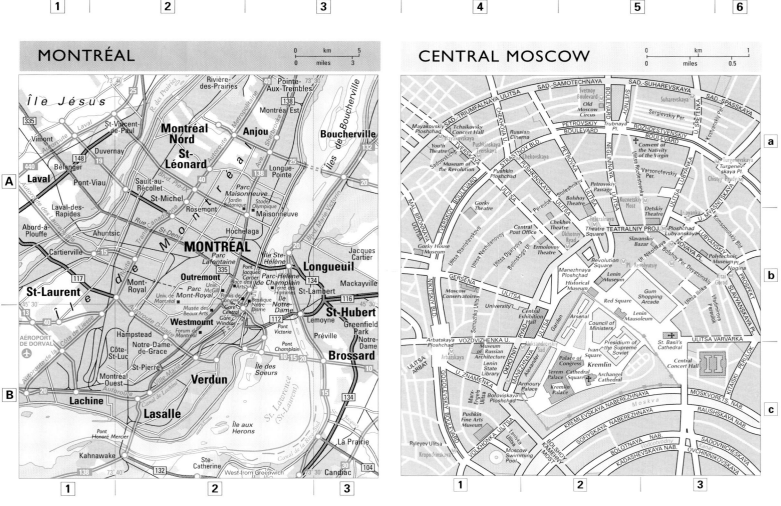

km 0–5 / miles 0–3

Île Jésus, Rivière-des-Prairies, Pointe-Aux-Trembles, Boucherville, Montréal Est, Montréal Nord, St-Léonard, Anjou, Longue-Pointe, Laval, Vimont, Duvernay, Bélanger, Pont-Viau, Sault-au-Récollet, Parc Maisonneuve, Jardin Botanique, Stade Olympique, Maisonneuve, Abord-à-Plouffe, St-Michel, Rosemont, Hochelaga, Cartierville, Ahuntsic, MONTRÉAL, Parc Lafontaine, Île Ste-Hélène, Jacques Cartier, St-Laurent, Mont-Royal, Outremont, Parc du Mont-Royal, Univ. McGill, Univ. de Montréal, Place des Arts, Longueuil, Mackayville, St-Lambert, Hampstead, Musée des Beaux Arts, Westmount, Forum de Montréal, Basilique Notre-Dame, Gare Central, Gare Windsor, Île Notre-Dame, St-Hubert, Lemoyne, Greenfield Park, Préville, Notre-Dame-de-Grace, Côte-St-Luc, St-Pierre, Montréal Ouest, Verdun, Île des Soeurs, Brossard, AÉROPORT DE DORVAL, Lachine, Lasalle, Canal de Lachine, St. Laurent (St-Laurent), Île aux Herons, Kahnawake, Pont Honoré Mercier, Ste-Catherine, West from Greenwich, Candiac

---

CENTRAL MOSCOW

km 0–1 / miles 0–0.5

Sad-Samotechnaya, Sad-Suharevskaya, Svetnoy Boulevard, Old Moscow Circus, Suharevskaya, Sergievskiy Per, Sad-Spasskaya, Mayakovski Ploshchad, Tchaikovsky Concert Hall, Russian Cinema, Petrovskiy Boulevard, Trubnaya Pl, Rozhdestvenskiy Boulevard, U.Sretenka, Youth Theatre, Pushkinskaya, Tverskaya, Chekhovskaya, Petrovka, Neglinnaya, Ulitsa Rozhdestvenka, Convent of the Nativity of the Virgin, Turgenevskaya Pl, Chisty Prudy, Museum of the Revolution, Pushkin Ploshchad, Stoleshnikov, Perdolov, Bolshoi Theatre, Petrovskiy Passage, Varsonofevskiy Per, Kuznetskiy Most, Detskiy Theatre, Lubyanka, Gorky Theatre, Chekhov Theatre, Ermolovy Theatre, Teatralnaya, Theatre Square, TEATRALNIY PROJ., Ploshchad Lubyanskaya, Novaya Pl, Polytechnic Museum, Nogina, Gorky House Museum, Okhotnyy Ryad, Slavyanski Bazar, Moscow Conservatoire, GERSENA, University, Central Exhibition Hall, Revolution Square, Lenin Museum, Gum Shopping Arcade, Lenin Mausoleum, Manezhnaya Ploshchad, Historical Museum, Red Square, Council of Ministers, St Basil's Cathedral, ULITSA VARVARKA, Arbatskaya Ploshchad, VOZDVIZHENKA U., Museum of Russian Architecture, Alexandrovski Sad, Ivan Square, Presidium of the Supreme Soviet, Central Concert Hall, ULITSA ARBAT, Lenin State Library, Kremlin, Arsenal, Palace of Congress, Terem Palace, Cathedral Square, Armoury Palace, Kremlin Palace, Archangel Cathedral, Marx Engels Ulitsa, Borovitskaya Ploshchad, Pushkin Fine Arts Museum, Kremlevskaya Naberezhnaya, Moskvoretskiy Most, Ryleyev Ulitsa, Kropotkinskaya, Moscow Swimming Pool, Bolshoy Kamenni Most, Bolotnaya Nab, Vodootvodny, Sadovnicheskaya, Ovchinnikovskaya, Raushskaya Nab, Kadashevskaya Nab

COPYRIGHT GEORGE PHILIP LTD

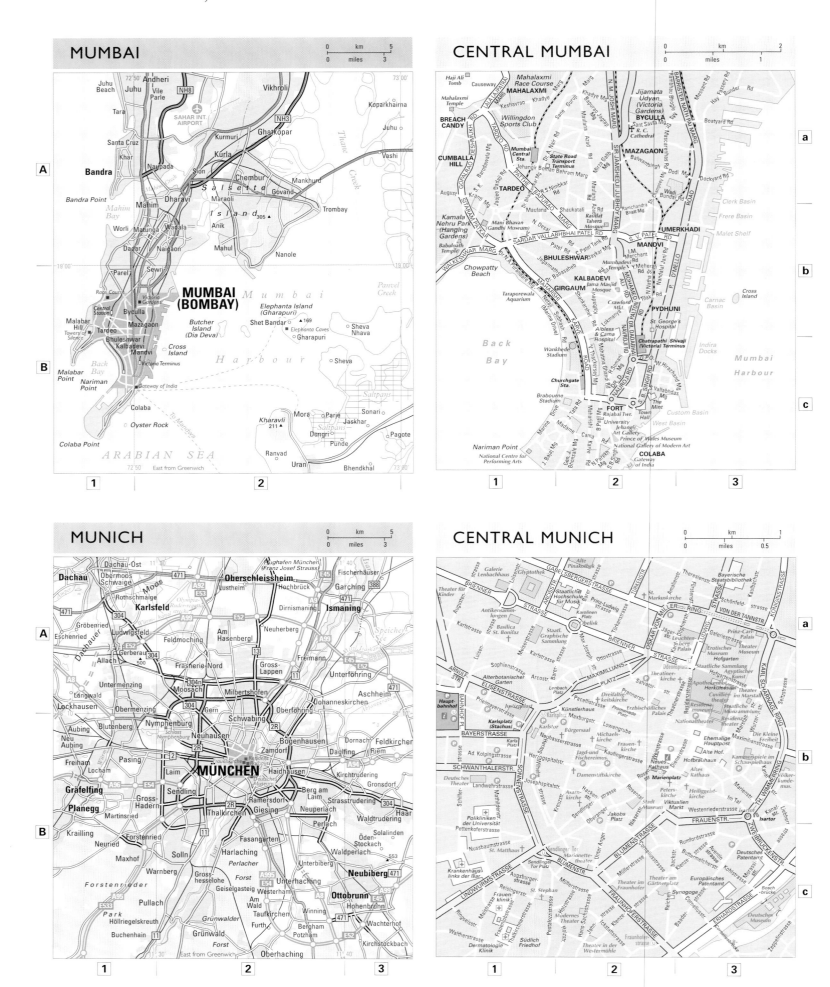

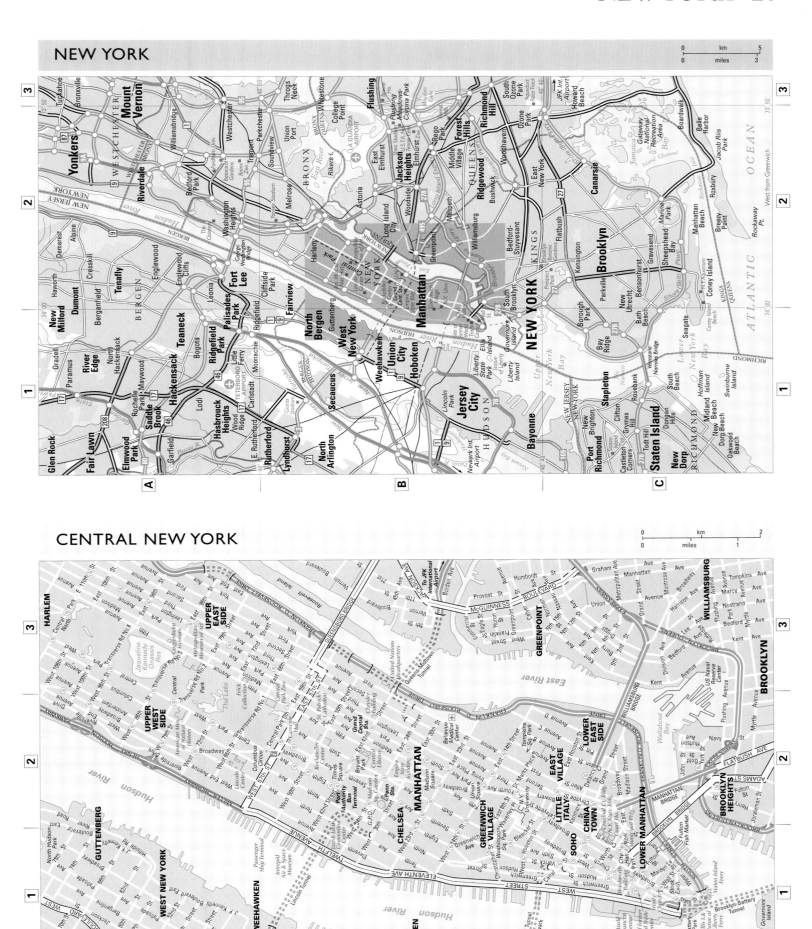

NEW YORK

km 5
miles 3

NEW JERSEY
NEW YORK

Tuckahoe · Bronxville · Williamsbridge
Yonkers · **WESTCHESTER** · **Mount Vernon**
Riverdale · Bedford Park · Westchester · Parkchester · Soundview · Throgs Neck · Whitestone · College Point · **Flushing** · Flushing Meadows-Corona Park
BRONX · East River · Rikers I. · **LA GUARDIA AIRPORT** · Union Port · Astoria · Long Island City · East Elmhurst · Jackson Heights · Woodside · Elmhurst · **Forest Hills** · **Richmond Hill** · Ozone Park · **JFK Int. Airport** · Howard Beach
Demarest · Alpine · Cresskill · Englewood · Englewood Cliffs · Leonia · Fort Lee · Cliffside Park · Fairview · Ridgefield · **North Bergen** · Guttenberg · **West New York** · Weehawken · **Union City** · **Hoboken** · **Manhattan** · Harlem · Central Park · **NEW YORK** · **Brooklyn** · Bedford-Stuyvesant · Bushwick · **Ridgewood** · East New York · **Canarsie** · Flatbush · Kensington · Parkville · Borough Park · New Utrecht · Bensonhurst · Gravesend · Sheepshead Bay · **Coney Island** · Manhattan Beach · Breezy Point · Rockaway Pt. · Jacob Riis Park · Belle Harbor
ATLANTIC OCEAN
New Milford · River Edge · Dumont · Tenafly · Teaneck · Hackensack · Ridgefield Park · Palisades Park · Secaucus · **Jersey City** · **Bayonne** · **Staten Island** · **Port Richmond** · **New Dorp** · Stapleton · Clifton · **RICHMOND**

A · B · C

CENTRAL NEW YORK

km 2
miles 1

HARLEM · **UPPER EAST SIDE** · **UPPER WEST SIDE** · **MANHATTAN** · **GREENPOINT** · **WILLIAMSBURG** · **BROOKLYN** · **Hudson River** · **East River** · **WEST NEW YORK** · **GUTTENBERG** · **WEEHAWKEN** · **UNION CITY** · **HOBOKEN** · **CHELSEA** · **GREENWICH VILLAGE** · **LITTLE ITALY** · **SOHO** · **CHINA TOWN** · **LOWER EAST SIDE** · **EAST VILLAGE** · **BROOKLYN HEIGHTS** · **LOWER MANHATTAN**
Central Park · The Lake · Jacqueline Kennedy Onassis Res.
Queensboro Bridge · Williamsburg Bridge · Manhattan Bridge · Brooklyn Bridge · Brooklyn-Battery Tunnel · Holland Tunnel · Lincoln Tunnel

a · b · c · d · e · f

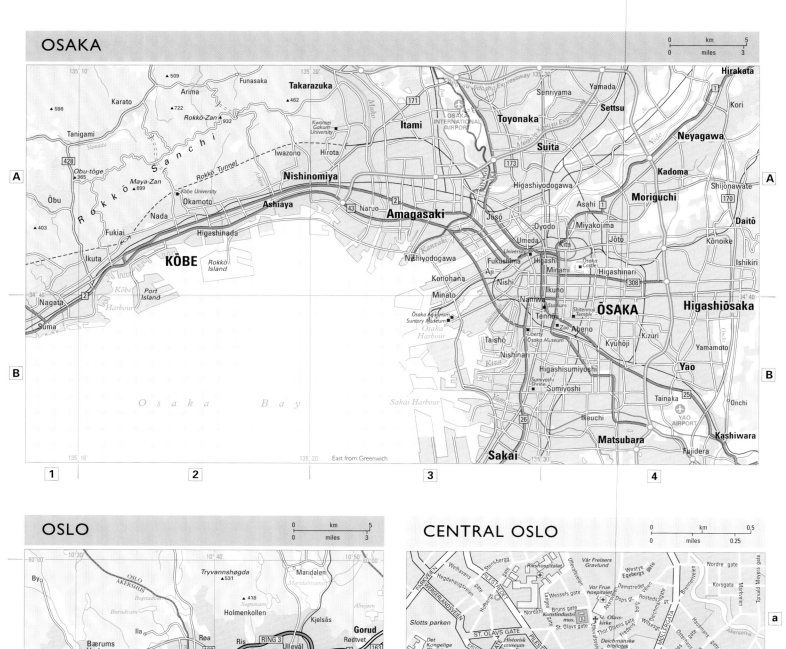

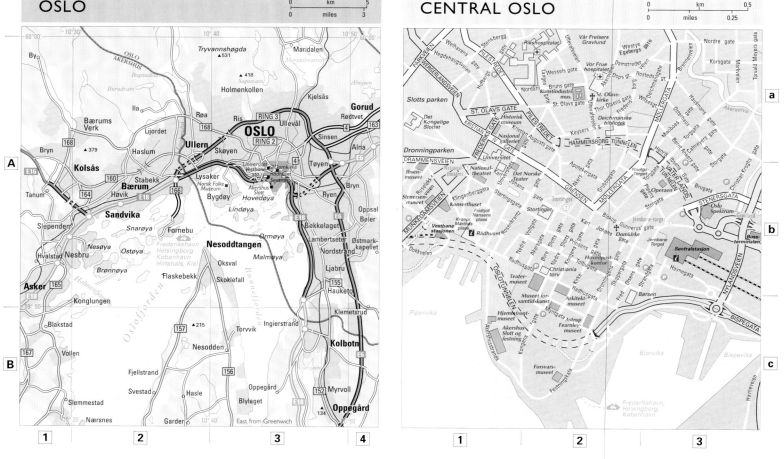

PARIS

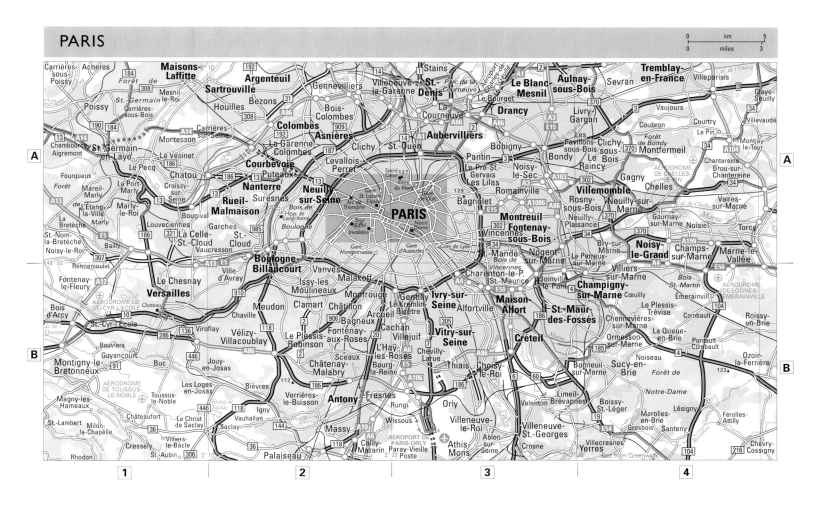

CENTRAL PARIS

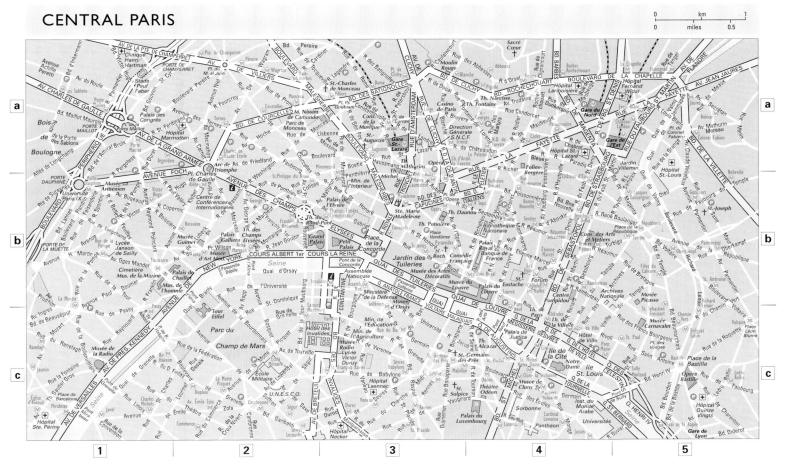

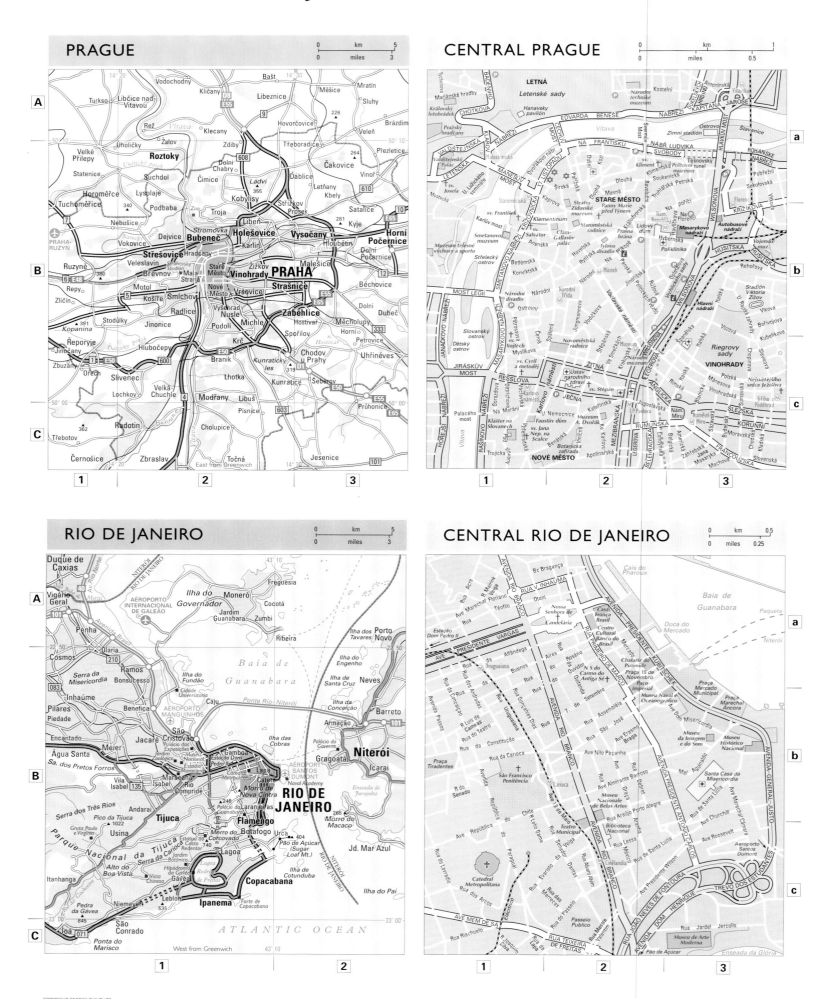

ROME

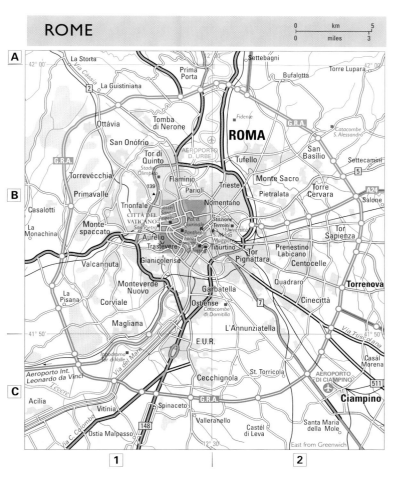

CENTRAL ROME

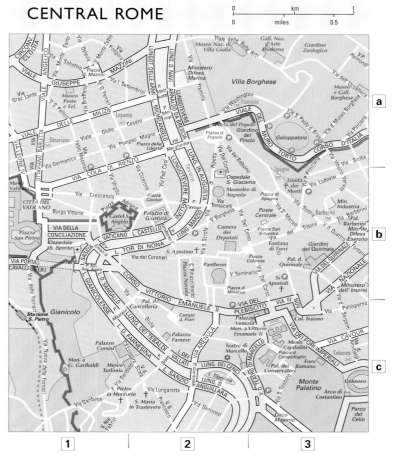

SAN FRANCISCO

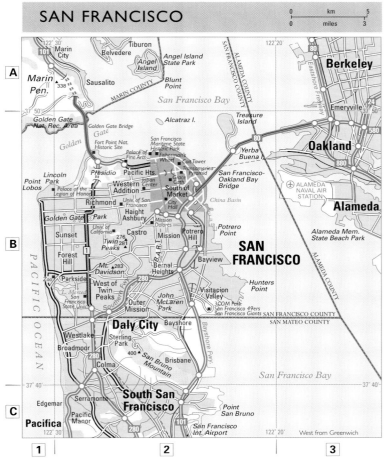

CENTRAL SAN FRANCISCO

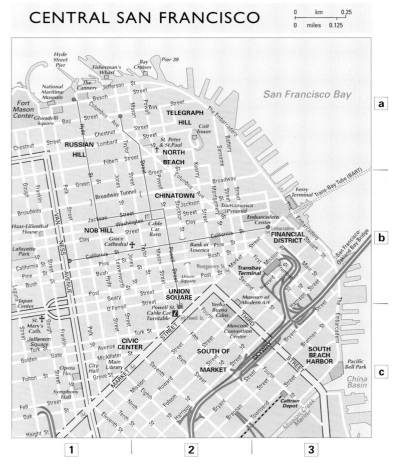

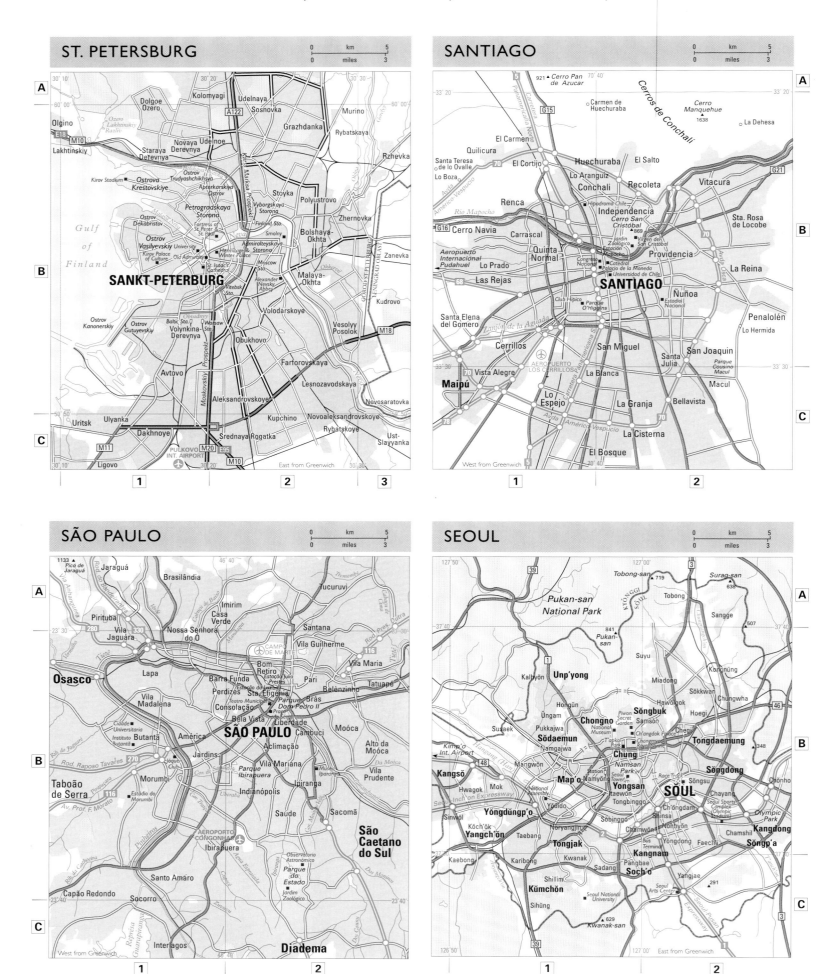

SHANGHAI

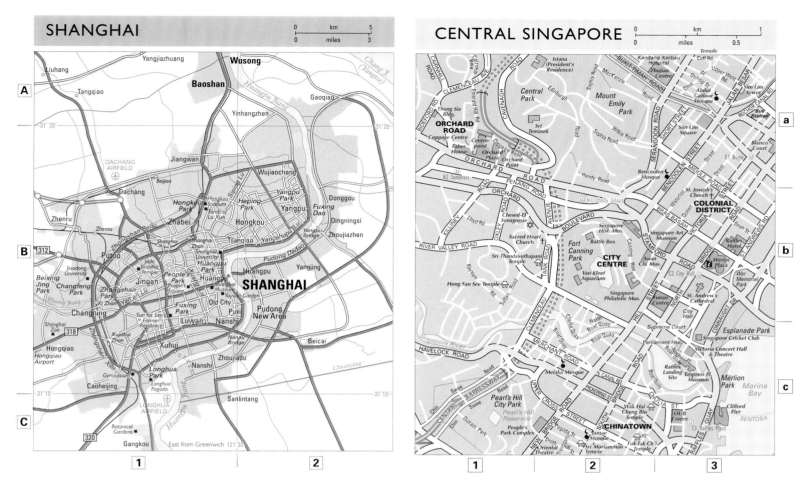

CENTRAL SINGAPORE

SINGAPORE

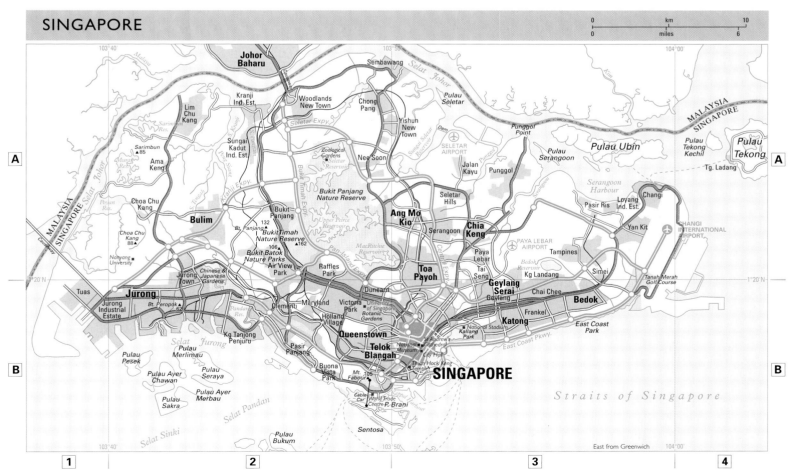

STOCKHOLM

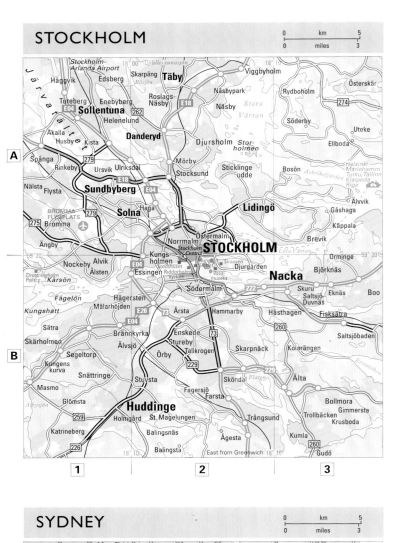

CENTRAL STOCKHOLM

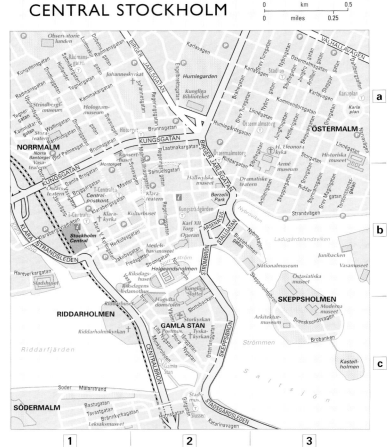

SYDNEY

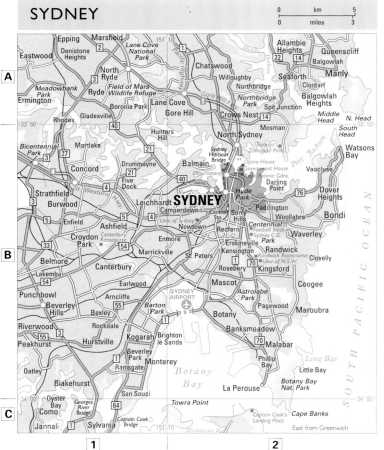

CENTRAL SYDNEY

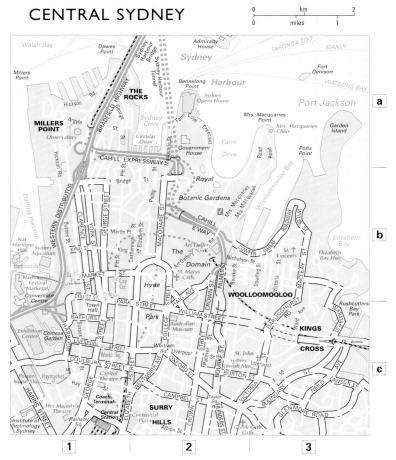

TOKYO

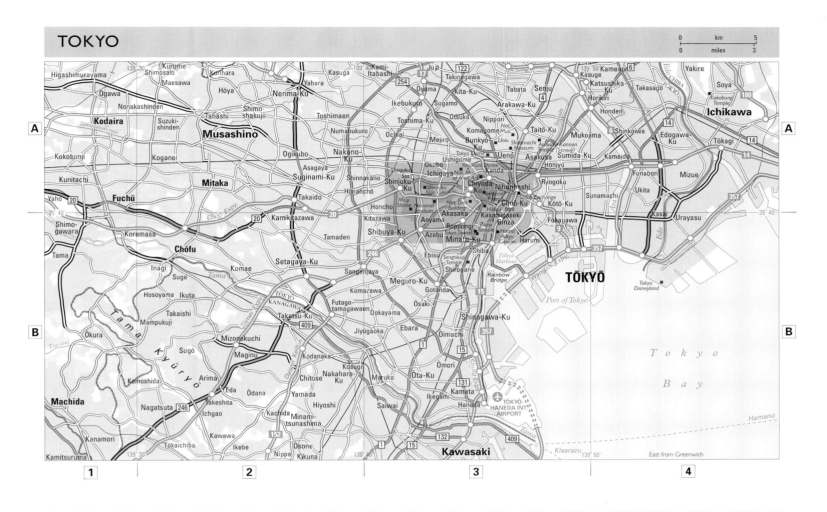

CENTRAL TOKYO

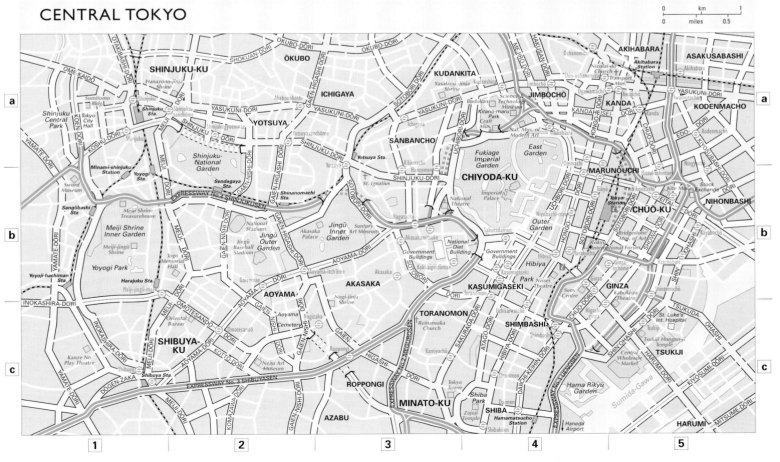

TEHRAN

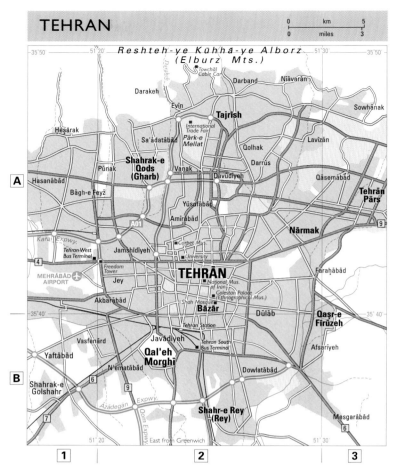

TIANJIN

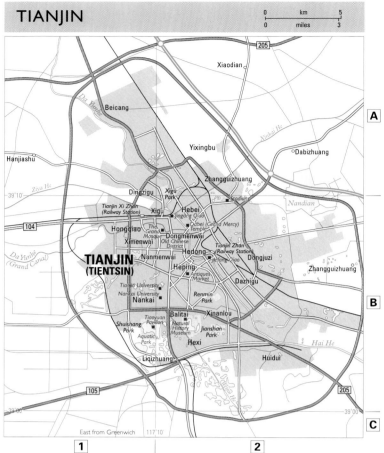

TORONTO

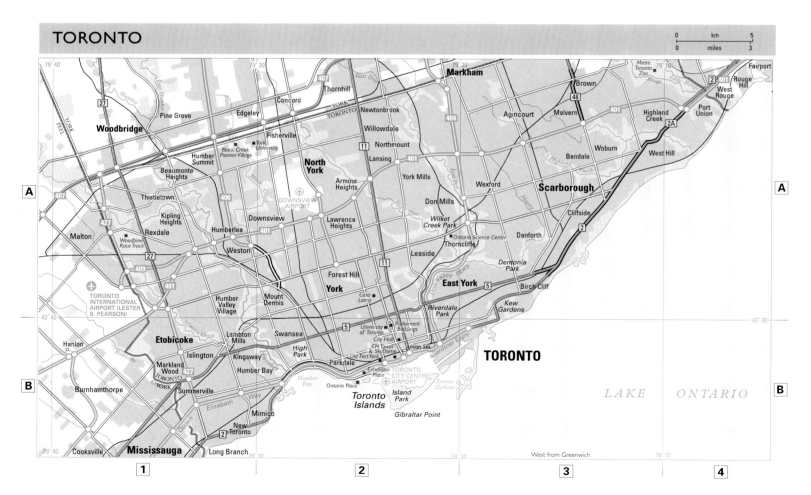

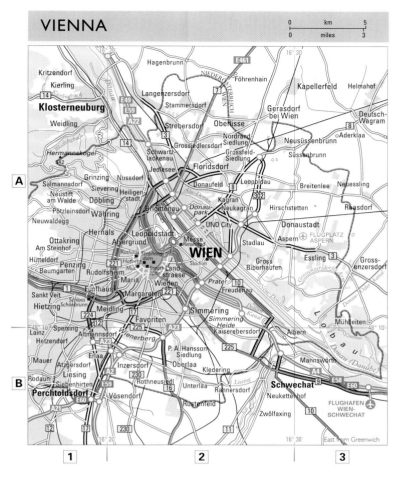

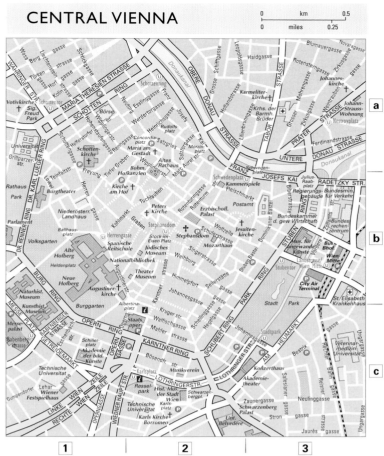

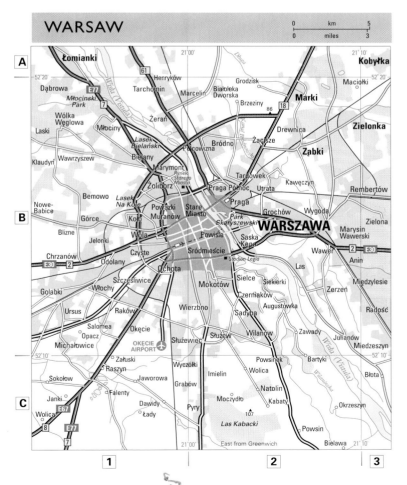

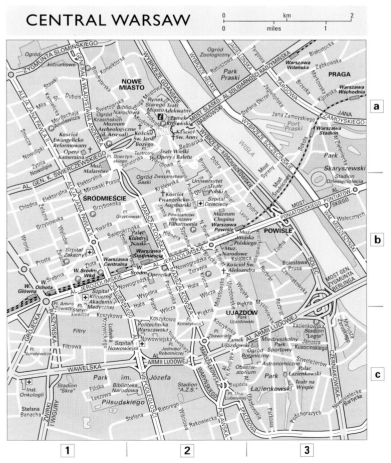

WASHINGTON

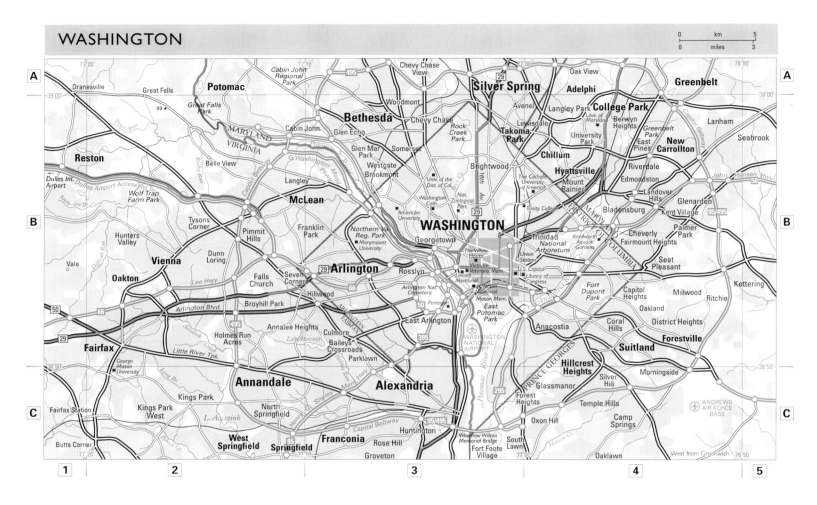

CENTRAL WASHINGTON

WELLINGTON

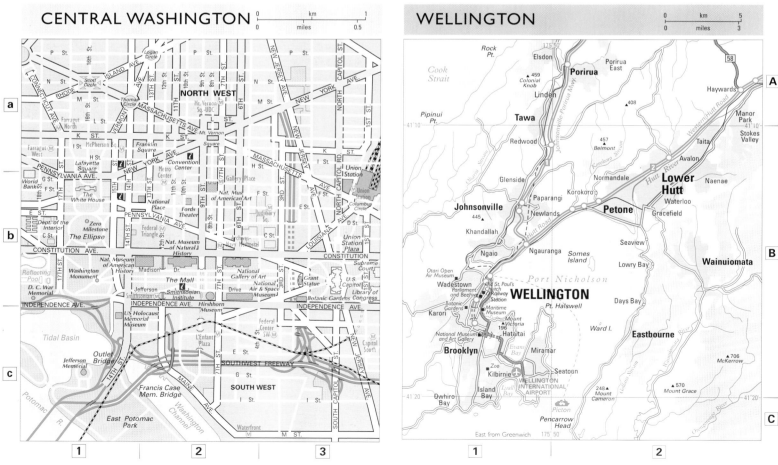

INDEX TO CITY MAPS

The index contains the names of all the principal places and features shown on the City Maps. Each name is followed by an additional entry in italics giving the name of the City Map within which it is located.

The number in bold type which follows each name refers to the number of the City Map page where that feature or place will be found.

The letter and figure which are immediately after the page number give the grid square on the map within which the feature or place is situated. The letter represents the latitude and the figure the longitude. Upper case letters refer to the City Maps, lower case letters to the Central Area Maps. The full geographic reference is provided in the border of the City Maps.

The location given is the centre of the city, suburb or feature and is not necessarily the name. Rivers, canals and roads are indexed to their name. Rivers carry the symbol → after their name.

An explanation of the alphabetical order rules and a list of the abbreviations used are to be found at the beginning of the World Map Index.

A

Aalām, *Baghdad* **3** B2
Aalsmeer, *Amsterdam* **2** B1
Abbey Wood, *London* **15** B4
Abcoude, *Amsterdam* **2** B2
Âbdin, *Cairo* **7** A2
Abeno, *Osaka* **22** B4
Aberdeen, *Hong Kong* **12** B2
Aberdour, *Edinburgh* **11** A2
Aberdour Castle, *Edinburgh* **11** A2
Abfanggraben →, *Munich* **20** A3
Ablon-sur-Seine, *Paris* **23** B3
Abord-à-Plouffe, *Montreal* **19** A1
Abramtsevo, *Moscow* **19** B4
Abu Dis, *Jerusalem* **13** B2
Abû en Numrus, *Cairo* **7** B2
Abu Ghosh, *Jerusalem* **13** B1
Acacias, *Madrid* **17** c2
Acassuso, *Buenos Aires* **7** A1
Accotink Cr. →, *Washington* **32** B2
Acheres, *Paris* **23** A1
Acília, *Rome* **25** C1
Aclimação, *São Paulo* **26** B2
Acton, *London* **15** A2
Açúcar, Pão de,
Rio de Janeiro **24** B2
Ada Beja, *Lisbon* **14** A1
Adams Park, *Atlanta* **3** B2
Adams Shore, *Boston* **6** B4
Addiscombe, *London* **15** B3
Adelphi, *Washington* **32** A4
Aderklaa, *Vienna* **31** A3
Admiralteyskaya Storona,
St. Petersburg **26** B2
Áffori, *Milan* **18** A2
Aflandshage, *Copenhagen* **10** B3
Afsarīyeh, *Tehran* **30** B2
Agboyi Cr. →, *Lagos* **14** A2
Ågerup, *Copenhagen* **10** A1
Ågesta, *Stockholm* **28** B2
Agincourt, *Toronto* **30** A3
Agora, Arhéa, *Athens* **2** c1
Agra Canal, *Delhi* **10** B2
Agricola Oriental,
Mexico City **18** B2
Agua Espraiada →,
São Paulo **26** B2
Agualva-Cacem, *Lisbon* **14** A1
Agustino, Cerro El, *Lima* **16** B2
Ahrensfelde, *Berlin* **5** A4
Ahuntsic, *Montreal* **19** A1
Ai →, *Osaka* **22** A4
Aigremont, *Paris* **23** A1
Air View Park, *Singapore* **27** A2
Airport West, *Melbourne* **17** A1
Aiyaleo, *Athens* **2** B2
Aiyáleos, Óros, *Athens* **2** B1
Ajegunle, *Lagos* **14** B2
Aji, *Osaka* **22** A3
Ajuda, *Lisbon* **14** A1
Akalla, *Stockholm* **28** A1
Akasaka, *Tokyo* **29** b3
Akbarābād, *Tehran* **30** A2
Akershus Slott, *Oslo* **22** A3
Akihabara, *Tokyo* **29** a5
Akrópolis, *Athens* **2** c2
Al 'Azamiyah, *Baghdad* **3** A2
Al Quds = Jerusalem,
Jerusalem **13** B2
Alaguntan, *Lagos* **14** B2
Alameda, *San Francisco* **25** B3
Alameda, Parque,
Mexico City **18** b2
Alameda Memorial State
Beach Park, *San Francisco* **25** B3
Albern, *Vienna* **31** B2
Albert Park, *Melbourne* **17** B1
Alberton, *Johannesburg* **13** B2
Albertslund, *Copenhagen* **10** B2
Albysjön, *Stockholm* **28** B1
Alcantara, *Lisbon* **14** A1
Alcatraz I., *San Francisco* **25** B2
Alcobendas, *Madrid* **17** A2
Alcorcón, *Madrid* **17** B1
Aldershof, *Berlin* **5** B4
Aldo Bonzi, *Buenos Aires* **7** C1
Aleksandrovskoye,
St. Petersburg **26** B2
Alexander Nevsky Abbey,
St. Petersburg **26** B2
Alexander Soutzos Moussío,
Athens **2** b3
Alexandra, *Johannesburg* **13** A2
Alexandra, *Singapore* **27** B2
Alexandria, *Washington* **32** C3
Alfama, *Lisbon* **14** c3
Alfortville, *Paris* **23** B3
Algés, *Lisbon* **14** A1
Alhambra, *Los Angeles* **16** B4
Alibey →, *Istanbul* **12** B1
Alibey Barajı, *Istanbul* **12** B1
Alibeyköy, *Istanbul* **12** B1
Alimos, *Athens* **2** B2
Alipur, *Calcutta* **8** B1
Allach, *Munich* **20** A1
Allambie Heights, *Sydney* **28** A2
Allard Pierson Museum,
Amsterdam **2** b2
Allermuir Hill, *Edinburgh* **11** B2
Allerton, Pt., *Boston* **6** B4
Allston, *Boston* **6** A3
Almada, *Lisbon* **14** A2
Almagro, *Buenos Aires* **7** B2
Almargem do Bispo, *Lisbon* **14** A1
Almazovo, *Moscow* **19** A6
Almirante G. Brown, Parque,
Buenos Aires **7** C2
Almon, *Jerusalem* **13** B2
Almond →, *Edinburgh* **11** B2
Alnabru, *Oslo* **22** A4
Alnsjøen, *Oslo* **22** A4
Alperton, *London* **15** A2
Alpine, *New York* **21** A2
Alrode, *Johannesburg* **13** B2
Alsemerg, *Brussels* **6** B1
Alsergrund, *Vienna* **31** A2
Alsip, *Chicago* **9** C2
Ålsten, *Stockholm* **28** B1
Älta, *Stockholm* **28** B3
Altadena, *Los Angeles* **16** A4
Alte-Donau →, *Vienna* **31** A2
Alte Hofburg, *Vienna* **31** b1
Alter Finkenkrug, *Berlin* **5** A1
Altes Rathaus, *Munich* **20** b3
Altglienicke, *Berlin* **5** B4
Altlandsberg, *Berlin* **5** A5
Altlandsberg Nord, *Berlin* **5** A5
Altmannsdorf, *Vienna* **31** B1
Alto da Moóca, *São Paulo* **26** B2
Alto do Pina, *Lisbon* **14** A2
Altona, *Melbourne* **17** B1
Alvaro Obregon, *Mexico City* **18** B1
Alvik, *Stockholm* **28** B1
Älvsjo, *Stockholm* **28** B2
Älvvik, *Stockholm* **28** A3
Am Hasenbergl, *Munich* **20** A2
Am Steinhof, *Vienna* **31** A1
Am Wald, *Munich* **20** B2
Ama Keng, *Singapore* **27** A2
Amadora, *Lisbon* **14** A1
Amagasaki, *Osaka* **22** A3
Amager, *Copenhagen* **10** B3
Amāl Qādisiya, *Baghdad* **3** B2
Amalienborg, *Copenhagen* **10** b3
Amata, *Milan* **18** A1
Ameixoeira, *Lisbon* **14** A2
América, *São Paulo* **26** B1
Amin, *Baghdad* **3** B2
Aminadov, *Jerusalem* **13** B1
Aminyevo, *Moscow* **19** B2
Amīrābād, *Tehran* **30** A2
Amora, *Lisbon* **14** B2
Amoreira, *Lisbon* **14** A1
Ampelokipi, *Athens* **2** B2
Amper →, *Munich* **20** A1
Amstel, *Amsterdam* **2** b2
Amstel →, *Amsterdam* **2** c2
Amstel-Drecht-Kanaal,
Amsterdam **2** B2
Amstel Station, *Amsterdam* **2** c3
Amstelhof, *Amsterdam* **2** b2
Amstelveen, *Amsterdam* **2** B2
Amsterdam, *Amsterdam* **2** A2
Amsterdam-Rijnkanaal,
Amsterdam **2** B3
Amsterdam Zoo, *Amsterdam* **2** b3
Amsterdam Zuidoost,
Amsterdam **2** B2
Amsterdamse Bos,
Amsterdam **2** B1
Anacostia, *Washington* **32** B4
Anadoluhisarı, *Istanbul* **12** B2
Anadolukavağı, *Istanbul* **12** A2
Anata, *Jerusalem* **13** B2
Ancol, *Jakarta* **13** A1
'Andalus, *Baghdad* **3** B1
Andarai, *Rio de Janeiro* **24** B1
Anderlecht, *Brussels* **6** A1
Anderson Park, *Atlanta* **3** B2
Andingmen, *Beijing* **4** B2
Andrews Air Force Base,
Washington **32** C4
Ang Mo Kio, *Singapore* **27** A3
Ängby, *Stockholm* **28** A1
Angel I., *San Francisco* **25** A2
Angel Island State Park,
San Francisco **25** A2
Angke, Kali →, *Jakarta* **13** A1
Angyalföld, *Budapest* **7** A2
Anik, *Mumbai* **20** A2
Anin, *Warsaw* **31** B2
Anjou, *Montreal* **19** A2
Annalee Heights, *Washington* **32** B2
Annandale, *Washington* **32** C2
Anne Frankhuis, *Amsterdam* **2** a1
Antony, *Paris* **23** B2
Anyangch'on, *Seoul* **26** C1
Aoyama, *Tokyo* **29** b2
Ap Lei Chau, *Hong Kong* **12** B1
Apapa, *Lagos* **14** B2
Apelacão, *Lisbon* **14** A2
Apterkarskiy Ostrov,
St. Petersburg **26** B2
Ar Kazimiyah, *Baghdad* **3** B1
Ara →, *Tokyo* **29** A4
Arakawa-Ku, *Tokyo* **29** A3
Arany-hegyi-patak →,
Budapest **7** A2
Aravaca, *Madrid* **17** B1
Arbataash, *Baghdad* **3** A1
Arc de Triomphe, *Paris* **23** a2
Arcadia, *Los Angeles* **16** B4
Arceuil, *Paris* **23** B2
Arco Plaza, *Los Angeles* **16** b1
Arese, *Milan* **18** A1
Arganzuela, *Madrid* **17** B1
Argenteuil, *Paris* **23** A2
Argonne Forest, *Chicago* **9** C1
Argüelles, *Madrid* **17** a1
Arima, *Osaka* **22** A2
Arima, *Tokyo* **29** B2
Ários Págos, *Athens* **2** c1
Arkhangelyskoye, *Moscow* **19** B1
Arlington, *Boston* **6** A2
Arlington, *Washington* **32** B3
Arlington Heights, *Boston* **6** A2
Arlington Nat. Cemetery,
Washington **32** B3
Armação, *Rio de Janeiro* **24** B2
Armadale, *Melbourne* **17** B2
Armenian Quarter, *Jerusalem* **13** b3
Armour Heights, *Toronto* **30** A2
Arncliffe, *Sydney* **28** B1
Arnold Arboretum, *Boston* **6** B3
Árpádföld, *Budapest* **7** A3
Arrentela, *Lisbon* **14** B2
Årsta, *Stockholm* **28** B2
Art Institute, *Chicago* **9** c2
Artane, *Dublin* **11** A2
Artas, *Jerusalem* **13** B2
Arthur's Seat, *Edinburgh* **11** B3
Aryiróupolis, *Athens* **2** B2
Asagaya, *Tokyo* **29** A2
Asahi, *Osaka* **22** A4
Asakusa, *Tokyo* **29** A3
Asakusabashi, *Tokyo* **29** a5
Asati, *Calcutta* **8** C1
Aschheim, *Munich* **20** A3
Ascot Vale, *Melbourne* **17** A1
Ashburn, *Chicago* **9** C2
Ashburton, *Melbourne* **17** B2
Ashfield, *Sydney* **28** B1
Ashford, *London* **15** B1
Ashiya, *Osaka* **22** A2
Ashiya →, *Osaka* **22** A2
Ashtown, *Dublin* **11** A2
Askisto, *Helsinki* **12** B1
Askrikefjärden, *Stockholm* **28** A3
Asnières, *Paris* **23** A2
Aspern, *Vienna* **31** A2
Aspern, Flugplatz, *Vienna* **31** A3
Assago, *Milan* **18** B1
Assemblée Nationale, *Paris* **23** b3
Assendelft, *Amsterdam* **2** A1
Assiano, *Milan* **18** B1
Astoria, *New York* **21** B2
Astrolabe Park, *Sydney* **28** B2
Atarot Airport, *Jerusalem* **13** A2
Atghara, *Calcutta* **8** B2
Athens = Athínai, *Athens* **2** B2
Athínai, *Athens* **2** B2
Athinai-Ellinikón Airport,
Athens **2** B2
Athis-Mons, *Paris* **23** B3
Athlone, *Cape Town* **8** A2
Atholl, *Johannesburg* **13** A2
Atīfīya, *Baghdad* **3** A2
Atişalen, *Istanbul* **12** B1
Atlanta, *Atlanta* **3** B2
Atlanta History Center,
Atlanta **3** B2
Atomium, *Brussels* **6** A2
Attiki, *Athens* **2** A2
Atzgersdorf, *Vienna* **31** B1
Aubervilliers, *Paris* **23** A3
Aubing, *Munich* **20** B1
Auburndale, *Boston* **6** A2
Aucherdinny, *Edinburgh* **11** B2
Auckland Park, *Johannesburg* **13** B2
Auderghem, *Brussels* **6** B2
Augusta, Mausoleo di, *Rome* **25** b2
Augustówka, *Warsaw* **31** B2
Aulnay-sous-Bois, *Paris* **23** A3
Aurelio, *Rome* **25** B1
Ausîm, *Cairo* **7** A1
Austerlitz, Gare d', *Paris* **23** A3
Austin, *Chicago* **9** B2
Avalon, *Wellington* **32** B2
Avedøre, *Copenhagen* **10** B2
Avellaneda, *Buenos Aires* **7** C2
Avenel, *Washington* **32** B4
Avondale, *Chicago* **9** B2
Avondale Heights, *Melbourne* **17** A1
Avtovo, *St. Petersburg* **26** B1
Ayazağa, *Istanbul* **12** B1
Ayer Chawan, P., *Singapore* **27** B2
Ayer Merbau, P., *Singapore* **27** B2
Ayía Marina, *Athens* **2** C3
Ayía Paraskevi, *Athens* **2** A2
Áyios Dhimitrios, *Athens* **2** B2
Áyios Ioánnis Rendis, *Athens* **2** B1
Azabu, *Tokyo* **29** c3
Azcapotzalco, *Mexico City* **18** B1
Azteca, Estadia, *Mexico City* **18** C2
Azucar, Cerro Pan de,
Santiago **26** A1

B

Baambrugge, *Amsterdam* **2** B2
Baba I., *Karachi* **14** B1
Babarpur, *Delhi* **10** A2
Babushkin, *Moscow* **19** A4
Back B., *Mumbai* **20** B1
Baclaran, *Manila* **17** B2
Bacoor, *Manila* **17** C1
Bacoor B., *Manila* **17** C1
Badalona, *Barcelona* **4** A2
Badhoevedorp, *Amsterdam* **2** A1
Badli, *Delhi* **10** A1
Bærum, *Oslo* **22** A2
Bağcılar, *Istanbul* **12** B1
Bággio, *Milan* **18** B1
Bāgh-e-Feyz, *Tehran* **30** A1
Baghdād, *Baghdad* **3** A2
Bagmari, *Calcutta* **8** B2
Bagneux, *Paris* **23** B2
Bagnolet, *Paris* **23** A3
Bagsværd, *Copenhagen* **10** A2
Bagsværd Sø, *Copenhagen* **10** A2
Baguiati, *Calcutta* **8** B2
Bagumbayan, *Manila* **17** C2
Bahçeköy, *Istanbul* **12** A1
Bahtîm, *Cairo* **7** A2
Baileys Crossroads,
Washington **32** B3
Bailly, *Paris* **23** A1
Bairro Alto, *Lisbon* **14** c1
Bairro Lopes, *Lisbon* **14** b3
Baisha, *Canton* **8** B2
Baisha →, *Canton* **8** B2
Baixa, *Lisbon* **14** c2
Baiyun Airport, *Canton* **8** A2
Baiyun Hill Scenic Spot,
Canton **8** B2
Bakırköy, *Istanbul* **12** C1
Bakovka, *Moscow* **19** B2
Bal Harbor, *Miami* **18** A2
Balara, *Manila* **17** B2
Balashikha, *Moscow* **19** B5
Baldia, *Karachi* **14** A1
Baldoyle, *Dublin* **11** A3
Baldwin Hills, *Los Angeles* **16** B2
Baldwin Hills Res.,
Los Angeles **16** B2
Balgowlah, *Sydney* **28** A2
Balgowlah Heights, *Sydney* **28** A2
Balham, *London* **15** B3
Bali, *Calcutta* **8** B1
Baliganja, *Calcutta* **8** B2
Balingsnäs, *Stockholm* **28** B2
Balingsta, *Stockholm* **28** B2
Balintawak, *Manila* **17** B1
Balitai, *Tianjin* **30** B2
Ballerup, *Copenhagen* **10** A2
Ballinteer, *Dublin* **11** B2
Ballyboden, *Dublin* **11** B2
Ballybrack, *Dublin* **11** B3
Ballyfermot, *Dublin* **11** A1
Ballymorefinn Hill, *Dublin* **11** B1
Ballymun, *Dublin* **11** A2
Balmain, *Sydney* **28** B2
Baluhati, *Calcutta* **8** B1
Balvanera, *Buenos Aires* **7** B2
Balwyn, *Melbourne* **17** A2
Balwyn North, *Melbourne* **17** A2
Banática, *Lisbon* **14** A1
Banco do Brasil, Centro
Cultural, *Rio de Janeiro* **24** a2
Bandra, *Mumbai* **20** A1
Bandra Pt., *Mumbai* **20** A1
Bang Kapi, *Bangkok* **3** B2
Bang Kholaem, *Bangkok* **3** A2
Bang Na, *Bangkok* **3** B2
Bang Phlad, *Bangkok* **3** a1
Bangkhen, *Bangkok* **3** A2
Bangkok = Krung Thep,
Bangkok **3** B2
Bangkok Noi, *Bangkok* **3** B1
Bangkok Yai, *Bangkok* **3** B1
Banglamphoo, *Bangkok* **3** b2
Banglo, *Calcutta* **8** B1
Bangrak, *Bangkok* **3** B2
Bangsu, *Bangkok* **3** B2
Bank, *London* **15** b5
Bank of America,
San Francisco **25** b2
Bank of China Tower,
Hong Kong **12** c1
Banks, C., *Sydney* **28** C2
Banksmeadow, *Sydney* **28** B2
Banstala, *Calcutta* **8** B2
Bantra, *Calcutta* **8** B1
Baoshan, *Shanghai* **27** A1
Bar Giyora, *Jerusalem* **13** B1
Barahanagar, *Calcutta* **8** B2
Barajas, *Madrid* **17** B2
Barajas, Aeropuerto
Transoceanico de, *Madrid* **17** B2
Barakpur, *Calcutta* **8** A2
Barberini, Palazzo, *Rome* **25** b3
Barbican, *London* **15** a4
Barcarena, *Lisbon* **14** A1
Barcarena, Rib. de →, *Lisbon* **14** A1
Barcelona, *Barcelona* **4** A2
Barcelona-Prat, Aeropuerta
de, *Barcelona* **4** B1
Barceloneta, *Barcelona* **4** A2
Barking, *London* **15** A4
Barkingside, *London* **15** A4
Barnes, *London* **15** B2
Barnet, *London* **15** A2
Barra Andai, *Karachi* **14** B2
Barra Funda, *São Paulo* **26** B2
Barracas, *Buenos Aires* **7** B2
Barranco, *Lima* **16** B2
Barreiro, *Lisbon* **14** B2
Barreto, *Rio de Janeiro* **24** B2
Bartala, *Calcutta* **8** B1
Barton Park, *Sydney* **28** B1
Bartyki, *Warsaw* **31** C2
Barvikha, *Moscow* **19** B1
Bastille, Place de la, *Paris* **23** c5
Basus, *Cairo* **7** A2
Batanagar, *Calcutta* **8** B1
Bath Beach, *New York* **21** C1
Bath I., *Karachi* **14** B2
Batir, *Jerusalem* **13** B1
Batok, Bukit, *Singapore* **27** A2
Battersea, *London* **15** B3
Battery Park, *New York* **21** f1
Bauman, *Moscow* **19** B4
Baumgarten, *Vienna* **31** A1
Bay Harbour Islands, *Miami* **18** A2
Bay Ridge, *New York* **21** C1
Bayonne, *New York* **21** B1
Bayshore, *San Francisco* **25** B3
Bayswater, *London* **15** b2
Bayt Lahm = Bethlehem,
Jerusalem **13** B2
Bayview, *San Francisco* **25** B2
Bāzār, *Tehran* **30** A2
Beachmont, *Boston* **6** A4
Beacon Hill, *Hong Kong* **12** A2
Beato, *Lisbon* **14** A2
Beaumont, *Dublin* **11** A2
Beaumonte Heights, *Toronto* **30** A1
Bebek, *Istanbul* **12** B2
Běchovice, *Prague* **24** B3
Beck L., *Chicago* **9** A1
Beckenham, *London* **15** B3
Beckton, *London* **15** A4
Becontree, *London* **15** A4
Beddington Corner, *London* **15** B3
Bedford, *Boston* **6** A2
Bedford Park, *Chicago* **9** C2
Bedford Park, *New York* **21** A2
Bedford Stuyvesant,
New York **21** B2
Bedford View, *Johannesburg* **13** B2
Bedok, *Singapore* **27** B3
Bedok, Res., *Singapore* **27** A3
Beersel, *Brussels* **6** B1
Behala, *Calcutta* **8** B1
Bei Hai, *Beijing* **4** B2
Beicai, *Shanghai* **27** B2
Beicang, *Tianjin* **30** A1
Beihai Park, *Beijing* **4** b2
Beijing, *Beijing* **4** B1
Beit Ghur el-Fawqa,
Jerusalem **13** A1
Beit Hanina, *Jerusalem* **13** B2
Beit Iksa, *Jerusalem* **13** B2
Beit I'nan, *Jerusalem* **13** A1
Beit Jala, *Jerusalem* **13** B2
Beit Lekhem = Bethlehem,
Jerusalem **13** B2
Beit Nekofa, *Jerusalem* **13** B1
Beit Sahur, *Jerusalem* **13** B2
Beit Surik, *Jerusalem* **13** B1
Beit Zayit, *Jerusalem* **13** B1
Beitaipingzhuan, *Beijing* **4** B1
Beitar Ilit, *Jerusalem* **13** B1
Beitsun, *Canton* **8** B2
Beitunya, *Jerusalem* **13** A2
Beixing Jing Park, *Shanghai* **27** B1
Békásmegyer, *Budapest* **7** A2
Bekkelaget, *Oslo* **22** A3
Bel Air, *Los Angeles* **16** B2
Bela Vista, *São Paulo* **26** B2
Bélanger, *Montreal* **19** A1
Belas, *Lisbon* **14** A1
Belas Artes, Museu Nacionale
de, *Rio de Janeiro* **24** b2
Beleghata, *Calcutta* **8** B2
Belém, *Lisbon* **14** A1
Belém, Torre de, *Lisbon* **14** A1
Belènzinho, *São Paulo* **26** B2
Belgachiya, *Calcutta* **8** B2
Belgharia, *Calcutta* **8** B2
Belgrano, *Buenos Aires* **7** B2
Belgravia, *London* **15** c3
Bell, *Los Angeles* **16** C3
Bell Gardens, *Los Angeles* **16** C4
Bell Tower, *Beijing* **4** a2
Bellavista, *Lima* **16** B2
Bellavista, *Santiago* **26** C2
Belle Harbor, *New York* **21** C2
Belle View, *Washington* **32** B2
Bellevue, Schloss, *Berlin* **5** a2
Bellingham, *London* **15** B3
Bellwood, *Chicago* **9** B1
Belmont, *Boston* **6** A2
Belmont, *London* **15** A2
Belmont, *Wellington* **32** B2
Belmont Harbor, *Chicago* **9** B3
Belmore, *Sydney* **28** B1
Belur, *Calcutta* **8** B2
Belvedere, *Atlanta* **3** B3
Belvedere, *London* **15** B4
Belvedere, *San Francisco* **25** A2
Belyayevo Bogorodskoye,
Moscow **19** C3
Bemowo, *Warsaw* **31** B1
Benaki, Moussío, *Athens* **2** b3
Bendale, *Toronto* **30** A3
Bendkhal, *Mumbai* **20** B2
Benefica, *Rio de Janeiro* **24** B1
Benfica, *Lisbon* **14** A1
Benito Juárez, *Mexico City* **18** B2
Benito Juárez, Aeropuerto
Int., *Mexico City* **18** B2
Bensonhurst, *New York* **21** C2
Berchem-Sainte-Agathe,
Brussels **6** A1
Berg am Laim, *Munich* **20** B2
Bergenfield, *New York* **21** A2
Bergham, *Munich* **20** B2
Bergvliet, *Cape Town* **8** B1
Beri, *Barcelona* **4** A1
Berkeley, *San Francisco* **25** A3
Berlin, *Berlin* **5** A3
Bermondsey, *London* **15** B3
Bernabeu, Estadio, *Madrid* **17** B1
Bernal Heights, *San Francisco* **25** B2
Berwyn, *Chicago* **9** B2
Berwyn Heights, *Washington* **32** B4
Besiktas, *Istanbul* **12** B2
Besós →, *Barcelona* **4** A2
Bethesda, *Washington* **32** B3
Bethlehem, *Jerusalem* **13** B2
Bethnal Green, *London* **15** A3
Betor, *Calcutta* **8** B1
Beurs, *Amsterdam* **2** b2
Beverley Hills, *Sydney* **28** B1
Beverley Park, *Sydney* **28** B1
Beverly, *Chicago* **9** C3
Beverly Glen, *Los Angeles* **16** B2
Beverly Hills, *Los Angeles* **16** B2
Bexley, *London* **15** B4
Bexley, *Sydney* **28** B1
Bexleyheath, *London* **15** B4
Beykoz, *Istanbul* **12** B2
Beylerbeyi, *Istanbul* **12** B2
Beyoğlu, *Istanbul* **12** B1
Bezons, *Paris* **23** A2
Bezuidenhout Park,
Johannesburg **13** B2
Bhadrakali, *Calcutta* **8** A2
Bhalswa, *Delhi* **10** A2
Bhambo Khan Qarmati,
Karachi **14** B2
Bhatsala, *Calcutta* **8** B1
Bhawanipur, *Calcutta* **8** B2
Bhuleshwar, *Mumbai* **20** b2
Białołeka Dworska, *Warsaw* **31** B2
Biblioteca Nacional,
Rio de Janeiro **24** c2
Bicentennial Park, *Sydney* **28** B1
Bickley, *London* **15** B4
Bidu, *Jerusalem* **13** B1
Bielany, *Warsaw* **31** B1
Bielawa, *Warsaw* **31** C2
Biesdorf, *Berlin* **5** A4
Bièvre →, *Paris* **23** B1
Bièvres, *Paris* **23** B2
Bilston, *Edinburgh* **11** B2
Binacayan, *Manila* **17** C1
Binondo, *Manila* **17** B1
Birak el Kiyam, *Cairo* **7** A1
Birch Cliff, *Toronto* **30** A3
Birkenstein, *Berlin* **5** A5
Birkholz, *Berlin* **5** A4
Birkholzaue, *Berlin* **5** A4
Birrarrung Park, *Melbourne* **17** A2
Biscayne Bay, *Miami* **18** B2
Biscayne Park, *Miami* **18** A2
Bishop Lavis, *Cape Town* **8** A2
Bishopscourt, *Cape Town* **8** A1
Bispebjerg, *Copenhagen* **10** A3
Biwon Secret Garden, *Seoul* **26** B1
Björknas, *Stockholm* **28** B3
Black Cr. →, *Toronto* **30** A2
Blackfen, *London* **15** B4
Blackheath, *London* **15** B4
Blackrock, *Dublin* **11** B2
Bladensburg, *Washington* **32** B4
Blair Village, *Atlanta* **3** C2
Blairgowrie, *Johannesburg* **13** A2
Blakehurst, *Sydney* **28** B1
Blakstad, *Oslo* **22** B1
Blankenburg, *Berlin* **5** A3
Blankenfelde, *Berlin* **5** A3
Blizne, *Warsaw* **31** B1
Bloomsbury, *London* **15** a3
Błota, *Warsaw* **31** C3
Blue Island, *Chicago* **9** C2
Bluebell, *Dublin* **11** B1
Bluff Hd., *Hong Kong* **12** B2
Blumberg, *Berlin* **5** A4
Blunt Pt., *San Francisco* **25** A2
Blutenberg, *Munich* **20** B1
Blylaget, *Oslo* **22** B3
Bo-Kaap Museum,
Cape Town **8** c2
Boa Vista, Alto do,
Rio de Janeiro **24** B1
Boardwalk, *New York* **21** C3
Boavista, *Lisbon* **14** A2
Bobigny, *Paris* **23** A3
Bocanegra, *Lima* **16** A2
Boedo, *Buenos Aires* **7** B2
Bogenhausen, *Munich* **20** B2
Bogorodskoye, *Moscow* **19** B4
Bogota, *New York* **21** A1
Bogstadvatnet, *Oslo* **22** A2
Bohnsdorf, *Berlin* **5** B4
Bois-Colombes, *Paris* **23** A2
Bois-d'Arcy, *Paris* **23** B1
Boissy-St.-Léger, *Paris* **23** B4
Boldinasco, *Milan* **18** B1
Bøler, *Oslo* **22** A4
Bollate, *Milan* **18** A1
Bollebeek, *Brussels* **6** A1
Bollensdorf, *Berlin* **5** A5
Bollmora, *Stockholm* **28** B3
Bolshaya-Okhta,
St. Petersburg **26** B2
Bolton, *Atlanta* **3** B2
Bom Retiro, *São Paulo* **26** B2
Bombay = Mumbai, *Mumbai* **20** B2
Bondi, *Sydney* **28** B2
Bondy, *Paris* **23** A3
Bondy, Forêt de, *Paris* **23** A4
Bonifacio Monument, *Manila* **17** B1
Bonneuil-sur-Marne, *Paris* **23** B4
Bonnington, *Edinburgh* **11** B1
Bonnyrig and Lasswade,
Edinburgh **11** B3
Bonsucesso, *Rio de Janeiro* **24** B1
Bonteheuwel, *Cape Town* **8** A2
Boo, *Stockholm* **28** A3
Booterstown, *Dublin* **11** B2
Borisovo, *Moscow* **19** C4
Borle, *Mumbai* **20** A2
Boronia Park, *Sydney* **28** A1
Borough Park, *New York* **21** C2
Bosmont, *Johannesburg* **13** B1
Bosön, *Stockholm* **28** A3
Bosporus = Istanbul Boğazi,
Istanbul **12** B2
Bostancı, *Istanbul* **12** C2
Boston Harbor, *Boston* **6** A4
Botafogo, *Rio de Janeiro* **24** B1
Botanisk Have, *Copenhagen* **10** b2
Botany, *Sydney* **28** B2
Botany B., *Sydney* **28** B2
Botany Bay Nat. Park, *Sydney* **28** B2
Botič →, *Prague* **24** B3
Botica Sete, *Lisbon* **14** A1
Boucherville, *Montreal* **19** A3
Boucherville, Îs. de, *Montreal* **19** A3
Bougival, *Paris* **23** A1
Boulder Pt., *Hong Kong* **12** B1
Boulogne, Bois de, *Paris* **23** A2
Boulogne-Billancourt, *Paris* **23** A2
Bourg-la-Reine, *Paris* **23** B2
Bouviers, *Paris* **23** B1
Bovenkerk, *Amsterdam* **2** B2
Bovenkerker Polder,
Amsterdam **2** B2
Bovisa, *Milan* **18** A2
Bow, *London* **15** A3
Bowery, *New York* **21** e2
Boyacıköy, *Istanbul* **12** B2
Boyle Heights, *Los Angeles* **16** B3
Bradbury Building,
Los Angeles **16** b2
Braepark, *Edinburgh* **11** B2
Braid, *Edinburgh* **11** B2
Bramley, *Johannesburg* **13** A2
Brandenburger Tor, *Berlin* **5** A3
Brani, P., *Singapore* **27** B3
Branik, *Prague* **24** B2
Brännkyrka, *Stockholm* **28** B2
Brás, *São Paulo* **26** B2
Brasilândia, *São Paulo* **26** A1
Brateyevo, *Moscow* **19** C4
Bratsevo, *Moscow* **19** A2
Bray, *Dublin* **11** B3
Braybrook, *Melbourne* **17** A1
Brázdim, *Prague* **24** A3
Breach Candy, *Mumbai* **20** a1
Breakheart Reservation,
Boston **6** A3
Brede, *Copenhagen* **10** A3
Breeds Pond, *Boston* **6** A4
Breezy Point, *New York* **21** C2
Breitenlee, *Vienna* **31** A3
Breña, *Lima* **16** B2
Brent, *London* **15** A2
Brent Res., *London* **15** A2
Brentford, *London* **15** B2
Brentwood Park, *Los Angeles* **16** B2
Brera, *Milan* **18** B2
Bresso, *Milan* **18** A2
Brevik, *Stockholm* **28** A3
Břevnov, *Prague* **24** B2
Bridgeport, *Chicago* **9** B3
Bridgetown, *Cape Town* **8** A2
Bridgeview, *Chicago* **9** C2
Brighton, *Boston* **6** A3
Brighton, *Melbourne* **17** B1
Brighton le Sands, *Sydney* **28** B1
Brighton Park, *Chicago* **9** C2
Brightwood, *Washington* **32** B3
Brigittenau, *Vienna* **31** A2
Brimbank Park, *Melbourne* **17** A1
Brisbane, *San Francisco* **25** B2
British Museum, *London* **15** a3
Britz, *Berlin* **5** B3
Brixton, *London* **15** B3
Broad Sd., *Boston* **6** A4
Broadmeadows, *Melbourne* **17** A1
Broadmoor, *San Francisco* **25** B2
Broadview, *Chicago* **9** B1
Broadway, *New York* **21** e1
Brockley, *London* **15** B3
Bródno, *Warsaw* **31** B2
Bródnowski, Kanal, *Warsaw* **31** B2
Broek in Waterland,
Amsterdam **2** A2
Bromley, *London* **15** B4
Bromley Common, *London* **15** B4
Bromma, *Stockholm* **28** A1
Bromma flygplats, *Stockholm* **28** A1
Brompton, *London* **15** c2
Brøndby Strand, *Copenhagen* **10** B2
Brøndbyøster, *Copenhagen* **10** B2
Brøndbyvester, *Copenhagen* **10** B2
Brondesbury, *London* **15** A2
Brønnøya, *Oslo* **22** A2
Brønshøj, *Copenhagen* **10** A2

BRONXVILLE

Bronxville, *New York* 21 A3
Brookfield, *Chicago* 9 C1
Brookhaven, *Atlanta* 3 A2
Brookline, *Boston* 6 B3
Brooklyn, *Cape Town* 8 A1
Brooklyn, *New York* 21 C2
Brooklyn, *Wellington* 32 B1
Brooklyn Bridge, *New York* 21 f2
Brookmont, *Washington* 32 B3
Brossard, *Montreal* 19 B3
Brou-sur-Chantereine, *Paris* 23 A4
Brown, *Toronto* 30 A3
Broyhill Park, *Washington* 32 B2
Brughério, *Milan* 18 A2
Brunswick, *Melbourne* 17 A1
Brush Hill, *Boston* 6 B1
Brussegem, *Brussels* 6 A1
Brussel Nat. Luchthaven, *Brussels* 6 A2
Brussels = Bruxelles, *Brussels* 6 A2
Bruxelles, *Brussels* 6 A2
Bruzzano, *Milan* 18 A2
Bry-sur-Marne, *Paris* 23 A4
Bryanston, *Johannesburg* 13 A1
Bryn, *Oslo* 22 A1
Brzeziny, *Warsaw* 31 B2
Bubeneč, *Prague* 24 B2
Buc, *Paris* 23 B1
Buchenhain, *Munich* 20 B1
Buchholz, *Berlin* 5 A3
Buckhead, *Atlanta* 3 A2
Buckingham Palace, *London* 15 b3
Buckow, *Berlin* 5 B3
Buda, *Budapest* 7 A2
Budafok, *Budapest* 7 B2
Budaörs, *Budapest* 7 B1
Budapest, *Budapest* 7 B2
Budatétény, *Budapest* 7 B2
Budavaripalota, *Budapest* 7 b2
Buddinge, *Copenhagen* 10 A3
Budokan, *Tokyo* 29 a4
Buena Vista, *San Francisco* 25 B2
Buenos Aires, *Buenos Aires* 7 B2
Bufalotta, *Rome* 25 B2
Bugio, *Lisbon* 14 B1
Buiksloot, *Amsterdam* 2 A2
Buitenveldert, *Amsterdam* 2 B2
Buizingen, *Brussels* 6 B1
Bukit Panjang Nature Reserve, *Singapore* 27 A2
Bukit Timah Nature Reserve, *Singapore* 27 A2
Bukum, P., *Singapore* 27 B2
Bûlâq, *Cairo* 7 A2
Bule, *Manila* 17 C2
Bulim, *Singapore* 27 A2
Bullen Park, *Melbourne* 17 A2
Bundoora North, *Melbourne* 17 A2
Bundoora Park, *Melbourne* 17 A2
Bunker I., *Karachi* 14 B1
Bunkyo-Ku, *Tokyo* 29 A3
Bunnefjorden, *Oslo* 22 A3
Buona Vista Park, *Singapore* 27 B2
Burbank, *Chicago* 9 C2
Burbank, *Los Angeles* 16 A3
Burlington, *Boston* 6 A2
Burnham Park, *Chicago* 9 c2
Burnham Park Harbor, *Chicago* 9 B3
Burnhamthorpe, *Toronto* 30 B1
Burnt Oak, *London* 15 A2
Burntisland, *Edinburgh* 11 A2
Burnwynd, *Edinburgh* 11 B1
Burqa, *Jerusalem* 13 A2
Burtus, *Cairo* 7 A1
Burudvatn, *Oslo* 22 A2
Burwood, *Sydney* 28 B1
Bushwick, *New York* 21 B2
Bushy Park, *London* 15 B1
Butantã, *São Paulo* 26 B1
Butcher I., *Mumbai* 20 B2
Butts Corner, *Washington* 32 C2
Büyükdere, *Istanbul* 12 B2
Byculla, *Mumbai* 20 B2
Bygdøy, *Oslo* 22 A3

C

C.N. Tower, *Toronto* 30 B2
Cabaçu de Cima →, *São Paulo* 26 A2
Caballito, *Buenos Aires* 7 B2
Cabin John, *Washington* 32 B2
Cabin John Regional Park, *Washington* 32 A2
Cabinteely, *Dublin* 11 B3
Cabra, *Dublin* 11 A2
Cabuçú de Baixo →, *São Paulo* 26 A1
Cachan, *Paris* 23 B2
Cachenka →, *Moscow* 19 B1
Cachoeira, Rib. da →, *São Paulo* 26 B1
Cacilhas, *Lisbon* 14 A2
Cahuenga Pk., *Los Angeles* 16 B3
Cairo = El Qâhira, *Cairo* 7 A2
Caju, *Rio de Janeiro* 24 B1
Čakovice, *Prague* 24 B3
Calcutta = Kolkata, *Calcutta* 8 B2
California Inst. of Tech., *Los Angeles* 16 B4
California Plaza, *Los Angeles* 16 b1
California State Univ., *Los Angeles* 16 B3
Callao, *Lima* 16 B2
Caloocan, *Manila* 17 B1
Calumet Park, *Chicago* 9 C3
Calumet Sag Channel →, *Chicago* 9 C2
Calumpang, *Manila* 17 B2
Calvairate, *Milan* 18 B2
Camarate, *Lisbon* 14 A2
Camaroes, *Lisbon* 14 A1
Camberwell, *London* 15 B3
Camberwell, *Melbourne* 17 B2
Cambridge, *Boston* 6 A3
Cambridge Res., *Boston* 6 A2
Cambuci, *São Paulo* 26 B2
Camden, *London* 15 A3
Cameron, Mt., *Wellington* 32 B2
Çamlıca, *Istanbul* 12 B2
Camp Springs, *Washington* 32 C4
Campamento, *Madrid* 17 B1
Campbellfield, *Melbourne* 17 A1
Camperdown, *Sydney* 28 B2
Campidoglio, *Rome* 25 c3
Campo, Casa de, *Madrid* 17 B1
Campo F.C. Barcelona, *Barcelona* 4 A1
Campo Grando, *Lisbon* 14 A2
Campo Pequeño, *Lisbon* 14 A2
Campolide, *Lisbon* 14 A2
Camps Bay, *Cape Town* 8 A1
C'an San Joan, *Barcelona* 4 A2
Cañacao B., *Manila* 17 C1
Canarsie, *New York* 21 C2
Cancelleria, Palazzo dei, *Rome* 25 c2
Candiac, *Montreal* 19 B3
Caneças, *Lisbon* 14 A1
Canillas, *Madrid* 17 B2
Canillejas, *Madrid* 17 B2
Canning Town, *London* 15 A4
Canteras de Vallecas, *Madrid* 17 B2
Canterbury, *Melbourne* 17 A2
Canterbury, *Sydney* 28 B1
Canton = Guangzhou, *Canton* 8 B2
Caoheijing, *Shanghai* 27 B1
Capão Redondo, *São Paulo* 26 B1
Caparica, *Lisbon* 14 A2
Caparica, Costa da, *Lisbon* 14 B1
Cape Flats, *Cape Town* 8 B2
Cape Town, *Cape Town* 8 A1
Capitol Heights, *Washington* 32 B4
Capitol Hill, *Washington* 32 B4
Capitolini, Musei, *Rome* 25 c3
Captain Cook Bridge, *Sydney* 28 C1
Captain Cook Landing Place Park, *Sydney* 28 C2
Capuchos, *Lisbon* 14 B1
Carabanchel Alto, *Madrid* 17 B1
Carabanchel Bajo, *Madrid* 17 B1
Carapachay, *Buenos Aires* 7 B1
Caraza, *Buenos Aires* 7 C2
Caridad, *Manila* 17 C1
Carioca, Sa. da, *Rio de Janeiro* 24 B1
Carlstadt, *New York* 21 A1
Carlton, *Melbourne* 17 A1
Carmen de Huechuraba, *Santiago* 26 B1
Carmen de la Legua, *Lima* 16 B2
Carnaxide, *Lisbon* 14 A1
Carnegie, *Melbourne* 17 B2
Carnegie Hall, *New York* 21 c2
Carnide, *Lisbon* 14 A1
Carol City, *Miami* 18 A1
Carrascal, *Santiago* 26 B1
Carrickmines, *Dublin* 11 B3
Carrières-sous-Bois, *Paris* 23 A1
Carrières-sous-Poissy, *Paris* 23 A1
Carrières-sur-Seine, *Paris* 23 A2
Carrigeen Bay, *Dublin* 11 A3
Cartierville, *Montreal* 19 A1
Casa Verde, *São Paulo* 26 A1
Casál Morena, *Rome* 25 C2
Casalotti, *Rome* 25 B1
Cascade Heights, *Atlanta* 3 B2
Castél di Leva, *Rome* 25 C2
Castel Sant'Angelo, *Rome* 25 B1
Castle, *Dublin* 11 c2
Castle, *Edinburgh* 11 b2
Castle of Good Hope, *Cape Town* 8 c3
Castleknock, *Dublin* 11 A1
Castleton Corners, *New York* 21 C1
Catedral Metropolitana, *Mexico City* 18 b3
Catedral Metropolitana, *Rio de Janeiro* 24 c1
Catete, *Rio de Janeiro* 24 B1
Catford, *London* 15 B3
Caulfield, *Melbourne* 17 B2
Causeway Bay, *Hong Kong* 12 c3
Cavite, *Manila* 17 C1
Caxias, *Lisbon* 14 A1
Cebecci, *Istanbul* 12 B1
Cecchignola, *Rome* 25 C2
Cecilienhof, Schloss, *Berlin* 5 B1
Cedar Grove, *Atlanta* 3 C3
Cempaka Putih, *Jakarta* 13 B2
Çengelköy, *Istanbul* 12 B2
Cengkareng, *Jakarta* 13 A1
Centennial Park, *Sydney* 28 B2
Center Hill, *Atlanta* 3 B2
Centocelle, *Rome* 25 B2
Centraal Station, *Amsterdam* 2 a2
Central Park, *New York* 21 B2
Cerillos, *Santiago* 26 B1
Cerro de la Estrella, *Mexico City* 18 B2
Cerro de los Angeles, *Madrid* 17 C1
Cerro Navia, *Santiago* 26 B1
Certanovka →, *Moscow* 19 C3
Certanovo, *Moscow* 19 C3
Cesano Boscone, *Milan* 18 B1
Cesate, *Milan* 18 A1
Cha Kwo Ling, *Hong Kong* 12 B2
Chacarrita, *Buenos Aires* 7 B2
Chadwell Heath, *London* 15 A4
Chai Chee, *Singapore* 27 B3
Chai Wan, *Hong Kong* 12 B2
Chai Wan Kok, *Hong Kong* 12 A1
Chaillot, Palais de, *Paris* 23 b2
Chakdaha, *Calcutta* 8 C1
Chamartin, *Madrid* 17 B1
Chamberi, *Madrid* 17 B1
Chambourcy, *Paris* 23 A1
Champ de Mars, Parc du, *Paris* 23 c2
Champigny-sur-Marne, *Paris* 23 B4
Champlain, Pont, *Montreal* 19 B2
Champs Elysées, Avenue des, *Paris* 23 b2
Champs-sur-Marne, *Paris* 23 A4
Chamrail, *Calcutta* 8 B1
Chamshil, *Seoul* 26 B2
Chamwŏn, *Seoul* 26 B2
Chanakyapuri, *Delhi* 10 B2
Chanditala, *Calcutta* 8 A1
Changfeng Park, *Shanghai* 27 B1
Changi, *Singapore* 27 A3
Changi Int. Airport, *Singapore* 27 A3
Changning, *Shanghai* 27 B1
Chantereine, *Paris* 23 A4
Chantian, *Canton* 8 A2
Chao Phraya →, *Bangkok* 3 B2
Chaoyang, *Beijing* 4 B2
Chaoyangmen, *Beijing* 4 B2
Chapelizod, *Dublin* 11 A1
Chapultepec, Bosque de, *Mexico City* 18 B1
Chapultepec, Castillo de, *Mexico City* 18 B1
Charenton-le-Pont, *Paris* 23 B3
Charing Cross, *London* 15 b4
Charleroi, Kanal de →, *Brussels* 6 B1
Charles Bridge, *Prague* 24 b1
Charles Square, *Prague* 24 c1
Charlestown, *Boston* 6 A3
Charlottenburg, *Berlin* 5 A2
Charlottenburg, Schloss, *Berlin* 5 A2
Charlottenlund, *Copenhagen* 10 A3
Charlton, *London* 15 B4
Charneca, *Lisbon* 14 A2
Charneca, *Lisbon* 14 B1
Châteaufort, *Paris* 23 B1
Châtenay-Malabry, *Paris* 23 B2
Chatham, *Chicago* 9 C3
Châtillon, *Paris* 23 B2
Chatou, *Paris* 23 A1
Chatpur, *Calcutta* 8 B2
Chatswood, *Sydney* 28 A2
Chatuchak, *Bangkok* 3 B2
Chatuchak Park, *Bangkok* 3 B2
Chauki, *Karachi* 14 A1
Chavarria, *Lima* 16 B2
Chaville, *Paris* 23 B2
Chayang, *Seoul* 26 B2
Chegi, *Seoul* 26 B2
Chelles, *Paris* 23 A4
Chelles, Canal de, *Paris* 23 A4
Chells-le-Pin, Aérodrome, *Paris* 23 A4
Chelsea, *Boston* 6 A3
Chelsea, *London* 15 B2
Chelsea, *New York* 21 c1
Chembur, *Mumbai* 20 A2
Chennevières-sur-Marne, *Paris* 23 B4
Cheops, *Cairo* 7 B1
Cherepkovo, *Moscow* 19 B2
Chernyovo, *Moscow* 19 A1
Cheryomushki, *Moscow* 19 B3
Chestnut Hill, *Boston* 6 B2
Cheung Sha Wan, *Hong Kong* 12 A1
Cheverly, *Washington* 32 B4
Chevilly-Larue, *Paris* 23 B3
Chevry-Cossigny, *Paris* 23 B4
Chevy Chase, *Washington* 32 B3
Chevy Chase View, *Washington* 32 A3
Chia Keng, *Singapore* 27 A3
Chiaravalle Milanese, *Milan* 18 B2
Chicago, *Chicago* 9 B3
Chicago Harbor, *Chicago* 9 B3
Chicago Lawn, *Chicago* 9 C2
Chicago-Midway Airport, *Chicago* 9 C2
Chicago-O'Hare Int. Airport, *Chicago* 9 B1
Chicago Ridge, *Chicago* 9 C2
Chicago Sanitary and Ship Canal, *Chicago* 9 C2
Chienzui, *Canton* 8 A3
Chik Sha, *Hong Kong* 12 B2
Child's Hill, *London* 15 A2
Chilla Saroda, *Delhi* 10 B2
Chillum, *Washington* 32 B4
Chilly-Mazarin, *Paris* 23 B2
Chinatown, *Los Angeles* 16 a3
Chinatown, *New York* 21 e2
Chinatown, *San Francisco* 25 b2
Chinatown, *Singapore* 27 c2
Chingupota, *Calcutta* 8 C1
Chislehurst, *London* 15 B4
Chiswick, *London* 15 B2
Chiswick House, *London* 15 B2
Chitose, *Tokyo* 29 B2
Chitralada Palace, *Bangkok* 3 B2
Chiyoda-Ku, *Tokyo* 29 b4
Chkalova, *Moscow* 19 C5
Choa Chu Kang, *Singapore* 27 A2
Choboty, *Moscow* 19 C2
Chodov u Prahy, *Prague* 24 B3
Chōfu, *Tokyo* 29 B2
Choisy-le-Roi, *Paris* 23 B3
Cholupice, *Prague* 24 C2
Chom Thong, *Bangkok* 3 B1
Chong Pang, *Singapore* 27 A2
Ch'ŏngdam, *Seoul* 26 B2
Chongmyo Royal Shrine, *Seoul* 26 B1
Chongno, *Seoul* 26 B1
Chongwen, *Beijing* 4 B2
Chŏnho, *Seoul* 26 B2
Chopin, Muzeum, *Warsaw* 31 b2
Chornaya →, *Moscow* 19 B6
Chorrillos, *Lima* 16 C2
Chowpatty Beach, *Mumbai* 20 b1
Christian Quarter, *Jerusalem* 13 b3
Christiansborg, *Copenhagen* 10 c2
Christianshavn, *Copenhagen* 10 A3
Chrysler Building, *New York* 21 c2
Chrzanów, *Warsaw* 31 B1
Chuen Lung, *Hong Kong* 12 A1
Chuk Kok, *Hong Kong* 12 A2
Chulalongkom Univ., *Bangkok* 3 B2
Chung, *Seoul* 26 B1
Chunghwa, *Seoul* 26 B2
Chungnangch'on →, *Seoul* 26 B1
Chūō-Ku, *Tokyo* 29 b5
Church End, *London* 15 A2
Churchtown, *Dublin* 11 B2
Ciampino, *Rome* 25 C2
Ciampino, Aeroporto di, *Rome* 25 C2
Cicero, *Chicago* 9 B2
Cilandak, *Jakarta* 13 B1
Cilincing, *Jakarta* 13 A2
Ciliwung →, *Jakarta* 13 B2
Čimice, *Prague* 24 B2
Cinecittà, *Rome* 25 B2
Cinisello Bálsamo, *Milan* 18 A2
Cinkota, *Budapest* 7 A3
Cipete, *Jakarta* 13 B1
Citadella, *Budapest* 7 c2
Citta degli Studi, *Milan* 18 B2
Città del Vaticano, *Rome* 25 B1
City, *London* 15 A3
City Hall, *New York* 21 e1
Ciudad Deportiva, *Mexico City* 18 B2
Ciudad Fin de Semana, *Madrid* 17 B2
Ciudad General Belgrano, *Buenos Aires* 7 C1
Ciudad Lineál, *Madrid* 17 B2
Ciudad Satélite, *Mexico City* 18 A1
Ciudad Universitaria, *Buenos Aires* 7 B2
Ciudad Universitaria, *Mexico City* 18 C1
Ciutadella, Parc de la, *Barcelona* 4 b3
Civic Center, *Los Angeles* 16 b2
Clamart, *Paris* 23 B2
Clapham, *London* 15 B3
Clapton, *London* 15 A3
Claremont, *Cape Town* 8 A1
Clayhall, *London* 15 A4
Clerkenwell, *London* 15 a4
Clermiston, *Edinburgh* 11 B2
Clichy, *Paris* 23 A2
Clichy-sous-Bois, *Paris* 23 A4
Cliffside, *Toronto* 30 A3
Cliffside Park, *New York* 21 B2
Clifton, *Boston* 6 A4
Clifton, *Karachi* 14 B2
Clifton, *New York* 21 C1
Cliftondale, *Boston* 6 A3
Cloghran, *Dublin* 11 A2
Clonskeagh, *Dublin* 11 B2
Clontarf, *Dublin* 11 A2
Clontarf, *Sydney* 28 A2
Clovelly, *Sydney* 28 B2
Cobras, I. das, *Rio de Janeiro* 24 B2
Coburg, *Melbourne* 17 A1
Cochituate, *Boston* 6 A1
Cochituate, L., *Boston* 6 B1
Cocotá, *Rio de Janeiro* 24 A1
Cœuilly, *Paris* 23 B4
Coina, *Lisbon* 14 B2
Coit Tower, *San Francisco* 25 a2
Coker, *Lagos* 14 B2
Colaba, *Mumbai* 20 B1
Colaba Pt., *Mumbai* 20 B1
Colegiales, *Buenos Aires* 7 B2
Colindale, *London* 15 A2
Colinton, *Edinburgh* 11 B2
College Park, *Atlanta* 3 C2
College Park, *Washington* 32 B4
College Point, *New York* 21 B2
Collégien, *Paris* 23 A4
Collier Row, *London* 15 A4
Colliers Wood, *London* 15 B2
Colma, *San Francisco* 25 B2
Colney Hatch, *London* 15 A3
Cologno Monzese, *Milan* 18 A2
Colombes, *Paris* 23 A2
Colón, Monumente, *Barcelona* 4 c3
Colon, Plaza de, *Madrid* 17 a3
Colonia Güell, *Barcelona* 4 A1
Colonial Knob, *Wellington* 32 A1
Colosseo, *Rome* 25 c3
Columbus Circus, *New York* 21 b2
Combault, *Paris* 23 B4
Comércio, Praça do, *Lisbon* 14 A2
Commerce, *Los Angeles* 16 B4
Como, *Sydney* 28 C1
Company's Gardens, *Cape Town* 8 c2
Conceição, I. da, *Rio de Janeiro* 24 B2
Concertgebouw, *Amsterdam* 2 c1
Conchali, *Santiago* 26 B2
Concord, *Boston* 6 A1
Concord, *Sydney* 28 B1
Concord, *Toronto* 30 A2
Concorde, Place de la, *Paris* 23 b3
Concorezzo, *Milan* 18 A2
Coney Island, *New York* 21 C2
Congonhas, Aéroporto, *São Paulo* 26 B2
Connaught Place, *Delhi* 10 B2
Conservatori, Palazzo dei, *Rome* 25 c3
Consolação, *São Paulo* 26 B2
Constantia, *Cape Town* 8 B1
Constitución, *Buenos Aires* 7 B2
Constitution, *Atlanta* 3 B2
Convention and Exhibition Centre, *Hong Kong* 12 b2
Coogee, *Sydney* 28 B2
Cook Str., *Wellington* 32 A1
Cooksville, *Toronto* 30 B1
Coolock, *Dublin* 11 A2
Copacabana, *Rio de Janeiro* 24 B1
Copenhagen = København, *Copenhagen* 10 A2
Coral Gables, *Miami* 18 B2
Coral Hills, *Washington* 32 B4
Corcovado, Morro do, *Rio de Janeiro* 24 B1
Corduff, *Dublin* 11 A1
Cormano, *Milan* 18 A2
Cornaredo, *Milan* 18 A1
Córsico, *Milan* 18 B1
Corsini, Palazzo, *Rome* 25 c1
Corviale, *Rome* 25 B1
Coslada, *Madrid* 17 B2
Cossigny, *Paris* 23 B4
Cossipore, *Calcutta* 8 B2
Costantino, Arco di, *Rome* 25 c3
Costorphine, *Edinburgh* 11 B2
Cotao, *Lisbon* 14 A1
Côte St.-Luc, *Montreal* 19 B2
Cotunduba, I. de, *Rio de Janeiro* 24 B2
Coubron, *Paris* 23 A4
Countryside, *Chicago* 9 C1
Courbevoie, *Paris* 23 A2
Courtry, *Paris* 23 A4
Covent Garden, *London* 15 b4
Cowgate, *Edinburgh* 11 b3
Cowley, *London* 15 A1
Coyoacán, *Mexico City* 18 B2
Cragin, *Chicago* 9 B2
Craighall Park, *Johannesburg* 13 A2
Craiglockhart, *Edinburgh* 11 B2
Craigmillar, *Edinburgh* 11 B3
Cramond, *Edinburgh* 11 B2
Cramond Bridge, *Edinburgh* 11 B1
Cramond I., *Edinburgh* 11 B2
Cranford, *London* 15 B1
Crawford, *Cape Town* 8 A2
Crayford, *London* 15 B5
Creekmouth, *London* 15 A4
Crescenzago, *Milan* 18 A2
Cressely, *Paris* 23 B1
Cresskill, *New York* 21 A2
Creteil, *Paris* 23 B3
Cricklewood, *London* 15 A2
Cristo Redentor, Estatua do, *Rio de Janeiro* 24 B1
Crockenhill, *London* 15 B4
Croissy-Beaubourg, *Paris* 23 B4
Croissy-sur-Seine, *Paris* 23 A1
Crosby, *Johannesburg* 13 B1
Crosne, *Paris* 23 B3
Cross I., *Mumbai* 20 B2
Crouch End, *London* 15 A3
Crown Mine, *Johannesburg* 13 B1
Crows Nest, *Sydney* 28 A2
Croydon, *London* 15 B3
Croydon Park, *Sydney* 28 B1
Cruagh Mt., *Dublin* 11 B2
Crumlin, *Dublin* 11 B2
Cruz de Pau, *Lisbon* 14 B2
Crystal Palace, *London* 15 B3
Csepel, *Budapest* 7 B2
Csepelsziget, *Budapest* 7 B2
Csillaghegy, *Budapest* 7 A2
Csillagtelep, *Budapest* 7 B2
Csömör, *Budapest* 7 A3
Csömöri-patak →, *Budapest* 7 A3
Cuatro Vientos, *Madrid* 17 B1
Cuauhtémoc, *Mexico City* 18 B2
Cubao, *Manila* 17 B2
Çubuklu, *Istanbul* 12 B2
Cudahy, *Los Angeles* 16 C3
Cuicuilco, Pirámido de, *Mexico City* 18 C1
Culver City, *Los Angeles* 16 B2
Cumballa Hill, *Mumbai* 20 a1
Cumbres de Vallecas, *Madrid* 17 B2
Cupecé, *São Paulo* 26 B1
Currie, *Edinburgh* 11 B2
Cusago, *Milan* 18 B1
Cusano Milanino, *Milan* 18 A2
Custom House, *Dublin* 11 b3
Çuvuşabaşi →, *Istanbul* 12 B1
Czernriaków, *Warsaw* 31 B2
Czyste, *Warsaw* 31 B1

D

D.F. Malan Airport, *Cape Town* 8 A2
Da Moóca →, *São Paulo* 26 B2
Da Yunhe →, *Tianjin* 30 A1
Dabizhuang, *Tianjin* 30 A2
Ďablice, *Prague* 24 B2
Dąbrowa, *Warsaw* 31 B1
Dachang, *Shanghai* 27 B1
Dachang Airfield, *Shanghai* 27 B1
Dachau-Ost, *Munich* 20 A1
Dachauer Moos, *Munich* 20 A1
Dadar, *Mumbai* 20 A1
Dagenham, *London* 15 A4
Daglfing, *Munich* 20 B2
Daheisha, *Jerusalem* 13 B2
Dahlem, *Berlin* 5 B2
Dahlwitz-Hoppegarten, *Berlin* 5 A5
Dahongmen, *Beijing* 4 C2
Daitō, *Osaka* 22 A4
Dajiaoting, *Beijing* 4 B2
Dakhnoye, *St. Petersburg* 26 C1
Dalejsky potok →, *Prague* 24 B2
Dalgety Bay, *Edinburgh* 11 A1
Dalkeith, *Edinburgh* 11 B3
Dalkey, *Dublin* 11 B3
Dalkey Island, *Dublin* 11 B3
Dallgow, *Berlin* 5 A1
Dalmeny, *Edinburgh* 11 B1
Dalston, *London* 15 A3
Daly City, *San Francisco* 25 B2
Dam, *Amsterdam* 2 b2
Dam Rak, *Amsterdam* 2 a2
Damaia, *Lisbon* 14 A1
Dämeritzsee, *Berlin* 5 B5
Dan Ryan Woods, *Chicago* 9 C2
Danderhall, *Edinburgh* 11 B3
Danderyd, *Stockholm* 28 A2
Danforth, *Toronto* 30 A3
Darakeh, *Tehran* 30 A2
Darband, *Tehran* 30 A2
Darling Harbour, *Sydney* 28 b1
Darling Point, *Sydney* 28 B2
Darndale, *Dublin* 11 A2
Darrūs, *Tehran* 30 A2
Dartford, *London* 15 B5
Darya Ganj, *Delhi* 1 a3
Dashi, *Canton* 8 B2
Datansha, *Canton* 8 B2
Datun, *Beijing* 4 B2
Daulatpur, *Delhi* 10 A1
David's Citadel, *Jerusalem* 13 b3
David's Tomb, *Jerusalem* 13 b3
Davidson, Mt., *San Francisco* 25 B2
Davidson's Mains, *Edinburgh* 11 B2
Dāvūdiyeh, *Tehran* 30 A2
Davydkovo, *Moscow* 19 B2
Dawidy, *Warsaw* 31 C1
Days Bay, *Wellington* 32 B2
Dazhigu, *Tianjin* 30 B2
De Waag, *Amsterdam* 2 b2
Decatur, *Atlanta* 3 B3
Dedham, *Boston* 6 B2
Deer I., *Boston* 6 A4
Degunino, *Moscow* 19 A3
Deir Dibwan, *Jerusalem* 13 A2
Deir Ibzi'e, *Jerusalem* 13 A1
Dejvice, *Prague* 24 B2
Dekabristov, Ostrov, *St. Petersburg* 26 B1
Delhi, *Delhi* 10 B2
Delhi Gate, *Delhi* 1 b3
Demarest, *New York* 21 A2
Den Ilp, *Amsterdam* 2 A2
Denistone Heights, *Sydney* 28 A1
Dentonia Park, *Toronto* 30 A3
Deptford, *London* 15 B3
Deputati, Camera dei, *Rome* 25 b2
Des Plaines, *Chicago* 9 A1
Des Plaines →, *Chicago* 9 B1
Deshengmen, *Beijing* 4 B2
Deutsch-Wagram, *Vienna* 31 A3
Deutsche Oper, *Berlin* 5 A2
Deutscher Museum, *Munich* 20 B2
Devil's Peak, *Cape Town* 8 A1
Dháfni, *Athens* 2 B2
Dhakuria, *Calcutta* 8 B2
Dhamarakia, *Athens* 2 B1
Dharavi, *Mumbai* 20 A2
Dhrapersón, *Athens* 2 B1
Diadema, *São Paulo* 26 C2
Diegen, *Brussels* 6 A2
Diemen, *Amsterdam* 2 A2
Diepkloof, *Johannesburg* 13 B1
Dieprivier, *Cape Town* 8 B1
Difficult Run →, *Washington* 32 B2
Dilbeek, *Brussels* 6 A1
Dinzigu, *Tianjin* 30 A1
Dirnismaning, *Munich* 20 A2
District Heights, *Washington* 32 B4
Ditan Park, *Beijing* 4 a2
Diyāla →, *Baghdad* 3 B3
Djursholm, *Stockholm* 28 A2
Döberitz, *Berlin* 5 A1
Döbling, *Vienna* 31 A2
Docklands, *London* 15 A3
Dodder, R. →, *Dublin* 11 B1
Dodger Stadium, *Los Angeles* 16 B3
Dolgoe Ozero, *St. Petersburg* 26 A1
Doll Museum, *Delhi* 1 b3
Dollis Hill, *London* 15 A2
Dollymount, *Dublin* 11 A2
Dolni, *Prague* 24 B3
Dolni Chabry, *Prague* 24 B2
Dolni Počernice, *Prague* 24 B3
Dolphins Barn, *Dublin* 11 B2
Dom Pedro II, Parque, *São Paulo* 26 B2
Domain, The, *Sydney* 28 b2
Dome of the Rock, *Jerusalem* 13 b3
Don Mills, *Toronto* 30 A2
Don Muang Int. Airport, *Bangkok* 3 A2
Donaghmede, *Dublin* 11 A3
Donau-Oder Kanal, *Vienna* 31 A3
Donaufeld, *Vienna* 31 A2
Donaupark, *Vienna* 31 A2
Donaustadt, *Vienna* 31 A2
Dongan Hills, *New York* 21 C1
Dongcheng, *Beijing* 4 B2
Donggou, *Shanghai* 27 B2
Dongjiao, *Canton* 8 B2
Dongjuzi, *Tianjin* 30 B2
Dongmenwai, *Tianjin* 30 B2
Dongri, *Mumbai* 20 B2
Dongshanhu Park, *Canton* 8 B2
Dongzhimen, *Beijing* 4 B2
Donnybrook, *Dublin* 11 B2
Doornfontein, *Johannesburg* 13 B2
Dorchester, *Boston* 6 B3
Dorchester B., *Boston* 6 B3
Dornach, *Munich* 20 B3
Dorval, Aéroport de, *Montreal* 19 B1
Dos Couros →, *São Paulo* 26 C2
Dos Moninos →, *São Paulo* 26 C2
Douglas Park, *Chicago* 9 B2
Dover Heights, *Sydney* 28 B2
Dowlatābād, *Tehran* 30 B2
Downey, *Los Angeles* 16 C4
Downsview, *Toronto* 30 A1
Dragør, *Copenhagen* 10 B3
Drancy, *Paris* 23 A3
Dranesville, *Washington* 32 A1
Dreilinden, *Berlin* 5 B2
Drewnica, *Warsaw* 31 B2
Drigh Road, *Karachi* 14 A2
Drimnagh, *Dublin* 11 B2
Drogenbos, *Brussels* 6 B1
Druid Hills, *Atlanta* 3 B2
Drum Towwer, *Beijing* 4 a2
Drumcondra, *Dublin* 11 A2
Drummoyne, *Sydney* 28 B1
Drylaw, *Edinburgh* 11 B2
Dubeč, *Prague* 24 B3
Dublin, *Dublin* 11 A2
Dublin Airport, *Dublin* 11 A2
Dublin Bay, *Dublin* 11 B3
Dublin Harbour, *Dublin* 11 A2
Duddingston, *Edinburgh* 11 B3
Dugnano, *Milan* 18 A2
Dūlāb, *Tehran* 30 B2
Dulwich, *London* 15 B3
Dum Dum, *Calcutta* 8 B2
Dum Dum Int. Airport, *Calcutta* 8 B2
Dumont, *New York* 21 A2
Dún Laoghaire, *Dublin* 11 B3
Duna →, *Budapest* 7 A2
Duncan Dock, *Cape Town* 8 a3
Dundrum, *Dublin* 11 B2
Dunearn, *Singapore* 27 B2
Dunfermline, *Edinburgh* 11 A1
Dunn Loring, *Washington* 32 B2
Dunning, *Chicago* 9 B2
Dunvegan, *Johannesburg* 13 A2
Duomo, *Milan* 18 B2
Duque de Caxias, *Rio de Janeiro* 24 A1
Dusit, *Bangkok* 3 B2
Dusit Zoo, *Bangkok* 3 a2
Duvernay, *Montreal* 19 A1
Dworp, *Brussels* 6 B1
Dyakovo, *Moscow* 19 B3
Dzerzhinskiy, *Moscow* 19 C5
Dzerzhinskiy, *Moscow* 19 B3
Dzerzhinskiy Park, *Moscow* 19 B3

E

Eagle Rock, *Los Angeles* 16 B3
Ealing, *London* 15 A2
Earl's Court, *London* 15 c1
Earlsfield, *London* 15 B2
Earlwood, *Sydney* 28 B1
East Acton, *Boston* 6 A1
East Arlington, *Boston* 6 A3
East Arlington, *Washington* 32 B3
East Bedfont, *London* 15 B1
East Boston, *Boston* 6 A3
East Don →, *Toronto* 30 A2
East Elmhurst, *New York* 21 B2
East Finchley, *London* 15 A2
East Ham, *London* 15 A4
East Humber →, *Toronto* 30 A1
East Lamma Channel, *Hong Kong* 12 B1
East Lexington, *Boston* 6 A2
East Los Angeles, *Los Angeles* 16 B3
East Molesey, *London* 15 B1
East New York, *New York* 21 B2
East Pines, *Washington* 32 B4
East Point, *Atlanta* 3 B2
East Potomac Park, *Washington* 32 B3
East Pt., *Boston* 6 A4
East River →, *New York* 21 B2
East Rutherford, *New York* 21 A1
East Sheen, *London* 15 B2
East Village, *New York* 21 e2
East Wickham, *London* 15 B4
East York, *Toronto* 30 A2
Eastbourne, *Wellington* 32 B2
Eastcote, *London* 15 A1
Easter Howgate, *Edinburgh* 11 B2
Eastwood, *Sydney* 28 A1
Ebara, *Tokyo* 29 B3
Ebisu, *Tokyo* 29 B3
Ebute-Ikorodu, *Lagos* 14 A2
Ebute-Metta, *Lagos* 14 B2
Echo Park, *Los Angeles* 16 a1
Eda, *Tokyo* 29 B2
Edendale, *Johannesburg* 13 A2
Edenmore, *Dublin* 11 A2
Edgars Cr. →, *Melbourne* 17 A1
Edgeley, *Toronto* 30 A1
Edgemar, *San Francisco* 25 C2
Edinburgh, *Edinburgh* 11 B2
Edison Park, *Chicago* 9 A2
Edmondston, *Washington* 32 B4
Edmondstown, *Dublin* 11 B2
Edo →, *Tokyo* 29 B4
Edogawa-Ku, *Tokyo* 29 A4
Edsberg, *Stockholm* 28 A1
Edwards L., *Melbourne* 17 A1
Eiche, *Berlin* 5 A4
Eiche Sud, *Berlin* 5 A4
Eiffel, Tour, *Paris* 23 A2
Ein Arik, *Jerusalem* 13 A1
Ein Naquba, *Jerusalem* 13 B1
Ein Rafa, *Jerusalem* 13 B1
Eizariya, *Jerusalem* 13 B2
Ejby, *Copenhagen* 10 A2
Ejigbo, *Lagos* 14 A1
Ekeberg, *Oslo* 22 A3
Eknäs, *Stockholm* 28 B3
El 'Abbasiya, *Cairo* 7 A2
El Agustino, *Lima* 16 B2
El Baragil, *Cairo* 7 A1
El Basâtîn, *Cairo* 7 B2
El-Bira, *Jerusalem* 13 A2
El Bosque, *Santiago* 26 C2
El Carmen, *Santiago* 26 B1
El Cortijo, *Santiago* 26 B1
El Duqqi, *Cairo* 7 A2
El Encinar de los Reyes, *Madrid* 17 A2
El Ghurîya, *Cairo* 7 A2
El Gîza, *Cairo* 7 A2
El-Khadr, *Jerusalem* 13 B1
El Khalîfa, *Cairo* 7 A2
El Kôm el Ahmar, *Cairo* 7 A2
El Ma'âdi, *Cairo* 7 B2
El Matarîya, *Cairo* 7 A2
El Mohandessin, *Cairo* 7 A2
El Monte, *Los Angeles* 16 B4
El Mûskî, *Cairo* 7 A2
El Pardo, *Madrid* 17 A1
El Portal, *Miami* 18 A2
El Prat de Llobregat, *Barcelona* 4 B1
El Pueblo de L.A. Historic Park, *Los Angeles* 16 b2
El Qâhira, *Cairo* 7 A2
El Qubba, *Cairo* 7 A2
El Reloj, *Mexico City* 18 C2
El Retiro, *Madrid* 17 B1
El Salto, *Santiago* 26 B2
El Sereno, *Los Angeles* 16 B3
El Talibîya, *Cairo* 7 B2
El Vergel, *Mexico City* 18 C2
El Wâhli, *Cairo* 7 A2
El Zamâlik, *Cairo* 7 A2
El Zeitûn, *Cairo* 7 A2
Elephanta Caves, *Mumbai* 20 B2
Elephanta I., *Mumbai* 20 B2
Ellboda, *Stockholm* 28 A3
Ellinikón, *Athens* 2 B2
Ellis I., *New York* 21 B1
Elm Park, *London* 15 A5
Elmers End, *London* 15 B3
Elmhurst, *New York* 21 B2
Elmstead, *London* 15 B4
Elmwood Park, *Chicago* 9 B2
Elmwood Park, *New York* 21 A1
Elsdon, *Wellington* 32 A1
Elsiesrivier, *Cape Town* 8 A2
Elsternwick, *Melbourne* 17 B2
Eltham, *London* 15 B4
Elwood, *Melbourne* 17 B1
Élysée, *Paris* 23 A2
Elysian Park, *Los Angeles* 16 a3
Embajadores, *Madrid* 17 c2
Embarcadero Center, *San Francisco* 25 b3
Emek Refa'im, *Jerusalem* 13 c2
Émerainville, *Paris* 23 B4
Emeryville, *San Francisco* 25 A3
Eminönü, *Istanbul* 12 B1
Emmarentia, *Johannesburg* 13 A2
Empire State Building, *New York* 21 c2
Encantado, *Rio de Janeiro* 24 B1
Encino, *Los Angeles* 16 B2
Encino Res., *Los Angeles* 16 B1
Enebyberg, *Stockholm* 28 A1
Enfield, *Sydney* 28 B1
Engenho, I. do, *Rio de Janeiro* 24 B2
Englewood, *Chicago* 9 C3
Englewood, *New York* 21 A2
Englewood Cliffs, *New York* 21 A2
Enmore, *Sydney* 28 B2
Enskede, *Stockholm* 28 B2
Entrevias, *Madrid* 17 B1
Epping, *Sydney* 28 A1
Erawan Shrine, *Bangkok* 3 c3
Eregun, *Lagos* 14 A2
Erenköy, *Istanbul* 12 C2
Erith, *London* 15 B5
Erlaa, *Vienna* 31 B1
Ermington, *Sydney* 28 A1
Ermita, *Manila* 17 B1
Ershatou, *Canton* 8 B2
Erskineville, *Sydney* 28 B2
Erunkan, *Lagos* 14 A2
Erzsébet-Telep, *Budapest* 7 B3
Eschenried, *Munich* 20 A1
Esenler, *Istanbul* 12 B1
Esher, *London* 15 B1
Eskbank, *Edinburgh* 11 B3
Esperanza, *Mexico City* 18 c3
Esplanade Park, *Singapore* 27 c3
Esplugas, *Barcelona* 4 A1
Esposizione Univ. di Roma (E.U.R.), *Rome* 25 C1
Essendon, *Melbourne* 17 A1
Essendon Airport, *Melbourne* 17 A1
Essingen, *Stockholm* 28 B1
Essling, *Vienna* 31 A3
Est, Gare de l', *Paris* 23 a5
Estadio Maracanã, *Rio de Janeiro* 24 B1
Estado, Parque do, *São Paulo* 26 B2
Estefânia, *Lisbon* 14 a2
Estrela, Basilica da, *Lisbon* 14 A2
Ethnikó Arheologiko Moussío, *Athens* 2 a2
Etobicoke, *Toronto* 30 B1
Etobicoke Cr. →, *Toronto* 30 B1
Etterbeek, *Brussels* 6 B2
Euston, *London* 15 a3
Evanston, *Chicago* 9 A2
Even Sapir, *Jerusalem* 13 B1
Evere, *Brussels* 6 A2
Everett, *Boston* 6 A3
Evergreen Park, *Chicago* 9 C2
Evīn, *Tehran* 30 A2
Évzonos, *Athens* 2 B2
Ewu, *Lagos* 14 A1
Exchange Square, *Hong Kong* 12 c1
Exposições, Palácio das, *Rio de Janeiro* 24 B1
Eyüp, *Istanbul* 12 B1

F

Fabour, Mt., *Singapore* 27 B2
Faechi, *Seoul* 26 B2
Fælledparken, *Copenhagen* 10 A3
Fågelön, *Stockholm* 28 B1
Fagersjö, *Stockholm* 28 B2
Fair Lawn, *New York* 21 A1
Fairfax, *Washington* 32 B2
Fairfax Station, *Washington* 32 C2
Fairhaven Bay, *Boston* 6 A1
Fairhaven Hill, *Boston* 6 A1
Fairland, *Johannesburg* 13 A1
Fairmilehead, *Edinburgh* 11 B2
Fairmount Heights, *Washington* 32 B4
Fairport, *Toronto* 30 A4
Fairview, *New York* 21 B2
Falenty, *Warsaw* 31 C1
Fálirou, Órmos, *Athens* 2 B2
Falkenburg, *Berlin* 5 A4
Falkenhagen, *Berlin* 5 A1
Falkensee, *Berlin* 5 A1
Falls Church, *Washington* 32 B2
Falomo, *Lagos* 14 B2
False Bay, *Cape Town* 8 B2
Fangcun, *Canton* 8 B2
Farahābād, *Tehran* 30 A2
Farforovskaya, *St. Petersburg* 26 B2
Farningham, *London* 15 B5
Farrar Pond, *Boston* 6 A1
Farsta, *Stockholm* 28 B2
Fasanerie-Nord, *Munich* 20 A2
Fasangarten, *Munich* 20 B2
Fasting Palace, *Beijing* 4 c2
Fatih, *Istanbul* 12 B1
Favoriten, *Vienna* 31 B2
Fawkner, *Melbourne* 17 A1

KÁPOSZTÁSMEGYER

Káposztásmegyer, *Budapest* 7 A2
Kapotnya, *Moscow* 19 C4
Käppala, *Stockholm* 28 A3
Käpylä, *Helsinki* 12 B2
Karachi, *Karachi* 14 A2
Karachi Int. Airport, *Karachi* 14 A2
Karato, *Osaka* 22 A2
Karibong, *Seoul* 26 C1
Karkh, *Baghdad* 3 A2
Karlin, *Prague* 24 B2
Karlsfeld, *Munich* 20 A1
Karlshorst, *Berlin* 5 B4
Karlsplatz, *Munich* 20 b1
Karntner Strasse, *Vienna* 31 b2
Karol Bagh, *Delhi* 10 B2
Karolinenhof, *Berlin* 5 B4
Karori, *Wellington* 32 B1
Karow, *Berlin* 5 A3
Karrādah, *Baghdad* 3 B2
Kärsön, *Stockholm* 28 B1
Kasai, *Tokyo* 29 B4
Kashiwara, *Osaka* 22 B4
Kastellet, *Copenhagen* 10 a3
Kastrup, *Copenhagen* 10 B3
Kastrup Lufthavn, *Copenhagen* 10 B3
Kasuga, *Tokyo* 29 A2
Kasuge, *Tokyo* 29 A3
Kasumigaseki, *Tokyo* 29 b4
Katong, *Singapore* 27 B3
Katrineberg, *Stockholm* 28 B1
Katsushika-Ku, *Tokyo* 29 A4
Kau Pei Chau, *Hong Kong* 12 B2
Kau Yi Chau, *Hong Kong* 12 B1
Kaulsdorf, *Berlin* 5 B4
Kauniainen, *Helsinki* 12 B1
Kawasaki, *Tokyo* 29 B3
Kawawa, *Tokyo* 29 B2
Kawęczyn, *Warsaw* 31 B2
Kayu Putih, *Jakarta* 13 B2
Kbely, *Prague* 24 B3
Kebayoran Baru, *Jakarta* 13 B1
Kebayoran Lama, *Jakarta* 13 B1
Kebon Jeruk, *Jakarta* 13 B1
Kedar, *Jerusalem* 13 B2
Keilor, *Melbourne* 17 A1
Keilor North, *Melbourne* 17 A1
Keimola, *Helsinki* 12 A1
Kelenföld, *Budapest* 7 B2
Kelvin, *Johannesburg* 13 A2
Kemang, *Jakarta* 13 B1
Kemayoran, *Jakarta* 13 B2
Kemerburgaz, *Istanbul* 12 B1
Kempton Park Races, *London* 15 B1
Kendall Green, *Boston* 6 A2
Kenilworth, *Cape Town* 8 A1
Kennedy Town, *Hong Kong* 12 B1
Kennington, *London* 15 c4
Kensal Green, *London* 15 A2
Kensal Rise, *London* 15 a1
Kensington, *Johannesburg* 13 B2
Kensington, *London* 15 B2
Kensington, *New York* 21 C2
Kensington, *Sydney* 28 B2
Kensington Palace, *London* 15 A2
Kent Village, *Washington* 32 B4
Kentish Town, *London* 15 A3
Kenton, *London* 15 A2
Kenwood House, *London* 15 A3
Kepa, *Warsaw* 31 B2
Keppel Harbour, *Singapore* 27 B2
Keramíkos, *Athens* 2 b1
Kettering, *Washington* 32 B5
Kew, *London* 15 B2
Kew, *Melbourne* 17 A2
Kew Gardens, *London* 15 B2
Kew Gardens, *Toronto* 30 B3
Key Biscayne, *Miami* 18 B2
Khaidhárion, *Athens* 2 A1
Khalándrion, *Athens* 2 A2
Khalīj, *Baghdad* 3 B2
Khandallah, *Wellington* 32 B1
Khansā', *Baghdad* 3 A2
Kharavli, *Mumbai* 20 B2
Khefren, *Cairo* 7 B1
Khichripur, *Delhi* 10 B2
Khidirpur, *Calcutta* 8 B1
Khimki-Khovrino, *Moscow* 19 A3
Khirbet Jub e-Rum, *Jerusalem* 13 B2
Khlong San, *Bangkok* 3 B2
Khlong Toey, *Bangkok* 3 B2
Kholargós, *Athens* 2 B2
Khorel, *Calcutta* 8 A1
Khorosovo, *Moscow* 19 B2
Kiamari, *Karachi* 14 B1
Kierling, *Vienna* 31 A1
Kierlingbach →, *Vienna* 31 A1
Kifisós →, *Athens* 2 B2
Kikuna, *Tokyo* 29 B2
Kilbarrack, *Dublin* 11 A3
Kilbirnie, *Wellington* 32 B1
Kilburn, *London* 15 A2
Killakee, *Dublin* 11 B2
Killester, *Dublin* 11 A2
Killiney, *Dublin* 11 B3
Killiney Bay, *Dublin* 11 B3
Kilmacud, *Dublin* 11 B2
Kilmainham, *Dublin* 11 A2
Kilmashogue Mt., *Dublin* 11 B2
Kilmore, *Dublin* 11 A2
Kilnamanagh, *Dublin* 11 B1
Kilo, *Helsinki* 12 B1
Kilokri, *Delhi* 10 B2
Kiltiernan, *Dublin* 11 B2
Kimmage, *Dublin* 11 B2
Kindi, *Baghdad* 3 B2
Kinghorn, *Edinburgh* 11 A2
King's Cross, *London* 15 a4
Kings Cross, *Sydney* 28 c3
Kings Domain, *Melbourne* 17 A1
Kings Park, *Washington* 32 C2
Kings Park West, *Washington* 32 C2
Kingsbury, *London* 15 A2
Kingsbury, *Melbourne* 17 A2
Kingsford, *Sydney* 28 B2
Kingston upon Thames, *London* 15 B2
Kingston Vale, *London* 15 B2
Kingsway, *Toronto* 30 B1
Kinsaley, *Dublin* 11 A2
Kipling Heights, *Toronto* 30 A1
Kipséli, *Athens* 2 B2
Kirchstockbach, *Munich* 20 B3
Kirchtrudering, *Munich* 20 B3
Kirikiri, *Lagos* 14 B1
Kirke Værløse, *Copenhagen* 10 A1
Kirkhill, *Edinburgh* 11 B2
Kirkliston, *Edinburgh* 11 B1
Kirknewton, *Edinburgh* 11 B1
Kirov Palace of Culture, *St. Petersburg* 26 B1
Kısıklı, *Istanbul* 12 B2
Kispest, *Budapest* 7 B2
Kista, *Stockholm* 28 A1
Kita, *Osaka* 22 A4
Kita-Ku, *Tokyo* 29 A3
Kitazawa, *Tokyo* 29 B3
Kiu Tsiu, *Hong Kong* 12 A2
Kivistö, *Helsinki* 12 B2
Kızıltoprak, *Istanbul* 12 C2
Kizu →, *Osaka* 22 B3
Kizuri, *Osaka* 22 B4
Kjelsås, *Oslo* 22 A3
Kladow, *Berlin* 5 B1
Klampenborg, *Copenhagen* 10 A3
Klaudyń, *Warsaw* 31 B1
Klecany, *Prague* 24 A2
Kledering, *Vienna* 31 B2
Klein Jukskei →, *Johannesburg* 13 A1
Kleinmachnow, *Berlin* 5 B2
Kleinschönebeck, *Berlin* 5 B5
Klemetsrud, *Oslo* 22 A4
Kličany, *Prague* 24 A2
Klipriviersberg Nature Reserve, *Johannesburg* 13 B2
Klosterneuburg, *Vienna* 31 A1
Knesset, *Jerusalem* 13 b1
Knightsbridge, *London* 15 c2
Köbánya, *Budapest* 7 B2
Kobbegem, *Brussels* 6 A1
Kōbe, *Osaka* 22 A2
Kōbe Harbour, *Osaka* 22 B2
København, *Copenhagen* 10 A2
Kobylisy, *Prague* 24 B2
Kobyłka, *Warsaw* 31 A3
Kŏch'ŏk, *Seoul* 26 B1
Kodaira, *Tokyo* 29 A1
Kodanaka, *Tokyo* 29 B2
Kodenmacho, *Tokyo* 29 a5
Koekelberg, *Brussels* 6 A1
Koganei, *Tokyo* 29 A2
Kogarah, *Sydney* 28 B1
Køge Bugt, *Copenhagen* 10 B2
Koivupää, *Helsinki* 12 B2
Koja, *Jakarta* 13 A2
Koja Utara, *Jakarta* 13 A2
Kokobunji, *Tokyo* 29 A1
Kokobunji-Temple, *Tokyo* 29 A4
Kolarängen, *Stockholm* 28 B3
Kolbotn, *Oslo* 22 B3
Kolkata, *Calcutta* 8 B2
Koło, *Warsaw* 31 B1
Kolokinthóu, *Athens* 2 B2
Kolomyagi, *St. Petersburg* 26 A1
Kolónos, *Athens* 2 B2
Kolsås, *Oslo* 22 A2
Komae, *Tokyo* 29 B2
Komagome, *Tokyo* 29 A3
Komazawa, *Tokyo* 29 B3
Kona, *Calcutta* 8 B1
Konala, *Helsinki* 12 B2
Kondli, *Delhi* 10 B2
Kongelige Slottet, *Oslo* 22 a1
Kongelunden, *Copenhagen* 10 B3
Kongens Lyngby, *Copenhagen* 10 A3
Kongnŭng, *Seoul* 26 B2
Kongo, *Helsinki* 12 A1
Koninklijk Paleis, *Amsterdam* 2 b2
Konnagar, *Calcutta* 8 A2
Konohana, *Osaka* 22 A3
Kōnoike, *Osaka* 22 A4
Konradshöhe, *Berlin* 5 A2
Kopanina, *Prague* 24 B1
Koparkhairna, *Mumbai* 20 A2
Köpenick, *Berlin* 5 B4
Korangi, *Karachi* 14 B2
Koremasa, *Tokyo* 29 B1
Korenevo, *Moscow* 19 B6
Kori, *Osaka* 22 A4
Koridhallós, *Athens* 2 B1
Korokoro, *Wellington* 32 B2
Korokoro Stream →, *Wellington* 32 B2
Kosino, *Moscow* 19 B5
Kosugi, *Tokyo* 29 B2
Kota, *Jakarta* 13 A1
Kotelyniki, *Moscow* 19 C5
Kōtō-Ku, *Tokyo* 29 A3
Kotrung, *Calcutta* 8 A2
Kouponia, *Athens* 2 B2
Kowloon, *Hong Kong* 12 B1
Kowloon Park, *Hong Kong* 12 a2
Kowloon Peak, *Hong Kong* 12 A2
Kowloon Res., *Hong Kong* 12 A1
Kowloon Tong, *Hong Kong* 12 A2
Kozhukhovo, *Moscow* 19 B5
Kraainem, *Brussels* 6 A2
Krailling, *Munich* 20 B1
Krampnitz, *Berlin* 5 B1
Krampnitzsee, *Berlin* 5 B1
Kranji, Sungei →, *Singapore* 27 A2
Kranji Industrial Estate, *Singapore* 27 A2
Kraskovo, *Moscow* 19 C5
Krasno-Presnenskaya, *Moscow* 19 B3
Krasnogorsk, *Moscow* 19 B1
Krč, *Prague* 24 B2
Krestovskiye, Ostrov, *St. Petersburg* 26 B1
Kreuzberg, *Berlin* 5 A3
Kritzendorf, *Vienna* 31 A1
Krumme Lanke, *Berlin* 5 B2
Krummensee, *Berlin* 5 A5
Krung Thep, *Bangkok* 3 B2
Krusboda, *Stockholm* 28 B3
Krylatskoye, *Moscow* 19 B2
Küçükköy, *Istanbul* 12 B1
Kudankita, *Tokyo* 29 a3
Kudrovo, *St. Petersburg* 26 B3
Kulosaari, *Helsinki* 12 B3
Kulturforum, *Berlin* 5 b3
Kultury i Nauki, Palac, *Warsaw* 31 b2
Kŭmch'ŏn, *Seoul* 26 C1
Kumla, *Stockholm* 28 B3
Kungens kurva, *Stockholm* 28 B1
Kungliga Slottet, *Stockholm* 28 b2
Kungshatt, *Stockholm* 28 B1
Kungsholmen, *Stockholm* 28 A2
Kuningan, *Jakarta* 13 B1
Kunitachi, *Tokyo* 29 A1
Kunming Hu, *Beijing* 4 B1
Kunratice, *Prague* 24 B2
Kunsthistorischesmuseum, *Vienna* 31 b1
Kuntsevo, *Moscow* 19 B2
Kupchino, *St. Petersburg* 26 B2
Kurbağalı →, *Istanbul* 12 C2
Kurihara, *Tokyo* 29 A2
Kurla, *Mumbai* 20 A2
Kurmuri, *Mumbai* 20 A2
Kurume, *Tokyo* 29 A2
Kuryanovo, *Moscow* 19 C4
Kuskovo, *Moscow* 19 B4
Kustia, *Calcutta* 8 B2
Kutsino, *Moscow* 19 B5
Kuzguncuk, *Istanbul* 12 B2
Kuzyminki, *Moscow* 19 B4
Kwai Chung, *Hong Kong* 12 A1
Kwanak, *Seoul* 26 C1
Kwanak-san, *Seoul* 26 C1
Kyje, *Prague* 24 B3
Kyūhōji, *Osaka* 22 B4

L

La Blanca, *Santiago* 26 C2
La Boca, *Buenos Aires* 7 B2
La Bretèche, *Paris* 23 A1
La Campiña, *Lima* 16 C2
La Celle-St.-Cloud, *Paris* 23 A1
La Ciudadela, *Mexico City* 18 c2
La Courneuve, *Paris* 23 A3
La Dehesa, *Santiago* 26 B2
La Encantada, *Lima* 16 C2
La Estación, *Madrid* 17 B1
La Floresta, *Barcelona* 4 A1
La Fortuna, *Madrid* 17 B1
La Fransa, *Barcelona* 4 A1
La Garenne-Colombes, *Paris* 23 A2
La Giustiniana, *Rome* 25 B1
La Grange, *Chicago* 9 C1
La Grange Park, *Chicago* 9 C1
La Granja, *Santiago* 26 C2
La Guardia Airport, *New York* 21 B2
La Hulpe, *Brussels* 6 B2
La Llacuna, *Barcelona* 4 A2
La Loma, *Mexico City* 18 A1
La Lucila, *Buenos Aires* 7 B2
La Maladrerie, *Paris* 23 A1
La Milla, Cerro, *Lima* 16 B2
La Monachina, *Rome* 25 B1
La Moraleja, *Madrid* 17 A2
La Nopalera, *Mexico City* 18 C2
La Paternal, *Buenos Aires* 7 B2
La Perla, *Lima* 16 B2
La Perouse, *Sydney* 28 B2
La Pineda, *Barcelona* 4 B1
La Pisana, *Rome* 25 B1
La Prairie, *Montreal* 19 B3
La Punta, *Lima* 16 B1
La Puntigala, *Barcelona* 4 A2
La Queue-en-Brie, *Paris* 23 B4
La Reina, *Santiago* 26 B2
La Ribera, *Barcelona* 4 A1
La Sagrera, *Barcelona* 4 A2
La Salada, *Buenos Aires* 7 C2
La Scala, *Milan* 18 B2
La Storta, *Rome* 25 A1
La Taxonera, *Barcelona* 4 A2
La Victoria, *Lima* 16 B2
Laajalahti, *Helsinki* 12 B1
Laajasalo, *Helsinki* 12 B3
Laaksolahti, *Helsinki* 12 B1
Lablâba, W. el →, *Cairo* 7 A2
Lac Cisterna, *Santiago* 26 C2
Lachine, *Montreal* 19 B1
Lad Phrao, *Bangkok* 3 B2
Ladera Heights, *Los Angeles* 16 C2
Ládvi, *Prague* 24 B2
Łady, *Warsaw* 31 C1
Lafontaine, Parc, *Montreal* 19 A2
Lagoa, *Rio de Janeiro* 24 B1
Lagos, *Lagos* 14 B2
Lagos Harbour, *Lagos* 14 B2
Lagos-Ikeja Airport, *Lagos* 14 A1
Lagos Island, *Lagos* 14 B2
Lagos Lagoon, *Lagos* 14 B2
Laguna de B., *Manila* 17 C2
Laim, *Munich* 20 B2
Lainate, *Milan* 18 A1
Lainz, *Vienna* 31 B1
Lakemba, *Sydney* 28 B1
Lakeside, *Cape Town* 8 B1
Lakeside, *Johannesburg* 13 A2
Lakeview, *Chicago* 9 B3
Lakewood Park, *Atlanta* 3 B2
Lakhtinskiy, *St. Petersburg* 26 B1
Lakhtinskiy Razliv, Oz., *St. Petersburg* 26 B1
Lakshmanpur, *Calcutta* 8 B1
Lal Qila, *Delhi* 1 a3
Lam Tin, *Hong Kong* 12 B2
Lambert, *Oslo* 22 A3
Lambeth, *London* 15 B3
Lambrate, *Milan* 18 B2
Lambro, Parco, *Milan* 18 B2
Lambton Mills, *Toronto* 30 B1
Lamma I., *Hong Kong* 12 B1
Landover Hills, *Washington* 32 B4
Landsmeer, *Amsterdam* 2 A2
Landstrasse, *Vienna* 31 A2
Landwehr kanal, *Berlin* 5 B3
Lane Cove, *Sydney* 28 A1
Lane Cove National Park, *Sydney* 28 A1
Langa, *Cape Town* 8 A2
Langenzersdorf, *Vienna* 31 A2
Langer See, *Berlin* 5 B4
Langley, *Washington* 32 B2
Langley Park, *Washington* 32 B4
Langwald, *Munich* 20 A1
Lanham, *Washington* 32 B4
Lankwitz, *Berlin* 5 B3
L'Annunziatella, *Rome* 25 C2
Lansdowne, *Cape Town* 8 A2
Lansing, *Toronto* 30 A2
Lanús, *Buenos Aires* 7 C2
Lapa, *Rio de Janeiro* 24 B1
Laranjeiras, *Rio de Janeiro* 24 B1
Larísa Sta., *Athens* 2 a1
Las, *Warsaw* 31 B2
Las Corts, *Barcelona* 4 A1
Las Kabacki, *Warsaw* 31 C2
Las Pinas, *Manila* 17 C1
Las Rejas, *Santiago* 26 B1
Lasalle, *Montreal* 19 B2
Lasek Bielański, *Warsaw* 31 B1
Lasek Na Kole, *Warsaw* 31 B1
Laski, *Warsaw* 31 B1
Latina, *Madrid* 17 B1
Laurence G. Hanscom Field, *Boston* 6 A2
Lauttasaari, *Helsinki* 12 C2
Laval, *Montreal* 19 A1
Laval-des-Rapides, *Montreal* 19 A1
Lavīzān, *Tehran* 30 A2
Lavradio, *Lisbon* 14 A2
Lawndale, *Chicago* 9 B2
Lawrence Heights, *Toronto* 30 A2
Layari, *Karachi* 14 A2
Layari →, *Karachi* 14 A1
Lazare, Gare St., *Paris* 23 a3
Łazienkowski, Palac, *Warsaw* 31 c3
Łazienkowski Park, *Warsaw* 31 B2
Le Blanc-Mesnil, *Paris* 23 A3
Le Bourget, *Paris* 23 A3
Le Chenoi, *Brussels* 6 B2
Le Chesnay, *Paris* 23 B1
Le Christ de Saclay, *Paris* 23 B2
Le Kremlin-Bicêtre, *Paris* 23 B3
Le Mesnil-le-Roi, *Paris* 23 A1
Le Pecq, *Paris* 23 A1
Le Perreux, *Paris* 23 A3
Le Pin, *Paris* 23 A4
Le Plessis-Robinson, *Paris* 23 B2
Le Plessis-Trévise, *Paris* 23 B4
Le Port-Marly, *Paris* 23 A1
Le Pré-St.-Gervais, *Paris* 23 A3
Le Raincy, *Paris* 23 A4
Le Vésinet, *Paris* 23 A1
Lea Bridge, *London* 15 A3
Leaside, *Toronto* 30 A2
Leblon, *Rio de Janeiro* 24 B1
Lee, *London* 15 B4
Leganés, *Madrid* 17 C1
Legazpi, *Madrid* 17 B1
Lehtisaari, *Helsinki* 12 B2
Lei Yue Mun, *Hong Kong* 12 B2
Leião, *Lisbon* 14 A1
Leicester Square, *London* 15 b3
Leichhardt, *Sydney* 28 B1
Leith, *Edinburgh* 11 B3
Lemoyne, *Montreal* 19 B3
Lenin, *Moscow* 19 B3
Lenino, *Moscow* 19 C3
Leninskiye Gory, *Moscow* 19 B3
Lennox, *Los Angeles* 16 C2
Leonia, *New York* 21 A2
Leopardstown, *Dublin* 11 B2
Leopoldau, *Vienna* 31 A2
Leopoldstadt, *Vienna* 31 A2
Leportovo, *Moscow* 19 B4
Leppävaara, *Helsinki* 12 B1
Les Lilas, *Paris* 23 A3
Les Loges-en-Josas, *Paris* 23 B1
Les Pavillons-sous-Bois, *Paris* 23 A4
Lésigny, *Paris* 23 B4
Lesnozavodskaya, *St. Petersburg* 26 B2
L'Étang-la-Ville, *Paris* 23 A1
Letná, *Prague* 24 a1
Letňany, *Prague* 24 B3
Levallois-Perret, *Paris* 23 A2
Levent, *Istanbul* 12 B2
Lewisdale, *Washington* 32 B4
Lewisham, *London* 15 B3
Lexington, *Boston* 6 A2
Leyton, *London* 15 A3
Leytonstone, *London* 15 A4
L'Hay-les-Roses, *Paris* 23 B3
L'Hospitalet de Llobregat, *Barcelona* 4 A1
Lhotka, *Prague* 24 B2
Liangshui He →, *Beijing* 4 C2
Lianhua Chi, *Beijing* 4 B1
Lianhua He →, *Beijing* 4 B1
Libčice nad Vitavou, *Prague* 24 A2
Libeň, *Prague* 24 B2
Liberdade, *São Paulo* 26 B2
Liberdade, Ave da, *Lisbon* 14 b1
Liberton, *Edinburgh* 11 B3
Liberty I., *New York* 21 B1
Liberty State Park, *New York* 21 B1
Libeznice, *Prague* 24 A2
Library of Congress, *Washington* 32 c3
Libuš, *Prague* 24 B2
Lichiao, *Canton* 8 B2
Lichtenburg, *Berlin* 5 A4
Lichterfelde, *Berlin* 5 B2
Lidingö, *Stockholm* 28 A2
Lieshi Lingyuan, *Canton* 8 B2
Liesing, *Vienna* 31 B1
Liesing →, *Vienna* 31 B2
Liffey, R. →, *Dublin* 11 A1
Ligovo, *St. Petersburg* 26 C1
Lijordet, *Oslo* 22 A2
Likavitos, *Athens* 2 b3
Likhoborka →, *Moscow* 19 A3
Lilla Värtan, *Stockholm* 28 A3
Lille Værløse, *Copenhagen* 10 A2
Liluah, *Calcutta* 8 B1
Lim Chu Kang, *Singapore* 27 A2
Lima, *Lima* 16 B2
Limbiate, *Milan* 18 A1
Limehouse, *London* 15 A3
Limeil-Brévannes, *Paris* 23 B3
Linate, Aeroporto Internazionale di, *Milan* 18 B2
Linbropark, *Johannesburg* 13 A2
Lincoln, *Boston* 6 A2
Lincoln Center, *New York* 21 b2
Lincoln Heights, *Los Angeles* 16 B3
Lincoln Park, *Chicago* 9 B3
Lincoln Park, *New York* 21 B1
Lincoln Park, *San Francisco* 25 B1
Lincolnwood, *Chicago* 9 A2
Linda-a-Pastora, *Lisbon* 14 A1
Linden, *Johannesburg* 13 A2
Linden, *Wellington* 32 A1
Lindenberg, *Berlin* 5 A4
Lindøya, *Oslo* 22 A3
Liniers, *Buenos Aires* 7 B1
Linkebeek, *Brussels* 6 B2
Linksfield, *Johannesburg* 13 A2
Linmeyer, *Johannesburg* 13 B2
Linna, *Helsinki* 12 A2
Lintuvaara, *Helsinki* 12 B1
Lion Rock Country Park, *Hong Kong* 12 A2
Lioúmi, *Athens* 2 B2
Liqizhuang, *Tianjin* 30 B2
Lisboa, *Lisbon* 14 A2
Lisbon = Lisboa, *Lisbon* 14 A2
Lishui, *Canton* 8 A1
Little B., *Sydney* 28 B2
Little Calumet →, *Chicago* 9 D3
Little Ferry, *New York* 21 A1
Little Italy, *New York* 21 e2
Little Mermaid, *Copenhagen* 10 a3
Little Rouge →, *Toronto* 30 A4
Little Tokyo, *Los Angeles* 16 c2
Liuhang, *Shanghai* 27 A1
Liurong Temple, *Canton* 8 B2
Liuxi →, *Canton* 8 B2
Liverpool Street, *London* 15 a5
Livry-Gargan, *Paris* 23 A4
Ljan, *Oslo* 22 A3
Llano de Can Gineu, *Barcelona* 4 A2
Llobregat →, *Barcelona* 4 A1
Lo Aranguiz, *Santiago* 26 B2
Lo Boza, *Santiago* 26 B1
Lo Chau, *Hong Kong* 12 B2
Lo Espejo, *Santiago* 26 C1
Lo Hermida, *Santiago* 26 B2
Lo Prado, *Santiago* 26 B1
Lo So Shing, *Hong Kong* 12 B1
Lo Wai, *Hong Kong* 12 A1
Loanhead, *Edinburgh* 11 B3
Lobau, *Vienna* 31 A3
Lobos, Pt., *San Francisco* 25 B1
Locham, *Munich* 20 B1
Lochino, *Moscow* 19 B1
Lochkov, *Prague* 24 B2
Lockhausen, *Munich* 20 A1
Lodi, *New York* 21 A1
Lodi Estate, *Delhi* 10 B2
Logan Int. Airport, *Boston* 6 A4
Logan Square, *Chicago* 9 B2
Lognes-Émerainville, Aérodrome de, *Paris* 23 B4
Löhme, *Berlin* 5 A5
Lolokhet, *Karachi* 14 A2
Lomas Chapultepec, *Mexico City* 18 B1
Lomas de San Angel Inn, *Mexico City* 18 B1
Lomas de Zamora, *Buenos Aires* 7 C2
Lombardy East, *Johannesburg* 13 A2
Łomianki, *Warsaw* 31 A1
Lomus Reforma, *Mexico City* 18 B1
London, *London* 15 A3
London Bridge, *London* 15 b5
London City Airport, *London* 15 A4
London Zoo, *London* 15 A3
Long B., *Sydney* 28 B2
Long Branch, *Toronto* 30 B1
Long Brook →, *Washington* 32 C2
Long Ditton, *London* 15 B2
Long I., *Boston* 6 B4
Long Island City, *New York* 21 B2
Long Street, *Cape Town* 8 c2
Longchamp, Hippodrôme de, *Paris* 23 A2
Longhua Pagoda, *Shanghai* 27 B1
Longhua Park, *Shanghai* 27 B1
Longjohn Slough, *Chicago* 9 C1
Longtan Hu →, *Beijing* 4 B2
Longue-Pointe, *Montreal* 19 A2
Longueuil, *Montreal* 19 A3
Loni, *Delhi* 10 A2
Loop, The, *Chicago* 9 c1
Lord's Cricket Ground, *London* 15 A2
Loreto, *Milan* 18 B2
Los Angeles Int. Airport, *Los Angeles* 16 C2
Los Cerrillos, Aeropuerto, *Santiago* 26 B1
Los Nietos, *Los Angeles* 16 C4
Los Olivos, *Lima* 16 A2
Los Reyes, *Mexico City* 18 B2
Lot, *Brussels* 6 B1
Loughlinstown, *Dublin* 11 B3
Loures, *Lisbon* 14 A1
Louveciennes, *Paris* 23 A1
Louvre, Musée du, *Paris* 23 b4
Louvre, Palais du, *Paris* 23 b4
Lower East Side, *New York* 21 e2
Lower Hutt, *Wellington* 32 B2
Lower Manhattan, *New York* 21 e1
Lower New York B., *New York* 21 C1
Lower Shing Mun Res., *Hong Kong* 12 A1
Lowry Bay, *Wellington* 32 B2
Lu Xun Museum, *Beijing* 4 b1
Lübars, *Berlin* 5 A3
Ludwigsfeld, *Munich* 20 A1
Luhu, *Canton* 8 B2
Lumiar, *Lisbon* 14 A2
Lumphini Park, *Bangkok* 3 B2
Lundtofte, *Copenhagen* 10 A3
Lung Mei, *Hong Kong* 12 A2
Luojiang, *Canton* 8 B2
Lustheim, *Munich* 20 A2
Luwan, *Shanghai* 27 B1
Luxembourg, Palais du, *Paris* 23 c4
Luzhniki Sports Centre, *Moscow* 19 B3
Lyndhurst, *New York* 21 B1
Lynn, *Boston* 6 A4
Lynn Harbor, *Boston* 6 A4
Lynn Woods Res., *Boston* 6 A3
Lyon, Gare de, *Paris* 23 c5
Lyons, *Chicago* 9 C2
Lysaker, *Oslo* 22 A2
Lysakerselva →, *Oslo* 22 A2
Lysolaje, *Prague* 24 B2
Lyubertsy, *Moscow* 19 B5
Lyublino, *Moscow* 19 B4

M

Ma Nam Wat, *Hong Kong* 12 A2
Ma On Shan Country Park, *Hong Kong* 12 A2
Ma'ale Adumim, *Jerusalem* 13 B2
Ma'ale Ha Khamisha, *Jerusalem* 13 B1
Ma'ale Mikhmas, *Jerusalem* 13 A2
Maantiekylä, *Helsinki* 12 A3
Maarifa, *Baghdad* 3 B2
Mabato Pt., *Manila* 17 C2
Macaco, Morro do, *Rio de Janeiro* 24 B2
McCook, *Chicago* 9 C2
Machelen, *Brussels* 6 A2
Machida, *Tokyo* 29 B1
Maciołki, *Warsaw* 31 B2
Mackayville, *Montreal* 19 A3
McKerrow, *Wellington* 32 B2
McKinley Park, *Chicago* 9 C2
Mclean, *Washington* 32 B2
Macopocho, R. →, *Santiago* 26 B1
MacRitchie Res., *Singapore* 27 A2
Macul, *Santiago* 26 C2
Madame Tussaud's, *London* 15 a3
Madhudaha, *Calcutta* 8 B2
Madhyamgram, *Calcutta* 8 A2
Madīnah Al Mansūr, *Baghdad* 3 B2
Mâdinet Nasr, *Cairo* 7 A2
Madison Avenue, *New York* 21 c2
Madison Square, *New York* 21 d2
Madrid, *Madrid* 17 B1
Madrona, *Barcelona* 4 A1
Maesawa, *Tokyo* 29 A2
Magdalena, *Lima* 16 B2
Magdalena Contreras, *Mexico City* 18 C1
Maghreb, *Baghdad* 3 A2
Maginu, *Tokyo* 29 B2
Magliana, *Rome* 25 B1
Magny-les-Hameaux, *Paris* 23 B1
Magonoy, *Manila* 17 B2
Mahalaxmi, *Mumbai* 20 a1
Maheshtala, *Calcutta* 8 C1
Mahim, *Mumbai* 20 A2
Mahim B., *Mumbai* 20 A1
Mahlsdorf, *Berlin* 5 A4
Mahmoodabad, *Karachi* 14 A2
Mahrauli, *Delhi* 10 B1
Mahul, *Mumbai* 20 A2
Maida Vale, *London* 15 a1
Maidstone, *Melbourne* 17 A1
Maipú, *Santiago* 26 C1
Maisonneuve, Parc, *Montreal* 19 A2
Maisons-Alfort, *Paris* 23 B3
Maisons-Laffitte, *Paris* 23 A1
Maissoneuve, *Montreal* 19 A2
Maitland, *Cape Town* 8 A1
Makati, *Manila* 17 B2
Mäkiniitty, *Helsinki* 12 A2
Mala Straná, *Prague* 24 B2
Malabar, *Mumbai* 20 B1
Malabar, *Sydney* 28 B2
Malabar Hill, *Mumbai* 20 B1
Malabar Pt., *Mumbai* 20 B1
Malabon, *Manila* 17 B1
Malacañang Palace, *Manila* 17 B1
Malahide, *Dublin* 11 A3
Malakhovka, *Moscow* 19 C6
Malakoff, *Paris* 23 B2
Mälarhöjaen, *Stockholm* 28 B1
Malate, *Manila* 17 B1
Malay Quarter, *Cape Town* 8 c2
Malaya Neva, *St. Petersburg* 26 B1
Malaya-Okhta, *St. Petersburg* 26 B2
Malchow, *Berlin* 5 A3
Malden, *Boston* 6 A3
Malden, *London* 15 B2
Maleizen, *Brussels* 6 B3
Malešice, *Prague* 24 B3
Malir →, *Karachi* 14 B2
Mall, The, *Washington* 32 b2
Malleny Mills, *Edinburgh* 11 B2
Malmi, *Helsinki* 12 B2
Malmøya, *Oslo* 22 A3
Måløv, *Copenhagen* 10 A2
Malpasso, Ost., *Rome* 25 C1
Malton, *Toronto* 30 A1
Malvern, *Johannesburg* 13 B2
Malvern, *Melbourne* 17 B2
Malvern, *Toronto* 30 A3
Mamonovo, *Moscow* 19 B2
Mampang Prapatan, *Jakarta* 13 B1
Mampukuji, *Tokyo* 29 B2
Man Budrukh, *Mumbai* 20 A2
Man Khurd, *Mumbai* 20 A2
Mandaluyong, *Manila* 17 B2
Mandaoli, *Delhi* 10 B2
Mandaqui →, *São Paulo* 26 A2
Mandoli, *Delhi* 10 A2
Mandvi, *Mumbai* 20 B2
Manenberg, *Cape Town* 8 A2
Mang Kung Uk, *Hong Kong* 12 B2
Mangolpuri, *Delhi* 10 A1
Manguinhos, Aéroporto, *Rio de Janeiro* 24 B1
Mangwŏn, *Seoul* 26 B1
Manhattan, *New York* 21 B2
Manhattan Beach, *New York* 21 C2
Manila, *Manila* 17 B1
Manila B., *Manila* 17 B1
Manila Int. Airport, *Manila* 17 B2
Mankkaa, *Helsinki* 12 B1
Manly, *Sydney* 28 A2
Mannswörth, *Vienna* 31 B3
Manor Park, *London* 15 A4
Manor Park, *Wellington* 32 A2
Manora, *Karachi* 14 B1
Manquehue, Cerro, *Santiago* 26 B2
Manzanares, Canal de, *Madrid* 17 C2
Mao Mausoleum, *Beijing* 4 c2
Map'o, *Seoul* 26 B1
Maracanã, *Rio de Janeiro* 24 B1
Maraoli, *Mumbai* 20 A2
Marblehead, *Boston* 6 A4
Marcelin, *Warsaw* 31 B1
Mareil-Marly, *Paris* 23 A1
Margareten, *Vienna* 31 A2
Maria, *Vienna* 31 A2
Maridalen, *Oslo* 22 A3
Maridalsvatnet, *Oslo* 22 A3
Mariendorf, *Berlin* 5 B3
Marienfelde, *Berlin* 5 B3
Marienplatz, *Munich* 20 b2
Marikina →, *Manila* 17 B2
Marin City, *San Francisco* 25 A1
Marin Headlands State Park, *San Francisco* 25 A2
Marin Pen., *San Francisco* 25 A1
Marina del Rey, *Los Angeles* 16 C2
Marine Drive, *Mumbai* 20 b1
Marino, *Dublin* 11 A2
Maritim, Museu, *Barcelona* 4 c2
Markham, *Toronto* 30 A2
Marki, *Warsaw* 31 B2
Markland Wood, *Toronto* 30 B1
Marly, Forêt de, *Paris* 23 A1
Marly-le-Roi, *Paris* 23 A1
Marne →, *Paris* 23 B3
Marne-la-Vallée, *Paris* 23 A4
Marolles-en-Brie, *Paris* 23 B4
Maroubra, *Sydney* 28 B2
Marquette Park, *Chicago* 9 C2
Marrickville, *Sydney* 28 B1
Marsfield, *Sydney* 28 A1
Marshall Field's, *Chicago* 9 c2
Marte, Campo de, *São Paulo* 26 B2
Martesana, Navíglio della, *Milan* 18 A2
Martin Luther King National Historic Site, *Atlanta* 3 B2
Martinez, *Buenos Aires* 7 A1
Martinkylä, *Helsinki* 12 B2
Martinsried, *Munich* 20 B1
Maruko, *Tokyo* 29 B3
Marunouchi, *Tokyo* 29 b4
Marusino, *Moscow* 19 B5
Maryino, *Moscow* 19 B4
Maryland, *Singapore* 27 B2
Marylebone, *London* 15 A2
Marymont, *Warsaw* 31 B1
Marysin Wawerski, *Warsaw* 31 B2
Marzahn, *Berlin* 5 A4
Mascot, *Sydney* 28 B2
Masmo, *Stockholm* 28 B1
Maspeth, *New York* 21 B2
Masr el Gedida, *Cairo* 7 A2
Masr el Qadîma, *Cairo* 7 A2
Massachusetts B., *Boston* 6 A4
Massachusett's Inst. of Tech., *Boston* 6 A3
Massamá, *Lisbon* 14 A1
Massey →, *Toronto* 30 A3
Massy, *Paris* 23 B2
Matihutong, *Beijing* 4 B1
Matinha, *Lisbon* 14 A2
Matramam, *Jakarta* 13 B2
Matsubara, *Osaka* 22 B4
Mattapan, *Boston* 6 B3
Mátyásföld, *Budapest* 7 A3
Mátyástemplom, *Budapest* 7 b1
Mau Tso Ngam, *Hong Kong* 12 A2
Mauer, *Vienna* 31 B1
Mauripur, *Karachi* 14 A1
Maxhof, *Munich* 20 B1
Maya-Zan, *Osaka* 22 A2
Mayfair, *Johannesburg* 13 B2
Mayfair, *London* 15 b3
Mayor, Plaza, *Madrid* 17 b2
Maywood, *Chicago* 9 B1
Maywood, *Los Angeles* 16 C3
Maywood, *New York* 21 A1
Mazagaon, *Mumbai* 20 a2
Me'a She' Arim, *Jerusalem* 13 a2
Meadowbank Park, *Sydney* 28 A1
Měcholupy, *Prague* 24 B3
Měčice, *Prague* 24 A3
Mecidiyeköy, *Istanbul* 12 B2
Medford, *Boston* 6 A3
Mediodia, *Madrid* 17 B2
Medvezhiy Ozyora, *Moscow* 19 A5
Meguro →, *Tokyo* 29 B3
Meguro-Ku, *Tokyo* 29 B3
Mehpalpur, *Delhi* 10 B1
Mehrābād Airport, *Tehran* 30 A1
Mehram Nagar, *Delhi* 10 B1
Mehrow, *Berlin* 5 A4
Mei Lanfang, *Beijing* 4 a2
Meidling, *Vienna* 31 A2
Méier, *Rio de Janeiro* 24 B1
Meiji Shrine, *Tokyo* 29 b1
Meise, *Brussels* 6 A1
Mejiro, *Tokyo* 29 A3
Melbourne, *Melbourne* 17 A1
Melbourne Airport, *Melbourne* 17 A1
Melkki, *Helsinki* 12 C2
Mellunkylä, *Helsinki* 12 B3
Mellunmäki, *Helsinki* 12 B3
Melrose, *Boston* 6 A3
Melrose, *New York* 21 B2
Melrose Park, *Chicago* 9 B1
Melsbroek, *Brussels* 6 A2
Menteng, *Jakarta* 13 B1
Mérantaise →, *Paris* 23 B1
Mercamadrid, *Madrid* 17 B2
Merced, L., *San Francisco* 25 B2
Meredale, *Johannesburg* 13 B1
Merlimau, P., *Singapore* 27 B2
Merri Cr. →, *Melbourne* 17 A1
Merrion, *Dublin* 11 B2
Merrionette Park, *Chicago* 9 C2
Merton, *London* 15 B2
Mesgarābād, *Tehran* 30 B3
Meshcherskiy, *Moscow* 19 B2
Messe, *Vienna* 31 A2
Messe-palast, *Vienna* 31 c1
Metanópoli, *Milan* 18 B2
Metropolitan Museum of Art, *New York* 21 b3
Meudon, *Paris* 23 B2
Mevaseret Tsiyon, *Jerusalem* 13 B1
Mevo Beitar, *Jerusalem* 13 B1
México, Ciudad de, *Mexico City* 18 B1
Meyersdal, *Johannesburg* 13 B2
Mezzano, *Milan* 18 B2
Mezzate, *Milan* 18 B2
Miadong, *Seoul* 26 B2
Miami, *Miami* 18 B2
Miami Beach, *Miami* 18 B2
Miami Canal →, *Miami* 18 A1
Miami Int. Airport, *Miami* 18 B1
Miami Shores, *Miami* 18 A2
Miami Springs, *Miami* 18 B1
Miasto, *Warsaw* 31 B2
Michałowice, *Warsaw* 31 B1
Michigan Avenue, *Chicago* 9 b2
Michle, *Prague* 24 B2
Middle Harbour, *Sydney* 28 A2
Middle Hd., *Sydney* 28 A2
Middle Park, *Melbourne* 17 B1
Middle Village, *New York* 21 B2
Middlesex Fells Reservation, *Boston* 6 A3
Midi, Gare du, *Brussels* 6 c1
Midland Beach, *New York* 21 C1
Miedzeszyn, *Warsaw* 31 B3
Międzylesie, *Warsaw* 31 B3
Miessaari, *Helsinki* 12 C1
Miguel Hidalgo, *Mexico City* 18 B1
Mikhelysona, *Moscow* 19 B5
Milano, *Milan* 18 B1
Milano Due, *Milan* 18 B2
Milano San Felice, *Milan* 18 B2
Milbertshofen, *Munich* 20 A2
Mill Hill, *London* 15 A2
Millennium Dome, *London* 15 A4
Miller Meadow, *Chicago* 9 B2
Millerhill, *Edinburgh* 11 B3
Millers Point, *Sydney* 28 a1
Milltown, *Dublin* 11 B2
Millwood, *Washington* 32 B4
Milnerton, *Cape Town* 8 A1
Milon-la-Chapelle, *Paris* 23 B1
Milton, *Boston* 6 B3
Milton Bridge, *Edinburgh* 11 B2
Mimico, *Toronto* 30 B2
Minami, *Osaka* 22 A4
Minamitsunashima, *Tokyo* 29 B2
Minato, *Osaka* 22 B3
Minato-Ku, *Tokyo* 29 c3
Minshât el Bekkarî, *Cairo* 7 A1
Minute Man Nat. Hist. Park, *Boston* 6 A2
Miraflores, *Lima* 16 B2
Miramar, *Wellington* 32 B1
Misericordia, Sa. da, *Rio de Janeiro* 24 B1
Mission, *San Francisco* 25 B2
Mississauga, *Toronto* 30 B1
Mitaka, *Tokyo* 29 A2
Mitcham, *London* 15 B2
Mitcham Common, *London* 15 B3
Mitchell's Plain, *Cape Town* 8 B2
Mitino, *Moscow* 19 A2
Mitte, *Berlin* 5 A3
Mittel Isarkanal →, *Munich* 20 A3
Mixcoac, *Mexico City* 18 B1
Mixcoac, Presa de, *Mexico City* 18 B1
Miyakojima, *Osaka* 22 A4
Mizonokuchi, *Tokyo* 29 B2
Mizue, *Tokyo* 29 A4
Młocinski Park, *Warsaw* 31 B1
Młociny, *Warsaw* 31 B1
Mnevniki, *Moscow* 19 B2
Moba, *Lagos* 14 B2
Moczydło, *Warsaw* 31 C2
Modderfontein, *Johannesburg* 13 A2
Modřany, *Prague* 24 B2
Mogyoród, *Budapest* 7 A3
Moinho Velho, Cor. →, *São Paulo* 26 B2
Mok, *Seoul* 26 B1
Mokotów, *Warsaw* 31 B2
Molenbeek-Saint-Jean, *Brussels* 6 A1
Molino de Rosas, *Mexico City* 18 B1
Mollem, *Brussels* 6 A1
Mollins de Rey, *Barcelona* 4 A1
Mondeor, *Johannesburg* 13 B2
Moneda, Palacio de la, *Santiago* 26 B2
Moneró, *Rio de Janeiro* 24 A1
Mong Kok, *Hong Kong* 12 B2
Monkstown, *Dublin* 11 B3
Monnickendam, *Amsterdam* 2 A3
Monrovia, *Los Angeles* 16 B4
Monsanto, *Lisbon* 14 A1
Monsanto, Parque Florestal de, *Lisbon* 14 A1
Mont Royal, *Montreal* 19 A2
Mont-Royal, Parc, *Montreal* 19 A2
Montana de Montjuich, *Barcelona* 4 A1
Monte Chingolo, *Buenos Aires* 7 C2

RAFFLES PARK

Monte Palatino, *Rome* 25 c3
Montebello, *Los Angeles* 16 B4
Montemor, *Lisbon* 14 A1
Monterey Park, *Los Angeles* 16 B4
Montespaccato, *Rome* 25 B1
Montesson, *Paris* 23 A1
Monteverde Nuovo, *Rome* 25 B1
Montfermeil, *Paris* 23 A4
Montigny-le-Bretonneux, *Paris* 23 B1
Montjay-la-Tour, *Paris* 23 A4
Montjuic, Parc de, *Barcelona* 4 c1
Montparnasse, Gare, *Paris* 23 A2
Montréal, *Montreal* 19 A2
Montréal, Î. de, *Montreal* 19 A2
Montréal, Univ. de, *Montreal* 19 B2
Montréal Est, *Montreal* 19 A2
Montréal Nord, *Montreal* 19 A2
Montréal Ouest, *Montreal* 19 B1
Montreuil, *Paris* 23 A3
Montrouge, *Paris* 23 B2
Montserrat, *Buenos Aires* 7 B2
Monza, *Milan* 18 A2
Monzoro, *Milan* 18 B1
Moóca, *São Paulo* 26 B2
Moonachie, *New York* 21 B1
Moonee Ponds, *Melbourne* 17 A1
Moonee Valley Racecourse, *Melbourne* 17 A1
Moosach, *Munich* 20 A2
Mora, *Mumbai* 20 B2
Moratalaz, *Madrid* 17 B2
Mörby, *Stockholm* 28 A2
Morden, *London* 15 B2
Morée →, *Paris* 23 A3
Morgan Park, *Chicago* 9 C3
Moriguchi, *Osaka* 22 A4
Morivione, *Milan* 18 B2
Morningside, *Edinburgh* 11 B2
Morningside, *Johannesburg* 13 A2
Morningside, *Washington* 32 C4
Morro Solar, Cerro, *Lima* 16 C2
Mortlake, *London* 15 B2
Mortlake, *Sydney* 28 B1
Morton Grove, *Chicago* 9 A2
Morumbi, *São Paulo* 26 B1
Moscavide, *Lisbon* 14 A2
Moscow = Moskva, *Moscow* 19 B3
Moskhaton, *Athens* 2 B2
Moskva, *Moscow* 19 B3
Moskva →, *Moscow* 19 B2
Moskvoretskiy, *Moscow* 19 B3
Mosman, *Sydney* 28 A2
Móstoles, *Madrid* 17 C1
Moti Bagh, *Delhi* 10 B2
Motol, *Prague* 24 B1
Motsa, *Jerusalem* 13 B2
Motsa Ilit, *Jerusalem* 13 B1
Motspur Park, *London* 15 B2
Mottingham, *London* 15 B4
Moulin Rouge, *Paris* 23 a3
Mount Dennis, *Toronto* 30 A2
Mount Greenwood, *Chicago* 9 C2
Mount Hood Memorial Park, *Boston* 6 A3
Mount Merrion, *Dublin* 11 B2
Mount Rainier, *Washington* 32 B4
Mount Vernon, *New York* 21 A3
Mount Vernon Square, *Washington* 32 a2
Mount Zion, *Jerusalem* 13 b3
Mozarthaus, *Vienna* 31 b2
Müggelberge, *Berlin* 5 B4
Müggelheim, *Berlin* 5 B5
Muggiò, *Milan* 18 A2
Mughal Gardens, *Delhi* 1 c1
Mühleiten, *Vienna* 31 A3
Mühlenfliess →, *Berlin* 5 A5
Muiden, *Amsterdam* 2 A3
Muiderpoort Station, *Amsterdam* 2 b3
Muizenberg, *Cape Town* 8 B1
Mujahidpur, *Delhi* 10 B2
Mukandpur, *Delhi* 10 A2
Mukhmas, *Jerusalem* 13 A2
Muko →, *Osaka* 22 A3
Mukojima, *Tokyo* 29 A3
Mulbarton, *Johannesburg* 13 B2
Mumbai, *Mumbai* 20 B2
Mumbai Harbour, *Mumbai* 20 B2
Münchehofe, *Berlin* 5 B5
München, *Munich* 20 B2
Munich = München, *Munich* 20 B2
Munkkiniemi, *Helsinki* 12 B2
Munro, *Buenos Aires* 7 B1
Murai Res., *Singapore* 27 A2
Muranów, *Warsaw* 31 B1
Murino, *St. Petersburg* 26 B2
Murrayfield, *Edinburgh* 11 B2
Musashino, *Tokyo* 29 A2
Museu Nacional, *Rio de Janeiro* 24 B1
Mushin, *Lagos* 14 A2
Musiektheater, *Amsterdam* 2 b2
Muslim Quarter, *Jerusalem* 13 a3
Musocco, *Milan* 18 B1
Mustansirīya, *Baghdad* 3 A2
Musturud, *Cairo* 7 A2
Muswell Hill, *London* 15 A3
Mutanabi, *Baghdad* 3 B2
Muthana, *Baghdad* 3 B2
Myakinino, *Moscow* 19 B2
Mykerinos, *Cairo* 7 B1
Myllypuro, *Helsinki* 12 B3

N

Nacka, *Stockholm* 28 B3
Nada, *Osaka* 22 A2
Naenae, *Wellington* 32 B2
Nærsnes, *Oslo* 22 B1
Nagata, *Osaka* 22 B1
Nagatsuta, *Tokyo* 29 B2
Nagytétény, *Budapest* 7 B1
Nahant, *Boston* 6 A4
Nahant B., *Boston* 6 A4
Nahant Harbor, *Boston* 6 A4
Nahr Dijlah →, *Baghdad* 3 B2
Najafgarh Drain →, *Delhi* 10 B1
Nakahara-Ku, *Tokyo* 29 B2
Nakano-Ku, *Tokyo* 29 A2
Namgajwa, *Seoul* 26 B1
Namsan Park, *Seoul* 26 B1
Namyŏng, *Seoul* 26 B1
Nanbiancun, *Canton* 8 B1
Nanchang He →, *Beijing* 4 B1
Nandang, *Canton* 8 B2
Nandian, *Tianjin* 30 A2
Nangal Dewat, *Delhi* 10 B1
Naniwa, *Osaka* 22 B3
Nankai, *Tianjin* 30 B1
Nanmenwai, *Tianjin* 30 B2
Nanole, *Mumbai* 20 A2
Nanpu Bridge, *Shanghai* 27 B2
Nanshi, *Shanghai* 27 B1
Nantasket Beach, *Boston* 6 B4
Nanterre, *Paris* 23 A2
Naoabad, *Calcutta* 8 C2
Napier Mole, *Karachi* 14 B1
Naraina, *Delhi* 10 B1
Nariman Point, *Mumbai* 20 c1
Nariman Pt., *Mumbai* 20 B1
Nārmak, *Tehran* 30 A2
Naruo, *Osaka* 22 A3
Näsby, *Stockholm* 28 A2
Näsbypark, *Stockholm* 28 A2
Nathan Road, *Hong Kong* 12 a2
Natick, *Boston* 6 B2
National Maritime Museum, *San Francisco* 25 a1
National Museum, *Bangkok* 3 b1
Nationalmuseum, *Stockholm* 28 b2
Natolin, *Warsaw* 31 C2
Naturhistorischesmuseum, *Vienna* 31 b1
Naucalpan de Juárez, *Mexico City* 18 B1
Naupada, *Mumbai* 20 A2
Navíglio di Pavia, *Milan* 18 B1
Navíglio Grande, *Milan* 18 B1
Navona, Piazza, *Rome* 25 b2
Navotas, *Manila* 17 B1
Navy Pier, *Chicago* 9 b3
Nazal Hikmat Beg, *Baghdad* 3 A2
Nazimabad, *Karachi* 14 A2
Nazlet el Simmân, *Cairo* 7 B1
Néa Alexandhria, *Athens* 2 B2
Néa Faliron, *Athens* 2 B1
Néa Ionía, *Athens* 2 A2
Néa Liósia, *Athens* 2 A2
Néa Smírni, *Athens* 2 B2
Neapolis, *Athens* 2 B2
Near North, *Chicago* 9 b2
Nebušice, *Prague* 24 B1
Nederhorst, *Amsterdam* 2 B3
Nedlitz, *Berlin* 5 B1
Nee Soon, *Singapore* 27 A2
Needham Heights, *Boston* 6 B2
Nekrasovka, *Moscow* 19 B5
N'ematābād, *Tehran* 30 B2
Nemchinovka, *Moscow* 19 B1
Nemzeti Muz, *Budapest* 7 c3
Neponsit, *New York* 21 C2
Nerima-Ku, *Tokyo* 29 A3
Nesodden, *Oslo* 22 B3
Nesoddtangen, *Oslo* 22 A3
Nesøya, *Oslo* 22 A2
Neu Aubing, *Munich* 20 B1
Neu Buch, *Berlin* 5 A4
Neu Buchhorst, *Berlin* 5 B5
Neu Fahrland, *Berlin* 5 B1
Neu Lindenberg, *Berlin* 5 A4
Neubiberg, *Munich* 20 B3
Neue Hofburg, *Vienna* 31 b1
Neuenhagen, *Berlin* 5 A4
Neuessling, *Vienna* 31 A3
Neuhausen, *Munich* 20 B2
Neuherberg, *Munich* 20 A2
Neuhönow, *Berlin* 5 A5
Neuilly-Plaisance, *Paris* 23 A4
Neuilly-sur-Marne, *Paris* 23 A4
Neuilly-sur-Seine, *Paris* 23 A2
Neukagran, *Vienna* 31 A2
Neukettenhof, *Vienna* 31 B2
Neukölln, *Berlin* 5 B3
Neuperlach, *Munich* 20 B2
Neuried, *Munich* 20 B1
Neustift am Walde, *Vienna* 31 A1
Neusüssenbrunn, *Vienna* 31 A2
Neuwaldegg, *Vienna* 31 A1
Neva →, *St. Petersburg* 26 B2
Neves, *Rio de Janeiro* 24 B2
New Baghdād, *Baghdad* 3 B2
New Barakpur, *Calcutta* 8 A2
New Brighton, *New York* 21 C1
New Canada, *Johannesburg* 13 B1
New Canada Dam, *Johannesburg* 13 B1
New Carrollton, *Washington* 32 B4
New Cross, *London* 15 B3
New Delhi, *Delhi* 10 B2
New Dorp, *New York* 21 C1
New Dorp Beach, *New York* 21 C1
New Malden, *London* 15 B2
New Milford, *New York* 21 A1
New Territories, *Hong Kong* 12 A1
New Toronto, *Toronto* 30 B1
New Town, *Edinburgh* 11 B2
New Utrecht, *New York* 21 C2
Newark B., *New York* 21 B1
Newbattle, *Edinburgh* 11 B3
Newbury Park, *London* 15 A4
Newcraighall, *Edinburgh* 11 B3
Newham, *London* 15 A4
Newhaven, *Edinburgh* 11 B2
Newington, *Edinburgh* 11 B2
Newington, *London* 15 c5
Newlands, *Johannesburg* 13 B1
Newlands, *Wellington* 32 B1
Newport, *Melbourne* 17 B1
Newton, *Boston* 6 B2
Newtonbrook, *Toronto* 30 A2
Newtongrange, *Edinburgh* 11 B3
Newtonville, *Boston* 6 A2
Newtown, *Sydney* 28 B2
Neyagawa, *Osaka* 22 A4
Ngaio, *Wellington* 32 B1
Ngau Chi Wan, *Hong Kong* 12 A2
Ngau Tau Kok, *Hong Kong* 12 B2
Ngauranga, *Wellington* 32 B1
Ngong Shuen Chau, *Hong Kong* 12 B1
Ngua Kok Wan, *Hong Kong* 12 A1
Nīāvarān, *Tehran* 30 A2
Nibra, *Calcutta* 8 B1
Nidāl, *Baghdad* 3 B2
Niddrie, *Edinburgh* 11 B3
Niddrie, *Melbourne* 17 A1
Nieder Neuendorf, *Berlin* 5 A2
Niederschöneweide, *Berlin* 5 B3
Niederschönhausen, *Berlin* 5 A3
Niemeyer, *Rio de Janeiro* 24 B1
Nieuw Zuid, *Amsterdam* 2 c2
Nieuwe Kerk, *Amsterdam* 2 b2
Nieuwendam, *Amsterdam* 2 A2
Nihonbashi, *Tokyo* 29 b5
Niipperi, *Helsinki* 12 B1
Níkaia, *Athens* 2 B1
Nikolassee, *Berlin* 5 B2
Nikolskiy, *Moscow* 19 B2
Nikolyskoye, *Moscow* 19 B5
Nikulino, *Moscow* 19 B2
Nil, Nahr en →, *Cairo* 7 B2
Nile = Nil, Nahr en →, *Cairo* 7 B2
Niles, *Chicago* 9 A2
Nimta, *Calcutta* 8 A2
Ningyuan, *Tianjin* 30 B2
Nippa, *Tokyo* 29 B2
Nippori, *Tokyo* 29 A3
Nishi, *Osaka* 22 A3
Nishinari, *Osaka* 22 B3
Nishiyodogawa, *Osaka* 22 A3
Niterói, *Rio de Janeiro* 24 B2
Nob Hill, *San Francisco* 25 b1
Nockeby, *Stockholm* 28 B1
Noel Park, *London* 15 A3
Nogatino, *Moscow* 19 B4
Nogent-sur-Marne, *Paris* 23 A3
Noida, *Delhi* 10 B2
Noiseau, *Paris* 23 B4
Noisiel, *Paris* 23 A4
Noisy-le-Grand, *Paris* 23 A4
Noisy-le-Roi, *Paris* 23 A1
Noisy-le-Sec, *Paris* 23 A3
Nokkala, *Helsinki* 12 C1
Nomentano, *Rome* 25 B2
Nonakashinden, *Tokyo* 29 A2
Nongminyundong Jiangxisuo, *Canton* 8 B2
Nonhyŏn, *Seoul* 26 B2
Nonthaburi, *Bangkok* 3 A1
Noon Gun, *Cape Town* 8 b1
Noorder Kerk, *Amsterdam* 2 a1
Noordgesig, *Johannesburg* 13 B1
Noordzeekanaal, *Amsterdam* 2 A1
Nord, Gare du, *Paris* 23 a4
Nordrand-Siedlung, *Vienna* 31 A2
Nordstrand, *Oslo* 22 A3
Normandale, *Wellington* 32 B2
Nørrebro, *Copenhagen* 10 a1
Norridge, *Chicago* 9 B2
Norrmalm, *Stockholm* 28 a1
North Arlington, *New York* 21 B1
North Bay Village, *Miami* 18 A2
North Bergen, *New York* 21 B1
North Branch Chicago River →, *Chicago* 9 B2
North Bull Island, *Dublin* 11 A3
North Cambridge, *Boston* 6 A3
North Cheam, *London* 15 B2
North Cohasset, *Boston* 6 B4
North Cray, *London* 15 B4
North Decatur, *Atlanta* 3 B3
North Druid Hills, *Atlanta* 3 B3
North Esk →, *Edinburgh* 11 B2
North Gyle, *Edinburgh* 11 B2
North Hackensack, *New York* 21 A1
North Harbor, *Manila* 17 B1
North Hd., *Sydney* 28 A2
North Hollywood, *Los Angeles* 16 B2
North Lexington, *Boston* 6 A2
North Miami, *Miami* 18 A2
North Miami Beach, *Miami* 18 A2
North Nazimabad, *Karachi* 14 A2
North Pt., *Hong Kong* 12 B2
North Queensferry, *Edinburgh* 11 A1
North Quincy, *Boston* 6 B3
North Res., *Boston* 6 A3
North Riverside, *Chicago* 9 B2
North Saugus, *Boston* 6 A3
North Shore Channel →, *Chicago* 9 B2
North Springfield, *Washington* 32 C2
North Sudbury, *Boston* 6 A1
North Sydney, *Sydney* 28 B2
North Woolwich, *London* 15 A4
North York, *Toronto* 30 A2
Northbridge, *Sydney* 28 A2
Northbridge Park, *Sydney* 28 A2
Northcliff, *Johannesburg* 13 A1
Northcote, *Melbourne* 17 A2
Northlake, *Chicago* 9 B1
Northmount, *Toronto* 30 A2
Northolt, *London* 15 A1
Northumberland Heath, *London* 15 B5
Northwood, *London* 15 A1
Norumbega Res., *Boston* 6 B2
Norwood, *Johannesburg* 13 A2
Norwood Park, *Chicago* 9 B2
Noryangjin, *Seoul* 26 B1
Nossa Senhora de Candelária, *Rio de Janeiro* 24 a2
Nossa Senhora do Ó, *São Paulo* 26 B1
Nossegem, *Brussels* 6 A3
Notre-Dame, *Montreal* 19 B3
Notre-Dame, *Paris* 23 c4
Notre-Dame, Bois, *Paris* 23 B4
Notre-Dame-de-Grace, *Montreal* 19 B2
Notting Hill, *London* 15 b1
Nova Milanese, *Milan* 18 A2
Novate Milanese, *Milan* 18 A1
Novaya Derevnya, *St. Petersburg* 26 A1
Nové Město, *Prague* 24 B2
Novoaleksandrovskoye, *St. Petersburg* 26 B2
Novogireyevo, *Moscow* 19 B4
Novoivanovskoye, *Moscow* 19 B1
Novonikolyskoye, *Moscow* 19 A1
Novosaratovka, *St. Petersburg* 26 B3
Nowe-Babice, *Warsaw* 31 B1
Nöykkiö, *Helsinki* 12 B1
Nueva Atzacoalco, *Mexico City* 18 B2
Nueva Pompeya, *Buenos Aires* 7 C2
Nueva Tenochtitlán, *Mexico City* 18 B2
Nuijala, *Helsinki* 12 B1
Numabukuro, *Tokyo* 29 A2
Nunez, *Buenos Aires* 7 B2
Nunhead, *London* 15 B3
Ñuñoa, *Santiago* 26 B2
Nusle, *Prague* 24 B2
Nussdorf, *Vienna* 31 A2
Nyanga, *Cape Town* 8 A2
Nymphenburg, *Munich* 20 B2
Nymphenburg, Schloss, *Munich* 20 B2

O

Oak Grove, *Atlanta* 3 A3
Oak Island, *Boston* 6 A4
Oak Lawn, *Chicago* 9 C2
Oak Park, *Chicago* 9 B2
Oak View, *Washington* 32 A4
Oakdale, *Atlanta* 3 A2
Oakland, *San Francisco* 25 B3
Oakland, *Washington* 32 B4
Oaklawn, *Washington* 32 C4
Oakleigh, *Melbourne* 17 B2
Oakton, *Washington* 32 B2
Oakwood Beach, *New York* 21 C1
Oatley, *Sydney* 28 B1
Obalende, *Lagos* 14 B2
Oba's Palace, *Lagos* 14 B2
Oberföhring, *Munich* 20 B2
Oberhaching, *Munich* 20 B2
Oberlaa, *Vienna* 31 B2
Oberlisse, *Vienna* 31 A2
Obermenzing, *Munich* 20 A1
Obermoos Schwaige, *Munich* 20 A1
Oberschleissheim, *Munich* 20 A2
Oberschöneweide, *Berlin* 5 B4
Observatory, *Johannesburg* 13 B2
Observatory, *Sydney* 28 a1
Ōbu, *Osaka* 22 A1
Obu-tōge, *Osaka* 22 A1
Óbuda, *Budapest* 7 A2
Obukhovo, *St. Petersburg* 26 B2
Obvodnyy Kanal, *St. Petersburg* 26 B1
Ocean Park, *Hong Kong* 12 B2
Ochakovo, *Moscow* 19 B2
Ochota, *Warsaw* 31 B1
O'Connell Street, *Dublin* 11 b2
Ōdana, *Tokyo* 29 B2
Öden-Stockach, *Munich* 20 B3
Odilampi, *Helsinki* 12 B1
Odintsovo, *Moscow* 19 B1
Odivelas, *Lisbon* 14 A1
Odolany, *Warsaw* 31 B1
Oeiras, *Lisbon* 14 A1
Ofin, *Lagos* 14 A3
Ogawa, *Tokyo* 29 A1
Ogden Park, *Chicago* 9 C2
Ogikubo, *Tokyo* 29 A2
Ogogoro, *Lagos* 14 B2
Ogoyo, *Lagos* 14 B2
Ogudu, *Lagos* 14 A2
Ohariu Stream →, *Wellington* 32 B1
O'Higgins, Parque, *Santiago* 26 B2
Ōimachi, *Tokyo* 29 B3
Ojota, *Lagos* 14 A2
Okamoto, *Osaka* 22 A2
Okęcie, *Warsaw* 31 B1
Okęcie Airport, *Warsaw* 31 B1
Okelra, *Lagos* 14 B2
Okeogbe, *Lagos* 14 B2
Okha, *Delhi* 10 B2
Okhta →, *St. Petersburg* 26 B2
Okkervil →, *St. Petersburg* 26 B2
Okrzeszyn, *Warsaw* 31 C2
Oksval, *Oslo* 22 A3
Oktyabrskiy, *Moscow* 19 B3
Ōkubo, *Tokyo* 29 a2
Ōkura, *Tokyo* 29 B1
Olari, *Helsinki* 12 B1
Olaria, *Rio de Janeiro* 24 B1
Old Admiralty, *St. Petersburg* 26 B1
Old City, *Delhi* 1 a3
Old City, *Jerusalem* 13 b3
Old City, *Shanghai* 27 B1
Old Fort = Purana Qila, *Delhi* 1 c3
Old Harbor, *Boston* 6 B3
Old Town, *Chicago* 9 B3
Old Town, *Edinburgh* 11 B2
Oldbawn, *Dublin* 11 B1
Olgino, *St. Petersburg* 26 A1
Olimpico, Estadio, *Mexico City* 18 C1
Olivais, *Lisbon* 14 A2
Olivar de los Padres, *Mexico City* 18 B1
Olivar del Conde, *Mexico City* 18 B1
Olivos, *Buenos Aires* 7 B2
Olona →, *Milan* 18 B1
Olympia, *London* 15 c1
Olympic Stadium, *Helsinki* 12 B2
Olympique, Stade, *Montreal* 19 A2
Omonias, Pl., *Athens* 2 b1
Ōmori, *Tokyo* 29 B3
Onchi, *Osaka* 22 B4
Onchi →, *Osaka* 22 B4
Onisigun, *Lagos* 14 A2
Ōokayama, *Tokyo* 29 B3
Oosterpark, *Amsterdam* 2 b3
Oostzaan, *Amsterdam* 2 A2
Opa-Locka, *Miami* 18 A1
Opa-Locka Airport, *Miami* 18 A1
Opacz, *Warsaw* 31 B1
Opera House, *Sydney* 28 a2
Ophirton, *Johannesburg* 13 B2
Oppegård, *Oslo* 22 B3
Oppem, *Brussels* 6 A1
Oppsal, *Oslo* 22 A4
Ora, *Jerusalem* 13 B1
Oradell, *New York* 21 A1
Orange Bowl Stadium, *Miami* 18 B2
Orangi, *Karachi* 14 A2
Orchard Road, *Singapore* 27 a1
Ordrup, *Copenhagen* 10 A3
Orech, *Prague* 24 B1
Øresund, *Copenhagen* 10 A3
Orient Heights, *Boston* 6 A4
Orlando Dam, *Johannesburg* 13 B1
Orlando East, *Johannesburg* 13 B1
Orlovo, *Moscow* 19 C2
Orly, *Paris* 23 B3
Ormesson-sur-Marne, *Paris* 23 B4
Ormond, *Melbourne* 17 B2
Ormøya, *Oslo* 22 A3
Orpington, *London* 15 B4
Orsay, Musée d', *Paris* 23 b3
Országház, *Budapest* 7 b2
Országos Levétár, *Budapest* 7 b1
Ortaköy, *Istanbul* 12 B2
Ortica, *Milan* 18 B2
Oruba, *Lagos* 14 A2
Orvostörteneti Múz., *Budapest* 7 c2
Ōsaka, *Osaka* 22 B4
Osaka B., *Osaka* 22 B2
Osaka Castle, *Osaka* 22 A4
Osaka Harbour, *Osaka* 22 B3
Osaka International Airport, *Osaka* 22 A3
Ōsaki, *Tokyo* 29 B3
Osasco, *São Paulo* 26 B1
Osdorf, *Berlin* 5 B3
Osdorp, *Amsterdam* 2 A1
Oshodi, *Lagos* 14 A2
Oslo, *Oslo* 22 A3
Oslofjorden, *Oslo* 22 B2
Ōsone, *Tokyo* 29 B2
Osorun, *Lagos* 14 A2
Ospiate, *Milan* 18 A1
Ostankino, *Moscow* 19 B3
Östasiatiskamuséet, *Stockholm* 28 b3
Österalm, *Stockholm* 28 a3
Østerbro, *Copenhagen* 10 a1
Osterley, *London* 15 B1
Osterley Park, *London* 15 B1
Östermalm, *Stockholm* 28 A2
Österskär, *Stockholm* 28 A3
Ostiense, *Rome* 25 B1
Østmarkkapellet, *Oslo* 22 A4
Ostøya, *Oslo* 22 A2
Østre Aker, *Oslo* 22 A3
Ōta-Ku, *Tokyo* 29 B3
Otaniemi, *Helsinki* 12 B1
Otari Open Air Museum, *Wellington* 32 B1
Otsuka, *Tokyo* 29 A3
Ottakring, *Vienna* 31 A1
Ottávia, *Rome* 25 B1
Ottery, *Cape Town* 8 B2
Ottobrunn, *Munich* 20 B3
Oud Zuid, *Amsterdam* 2 b1
Oude Kerk, *Amsterdam* 2 b2
Ouderkerk, *Amsterdam* 2 B2
Oulunkylä, *Helsinki* 12 B2
Ourcq, Canal de l', *Paris* 23 A3
Outer Mission, *San Francisco* 25 B2
Outremont, *Montreal* 19 A2
Overijse, *Brussels* 6 B3
Owhiro Bay, *Wellington* 32 C1
Oworonsoki, *Lagos* 14 A2
Oxford Street, *London* 15 b3
Oxgangs, *Edinburgh* 11 B2
Oxon Hill, *Washington* 32 C4
Oyodo, *Osaka* 22 A3
Oyster B., *Sydney* 28 C1
Oyster Rock, *Mumbai* 20 B1
Oyster Rocks, *Karachi* 14 B2
Ozoir-la-Ferrière, *Paris* 23 B4
Ozone Park, *New York* 21 B2

P

Pacific Heights, *San Francisco* 25 B2
Pacific Manor, *San Francisco* 25 C2
Pacific Palisades, *Los Angeles* 16 B1
Pacifica, *San Francisco* 25 C2
Paco, *Manila* 17 B1
Paco de Arcos, *Lisbon* 14 A1
Paco Imperial, *Rio de Janeiro* 24 a2
Paddington, *London* 15 b2
Paddington, *Sydney* 28 B2
Paderno, *Milan* 18 A1
Pagewood, *Sydney* 28 B2
Pagote, *Mumbai* 20 B2
Pai, I. do, *Rio de Janeiro* 24 B2
Pak Kong, *Hong Kong* 12 A2
Pakila, *Helsinki* 12 B2
Palacio de Bellas Artes, *Mexico City* 18 b2
Palacio de Communicaciones, *Madrid* 17 a3
Palacio Nacional, *Mexico City* 18 b3
Palacio Real, *Barcelona* 4 b3
Palacio Real, *Madrid* 17 b1
Palaión Fáliron, *Athens* 2 B2
Palais de Justice, *Brussels* 6 c2
Palais Royal, *Paris* 23 b4
Palais Royale, *Brussels* 6 b3
Palaiseau, *Paris* 23 B2
Palau Nacional Museu d'Art, *Barcelona* 4 c1
Palazzolo, *Milan* 18 A1
Palermo, *Buenos Aires* 7 B2
Palhais, *Lisbon* 14 B2
Palisades Park, *New York* 21 A1
Palmer Park, *Washington* 32 B4
Palmerston, *Dublin* 11 A1
Paloheinä, *Helsinki* 12 B2
Palomeras, *Madrid* 17 B2
Palos Heights, *Chicago* 9 D2
Palos Hills, *Chicago* 9 C2
Palos Hills Forest, *Chicago* 9 C1
Palos Park, *Chicago* 9 C1
Palpara, *Calcutta* 8 B2
Panchur, *Calcutta* 8 B1
Pandacan, *Manila* 17 B2
Pandan, Selat, *Singapore* 27 B2
Pandan Res., *Singapore* 27 B2
Panepistimio, *Athens* 2 b2
Pangbae, *Seoul* 26 C1
Pangrati, *Athens* 2 B2
Pangsua, Sungei →, *Singapore* 27 A2
Panihati, *Calcutta* 8 A2
Panjang, Bukit, *Singapore* 27 A2
Panje, *Mumbai* 20 B2
Panke →, *Berlin* 5 A3
Pankow, *Berlin* 5 A3
Panthéon, *Paris* 23 c4
Pantheon, *Rome* 25 b2
Pantin, *Paris* 23 A3
Pantitlán, *Mexico City* 18 B2
Panvel Cr. →, *Mumbai* 20 B2
Paparangi, *Wellington* 32 B1
Papiol, *Barcelona* 4 A1
Paramus, *New York* 21 A1
Paranaque, *Manila* 17 B1
Paray-Vieille-Poste, *Paris* 23 B3
Parco Regionale, *Milan* 18 A1
Parel, *Mumbai* 20 B1
Pari, *São Paulo* 26 B2
Parioli, *Rome* 25 B1
Paris, *Paris* 23 A3
Paris-Orly, Aéroport de, *Paris* 23 B3
Pārk-e Mellat, *Tehran* 30 A2
Park Ridge, *Chicago* 9 A1
Park Royal, *London* 15 A2
Parkchester, *New York* 21 B2
Parkdale, *Toronto* 30 B2
Parkhurst, *Johannesburg* 13 A2
Parklawn, *Washington* 32 B3
Parkmore, *Johannesburg* 13 A2
Parkside, *San Francisco* 25 B2
Parktown, *Johannesburg* 13 B2
Parktown North, *Johannesburg* 13 A2
Parkview, *Johannesburg* 13 A2
Parkville, *New York* 21 C2
Parkwood, *Cape Town* 8 B1
Parkwood, *Johannesburg* 13 A2
Parow, *Cape Town* 8 A2
Parque Chabuco, *Buenos Aires* 7 B2
Parque Patricios, *Buenos Aires* 7 B2
Parramatta →, *Sydney* 28 A1
Parthenon, *Athens* 2 c2
Paşabahçe, *Istanbul* 12 B2
Pasadena, *Los Angeles* 16 B4
Pasar Minggu, *Jakarta* 13 B1
Pasay, *Manila* 17 B1
Pascoe Vale, *Melbourne* 17 A1
Paseo de la Reforma, *Mexico City* 18 b2
Pasig, *Manila* 17 B2
Pasig →, *Manila* 17 B2
Pasila, *Helsinki* 12 B2
Pasing, *Munich* 20 B1
Pasir Panjang, *Singapore* 27 B2
Pasir Ris, *Singapore* 27 A3
Passaic →, *New York* 21 B1
Passirana, *Milan* 18 A1
Patel Nagar, *Delhi* 10 B1
Pateros, *Manila* 17 B2
Pathersville, *Atlanta* 3 B3
Pathumwan, *Bangkok* 3 B2
Patipukur, *Calcutta* 8 B2
Patisia, *Athens* 2 A2
Paulo E. Virginia, Gruta, *Rio de Janeiro* 24 B1
Paulshof, *Berlin* 5 A5
Pavshino, *Moscow* 19 B1
Paya Lebar, *Singapore* 27 A3
Peachtree →, *Atlanta* 3 B2
Peakhurst, *Sydney* 28 B1
Peania, *Athens* 2 B3
Peckham, *London* 15 B3
Peddocks I., *Boston* 6 B4
Pederstrup, *Copenhagen* 10 A2
Pedralbes, *Barcelona* 4 A1
Pedregal de San Angel, Jardines del, *Mexico City* 18 C1
Pekhorka →, *Moscow* 19 C6
Pekhra-Pokrovskoye, *Moscow* 19 A5
Pekhra-Yakovievskaya, *Moscow* 19 B5
Peking = Beijing, *Beijing* 4 B1
Pelcowizna, *Warsaw* 31 B2
Pelopónnisos Sta., *Athens* 2 a1
Penalolén, *Santiago* 26 B2
Pencarrow Hd., *Wellington* 32 C2
Peng Siang →, *Singapore* 27 A2
Penge, *London* 15 B3
Penha, *Rio de Janeiro* 24 A1
Penicuik, *Edinburgh* 11 B2
Penjaringan, *Jakarta* 13 A1
Penn Station, *New York* 21 c2
Pennsylvania Avenue, *Washington* 32 b1
Pentland Hills, *Edinburgh* 11 B1
Penyagino, *Moscow* 19 A2
Penzing, *Vienna* 31 A1
People's Park, *Shanghai* 27 B1
People's Square, *Shanghai* 27 B1
Perales del Rio, *Madrid* 17 C2
Peravillo, *Mexico City* 18 a3
Perchtoldsdorf, *Vienna* 31 B1
Perdizes, *São Paulo* 26 B2
Peredelkino, *Moscow* 19 C2
Pergamon Museum, *Berlin* 5 a4
Peristérion, *Athens* 2 A2
Perivale, *London* 15 A2
Perk, *Brussels* 6 A2
Perlach, *Munich* 20 B2
Perlacher Forst, *Munich* 20 B2
Pero, *Milan* 18 A1
Peropok, Bukit, *Singapore* 27 B2
Perovo, *Moscow* 19 B4
Pershing Square, *Los Angeles* 16 c1
Pertusella, *Milan* 18 A1
Pesagot, *Jerusalem* 13 A2
Pesanggrahag, Kali →, *Jakarta* 13 B1
Peschiera Borromeo, *Milan* 18 B2
Pesek, P., *Singapore* 27 B2
Pest, *Budapest* 7 B2
Pesterzsébet, *Budapest* 7 B2
Pesthidegkút, *Budapest* 7 A1
Pestimre, *Budapest* 7 B3
Pestlörinc, *Budapest* 7 B3
Pestújhely, *Budapest* 7 A2
Petas, *Helsinki* 12 B2
Petone, *Wellington* 32 B2
Petrogradskaya Storona, *St. Petersburg* 26 B2
Petroúpolis, *Athens* 2 A2
Petrovice, *Prague* 24 B3
Petrovskiy Park, *Moscow* 19 B3
Petrovsko-Razumovskoye, *Moscow* 19 B3
Pettycur, *Edinburgh* 11 A2
Peutie, *Brussels* 6 A2
Pfaueninsel, *Berlin* 5 B1
Phaya Thai, *Bangkok* 3 B2
Phihai, *Karachi* 14 A2
Phillip B., *Sydney* 28 B2
Phoenix Park, *Dublin* 11 A2
Phra Khanong, *Bangkok* 3 B2
Phra Pradaeng, *Bangkok* 3 C2
Phranakhon, *Bangkok* 3 B1
Picasso, Museu, *Barcelona* 4 c2
Piccadilly, *London* 15 b3
Pico Rivera, *Los Angeles* 16 C4
Piedade, *Lisbon* 14 A1
Piedade, *Rio de Janeiro* 24 B1
Piedade, Cova da, *Lisbon* 14 A2
Piedmont Park, *Atlanta* 3 B2
Pietralata, *Rome* 25 B2
Pihlajamäki, *Helsinki* 12 B2
Pihlajasaari, *Helsinki* 12 C2
Pilares, *Rio de Janeiro* 24 B1
Pilton, *Edinburgh* 11 B2
Pimlico, *London* 15 c3
Pimmit Hills, *Washington* 32 B2
Pine Grove, *Toronto* 30 A1
Pinewood, *Miami* 18 A2
Piney Run →, *Washington* 32 B2
Pinganli, *Beijing* 4 B2
Pingzhou, *Canton* 8 B2
Pinheiros →, *São Paulo* 26 B1
Pinjrapur, *Karachi* 14 A2
Pinner, *London* 15 A1
Pinner Green, *London* 15 A1
Pioltello, *Milan* 18 A2
Pipinui Pt., *Wellington* 32 A1
Piraévs, *Athens* 2 B1
Pirajuçara →, *São Paulo* 26 B1
Pirinççi, *Istanbul* 12 B1
Pirituba, *São Paulo* 26 A1
Pirkkola, *Helsinki* 12 B2
Písnice, *Prague* 24 C2
Pitampura, *Delhi* 10 A1
Pitkäjärvi, *Helsinki* 12 B1
Planegg, *Munich* 20 B1
Plumstead, *Cape Town* 8 B1
Plumstead, *London* 15 B4
Plyushchevo, *Moscow* 19 B4
Pníka, *Athens* 2 c1
Po Toi I., *Hong Kong* 12 B2
Po Toi O, *Hong Kong* 12 B2
Poasco, *Milan* 18 B2
Podbaba, *Prague* 24 B2
Podoli, *Prague* 24 B2
Poduskino, *Moscow* 19 B1
Pointe-Aux-Trembles, *Montreal* 19 A2
Poissy, *Paris* 23 A1
Pok Fu Lam, *Hong Kong* 12 B1
Pokrovsko-Sresnevo, *Moscow* 19 B2
Polton, *Edinburgh* 11 B3
Polyustrovo, *St. Petersburg* 26 B2
Pompidou, Centre, *Paris* 23 b4
Pomprap, *Bangkok* 3 B2
Pondok Indah, *Jakarta* 13 B1
Pont-Viau, *Montreal* 19 A1
Ponta do Marisco, *Rio de Janeiro* 24 C1
Pontault-Combault, *Paris* 23 B4
Pontinha, *Lisbon* 14 A1
Poplar, *London* 15 A3
Popolo, Porta del, *Rome* 25 a2
Poppintree, *Dublin* 11 A2
Porirua, *Wellington* 32 A2
Porirua East, *Wellington* 32 A2
Port I., *Osaka* 22 A2
Port Melbourne, *Melbourne* 17 B1
Port Nicholson, *Wellington* 32 B2
Port Philip Bay, *Melbourne* 17 B1
Port Richmond, *New York* 21 C1
Port Shelter, *Hong Kong* 12 A2
Port Union, *Toronto* 30 A4
Portage Park, *Chicago* 9 B2
Portal de la Pau, Pl., *Barcelona* 4 c2
Portela, Aeroporto da, *Lisbon* 14 A2
Portmarnock, *Dublin* 11 A3
Porto Brandão, *Lisbon* 14 A1
Porto Novo, *Rio de Janeiro* 24 A2
Porto Novo Cr. →, *Lagos* 14 B2
Portobello, *Edinburgh* 11 B3
Portrero, *San Francisco* 25 B3
Potomac, *Washington* 32 A2
Potomac →, *Washington* 32 B3
Potrero Pt., *San Francisco* 25 B2
Potsdam, *Berlin* 5 B1
Potsdamer Platz, *Berlin* 5 b3
Potzham, *Munich* 20 B2
Pötzleinsdorf, *Vienna* 31 A1
Povoa de Santo Adriao, *Lisbon* 14 A2
Powązki, *Warsaw* 31 B1
Powiśle, *Warsaw* 31 B2
Powsin, *Warsaw* 31 C2
Powsinek, *Warsaw* 31 C2
Poyan Res., *Singapore* 27 A2
Pozuelo de Alarcon, *Madrid* 17 B1
Prado, Museo del, *Madrid* 17 b3
Prado Churubusco, *Mexico City* 18 B2
Praga, *Warsaw* 31 B2
Prague = Praha, *Prague* 24 B2
Praha, *Prague* 24 B2
Praha-Ruzyně Airport, *Prague* 24 B1
Praires, R. des →, *Montreal* 19 A2
Prater, *Vienna* 31 A2
Precotto, *Milan* 18 A2
Prenestino Labicano, *Rome* 25 B2
Prenzlauerberg, *Berlin* 5 A3
Preston, *Melbourne* 17 A1
Pretos Forros, Sa. dos, *Rio de Janeiro* 24 B1
Préville, *Montreal* 19 B3
Přezletice, *Prague* 24 B3
Prima Porta, *Rome* 25 B1
Primavalle, *Rome* 25 B1
Primrose, *Johannesburg* 13 B2
Princes Street, *Edinburgh* 11 b2
Printer's Row, *Chicago* 9 d2
Progreso Nacional, *Mexico City* 18 A2
Prosek, *Prague* 24 B3
Prospect Hill Park, *Boston* 6 A2
Providencia, *Santiago* 26 B2
Prudential Building, *Chicago* 9 c2
Průhonice, *Prague* 24 C3
Psikhikón, *Athens* 2 A2
Pudong New Area, *Shanghai* 27 B2
Pueblo Libre, *Lima* 16 B2
Pueblo Nuevo, *Barcelona* 4 A2
Pueblo Nuevo, *Madrid* 17 B2
Puerta del Sol, Plaza, *Madrid* 17 b2
Puerto Madero, *Buenos Aires* 7 B2
Puerto Retiro, *Buenos Aires* 7 B2
Puhuangyu, *Beijing* 4 B2
Puistola, *Helsinki* 12 B3
Pukan-san, *Seoul* 26 B1
Pukinmäki, *Helsinki* 12 B2
Pukkajwa, *Seoul* 26 B1
Pulkovo Int. Airport, *St. Petersburg* 26 C1
Pullach, *Munich* 20 B1
Pulo Gadung, *Jakarta* 13 B2
Pūnak, *Tehran* 30 A2
Punchbowl, *Sydney* 28 B1
Punde, *Mumbai* 20 B2
Punggol, *Singapore* 27 A3
Punggol, Sungei →, *Singapore* 27 A3
Punggol Pt., *Singapore* 27 A3
Punjabi Bagh, *Delhi* 10 A1
Puotila, *Helsinki* 12 B3
Purana Qila, *Delhi* 1 c3
Puteaux, *Paris* 23 A2
Putilkovo, *Moscow* 19 A2
Putney, *London* 15 B2
Putuo, *Shanghai* 27 B1
Putxet, *Barcelona* 4 A1
Puxi, *Shanghai* 27 B1
Pydhuni, *Mumbai* 20 b2
Pyramids, *Cairo* 7 B1
Pyry, *Warsaw* 31 C1

Q

Qalandya, *Jerusalem* 13 A2
Qal'eh Morghī, *Tehran* 30 B2
Qanâ el Ismâ'ilîya, *Cairo* 7 A2
Qāsemābād, *Tehran* 30 A3
Qasr-e Firūzeh, *Tehran* 30 B3
Qatane, *Jerusalem* 13 B1
Qianmen, *Beijing* 4 B2
Qinghuayuan, *Beijing* 4 B1
Qingningsi, *Shanghai* 27 B2
Qolhak, *Tehran* 30 A2
Quadraro, *Rome* 25 B2
Quaid-i-Azam, *Karachi* 14 A1
Quartiere Zingone, *Milan* 18 B1
Quds, *Baghdad* 3 A2
Queen Mary Res., *London* 15 B1
Queen Street, *Edinburgh* 11 a1
Queensbury, *London* 15 A2
Queenscliffe, *Sydney* 28 A2
Queensferry, *Edinburgh* 11 B1
Queenstown, *Singapore* 27 B2
Quellerina, *Johannesburg* 13 A1
Queluz, *Lisbon* 14 A1
Quezon City, *Manila* 17 B2
Quezon Memorial Circle, *Manila* 17 B2
Quilicura, *Santiago* 26 B1
Quincy, *Boston* 6 B3
Quincy B., *Boston* 6 B4
Quinta Normal, *Santiago* 26 B1
Quinto de Stampi, *Milan* 18 B2
Quinto Romano, *Milan* 18 B1
Quirinale, *Rome* 25 B1
Quirinale, Palazzo dei, *Rome* 25 b3

R

Raasdorf, *Vienna* 31 A3
Rådhuset, *Oslo* 22 A3
Radlice, *Prague* 24 B2
Radość, *Warsaw* 31 B3
Radotin, *Prague* 24 C2
Rafat, *Jerusalem* 13 A2
Raffles Hotel, *Singapore* 27 b3
Raffles Park, *Singapore* 27 B2

RAHENY

Raheny, *Dublin* 11 A3
Rahnsdorf, *Berlin* 5 B5
Rainham, *London* 15 A5
Raj Ghat, *Delhi* 1 b3
Rajakylä, *Helsinki* 12 B3
Rajpath, *Delhi* 1 c2
Rajpura, *Delhi* 10 A2
Rákos-patak →, *Budapest* 7 B3
Rákoshegy, *Budapest* 7 B3
Rákoskeresztúr, *Budapest* 7 B3
Rákoskert, *Budapest* 7 B3
Rákosliget, *Budapest* 7 B3
Rákospalota, *Budapest* 7 A2
Rákosszentmihály, *Budapest* 7 A2
Raków, *Warsaw* 31 B1
Ram, *Jerusalem* 13 A2
Rām Allāh, *Jerusalem* 13 A2
Ramadān, *Baghdad* 3 B2
Ramakrishna Puram, *Delhi* 10 B1
Ramanathpur, *Calcutta* 8 A1
Rambla, La, *Barcelona* 4 b2
Rambler Channel, *Hong Kong* 12 A1
Ramenki, *Moscow* 19 B2
Ramersdorf, *Munich* 20 B2
Ramos, *Rio de Janeiro* 24 B1
Ramos Mejia, *Buenos Aires* 7 B1
Ramot, *Jerusalem* 13 B2
Rampur, *Delhi* 10 A2
Ramsgate, *Sydney* 28 B1
Rand Afrikaans Univ., *Johannesburg* 13 B2
Rand Airport, *Johannesburg* 13 B2
Randburg, *Johannesburg* 13 A1
Randhart, *Johannesburg* 13 B2
Randpark Ridge, *Johannesburg* 13 A1
Randwick, *Sydney* 28 B2
Ranelagh, *Dublin* 11 A2
Rannersdorf, *Vienna* 31 B2
Ransbèche, *Brussels* 6 B2
Ransdorp, *Amsterdam* 2 A2
Ranvad, *Mumbai* 20 B2
Raposo, *Lisbon* 14 A1
Rashtrapati Bhawan, *Delhi* 1 c1
Rasskazovka, *Moscow* 19 C2
Rastaala, *Helsinki* 12 B1
Rastila, *Helsinki* 12 B3
Raszyn, *Warsaw* 31 C1
Ratcha Thewi, *Bangkok* 3 b3
Rathfarnham, *Dublin* 11 B2
Ratho, *Edinburgh* 11 B1
Ratho Station, *Edinburgh* 11 B1
Rato, *Lisbon* 14 A2
Ravelston, *Edinburgh* 11 B2
Rawamangun, *Jakarta* 13 B2
Rayners Lane, *London* 15 A1
Raynes Park, *London* 15 B2
Raypur, *Calcutta* 8 C2
Razdory, *Moscow* 19 B1
Real Felipe, Fuerte, *Lima* 16 B2
Recoleta, *Buenos Aires* 7 B2
Recoleta, *Santiago* 26 B2
Red Fort = Lal Qila, *Delhi* 1 a3
Redbridge, *London* 15 A4
Redfern, *Sydney* 28 B2
Redwood, *Wellington* 32 B1
Reeves Hill, *Boston* 6 A1
Refshaleøen, *Copenhagen* 10 A3
Regents Park, *Johannesburg* 13 B2
Regent's Park, *London* 15 a2
Rego Park, *New York* 21 B2
Reichstag, *Berlin* 5 a3
Reina Sofia, Centro de Arte, *Madrid* 17 c3
Reinickendorf, *Berlin* 5 A3
Rekola, *Helsinki* 12 B3
Rembertów, *Warsaw* 31 B2
Rembrandthuis, *Amsterdam* 2 b2
Rembrandtpark, *Amsterdam* 2 A2
Rembrandtsplein, *Amsterdam* 2 b2
Remedios, Parque Nacional de los, *Mexico City* 18 B1
Remedios de Escalada, *Buenos Aires* 7 C2
Rémola, Laguna del, *Barcelona* 4 B1
Renca, *Santiago* 26 B1
Renmin Park, *Tianjin* 30 B2
Rennemoulin, *Paris* 23 A1
Řeporyje, *Prague* 24 B1
Republica, Plaza de la, *Mexico City* 18 b1
République, Place de la, *Paris* 23 b5
Repulse Bay, *Hong Kong* 12 B2
Repy, *Prague* 24 B1
Residenz, *Munich* 20 B2
Residenzmuseum, *Munich* 20 b3
Reston, *Washington* 32 B2
Retiro, *Buenos Aires* 7 B2
Retiro, *Madrid* 17 B1
Retreat, *Cape Town* 8 B1
Reutov, *Moscow* 19 B5
Réveillon →, *Paris* 23 B4
Revere, *Boston* 6 A3
Rexdale, *Toronto* 30 A1
Reynosa Tamaulipas, *Mexico City* 18 A1
Rho, *Milan* 18 A1
Rhodes, *Sydney* 28 A1
Rhodon, *Paris* 23 B1
Rhodon →, *Paris* 23 B1
Ribeira, *Rio de Janeiro* 24 A1
Ricarda, Laguna de la, *Barcelona* 4 B1
Richmond, *Melbourne* 17 A2
Richmond, *San Francisco* 25 B2
Richmond Hill, *New York* 21 B2
Richmond Park, *London* 15 B2
Richmond upon Thames, *London* 15 B2
Riddarholmen, *Stockholm* 28 c1
Riddarhuset, *Stockholm* 28 c2
Ridgefield, *New York* 21 B1
Ridgefield Park, *New York* 21 A1
Ridgewood, *New York* 21 B2
Riem, *Munich* 20 B3
Rijksmuseum, *Amsterdam* 2 b1
Rikers I., *New York* 21 B2
Riksdagensledamothus, *Stockholm* 28 b2
Riksdagshuset, *Stockholm* 28 b2
Rimac, *Lima* 16 B2
Ringsend, *Dublin* 11 A2
Rinkeby, *Stockholm* 28 A1
Rio Compride, *Rio de Janeiro* 24 B1
Rio de Janeiro, *Rio de Janeiro* 24 B1
Rio de la Plata, *Buenos Aires* 7 B2
Rio de Mouro, *Lisbon* 14 A1
Ripollet, *Barcelona* 4 A1
Ris, *Oslo* 22 A3
Risby, *Copenhagen* 10 A1
Rishra, *Calcutta* 8 A2
Ritchie, *Washington* 32 B4
Rithala, *Delhi* 10 A1
Rive Sud, Canal de la, *Montreal* 19 B2
River Edge, *New York* 21 A1
River Forest, *Chicago* 9 B2
River Grove, *Chicago* 9 B1
Riverdale, *New York* 21 A2
Riverdale, *Washington* 32 B4
Riverdale Park, *Toronto* 30 A2
Riverlea, *Johannesburg* 13 B1
Riverside, *Chicago* 9 C2
Riverwood, *Sydney* 28 B1
Rivière-des-Praires, *Montreal* 19 A2
Rixensart, *Brussels* 6 B3
Riyad, *Baghdad* 3 B2
Rizal Park, *Manila* 17 B1
Rizal Stadium, *Manila* 17 B1
Røa, *Oslo* 22 A2
Robbins, *Chicago* 9 D2
Robertsham, *Johannesburg* 13 B2
Rochelle Park, *New York* 21 A1
Rock Cr. →, *Washington* 32 B3
Rock Creek Park, *Washington* 32 B3
Rock Pt., *Wellington* 32 A1
Rockaway Pt., *New York* 21 C2
Rockdale, *Sydney* 28 B1
Rockefeller Center, *New York* 21 c2
Rodaon, *Vienna* 31 B1
Rødovre, *Copenhagen* 10 A2
Rodrigo de Freitas, L., *Rio de Janeiro* 24 B1
Roehampton, *London* 15 B2
Rogers Park, *Chicago* 9 A2
Roihuvuori, *Helsinki* 12 B3
Roissy-en-Brie, *Paris* 23 B4
Rokin, *Amsterdam* 2 b2
Rokkō I., *Osaka* 22 A2
Rokkō Sanchi, *Osaka* 22 A2
Rokkō-Zan, *Osaka* 22 A2
Rokytka →, *Prague* 24 B3
Roma, *Rome* 25 B1
Római-Fürdö, *Budapest* 7 A2
Romainville, *Paris* 23 A3
Romano Banco, *Milan* 18 B1
Romashkovo, *Moscow* 19 B1
Rome = Roma, *Rome* 25 B1
Romford, *London* 15 A5
Rondebosch, *Cape Town* 8 A1
Roppongi, *Tokyo* 29 c3
Rose Hill, *Washington* 32 C3
Rosebank, *New York* 21 C1
Rosebery, *Sydney* 28 B2
Rosedal La Candelaria, *Mexico City* 18 B2
Roseland, *Chicago* 9 C3
Rosemead, *Los Angeles* 16 B4
Rosemont, *Montreal* 19 A2
Rosenborg Have, *Copenhagen* 10 A3
Rosenthal, *Berlin* 5 A3
Rosettenville, *Johannesburg* 13 B2
Rosewell, *Edinburgh* 11 B3
Rosherville Dam, *Johannesburg* 13 B2
Rösjön, *Stockholm* 28 A2
Roslags-Näsby, *Stockholm* 28 A2
Roslin, *Edinburgh* 11 B3
Roslindale, *Boston* 6 B3
Rosny-sous-Bois, *Paris* 23 A4
Rosslyn, *Washington* 32 B3
Rosyth, *Edinburgh* 11 A1
Rotherhithe, *London* 15 B3
Rothneusiedl, *Vienna* 31 B2
Rothschmaige, *Munich* 20 A1
Rouge Hill, *Toronto* 30 A4
Round I., *Hong Kong* 12 B2
Roxbury, *Boston* 6 B3
Roxeth, *London* 15 A1
Royal Botanic Garden, *Edinburgh* 11 B2
Royal Botanic Gardens, *Sydney* 28 b2
Royal Grand Palace, *Bangkok* 3 b1
Royal Observatory, *Edinburgh* 11 B2
Royal Park, *Melbourne* 17 A1
Royal Turf Club, *Bangkok* 3 b2
Röylä, *Helsinki* 12 B1
Rozas, Portilleros de las, *Madrid* 17 B1
Roztoky, *Prague* 24 B2
Rozzano, *Milan* 18 B1
Rubi →, *Barcelona* 4 A1
Rublovo, *Moscow* 19 B2
Rudnevka →, *Moscow* 19 B5
Rudolfsheim, *Vienna* 31 A2
Rudolfshöhe, *Berlin* 5 A5
Rudow, *Berlin* 5 B3
Rueil-Malmaison, *Paris* 23 A2
Ruisbroek, *Brussels* 6 B1
Ruislip, *London* 15 A1
Rumelihisarı, *Istanbul* 12 B2
Rumyantsevo, *Moscow* 19 C2
Rungis, *Paris* 23 B3
Rusāfa, *Baghdad* 3 A2
Rush Green, *London* 15 A5
Russa, *Calcutta* 8 C2
Russian Hill, *San Francisco* 25 a1
Rustenfeld, *Vienna* 31 B2
Rutherford, *New York* 21 B1
Ruzyně, *Prague* 24 B1
Rybatskaya, *St. Petersburg* 26 B2
Rydboholm, *Stockholm* 28 A3
Ryde, *Sydney* 28 A1
Rynek, *Warsaw* 31 a2
Ryogoku, *Tokyo* 29 A3
Rzhevka, *St. Petersburg* 26 B3

S

Sa'ādatābād, *Tehran* 30 A2
Saadūn, *Baghdad* 3 B2
Saavedra, *Buenos Aires* 7 B2
Saboli, *Delhi* 10 A2
Sabugo, *Lisbon* 14 A1
Sabzi Mand, *Delhi* 10 A2
Sacavém, *Lisbon* 14 A2
Saclay, *Paris* 23 B2
Saclay, Étang de, *Paris* 23 B1
Sacomã, *São Paulo* 26 B2
Sacré Cœur, *Paris* 23 a4
Sacrow, *Berlin* 5 B1
Sacrower See, *Berlin* 5 B1
Sadang, *Seoul* 26 C1
Sadar Bazar, *Delhi* 1 a1
Saddām City, *Baghdad* 3 A2
Saddle Brook, *New York* 21 A1
Sadr, *Karachi* 14 A2
Sadyba, *Warsaw* 31 B2
Saft el Laban, *Cairo* 7 A2
Saganashkee Slough, *Chicago* 9 C1
Sagene, *Oslo* 22 A3
Sagrada Família, Templo de, *Barcelona* 4 A2
Sagrado Familia, Templo de, *Barcelona* 4 a2
Sahar Int. Airport, *Mumbai* 20 A2
Sai Kung, *Hong Kong* 12 A2
Sai Wan Ho, *Hong Kong* 12 B2
Sai Ying Pun, *Hong Kong* 12 B1
St.-Aubin, *Paris* 23 B1
St.-Cloud, *Paris* 23 A2
St.-Cyr-l'École, *Paris* 23 B1
St.-Cyr-l'École, Aérodrome de, *Paris* 23 B1
St.-Denis, *Paris* 23 A3
St.-Germain, Forêt de, *Paris* 23 A1
St.-Germain-en-Laye, *Paris* 23 A1
St. Giles Cathedral, *Edinburgh* 11 b2
St. Helier, *London* 15 B2
St.-Hubert, *Montreal* 19 B3
St. Hubert, Galerie, *Brussels* 6 b2
St. Isaac's Cathedral, *St. Petersburg* 26 B1
St. Jacques →, *Montreal* 19 B3
St. James's, *London* 15 b3
St. John's Cathedral, *Hong Kong* 12 c1
St. Kilda, *Melbourne* 17 B1
St. Lambert, *Montreal* 19 A3
St.-Lambert, *Paris* 23 B1
St.-Laurent, *Montreal* 19 A1
St. Lawrence →, *Montreal* 19 B2
St.-Lazare, Gare, *Paris* 23 A2
St.-Léonard, *Montreal* 19 A2
St. Magelungen, *Stockholm* 28 B2
St.-Mandé, *Paris* 23 A3
St. Margaret's, *Dublin* 11 A2
St.-Martin, Bois, *Paris* 23 B4
St. Mary Cray, *London* 15 B4
St.-Maur-des-Fossés, *Paris* 23 B3
St.-Maurice, *Paris* 23 B3
St.-Michel, *Montreal* 19 A2
St. Nikolaus-Kirken, *Prague* 24 B2
St.-Ouen, *Paris* 23 A3
St. Patrick's Cathedral, *Dublin* 11 c1
St. Patrick's Cathedral, *New York* 21 c2
St. Paul's Cathedral, *London* 15 b4
St. Paul's Cray, *London* 15 B4
St. Peters, *Sydney* 28 B2
St. Petersburg = Sankt Peterburg, *St. Petersburg* 26 B1
St.-Pierre, *Montreal* 19 B2
St.-Quentin, Étang de, *Paris* 23 B1
St. Stephen's Green, *Dublin* 11 c3
St.-Vincent-de-Paul, *Montreal* 19 A2
Ste.-Catherine, *Montreal* 19 B2
Ste.-Hélène, Î., *Montreal* 19 A2
Saiwai, *Tokyo* 29 B3
Sakai, *Osaka* 22 B3
Sakai Harbour, *Osaka* 22 B3
Sakra, P., *Singapore* 27 B2
Salam, *Baghdad* 3 A2
Salamanca, *Madrid* 17 B1
Sâllynoggin, *Dublin* 11 B3
Salmannsdorf, *Vienna* 31 A1
Salmedina, *Madrid* 17 C2
Salomea, *Warsaw* 31 B1
Salsette I., *Mumbai* 20 A2
Salt Lake City, *Calcutta* 8 B2
Salt River, *Cape Town* 8 A1
Salt Water L., *Calcutta* 8 B2
Saltsjö-Duvnäs, *Stockholm* 28 B3
Saltykovka, *Moscow* 19 B5
Samatya, *Istanbul* 12 C1
Sampaloc, *Manila* 17 B1
Samphan Thawong, *Bangkok* 3 B2
Samsŏn, *Seoul* 26 B2
San Andrés, *Barcelona* 4 A2
San Angel, *Mexico City* 18 B1
San Angelo, Castel, *Rome* 25 b1
San Basilio, *Rome* 25 B2
San Borja, *Lima* 16 B3
San Bóvio, *Milan* 18 B2
San Bruno, Pt., *San Francisco* 25 C2
San Bruno Mt., *San Francisco* 25 B2
San Cristobal, *Buenos Aires* 7 B2
San Cristobal, *Madrid* 17 B2
San Cristóbal, Cerro, *Santiago* 26 B2
San Cristoforo, *Milan* 18 B1
San Donato Milanese, *Milan* 18 B2
San Francisco, *San Francisco* 25 B2
San Francisco B., *San Francisco* 25 B3
San Francisco Culhuacán, *Mexico City* 18 C2
San Fruttuoso, *Milan* 18 A2
San Gabriel, *Los Angeles* 16 B4
San Giuliano Milanese, *Milan* 18 B2
San Isidro, *Lima* 16 B2
San Jerónimo Lidice, *Mexico City* 18 C1
San Joaquin, *Santiago* 26 B2
San José Rio Hondo, *Mexico City* 18 B1
San Juan →, *Manila* 17 B2
San Juan de Aragón, *Mexico City* 18 B2
San Juan de Aragón, Parque, *Mexico City* 18 B2
San Juan de Lurigancho, *Lima* 16 A2
San Juan del Monte, *Manila* 17 B2
San Juan Ixtacala, *Mexico City* 18 A1
San Juan Toltotepec, *Mexico City* 18 B1
San Just Desvern, *Barcelona* 4 A1
San Justo, *Buenos Aires* 7 C1
San Lorenzo Tezonco, *Mexico City* 18 C2
San Luis, *Lima* 16 B2
San Marino, *Los Angeles* 16 B4
San Martin, *Barcelona* 4 A2
San Martin de Porras, *Lima* 16 B2
San Miguel, *Lima* 16 B2
San Miguel, *Santiago* 26 B2
San Nicolas, *Buenos Aires* 7 B2
San Onófrio, *Rome* 25 B1
San Pedro Martir, *Barcelona* 4 A1
San Pedro Zacatenco, *Mexico City* 18 A2
San Pietro, Piazza, *Rome* 25 b1
San Po Kong, *Hong Kong* 12 A2
San Rafael Chamapa, *Mexico City* 18 B1
San Rafael Hills, *Los Angeles* 16 A3
San Roque, *Manila* 17 B2
San Siro, *Milan* 18 B1
San Souci, *Sydney* 28 B1
San Telmo, *Buenos Aires* 7 B2
San Vicenc dels Horts, *Barcelona* 4 A1
Sanbancho, *Tokyo* 29 a3
Sandown, *Johannesburg* 13 A2
Sandown Park Races, *London* 15 B1
Sandton, *Johannesburg* 13 A2
Sandvika, *Oslo* 22 A2
Sandy Pond, *Boston* 6 A2
Sandyford, *Dublin* 11 B2
Sandymount, *Dublin* 11 B2
Sangenjaya, *Tokyo* 29 B2
Sangge, *Seoul* 26 B2
Sangley Pt., *Manila* 17 C1
Sankrail, *Calcutta* 8 B1
Sankt Peterburg, *St. Petersburg* 26 B1
Sankt Veit, *Vienna* 31 A1
Sanlihe, *Beijing* 4 B1
Sanlintang, *Shanghai* 27 C1
Sans, *Barcelona* 4 A1
Sant Agusti, *Barcelona* 4 c2
Sant Ambrogio, Basilica di, *Milan* 18 B2
Sant Boi de Llobregat, *Barcelona* 4 A1
Sant Cugat, *Barcelona* 4 A1
Sant Feliu de Llobregat, *Barcelona* 4 A1
Sant Joan Despi, *Barcelona* 4 A1
Sant Maria del Mar, *Barcelona* 4 b3
Sant Pau del Camp, *Barcelona* 4 c2
Santa Ana, *Manila* 17 B2
Santa Coloma de Gramanet, *Barcelona* 4 A2
Santa Cruz, *Manila* 17 B1
Santa Cruz, *Mumbai* 20 A1
Santa Cruz, I. de, *Rio de Janeiro* 24 B2
Santa Cruz de Olorde, *Barcelona* 4 A1
Santa Efigénia, *São Paulo* 26 B2
Santa Elena, *Manila* 17 B2
Santa Elena del Gomero, *Santiago* 26 B1
Santa Eulalia, *Barcelona* 4 A2
Santa Fe Springs, *Los Angeles* 16 C4
Santa Iria da Azóia, *Lisbon* 14 A2
Santa Julia, *Santiago* 26 C2
Santa Maria, *Mexico City* 18 a1
Santa Monica, *Los Angeles* 16 B2
Santa Monica Mts., *Los Angeles* 16 B2
Santa Rosa De Locobe, *Santiago* 26 B2
Santa Teresa de la Ovalle, *Santiago* 26 B1
Santahamina, *Helsinki* 12 C3
Santana, *São Paulo* 26 A2
Santeny, *Paris* 23 B4
Santiago, *Santiago* 26 B2
Santiago de Surco, *Lima* 16 B2
Santo Amaro, *Lisbon* 14 A1
Santo Amaro, *São Paulo* 26 B1
Santo Andre, *Lisbon* 14 B2
Santo Antão do Tojal, *Lisbon* 14 A2
Santo António, Qta. de, *Lisbon* 14 B1
Santo Tomas, Univ. of, *Manila* 17 B1
Santos Dumont, Aéroport, *Rio de Janeiro* 24 B2
Santoshpur, *Calcutta* 8 B1
Santragachi, *Calcutta* 8 B1
Santry, *Dublin* 11 A2
Sanyuanli, *Canton* 8 B2
São Caetano do Sul, *São Paulo* 26 B2
São Conrado, *Rio de Janeiro* 24 C1
São Cristovão, *Rio de Janeiro* 24 B1
São Francisco Penitência, *Rio de Janeiro* 24 b1
São Jorge, Castelo de, *Lisbon* 14 A2
São Juliao do Tojal, *Lisbon* 14 A2
São Paulo, *São Paulo* 26 B2
Sapa, *Calcutta* 8 B1
Sapateiro, Cor. do →, *São Paulo* 26 B1
Sarandi, *Buenos Aires* 7 C2
Saraswati →, *Calcutta* 8 A1
Sarecky potok →, *Prague* 24 B2
Sarimbun, *Singapore* 27 A2
Sarimbun Res., *Singapore* 27 A2
Sarıyer, *Istanbul* 12 A2
Saronikós Kólpos, *Athens* 2 B1
Sarriá, *Barcelona* 4 A1
Sarsuna, *Calcutta* 8 C1
Sartrouville, *Paris* 23 A2
Sasad, *Budapest* 7 B2
Sashalom, *Budapest* 7 A3
Saska, *Warsaw* 31 B2
Satalice, *Prague* 24 B3
Satgachi, *Calcutta* 8 B2
Sathorn, *Bangkok* 3 B2
Satpukur, *Calcutta* 8 B2
Sätra, *Stockholm* 28 B1
Sattru Pha, *Bangkok* 3 b2
Saúde, *São Paulo* 26 B2
Saugus, *Boston* 6 A3
Saugus →, *Boston* 6 A3
Sault-au-Récollet, *Montreal* 19 A2
Sausalito, *San Francisco* 25 A2
Sawah Besar, *Jakarta* 13 A1
Saxonville, *Boston* 6 B1
Scald Law, *Edinburgh* 11 B2
Scarborough, *Toronto* 30 A3
Sceaux, *Paris* 23 B2
Schaerbeek, *Brussels* 6 A2
Scharfenberg, *Berlin* 5 A2
Scheepvartmuseum, *Amsterdam* 2 b3
Schiller Park, *Chicago* 9 B1
Schiller Woods, *Chicago* 9 B1
Schiphol, Luchthaven, *Amsterdam* 2 B1
Schlachtensee, *Berlin* 5 B2
Schlossgarten, *Berlin* 5 A2
Schmargendorf, *Berlin* 5 B2
Schönblick, *Berlin* 5 B5
Schönbrunn, Schloss, *Vienna* 31 A1
Schöneberg, *Berlin* 5 B3
Schöneiche, *Berlin* 5 B5
Schönwalde, *Berlin* 5 A1
Schotschekloof, *Cape Town* 8 b1
Schulzendorf, *Berlin* 5 A2
Schwabing, *Munich* 20 B2
Schwanebeck, *Berlin* 5 A4
Schwanenwerder, *Berlin* 5 B2
Schwarzlackenau, *Vienna* 31 A2
Schwechat, *Vienna* 31 B2
Scitrek Museum, *Atlanta* 3 B2
Scott Monument, *Edinburgh* 11 b2
Scottdale, *Atlanta* 3 B3
Sea Point, *Cape Town* 8 A1
Seabrook, *Washington* 32 B5
Seacliff, *San Francisco* 25 B2
Seaforth, *Sydney* 28 A2
Seagate, *New York* 21 C1
Sears Tower, *Chicago* 9 c1
Seat Pleasant, *Washington* 32 B4
Seaview, *Wellington* 32 B2
Šeberov, *Prague* 24 B3
Secaucus, *New York* 21 B1
Seddinsee, *Berlin* 5 B5
Seeberg, *Berlin* 5 A5
Seeburg, *Berlin* 5 A1
Seefeld, *Berlin* 5 A5
Seegefeld, *Berlin* 5 A1
Seehof, *Berlin* 5 B2
Segeltorp, *Stockholm* 28 B1
Segrate, *Milan* 18 B2
Seguro, *Milan* 18 B1
Seine →, *Paris* 23 B3
Seixal, *Lisbon* 14 B2
Selby, *Johannesburg* 13 B2
Seletar, P., *Singapore* 27 A3
Seletar Hills, *Singapore* 27 A3
Seletar Res., *Singapore* 27 A2
Selhurst, *London* 15 B3
Sembawang, *Singapore* 27 A2
Senago, *Milan* 18 A1
Sendinger Tor Platz, *Munich* 20 c1
Sendling, *Munich* 20 B2
Senju, *Tokyo* 29 A3
Senriyama, *Osaka* 22 A4
Sentosa, P., *Singapore* 27 B2
Seoul = Sŏul, *Seoul* 26 B2
Seoul National Univ., *Seoul* 26 C1
Seoul Tower, *Seoul* 26 B1
Sepolia, *Athens* 2 A2
Sepulveda Flood Control Basin, *Los Angeles* 16 A2
Serangoon, *Singapore* 27 A3
Serangoon, P., *Singapore* 27 A3
Serangoon, Sungei →, *Singapore* 27 A3
Serangoon Harbour, *Singapore* 27 A3
Seraya, P., *Singapore* 27 B2
Serebryanka, *Moscow* 19 B5
Serebryanka →, *Moscow* 19 B4
Serramonte, *San Francisco* 25 C2
Sesto San Giovanni, *Milan* 18 A2
Sesto Ulteriano, *Milan* 18 B2
Setagaya-Ku, *Tokyo* 29 B2
Seter, *Oslo* 22 A3
Setia Budi, *Jakarta* 13 B1
Settebagni, *Rome* 25 A2
Settecamini, *Rome* 25 B2
Séttimo Milanese, *Milan* 18 B1
Settsu, *Osaka* 22 A4
Setuny →, *Moscow* 19 B2
Seutula, *Helsinki* 12 A2
Seven Corners, *Washington* 32 B3
Seven Kings, *London* 15 A4
Sévesco →, *Milan* 18 A1
Sevran, *Paris* 23 A4
Sewri, *Mumbai* 20 B2
Sforzesso, Castello, *Milan* 18 B2
Sha Kok Mei, *Hong Kong* 12 A2
Sha Tin, *Hong Kong* 12 A2
Sha Tin Wai, *Hong Kong* 12 A2
Shabrâmant, *Cairo* 7 B2
Shahdara, *Delhi* 10 A2
Shahe, *Canton* 8 B2
Shahr-e Rey, *Tehran* 30 B2
Shahrak-e Golshahr, *Tehran* 30 B1
Shahrak-e Qods, *Tehran* 30 A2
Shaikh Aomar, *Baghdad* 3 A2
Shakurbasti, *Delhi* 10 A1
Shalkiya, *Calcutta* 8 B2
Sham Shui Po, *Hong Kong* 12 B1
Shamapur, *Delhi* 10 A1
Shamian, *Canton* 8 B2
Shan Mei, *Hong Kong* 12 A2
Shanghai, *Shanghai* 27 B2
Shankill, *Dublin* 11 B3
Sharp I., *Hong Kong* 12 A2
Shastrinagar, *Delhi* 10 A2
Shau Kei Wan, *Hong Kong* 12 B2
Shawocun, *Beijing* 4 B1
Shayuan, *Canton* 8 B2
Sheepshead Bay, *New York* 21 C2
Shek O, *Hong Kong* 12 B2
Shelter I., *Hong Kong* 12 B2
Sheng Fa Shan, *Hong Kong* 12 A1
Shepherds Bush, *London* 15 A2
Shepperton, *London* 15 B1
Sherman Oaks, *Los Angeles* 16 B2
Sherman Park, *Chicago* 9 C2
Shet Bandar, *Mumbai* 20 B2
Sheung Lau Wan, *Hong Kong* 12 B2
Sheung Wan, *Hong Kong* 12 B1
Sheva, *Mumbai* 20 B2
Sheva Nhava, *Mumbai* 20 B2
Shiba, *Tokyo* 29 c4
Shibpur, *Calcutta* 8 B1
Shibuya-Ku, *Tokyo* 29 c1
Shijōnawate, *Osaka* 22 A4
Shillim, *Seoul* 26 C1
Shimogawara, *Tokyo* 29 B1
Shimosalo, *Tokyo* 29 A2
Shimoshakujii, *Tokyo* 29 A2
Shinagawa-Ku, *Tokyo* 29 B3
Shing Mun Res., *Hong Kong* 12 A1
Shinjuku-Ku, *Tokyo* 29 a1
Shinjuku National Garden, *Tokyo* 29 a2
Shinkoiwa, *Tokyo* 29 A4
Shinnakano, *Tokyo* 29 A3
Shinsa, *Seoul* 26 B2
Shipai, *Canton* 8 B3
Shirinashi →, *Osaka* 22 B3
Shirogane, *Tokyo* 29 B3
Shiweitang, *Canton* 8 B2
Shogunle, *Lagos* 14 A2
Shomolu, *Lagos* 14 A2
Shooters Hill, *London* 15 B4
Shoreditch, *London* 15 a5
Shortlands, *London* 15 B4
Shu' afat, *Jerusalem* 13 B2
Shubrâ, *Cairo* 7 A2
Shubrâ el Kheima, *Cairo* 7 A2
Shuikuo, *Canton* 8 A2
Shuishang Park, *Tianjin* 30 B1
Sidcup, *London* 15 B4
Siebenhirten, *Vienna* 31 B1
Siedlung, *Berlin* 5 A1
Siekierki, *Warsaw* 31 B2
Sielce, *Warsaw* 31 B2
Siemensstadt, *Berlin* 5 A2
Sierra Madre, *Los Angeles* 16 B4
Sievering, *Vienna* 31 A2
Sighthill, *Edinburgh* 11 B2
Signal Hill, *Cape Town* 8 A1
Sihŭng, *Seoul* 26 C1
Sikátorpuszta, *Budapest* 7 A3
Silampur, *Delhi* 10 B2
Silver Hill, *Boston* 6 A2
Silver Hill, *Washington* 32 C4
Silver Spring, *Washington* 32 A3
Silvermine Nature Reserve, *Cape Town* 8 B1
Silvolantekojärvi, *Helsinki* 12 B2
Simei, *Singapore* 27 A3
Simla, *Calcutta* 8 B2
Simmering, *Vienna* 31 A2
Simmering Heide, *Vienna* 31 A2
Simonkylä, *Helsinki* 12 B3
Singapore, *Singapore* 27 B3
Singapore, Univ. of, *Singapore* 27 B2
Sinicka →, *Moscow* 19 A1
Sinki, Selat, *Singapore* 27 B2
Sint-Genesius-Rode, *Brussels* 6 B2
Sinwŏl, *Seoul* 26 B1
Sion, *Mumbai* 20 A2
Sipson, *London* 15 B1
Siqeil, *Cairo* 7 A1
Şişli, *Istanbul* 12 B1
Skansen, *Stockholm* 28 B2
Skärholmen, *Stockholm* 28 B1
Skarpäng, *Stockholm* 28 A2
Skarpnäck, *Stockholm* 28 B2
Skaryszewski Park, *Warsaw* 31 B2
Skeppsholmen, *Stockholm* 28 c3
Skokie, *Chicago* 9 A2
Skokie →, *Chicago* 9 A2
Skoklefall, *Oslo* 22 A3
Sköndal, *Stockholm* 28 B2
Skovlunde, *Copenhagen* 10 A2
Skovshoved, *Copenhagen* 10 A3
Skuru, *Stockholm* 28 B3
Skyland, *Atlanta* 3 A3
Slade Green, *London* 15 B5
Slemmestad, *Oslo* 22 B1
Slependen, *Oslo* 22 A2
Slipi, *Jakarta* 13 B1
Slivenec, *Prague* 24 B2
Sloten, *Amsterdam* 2 A1
Sloterpark, *Amsterdam* 2 A1
Sluhy, *Prague* 24 A3
Służew, *Warsaw* 31 B2
Służewiec, *Warsaw* 31 B2
Smíchov, *Prague* 24 B2
Smith Forest Preserve, *Chicago* 9 B2
Smithsonian Institute, *Washington* 32 b2
Smolny, *St. Petersburg* 26 B2
Snake Creek Canal →, *Miami* 18 A2
Snarøya, *Oslo* 22 A2
Snättringe, *Stockholm* 28 B1
Sŏbinggo, *Seoul* 26 B1
Søborg, *Copenhagen* 10 A2
Sobreda, *Lisbon* 14 B1
Soch'o, *Seoul* 26 C1
Sŏdaemun, *Seoul* 26 B1
Söderby, *Stockholm* 28 A3
Södermalm, *Stockholm* 28 B2
Sodpur, *Calcutta* 8 A2
Soeurs, Î. des, *Montreal* 19 B2
Sognsvatn, *Oslo* 22 A3
Soho, *London* 15 b3
Soho, *New York* 21 e1
Soignes, Forêt de, *Brussels* 6 B2
Sok Kwu Wan, *Hong Kong* 12 B1
Sŏkkwan, *Seoul* 26 B2
Sokolniki, *Moscow* 19 B4
Sokolniki Park, *Moscow* 19 B4
Sokołów, *Warsaw* 31 C1
Solalinden, *Munich* 20 B3
Soldier Field, *Chicago* 9 e3
Sollentuna, *Stockholm* 28 A1
Solln, *Munich* 20 B2
Solna, *Stockholm* 28 A1
Solntsevo, *Moscow* 19 C2
Somerset, *Washington* 32 B3
Somerville, *Boston* 6 A3
Somes Is., *Wellington* 32 B2
Sonari, *Mumbai* 20 B2
Søndersø, *Copenhagen* 10 A2
Sŏngbuk, *Seoul* 26 B2
Sŏngdong, *Seoul* 26 B2
Sŏngp'a, *Seoul* 26 B2
Sŏngsu, *Seoul* 26 B2
Soong Qingling, Former Res. of, *Beijing* 4 a2
Soroksár, *Budapest* 7 B2
Soroksari Duna →, *Budapest* 7 B2
Sosenka →, *Moscow* 19 B4
Sosnovka, *St. Petersburg* 26 B2
Sŏul, *Seoul* 26 B2
Soundview, *New York* 21 B2
South Beach, *New York* 21 C1
South Beach Harbor, *San Francisco* 25 c3
South Bend Park, *Atlanta* 3 B2
South Boston, *Boston* 6 A3
South Brooklyn, *New York* 21 B2
South Decatur, *Atlanta* 3 B3
South Deering, *Chicago* 9 C3
South El Monte, *Los Angeles* 16 B4
South Gate, *Los Angeles* 16 C3
South Harbor, *Manila* 17 B1
South Harrow, *London* 15 A1
South Hd., *Sydney* 28 B2
South Hills, *Johannesburg* 13 B2
South Hornchurch, *London* 15 A5
South Kensington, *London* 15 c2
South Lawn, *Washington* 32 C3
South Lincoln, *Boston* 6 A2
South Miami, *Miami* 18 B1
South Norwood, *London* 15 B3
South of Market, *San Francisco* 25 B2
South Ozone Park, *New York* 21 B3
South Pasadena, *Los Angeles* 16 B4
South Res., *Boston* 6 A3
South Ruislip, *London* 15 A1
South San Francisco, *San Francisco* 25 C2
South San Gabriel, *Los Angeles* 16 B4
South Shore, *Chicago* 9 C3
South Sudbury, *Boston* 6 A1
Southall, *London* 15 A1
Southborough, *London* 15 B4
Southend, *London* 15 B3
Southfields, *London* 15 B2
Southwark, *London* 15 B3
Søvang, *Copenhagen* 10 B3
Soweto, *Johannesburg* 13 B1
Sowhānak, *Tehran* 30 A3
Soya, *Tokyo* 29 A4
Spandau, *Berlin* 5 A1
Spånga, *Stockholm* 28 A1
Spanische Reitschule, *Vienna* 31 b1
Spectacle I., *Boston* 6 A4
Speicher-See, *Munich* 20 A3
Speising, *Vienna* 31 B1
Sphinx, *Cairo* 7 B1
Spinaceto, *Rome* 25 C1
Spit Junction, *Sydney* 28 A2
Spořilov, *Prague* 24 B3
Spot Pond, *Boston* 6 A3
Spotswood, *Melbourne* 17 B1
Spree →, *Berlin* 5 A2
Spring Pond, *Boston* 6 A4
Springeberg, *Berlin* 5 B5
Springfield, *Washington* 32 C2
Squantum, *Boston* 6 B3
Srednaya Rogatka, *St. Petersburg* 26 C2
Śródmieście, *Warsaw* 31 B2
Saint-Gilles, *Brussels* 6 B2
Saint-Joose-Ten-Noode, *Brussels* 6 A2
Saint-Pieters-Leeuw, *Brussels* 6 B1
Saint-Stevens-Woluwe, *Brussels* 6 A2
Staaken, *Berlin* 5 A1
Stabekk, *Oslo* 22 A2
Stadhion, *Athens* 2 c3
Stadhuis, *Amsterdam* 2 b2
Stadlau, *Vienna* 31 A2
Stadshuset, *Stockholm* 28 b1
Stains, *Paris* 23 A3
Stamford Hill, *London* 15 A3
Stammersdorf, *Vienna* 31 A2
Stanley, *Hong Kong* 12 B2
Stanley Mound, *Hong Kong* 12 B2
Stanley Pen., *Hong Kong* 12 B2
Stanmore, *London* 15 A2
Stapleton, *New York* 21 C1
Star Ferry, *Hong Kong* 12 a2
Staraya Derevnya, *St. Petersburg* 26 B1
Stare, *Warsaw* 31 B2
Staré Město, *Prague* 24 B2
Starego Miasto, *Warsaw* 31 a2
Staten Island Zoo, *New York* 21 C1
Statenice, *Prague* 24 B1
Statue Square, *Hong Kong* 12 c1
Stedelijk Museum, *Amsterdam* 2 c1
Steele Creek, *Melbourne* 17 A1
Steenokkerzeel, *Brussels* 6 A2
Steglitz, *Berlin* 5 B2
Stepaside, *Dublin* 11 B2
Stephansdom, *Vienna* 31 b2
Stepney, *London* 15 A3
Sterling Park, *San Francisco* 25 B2
Sticklinge udde, *Stockholm* 28 A2
Stickney, *Chicago* 9 C2
Stillorgan, *Dublin* 11 B2
Stockholm, *Stockholm* 28 B2
Stocksund, *Stockholm* 28 A2
Stodůlky, *Prague* 24 B1
Stoke Newington, *London* 15 A3
Stokes Valley, *Wellington* 32 B2
Stone Canyon Res., *Los Angeles* 16 B2
Stone Park, *Chicago* 9 B1
Stonebridge, *London* 15 A2
Stoneham, *Boston* 6 A3
Stony Brook Res., *Boston* 6 B3
Stora Värtan, *Stockholm* 28 A2
Store Hareskov, *Copenhagen* 10 A2
Store Magleby, *Copenhagen* 10 B3
Storholmen, *Stockholm* 28 A2
Stoyka, *St. Petersburg* 26 B2
Straiton, *Edinburgh* 11 B3
Strand, *London* 15 b4
Strandfontein, *Cape Town* 8 B2
Strašnice, *Prague* 24 B2
Strasstrudering, *Munich* 20 B3
Stratford, *London* 15 A4
Strathfield, *Sydney* 28 B1
Streatham, *London* 15 B3
Streatham Vale, *London* 15 B3
Strebersdorf, *Vienna* 31 A2
Střešovice, *Prague* 24 B2
Stříżkov, *Prague* 24 B2
Strogino, *Moscow* 19 B2
Strombeek-Bever, *Brussels* 6 A2
Stromovka, *Prague* 24 B2
Studio City, *Los Angeles* 16 B2
Stureby, *Stockholm* 28 B2
Stuvsta, *Stockholm* 28 B2
Subhepur, *Delhi* 10 A2
Sucat, *Manila* 17 C2
Suchdol, *Prague* 24 B2
Sucy-en-Brie, *Paris* 23 B4
Sudbury, *Boston* 6 A1
Sugamo, *Tokyo* 29 A3
Sugar Loaf Mt. = Açúcar, Pão de, *Rio de Janeiro* 24 B2
Suge, *Tokyo* 29 B2
Suginami-Ku, *Tokyo* 29 A2
Sugō, *Tokyo* 29 B2
Suita, *Osaka* 22 A4
Suitland, *Washington* 32 B4
Sukchar, *Calcutta* 8 A2
Suma, *Osaka* 22 B1
Sumida →, *Tokyo* 29 A3
Sumida-Ku, *Tokyo* 29 A3
Sumiyoshi, *Osaka* 22 B4
Summerville, *Toronto* 30 B1
Summit, *Chicago* 9 C2
Sunamachi, *Tokyo* 29 A4
Sunbury-on-Thames, *London* 15 B1
Sundbyberg, *Stockholm* 28 A1
Sundbyerne, *Copenhagen* 10 B3
Sung Kong, *Hong Kong* 12 B2
Sungei Kadut Industrial Estate, *Singapore* 27 A2
Sungei Selatar Res., *Singapore* 27 A3
Sunter, *Jakarta* 13 A2
Sunter, Kali →, *Jakarta* 13 B2
Suomenlinna, *Helsinki* 12 C2
Supreme Court, *Washington* 32 b3
Sura, *Calcutta* 8 B2
Surag-san, *Seoul* 26 A2
Surbiton, *London* 15 B2
Suresnes, *Paris* 23 A2
Surfside, *Miami* 18 A2
Surquillo, *Lima* 16 B2
Surrey Hills, *Sydney* 28 B2
Susaek, *Seoul* 26 B1
Süssenbrunn, *Vienna* 31 A2
Sutton, *Dublin* 11 A3
Sutton, *London* 15 B2
Suyu, *Seoul* 26 B2
Suzukishinden, *Tokyo* 29 A2
Svanemøllen, *Copenhagen* 10 A3
Sverdlov, *Moscow* 19 B3
Svestad, *Oslo* 22 B2
Svinö, *Helsinki* 12 C1
Swampscott, *Boston* 6 A4
Swanley, *London* 15 B4
Swansea, *Toronto* 30 B2
Swinburne I., *New York* 21 C1
Swords, *Dublin* 11 A2
Sydenham, *Johannesburg* 13 A2
Sydney, *Sydney* 28 B2
Sydney, Univ. of, *Sydney* 28 B2
Sydney Airport, *Sydney* 28 B2
Sydney Harbour Bridge, *Sydney* 28 B2
Sydstranden, *Copenhagen* 10 B3
Sylvania, *Sydney* 28 C1
Syntagma, Pl., *Athens* 2 b3
Syon Park, *London* 15 B2
Szczęsliwice, *Warsaw* 31 B1
Széchnenyi-hegy, *Budapest* 7 B1
Szent Istvánbaz, *Budapest* 7 b2
Széphalom, *Budapest* 7 A1

T

Tabata, *Tokyo* 29 A3
Tablada, *Buenos Aires* 7 C1
Table Bay, *Cape Town* 8 A1
Table Mountain, *Cape Town* 8 A1
Taboão da Serra, *São Paulo* 26 B1
Täby, *Stockholm* 28 A2

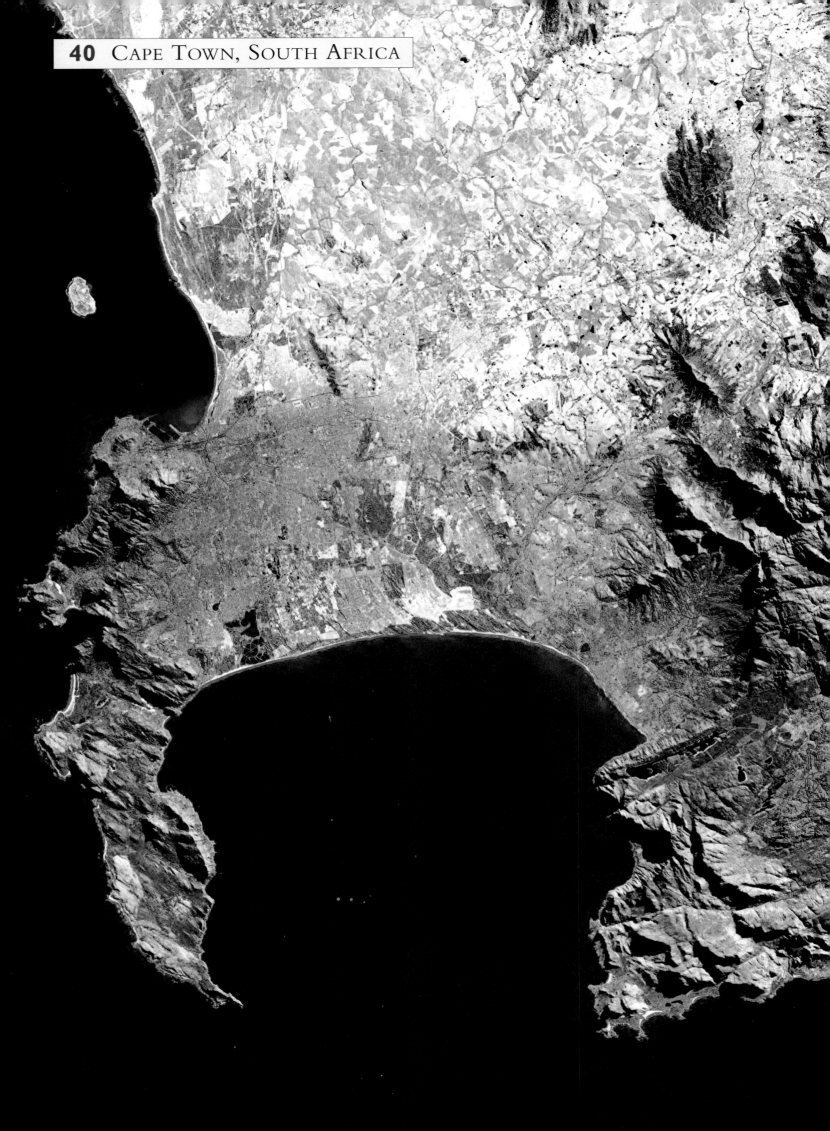

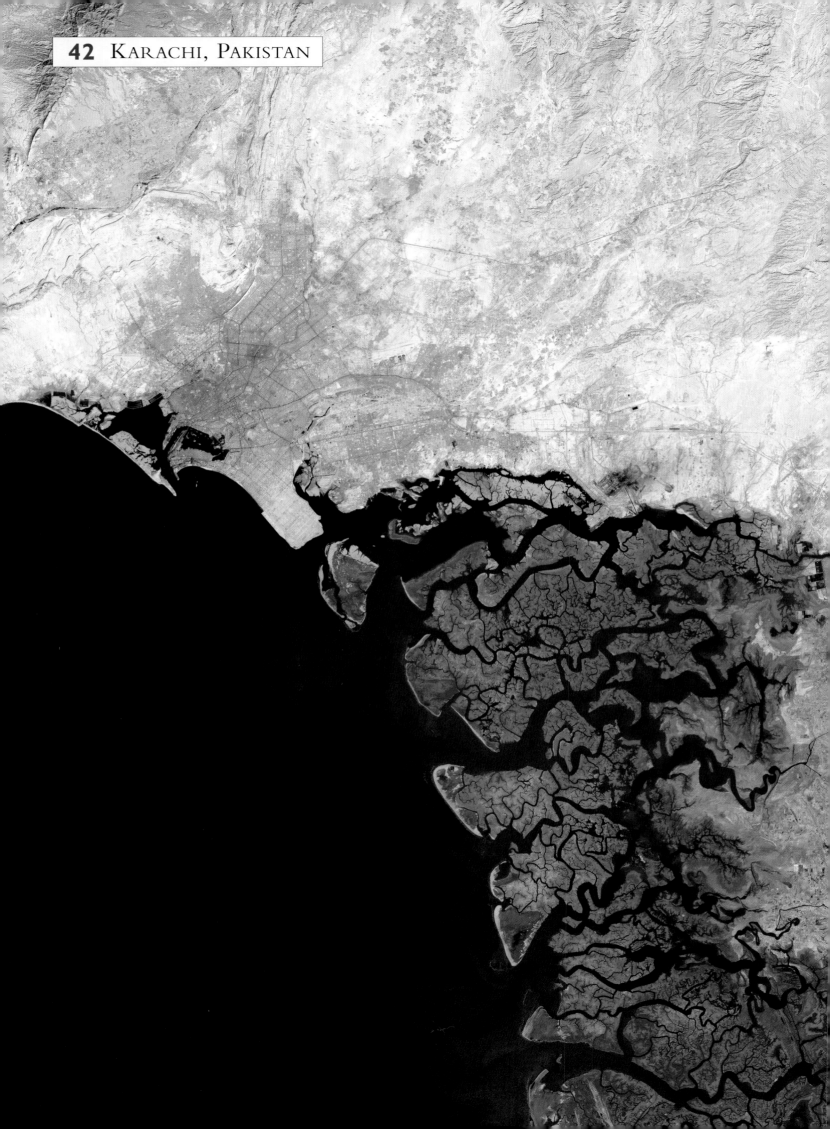

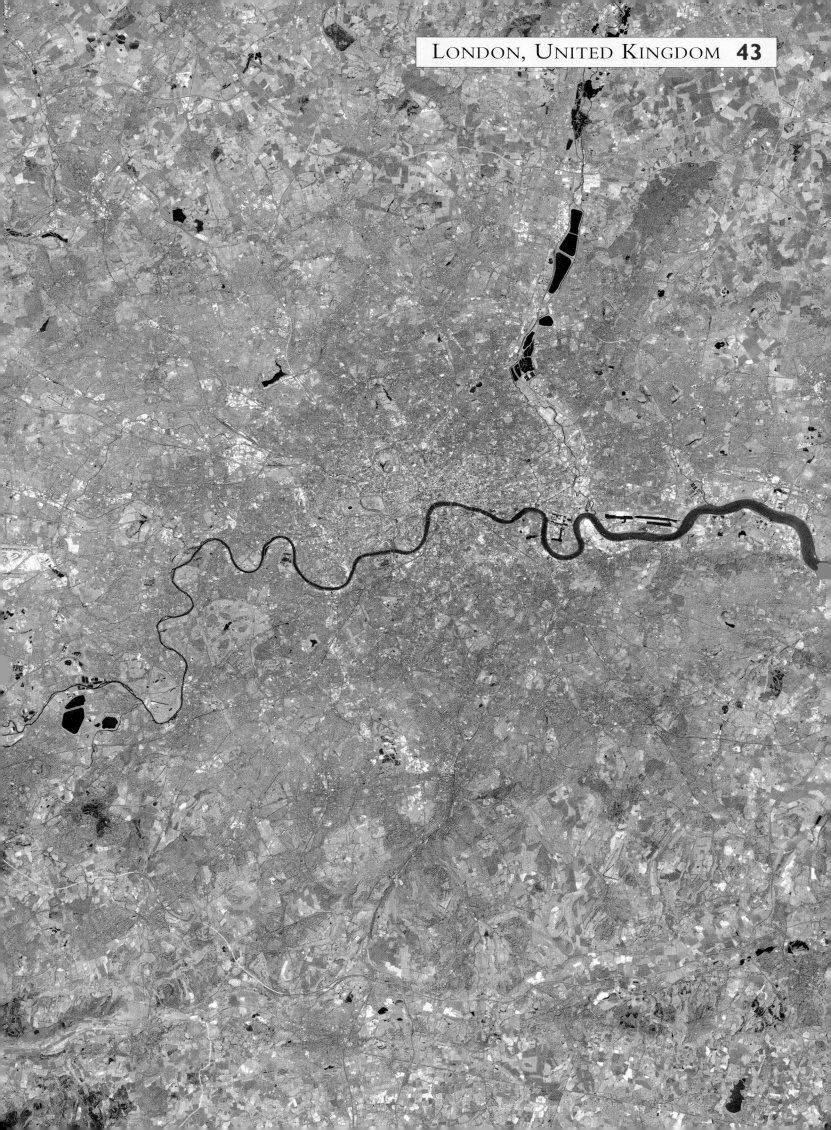

THE WORLD
AND
CONTINENTS

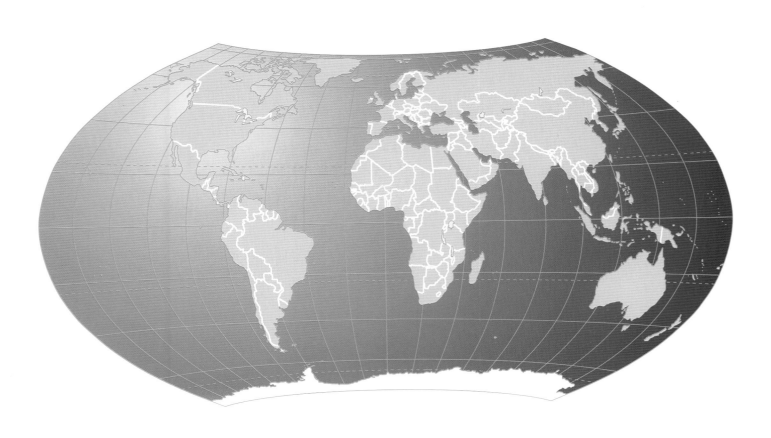

Projection: *Hammer Equal Area*

Hanoi ● Capital Cities

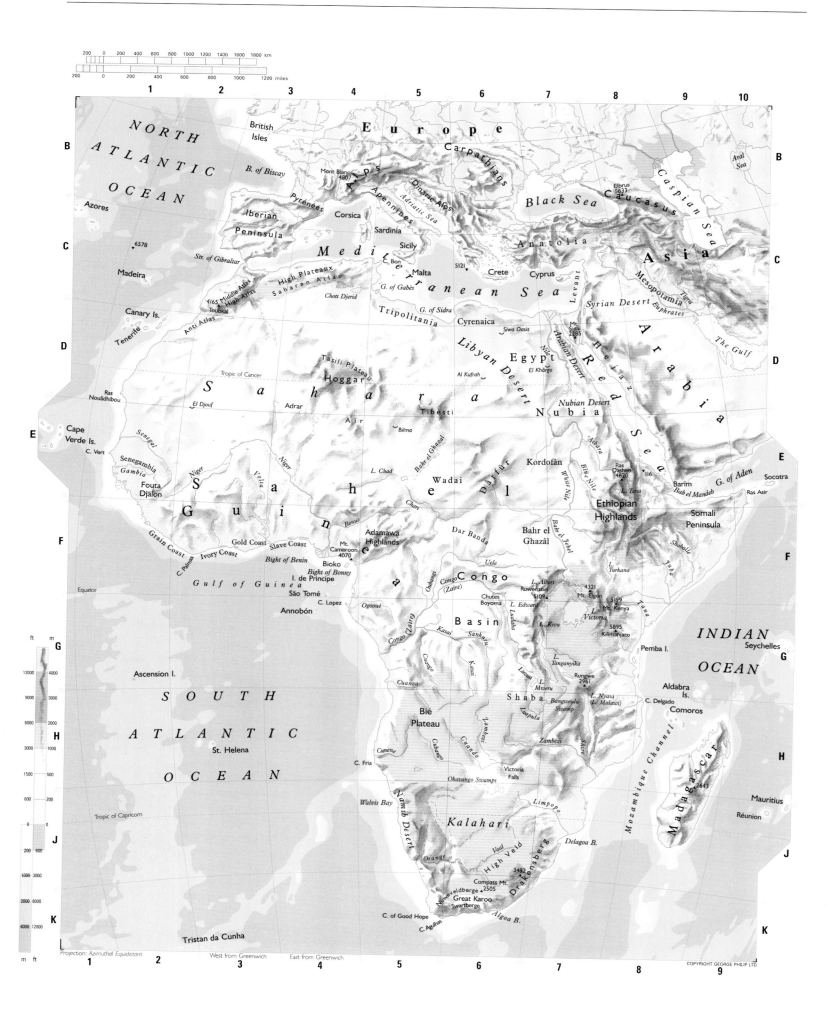

Projection: Azimuthal Equidistant

COPYRIGHT GEORGE PHILIP LTD.

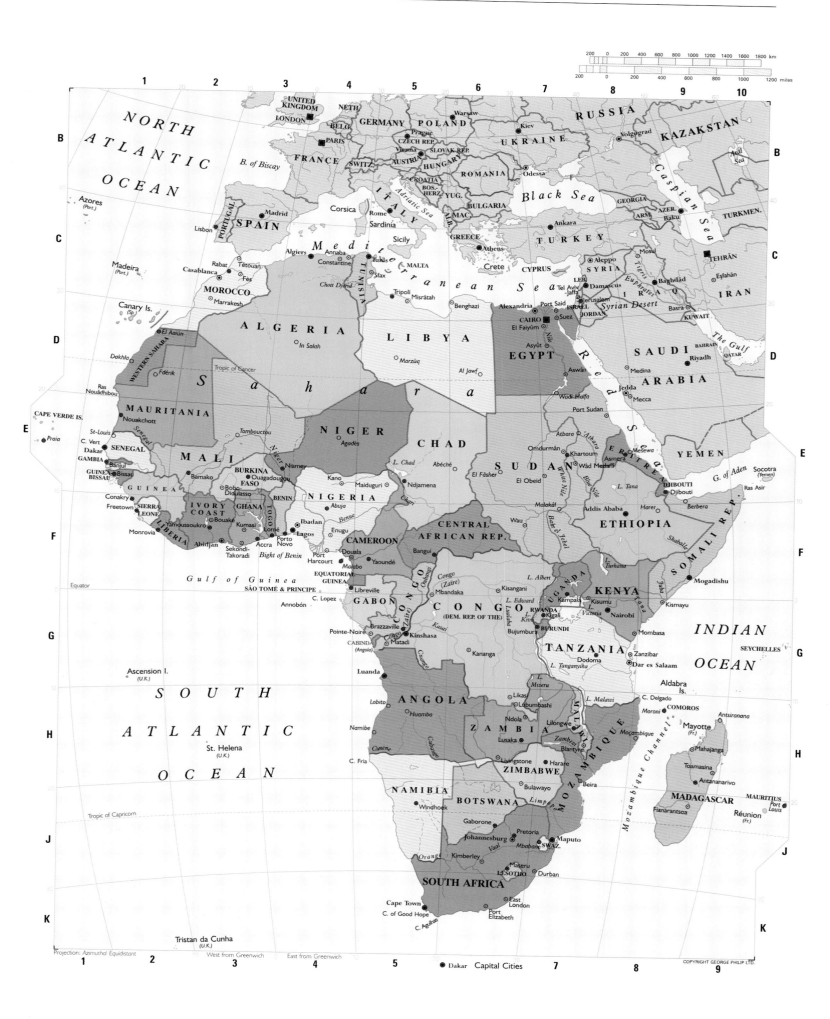

200 0 200 400 600 800 1000 1200 1400 1600 1800 km
200 0 200 400 600 800 1000 1200 miles

NORTH ATLANTIC OCEAN

UNITED KINGDOM
LONDON
NETH.
BELG.
GERMANY POLAND Warsaw
PARIS Prague
CZECH REP. Vienna Kiev
FRANCE SWITZ. AUSTRIA SLOVAK REP.
B. of Biscay HUNGARY ROMANIA Odessa
CROATIA BULGARIA
BOS.
HERZ. YUG.
ALB. MAC.

RUSSIA

UKRAINE

KAZAKSTAN

Volgograd

Aral Sea

Azores
(Port.)

Madrid
Lisbon
PORTUGAL SPAIN

Corsica
Rome
Sardinia
Sicily

Adriatic Sea
ITALY

Black Sea

GEORGIA
ARM.
Baku
AZER.

Caspian Sea

TURKMEN.

Madeira
(Port.)

Algiers
Annaba
Constantine
Rabat
Casablanca
Tétouan
Fès
MOROCCO
Marrakesh

Mediterranean Sea

TUNISIA
Tunis
Sfax

MALTA

Tripoli
Misrātah

Crete

GREECE
Athens

CYPRUS

Ankara
TURKEY

Aleppo
SYRIA
LEB.
Tel Aviv
-Jaffa
ISRAEL
JORDAN

Mosul
Tigris
Damascus
Syrian Desert

Euphrates
Baghdad

IRAQ

Esfahān

TEHRĀN

IRAN

Canary Is.
(Sp.)

Dakhla

Ras Nouâdhibou

C. Vert
Dakar

St-Louis

Nouakchott

CAPE VERDE IS.

Praia

El Aaiún

Fdérik

WESTERN SAHARA

Tropic of Cancer

ALGERIA

In Salah

Sahara

LIBYA

Marzūq

Al Jawf

Benghazi
Alexandria
Port Said
CAIRO
El Faiyûm
Suez
Asyût

EGYPT

Aswân

Medina

Jedda
Mecca

SAUDI ARABIA

Riyadh

BAHRAIN
QATAR

The Gulf

KUWAIT
Basra

MAURITANIA

Tombouctou

NIGER

Agades

CHAD

Abéché

L. Chad

Ndjamena

Wadi Halfa
Port Sudan

Atbara
Omdurmán
Khartoum
Wād Medani

SUDAN

El Obeid
El Fâsher

Atbara

Mesewa
Asmera
ERITREA

YEMEN

DJIBOUTI
Djibouti

G. of Aden

Socotra
(Yemen)

Ras Asir

MALI

Bamako

BURKINA FASO
Ouagadougou
Bobo Dioulasso

Niamey
Kano
Maiduguri

NIGERIA
Abuja

Benue

Malakâl
Wau

White Nile

Blue Nile
L. Tana

Berbera

Senegal
SENEGAL
Banjul
GAMBIA
Bissau
GUINEA-BISSAU
Conakry
Freetown
SIERRA LEONE
Monrovia
LIBERIA

GUINEA

IVORY COAST
Yamoussoukro
Bouaké
Kumasi
GHANA
Abidjan
Accra
Sekondi-Takoradi

BENIN
TOGO
Lomé
Porto Novo

Ibadan
Lagos
Enugu
Porto Novo

Bight of Benin

Abéché

CENTRAL AFRICAN REP.

Bangui

Addis Ababa
Harer

ETHIOPIA

Shabelle

SOMALI REP.

Mogadishu

Kismayu

Equator

Gulf of Guinea

SÃO TOMÉ & PRINCIPE

C. Lopez

Annobón

CAMEROON
Douala
Yaoundé
Malabo
Port Harcourt

EQUATORIAL GUINEA
Libreville

GABON

Chari

Oubangui

Congo
(Zaïre)

Mbandaka
Kisangani

CONGO
(DEM. REP. OF THE)

Bahr el Jebel

L. Turkana

UGANDA
Kampala
L. Albert
L. Edward
RWANDA
Kigali
L. Kivu
BURUNDI
Bujumbura

KENYA
Kisumu
Nairobi
L. Victoria

Juba
Tana

Mombasa

Brazzaville
Pointe-Noire
Kinshasa
Matadi
CABINDA
(Angola)

CONGO

Kasai

Kananga

Kuango

TANZANIA
Dodoma
Dar es Salaam

Zanzibar

L. Tanganyika

INDIAN OCEAN

SEYCHELLES

Luanda

SOUTH ATLANTIC OCEAN

Ascension I.
(U.K.)

St. Helena
(U.K.)

Lobito

Namibe

C. Fria

Huambo

ANGOLA

Cuanza

Cunene

Likasi
Lubumbashi

L. Mweru

L. Malawi

Ndola

ZAMBIA

Lusaka

Kafue

Livingstone

Zambezi

MALAWI
Lilongwe
Blantyre

C. Delgado

Moçambique

MOZAMBIQUE

Mozambique Channel

COMOROS
Moroni

Mayotte
(Fr.)

Antsiranana

Mahajanga

Toamasina

Aldabra Is.

NAMIBIA

Windhoek

BOTSWANA

Gaborone

Harare
Bulawayo

ZIMBABWE

Beira

Limpopo

Antananarivo

MADAGASCAR

Fianarantsoa

MAURITIUS
Port Louis

Réunion
(Fr.)

Tropic of Capricorn

Johannesburg
Pretoria
SWAZ.
Mbabane
Maputo
Vaal
Kimberley
Maseru
LESOTHO
Durban

Orange

SOUTH AFRICA

Cape Town
C. of Good Hope
C. Agulhas

East London

Port Elizabeth

Tristan da Cunha
(U.K.)

● Dakar   Capital Cities

COPYRIGHT GEORGE PHILIP LTD.

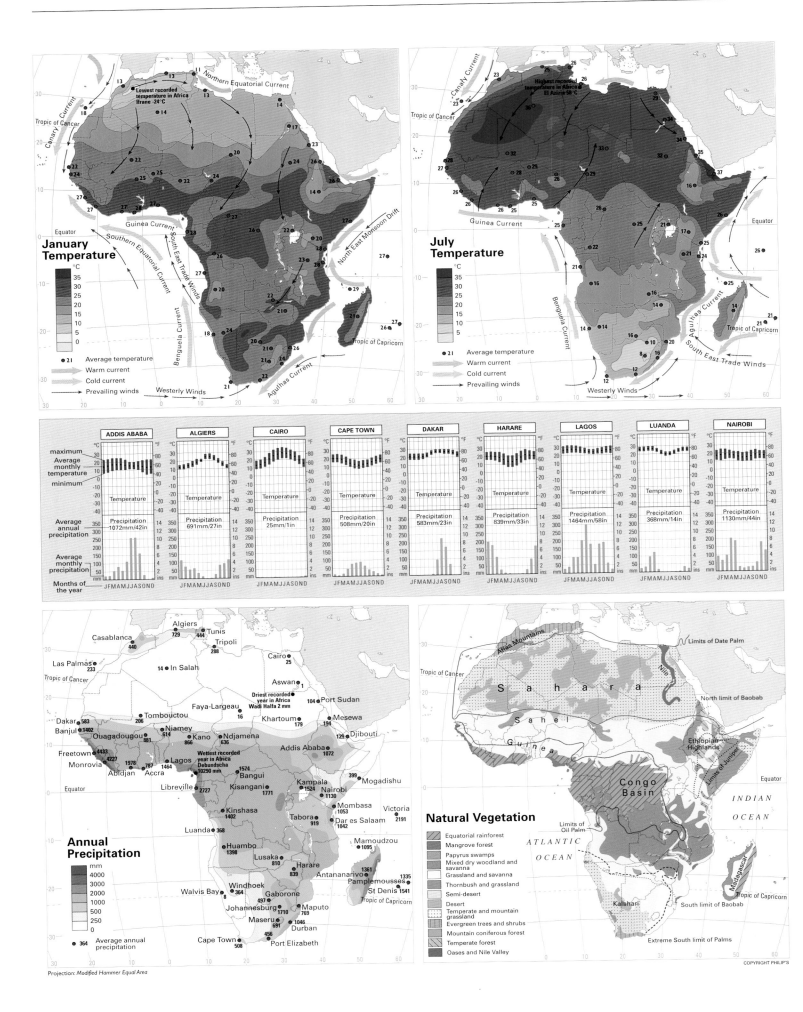

January Temperature

°C
35
30
25
20
15
10
5
0

- 21 Average temperature
- Warm current
- Cold current
- Prevailing winds

Lowest recorded temperature in Africa Ifrane -24°C

Northern Equatorial Current
Canary Current
Tropic of Cancer
Guinea Current
Southern Equatorial Current
South East Trade Winds
Benguela Current
North East Monsoon Drift
Equator
Westerly Winds
Agulhas Current

July Temperature

°C
35
30
25
20
15
10
5

- 21 Average temperature
- Warm current
- Cold current
- Prevailing winds

Highest recorded temperature in Africa El Azizia 58°C

Canary Current
Tropic of Cancer
Guinea Current
Benguela Current
Agulhas Current
Equator
South East Trade Winds
Westerly Winds
Tropic of Capricorn

Climate graphs

ADDIS ABABA — Temperature; Precipitation 1072mm/42in

maximum
Average monthly temperature
minimum

Average annual precipitation
Average monthly precipitation
Months of the year: JFMAMJJASOND

ALGIERS — Temperature; Precipitation 691mm/27in

CAIRO — Temperature; Precipitation 25mm/1in

CAPE TOWN — Temperature; Precipitation 508mm/20in

DAKAR — Temperature; Precipitation 583mm/23in

HARARE — Temperature; Precipitation 839mm/33in

LAGOS — Temperature; Precipitation 1464mm/58in

LUANDA — Temperature; Precipitation 368mm/14in

NAIROBI — Temperature; Precipitation 1130mm/44in

Annual Precipitation

mm
4000
3000
2000
1000
500
250
0

- 364 Average annual precipitation

Algiers 729
Tunis 444
Tripoli 288
Casablanca 440
Las Palmas 233
Cairo 25
Aswan 1
In Salah 14
Driest recorded year in Africa Wadi Halfa 2 mm
Faya-Largeau 16
Port Sudan 104
Dakar 583
Tombouctou 206
Khartoum 179
Mesewa 194
Banjul 1402
Niamey 614
Ouagadougou 881
Kano 866
Ndjamena 636
Djibouti 129
Freetown 4433
Addis Ababa 1072
Monrovia 4227
1978
787
Lagos 1464
Wettest recorded year in Africa Debundscha 10290 mm
Bangui 1574
Kampala 1524
Mogadishu 399
Abidjan Accra
Libreville 2727
Kisangani 1402
Nairobi 1771 1130
Kinshasa 1402
Tabora 919
Mombasa 1053
Dar es Salaam 1042
Victoria 2191
Luanda 368
Mamoudzou 1095
Huambo 1398
Lusaka 810
Harare 839
Antananarivo 1361
Pamplemousses 1335
St Denis 1541
Walvis Bay 8
Windhoek 364
Gaborone 497
Johannesburg 1710
Maputo 769
Maseru 1046
Durban 456 691
Cape Town 508
Port Elizabeth

Projection: Modified Hammer Equal Area

Natural Vegetation

- Equatorial rainforest
- Mangrove forest
- Papyrus swamps
- Mixed dry woodland and savanna
- Grassland and savanna
- Thornbush and grassland
- Semi-desert
- Desert
- Temperate and mountain grassland
- Evergreen trees and shrubs
- Mountain coniferous forest
- Temperate forest
- Oases and Nile Valley

Atlas Mountains
Limits of Date Palm
Sahara
Nile
North limit of Baobab
Sahel
Guinea
Ethiopian Highlands
Limits of Juniper
Congo Basin
Equator
INDIAN OCEAN
Limits of Oil Palm
ATLANTIC OCEAN
Kalahari
South limit of Baobab
Madagascar
Tropic of Capricorn
Extreme South limit of Palms

COPYRIGHT PHILIP'S

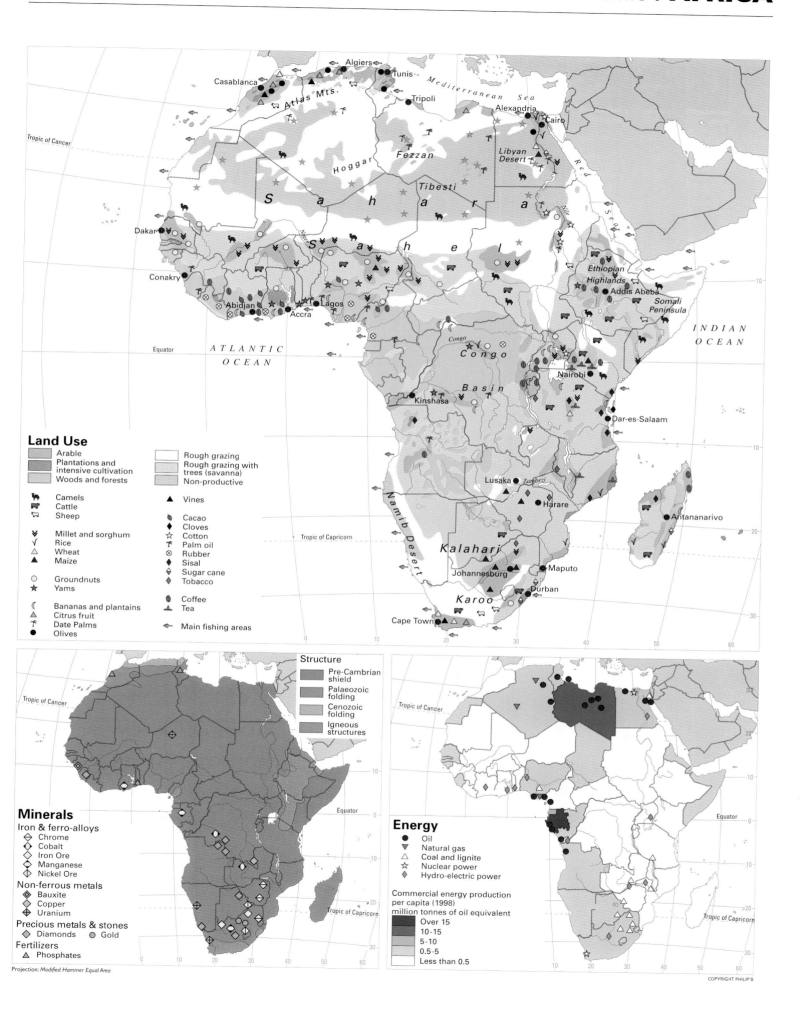

Land Use

- Arable
- Plantations and intensive cultivation
- Woods and forests
- Rough grazing
- Rough grazing with trees (savanna)
- Non-productive

- Camels
- Cattle
- Sheep

- Millet and sorghum
- Rice
- Wheat
- Maize

- Groundnuts
- Yams

- Bananas and plantains
- Citrus fruit
- Date Palms
- Olives

- Vines
- Cacao
- Cloves
- Cotton
- Palm oil
- Rubber
- Sisal
- Sugar cane
- Tobacco

- Coffee
- Tea

- Main fishing areas

Labels on main map
Algiers, Tunis, Casablanca, Tripoli, Alexandria, Cairo, *Mediterranean Sea*, *Hoggar*, *Fezzan*, *Tibesti*, *Libyan Desert*, *Nile*, *Red Sea*, *S a h a r a*, Dakar, *S a h e l*, Conakry, *Niger*, Abidjan, Lagos, Accra, *Ethiopian Highlands*, Addis Abeba, *Somali Peninsula*, *INDIAN OCEAN*, *ATLANTIC OCEAN*, Equator, *Congo*, *Congo Basin*, Kinshasa, Nairobi, Dar-es-Salaam, Lusaka, *Zambezi*, Harare, Antananarivo, *Namib Desert*, Tropic of Capricorn, *Kalahari*, Johannesburg, Maputo, *Karoo*, Durban, Cape Town, *Atlas Mts.*, Tropic of Cancer

Minerals

Iron & ferro-alloys
- Chrome
- Cobalt
- Iron Ore
- Manganese
- Nickel Ore

Non-ferrous metals
- Bauxite
- Copper
- Uranium

Precious metals & stones
- Diamonds
- Gold

Fertilizers
- Phosphates

Projection: *Modified Hammer Equal Area*

Structure
- Pre-Cambrian shield
- Palaeozoic folding
- Cenozoic folding
- Igneous structures

Energy

- Oil
- Natural gas
- Coal and lignite
- Nuclear power
- Hydro-electric power

Commercial energy production per capita (1998) million tonnes of oil equivalent
- Over 15
- 10-15
- 5-10
- 0.5-5
- Less than 0.5

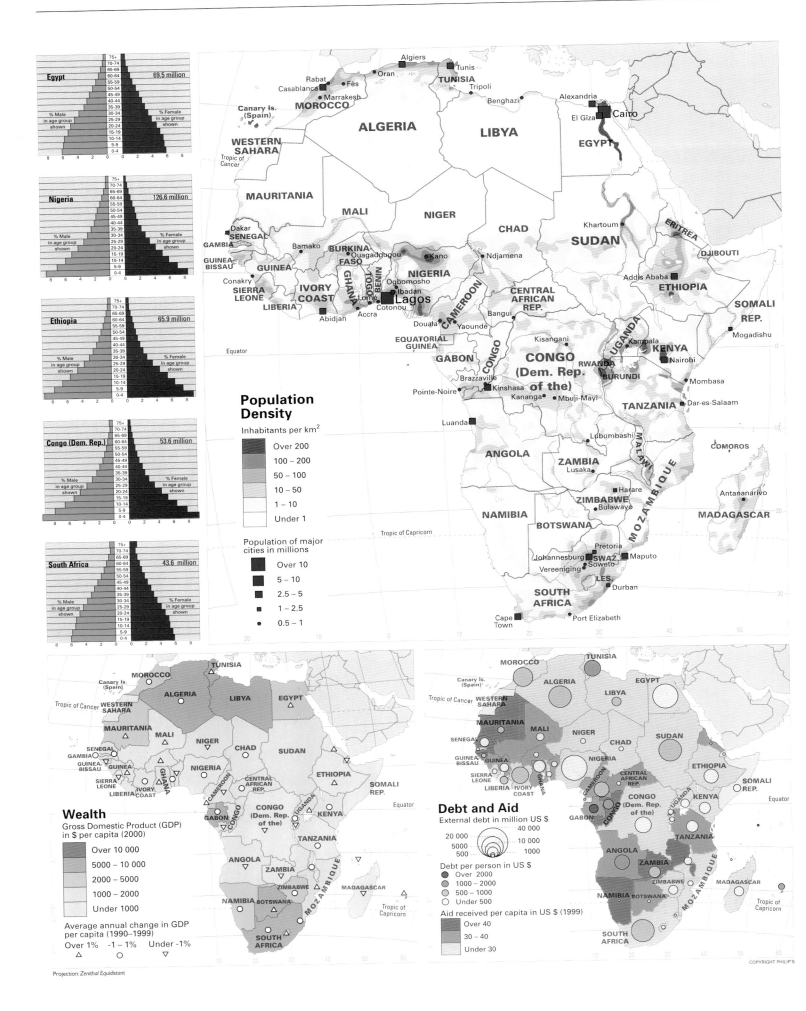

Egypt 69.5 million
75+ 70-74 65-69 60-64 55-59 50-54 45-49 40-44 35-39 30-34 25-29 20-24 15-19 10-14 5-9 0-4
% Male in age group shown % Female in age group shown
8 6 4 2 0 0 2 4 6 8

Nigeria 126.6 million
75+ 70-74 65-69 60-64 55-59 50-54 45-49 40-44 35-39 30-34 25-29 20-24 15-19 10-14 5-9 0-4
% Male in age group shown % Female in age group shown
8 6 4 2 0 0 2 4 6 8

Ethiopia 65.9 million
75+ 70-74 65-69 60-64 55-59 50-54 45-49 40-44 35-39 30-34 25-29 20-24 15-19 10-14 5-9 0-4
% Male in age group shown % Female in age group shown
8 6 4 2 0 0 2 4 6 8

Congo (Dem. Rep.) 53.6 million
75+ 70-74 65-69 60-64 55-59 50-54 45-49 40-44 35-39 30-34 25-29 20-24 15-19 10-14 5-9 0-4
% Male in age group shown % Female in age group shown
8 6 4 2 0 0 2 4 6 8

South Africa 43.6 million
75+ 70-74 65-69 60-64 55-59 50-54 45-49 40-44 35-39 30-34 25-29 20-24 15-19 10-14 5-9 0-4
% Male in age group shown % Female in age group shown
8 6 4 2 0 0 2 4 6 8

Population Density

Inhabitants per km²

- Over 200
- 100 – 200
- 50 – 100
- 10 – 50
- 1 – 10
- Under 1

Population of major cities in millions
- Over 10
- 5 – 10
- 2.5 – 5
- 1 – 2.5
- 0.5 – 1

Wealth

Gross Domestic Product (GDP) in $ per capita (2000)

- Over 10 000
- 5000 – 10 000
- 2000 – 5000
- 1000 – 2000
- Under 1000

Average annual change in GDP per capita (1990–1999)
- Over 1% △
- -1 – 1% ○
- Under -1% ▽

Debt and Aid

External debt in million US $
- 40 000
- 20 000
- 10 000
- 5000
- 1000
- 500

Debt per person in US $
- Over 2000
- 1000 – 2000
- 500 – 1000
- Under 500

Aid received per capita in US $ (1999)
- Over 40
- 30 – 40
- Under 30

Projection: Zenithal Equidistant

COPYRIGHT PHILIP'S

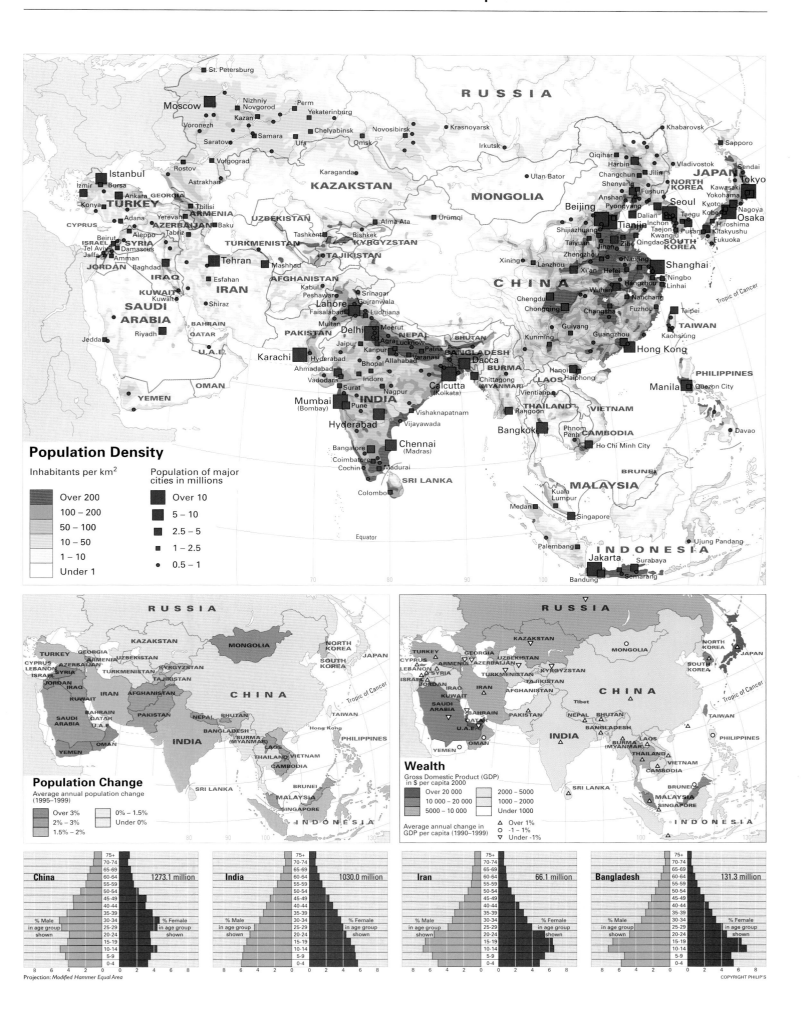

Population Density

Inhabitants per km²

	Over 200
	100 – 200
	50 – 100
	10 – 50
	1 – 10
	Under 1

Population of major cities in millions

■	Over 10
■	5 – 10
■	2.5 – 5
▪	1 – 2.5
•	0.5 – 1

Population Change

Average annual population change (1995–1999)

	Over 3%
	2% – 3%
	1.5% – 2%
	0% – 1.5%
	Under 0%

Wealth

Gross Domestic Product (GDP) in $ per capita 2000

	Over 20 000	2000 – 5000
	10 000 – 20 000	1000 – 2000
	5000 – 10 000	Under 1000

Average annual change in GDP per capita (1990–1999)

△ Over 1%
○ -1 – 1%
▽ Under -1%

China 1273.1 million

% Male in age group shown | % Female in age group shown

75+, 70-74, 65-69, 60-64, 55-59, 50-54, 45-49, 40-44, 35-39, 30-34, 25-29, 20-24, 15-19, 10-14, 5-9, 0-4

8 6 4 2 0 2 4 6 8

India 1030.0 million

% Male in age group shown | % Female in age group shown

8 6 4 2 0 2 4 6 8

Iran 66.1 million

% Male in age group shown | % Female in age group shown

8 6 4 2 0 2 4 6 8

Bangladesh 131.3 million

% Male in age group shown | % Female in age group shown

8 6 4 2 0 2 4 6 8

Projection: *Modified Hammer Equal Area*

COPYRIGHT PHILIP'S

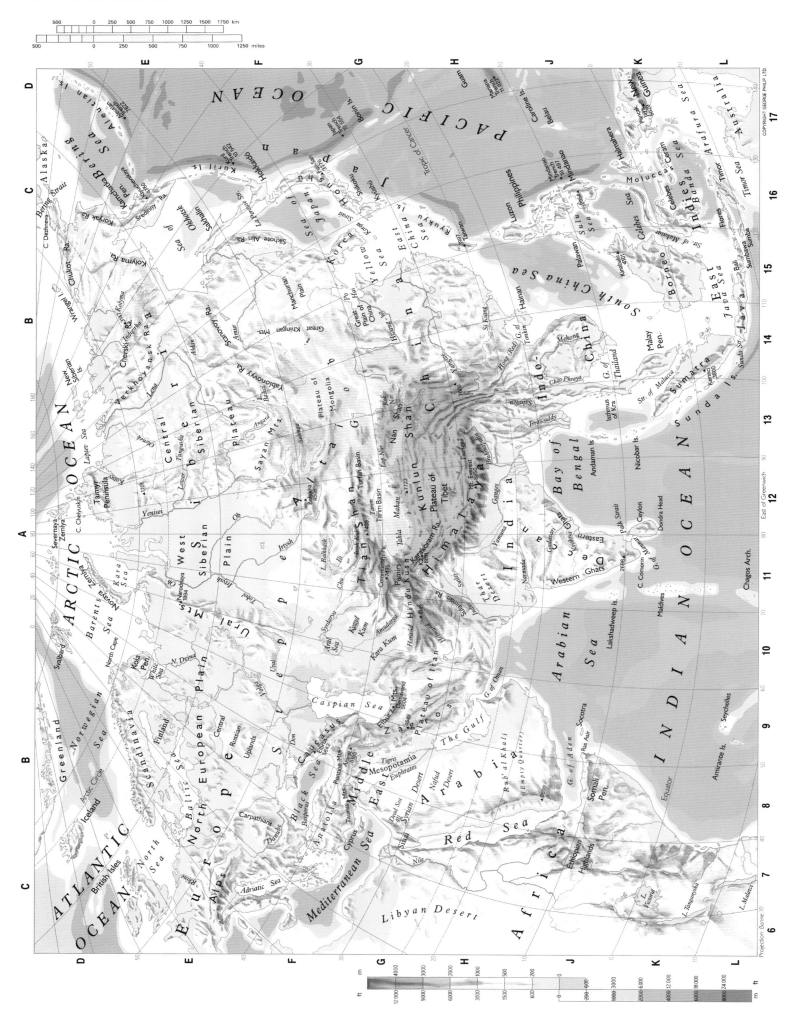

Projection Bonne

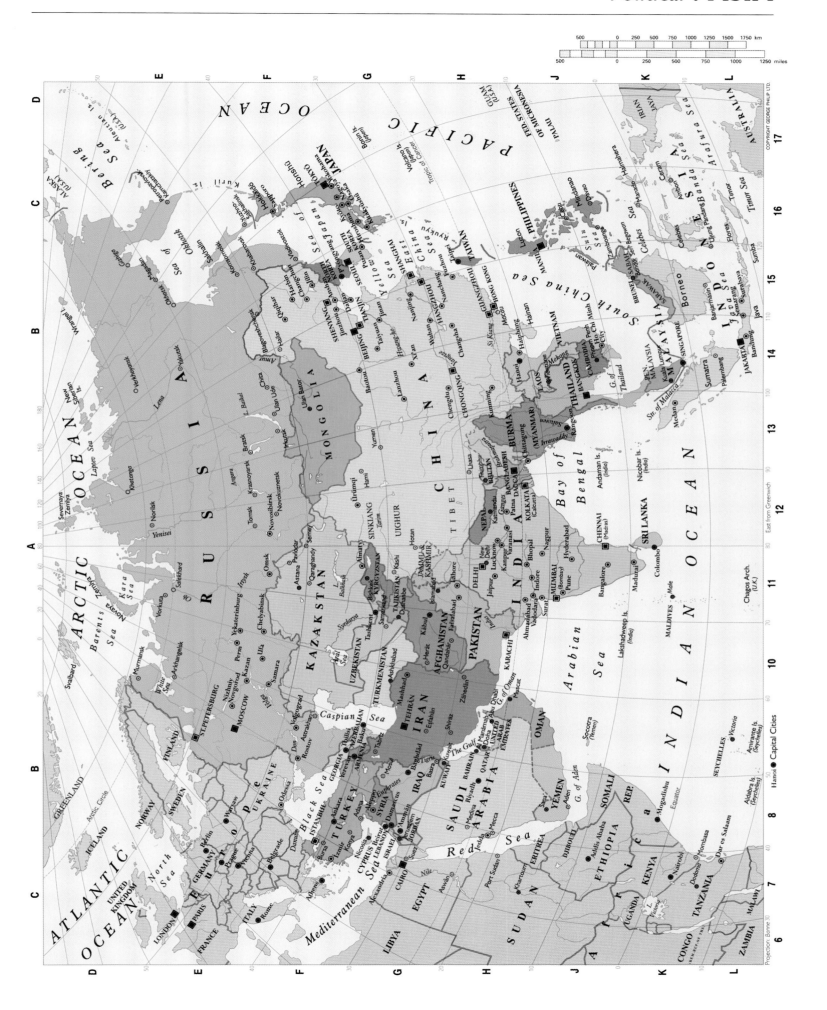

ASIA : Climate and Natural Vegetation

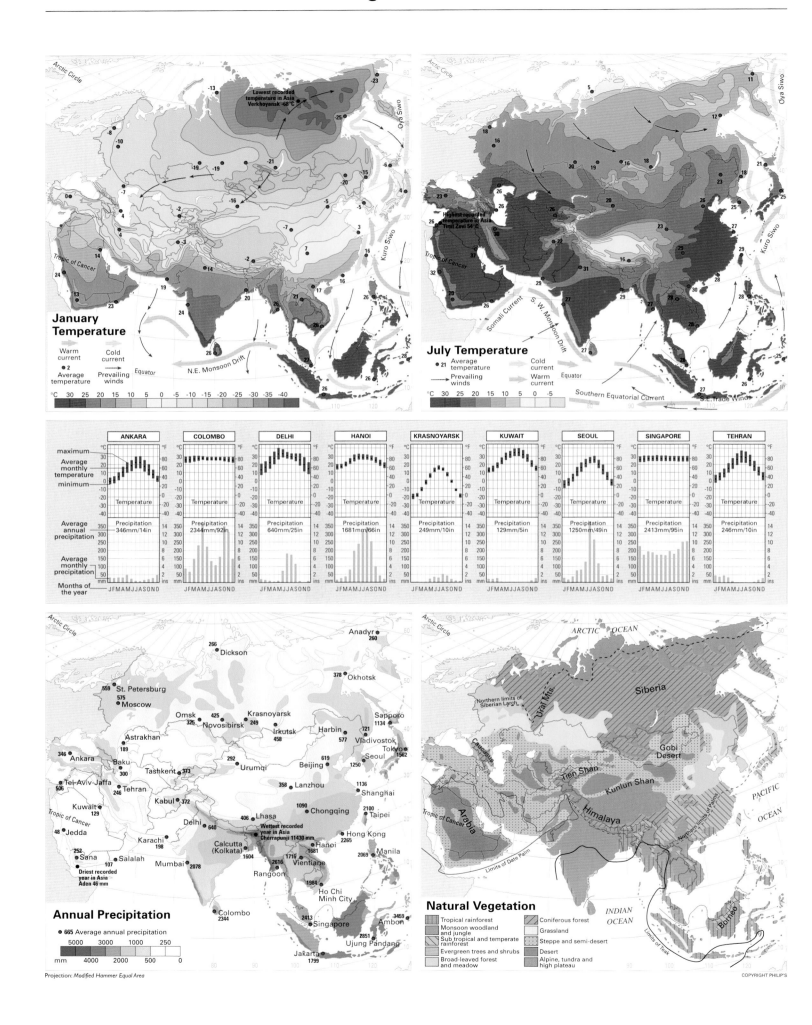

January Temperature

Lowest recorded temperature in Asia Verkhoyansk -68°C

- Warm current
- Cold current
- 2 Average temperature
- → Prevailing winds

N.E. Monsoon Drift

°C 30 25 20 15 10 5 0 -5 -10 -15 -20 -25 -30 -35 -40

July Temperature

Highest recorded temperature in Asia Tirat Zevi 54°C

- 21 Average temperature
- → Prevailing winds
- Cold current
- Warm current

Somali Current — S. W. Monsoon Drift — Southern Equatorial Current — S.E. Trade Winds

°C 30 25 20 15 10 5 0 -5

Climate graphs

	ANKARA	COLOMBO	DELHI	HANOI	KRASNOYARSK	KUWAIT	SEOUL	SINGAPORE	TEHRAN
Average annual precipitation	346mm/14in	2344mm/92in	640mm/25in	1681mm/66in	249mm/10in	129mm/5in	1250mm/49in	2413mm/95in	246mm/10in

maximum · Average monthly temperature · minimum

Temperature · Precipitation · Average monthly precipitation

Months of the year: J F M A M J J A S O N D

Annual Precipitation

- Anadyr 260
- Dickson 266
- Okhotsk 378
- St. Petersburg 559
- Moscow 575
- Omsk 425
- Novosibirsk 325
- Krasnoyarsk 249
- Irkutsk 458
- Harbin 577
- Sapporo 1134
- Vladivostok 721
- Astrakhan 189
- Ankara 346
- Baku 300
- Tashkent 373
- Urumqi 292
- Beijing 619
- Seoul 1250
- Tokyo 1562
- Tel-Aviv-Jaffa 506
- Tehran 246
- Kabul 372
- Lanzhou 358
- Shanghai 1136
- Kuwait 129
- Jedda 48
- Delhi 640
- Lhasa 406
- Chongqing 1090
- Taipei 2100
- Karachi 198
- Calcutta (Kolkata) 1604
- Hong Kong 2265
- Sana 252
- Salalah 107
- Mumbai 2078
- Rangoon 2616
- Vientiane 1716
- Hanoi 1681
- Manila 2069
- Wettest recorded year in Asia Cherrapunji 11430 mm
- Driest recorded year in Asia Aden 46 mm
- Ho Chi Minh City 1984
- Colombo 2344
- Singapore 2413
- Ambon 3459
- Ujung Pandang 2851
- Jakarta 1799

- 665 Average annual precipitation

mm: 5000 / 4000 / 3000 / 2000 / 1000 / 500 / 250 / 0

Projection: Modified Hammer Equal Area

Natural Vegetation

ARCTIC OCEAN · Siberia · Ural Mts. · Caucasus · Gobi Desert · Tien Shan · Kunlun Shan · Himalaya · Arabia · Northern limits of Siberian Larch · Northern limits of Palms · Limits of Date Palm · Limits of Teak · Borneo · INDIAN OCEAN · PACIFIC OCEAN

- Tropical rainforest
- Monsoon woodland and jungle
- Sub tropical and temperate rainforest
- Evergreen trees and shrubs
- Broad-leaved forest and meadow
- Coniferous forest
- Grassland
- Steppe and semi-desert
- Desert
- Alpine, tundra and high plateau

Oya Siwo · Kuro Siwo · Tropic of Cancer · Equator · Arctic Circle

COPYRIGHT PHILIP'S

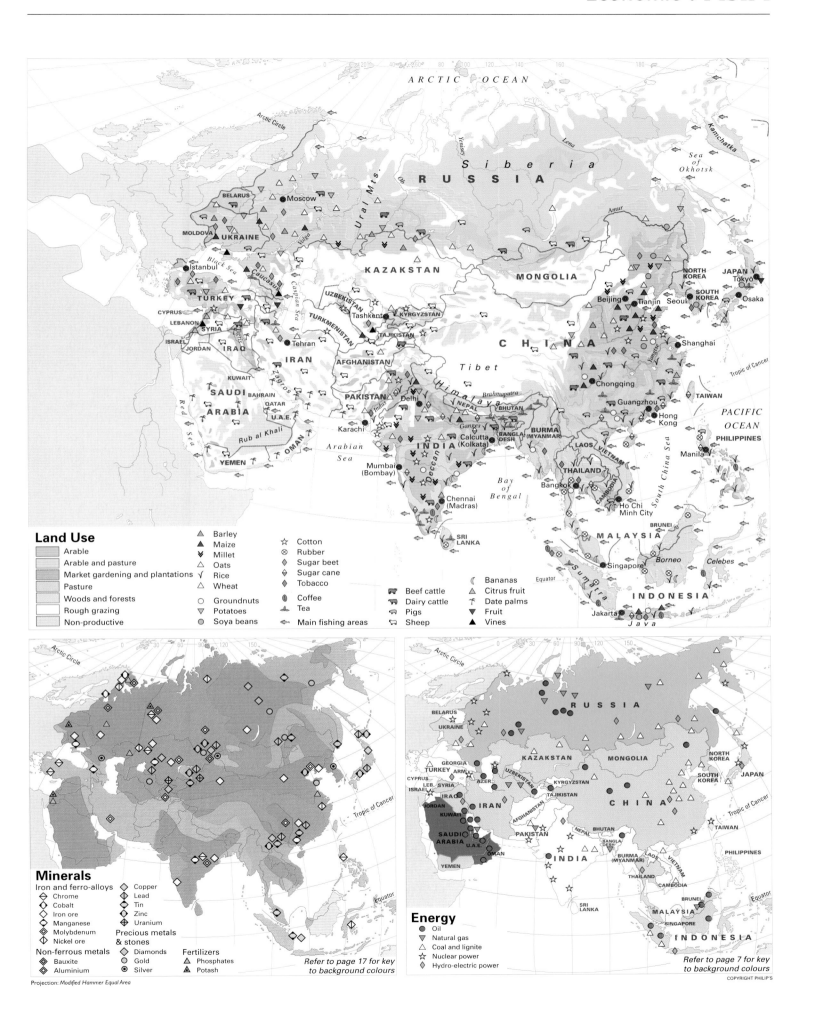

Land Use

- Arable
- Arable and pasture
- Market gardening and plantations
- Pasture
- Woods and forests
- Rough grazing
- Non-productive

- △ Barley
- ▲ Maize
- ⋎ Millet
- △ Oats
- √ Rice
- △ Wheat
- ○ Groundnuts
- ▽ Potatoes
- ○ Soya beans

- ☆ Cotton
- ⊗ Rubber
- ◇ Sugar beet
- ◇ Sugar cane
- ◇ Tobacco
- ◖ Coffee
- ⚘ Tea
- ⇒ Main fishing areas

- ☾ Bananas
- ⊗ Citrus fruit
- ⊤ Date palms
- ▼ Fruit
- ▲ Vines

- 🐄 Beef cattle
- 🐄 Dairy cattle
- 🐖 Pigs
- 🐑 Sheep

Minerals

Iron and ferro-alloys
- ⊼ Chrome
- ◇ Cobalt
- ◇ Iron ore
- ◇ Manganese
- ◈ Molybdenum
- ◈ Nickel ore

Non-ferrous metals
- ◈ Bauxite
- ◈ Aluminium

- ◇ Copper
- ◇ Lead
- ◇ Tin
- ◇ Zinc
- ⊕ Uranium

Precious metals & stones
- ◇ Diamonds
- ○ Gold
- ⊙ Silver

Fertilizers
- △ Phosphates
- △ Potash

Refer to page 17 for key to background colours

Projection: *Modified Hammer Equal Area*

Energy

- ● Oil
- ▽ Natural gas
- △ Coal and lignite
- ☆ Nuclear power
- ◇ Hydro-electric power

Refer to page 7 for key to background colours

COPYRIGHT PHILIP'S

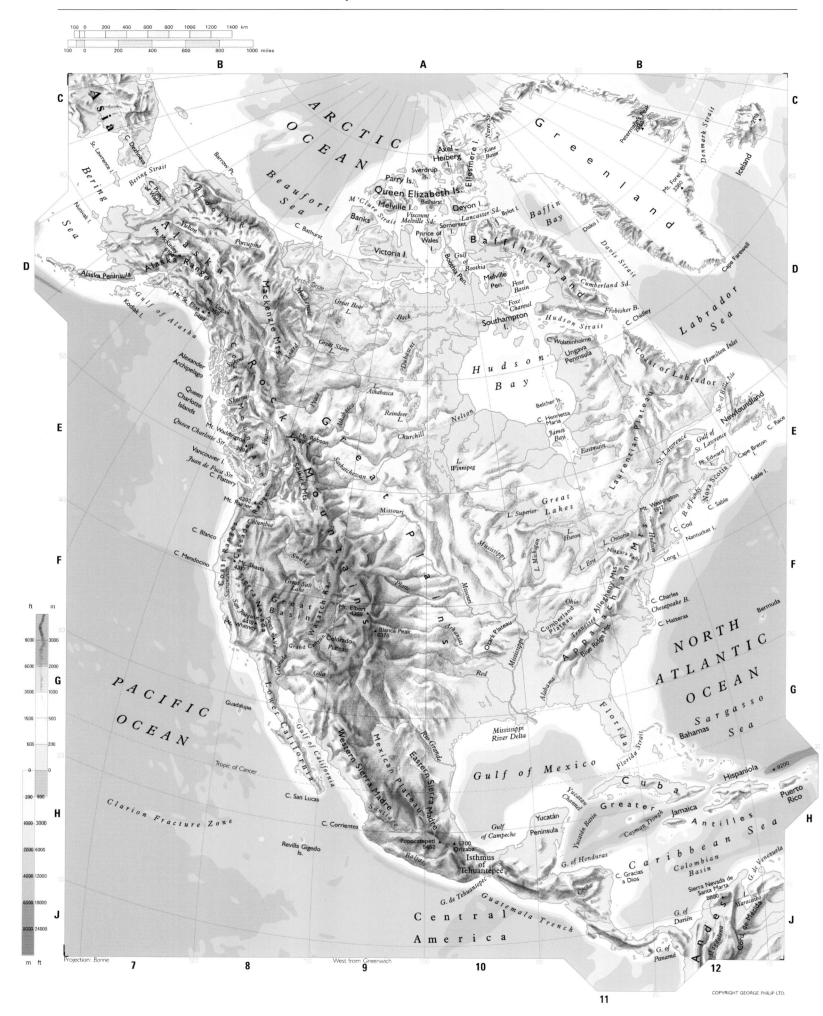

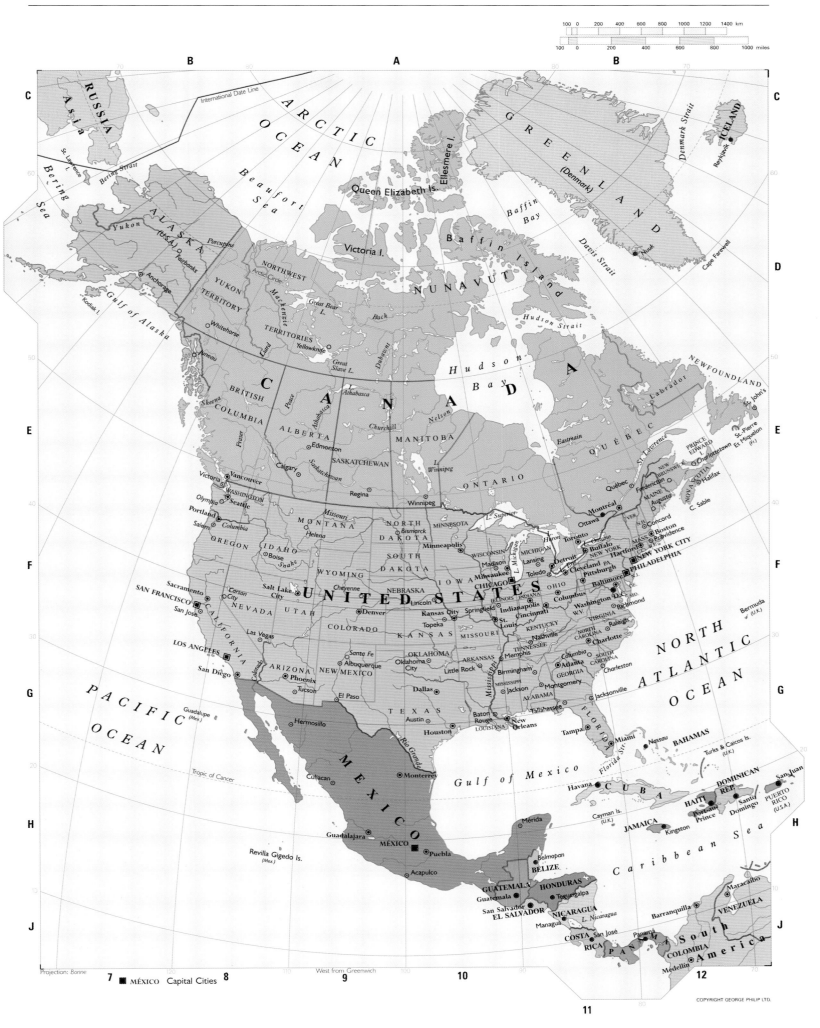

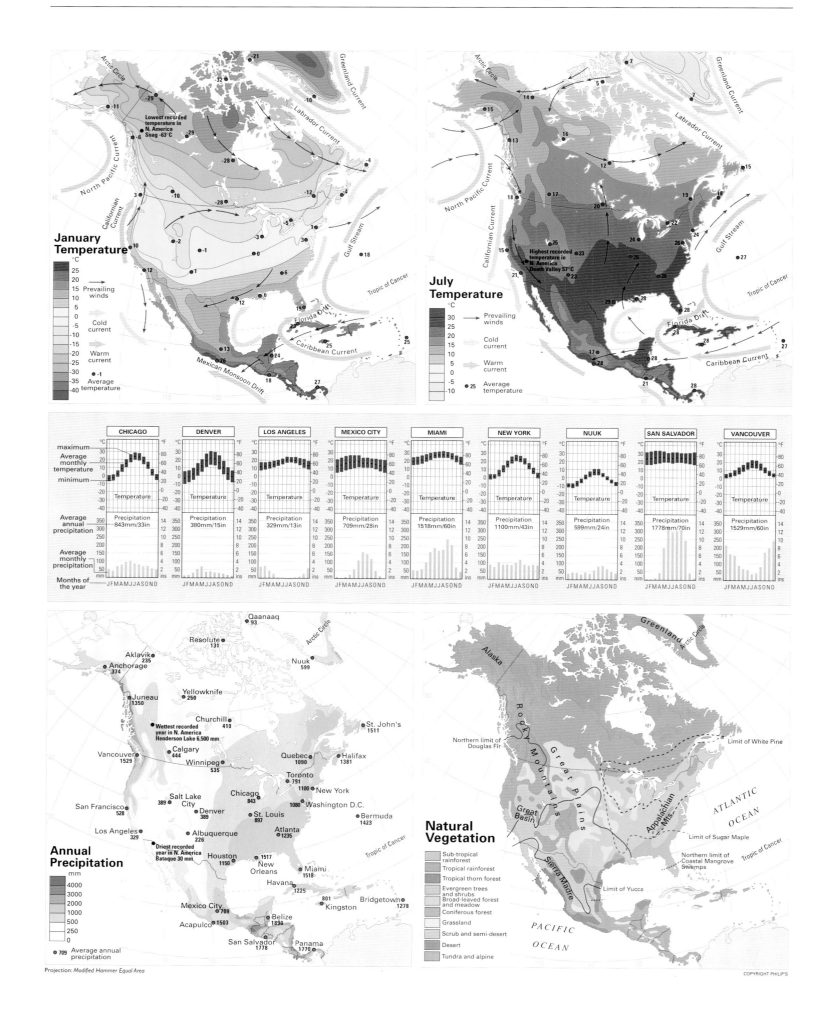

January Temperature

°C
25
20 — Prevailing winds
15
10
5
0
-5 — Cold current
-10
-15
-20 — Warm current
-25
-30
-35 ● -1 Average temperature
-40

Lowest recorded temperature in N. America Snag -63°C

July Temperature

°C
30 — Prevailing winds
25
20
15 — Cold current
10
5
0 — Warm current
-5
-10 ● 25 Average temperature

Highest recorded temperature in N. America Death Valley 57°C

CHICAGO	DENVER	LOS ANGELES	MEXICO CITY	MIAMI	NEW YORK	NUUK	SAN SALVADOR	VANCOUVER

maximum
Average monthly temperature
minimum

Temperature

Precipitation 843mm/33in | Precipitation 380mm/15in | Precipitation 329mm/13in | Precipitation 709mm/28in | Precipitation 1518mm/60in | Precipitation 1100mm/43in | Precipitation 599mm/24in | Precipitation 1778mm/70in | Precipitation 1529mm/60in

Average annual precipitation
Average monthly precipitation

Months of the year: JFMAMJJASOND

Annual Precipitation

Qaanaaq 93
Resolute 131
Aklavik 235
Anchorage 374
Nuuk 599
Juneau 1350
Yellowknife 250
Churchill 410
St. John's 1511
Wettest recorded year in N. America Henderson Lake 6,500 mm
Calgary 444
Vancouver 1529
Quebec 1090
Halifax 1381
Winnipeg 535
Toronto 791
Salt Lake City 389
Chicago 843
New York 1100
San Francisco 528
Denver 389
Washington D.C. 1080
St. Louis 897
Bermuda 1423
Los Angeles 329
Albuquerque 226
Atlanta 1235
Driest recorded year in N. America Bataque 30 mm
Houston 1150
New Orleans 1517
Miami 1518
Havana 1225
Mexico City 709
Kingston 801
Bridgetown 1278
Acapulco 1503
Belize 1890
San Salvador 1778
Panama 1770

mm
4000
3000
2000
1000
500
250
0
● 709 Average annual precipitation

Natural Vegetation

Northern limit of Douglas Fir
Limit of White Pine
Rocky Mountains
Great Plains
Great Basin
Appalachian Mts.
ATLANTIC OCEAN
Sierra Madre
Limit of Sugar Maple
Northern limit of Coastal Mangrove Swamps
Limit of Yucca
PACIFIC OCEAN

Sub-tropical rainforest
Tropical rainforest
Tropical thorn forest
Evergreen trees and shrubs
Broad-leaved forest and meadow
Coniferous forest
Grassland
Scrub and semi-desert
Desert
Tundra and alpine

Projection: Modified Hammer Equal Area

COPYRIGHT PHILIP'S

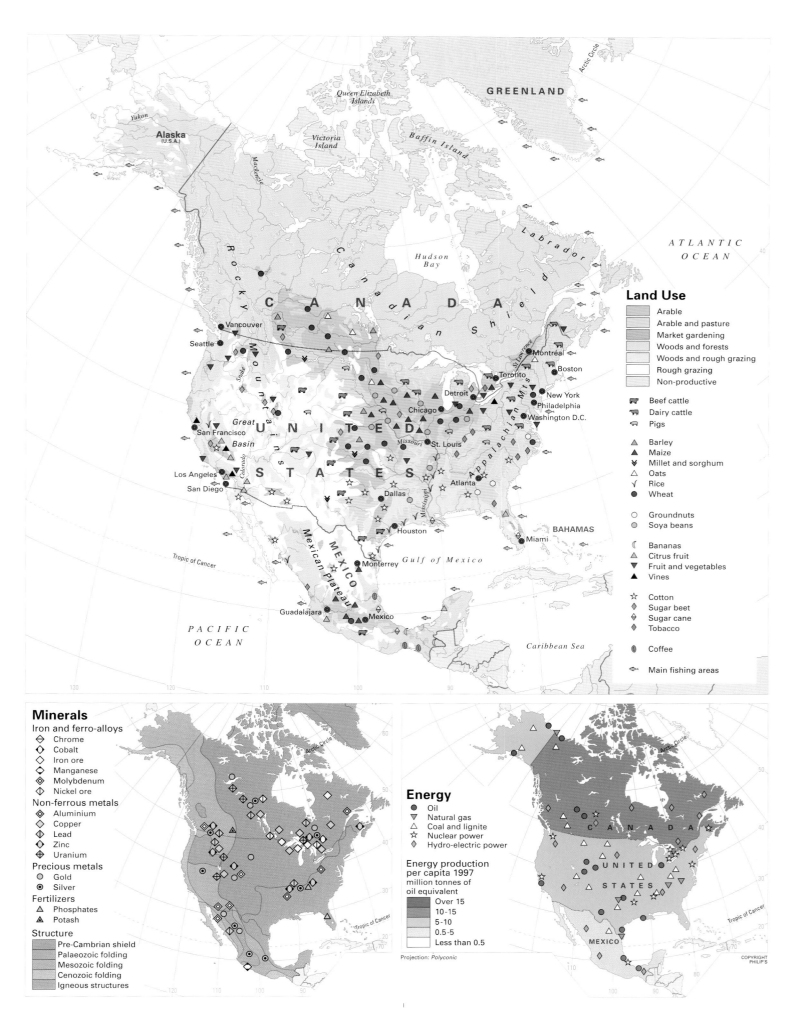

Land Use

- Arable
- Arable and pasture
- Market gardening
- Woods and forests
- Woods and rough grazing
- Rough grazing
- Non-productive

- Beef cattle
- Dairy cattle
- Pigs

- Barley
- Maize
- Millet and sorghum
- Oats
- Rice
- Wheat

- Groundnuts
- Soya beans

- Bananas
- Citrus fruit
- Fruit and vegetables
- Vines

- Cotton
- Sugar beet
- Sugar cane
- Tobacco

- Coffee

- Main fishing areas

Minerals

Iron and ferro-alloys
- Chrome
- Cobalt
- Iron ore
- Manganese
- Molybdenum
- Nickel ore

Non-ferrous metals
- Aluminium
- Copper
- Lead
- Zinc
- Uranium

Precious metals
- Gold
- Silver

Fertilizers
- Phosphates
- Potash

Structure
- Pre-Cambrian shield
- Palaeozoic folding
- Mesozoic folding
- Cenozoic folding
- Igneous structures

Energy
- Oil
- Natural gas
- Coal and lignite
- Nuclear power
- Hydro-electric power

Energy production per capita 1997
million tonnes of oil equivalent
- Over 15
- 10–15
- 5–10
- 0.5–5
- Less than 0.5

Projection: *Polyconic*

COPYRIGHT PHILIP'S

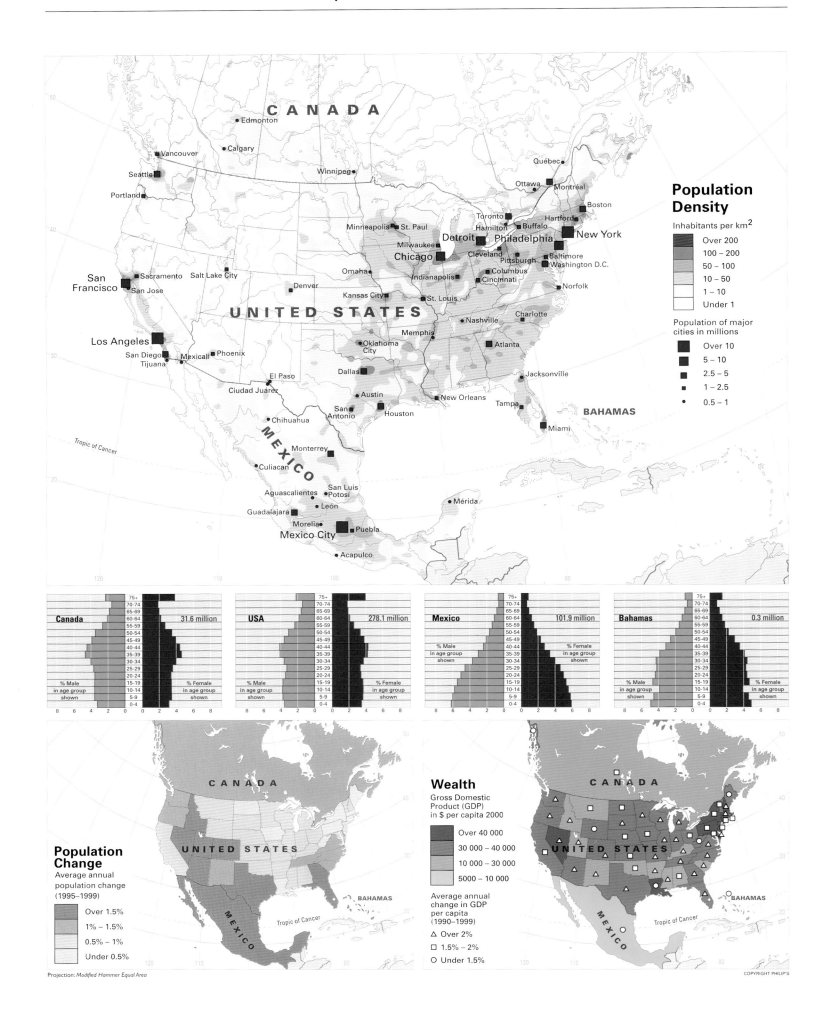

Population Density

Inhabitants per km²

- Over 200
- 100 – 200
- 50 – 100
- 10 – 50
- 1 – 10
- Under 1

Population of major cities in millions

- Over 10
- 5 – 10
- 2.5 – 5
- 1 – 2.5
- 0.5 – 1

Canada — 31.6 million

USA — 278.1 million

Mexico — 101.9 million

Bahamas — 0.3 million

% Male in age group shown / % Female in age group shown

Population Change

Average annual population change (1995–1999)

- Over 1.5%
- 1% – 1.5%
- 0.5% – 1%
- Under 0.5%

Wealth

Gross Domestic Product (GDP) in $ per capita 2000

- Over 40 000
- 30 000 – 40 000
- 10 000 – 30 000
- 5000 – 10 000

Average annual change in GDP per capita (1990–1999)

- △ Over 2%
- ▢ 1.5% – 2%
- ○ Under 1.5%

Projection: Modified Hammer Equal Area

COPYRIGHT PHILIP'S

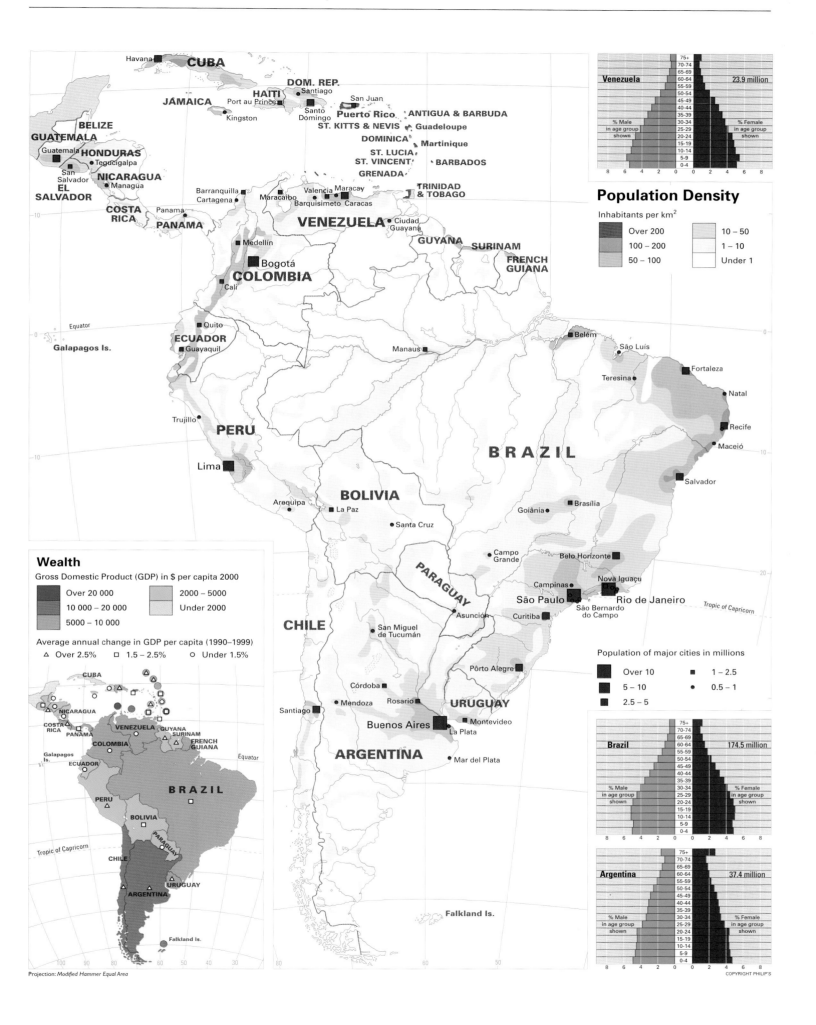

Venezuela 23.9 million

| 75+ |
| 70-74 |
| 65-69 |
| 60-64 |
| 55-59 |
| 50-54 |
| 45-49 |
| 40-44 |
| 35-39 |
| 30-34 |
| 25-29 |
| 20-24 |
| 15-19 |
| 10-14 |
| 5-9 |
| 0-4 |

% Male in age group shown — % Female in age group shown

8 6 4 2 0 2 4 6 8

Population Density

Inhabitants per km²

Over 200
100 – 200
50 – 100
10 – 50
1 – 10
Under 1

Wealth

Gross Domestic Product (GDP) in $ per capita 2000

Over 20 000
10 000 – 20 000
5000 – 10 000
2000 – 5000
Under 2000

Average annual change in GDP per capita (1990–1999)

△ Over 2.5%   □ 1.5 – 2.5%   ○ Under 1.5%

Population of major cities in millions

■ Over 10   ■ 1 – 2.5
■ 5 – 10   ● 0.5 – 1
■ 2.5 – 5

Brazil 174.5 million

Argentina 37.4 million

Projection: Modified Hammer Equal Area

COPYRIGHT PHILIP'S

19

SOUTH AMERICA : Physical

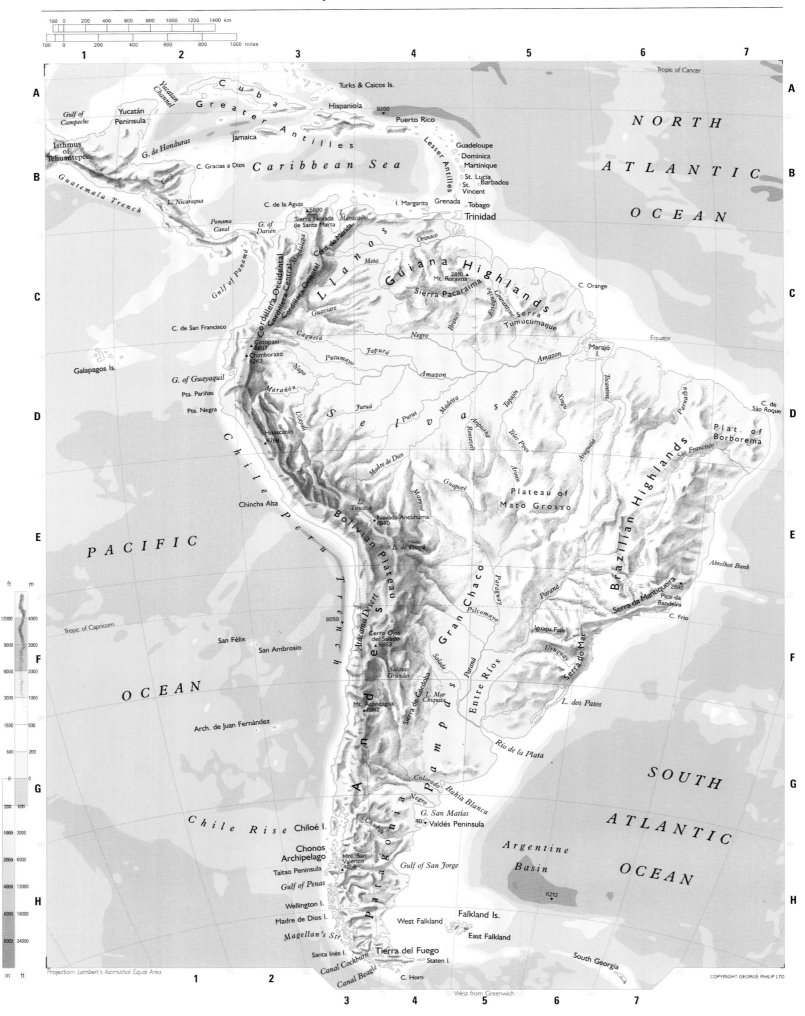

Projection: Lambert's Azimuthal Equal Area

COPYRIGHT GEORGE PHILIP LTD.

West from Greenwich

Projection: Lambert's Azimuthal Equal Area

■ LIMA   Capital Cities

COPYRIGHT GEORGE PHILIP LTD.

West from Greenwich

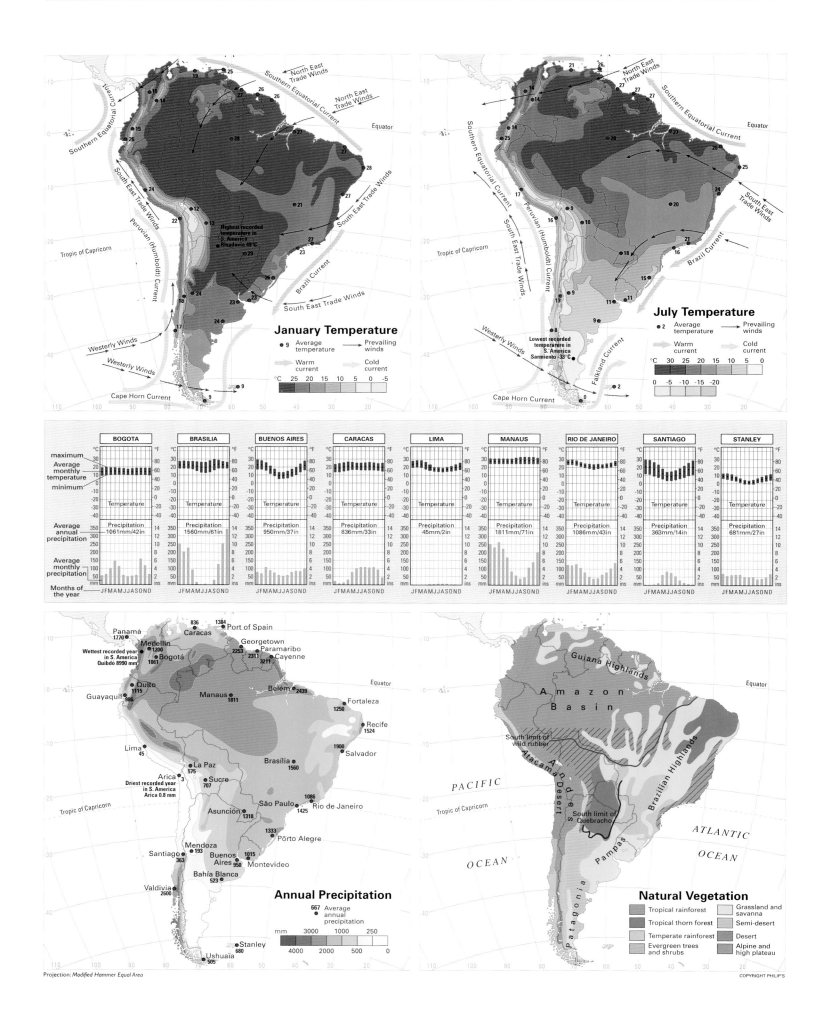

January Temperature

- 9 Average temperature
- → Prevailing winds
- Warm current
- Cold current

°C 25 20 15 10 5 0 -5

Highest recorded temperature in S. America Rivadavia 49°C

July Temperature

- 2 Average temperature
- → Prevailing winds
- Warm current
- Cold current

°C 30 25 20 15 10 5 0

0 -5 -10 -15 -20

Lowest recorded temperature in S. America Sarmiento -33°C

	BOGOTA	BRASILIA	BUENOS AIRES	CARACAS	LIMA	MANAUS	RIO DE JANEIRO	SANTIAGO	STANLEY

Temperature charts for each city

Average annual precipitation:
- BOGOTA: Precipitation 1061mm/42in
- BRASILIA: Precipitation 1560mm/61in
- BUENOS AIRES: Precipitation 950mm/37in
- CARACAS: Precipitation 836mm/33in
- LIMA: Precipitation 45mm/2in
- MANAUS: Precipitation 1811mm/71in
- RIO DE JANEIRO: Precipitation 1086mm/43in
- SANTIAGO: Precipitation 363mm/14in
- STANLEY: Precipitation 681mm/27in

Months of the year: JFMAMJJASOND

Annual Precipitation

Panamá 1770
Caracas 836
Port of Spain 1384
Medellín 1200
Bogotá 1061
Wettest recorded year in S. America Quibdó 8990 mm
Georgetown 2253
Paramaribo 2311
Cayenne 3211
Quito 1115
Guayaquil 986
Manaus 1811
Belém 2439
Fortaleza 1250
Recife 1524
Lima 45
Salvador 1900
La Paz 575
Brasília 1560
Arica 3
Driest recorded year in S. America Arica 0.8 mm
Sucre 707
São Paulo 1086
Rio de Janeiro 1425
Asunción 1318
Pôrto Alegre 1333
Mendoza 193
Santiago 363
Buenos Aires 1015
Montevideo 950
Bahía Blanca 523
Valdivia 2600
Stanley 680
Ushuaia 505

- 667 Average annual precipitation

mm 3000 1000 250
4000 2000 500 0

Natural Vegetation

Guiana Highlands
Amazon Basin
South limit of wild rubber
Andes
Atacama Desert
South limit of Quebracho
Pampas
Brazilian Highlands
Patagonia
PACIFIC OCEAN
ATLANTIC OCEAN

- Tropical rainforest
- Tropical thorn forest
- Temperate rainforest
- Evergreen trees and shrubs
- Grassland and savanna
- Semi-desert
- Desert
- Alpine and high plateau

Projection: Modified Hammer Equal Area

COPYRIGHT PHILIP'S

22

Land Use

- Arable
- Market gardening and plantations
- Pasture
- Woods and forests
- Rough grazing
- Non-productive
- Main fishing areas

Beef cattle	Bananas
Dairy cattle	Citrus fruit
Pigs	Fruit and vegetables
Sheep	Vines
Maize	Cacao
Millet and sorghum	Coconut palms
Rice	Cotton
Wheat	Sugar cane
Groundnuts	Tobacco
Potatoes	Coffee
Soya beans	Tea

Falkland Islands (U.K.)

Minerals

Iron and ferro-alloys
- Chrome
- Cobalt
- Iron ore
- Manganese
- Molybdenum
- Nickel ore

Non-ferrous metals
- Aluminium
- Bauxite
- Copper
- Tin

Precious metals & stones
- Diamonds
- Gold
- Silver

Fertilizers
- Phosphates

Structure
- Pre-Cambrian shield
- Palaeozoic folding
- Mesozoic folding
- Cenozoic folding
- Igneous structures

Energy
- Oil
- Natural gas
- Coal and lignite
- Nuclear power
- Hydro-electric power

Energy production per capita 1998
million tonnes of oil equivalent
- Over 15
- 10–15
- 5–10
- 0.5–5
- Less than 0.5

Projection: Modified Hammer Equal Area

COPYRIGHT PHILIP'S

AUSTRALIA & OCEANIA : Physical and Political

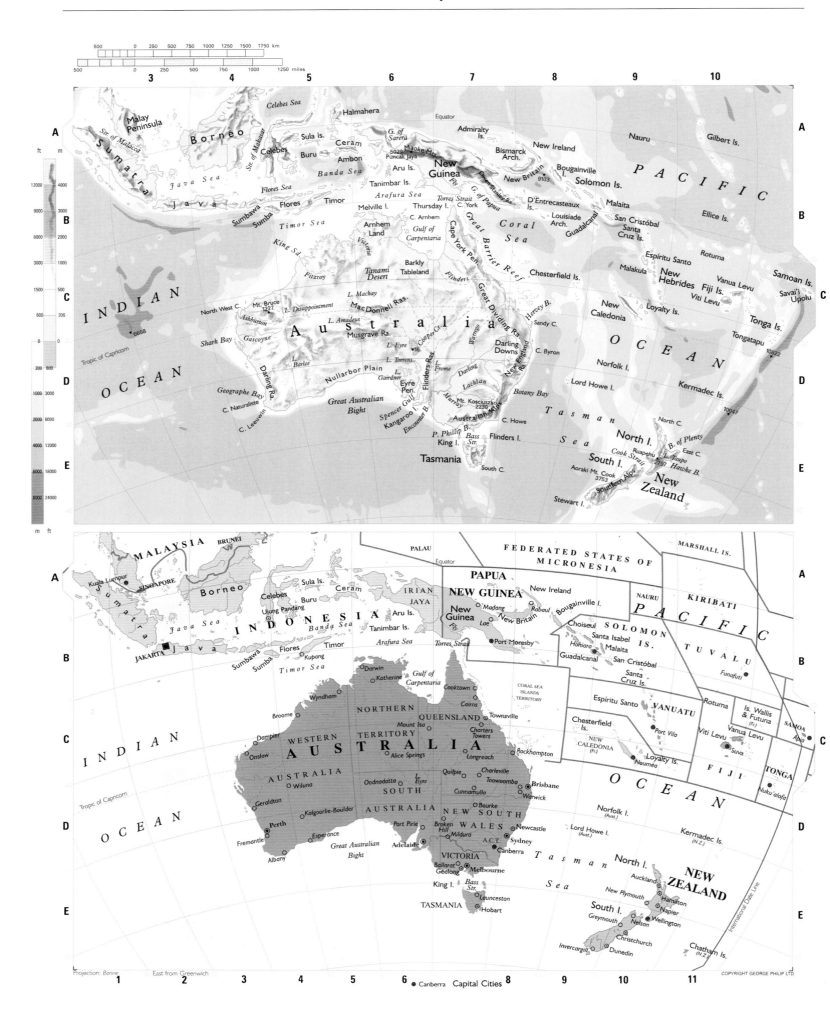

Physical map (top):

500 250 0 250 500 750 1000 1250 1500 1750 km
500 0 250 500 750 1000 1250 miles

Malay Peninsula
Str. of Malacca
Borneo
Celebes Sea
Halmahera
Equator
Admiralty Is.
Nauru
Gilbert Is.
PACIFIC
Sumatra
Celebes
Sula Is.
Ceram
G. of Sarera
5029 Maoke Mts.
Puncak Jaya
New Ireland
Bismarck Arch.
Buru
Ambon
Aru Is.
New Guinea
New Britain 9103
Bougainville I.
Solomon Is.
Java Sea
Banda Sea
Tanimbar Is.
Owen Stanley Ra.
D'Entrecasteaux Is.
Malaita
Ellice Is.
Flores Sea
Arafura Sea
Torres Strait
G. of Papua
C. York
San Cristóbal
Santa Cruz Is.
Sumbawa Sumba
Flores
Timor
Melville I.
Thursday I.
Coral Sea
Espíritu Santo
Rotuma
Samoan Is.
Timor Sea
Arnhem Land
C. Arnhem
Gulf of Carpentaria
Cape York Pen.
Great Barrier Reef
Chesterfield Is.
Malakula
New Hebrides
Vanua Levu
Savai'i Upolu
King Sd.
Victoria
Barkly Tableland
Flinders
Viti Levu
INDIAN
Fitzroy
Tanami Desert
Great Dividing Ra.
Hervey B.
New Caledonia
Loyalty Is.
Tonga Is.
North West C.
Mt. Bruce 1227
L. Mackay
MacDonnell Ras.
OCEAN
Ashburton
L. Disappointment
Australia
Sandy C.
Tongatapu 10822
6658
Shark Bay
Gascoyne
L. Amadeus
Musgrave Ra.
Cooper Cr.
Warrego
Darling Downs
C. Byron
OCEAN
Tropic of Capricorn
L. Eyre 16.
New England Ra.
Norfolk I.
Darling Ra.
L. Barlee
L. Torrens
L. Frome
Darling
Lord Howe I.
Kermadec Is.
Geographe Bay
Nullarbor Plain
Gairdner
Flinders Ras.
Lachlan
Botany Bay
10047
C. Naturaliste
Great Australian Bight
Eyre Pen.
Murray
Mt. Kosciuszko 2230
Tasman Sea
North C.
C. Leeuwin
Spencer Gulf
Kangaroo I.
Encounter B.
Australian Alps
C. Howe
North I.
B. of Plenty
East C.
P. Phillip B.
King I.
Bass Str.
Flinders I.
Cook Strait
Ruapehu 2797
L. Taupo
Hawke B.
Tasmania
South C.
South I.
Aoraki Mt. Cook 3753
Southern Alps
New Zealand
Stewart I.

Political map (bottom):

MALAYSIA
BRUNEI
PALAU
FEDERATED STATES OF MICRONESIA
MARSHALL IS.
Kuala Lumpur
SINGAPORE
Borneo
Sula Is.
Ceram
IRIAN JAYA
PAPUA NEW GUINEA
New Ireland
NAURU
KIRIBATI
Sumatra
Celebes
Buru
New Guinea
Madang
Rabaul
Bougainville I.
PACIFIC
Ujung Pandang
INDONESIA
Aru Is.
New Britain
Choiseul
SOLOMON IS.
Java Sea
Banda Sea
Tanimbar Is.
Lae
Santa Isabel
TUVALU
JAKARTA
Java
Sumbawa
Flores
Timor
Kupang
Arafura Sea
Torres Strait
Port Moresby
Honiara
Malaita
Funafuti
Sumba
Timor Sea
Darwin
Katherine
Gulf of Carpentaria
Guadalcanal
San Cristóbal
Santa Cruz Is.
Wyndham
Cooktown
CORAL SEA ISLANDS TERRITORY
Espíritu Santo
VANUATU
Rotuma
Is. Wallis & Futuna (Fr.)
SAMOA
INDIAN
Broome
NORTHERN
Cairns
Chesterfield Is.
Port Vila
Vanua Levu
Apia
Dampier
TERRITORY
QUEENSLAND
Townsville
NEW CALEDONIA (Fr.)
Viti Levu
Onslow
WESTERN
Mount Isa
Charters Towers
Port Vila
Suva
TONGA
AUSTRALIA
Alice Springs
Longreach
Rockhampton
Loyalty Is.
FIJI
OCEAN
AUSTRALIA
Wiluna
Oodnadatta
Quilpie
Charleville
Toowoomba
Nouméa
OCEAN
Nuku'alofa
Tropic of Capricorn
L. Eyre
SOUTH
Cunnamulla
Brisbane
Geraldton
Kalgoorlie-Boulder
AUSTRALIA
Bourke
Warwick
Norfolk I. (Aust.)
Kermadec Is. (N.Z.)
Perth
NEW SOUTH
Lord Howe I. (Aust.)
Fremantle
Esperance
Port Pirie
Broken Hill
WALES
Newcastle
North I.
NEW ZEALAND
Albany
Great Australian Bight
Mildura
A.C.T.
Sydney
Tasman
Auckland
Adelaide
Canberra
Sea
New Plymouth
Hamilton
VICTORIA
Ballarat
Geelong
Melbourne
Napier
Wellington
King I.
Bass Str.
South I.
Nelson
Launceston
Greymouth
TASMANIA
Hobart
Christchurch
Chatham Is. (N.Z.)
Invercargill
Dunedin

Projection: Bonne
East from Greenwich
International Date Line
COPYRIGHT GEORGE PHILIP LTD.

• Canberra   Capital Cities

24

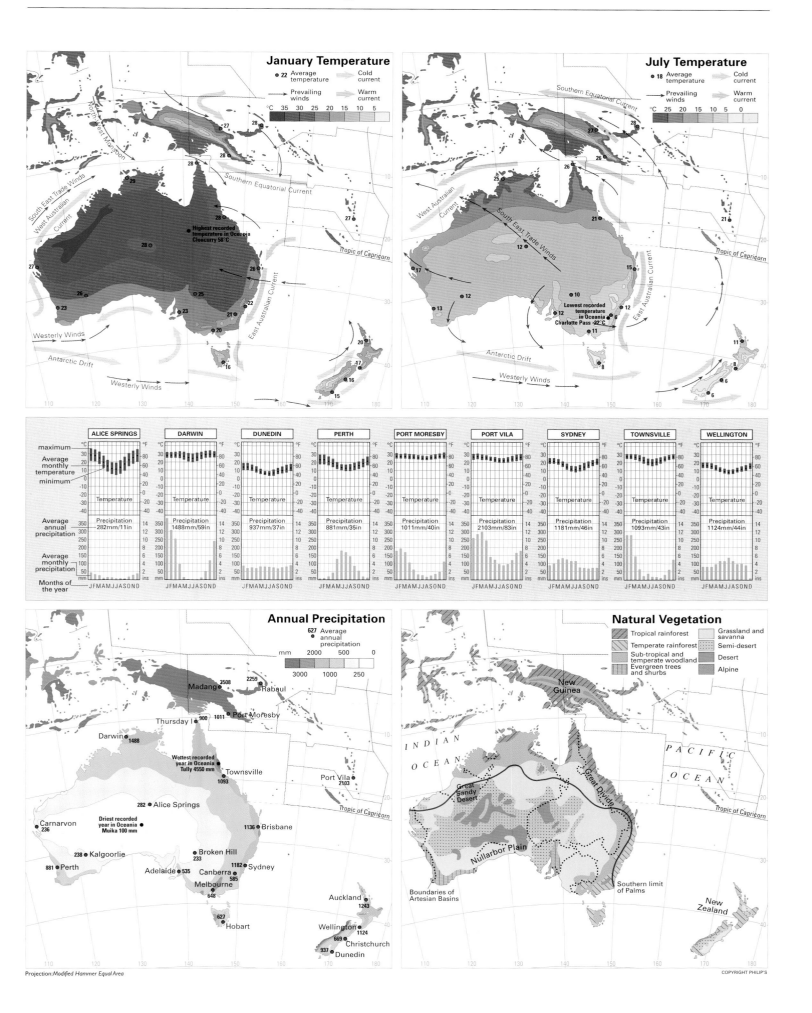

January Temperature

- • 22 Average temperature
- Prevailing winds
- Cold current
- Warm current

°C 35 30 25 20 15 10 5

Highest recorded temperature in Oceania Cloncurry 58°C

July Temperature

- • 18 Average temperature
- Prevailing winds
- Cold current
- Warm current

°C 25 20 15 10 5 0

Lowest recorded temperature in Oceania Charlotte Pass -22°C

	ALICE SPRINGS	DARWIN	DUNEDIN	PERTH	PORT MORESBY	PORT VILA	SYDNEY	TOWNSVILLE	WELLINGTON
Average annual precipitation	282mm/11in	1488mm/59in	937mm/37in	881mm/35in	1011mm/40in	2103mm/83in	1181mm/46in	1093mm/43in	1124mm/44in

Annual Precipitation

- • 627 Average annual precipitation

mm 2000 500 0
3000 1000 250

Madang 3508
Rabaul 2259
Thursday I 900 1011 Port Moresby
Darwin 1488
Wettest recorded year in Oceania Tully 4550 mm
Townsville 1093
Port Vila 2103
282 • Alice Springs
Carnarvon 236
Driest recorded year in Oceania Muika 100 mm
1136 • Brisbane
238 • Kalgoorlie
Broken Hill 233
881 • Perth
Adelaide • 535
Canberra 585
1182 Sydney
Melbourne 648
Auckland 1243
627 Hobart
Wellington 669 1124
Christchurch
937 Dunedin

Natural Vegetation

- Tropical rainforest
- Temperate rainforest
- Sub-tropical and temperate woodland
- Evergreen trees and shrubs
- Grassland and savanna
- Semi-desert
- Desert
- Alpine

New Guinea
INDIAN OCEAN
PACIFIC OCEAN
Great Sandy Desert
Great Divide
Nullarbor Plain
Boundaries of Artesian Basins
Southern limit of Palms
New Zealand

Projection: Modified Hammer Equal Area

COPYRIGHT PHILIP'S

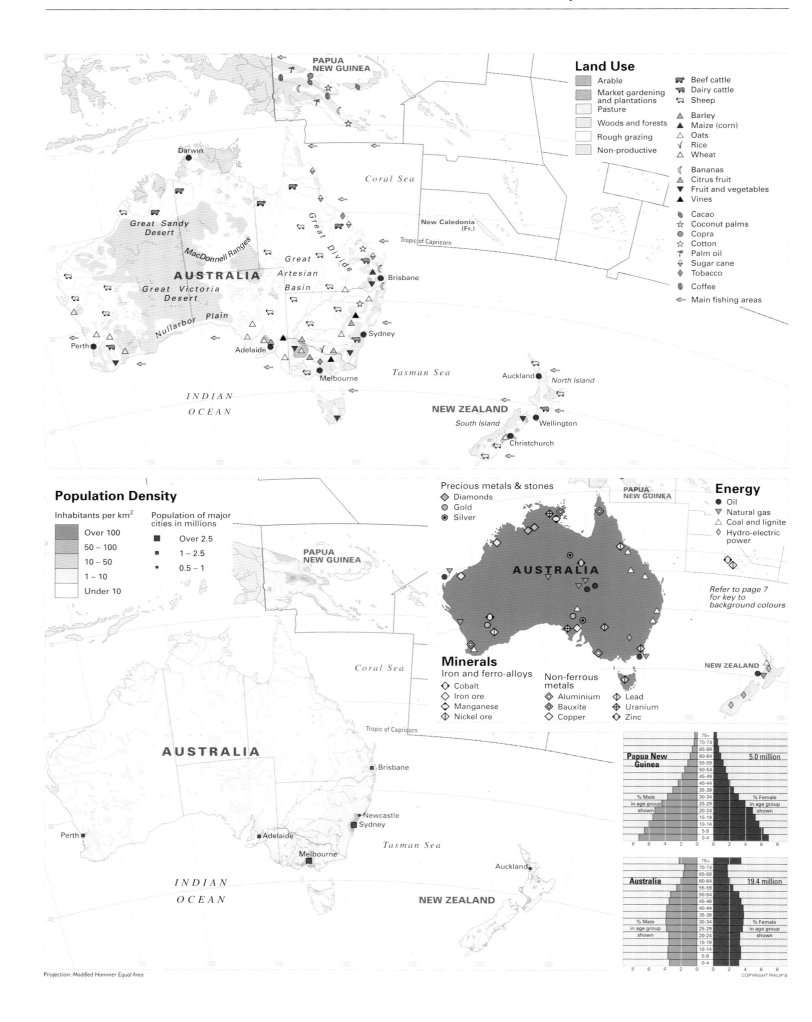

Land Use

Arable
Market gardening and plantations
Pasture
Woods and forests
Rough grazing
Non-productive

Beef cattle
Dairy cattle
Sheep

△ Barley
▲ Maize (corn)
△ Oats
Y Rice
△ Wheat

☾ Bananas
△ Citrus fruit
▼ Fruit and vegetables
▲ Vines

Cacao
☆ Coconut palms
● Copra
☆ Cotton
⊤ Palm oil
⬦ Sugar cane
⬦ Tobacco

● Coffee

◁◦ Main fishing areas

Population Density

Inhabitants per km²

Over 100
50 – 100
10 – 50
1 – 10
Under 10

Population of major cities in millions

■ Over 2.5
■ 1 – 2.5
• 0.5 – 1

Precious metals & stones

⬦ Diamonds
● Gold
◉ Silver

Minerals

Iron and ferro-alloys
◇ Cobalt
◇ Iron ore
◇ Manganese
◈ Nickel ore

Non-ferrous metals
◈ Aluminium
◈ Bauxite
◇ Copper
◇ Lead
✛ Uranium
◇ Zinc

Energy

● Oil
▽ Natural gas
△ Coal and lignite
◇ Hydro-electric power

Refer to page 7 for key to background colours

Projection: Modified Hammer Equal Area

COPYRIGHT PHILIP'S

26

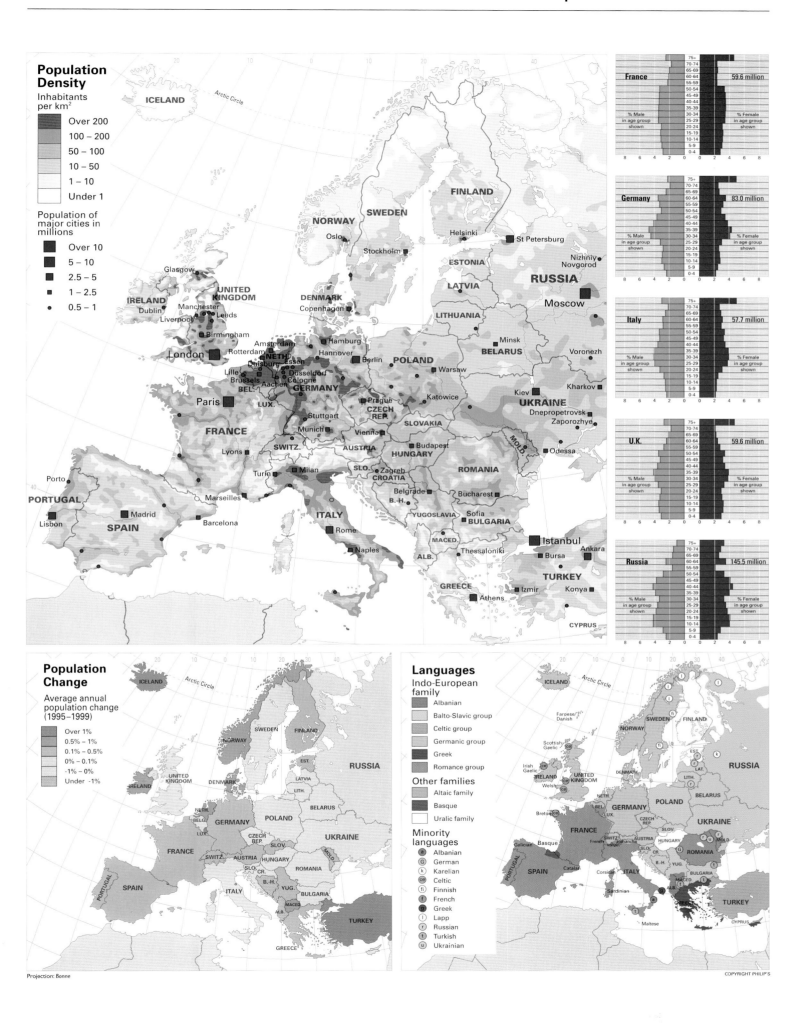

Population Density

Inhabitants per km²

Over 200
100 – 200
50 – 100
10 – 50
1 – 10
Under 1

Population of major cities in millions

Over 10
5 – 10
2.5 – 5
1 – 2.5
0.5 – 1

Population Change

Average annual population change (1995–1999)

Over 1%
0.5% – 1%
0.1% – 0.5%
0% – 0.1%
-1% – 0%
Under -1%

Languages

Indo-European family

Albanian
Balto-Slavic group
Celtic group
Germanic group
Greek
Romance group

Other families

Altaic family
Basque
Uralic family

Minority languages

ⓐ Albanian
ⓖ German
ⓚ Karelian
ⓒ Celtic
ⓕⁱ Finnish
ⓕ French
ⓖ Greek
ⓛ Lapp
ⓡ Russian
ⓣ Turkish
ⓤ Ukrainian

France 59.6 million
Germany 83.0 million
Italy 57.7 million
U.K. 59.6 million
Russia 145.5 million

Projection: Bonne

COPYRIGHT PHILIP'S

27

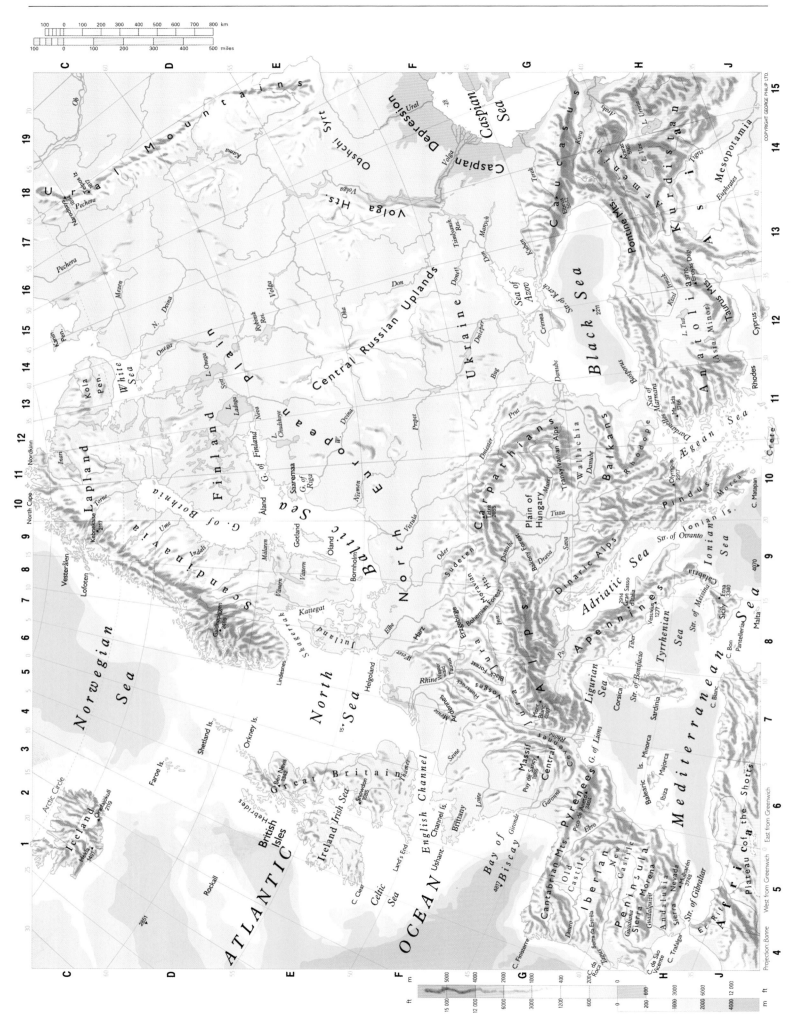

Projection Bonne — West from Greenwich — East from Greenwich

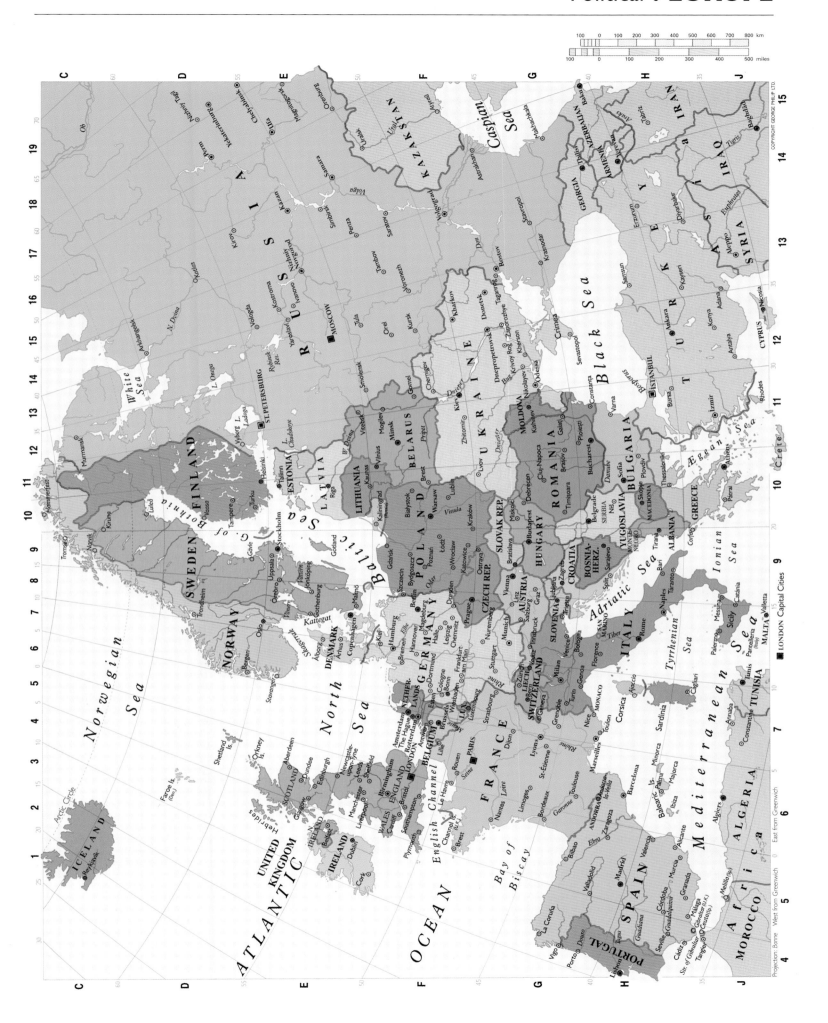

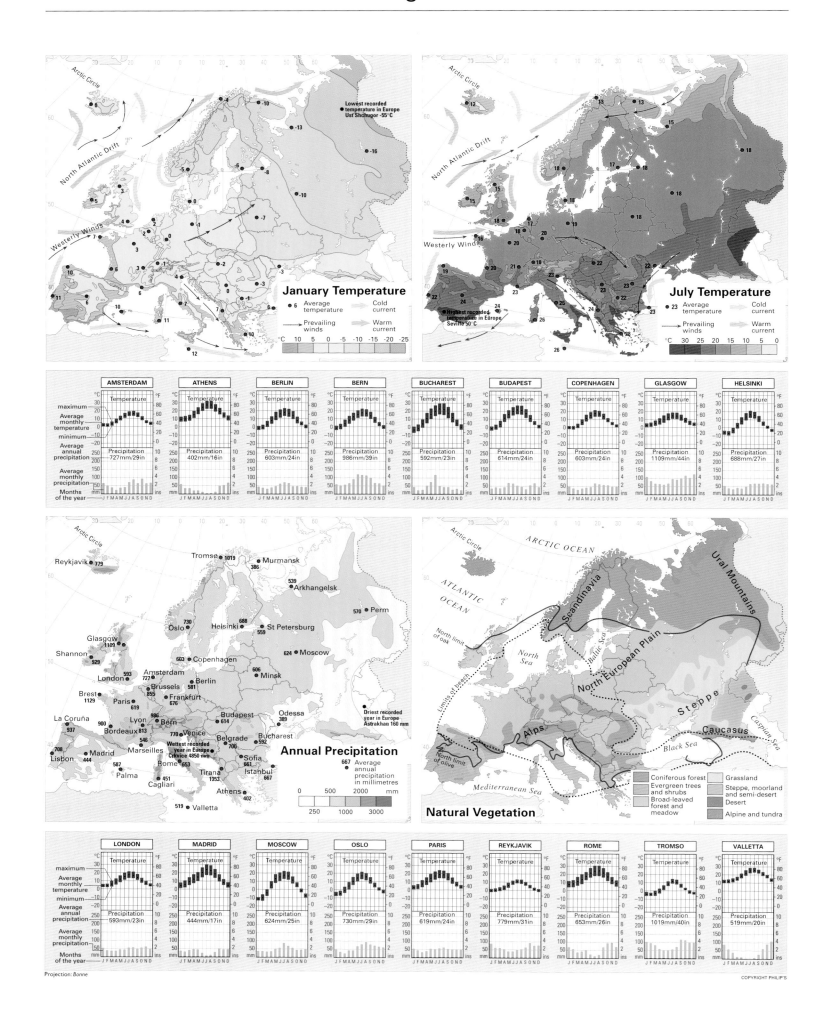

January Temperature
- 6 Average temperature
- Prevailing winds
- Cold current
- Warm current
°C 10 5 0 -5 -10 -15 -20 -25

Lowest recorded temperature in Europe Ust Shchugor -55°C

July Temperature
- 23 Average temperature
- Prevailing winds
- Cold current
- Warm current
°C 30 25 20 15 10 5 0

Highest recorded temperature in Europe Seville 50°C

AMSTERDAM | ATHENS | BERLIN | BERN | BUCHAREST | BUDAPEST | COPENHAGEN | GLASGOW | HELSINKI

maximum
Average monthly temperature
minimum
Average annual precipitation
Average monthly precipitation
Months of the year

Precipitation 727mm/29in | Precipitation 402mm/16in | Precipitation 603mm/24in | Precipitation 986mm/39in | Precipitation 592mm/23in | Precipitation 614mm/24in | Precipitation 603mm/24in | Precipitation 1109mm/44in | Precipitation 688mm/27in

Annual Precipitation
- 667 Average annual precipitation in millimetres
0 500 2000 mm
250 1000 3000

Reykjavik 779
Tromso 1019
Murmansk 386
Arkhangelsk 539
Perm 570
Oslo 730
Helsinki 688
St Petersburg 559
Glasgow 1109
Shannon 929
Amsterdam 727
London 593
Brussels 855
Berlin 581
Frankfurt 676
Minsk 606
Moscow 624
Brest 1129
Paris 619
La Coruña 937
Lyon 900
Bern 986
Bordeaux 813
Venice 770
Budapest 614
Odessa 389
Belgrade 700
Bucharest 592
Lisbon 708
Madrid 444
Marseilles 546
Rome 653
Sofia 661
Istanbul 667
Palma 587
Tirana 1353
Athens 402
Cagliari 451
Valletta 519

Driest recorded year in Europe Astrakhan 160 mm
Wettest recorded year in Europe Crkvice 4850 mm

Natural Vegetation
- Coniferous forest
- Evergreen trees and shrubs
- Broad-leaved forest and meadow
- Grassland
- Steppe, moorland and semi-desert
- Desert
- Alpine and tundra

Arctic Circle
ARCTIC OCEAN
ATLANTIC OCEAN
Scandinavia
Ural Mountains
North limit of oak
North Sea
Baltic Sea
North European Plain
Steppe
Limits of beech
Alps
Caucasus
Caspian Sea
Black Sea
North limit of olive
Mediterranean Sea

LONDON | MADRID | MOSCOW | OSLO | PARIS | REYKJAVIK | ROME | TROMSO | VALLETTA

maximum
Average monthly temperature
minimum
Average annual precipitation
Average monthly precipitation
Months of the year

Precipitation 593mm/23in | Precipitation 444mm/17in | Precipitation 624mm/25in | Precipitation 730mm/29in | Precipitation 619mm/24in | Precipitation 779mm/31in | Precipitation 653mm/26in | Precipitation 1019mm/40in | Precipitation 519mm/20in

Projection: Bonne

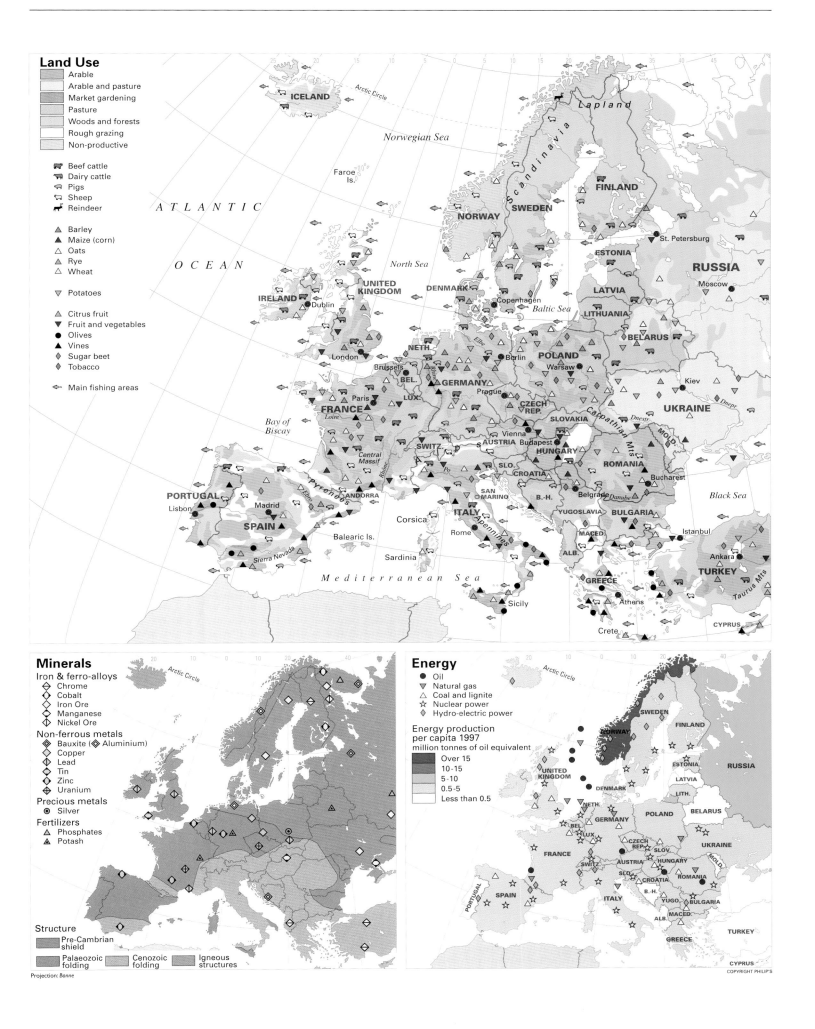

Land Use

Arable
Arable and pasture
Market gardening
Pasture
Woods and forests
Rough grazing
Non-productive

Beef cattle
Dairy cattle
Pigs
Sheep
Reindeer

Barley
Maize (corn)
Oats
Rye
Wheat

Potatoes

Citrus fruit
Fruit and vegetables
Olives
Vines
Sugar beet
Tobacco

Main fishing areas

Minerals

Iron & ferro-alloys
Chrome
Cobalt
Iron Ore
Manganese
Nickel Ore

Non-ferrous metals
Bauxite (◈ Aluminium)
Copper
Lead
Tin
Zinc
Uranium

Precious metals
Silver

Fertilizers
Phosphates
Potash

Structure
Pre-Cambrian shield
Palaeozoic folding
Cenozoic folding
Igneous structures

Projection: Bonne

Energy
Oil
Natural gas
Coal and lignite
Nuclear power
Hydro-electric power

Energy production per capita 1997
million tonnes of oil equivalent

Over 15
10-15
5-10
0.5-5
Less than 0.5

COPYRIGHT PHILIP'S

31

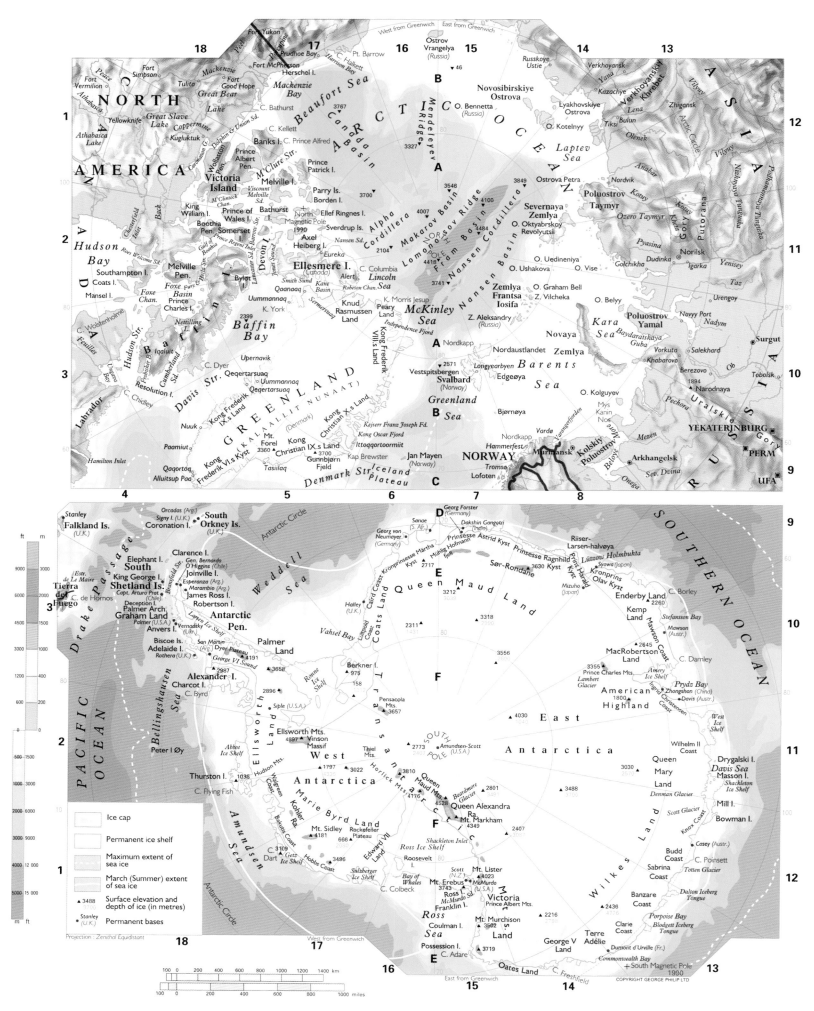

A–Z
COUNTRY
BY
COUNTRY

SETTLEMENTS

▣ **PARIS**   ▪ **Berne**   ◉ **Livorno**   ◉ Brugge   ◎ Algeciras   ○ *Frejus*   ○ *Oberammergau*   ○ Thira

Settlement symbols and type styles vary according to the scale of each map and indicate the importance
of towns on the map rather than specific population figures

∴ Ruins or archaeological sites   ॱ Wells in desert

ADMINISTRATION

▬▬▬ International boundaries	Country names	Administrative area names
▬ ▬ ▬. International boundaries (undefined or disputed)	NICARAGUA	LOUISIANA
┄┄┄ Internal boundaries		

International boundaries show the *de facto* situation where there are rival claims to territory

COMMUNICATIONS

▬▬▬ Principal roads	⊕ Airfields	⌒⌒ Other railways
⌒⌒ Other roads	▬⌒▬ Principal railways	┤┄┤ Railway tunnels
┤┄┤ Road tunnels	▬ ⌒ ▬ Railways under construction	⋯⋯ Principal canals
⋊⋉ Passes		

PHYSICAL FEATURES

⌒⌒ Perennial streams	⬭ Intermittent lakes	▲ 8848 Elevations in metres
⋯⌒⋯ Intermittent streams	Swamps and marshes	▼ 8500 Sea depths in metres
⬭ Perennial lakes	Permanent ice and glaciers	*1134* Height of lake surface above sea level in metres

Introduced in January 2002, this flag replaces that of the Mujaheddin ('holy warriors'), who defeated Afghanistan's socialist government but lost power at the end of 2001. The flag is the 19th different design used by the country since 1901.

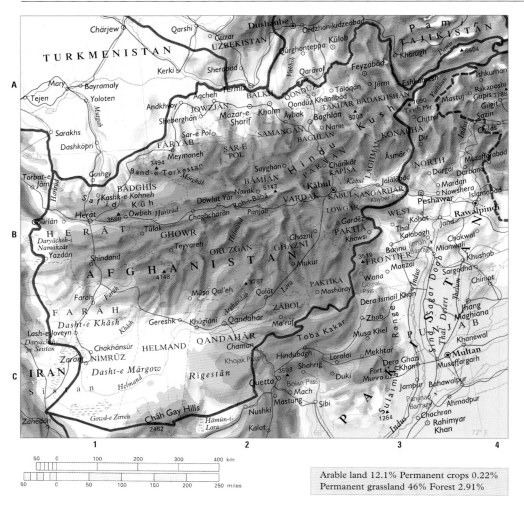

Arable land 12.1% Permanent crops 0.22%
Permanent grassland 46% Forest 2.91%

introduced Islam in the late 7th century. Afghanistan has always occupied a strategic position, because the Khyber Pass was both the gateway to India and the back door to Russia. Its modern history began in 1747, when local tribes united for the first time, though a civil war was fought between 1819 and 1835 as factions struggled for power. In 1839, British troops invaded Afghanistan, in an attempt to reduce Russian influence. Over the next 80 years, Britain fought three Anglo-Afghan wars to maintain control over the region. The British finally withdrew in 1921, when Afghanistan became independent.

Politics

In 1964, Afghanistan adopted a democratic constitution, but the country's ruler, King Zahir, and the legislature failed to agree on reforms. In 1973, Muhammad Daoud Khan, the king's cousin, seized power and abolished the monarchy. He ruled as president until 1978, when he was killed during a left-wing coup. The new regime's socialist policies conflicted with Islam and provoked a rebellion. On 25 December 1987, Soviet troops invaded Afghanistan to support the left-wing regime. The Soviet occupation led to a protracted civil war. Various Muslim groups united behind the banner of the Mujaheddin ('holy warriors') to wage a guerrilla campaign, financed by the United States and aided by Pakistan. Soviet forces were forced to withdraw in 1989. By 1992, the Mujaheddin had overthrown the government. The fundamentalist Muslim Taliban ('students') became the dominant group and, by 2000, the Taliban regime controlled 90% of the land. However, in October 2001, following the refusal of the Taliban regime to hand over the Saudi-born Osama bin Laden, who was suspected of masterminding the attacks on New York City and Washington D.C. on 11 September 2001, international action, led by the United States, was taken against Afghanistan. The objective was to destroy both bin Laden's terrorist organization, al Qaida, and the Taliban. In November, the Taliban regime collapsed and a coalition government, led by Hamid Karzai, was set up in Kabul. However, conflict continued into 2002.

Geography

Afghanistan is a landlocked country. The main regions are the northern plains, the central highlands, and the south-western lowlands. The central highlands, comprising most of the Hindu Kush and its foothills, with peaks rising to more than 6,400 m [21,000 ft], cover nearly three-quarters of the land. Many Afghans live in the deep valleys of the highlands. Much of the south-west is desert, while the northern plains contain most of the country's limited agricultural land.

Climate

The height of the land and the country's remote position have a great effect on the climate. In winter, northerly winds bring cold, snowy weather in the mountains, but summers are hot and dry.

History

In ancient times, the area was invaded by Aryans, Persians, Greeks and Macedonians, and warrior armies from central Asia. Arab armies

Economy

Afghanistan is one of the world's poorest countries. About 60% of the people are farmers, many of whom are semi-nomadic herders. Wheat is the chief crop. Natural gas is produced, but most mineral deposits are undeveloped. There are few factories. Exports include karakul skins (which are used to make hats and jackets), carpets, dried fruit and nuts.

AFGHANISTAN (KABUL)

The climate of Afghanistan is governed more by altitude than by latitude. From December to March, air masses come from the continental north, bringing cold weather and snow on the mountains. June to September is hot and dry, with the east getting rain from a weakened monsoon. The temperature at Kabul, at 2,000 m [6,000 ft], ranges from −5°C to 25°C [23–77°F]. There are over 10 hours of sunshine daily, May to August.

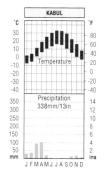

AREA
652,090 sq km
[251,772 sq mi]
POPULATION
26,813,000
CAPITAL (POPULATION)
Kabul (1,565,000)
GOVERNMENT
Transitional regime
ETHNIC GROUPS
Pashtun ('Pathan') 38%,

Tajik 25%, Hazara 19%,
Uzbek 6%, others 12%
LANGUAGES
Pashtu, Dari/Persian
(both official),
Uzbek
RELIGIONS
Islam (Sunni Muslim 84%,
Shiite Muslim 15%)
CURRENCY
Afghani = 100 puls

ALBANIA

Albania's official name, Shqiperia, means 'Land of the Eagle', and the black double eagle was the emblem of the 15th-century hero Scanderbeg. A star placed above the eagle in 1946 was removed in 1992 when a non-Communist government was formed.

Geography

The Republic of Albania lies in the Balkan Peninsula. It faces the Adriatic Sea in the west and is bordered by Yugoslavia (Serbia and Montenegro), Macedonia and Greece. About 70% of the land is mountainous, with the highest point, Korab, reaching 2,764 m [9,068 ft] on the Macedonian border. Most Albanians live in the west on the coastal lowlands. This is the main farming region. Albania lies in an earthquake zone and severe earthquakes occur occasionally.

Climate

The coastal areas of Albania have a typical Mediterranean climate, with fairly dry, sunny summers and cool, moist winters. The mountains have a severe climate, with heavy winter snowfalls.

History

In ancient times, Albania was part of a region called Illyria. In 167 BC, it became part of the Roman Empire. When the Roman Empire broke up in 395, much of Albania became part of the Eastern Roman, or Byzantine, Empire. The country was subsequently conquered by Goths, Bulgarians, Slavs and Normans, although southern Albania remained part of the Byzantine Empire until 1204. In the 14th century, much of Albania became part of the Serbian Empire. In the 15th century, a leader named Scanderbeg, now regarded as a national hero, successfully led the Albanians against the invading Ottoman Turks. But after he died in 1468, the Turks took over the country. Albania became part of the Ottoman Empire until 1912, when Albania declared its independence.

Italy invaded Albania in 1939, but German forces took over the country in 1943. At the end of World War II, an Albanian People's Republic was formed under the Communist leaders who had led the partisans against the Germans. Pursuing a modernization programme on rigid Stalinist lines, the regime of Enver Hoxha at various times associated politically and often economically with Yugoslavia (up to 1948), the Soviet Union (1948–61) and China (1961–77), before following a fiercely independent policy. After Hoxha died in 1985, his successor, Ramiz Alia, continued the dictator's austere policies, but by the end of the decade, even Albania was affected by the sweeping changes in Eastern Europe.

Politics

In 1990, the more progressive wing of the Communist Party, led by Ramiz Alia, won the struggle for power. The new government instituted a wide programme of reform, including the legalization of religion, the encouragement of foreign investment, the introduction of a free market for peasants' produce, and the establishment of pluralist democracy. The Communists comfortably retained their majority in elections in April 1991, but the government was brought down two months later by a general strike. An interim coalition 'national salvation' committee took over, but collapsed within six months. Elections in 1992 finally brought to an end the last Communist regime in Europe when the non-Communist Democratic Party won power. In 1997, amid a financial crisis caused by the collapse of fraudulent pyramid-selling schemes, fresh elections took place. The socialist-led government that took power was re-elected in 2001.

Economy

Albania is Europe's poorest country. In the early 1990s, agriculture employed 56% of the people. The land was divided into large collective and state farms, but private ownership has been encouraged since 1991. Major crops include fruits, maize, olives, potatoes, sugar beet, vegetables and wheat. Livestock farming is also important.

Albania has some mineral reserves, such as chromite, copper and nickel, which are exported. The country also has some oil, brown coal and hydroelectricity, and a few heavy industries.

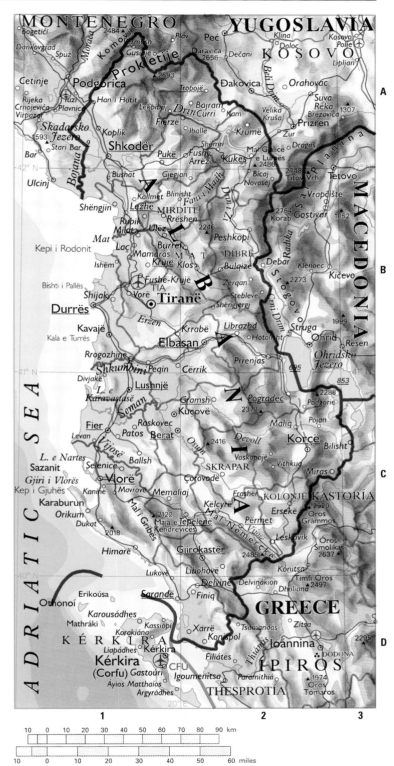

AREA	Macedonian, Vlachs, Gypsy
28,750 sq km [11,100 sq mi]	**LANGUAGES**
POPULATION	Albanian (official)
3,510,000	**RELIGIONS**
CAPITAL (POPULATION)	Many are non-believers; of the
Tirana (Tiranë, 251,000)	believers, 65% follow Islam
GOVERNMENT	and 33% follow Christianity
Multiparty republic	(Orthodox 20%, R. Catholic 13%)
ETHNIC GROUPS	**CURRENCY**
Albanian 95%, Greek 3%,	Lek = 100 qindars

The star and crescent and the colour green on Algeria's flag are traditional symbols of the Islamic religion. The liberation movement which fought for independence from French rule from 1954 used this flag. It became the national flag when Algeria became independent in 1962.

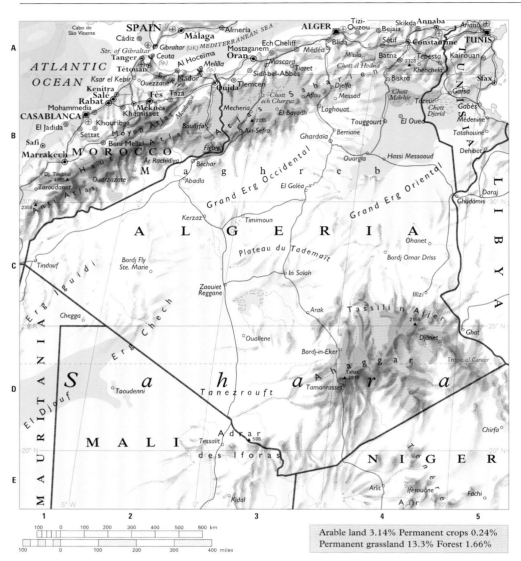

Arable land 3.14% Permanent crops 0.24%
Permanent grassland 13.3% Forest 1.66%

History

In early times, the region came under such rulers as the Phoenicians, Carthaginians, Romans and Vandals. Arabs invaded the area in the AD 600s, converting the local Berbers to Islam and introducing Arabic. Inter marriage has made it difficult to distinguish Arabs from Berbers by ancestry, though Berber dialects are still spoken. A law, effective from July 1998 making Arabic the only language allowed in public life, met with much opposition in Berber-speaking areas.

Politics

Like its neighbours Morocco and Tunisia, Algeria experienced French colonial rule and colonization by settlers. Algeria achieved independence in 1962, following years of bitter warfare between nationalist guerrillas and French armed forces. After independence, the socialist FLN (National Liberation Party) formed a one-party government. Opposition parties were permitted in 1989 and, in 1991, a Muslim party, the FIS (Islamic Salvation Front) won an election. The FLN cancelled the election results and declared a state of emergency. Terrorist activities mounted and, between 1991 and 1999, about 100,000 people were killed. A proposal to ban political parties based on religion was approved in a referendum in 1996. In 1999, Abdelaziz Bouteflika, the candidate who was thought to be favoured by the army, was elected president. In the early 2000s, the scale of the violence was reduced, but anti-government protests and killings continued.

Economy

Algeria is a developing country, whose main income comes from its two main natural resources, oil and natural gas, which were discovered in the Sahara in 1956. Its natural gas reserves are among the world's largest. Since independence, oil and gas have accounted for around two-thirds of the country's total revenues and more than 90% of the exports. Algeria's crude oil refining capacity is the biggest in Africa. Other manufactured products include cement, iron and steel, textiles and vehicles. While most larger industries are state-owned, much light industry is under private control.

Agriculture employs about 16% of the population. Barley, citrus fruits, dates, potatoes and wheat are the major crops. Cattle, goats and sheep are raised by Berber nomads, who live in the north-east. Many people work abroad due to the high level of unemployment.

Geography

The People's Democratic Republic of Algeria is Africa's second largest country after Sudan. Most Algerians live in the north, on the fertile coastal plains and hill country. South of this region lie high plateaux and ranges of the Atlas Mountains. Four-fifths of Algeria is in the Sahara, the world's largest desert. Most people in the Sahara live at oases, where springs and wells supply water.

Climate

The coast has a Mediterranean climate, with warm and dry summers and mild and moist winters. The northern highlands have warmer summers and colder winters. The arid Sahara is hot by day and cool at night. The yearly rainfall is less than 200 mm [8 in].

ALGERIA (ALGIERS)

Algiers is exposed to the maritime influences of the Mediterranean Sea, but is sheltered from the Sahara to the south by the Atlas Mountains. The temperature range is very small: annual 13°C [23°F]; diurnal 6°C [11°F]. Frosts have not been recorded. Rainfall has a winter maximum typical of the Mediterranean region, with amounts varying greatly from year to year. The mountains to the south are often snow-covered in winter.

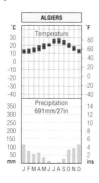

AREA	ETHNIC GROUPS
2,381,740 sq km	Arab-Berber 99%
[919,590 sq mi]	**LANGUAGES**
POPULATION	Arabic and Berber
31,736,000	(both official), French
CAPITAL (POPULATION)	**RELIGIONS**
Algiers (Alger, 1,722,000)	Sunni Muslim 99%
GOVERNMENT	**CURRENCY**
Socialist republic	Algerian dinar = 100 centimes

AMERICAN SAMOA – SEE PACIFIC OCEAN, PAGES 174–178;
ANDORRA – SEE SPAIN, PAGES 206–208

ANGOLA

The flag is based on the flag of the MPLA (the Popular Movement for the Liberation of Angola) during the independence struggle. The emblem includes a star symbolizing socialism, one half of a gearwheel to represent industry, and a machete symbolizing agriculture.

Geography

The Republic of Angola is a large country, more than twice the size of France, on the south-western coast of Africa. Most of the country is part of the plateau that forms most of southern Africa, with a narrow coastal plain in the west.

Angola has many rivers. In the north-east, several rivers flow northwards to become tributaries of the River Congo, while in the south, some rivers, including the Cubango (Okavango) and the Cuanda, flow south-eastwards into inland drainage basins in the interior of Africa.

Climate

Angola has a tropical climate, with temperatures of over 20°C [68°F] all year round, though upland areas are cooler. The coastal regions are dry, increasingly so to the south of Luanda, but the rainfall increases to the north and east. The rainy season is between November and April. Tropical forests flourish in the north, but the vegetation along the coast is sparse, with semi-desert in the south.

History

Bantu-speaking peoples from the north settled in Angola around 2,000 years ago. In the late 15th century, Portuguese navigators, seeking a route to Asia around Africa, explored the coast and, in the early 16th century, the Portuguese set up bases.

Angola became important as a source of slaves for Brazil, Portugal's huge colony in South America. After the decline of the slave trade, Portuguese settlers began to develop the land. The Portuguese population increased gently in the 20th century.

In the 1950s, local nationalists began to demand independence. In 1956, the MPLA (Popular Movement for the Liberation of Angola) was founded with support from the Mbundu and mestizos (people of African and European descent). The MPLA led a revolt in Luanda in 1961, but it was put down by Portuguese troops.

Other opposition groups developed. In the north, the Kongo set up the FNLA (Front for the Liberation of Angola), while, in 1966, southern peoples, including many Ovimbundu, formed UNITA (National Union for the Total Independence of Angola).

Politics

The Portuguese agreed to grant Angola independence in 1975, after which rival nationalist forces began a struggle for power. A long-running civil war developed between the government forces, which received aid from the Soviet Union and Cuba, the FNLA in the north and UNITA in the south. As the war developed, both the FNLA and UNITA turned to the West for support, while UNITA received support from South Africa. FNLA guerrilla activity ended in 1984, but UNITA took control of large areas. Economic progress was hampered not only by the vast spending on defence and security, but also by the MPLA government's austere Marxist policies.

In 1991, a peace accord was agreed and multiparty elections were held, in which the MPLA, which had renounced Marxism-Leninism, won a majority. But UNITA's leaders rejected the election result and civil war resumed in 1994. In 1997, the government invited UNITA leader, Jonas Savimbi, to join a coalition but he refused. Savimbi was killed in action in February 2002, raising hopes of peace.

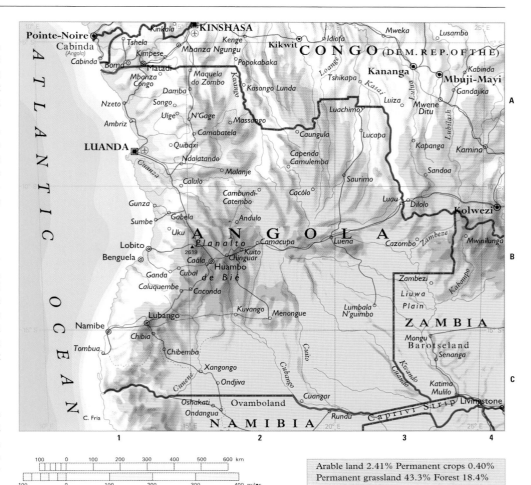

Arable land 2.41% Permanent crops 0.40%
Permanent grassland 43.3% Forest 18.4%

Economy

Angola is a developing country, where 70% of the people are poor farmers, although agriculture contributes only about 9% of the gross domestic product. The main food crops include cassava, maize, sweet potatoes and beans, while bananas, coffee, palm products, seed cotton and sugar cane are grown for export. Cattle are the leading livestock, but sheep and goats are raised in drier areas.

Despite the poverty of most of its people and its low per capita GNP ($270 in 1999), Angola has much economic potential. It has oil reserves near Luanda and in the enclave of Cabinda, which is separated from Angola by a strip of land belonging to the Democratic Republic of Congo. Oil and mineral fuels are the leading exports. Other resources include diamonds (the second most important export), copper and manganese. Angola also has a growing industrial sector. Manufactures include cement, chemicals, processed food and textiles.

AREA	Kimbundu 25%,
1,246,700 sq km	Bakongo 13%, others 25%
[481,351 sq mi]	**LANGUAGES**
POPULATION	Portuguese (official),
10,366,000	many others
CAPITAL (POPULATION)	**RELIGIONS**
Luanda (2,250,000)	Traditional beliefs 47%,
GOVERNMENT	Roman Catholic 38%,
Multiparty republic	Protestant 15%
ETHNIC GROUPS	**CURRENCY**
Ovimbundu 37%,	Kwanza = 100 lwei

ANGUILLA – SEE CARIBBEAN SEA, PAGES 71–76;
ANTIGUA AND BARBUDA – SEE CARIBBEAN SEA, PAGES 71–76

The 'celeste' (sky blue) and white stripes were the symbols of independence around the city of Buenos Aires, where an independent government was set up in 1810. It became the national flag in 1816. The gold May Sun was added two years later.

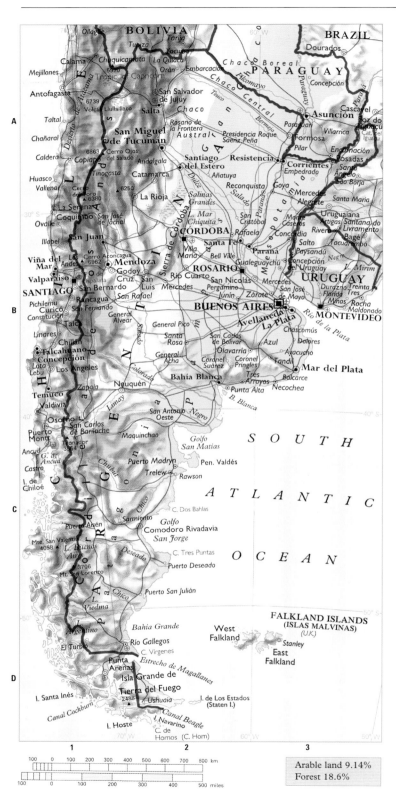

Arable land 9.14%
Forest 18.6%

Geography

The Argentine Republic, the largest of South America's Spanish-speaking countries, is less than a third of the size of Brazil. Its western boundary lies in the Andes, which includes basins, ridges and peaks of more than 6,000 m [19,685 ft] in the north. South of latitude 27°S, the ridges merge into a single high cordillera, where Aconcagua, at 6,962 m [22,849 ft], is the tallest mountain in the western hemisphere. In the south, the Andes are lower, with glaciers and volcanoes. Eastern Argentina is a series of alluvial plains, stretching from the Andean foothills to the sea. The Gran Chaco in the north slopes down to the Paraná River, from the high desert in the Andean foothills to lowland swamp forest. Between the Paraná and Uruguay rivers is Mesopotamia, a fertile region. Further south are the pampa grasslands, which are damp and fertile near Buenos Aires and drier, but still productive, elsewhere. To the south, the pampa gives way to the dry, windswept plateaux of Patagonia that extend towards Tierra del Fuego.

Climate

The climate varies from subtropical in the north to temperate in the south. Rainfall is abundant in the north-east, but is lower to the west and south. Patagonia is a dry region, crossed by rivers that rise in the Andes.

ARGENTINA (BUENOS AIRES)

Argentina, which stretches from the tropics almost into Antarctica, with the Andes to the west and lying between the two oceans, experiences a number of climates. The north is subtropical, with temperatures around 20°C [68°F] in June and 25°C [77°F] in January. The south is temperate, with May to August above freezing, and 10°C [50°F] in January or February. Rainfall is heaviest in the subtropical north-east.

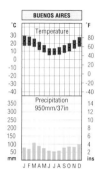

History

The first inhabitants of Argentina were Native Americans, though population densities were low by comparison with most of the rest of South America. In the pampa and in Patagonia, the people were nomadic hunters and gatherers, but farming communities existed in the north-west and the north-eastern forests. Spanish explorers first reached the coast in 1516, landing on the shores of the Rio de la Plata. They were soon followed by others in search of gold and silver. European settlement in Argentina, a name meaning 'land of silver', was concentrated at first in the north-west around Salta and San Miguel de Tucumán, which had strong links to Peru. This area is unusual today in retaining a large mestizo (mixed Amerindian and Spanish) population, a remnant of colonial times. Buenos Aires was founded in 1580. When it was accepted that the new Spanish territory lacked mineral wealth, the Spaniards began to develop agriculture by introducing cattle, horses and sheep. Before long, the settlements in the north-west began to develop economically by supplying animals, cloth and food to the mining settlements in Peru.

In 1776, Argentina, Paraguay, Uruguay and southern Bolivia were disengaged from Peru to form a separate viceroyalty, with its administrative centre at Buenos Aires which became a major trading city. In 1810, Buenos Aires declared itself independent and set up a government to administer the United Provinces of the Rio de la Plata, as the region was called, but Uruguay, Bolivia and Paraguay eventually broke away. In 1812, an Argentine general, José de San Martín, began an armed struggle against Spain and, in 1816, representatives of the Argentine provinces officially declared the country's independence. The new nation was then named the United Provinces of La Plata. In 1817, San Martín led an expedition across the Andes and defeated the Spaniards in Chile. His forces went on to conquer the Spaniards in Peru. Following independence, the people in Buenos Aires were in conflict with rural landowners, who wanted more control over their affairs. Following a period of dictatorship between 1829 and 1852, the country adopted a new constitution in 1853. This constitution, based largely on that of the USA, gave the provinces the right to control their own affairs. At first, Buenos Aires refused to enter the confederation, but it joined in 1862, becoming capital of the country, which had been renamed Argentina in 1860.

Early prosperity, based on stock raising and farming, combined with stable government, was boosted from 1870 by a massive influx of European immigrants, particularly Italians and Spaniards, for whom Argentina was a viable alternative to the United States. They settled lands recently cleared of Native Americans and often organized by huge land companies. Britain provided much of the capital and some of the immigrants, especially people from Wales, who are still identifiable in Patagonia today, speaking their own language. Development of a good railway network to the ports, plus steamship services to Europe, and, from 1877, refrigerated vessels, helped to create the strong meat, wool and wheat economy that carried Argentina through its formative years and into the 20th century. Before the Great Depression in the 1930s, Argentina was one of the world's more prosperous nations.

Politics

The collapse in the economy during the Great Depression led to a military coup in 1930. This started a long period of military intervention in the politics of the country. During World War II, Argentina openly favoured Germany, Italy and Japan, though it declared war on the Axis powers in March 1945. In 1943, another coup enabled Colonel Juan Peron, the minister of labour, to win popular support, because he then strengthened the unions and helped urban workers to obtain higher wages and better working conditions. Peron was elected president in 1946 and his second wife, Eva, served as his assistant until her death in 1952. Peron greatly increased government expenditure and, as the economic situation worsened, he restricted civil rights. Peron began his second term in 1952, but he lost the support of the Roman Catholic Church after he restricted its authority. In 1955, Peron fled the country after a rebellion by the armed forces. Elections were held in 1958, but another coup occurred in 1962. A series of military and civilian governments then held power until 1972. In 1973, a supporter of Peron, Hector Jose Campora, was elected president, but he resigned later in the year when Peron returned to Argentina. Peron was elected president, but following his death in 1974, his third wife, Isabel, took office. By then the economy was out of control. Soaring inflation and terrorism by extremist groups became widespread. Isabel Peron was arrested in 1976 and a military government was established.

The period from 1976 – the so-called 'dirty war' – saw the torture, wrongful imprisonment and murder ('disappearance') of up to 15,000 people by the military. Up to 2 million people fled the country. In 1982, the government, blamed for the poor state of the economy, launched an invasion of the Falkland Islands, which they had claimed since 1820. Britain regained the islands, which Argentines call Islas Malvinas, by sending an expeditionary force. Argentina's President Galtieri resigned. Constitutional government was restored in 1983 under President Raul Alfonsin, leader of the Radical Party, though the army remained influential. Argentina's economic problems – with their classic Latin American causes of reliance on certain commodities, big borrowing and maladministration – were inherited by his Peronist successor, Carlos Menem, in 1989. His austerity programme took Argentina through inflation rates of 3,084% and 2,314% down to 85% by 1991. This was stable money by previous standards. Menem also granted pardons to some people who had been imprisoned, and sold off many government businesses to private companies.

For much of the decade, the economy boomed. Menem was re-elected in 1995, but he stood down in 1999 after the onset of a severe economic depression. The conservative Ferdinand de la Rua, head of the Alianza Party, defeated Menem's chosen successor, Eduardo Duhalde, in the ensuing elections. But his regime failed to stop the economic decline. In December 2001, violent protests broke out when the government introduced severe austerity measures. De la Rua resigned and, in January, Duhalde became president. He devalued the peso and announced policies aimed at restoring the economy.

In 1999, Argentina and Britain signed an agreement concerning the Falkland Islands, the first since 1982. Under the agreement, Argentines were allowed to visit the Falkland Islands and erect a memorial to their war dead, while Argentina agreed to allow flights from the Falkland Islands to Chile.

Economy

According to the World Bank, Argentina is an 'upper-middle-income' developing country. It is one of the richest countries in South America in terms of natural resources, especially its fertile farmland, while its population – though remarkably urban, with 87% living in cities and towns – is not growing at anything like the rates seen in most of Africa and Asia. (In the 1990s, the rate of population increase was about 1.2% per annum, as compared with the world average of 1.57%.)

Argentina's population, predominantly European and predominantly middle-class, nevertheless relies on an economic base that is mainly agricultural. The richest farmland is found in the pampa and Mesopotamia, where the chief products are beef, maize and wheat. Sheep are raised in drier parts of the country, while other crops include citrus fruits, cotton, flax, grapes, potatoes, sorghum, sugar cane, sunflower seeds and tea. Many of the farms in Argentina are huge and mechanized. The owners of most of the large estates rent land to tenant farmers. However, many of the small farms in the north produce little more than what the farmers' families need to survive.

Oilfields in Patagonia and the Piedmont make Argentina almost self-sufficient in oil and natural gas, although much of the country's electricity supply is produced by hydroelectric plants. The country lacks the coal, iron ore and most of the minerals needed for industry, though some deposits of iron ore, lead, uranium and zinc are also mined. The chief industries are based on food products, such as beef, beer, flour, sugar, vegetable oil, wine, wool and hides. Other industries include the manufacture of cars, electrical equipment and textiles. Most consumer goods, such as food and household equipment, are produced in Argentina. However, many manufactures, including machinery, iron and steel and other items needed for production, together with transport equipment and chemical products, are imported. More than two-thirds of the country's factories are situated in or around Buenos Aires. Córdoba and Rosario are other industrial cities. Service industries, including transport and banking, which are heavily dependent on agriculture, employ more than half of the population.

The Pampas

'Pampa', or 'pampas', is a South American Quechua Indian term describing a flat featureless expanse. Although the term is applied to other flat areas in South America, including the desert in northern Chile, pampa is the most commonly used name for the broad grassy plains of central Argentina, between the Gran Chaco to the north and Patagonia to the south. From west to east, they stretch between the eastern flanks of the Andes to the Atlantic Ocean. Covering an area of about 760,000 sq km [295,000 sq mi], the Argentine pampa represents, geologically, outwash fans of rubble, sand, silt and clay, eroded from the Andes, washed down by torrents and redistributed by wind and water. Fine soils cover huge expanses of the pampa, providing good deep soils in the well-watered areas, such as the Buenos Aires region in the east. But where rainfall and ground water are lacking, scrub and sandy desert are the result, such as the dry pampa in the west, including most of La Pampa Province, which is largely barren, with sandy deserts and large saline areas.

Spanish settlers introduced horses and cattle, and later the best areas of pampa were enclosed for cattle ranching and cultivation. Now the pampas are almost entirely converted to rangelands growing turf grasses, or to huge fields producing alfalfa, maize, wheat and flax.

AREA	ETHNIC GROUPS
2,766,890 sq km	European 97%,
[1,068,296 sq mi]	Mestizo, Amerindian
POPULATION	**LANGUAGES**
37,385,000	Spanish (official)
CAPITAL (POPULATION)	**RELIGIONS**
Buenos Aires	Roman Catholic 92%,
(10,990,000)	Protestant 2%, Jewish 2%
GOVERNMENT	**CURRENCY**
Federal republic	Peso = 10,000 australs

Armenia's flag was first used between 1918 and 1922, when the country was an independent republic. It was readopted on 24 August 1990. The red represents the blood shed in the past, the blue the land of Armenia, and the orange the courage of the people.

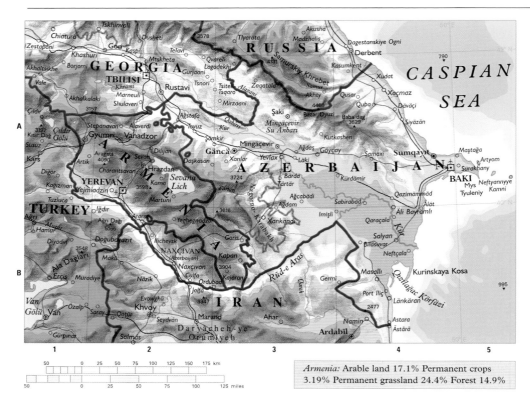

Armenia: Arable land 17.1% Permanent crops 3.19% Permanent grassland 24.4% Forest 14.9%

Geography and Climate

The Republic of Armenia is a landlocked country, mostly consisting of a plateau, criss-crossed by faults. Movements along the faults cause earth tremors and occasionally major earthquakes. Armenia's highest point is Mount Aragats, at 4,090 m [13,149 ft].

The height of the land gives rise to severe winters and cool summers. The highest peaks are snow-capped, but the total yearly rainfall is low.

History, Politics and Economy

In the 19th century, Armenians suffered hardships under Turkish rule. The Turks killed hundreds of thousands of people. During World War I, the Turks deported many Armenians, fearing they would support Russia. An independent Armenian republic was set up in the area held by Russia in 1918, but the western part of historic Armenia remained in Turkey, and another area was held by Iran.

In 1920, Armenia became a Communist republic. In 1922, it became, with Azerbaijan and Georgia, part of the Transcaucasian Republic within the Soviet Union. But the three territories became separate Soviet Socialist Republics in 1936. After the break-up of the Soviet Union in 1991, Armenia became an independent republic. Fighting broke out over Nagorno-Karabakh, an area enclosed by Azerbaijan where the majority of the people are Armenians. In 1992, Armenia occupied the territory between itself and Nagorno-Karabakh. A cease-fire in 1994 left Armenia in control of about 20% of Azerbaijan's land area. Attempts to resolve the dispute in 2001 failed.

The World Bank classifies Armenia as a 'lower-middle-income' economy. Conflict with Azerbaijan in the early 1990s damaged the economy, but since 1991 the government has encouraged free enterprise.

AREA	**ETHNIC GROUPS**
29,800 sq km	Armenian 93%,
[11,506 sq mi]	Azerbaijani 3%,
POPULATION	Russian, Kurd
3,336,000	**LANGUAGES**
CAPITAL (POPULATION)	Armenian (official)
Yerevan	**RELIGIONS**
(1,256,000)	Armenian Orthodox
GOVERNMENT	**CURRENCY**
Multiparty republic	Dram = 100 couma

AZERBAIJAN

Geography and Climate

Azerbaijan lies in south-west Asia, facing the Caspian Sea to the east. It includes the Naxçivan Autonomous Republic, an area cut off from the rest of Azerbaijan by Armenian territory. The Caucasus Mountains border Russia in the north. Azerbaijan has hot summers and cool winters. The plains have low rainfall. The uplands are much wetter.

History and Politics

After the Russian Revolution of 1917, attempts were made to form a Transcaucasian Federation made up of Armenia, Azerbaijan and Georgia. When this failed, Azerbaijanis set up an independent state. But Russian forces occupied the area in 1920. In 1922, the Communists set up a Transcaucasian Republic consisting of Armenia, Azerbaijan and Georgia under Russian control. In 1936, the areas became separate Soviet Socialist Republics within the Soviet Union. Following the break-up of the Soviet Union in 1991, Azerbaijan became independent. Economic progress was slow, partly because of the conflict with Armenia over the enclave of Nagorno-Karabakh, a region in Azerbaijan where the majority of people are Armenians. A cease-fire in 1994 left Armenia in control of about 20% of Azerbaijan's land area. Talks held in 2001 in an attempt to resolve the dispute proved fruitless.

Economy

In the mid-1990s, the World Bank classified Azerbaijan as a 'lower-middle-income' economy. Yet, by the late 1990s, the oil reserves in the Baku area on the Caspian Sea, and in the sea itself, held great promise. Oil extraction and manufacturing, including oil refining and the production of chemicals, machinery and textiles, are now the most valuable activities.

AREA	**ETHNIC GROUPS**
86,600 sq km	Azeri 90%, Dagestani 3%,
[33,436 sq mi]	Russian, Armenian, other
POPULATION	**LANGUAGES**
7,771,000	Azerbaijani (official)
CAPITAL (POPULATION)	**RELIGIONS**
Baku (Baki, 1,713,000)	Islam 93%, Russian Orthodox 2%,
GOVERNMENT	Armenian Orthodox 2%
Federal multiparty	**CURRENCY**
republic	Manat = 100 gopik

ARUBA – SEE CARIBBEAN SEA, PAGES 71–76;
ASCENSION – SEE ATLANTIC OCEAN, PAGES 41–43

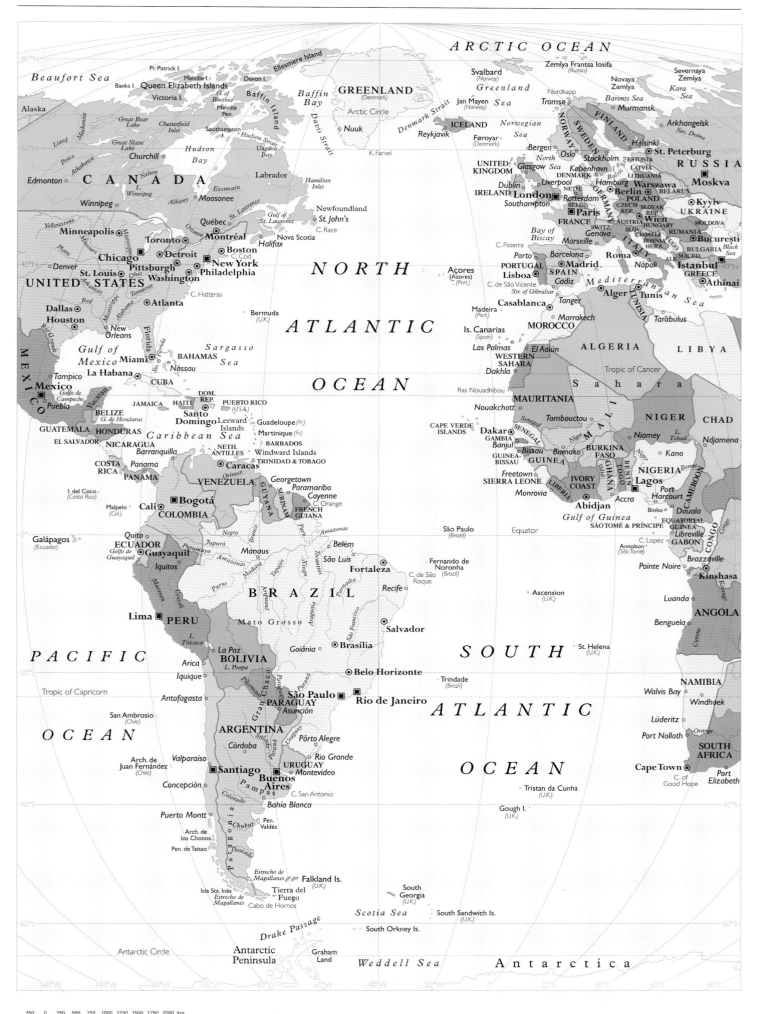

ATLANTIC OCEAN

ASCENSION

Ascension is a volcanic island of 88 sq km [34 sq mi], with a single high peak, Green Mountain (859 m [2,817 ft]), surrounded by ash and lava plains. The climate is cool and damp enough to support a farm which supplies vegetables for the local community of 700. Ascension has no native population. Administered from St Helena since 1922, its inhabitants are British, St Helenian or American.

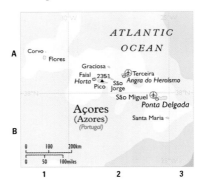

AZORES

The Azores is a group of nine large and several small islands in the North Atlantic Ocean. Part of the Mid-Atlantic Ridge, the islands are of relatively recent volcanic origin. The Azores have been Portuguese since the mid-15th century and, since 1976, they have been governed as three districts of Portugal, which form an autonomous region. Farming and fishing are the main occupations and tourism is growing.

AREA	CAPITAL
2,247 sq km [868 sq mi]	Ponta Delgada
POPULATION	**CURRENCY**
243,000	Port. escudo = 100 centavos

BERMUDA

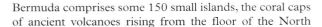

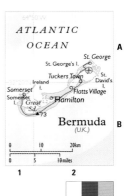

Bermuda comprises some 150 small islands, the coral caps of ancient volcanoes rising from the floor of the North Atlantic Ocean. Uninhabited when discovered in 1503 by the Spaniard Juan Mermúdez, the islands were taken over by the British over a century later, with slaves brought from Virginia. Bermuda is Britain's oldest overseas territory, but it has a long tradition of self-government. Tourism is the mainstay of the economy, but the islands are a tax haven for overseas companies.

AREA	CAPITAL
53 sq km [20 sq mi]	Hamilton
POPULATION	**CURRENCY**
64,000	Berm. dollar = 100 cents

CANARY ISLANDS

The Canary Islands contain seven large islands and many small volcanic islands situated off southern Morocco. The climate is subtropical, being dry at sea level, but wetter on the mountains. Claimed by Portugal in 1341, they were ceded to Spain in 1479. Since 1927, they formed two Spanish provinces. Tourism is a major occupation. Farming is important, as are food and fish processing, and boat building.

AREA	CAPITAL
7,273 sq km [2,807 sq mi]	Las Palmas/Santa Cruz
POPULATION	**CURRENCY**
1,577,000	Euro; Spanish peseta

CAPE VERDE

The Republic of Cape Verde consists of ten large and five small islands, divided into the Barlavento (windward) and Sotavento (leeward) groups. They are volcanic and mainly mountainous, with steep cliffs and rocky headlands.

The highest point is on the island of Fogo, an active volcano, which reaches 2,829 m [9,281 ft]. The climate is tropical, being hot for most of the year and mainly dry at sea level. The higher ground is cooler.

Portuguese since the 15th century, and used chiefly as a provisioning station and assembly point for slaves in the trade from West Africa, Cape Verde included Portuguese Guinea (now Guinea-Bissau) until 1879, when the mainland territory was separated. It was populated with slaves from Africa, and people from African and European origin.

Cape Verde became an overseas territory of Portugal in 1951 and fully independent in 1975. Linked with Guinea-Bissau in the fight against colonial rule, its socialist, single-party government flirted with union in 1980. But in 1991, the ruling party was soundly trounced in the country's first multiparty elections by a newly legalized opposition party, the Movement for Democracy (MPD). The MPD won further elections in 1996, but the former ruling African Independence Party (PAICV) regained power in 2001.

Poor soils and lack of water at the lower levels on the islands have inhibited development. But bananas, beans, coffee, fruit, groundnuts, maize and sugar cane are grown on the wetter, higher ground, when they are not ruined by endemic droughts, such as the one that killed 75,000 people in 1900. Cape Verde's exports comprise fish and fish preparations and bananas, but the country has to import much of the food it needs. The only significant minerals are salt and *pozzolana*, a volcanic rock used to make cement.

Much of the country's income comes from foreign aid and remittances which are sent home by the 600,000 Cape Verdeans who work abroad. In the last severe drought (1968–82), about 40,000 people emigrated to Portugal alone. Tourism is still in its infancy – the number of tourists reached 52,000 in 1998. Economic problems, including high unemployment levels, have been compounded by the arrival of thousands of Angolan refugees.

AREA	CAPITAL
4,030 sq km [1,556 sq mi]	Praia
POPULATION	**CURRENCY**
405,000	C. Verde escudo = 100 centavos

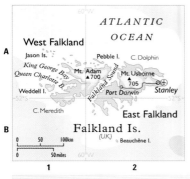

FALKLAND ISLANDS

The Falkland Islands, or the Islas Malvinas, as they are called in Argentina, which lies 480 km [300 mi] to the west, consist of two main islands, and more than 200 small ones.

The windswept islands were discovered in 1592 by the English navigator John Davis. The Falklands were first occupied nearly 200 years later by the French (East) in 1764 and the British (West). The French interest, bought by Spain in 1770, was assumed by Argentina in 1806. The British, who had withdrawn in 1774, returned in 1832. They dispossessed the Argentinian settlers and founded a settlement of their own – one that became a colony in 1892. In 1982, Argentinian forces invaded the islands, but two months later, the United Kingdom regained possession. In 1999, a formal agreement between Britain and Argentina permitted Argentinians to visit the islands. The economy is dominated by sheep-farming. The prospect of rich offshore oil and natural gas reserves remains enticing, but may be uneconomic to extract and export.

AREA	CAPITAL
12,170 sq km [4,699 sq mi]	Stanley
POPULATION	**CURRENCY**
2,895	F. Islands pound = 100 pence

GREENLAND

Greenland is regarded by geographers as the world's largest island. It is almost three times larger than the second largest island, New Guinea, but an ice sheet, the world's second largest after Antarctica, covers more than 85% of its area. Settlement is confined to the rocky coast. The warmer south-west coast, where the capital Nuuk (Godthaab) is situated, has more than seven months with average temperatures below freezing.

Greenland became a Danish possession in 1380 and an integral part of the Danish kingdom in 1953. It was taken into the European Economic Community (EEC) in 1973, despite a majority of Greenlanders voting against this. In 1979, after another referendum, home rule was introduced, with full internal self-government in 1981. In 1985, Greenland withdrew from the EEC, halving the Community's land area.

Greenland still relies heavily on Danish aid and Denmark is its main trading partner. The chief rural occupations are sheep-rearing and fishing, with shrimps, prawns and molluscs being exported. The only major manufacturing industry is fish canning, which has drawn many Inuit to the towns. Few Inuit now follow the traditional life of nomadic hunting. Most Greenlanders live precariously between the primitive and the modern. Yet a nationalist mood prevails, buoyed by rich fish stocks, lead and zinc from Uummannaq in the north-west, untapped uranium in the south and, possibly, oil in the east. In addition, an adventure-oriented tourist industry is expanding. In 1997, the nationalist resurgence was evident when Greenland made Inuit name forms official.

AREA	CAPITAL
2,175,600 sq km	Nuuk
[838,999 sq mi]	(Godthaab)
POPULATION	**CURRENCY**
56,000	Danish krone

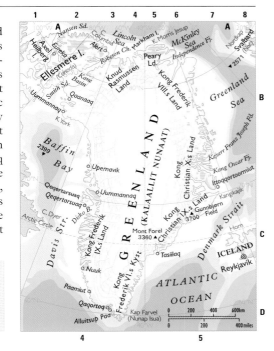

MADEIRA

Madeira is the largest of the group of volcanic islands lying 550 km [350 mi] west of the Moroccan coast and 900 km [560 mi] south-west of the national capital, Lisbon. Porto Santo, the uninhabited Islas Selvagens (not shown on the map) and the Desertas complete the group. The island of Madeira makes up more than 90% of the total area.

With a warm climate and fertile soils, the Madeira Islands are known for their rich exotic plant life. The abundance of species is all the more surprising because rainfall is confined to the winter months.

The present name, meaning 'wood', was given by the Portuguese when they first saw the forested islands in 1419. The forests were largely destroyed and a farming industry was established. Spain held the islands between 1580 and 1640, while Britain occupied the islands twice early in the 19th century.

Major crops include bananas, maize, mangoes, oranges and sugar cane. Grapes are grown to make the islands' best-known product, Madeira wine. Fishing is important, as also is tourism – the islands are a famous winter resort.

AREA	CAPITAL
813 sq km	Funchal
[314 sq mi]	**CURRENCY**
POPULATION	Euro; Spanish peseta
259,000	= 100 céntimos

ST HELENA

St Helena, which became a British colony in 1834, is an isolated volcanic island in the south Atlantic Ocean. Now a British overseas territory, it is also the administrative centre of Ascension and Tristan da Cunha.

TRISTAN DA CUNHA

Tristan da Cunha is the largest of four scattered islands to the southern end of the Mid-Atlantic Ridge. Like Ascension, which lies far to the north in the tropics, the islands are dependencies of St Helena. Tristan da Cunha has a population of about 300.

The national flag was adopted in 1901. It includes the British Union Flag, revealing Australia's historic links with Britain. In 1995, the Australian government put the flag used by the country's Aboriginal people (not shown here) on the same footing as the national flag.

Geography

The Commonwealth of Australia, the world's sixth largest country, is also a continent. It is primarily a land of low- to medium-altitude plateaux that form monotonous landscapes. The edges of the plateaux are more diverse, especially in the east, where gorges and waterfalls occur between the Great Dividing Range and the coast. Stunning gorge scenery is also found in the Hamersley Range and Kimberley Plateau.

Eastern Australia is the zone of greatest relief, highest rainfall, most abundant vegetation and largest population. Much of the region shows signs of volcanic activity in the relatively recent geological past and the young basaltic outcrops support nutrient-rich soils in contrast to the nutrient-poor, heavily weathered soils in the rest of Australia. The Great Dividing Range extends from the Cape York Peninsula to Victoria, while the mountains of Tasmania are its southernmost extension. The range contains many sub-ranges, one of which, the Snowy Mountains, contains Australia's highest peak, Mount Kosciuszko, which reaches 2,230 m [7,316 ft] above sea level.

Between the eastern highlands and the western plateaux lie the Carpentaria, central and Murray lowlands. The central lowlands drain to the internal river systems supplying Lake Eyre, or to the Bulloo system, or, through great inland deltas, to the Darling River. The parallel dune ridges of this area form part of the great continent-wide set of dune ridges extending in a huge anti-clockwise arc, eastwards through the Great Victoria Desert, northwards through the Simpson Desert and westwards to the Great Sandy Desert. All of these, though inhospitable, are only moderately arid, allowing widespread, if sparse, vegetation cover.

Ancient rocks form the western half of Australia. The area has little surface water and is essentially a landscape of worn-down ridges and plateaux, with depressions with sandy deserts and occasional salt lakes.

The Great Barrier Reef

When coral is alive it sways gently in the sea's currents, but when it dies it forms hard coral 'limestone' rock. The Great Barrier Reef, off the coast of Queensland in the Coral Sea and the world's biggest, is a maze of some 2,500 reefs exposed only at low tide, ranging in size from a few hundred hectares to 50 sq km [20 sq mi], and extending over an area of 250,000 sq km [100,000 sq mi]. The closest parts of the Great Barrier Reef are about 16 km [10 mi] from the coast, while other parts are 160 km [100 mi] out at sea.

The section extending for about 800 km [500 mi] north of Cairns forms a discontinuous wall of coral, through which narrow openings lead to areas of platform or patch reefs. South of Cairns, the reefs are less continuous, and extend further from the coast. Between the outer reef and the coast are many high islands, remnants of the mainland. These are coral cays, developed from coral sand on reefs and known locally as low islands, they are usually small and uninhabited, exceptions being Green Island and Heron Island.

A tourist attraction with more than 400 types of coral and over 1,500 species of fish, the modern reefs have evolved in the last 20,000 years, over older foundations exposed to the atmosphere during former low sea levels. Coral is susceptible to severe damage from tropical cyclones and also to damage by crown-of-thorns starfish, which feed on the living coral polyps. Scientists have not yet found the reason for these starfish invasions. Much of the area is now protected as the Great Barrier Reef Marine Park, which forms the world's largest protected sea area, but the existence of oil around and beneath the reef is a long-term threat to its ecological stability. The government has stopped oil companies drilling in the area and it is also illegal to collect coral from the reef.

Climate

Only 10% of Australia has an average yearly rainfall of over 1,000 mm [39 in]. These areas include the tropical north, where Darwin is situated, the north-east coast, and the south-east, where Sydney is located. The interior is dry, and water evaporates quickly in the heat.

The wettest part of the continent is the east coast of Queensland where the average annual rainfall reaches as much as 3,810 mm [150 in]. The coast is sometimes hit by typhoons.

AUSTRALIA – DARWIN

The wettest areas of Australia are the north, the east coast, Tasmania in the south-east, and the south-west tip of the continent. The northern half of Australia lies in the tropics. For example, Darwin has high temperatures that drop only very slightly during the dry winter. However, the monsoon brings much rain in the high sun period between December and March. Conditions during summer may be oppressive due to high humidity.

PERTH

The vast interior of Australia is very hot and dry. There are no great areas of high land that could form a barrier to the rain-bearing winds, or a relief to the high temperatures. Along the southern coast rainfall is slightly higher than in the interior. There is higher rainfall in the extreme south-west around Perth, which experiences a Mediterranean-type climate of hot, dry summers and warm, wet winters.

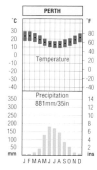

SYDNEY

In the south-east, annual rainfall is high, with a maximum from April to June. Rain falls on 12–13 days each month. The vast valleys inland of the Great Divide, in the lee of the rain-bearing winds, are drier. Temperatures are moderate, with winter night frosts in the south and the interior. Snow falls on the uplands of the south-east and Tasmania. Frosts are unknown in Sydney, the lowest temperatures being 2–4°C [36–39°F].

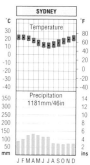

Vegetation

Luxuriant forests grow on the humid margins of Australia. They include the great jarrah forests of tall eucalyptus hardwoods in the extreme south-west of Western Australia; the temperate rainforests in Tasmania and on humid upland sites north through New South Wales to the Queensland border; and the tropical and subtropical rainforests found in the wetter areas along the coast, from the McIllwraith Range in the north to the vicinity of Mallacoota Inlet in the south.

Some rainforest areas are maintained as managed forests, others are in national parks, but most of the original cover has been cleared for agriculture, particularly for dairying and cattle fattening, and also for sugar- and banana-growing, north of Port Macquarie. The most adaptable tree genus is the *Eucalyptus*, which ranges from the tall flooded gum trees found on the edges of the rainforest to dry-living mallee species found on sand plains and inter-dune areas. Acacia species, especially the bright-yellow flowered wattles, are also highly adaptable.

Much of western Australia is desert, with some grasses and low shrubs. The central lowlands are grassy areas used to raise livestock. Water comes from the artesian wells that underlie the central plains.

AUSTRALIA

History

The Aboriginal people of Australia entered the continent from South-east Asia over 40,000 years ago. Fires, lit for hunting and allowed to burn uncontrolled, altered much of the vegetation, but the Aboriginal people understood their environment, protecting vital areas of natural food supply, restricting the use of certain desert waterholes which tradition taught would be reliable in a drought, and developing a resource-use policy which was aimed at living with nature.

European exploration began in 1606, when Willem Jansz, a Dutch navigator, sailed along the west coast of the Cape York Peninsula, thinking it was New Guinea. In 1642, another Dutchman, Abel Janszoon Tasman, circumnavigated Australia without sighting the mainland. But he did visit Van Diemen's Land, which was later renamed Tasmania in his honour. Other Dutch sailors who sighted the continent were unimpressed by its arid character and the hostility of its inhabitants. However, in 1770, the British Captain, James Cook, sighted the fertile east coast. He claimed the region for Britain and named it New South Wales. Between 1801 and 1803, a British navigator, Matthew Flinders, sailed around Australia, charting its coastline and proving that it was one landmass. He suggested that the area, which was known as New Holland, be renamed Australia after *Terra Australis* (Southern Continent), the name used for the supposed continent before its discovery. The name change took place in 1817.

European settlement in Australia began in 1788 as a penal colony at Botany Bay, in New South Wales. The settlement at this bay, which had been visited by Captain Cook, was the beginning of the city of Sydney. In 1813, the crossing of the Blue Mountains was the first of many expeditions to open up the grasslands beyond the Great Dividing Range. Other settlements were quickly established in Tasmania in 1803 and Queensland in 1824. The 1830s saw an increasing number of free, assisted immigrants arriving from Britain and also the beginning of the exploration of the interior. But Australia's population remained small until the 1851 gold rush in New South Wales brought a large influx of fortune hunters. Most of the prospectors were disappointed, but many stayed on, having earned less than they needed to buy their return ticket. As a result, Australia's population rose from about 400,000 in 1850 to 1,100,000 in 1860.

During the 19th century, the continent became divided into the colonies of New South Wales, Queensland (1859), South Australia (1836), Tasmania (1825), Victoria (1851) and Western Australia (1829). The area which now forms Northern Territory was under the control of South Australia. During the colonial period, the state seaports of Sydney, Brisbane, Adelaide, Hobart, Melbourne and Perth became established as the dominant manufacturing, commercial, administrative and legislative centres of their respective states. None of them has since relinquished these positions.

In 1901, the former colonies, which were redesignated as states, came together to create the Commonwealth of Australia with a federal constitution and Melbourne as its temporary capital. Trade between the states became free. External affairs, defence and immigration policy became federal responsibilities, but health, education, transport, mineral, agricultural and industrial development remained firmly in the hands of each state. Only gradually did powers of taxation give the federal government the opportunity to develop national policies.

The federal capital established at Canberra, in the new Australian Capital Territory, grew from a tiny settlement in 1911 to become a great seat of administration and learning, and the largest inland regional commercial centre. Building began in 1923 and a federal parliament opened in Canberra in 1927. The federal government's territorial responsibilities included the Northern Territory, which has been self-governing since 1978.

Immigration has changed the ethnic character of Australia since 1960. Australia now has Greek, Italian, Lebanese, South-east Asian, Turkish and Yugoslav communities alongside Aboriginal, British, Irish, Chinese, Dutch and German communities, though the culture remains strongly British in flavour. Almost 60% of the Australian population lives in Sydney, Melbourne, Adelaide, Brisbane, Perth and Hobart. Migration within states from inland rural areas to capital cities or coastal towns has left rural communities with ageing populations, while the new mining towns have young populations. The most rapid growth, outside mining towns, has been in coastal towns, which provide retirement homes and lifestyles differing from those of the cities.

From 1788, European settlement upset the ecological balance through the widespread clearing of coastal forests, overgrazing of inland pastures, and the introduction of exotic species, especially the destructive rabbit. But Europeans have also brought the technology which has enabled the mineral, water and soil resources of Australia to be developed. Soon after 1788, small-scale manufacturing began to supply domestic goods and machinery to the colonial community. Inevitably, manufacturing grew in the colonial seaport capitals, especially Sydney and Melbourne, which now have more than 60% of all manufacturing industries (though only 40% of the total population).

Much of Australia's growth since the beginning of European settlement has been related to the exploitation of mineral resources, which has led directly to the founding, growth and often eventual decline of the majority of inland towns. Broken Hill and Mount Isa are copper-, lead-, silver- and zinc-producing centres, while Kalgoorlie, Bendigo, Ballarat and Charters Towers all grew in the 19th-century gold rushes.

Today, less glamorous minerals support the Australian economy. In Western Australia, the great iron ore mines of Mount Tom Price, Mount Newman and Mount Goldsworthy are linked by new railways to special ports at Dampier and Port Hedland. Offshore are the oil and gas fields of the north-western continental shelf. Railways are vital for bulk freight, especially mineral ores, coal and wheat. However, most cattle and sheep are carried by 'road trains' – powerful units pulling several trailers. A rapidly improving highway system links all the major cities and towns, providing easy mobility for a largely car-owning population. Although 90% of all passenger transport is by road, air services provide much inter-state travel. Australia is also well-served by local broadcasting and television. The radio remains a lifeline for remote settlements dependent on the flying doctor or aerial ambulance, and for others when bush or forest fires threaten isolated communities.

Politics

Australia's close ties with Britain were evident during World Wars I and II, when Australia considered itself automatically on the side of Britain when the wars broke out. About 59,000 Australians died in World War I (the highest number of deaths in proportion to the total number of troops among all the Allies) and more than 29,000 died in battle or in prison camps in World War II.

After World War II, Australia began to redefine its global role and it began to play an increasingly important part in Asia and the Pacific region. In 1950, it helped to create the Colombo Plan for economic development in southern and south-eastern Asia. In 1952, it signed the ANZUS treaty, a mutual defence treaty with New Zealand and the United States. This led to Australia sending troops to Vietnam between 1964 and 1975, though, from 1966, Australia's involvement in the war and its alliance with the US, became a matter of heated debate.

Marsupials

Marsupials are mammals that give birth to their young at an early stage of development and attach them to their milk glands for a period, often inside a pouch (*marsupium*). Once widespread around the world, they have mostly been ousted by more advanced forms, but marsupials continue to flourish in Australia, New Guinea and South America.

Best known are the big red and grey kangaroos that range over the dry grasslands and forests of Australia. Standing up to 2 m [6.5 ft] tall, they are grazers that now compete for food with cattle and sheep. Bounding at speed they can clear fences of their own height. Wallabies – small species of the same family – live in the forests and mountains.

Australia has many other kinds of marsupials, though several have died out since the coming of Europeans. Tree-living koalas live exclusively on eucalyptus leaves. Heavily built wombats browse in the undergrowth like large rodents, and the fierce-sounding Tasmanian Devils are mild scavengers of the forest floor.

AUSTRALIA

PAPUA
NEW GUINEA

SOLOMON
ISLANDS

Guadalcanal
Honiara 2439

Misima I.
Louisade
Archipelago

Rossel I.
Tagula I.

C O R A L

S E A

C O R A L   S E A

I S L A N D S

TERRITORIES

Osprey Reef

Lihou Reefs
and Cays

P A C I F I C

I. de Sable

Is. Chesterfield
(France)

Kenn Reef

Saumarez Reef

Récifs Bellone

Wreck Reef

Cato I.

Tropic of Capricorn

O C E A N

Wessel
Is.
The English
Co. Is.
Nhulunbuy
Yirrkala
C. Wilberforce
Melville B.
C. Arnhem
Port Bradshaw
Caledon Bay
Blue Mud B.
C. Grey
Anguruga
C. Beatrice
Groote Eylandt

Gulf   of

Carpentaria

Limmen Bight
Maria I.
Sir Edward Pellew Group
Vanderlin I.

Borroloola

McArthur

arkly
Tableland

ORY

RN

Thursday I.
Prince of Wales I.
Banks I.
C. York

Shelburne Bay
C. Grenville
Temple B.
C. Weymouth

Endeavour Strait
Port Musgrave
Duifken Pt.
Albatross Bay
Weipa

Cape
Wenlock
York

Princess Charlotte Bay
Bathurst Bay
C. Melville

Coen
Holroyd

Peninsula
Coleman

Archer B.
C. Keer-Weer

Mornington I.
Wellesley Is.
Bentinck I.
C. Van Diemen
Karumba
Normanton
Burketown

Mitchell
Dunbar

Gilbert

Croydon

Mareeba
Chillagoe
Almaden
Atherton

Cairns
Bartle Frere 1612
Innisfail
Tully

Mossman

Great Barrier Reef

Laura
C. Bedford
Cooktown
C. Tribulation

C. Flattery

Normanby

Forsayth
Einasleigh

Ingham
Palm Is.
Halfax Bay
C. Cleveland
C. Bowling Green
Ayr

Hinchinbrook I.

Home
Hill
Charters
Towers
Collinsville

Townsville

Bowen   Whitsunday I.
Proserpine
Cumberland
Islands

Mackay
C. Palmerston
Broad Sd.

Arthur Pt.
Townshend I.

Swain
Reefs

Mount Isa
Cloncurry

Duchess
Dajarra

Selwyn Range

Julia
Creek
Kynuna

Richmond

Pentland

Hughenden

Great   Dividing   Range

Netherdale
Lake
Dairymple

Denham Ra.
Blair
Athol

Peak Ra.
Connors Ra.

Sarina

Q U E E N S L A N D

Great   Artesian   Basin

Boulia

Winton
Muttaburra

Longreach
Ilfracombe

Barcaldine

Aramac

Clermont

Emerald

Blackall

Springsure

Drummond Ra.

Nogoa

Mackenzie

Yeppoon
Rockhampton
Keppel B.
Mount
Morgan

Gladstone
Biloela

Capricorn Group
Curtis I.
Port Curtis

Bedourie

L. Machattie

Jundah

Barcoo

Yaraka

1312

Great   Dividing   Range

Theodore
Cracow
Taroom

Monto

Bundaberg
Hervey Bay
Childers
Sandy C.

Fraser I.
Hervey Bay

Windorah

Adavale
Augathella

Charleville

Mitchell

Injune

Roma

Gayndah
Wandoan
Murgon
Wondai

Maryborough
Gympie

Quilpie

Wyandra

Thargomindah

Bollon

Balonne

Warrego Ra.

Expedition Ra.
Dawson

Maranoa

Kingaroy
Nanango
Dalby

Nambour
Caloundra
Bribie I.
Moreton I.

Cunnamulla

St. George

Dirranbandi

Moonie

Goondiwindi

Toowoomba
Ipswich

BRISBANE
Gold Coast
Tweed Heads
Murwillumbah
Byron Bay

Warwick
Stanthorpe

1356
Kyogle
Casino
Lismore

Ballina

I M P S O N

D E S E R T

impson
Desert

The Macumba

Oodnadatta

na

L. Eyre
(North)
Lake Eyre
-16
Lake Eyre
(South)

Marree

L. Yamma-Yamma

L.
Gregory
Streletzki Cr.
Innamincka

Cooper Creek

Birdsville

Eyre Cr.

The Warburton

Tibooburra

L. Blanche

L. Callabonna

Bourke

Wanaaring

White Cliffs

Tenterfield
Glen
Innes 1586

Clarence
Maclean
Grafton

Coffs Harbour

Middleton Reef

Elizabeth Reef

T R A L I A

RALIA

Leigh Creek
Lake
Torrens

Harris
Pimba
Woomera

Lake
Gairdner

L. Macfarlane

Flinders   Ranges

St. Mary Pk.
1168
Hawker

Quorn
Mt. Brown
969

Lake Frome

Barrier Range

Wilcannia

Cobar

Nyngan

Broken
Hill

Menindee

Darling

Ivanhoe

Mt. Hope

N E W

S O U T H

Moree
Inverell

Narrabri

Gunnedah

Warialda

Gwydir

Bingara

Armidale

Namoi

New   England   Ra.

Nambucca Heads
Kempsey

Tamworth

Port Macquarie

Nundle

Coonamble

Gilgandra

Barrington Tops
1555
Muswellbrook

Taree

Port Augusta
Iron Knob
Whyalla

Peterborough
Jamestown
Mt. Bryan
934
Burra

Gladstone

Quom

Hawker

W A L E S

Cowal

Condobolin

Roto

Hillston

Parkes
Forbes

Orange

Mudgee

Singleton

P. Stephens

Maitland
Cessnock
Newcastle
Gosford

Lord Howe I.
Ball's Pyramid

Port
Pirie
Kimba
Kadina
Wallaroo

Spencer
Gulf

Renmark
Loxton

Wentworth

Mildura

Balranald

Ivanhoe

Hay

Lachlan

Murrumbidgee

Griffith

Leeton
Narrandera

Booligal

Gundagai

Young
Cowra

Goulburn
Yass

Bathurst
Lithgow
Katoomba

SYDNEY
Campbelltown
Wollongong
Shellharbour
Nowra-Bomaderry

Jervis Bay
(COMMONWEALTH TERRITORY)

Penrith

Eyre
Peninsula

Cleve

C. Spencer
Investigator Str.

ngaroo I.

Victor Harbor
Encounter Bay

Gawler
Elizabeth
ADELAIDE
Murray Bridge

Gulf
St.
Vincent

Pinnaroo

Alexandrina

Kingston S. E.

Bordertown

Keith

Swan Hill

Kerang

Cobram

Deniliquin

Shepparton
Benalla

Wagga Wagga

Junee
Tumut

Albury-
Wodonga

Wangaratta

Canberra
AUSTRALIAN
CAPITAL TERR.

Queanbeyan

Cooma

Mt.
Kosciuszko
2230

Bombala

Tivtfold B.

Batemans Bay

T A S M A N

S E A

Millicent
Penola

Mount Gambier

Naracoorte

Bendigo
Castlemaine

V I C T O R I A

Maryborough
Ararat

Ballarat

Horsham

Hamilton

C. Northumberland
Discovery Bay
C. Bridgewater
Portland
Port Fairy
Warrnambool

Heywood

Geelong

Colac

C. Otway

MELBOURNE

Moe
Wonthaggi
Foster

Morwell
Traralgon

Gippsland

Sale
Bairnsdale

Orbost

Snowy

Disaster B.
C. Howe
Mallacoota Inlet

Pt. Hicks

Phillip I.

Wilsons Promontory

Port Phillip

King Island
Currie

Bass   Strait

Cape Barren I.

Flinders I.
Furneaux
Group

Hunter I.

Devonport
George
Town

Clarke I.

Scottsdale

T A S M A N I A

Burnie
Ulverstone

Launceston

Zeehan

Mt. Ossa
1617
Queenstown
Strahan

St. Marys

1527
Ben Lomond

Bicheno
Freycinet
Pen.

New
Norfolk

Glenorchy

Hobart

P. Davey

Tasman Pen.
Port Arthur
Storm Bay

Bruny I.

Huonville

South East C.

47

Several other factors contributed to a reassessment by Australians of their role in the world and their relationship with Britain. These included the changes in Australia's population after World War II, when the country was seriously underpopulated, Britain's membership in the European Economic Community (now the European Union) which began in 1973, and changes in Australia's trade directions, with Japan and the United States replacing Europe as the country's chief trading partners. In 1986, the Australia Act abolished the remaining legislative, executive and judicial controls of the British parliament.

In 1999, a referendum was held on whether the country should remain a constitutional monarchy, with the British monarch as its head of state, or become a republic. The Australian Labor Party and much of the Liberal-National Party favoured the republican option. However, the issue put at the referendum meant that the president would have been chosen by the parliament. Hence, many people who favoured republicanism voted 'no' to the proposal, since they wanted a direct vote for the president. Only 45% of Australians voted in favour of change, and Australia remained a constitutional monarchy.

Another problem Australia faces is the status of the Aboriginal people who, for many years, were an unseen and unheard part of the population. However, in the 1960s, Aboriginal militants working on stations in the outback drew attention to their working conditions and achieved equal pay for black and white workers. In 1967, a large majority supported proposals in a constitutional referendum to grant the Aboriginals the right to vote. In 1971, they were included on the official census for the first time. This enabled them to vote and to receive social service benefits. Aboriginal campaigns for land rights began in the late 1960s, and they first proved successful in Northern Territory in 1976. In 1985, the title for Australia's best-known tourist attraction, Uluru (Ayers Rock), was handed to the traditional Aboriginal owners of the area. Campaigns for land rights continued through the 1990s, following a 1992 High Court ruling that Australia was not an 'empty land' when Europeans first arrived in 1788.

The country's leading political parties are the conservative Liberal Party, the Australian Labor Party, which is supported by the trade unions, and the National Party, which represents the rural population, including farmers.

Economy

Australia is a prosperous country, with a per capita GNP in 1999 of US $23,850, which was about the same as the per capita GNP of the United Kingdom. Crops can grow on only about 6% of the country, though dry pasture covers another 58%. Apart from the empty and largely unusable desert areas in Western Australia and the Simpson Desert, extensive cattle or sheep production dominates all of Australia, north and west of a line from Penong in South Australia, through Broken Hill in New South Wales to Bundaberg in Queensland, and east of a line from Geraldton to Esperance in Western Australia. Cattle and sheep populations in this zone are sparse, while individual pastoral holdings are large, with some covering more than 400,000 hectares [1 million acres].

Some of the Aboriginal people live by hunting and gathering in Arnhem Land and on the fringes of the deserts. But nearly all of them now live close to government settlements or mission stations. Many work as stockmen and seasonal agricultural workers, while thousands more have migrated to country towns or cities.

The intensive pastoral zones support the bulk of sheep and cattle of Australia. Wool, mutton and beef production is still the basic industry. The country is the world's largest producer of wool and ranks third in lamb and mutton. Wheat is cultivated in combination with sheep-raising over large tracts of the gentle inland slopes of the coastal ranges. Along the east coast are important cattle, dairy and sugar-cane industries. Sugar-cane production is especially important between Brisbane and Cairns. Irrigated areas also support cotton, rice, fruit and vegetable crops, largely for home consumption. Wine production around Perth, Adelaide, central Victoria and eastern New South Wales has expanded in recent decades, producing vintages of international renown.

Australia's mineral wealth is phenomenal. In 1995, it produced 38% of the world's diamonds, 14% of the world's manganese ore, 11% of the world's gold and uranium, 9% of the world's iron ore, 8% of the world's nickel, 7% of the world's silver, and 4–5% of the world's aluminium, lead, tin and zinc. In the east, the coal mines of central Queensland and eastern New South Wales are linked by rail to bulk-loading facilities at Sarina, Gladstone, Brisbane, Newcastle, Sydney and Port Kemble, which enable this high-grade coking coal to be shipped to worldwide markets. Bauxite mining has led to the development of new settlements at Nhulunby and Weipa on the Gulf of Carpentaria, with associated refineries at Kwinana, Gladstone and Bell Bay.

Rum Jungle, south of Darwin, became well known as one of the first uranium mines, but deposits further east in Arnhem Land are now being exploited. Meanwhile, new discoveries of ore bodies continue to be made in the ancient rocks in the western half of the country. Natural gas from Cooper Basin, just south of Innamincka on Cooper Creek, is piped to Adelaide and Sydney, while oil and gas from the Bass Strait and brown coal from the Yallourn-Morwell area have been vital to the industrial growth of Victoria. Fossil fuels are supported by hydro-electric power from projects in western Tasmania and the Snowy Mountains.

Although Australia's prosperity was based on farming and mining, manufacturing is now the leading economic activity. It accounted for nearly 16% of the gross domestic product in 1994–5, as compared with 3.3% from agriculture and 4.4% from mining. Many of Australia's factories concentrate on assembly work or light manufacturing, including the production of consumer products for domestic consumption. Leading manufactures include chemicals, clothing, processed food, metals, including iron and steel, paper, textiles and transport equipment. But Australia imports many producer goods, including machinery, construction equipment and other goods involved in production.

The leading sources of imports are the United States, Japan, the United Kingdom, Germany and China. Australia's leading exports include food and live animals, mineral fuels and lubricants, basic manufactures and metal ores and metal scrap. Major export destinations are Japan, South Korea, New Zealand, the United States, China, Singapore and Taiwan.

Australian Territories

Australia is responsible for a number of other territories. In the Indian Ocean, Britain transferred sovereignty of Heard Island and McDonald Island (both 1947), and further north the Cocos (Keeling) Islands (1955) and Christmas Island (1958). Australia also has jurisdiction over the Ashmore and Cartier Islands in the Timor Sea, the Coral Sea Islands Territory, and Norfolk Island in the south-west Pacific – while Lord Howe Island and Macquarie Island are administered by New South Wales and Tasmania, respectively. Of all these, only the Cocos Islands (600), Christmas Island (2,300), Norfolk Island (2,000) and Lord Howe Island (300) have permanent populations. The Coral Sea Islands Territory, which became an Australian territory in 1969, covers a sea area of about 1,000,000 sq km [386,100 sq mi], but its scattered reefs and islands are totally uninhabited apart from a meteorological station on Willis Island.

The country is also in charge of the largest sector of Antarctica, a continent protected from military and nuclear pollution under international agreement since 1991. A member of ANZUS since 1951, Australia has reviewed its own defence position since New Zealand banned US Navy nuclear warships in 1985.

AREA	Asian 7.5%,
7,686,850 sq km	Aboriginal 1.5%
[2,967,893 sq mi]	**LANGUAGES**
POPULATION	English (official)
19,358,000	**RELIGIONS**
CAPITAL (POPULATION)	Roman Catholic 26%,
Canberra (325,000)	Anglican 24%,
GOVERNMENT	other Christian 24%,
Federal constitutional monarchy	non-Christian 24%
ETHNIC GROUPS	**CURRENCY**
Caucasian 92%,	Australian dollar = 100 cents

AUSTRIA

According to legend, the colours on Austria's flag date back to a battle in 1191, during the Third Crusade, when an Austrian duke's tunic was stained with blood, except under his swordbelt, where it remained white. The flag was officially adopted in 1918.

Geography

The Republic of Austria is a landlocked country in the heart of Europe. About three-quarters of the land is mountainous, and tourism and winter sports are major activities in this scenic country. Northern Austria contains the valley of the River Danube, which rises in Germany and flows to the Black Sea, and the Vienna Basin. This is Austria's main farming region.

Southern Austria contains ranges of the Alps, which rise to their highest point at Grossglockner, at 3,797 m [12,457 ft] above sea level.

Climate

The climate of Austria is influenced both by westerly and easterly winds. The moist westerly winds bring rain and snow. They also moderate the temperatures. However, dry easterly winds bring very cold weather during the winter, and hot weather during the summer.

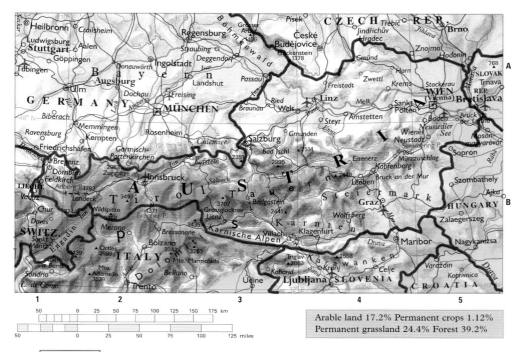

Arable land 17.2% Permanent crops 1.12%
Permanent grassland 24.4% Forest 39.2%

AUSTRIA (VIENNA)

Western Alpine regions have an Atlantic-type climate, while eastern lowlands are continental. The airflow is mainly from the west, which has twice the rainfall of the east at over 1,000 mm [40 in]. Winters are cold, and on the mountains there are glaciers and permanent snow in great depths. In Vienna, the January temperature is below freezing and is around 20°C [68°F] in July. From June to August, it is wetter and warmer.

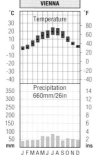

History

Following the collapse of the Roman Empire, of which Austria, south of the Danube formed a part, the area was invaded and settled by waves of Asian, Germanic and Slav peoples. In the late 8th century, Austria came under the rule of Charlemagne, but in the 10th century, the area was overrun by groups of Magyars.

In 955, the German king Otto I brought Austria under his rule, and in 962 it became part of what later became known as the Holy Roman Empire. German emperors ruled the area until 1806, when the Holy Roman Empire broke up. The Habsburg ruler of the Holy Roman Empire became Emperor Francis I of Austria. In 1867, Austria and Hungary set up the powerful dual monarchy of Austria-Hungary.

Austria-Hungary was allied to Germany in World War I, but the defeated empire collapsed in 1918. Austria's present boundaries derive from the Versailles Treaty which was signed in France in June 1919. In 1933, the Christian Socialist Chancellor Engelbert Dollfuss ended parliamentary democracy and ruled as a dictator. However, he was assassinated in 1934 because he opposed the Austrian Nazi Party's aim of uniting Austria and Germany.

The *Anschluss* (union with Germany) was achieved by the German invasion in March 1938. Austria became a province of the Third Reich called Ostmark until the defeat of the Axis powers in 1945.

Politics

After World War II, Austria was occupied by the Allies – Britain, France and the United States – and it paid reparations for a 10-year period. Finally, after agreeing to be permanently neutral, Austria became an independent federal republic in 1955.

Austria has been neutral since 1955 but, unlike Switzerland, it has not been frightened to take sides on certain issues. In 1994, two-thirds of the people voted in favour of joining the European Union and the country became a member on 1 January 1995. However, Austria became a centre of controversy in 1999, when the extreme right-wing Freedom Party, led by Jörg Haider, who had described Nazi Germany's employment policies as 'sound', came second in national elections to the ruling Social Democratic Party. In February 2000, a coalition government was formed consisting of equal numbers of ministers from the conservative People's Party, which had come third in the elections, and the Freedom Party. However, the Freedom Party suffered a setback in 2001 when its vote fell in city elections in Vienna.

Economy

Austria is a prosperous country. It has plenty of hydroelectric power, some oil and gas, and reserves of lignite (brown coal). However, these do not meet the country's needs, and fossil fuels are imported.

The country's leading economic activity is manufacturing metals and metal products, including iron and steel, vehicles, machinery, machine tools and ships. Vienna is the main industrial centre, though factories are found throughout the country. Many factories contain craft industries, making such things as fine glassware, jewellery and porcelain.

Crops are grown on 18% of the land and another 24% is pasture. Dairy and livestock farming are the leading activities. Major crops include barley, potatoes, rye, sugar beet and wheat.

AREA	ETHNIC GROUPS
83,850 sq km	Austrian 93%, Croatian, Slovene
[32,374 sq mi]	**LANGUAGES**
POPULATION	German (official)
8,151,000	**RELIGIONS**
CAPITAL (POPULATION)	Roman Catholic 78%,
Vienna (Wien, 1,560,000)	Protestant 5%, Islam
GOVERNMENT	**CURRENCY**
Federal republic	Euro = 100 cents

AZERBAIJAN – SEE ARMENIA, PAGE 40; AZORES – SEE ATLANTIC OCEAN, PAGES 41–43; BAHAMAS – SEE CARIBBEAN SEA, PAGES 71–76; BAHRAIN – SEE GULF STATES, PAGES 113–114

Bangladesh adopted this flag in 1971, following the country's break from Pakistan. The green is said to represent the fertility of the land. The red disc is the sun of independence. It commemorates the blood shed during the struggle for freedom.

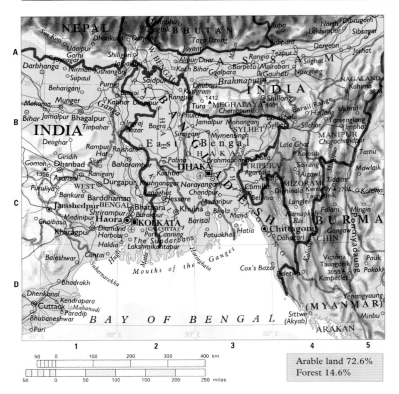

1	2	3	4	5

50 0 100 200 300 400 km

50 0 50 100 150 200 250 miles

Arable land 72.6%
Forest 14.6%

Geography

The People's Republic of Bangladesh is one of the world's most densely populated countries. Apart from the hilly regions in the far north-east and south-east, most of the land is flat and covered by fertile alluvium spread over the land by the Ganges, Brahmaputra and Meghna rivers. These rivers overflow when they are swollen by the annual monsoon rains. Floods also occur along the coast, 575 km [357 mi] long, when tropical cyclones (the name for hurricanes in this region) drive seawater inland. These periodic storms cause great human suffering. The world's most devastating tropical cyclone ever recorded occurred in Bangladesh in 1970, when an estimated 1 million people were killed.

Climate

Bangladesh has a tropical monsoon climate. Dry northerly winds blow during the winter, but, in summer, moist winds from the south bring monsoon rains. Heavy monsoon rains cause floods and in 1998, around two-thirds of the entire country was submerged, causing extensive damage.

BANGLADESH (DHAKA)

The Ganges delta has a monsoon climate. From June to September winds blow from the south over the Bay of Bengal, bringing heavy rain, over 240 mm [10 in] per month. On occasions, winds are so strong they pile seawater up against the outflowing river, bringing flood devastation. April is the hottest month and temperatures remain high through the monsoon season, though with little sunshine. January is the coldest month.

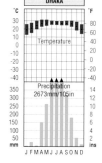

Vegetation

Most of Bangladesh is cultivated, but forests cover about 16% of the land. They include bamboo forests in the north-east and mangrove forests in the swampy Sundarbans region in the south-west, which is a sanctuary for the Royal Bengal tiger.

History

For 300 years after the mid-8th century AD, Buddhist rulers governed eastern Bengal, the area that now makes up Bangladesh. In the 13th century, Muslims from the north extended their rule into Bengal and, in 1576, the area became part of the Muslim Mughal Empire which was ruled by the emperor Akbar. This empire, which also included India, Pakistan and Afghanistan, began to break up in the early 18th century. Europeans, who had first made contact with the area in the 16th century, began to gain influence.

The East India Company, chartered by the English government in 1600 to develop trade in Asia, became the leading trade power in Bengal by the mid-18th century. In 1757, following the defeat of the nawab of Bengal in the Battle of Plessey, the East India Company effectively ruled Bengal. Discontent with the company led to the Sepoy Rebellion in 1857. In 1958, the British government took over the East India Company and its territory became known as British India.

Politics

In 1947, British India was partitioned between the mainly Hindu India and the Muslim Pakistan. Pakistan consisted of two parts, West and East Pakistan, which were separated by about 1,600 km [1,000 mi] of Indian territory. Differences developed between West and East Pakistan, since people in the east felt themselves victims of ethnic and economic discrimination by the Urdu- and Punjabi-speaking peoples of the west. In 1971, resentment turned to war when Bengali irregulars, aided by Indian troops, established the independent nation of 'Free Bengal', with Sheikh Mujibur Rahman as head of state. The Sheikh's assassination in 1975 – in one of the four military coups in the first 11 years of independence – led finally to a takeover by General Zia Rahman, who created an Islamic state before he, too, was assassinated in 1981. General Ershad took over in a coup in 1982. He resigned as army chief in 1986 to become a civilian president.

By 1990, protests from supporters of his two predecessors toppled Ershad from power and, after the first free parliamentary elections since independence, a coalition government was formed in 1991. Many problems arose in the 1990s, including the increasing strength of Muslim fundamentalism and the consequences of cyclone damage. In 1996, Sheikh Hasina Wajed of the Awami League became prime minister, but, in 1999, she was defeated by Khaleda Zia, leader of the Nationalist Party.

Economy

Bangladesh is one of the world's poorest countries. Its economy depends mainly on agriculture, which employs more than half of the people. Rice is the chief crop and Bangladesh is the world's fourth largest producer.

Other important crops include jute, sugar cane, tobacco and wheat. Jute processing is the leading manufacturing industry and jute is the leading export. Other manufactures include leather, paper and textiles. Some 60% of the internal trade is carried by boat.

AREA	ETHNIC GROUPS
144,000 sq km	Bengali 98%, tribal groups
[55,598 sq mi]	**LANGUAGES**
POPULATION	Bengali and English
131,270,000	(both official)
CAPITAL (POPULATION)	**RELIGIONS**
Dhaka	Islam 83%,
(7,832,000)	Hinduism 16%
GOVERNMENT	**CURRENCY**
Multiparty republic	Taka = 100 paisas

BARBADOS – SEE CARIBBEAN SEA, PAGES 71–76

BELARUS

In September 1991, Belarus adopted a red and white flag, replacing the flag used in the Soviet era. In June 1995, following a referendum in which Belarussians voted to improve relations with Russia, it was replaced with a design similar to the old flag, but without the hammer and sickle.

Geography

The Republic of Belarus, or Belorussia as it is also known, is a landlocked country in Eastern Europe. It was formerly part of the Soviet Union. The land is low-lying and mostly flat. In the south, much of the land is marshy. This area contains Europe's largest marsh and peat bog, the Pripet Marshes. A hilly region extends from north-east to south-west and includes the highest point in Belarus, situated near the capital Minsk. This hill reaches a height of 342 m [1,122 ft] above sea level. Over 1,000 lakes, mostly small, dot the land-scape. Forests cover large areas. Belarus and Poland jointly control a remnant of virgin forest, which contains a herd of rare wisent (European bison). This is the Belovezha Forest, which is known as the Bialowieza Forest in Poland.

Climate

The climate of Belarus is affected by both the moderating influence of the Baltic Sea and continental conditions to the east. The winters are cold and the summers warm.

History

Slavic people settled in what is now Belarus about 1,500 years ago. In the 9th century, the area became part of the first East Slavic state, Kievan Rus, which became a major European power in the 10th and 11th centuries. But, in the 13th century, Mongol invaders captured the eastern part of Kievan

Arable land 29.8% Permanent crops 0.67%
Permanent grassland 14.1% Forest 33.7%

Rus, while Germanic tribes threatened from the west. Belarus allied itself with Lithuania, which also became a powerful state. In 1386, the Lithuanian Grand Duke married the queen of Poland and Lithuanian-Polish kings ruled both countries until 1569, when Lithuania with Belarus merged with Poland. In the 18th century, Russia took most of eastern Poland, including Belarus. Yet the people of Belarus continued to maintain their individuality.

Following the Russian Revolution of 1917, a Communist govern-ment replaced tsarist rule in Russia, and, in March 1918, Belarus became an independent, non-Communist republic. However, later that year, Russian Communists invaded Belarus, which they renamed Byelorussia, a name derived from the Russian words *Belaya Rus*, or White Russia. They established a Communist government there in 1919, and, in 1922, the country became a founder republic of the Soviet Union. In 1939, Russia occupied what is now western Belarus, which had been part of Poland since 1919. Nazi troops occu-pied the area between 1941 and 1944, during which one in four of the population died. In 1945, Byelorussia became a founding member of the United Nations.

Politics

In 1990, the Byelorussian parliament declared that its laws took precedence over those of the Soviet Union. On 25 August 1991, many observers were very surprised that this most conservative and Communist-dominated of parliaments declared its independence. This quiet state of the Soviet Union played a supporting role in its decon-struction and the creation of the Commonwealth of Independent States (CIS). In September 1991, the republic changed its name back from the Russian form of Byelorussia to Belarus, its Belorussian form.

The Communists retained control in Belarus after independence. A new constitution introduced in 1994 led to presidential elections that brought Alyaksandr Lukashenka to power. This enabled economic reform to get under way, though the country remained pro-Russian. Lukashenka favoured a union with Russia and, in 1999, signed a union treaty committing the countries to setting up a confederal state. However, Russia insisted that a referendum would have to take place before any merger takes place. In 2001, Lukashenka was re-elected president amid accusations of electoral fraud.

Economy

The World Bank classifies Belarus as an 'upper-middle-income' econ-omy. Like other former republics of the Soviet Union, it faces many problems in turning from Communism to a free-market economy.

Under Communist rule, many manufacturing industries were set up, making such things as chemicals, trucks and tractors, machine tools and textiles. Farming is important and major products include barley, eggs, flax, meat, potatoes and other vegetables, rye and sugar beet. Leading exports include machinery and transport equipment, chemicals and food products.

AREA	Russian 11%, Polish,
207,600 sq km [80,154 sq mi]	Ukrainian
POPULATION	**LANGUAGES**
10,350,000	Belarussian and Russian
CAPITAL (POPULATION)	(both official)
Minsk (1,717,000)	**RELIGIONS**
GOVERNMENT	Eastern Orthodox 80%,
Multiparty republic	other 20%
ETHNIC GROUPS	**CURRENCY**
Belarussian 81%,	Belarussian rouble = 100 kopecks

Belgium's national flag was adopted in 1830, when the country won its independence from the Netherlands. The colours came from the arms of the province of Brabant, in central Belgium, which rebelled against Austrian rule in 1787.

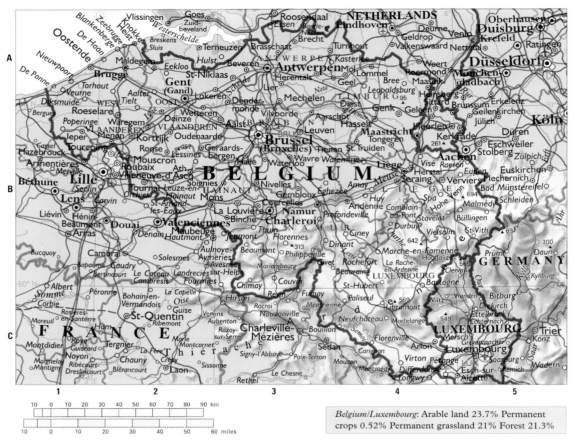

Belgium/Luxembourg: Arable land 23.7% Permanent crops 0.52% Permanent grassland 21% Forest 21.3%

Geography

The Kingdom of Belgium is a densely populated country situated in western Europe. Behind the coastline on the North Sea, which is 63 km [39 mi] long, lie its coastal plains. Some low-lying areas, called polders, are protected from the sea by dykes (or sea walls).

Central Belgium consists of low plateaux and the only highland region is the Ardennes in the south-east. The Ardennes, reaching a height of 694 m [2,277 ft], consists largely of moorland, peat bogs and woodland. The country's chief rivers are the Schelde, which flows through Tournai, Gent (or Ghent) and Antwerp in the west, and the Sambre and the Meuse, which flow between the central plateau and the Ardennes.

Climate

The moderating effects of the sea give much of Belgium a temperate climate, with mild winters and cool summers. Moist winds from the Atlantic Ocean bring significant amounts of rainfall throughout the year, especially in the Ardennes. During January and February, much snow falls in the Ardennes, where temperatures are more extreme than in the rest of the country. Brussels has mild winters and warm summers. The highland regions are much cooler.

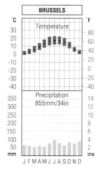

BELGIUM (BRUSSELS)

Belgium has a cool, temperate, maritime climate with weather systems moving eastwards from the Atlantic. Rainfall is heavy in the higher Ardennes plateau with snow from January to February. At Brussels, no month has a mean temperature below freezing and summer is warm. Temperatures over 30°C [86°F] have been recorded from May to September. Temperatures are lower at all seasons in the higher land to the south of the country.

History

Due to its strategic and stormy position, Belgium has often been called the 'cockpit of Europe'. In the Middle Ages, the area was split into small states, but, with the Netherlands and Luxembourg, it was united and made prosperous by the dukes of Burgundy in the 14th and 15th centuries. Later, at various times, Belgium, came under Austrian, Spanish and French rule.

From 1815, following the Napoleonic Wars, Belgium and the Netherlands were united as the 'Low Countries' but, in 1830, a National Congress proclaimed independence from the Dutch. In 1831, Prince Leopold of Saxe-Coburg became Belgium's king.

The division between Belgium and the Netherlands rested on history rather than geography. Belgium was a mainly Roman Catholic country while the Netherlands was mainly Protestant. Both were neutral in foreign policy, but both were occupied by the Nazis from 1940 until September 1944.

After World War II, Belgium achieved rapid economic progress, first through collaboration with the Netherlands and Luxembourg, which formed a customs union called Benelux, and later as a founder member of what is now the European Union. In 1960, Belgium granted independence to the Belgian Congo (now the Democratic Republic of the Congo) and, in 1962, its supervision of Ruanda-Urundi (now Rwanda and Burundi) was ended.

Politics

Belgium has always been an uneasy marriage of two peoples: the majority Flemings, who speak a language closely related to Dutch, and the Walloons, who speak French. The dividing line between the two communities runs east–west, just south of Brussels, although the capital is officially bilingual.

Since the inception of the country, the Flemings have caught up and overtaken the Walloons in cultural influence as well as in numbers. In 1971, the constitution was revised and three economic regions were established: Flanders (Vlaanderen), Wallonia (Wallonie) and Brussels, all shown on the administrative map on page 53. However, tensions remained. In 1993, Belgium adopted a federal system of government , with each of the three regions being granted its own regional assembly. Further changes in 2001 gave the regions greater tax-raising powers, plus responsibility for agriculture and the promotion of trade. Elections under this system were held in 1995 and 1999. Since 1995, the Chamber of Deputies has had 150 members, and the Senate 71. The regional assembly of Flanders had 118 deputies, while the assemblies of Brussels and Wallonia had 75 each.

Economy

Belgium is a major trading nation, with a highly developed economy. It imports most of the materials it needs for manufacturing, because it lacks minerals, except for coal. The textile industry, which has existed since medieval times in the towns of Flanders, Gent and Bruges, remains important. The steel industry, which was once situated in the Sambre-Meuse Valley, contained the main coalfield, but newer plants lie near the coast in Flanders. Chemicals, chemical products and processed foods are other leading manufactures.

Agriculture employs only 2.5% of the workforce, as compared with 24% in industry, but intensive farming methods produce most of the food needed by the country. Barley and wheat are the chief crops, followed by flax, hops, potatoes and sugar beet. However, the most valuable activities are dairy farming and livestock production.

AREA	ETHNIC GROUPS
30,150 sq km	Belgian 91% (Fleming 58%,
[11,780 sq mi]	Walloon 31%), other 11%
POPULATION	**LANGUAGES**
10,259,000	Dutch, French,
CAPITAL (POPULATION)	German (all official)
Brussels (Brussel or	**RELIGIONS**
Bruxelles, 948,000)	Roman Catholic 75%,
GOVERNMENT	other 25%
Federal constitutional	**CURRENCY**
monarchy	Euro = 100 cents

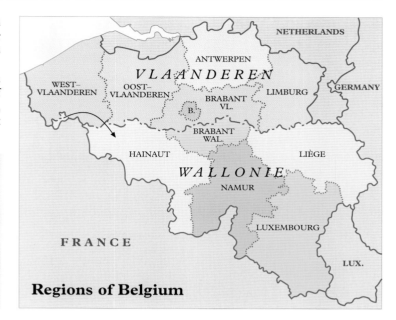

Regions of Belgium

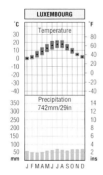

LUXEMBOURG

Geography

The Grand Duchy of Luxembourg is one of the smallest and oldest countries in Europe. The north belongs to an upland region which includes the Ardennes in Belgium and Luxembourg, and the Eiffel Highlands in Germany. This scenic region contains the country's highest point, a hill in the north which reaches 565 m [1,854 ft] above sea level. The southern two-thirds of Belgium, which is geographically part of French Lorraine, is a hilly or rolling plateau called the Bon Pays or Gut Land ('Good Land'). This region contains rich farmland, especially in the fertile Alzette, Moselle and Sûre (or Sauer) river valleys in the south and east.

Climate

Luxembourg experiences a temperate climate. The south of the country has warm summers and autumns, when grapes ripen in sheltered south-eastern valleys. Winters are sometimes severe, particularly in the Ardenne region, where snow can cover the land for some weeks.

LUXEMBOURG (LUXEMBOURG)

Luxembourg receives a reasonable amount of rain, sometimes snow, falling evenly throughout the year on about 200 days. The total is greater on the higher lands in the north. January is the coldest month with an average at freezing-point. The daytime temperatures exceed 20°C [68°F] from June to August. While the highest recorded temperature is 37°C [99°F], the lowest has reached –20°C [–4°F] on a number of occasions.

LUXEMBOURG	
Temperature	
Precipitation	
742mm/29in	

Vegetation

Forests cover about a fifth of Luxembourg, mainly in the north, where deer and wild boar are found. Farms cover about 25% of the land and pasture covers another 20%.

History

Luxembourg became an independent state in AD 963 and a duchy in 1354. In the 1440s, Luxembourg came under the House of Burgundy and, in the early 16th century, under the rule of the Habsburgs. From 1684, it came successively under France (1684–97), Spain (1697–1714) and Austria until 1795, when it reverted to French rule. In 1815, following the defeat of France, Luxembourg became a Grand Duchy under the Netherlands. This was because the Grand Duke

was also the king of the Netherlands. In 1890, when Wilhelmina became queen of the Netherlands, Luxembourg broke away because its laws did not permit a woman to rule. The Grand Duchy then passed to Adolphus, Duke of Nassau-Weilburg. But, in 1912, Luxembourg's laws were changed to allow Marie Adélaïde of Nassau to become the ruling grand duchess. Her sister Charlotte succeeded in 1919, but she abdicated in 1964 in favour of her son, Jean. In 2000, Grand Duke Jean handed over the role as head of state to his son, Prince Henri.

Germany occupied Luxembourg in World Wars I and II. In 1944–5, northern Luxembourg was the scene of the Battle of the Bulge. Following World War II, the economy recovered rapidly.

Politics

In 1948, Luxembourg joined Belgium and the Netherlands in a union called Benelux and, in the 1950s, it was one of the six founders of what is now the European Union. The country's capital, which is a major financial centre, contains the headquarters of several international agencies, including the European Coal and Steel Community and the European Court of Justice.

Economy

Luxembourg has iron-ore reserves and is a major steel producer. It also has many high-technology industries, producing electronic goods and computers. Steel and other manufactures, including chemicals, glass and rubber products, are exported. Other activities include tourism and financial services. Half the land area is farmed, but agriculture employs only 3% of workers. Crops include barley, fruits, oats, potatoes and wheat. Cattle, sheep, pigs and poultry are reared.

AREA	ETHNIC GROUPS
2,590 sq km	Luxembourger 71%,
[1,000 sq mi]	Portuguese 10%, Italian 5%,
POPULATION	French 3%, Belgian 3%
443,000	**LANGUAGES**
CAPITAL (POPULATION)	Luxembourgish (official),
Luxembourg	French, German
(76,000)	**RELIGIONS**
GOVERNMENT	Roman Catholic 95%
Constitutional monarchy	**CURRENCY**
(Grand Duchy)	Euro = 100 cents

BELIZE – SEE GUATEMALA, PAGE 110

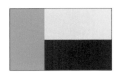

The colours on this flag, used by Africa's oldest independent nation, Ethiopia, symbolize African unity. Benin adopted this flag after independence in 1960. A flag with a red (Communist) star replaced it between 1975 and 1990, after which Benin dropped its Communist policies.

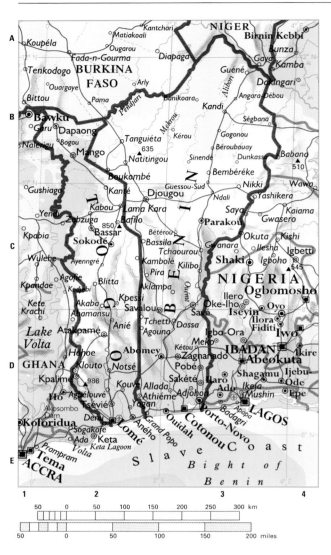

Geography and Climate

The Republic of Benin is one of Africa's smallest countries. It extends north–south for about 620 km [390 mi]. Lagoons line the short coastline, and the country has no natural harbours.

Benin has a hot, wet climate. The average annual temperature on the coast is about 25°C [77°F], and the average rainfall is about 1,330 mm [52 in]. The inland plains are wetter than the coast.

History and Politics

The ancient kingdom of Dahomey had its capital at Abomey. In the 17th century, the kings of Dahomey became involved in supplying slaves to European slave traders, including the Portuguese who shipped many Dahomeans to the Americas, particularly to Portugal's huge territory of Brazil.

After slavery was ended in the 19th century, the French began to gain influence in the area. Benin became self-governing in 1958 and fully independent in 1960. After much instability and many changes of government, a military group took over in 1972. The country, renamed Benin in 1975, became a one-party socialist state. Socialism was abandoned in 1989, and multiparty presidential elections were held in 1991, 1996 and 2001.

Economy

Benin is a poor developing country. Agriculture employs more than half of the people, though many live at subsistence level, making little contribution to the economy. Benin produces some petroleum, but industry is on a small scale. The main exports include cotton, crude petroleum, palm oil and palm kernels. Cocoa, coffee, groundnuts (peanuts), tobacco and shea nuts are also grown for export.

AREA	**ETHNIC GROUPS**
112,620 sq km	Fon, Adja, Bariba, Yoruba, Fulani
[43,483 sq mi]	**LANGUAGES**
POPULATION	French (official), Fon, Adja, Yoruba
6,591,000	**RELIGIONS**
CAPITAL (POPULATION)	Traditional beliefs 50%,
Porto-Novo (179,000)	Christianity 30%, Islam 20%
GOVERNMENT	**CURRENCY**
Multiparty republic	CFA franc = 100 centimes

TOGO

Geography and Climate

The Republic of Togo is a long, narrow country in West Africa. From north to south, it extends about 500 km [311 mi]. Its coastline on the Gulf of Guinea is only 64 km [40 mi] long, and it is only 145 km [90 mi] at its widest point.

Togo has year-round high temperatures. The main wet season runs from March to July, with a minor wet season in October and November.

History and Politics

Togo became a German protectorate in 1884. In 1919, Britain took over the western third of Togo, while France took over the eastern two-thirds. In 1956, the people of British Togoland voted to join Ghana, while French Togoland became an independent republic in 1960.

A military regime took power in 1963, and in 1967 General Gnassingbé Eyadéma became head of the government and suspended the constitution. A new constitution was adopted in 1992 and multi-party elections were held in 1994. However, in 1998, paramilitary police prevented the completion of the count in presidential elections when it became clear that Eyadéma had been defeated. Eyadéma continued in office and the main opposition parties boycotted the general elections in 1999.

Economy

Togo is a poor developing country. Farming employs 65% of the people, but most farmers grow little more than they need to feed their families. Major food crops include cassava, maize, millet and yams. The chief export crops are cocoa, coffee and cotton. But the leading export is phosphate rock, which is used to make fertilizers. Togo's small-scale manufacturing and mining industries employ about 6% of the people.

AREA	Tem-Kabre 26%,
56,790 sq km [21,927 sq mi]	Gurma 16%
POPULATION	**LANGUAGES**
5,153,000	French (official), Ewe,
CAPITAL (POPULATION)	Kabiye
Lomé (590,000)	**RELIGIONS**
GOVERNMENT	Traditional beliefs 50%,
Multiparty republic	Christianity 35%, Islam 15%
ETHNIC GROUPS	**CURRENCY**
Ewe-Adja 43%,	CFA franc = 100 centimes

BERMUDA – SEE ATLANTIC OCEAN, PAGES 41–43;
BHUTAN – SEE NEPAL, PAGE 164

BOLIVIA

This flag, which has been Bolivia's national and merchant flag since 1888, dates back to 1825 when Bolivia became independent. The red stands for Bolivia's animals and the courage of the army, the yellow for its mineral resources, and the green for its agricultural wealth.

Geography

The Republic of Bolivia is a landlocked country in central South America. The Andes in the west rise to a height of 6,542 m [21,463 ft] at Nevado Sajama. To the east lies the Altiplano, a high plateau that contains part of Lake Titicaca in the north and Lake Poopó in the south, while to the east lies the majestic Cordillera Real. More than half of all Bolivians live on the Altiplano. Eastern Bolivia is a vast lowland plain, drained by the headwaters of the River Madeira. The south-east is semi-arid, the centre is tropical savanna, while the north-east is forested.

Climate

The Bolivian climate is greatly affected by altitude, with the Andean peaks permanently snow-covered, while the eastern plains remain hot and humid.

BOLIVIA (LA PAZ)

Although within the tropics, La Paz lies at 3,625 m [11,893 ft] on the Bolivian plateau where altitude affects temperatures. The annual range is small (1°C [2°F]), but temperatures rise rapidly by day and fall sharply at night; the diurnal range is very large (10–15°C [18–27°F]), with frequent night frosts in winter. Rainfall, often thundery, occurs mainly in the summer. From April to October, rain falls on less than 10 days per month.

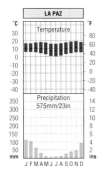

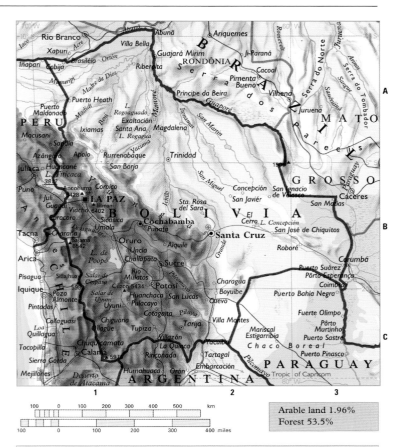

Arable land 1.96%
Forest 53.5%

History

American Indians have lived in Bolivia for at least 10,000 years. The main groups today are the Aymara and Quechua people.

When Spanish soldiers arrived in the early 16th century, Bolivia was part of the Inca empire. Following the defeat of the Incas, Spain ruled from 1532 to 1825, when Antonio José de Sucre, one of revolutionary leader Simón Bolívar's generals, defeated the Spaniards. Since independence, Bolivia has lost much territory to its neighbours. In 1932, Bolivia fought with Paraguay for control of the Gran Chaco region. Bolivia lost and most of this area passed to Paraguay in 1938.

Politics

Following the Chaco War, Bolivia entered a long period of instability. It had ten presidents, six of whom were members of the military, between 1936 and 1952, when the Revolutionary Movement replaced the military. The new government launched a series of reforms, which included the break-up of large estates and the granting of land to Amerindian farmers. Another military uprising occurred in 1964, heralding another period of instability. Elections were held in 1980, but the military again intervened until 1982, when civilian government was restored. Presidential elections were held in 1989, 1993 and 1997, when General Hugo Bánzer Suárez, who had ruled the country as a dictator in the 1970s, became president. Since the 1980s, Bolivia has followed free-enterprise policies, including privatization of formerly government-owned enterprises.

Economy

Bolivia is one of the poorest countries in South America. It has several natural resources, including tin, silver and natural gas, but the chief activity is agriculture, which employs 47% of the people. Potatoes, wheat and a grain called *quinoa* are important crops on the Altiplano, while bananas, cocoa, coffee and maize are grown at the lower, warmer levels. Manufacturing is small-scale and the main exports are mineral ores and fossil fuels. By the early 2000s, oil and natural gas had begun to replace coca, which is used to make cocaine, as the main export. The government is seeking to stamp out this illegal trade.

The Altiplano

A high, rolling plateau 3,600 m [12,000 ft] above sea level on the Peruvian border of Bolivia, the Altiplano stretches 400 km [250 mi] north to south between the eastern and western cordilleras of the Andes. Surrounded by high, snow-capped peaks, at its north end lies Lake Titicaca, the highest navigable body of water in the world. To the south are smaller lakes, and an extensive salt flat. Though tropical in latitude, the Altiplano is cold and bleak, yet over half the population of Bolivia, including many native Indians, make it their home.

The natural vegetation of the Altiplano is grassland with low trees and shrubs, merging at high levels to the harsh scrubland of the *puna*, the name for the higher and bleaker parts of the Altiplano. Summer rains and winter snows supply enough moisture to support pasture, and herds of llama and alpaca are raised as pack animals, while also providing meat and wool for peasant farmers. The northern part of the Altiplano contains various urban centres, such as Puno and Juliaca in the Lake Titicaca basin, and La Paz, which lies in a chasm that cuts the floor of the Altiplano. The arid conditions in the southern part of the Altiplano are hostile to human settlement, though the area is rich in minerals.

AREA
1,098,580 sq km [424,162 sq mi]
POPULATION
8,300,000
CAPITAL (POPULATION)
La Paz (1,126,000)
GOVERNMENT
Multiparty republic
ETHNIC GROUPS
Mestizo 30%,
Quechua 30%,
Aymara 25%,
White 15%
LANGUAGES
Spanish, Aymara,
Quechua (all official)
RELIGIONS
Roman Catholic 95%
CURRENCY
Boliviano = 100 centavos

Bosnia-Herzegovina adopted a new flag in 1998, because the previous flag was thought to be synonymous with the wartime Muslim regime. The blue background and white stars represent the country's links with the EU, and the triangle stands for the three ethnic groups in the country.

Arable land 11.8% Permanent crops 3.92% Forest 39.2%

Geography

The Republic of Bosnia-Herzegovina is one of the five republics to emerge from the former Federal People's Republic of Yugoslavia. Much of the country is mountainous or hilly, with an arid limestone plateau in the south-west. The River Sava, which forms most of the northern border with Croatia, is a tributary of the River Danube. Because of the country's odd shape, the coastline is limited to a short stretch of 20 km [13 mi] on the Adriatic coast.

Climate

A Mediterranean climate, with dry, sunny summers and moist, mild winters, prevails only near the coast. Inland, the weather becomes more severe, with hot, dry summers and bitterly cold, snowy winters. The north experiences the most severe weather.

History

Slavs settled in the area that is now Bosnia-Herzegovina around 1,400 years ago. In the late 15th century, the area was taken by the Ottoman Turks. In 1878, the dual monarchy of Austria-Hungary gained temporary control over Bosnia-Herzegovina and it formally took over the area in 1908. The assassination of Archduke Francis Ferdinand of Austria-Hungary in Sarajevo, in June 1914, was the catalyst that led to the start of World War I. In 1918, Bosnia-Herzegovina became part of the Kingdom of the Serbs, Croats and Slovenes, which was renamed Yugoslavia in 1929. Germany occupied Yugoslavia during World War II, and Bosnia-Herzegovina came under the control of a puppet regime in Croatia. A Communist government took over in Yugoslavia in 1945, and a new constitution in 1946 made the country a federal state, with Bosnia-Herzegovina as one of its six constituent republics.

Under Communist rule, Bosnia-Herzegovina was a potentially ex-plosive area because of its mixture of people, including Bosnian Muslims, Orthodox Christian Serbs and Roman Catholic Croats, as well as Albanian, gypsy and Ukrainian minorities. The ethnic and religious differences started to exert themselves after the death of Yugoslavia's president Josip Broz Tito in 1980, and the increasing indications that Communist economic policies were not working.

Politics

Free elections were held in 1990 and non-Communists won a majority, with a Muslim, Alija Izetbegovic, as president. In 1991, Croatia and Slovenia declared themselves independent republics and seceded from Yugoslavia. Bosnia-Herzegovina held a referendum on independence in 1992. While most Bosnian Serbs boycotted the vote, the Muslims and Croats voted in favour and Bosnia-Herzegovina proclaimed its independence. War then broke out.

At first, the Muslim-dominated government allied itself uneasily with the Croat minority, but it was at once under attack by local Serbs, supported by their co-nationals from beyond Bosnia-Herzegovina's borders. In their 'ethnic cleansing' campaign, heavily equipped Serb militias drove poorly-armed Muslims from towns they had long inhabited. By early 1993, the Muslims controlled less than a third of the former federal republic, and even the capital, Sarajevo, became disputed territory, with constant shelling.

The Muslim-Croat alliance rapidly disintegrated and refugees approached the million mark. Tougher economic sanctions on Serbia in April 1993 had little effect on the war in Bosnia. A small United Nations force attempted to deliver relief supplies to civilians and maintain 'safe' Muslim areas to no avail.

Finally, in 1995, the warring parties agreed to a solution to the conflict – the Dayton Peace Accord. This involved dividing the country into two self-governing provinces, one Bosnian Serb and the other Muslim-Croat, under a central, unified, multi-ethnic government. Elections were held in 1996 and 1998 under this new arrangement.

Economy

The economy of Bosnia-Herzegovina, the least developed of the six republics of the former Yugoslavia, apart from Macedonia, was shattered by the war during the early 1990s. Before the war started, manufactures were the main exports, including electrical equipment, machinery and transport equipment, and textiles.

Farm products include fruits, maize, tobacco, vegetables and wheat, but the country has to import food.

AREA	Croat 17%
51,129 sq km [19,745 sq mi]	**LANGUAGES**
POPULATION	Serbo-Croatian
3,922,000	**RELIGIONS**
CAPITAL (POPULATION)	Islam 40%,
Sarajevo (526,000)	Serbian Orthodox 31%,
GOVERNMENT	Roman Catholic 15%,
Federal republic	Protestant 4%
ETHNIC GROUPS	**CURRENCY**
Bosnian 49%, Serb 31%,	Convertible mark = 100 paras

The black-and-white zebra stripe in the centre of Botswana's flag symbolizes racial harmony. The blue represents rainwater, because water supply is the most vital need in this dry country. This flag was adopted in 1966, when Botswana became independent from Britain.

Geography

The Republic of Botswana is a landlocked country which lies in the heart of southern Africa. The majority of the land is flat or gently rolling, with an average height of about 1,000 m [3,280 ft]. More hilly country lies in the east. The Kalahari, a semi-desert area covers much of Botswana.

Most of the south has no permanent streams. But large depressions occur in the north. In one, the Okavango River, which flows from Angola, forms a large delta, an area of swampland. Another depression contains the Makgadikgadi Salt Pans. During floods, the Botletle River drains from the Okavango Swamps into the Makgadikgadi Salt Pans.

Climate

Temperatures are high in the summer months (October to April), but the winter months are much cooler. In winter, night-time temperatures sometimes drop below freezing point. The average annual rainfall ranges from over 400 mm [16 in] in the east to less than 200 mm [8 in] in the south-west.

Gaborone, the capital of Botswana, lies in the wetter eastern part of the country, where most of the people live. The rainy season occurs during summer, between the months of November and March. Frosts sometimes occur in parts of the east when the temperature drops below freezing.

History

The earliest inhabitants of the region were the San, who are also called Bushmen. They had a nomadic way of life, hunting wild animals and collecting plant foods.

The Tswana, who speak a Bantu language, now form the majority of the population. They are cattle owners, who settled in eastern Botswana more than 1,000 years ago. Their arrival led the San to move into the Kalahari region. Today, the San form a tiny minority, most of whom live in permanent settlements and work on cattle ranches.

Politics

Britain ruled the area as the Bechuanaland Protectorate between 1885 and 1966. When the country became independent, it adopted the name of Botswana. Since then, unlike many African countries, Botswana has been a stable multiparty democracy.

Under its first president, Sir Seretse Khama, who died in 1980, and his successor, Sir Ketumile Masire, who served from 1980 until 1998, when he retired in favour of Festus Mogae, the economy was steadily diversified. Despite a severe drought, the economy expanded and the government introduced major social programmes. Tourism also grew as huge national parks and reserves were established. However, by the early 2000s, Botswana had the world's highest rate of HIV infection – around one in five of the population had the virus. The average life expectancy fell from 60 to 40 years.

Economy

In 1966, Botswana was one of Africa's poorest countries, depending on meat and live cattle for its exports. But the discovery of minerals, including coal, cobalt, copper and nickel, has helped to diversify the economy. The mining of diamonds at Orapa, starting in 1971, was the chief factor in transforming the economy. By 1997, Botswana had become the world's leading producer, overtaking Australia and the Democratic Republic of the Congo. By 1997, diamonds accounted for about 74% of Botswana's exports, followed by copper-nickel matte, textiles and meat products. Another major source of income comes from tourists, the majority of whom come from South Africa, which continues to have a great influence on Botswana.

The development of mining and tourism has reduced the relative importance of farming, though agriculture still employs about a fifth of the population. The most important type of farming is livestock raising, particularly cattle, which are mostly reared in the wetter east. Crops include beans, maize, millet, sorghum and vegetables. Industry is still on a small scale.

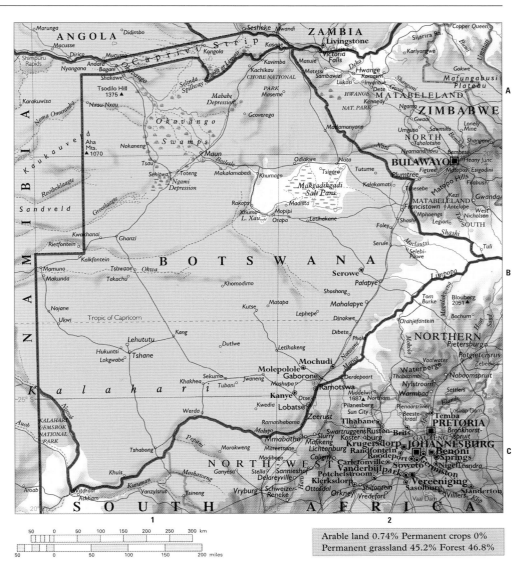

Arable land 0.74% Permanent crops 0%
Permanent grassland 45.2% Forest 46.8%

AREA	ETHNIC GROUPS
581,730 sq km	Tswana 75%, Shona 12%,
[224,606 sq mi]	San (Bushmen) 3%
POPULATION	**LANGUAGES**
1,586,000	English (official), Setswana
CAPITAL (POPULATION)	**RELIGIONS**
Gaborone	Traditional beliefs 50%,
(133,000)	Christianity 50%
GOVERNMENT	**CURRENCY**
Multiparty republic	Pula = 100 thebe

The green on the flag symbolizes Brazil's rainforests and the yellow diamond its mineral wealth. The blue sphere bears the motto 'Order and Progress'. The 27 stars, arranged in the pattern of the night sky over Rio de Janeiro, represent the states and the federal district.

| Arable land 5.11% Permanent crops 0.89% |
| Permanent grassland 21.9% Forest 57.7% |

Geography

The Federative Republic of Brazil is the world's fifth largest country. Structurally, it has two main regions. In the north is the vast Amazon basin, once an inland sea and now drained by a river system that carries one-fifth of the world's running water. The largest area of river plain is in the upper part of the basin, along the frontiers with Bolivia and Peru. Downstream, the flood plain is relatively narrow.

The Brazilian Highlands make up the country's second main region. It consists largely of hard crystalline rock dissected into rolling uplands.

It includes the heartland (Mato Grosso) and the whole western flank of the country from the bulge to the border with Uruguay. The undulating plateau of the northern highlands carries poor soils. The typical vegetation is thorny scrub which, in the south, merges into wooded savanna. Conditions are better in the south, where rainfall is more reliable. More than 60% of the country's population live in the four southern and south-eastern states, which are the most developed part of Brazil, though they account only for 17% of Brazil's total area.

Climate

Manaus has high temperatures all through the year. The rainfall is heavy, though the period from June to September is drier than the rest of the year. The capital, Brasília, and the city Rio de Janeiro also have tropical climates, with much more marked dry seasons than Manaus. The far south has a temperate climate. The north-eastern interior is the driest region, with an average annual rainfall of only 250 mm [10 in] in places. The rainfall is also unreliable and severe droughts are common in this region.

BRAZIL – BRASÍLIA

Brazil lies almost entirely within the tropics. The northern half of the country is dominated by the Amazon Basin and, excluding the highlands in the south-east, there are no mountains. Monthly temperatures are very high – over 25°C [77°F] – with very little annual variation. Brasília has only a 4°C [7°F] difference between July and October. The hottest part of the country is in the north-east. Frosts often occur in the eastern highlands and the extreme south.

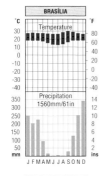

RIO DE JANEIRO

Rio de Janeiro experiences a high rainfall and a marked dry season from May to August – rain falls on only about 20 days from June to August – but not so marked as inland. Most of Brazil has moderate rainfall, but there are very heavy precipitation totals at the mouth and in the headwaters of the Amazon, and on the south-east coast below the highlands. There is an arid zone in the north-east. In Rio de Janeiro, the sun shines for 5–7 hours per day.

MANAUS

At Manaus, in the centre of the Amazon Basin, there is little difference between the temperature of the warmest month, October (29°C [84°F]), and the coolest, April (27°C [81°F]). Temperatures are not extremely high and the highest recorded was 37°C [99°F]; the lowest was 18°C [64°F]. Rainfall totals are high, especially December to March, with a distinct dry season from June to September, when rain falls, on average, only 5–10 days per month.

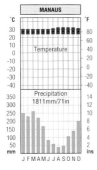

Vegetation

The Amazon basin contains the world's largest rainforests, which the Brazilians call the *selvas*. The forests contain an enormous variety of plant and animal species. But many species are threatened by loggers and others who want to exploit the forests. Forest destruction is also ruining the lives of the last surviving groups of Amazonian Indians.

Forests grow on the north-eastern coasts, but the dry interior has large areas of thorny scrub. The south-east contains fertile farmland and large ranches.

History

The Portuguese explorer Pedro Alvarez Cabral claimed Brazil for Portugal in 1500. While Spain was occupied in western South America, the first Portuguese colonists settled in the north-east in the 1530s. They were followed by other settlers, missionaries, explorers and prospectors who gradually penetrated the country during the 17th and 18th centuries. They encountered many groups of Amerindians, some of whom lived semi-nomadic lives, hunting, fishing and gathering fruits, while others lived in farming villages, growing cassava and other crops.

The Portuguese enslaved many Amerindians who were used for plantation work, while others were driven into the interior. The Portuguese also introduced about 4 million African slaves, notably in the sugar-cane-growing areas in the north-east. For many decades

---

Rio de Janeiro and São Paulo

Much of Brazil's population is concentrated in a small, highly developed 'corner' in the south-east of the country. Rio de Janeiro, discovered by the Portuguese in 1502, lies in a magnificent setting, stretching for 20 km [12 mi] along the coast between mountain and ocean. Though no longer the capital, it remains the focus of Brazil's cultural life, attracting visitors with the world's greatest pre-Lent festival at carnival time.

São Paulo, its early growth fuelled by the coffee boom of the late 19th century, is one of the most populous cities in the southern hemisphere. In both cities the gap between rich and poor is all too evident, the sprawling shanty towns (*favelas*) standing in sharp contrast to sophisticated metropolitan centres.

following the early settlements, Brazil was mainly a sugar-producing colony, with most plantations centred on the rich coastal plains of the north-east. These areas later produced cotton, cocoa, rice and other crops. In the south, colonists penetrated the interior in search of slaves and minerals, especially gold and diamonds. The city of Ouro Preto in Minas Gerais was built and Rio de Janeiro grew as a port for the area.

Initially little more than a group of rival provinces, Brazil began to unite in 1808, when the Portuguese royal court, seeking refuge from Napoleon's armies which had invaded Portugal in 1807, transferred from Lisbon to Rio de Janeiro. The eldest son of King Joas VI of Portugal was chosen as the 'Perpetual Defender' of Brazil by a national congress. In 1822, he proclaimed the independence of the country and was chosen as the constitutional emperor with the title of Pedro I. He became increasingly unpopular and was forced to abdicate in 1831. He was succeeded by his five-year-old son, Pedro II, who officially took office in 1841. Pedro's liberal policies included the gradual abolition of slavery (1888).

During the 19th century, São Paulo state became the centre of a huge coffee-growing industry. While the fortunes made in mining helped to develop Rio de Janeiro, profits from coffee were invested in the city of São Paulo. Immigrants from Italy and Germany settled in the south, introducing farming in the fertile valleys, in co-existence with the cattle ranchers and gauchos of the plains. The second half of the 19th century saw the development of the wild rubber industry in the Amazon basin, where the city of Manaus, with its world-famous opera house, served as a centre and market. Although Manaus lies 1,600 km [1,000 mi] from the mouth of the Amazon, rubber from the hinterland could be shipped out directly to world markets in ocean-going steamers. Brazil enjoyed a virtual monopoly of the rubber trade until the early 20th century, when Malaya began to compete, later with massive success.

The Amazon

Though not the world's longest river – 6,450 km [4,010 mi] – the Amazon is the mightiest, discharging 180,000 cu m/sec [6,350,000 cu ft/sec] into the Atlantic, more than four times the volume of its nearest rival, the Congo. The flow is so great that silt discolours the water up to 200 km [125 mi] out to sea.

The Amazon starts its journey in the Andes of Peru – only 150 km [95 mi] from the Pacific – at Lake Villafro, head of the Apurimac branch of the Ucayali, which then flows north to join the other main headstream, the Marañón. Navigable to ocean-going vessels of 6,600 tonnes up to the Peruvian jungle port of Iquitos, some 3,700 km [2,300 mi] from the sea, it then flows east – briefly forming the Peru-Colombian border – before entering Brazil. Here it becomes the Solimões, before joining the Negro (itself 18 km [11 mi] wide) at Manaus.

Along with more than 1,000 significant tributaries, seven of them more than 1,600 km [1,000 mi] long, the Amazon drains the largest river basin in the world – about 7 million sq km [2.7 million sq mi] – nearly two-fifths of South America and an area more than twice the size of India.

Regions of Brazil

Politics

A new constitution came into force in October 1988 – the eighth since Brazil became independent from Portugal in 1822. The constitution transferred powers from the president to the congress and paved the way for a return to democracy. In 1989, Fernando Collor de Mello was elected to cut inflation and combat corruption. But he made little progress and in 1992, with inflation soaring, his vice-president, Itamar Franco, took over as president. He served until 1994 when the Social Democrat Fernando Henrique Cardoso, a former finance minister, was elected president. Cardoso won a second term starting in 1999.

Today the country comprises 23 states, each with its own directly elected governor and legislature, three territories, and the Federal District of Brasília, which has been Brazil's capital since 1960. In 1991, Brazil, Argentina, Paraguay and Uruguay set up Mercosur, an alliance aimed at creating a free trade zone.

Economy

The United Nations has described Brazil as a 'Rapidly Industrializing Country', or RIC. Its total volume of production is one of the largest in the world. But many people, including poor farmers and residents of the *favelas* (city slums), do not share in the country's fast economic growth. Widespread poverty, together with high inflation and unemployment, cause political problems.

By the late 1990s, industry was the most valuable activity, employing about 20% of the people. Brazil is among the world's top producers of bauxite, chrome, diamonds, gold, iron ore, manganese and tin. It is also a major manufacturing country. Its products include aircraft, cars, chemicals, processed food, raw sugar, iron and steel, paper and textiles.

Brazil is one of the world's leading farming countries and agriculture employs 28% of the people. Coffee is a major export. Other leading products include bananas, citrus fruits, cocoa, maize, rice, soya beans and sugar cane. Brazil is also the top producer of eggs, meat and milk in South America.

Forestry is a major industry, though many people fear that the exploitation of the rainforests, with 1.5% to 4% of Brazil's forest being destroyed every year, is a disaster for the entire world.

Brazil's exports reflect its mixed economy. The leading items include iron and steel, non-electrical machinery and apparatus, mineral ores, motor vehicles, wood pulp, paper and paper products, coffee, sugar and confectionery, and aluminium and related products. Imports include machinery, chemicals and chemical products, and mineral fuels. Brazil's leading trading partners are the United States and Argentina.

A federal system was adopted for the United States of Brazil in the 1881 constitution and Brazil became a republic in 1889. Until 1930, the country experienced very strong economic expansion and prospered, but social unrest in 1930 resulted in a major revolt. From then on the country was under the control of President Getulio Vargas, who established a strong corporate state similar to that of fascist Italy, although Brazil entered World War II on the side of the Allies. Democracy, often corrupt, prevailed from 1956, 1964 and 1985. In between there were five military presidents of illiberal regimes.

The Amazon Rainforest

The world's largest and ecologically most important rainforest was still being destroyed at an alarming rate in the late 1990s, with somewhere between 1.5% and 4% disappearing each year in Brazil alone. Opening up the forest for many reasons – logging, mining, ranching, peasant resettlement – the Brazilian authorities did extremely little in real terms when confronted with a catalogue of indictments: decimation of a crucial world habitat; pollution of rivers; destruction of thousands of species of fauna and flora, especially medicinal plants; and the brutal ruination of the lives of the last remaining Amerindian tribes.

Once cut off from the rest of the world by impenetrable jungle, hundreds of thousands of Indians have been displaced in the provinces of Rondônia and Acre, principally by loggers and landless migrants, and in Para by mining, dams for HEP and ranching for beef cattle. It is estimated that five centuries ago the Amazon rainforest supported some 2 million Indians in more than 200 tribes; today the number has shrunk to a pitiful 50,000 or so, and many of the tribes have disappeared altogether.

A handful have been relatively lucky. The Yanomani, after huge international support, won their battle in 1991 for a reserve three times the size of Belgium – but for the majority of tribes a traditional lifestyle has vanished forever.

AREA	ETHNIC GROUPS
8,511,970 sq km	White 55%, Mulatto 38%,
[3,286,472 sq mi]	African American 6%, other 1%
POPULATION	**LANGUAGES**
174,469,000	Portuguese (official)
CAPITAL (POPULATION)	**RELIGIONS**
Brasília (2,051,000)	Roman Catholic 80%
GOVERNMENT	**CURRENCY**
Federal republic	Real = 100 centavos

BRUNEI – SEE MALAYSIA, PAGES 154–155

BULGARIA

This flag, first adopted in 1878, uses the colours associated with the Slav people. The national emblem, incorporating a lion – a symbol of Bulgaria since the 14th century – was first added to the flag in 1947. It is now added only for official government occasions.

Geography

The Republic of Bulgaria is a country in the Balkan Peninsula, facing the Black Sea in the east. There are two main lowland regions. The Danubian lowlands in the north consists of a plateau that descends to the Danube, which forms much of the boundary with Romania. The other lowland region is the warmer valley of the River Maritsa, where cotton, fruits, grains, rice, tobacco and vines are grown.

Separating the two lowland areas are the Balkan Mountains (Stara Planina), rising to heights of over 2,000 m [6,500 ft]. North of the capital Sofia (Sofiya), the Balkan Mountains contain rich mineral veins of iron and nonferrous metals. In south-facing valleys overlooking the Maritsa Plain, plums, tobacco and vines are grown. A feature of this area is Kazanluk, from which attar of roses is exported worldwide to the cosmetics industry. South and west of the Maritsa Valley are the Rhodope (or Rhodopi) Mountains, which contain lead, zinc and copper ores.

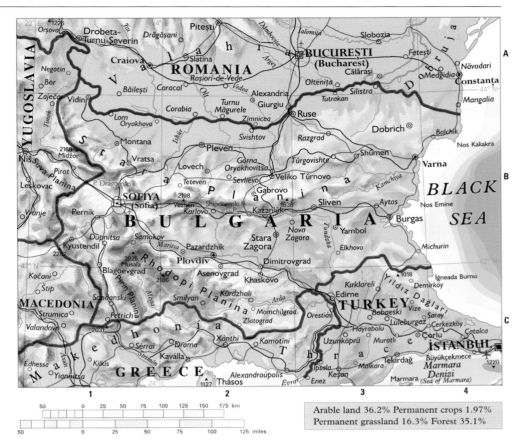

Arable land 36.2% Permanent crops 1.97%
Permanent grassland 16.3% Forest 35.1%

Climate

Summers are hot and winters are cold, but seldom severe. Rainfall is moderate all through the year.

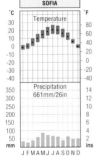

BULGARIA (SOFIA)

Bulgaria has hot summers, cold winters and moderate rainfall, with a summer maximum. This is changed by the influence of nearby seas and mountains. Eastern and southern lowlands have a much drier, warmer summer. Varna, on the coast, is usually 3–4°C [5–7°F] warmer than Sofia. The Danube lowlands are colder in winter with winds coming in from the continental interior. Temperatures are lower in the mountains.

History

Most of the Bulgarian people are descendants of Slavs and nomadic Bulgar tribes who arrived from the east in the 6th and 7th centuries. A powerful Bulgar kingdom was set up in 681, but the country became part of the Byzantine Empire in the 11th century.

Ottoman Turks ruled Bulgaria from 1396 and ethnic Turks still form a sizeable minority in the country. In 1879, Bulgaria became a monarchy, and in 1908 became fully independent. Bulgaria was an ally of Germany in World War I (1914–18) and again in World War II (1939–45). In 1944, Soviet troops invaded Bulgaria. After the war, the monarchy was abolished and the country became a Communist ally of the Soviet Union.

Politics

In the period after World War II, and especially under President Zhikov from 1954, Bulgaria became all too dependent on the Soviet Union. In 1990, the Communist Party held on to power under increasing pressure by ousting Zhikov, renouncing its leading role in the nation's affairs and changing its name to the Socialist Party, before winning the first free elections since the war, albeit unconvincingly and against confused opposition. With improved organization, the Union of Democratic Forces defeated the old guard in the following year

and began the unenviable task of making the transition to a free-market economy. Subsequent governments faced numerous problems, including inflation, food shortages, rising unemployment, strikes, a large foreign debt, a declining manufacturing industry, increased prices for raw materials, and a potential drop in the expanding tourist industry. In 2001, the former king, Siméon Saxe-Coburg-Gotha, who had left Bulgaria in 1948 when the monarchy was abolished, became prime minister after his coalition won victory in national elections.

Economy

According to the World Bank, Bulgaria in the 1990s was a 'lower-middle-income' developing country. Bulgaria has some deposits of minerals, including brown coal, manganese and iron ore. Manufacturing is the leading economic activity, though problems arose in the early 1990s, because much industrial technology was outdated. The main products are chemicals, processed foods, metal products, machinery and textiles. Manufactures are the leading exports. Bulgaria trades mainly with countries in Eastern Europe.

Wheat and maize are the chief crops of Bulgaria. Fruit, oilseeds, tobacco and vegetables are also important and these are grown in the south-facing valleys overlooking the Maritsa Plain. Livestock farming, particularly the rearing of dairy and beef cattle, sheep and pigs, is important.

AREA	Gypsy 3%, Macedonian,
110,910 sq km [42,822 sq mi]	Armenian, other
POPULATION	**LANGUAGES**
7,707,000	Bulgarian (official),
CAPITAL (POPULATION)	Turkish
Sofia (Sofiya, 1,139,000)	**RELIGIONS**
GOVERNMENT	Christianity (Eastern
Multiparty republic	Orthodox 87%), Islam 13%
ETHNIC GROUPS	**CURRENCY**
Bulgarian 83%, Turkish 8%,	Lev = 100 stotinki

BURKINA FASO

This flag was adopted in 1984, when Upper Volta was renamed Burkino Faso. The red, green and yellow colours used on this flag symbolize the desire for African unity. This is because they are used on the flag of Ethiopia, Africa's oldest independent country.

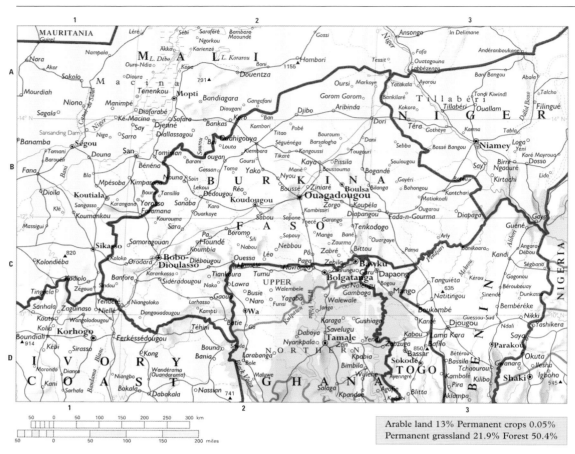

50 0 50 100 150 200 250 300 km	
50 0 50 100 150 200 miles	

Arable land 13% Permanent crops 0.05%
Permanent grassland 21.9% Forest 50.4%

Burkina Faso shares with Benin and Niger, and the Arly Park. A third wildlife area is the Po Park situated south of Ouagadougou.

History and Politics

The people of Burkina Faso are divided into two main groups. The Voltaic group includes the Mossi, who form the largest single group, and the Bobo. The other main group is the Mande family. Burkina Faso also contains some Fulani herders and Hausa traders, who are related to the people of northern Nigeria. In early times, the ethnic groups in Burkina Faso were divided into kingdoms and chiefdoms. The leading kingdom, which was ruled by an absolute monarch called the Moro Naba, was that of the Mossi. It has existed since the 13th century.

The French conquered the Mossi capital of Ouagadougou in 1897 and they made the area a protectorate. In 1919, the area became a French colony called Upper Volta.

After independence in 1960, Upper Volta became a one-party state. But it was unstable – military groups seized power several times and a number of political killings took place. In 1984, the country's name was changed to Burkina Faso. Elections were held in 1991. The victor, Captain Blaise Compaoré, the former military leader, was re-elected in 1998.

Economy

Burkina Faso is one of the world's 20 poorest countries and has become extremely dependent on foreign aid. Approximately 90% of the people earn their living by farming or by raising livestock. Grazing land covers around 37% of the land and farmland covers around 10%.

Most of Burkina Faso is dry with thin soils. The country's main food crops are beans, maize, millet, rice and sorghum. Cotton, groundnuts and shea nuts, whose seeds produce a fat used to make cooking oil and soap, are grown for sale abroad. Livestock are also an important export.

The country has few resources and manufacturing is on a small scale. There are some deposits of manganese, zinc, lead and nickel in the north of the country, but there is not yet a good enough transport route there. Many young men seek jobs abroad in Ghana and Ivory Coast. The money they send home to their families is important to the country's economy.

Geography and Climate

The Democratic People's Republic of Burkina Faso is a landlocked country, a little larger than the United Kingdom, in West Africa. But Burkina Faso has only one-sixth of the population of the UK.

Burkina Faso consists of a plateau, between about 300 m and 700 m [650–2,300 ft] above sea level. The plateau is cut by several rivers. Most of the rivers flow south into Ghana or east into the River Niger. During droughts, some of the rivers stop flowing, becoming marshes.

Burkina Faso has three main seasons. From October to February, it is relatively cool and dry. From March to April, it is hot and dry, while it is hot and humid from May to September.

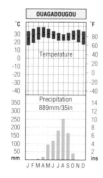

BURKINA FASO (OUAGADOUGOU)

The country's capital city, Ouagadougou, situated in central Burkina Faso, experiences uniformly high temperatures throughout the year. Most of the rain falls during the summer between May and September, but the rainfall is extremely erratic and droughts are common. The average annual rainfall in Ouagadougou is around 900 mm [35 in], with as much as 830 mm [33 in] falling from between May and September.

Vegetation

The northern part of the country is covered by savanna, consisting of grassland with stunted trees and shrubs. It is part of a region called the Sahel, where the land merges into the Sahara Desert. Overgrazing of the land and deforestation (that is, the chopping down of trees to clear land) are common problems here.

Woodlands border the rivers and parts of the south-east region are swampy. The south-east contains the 'W' National Park, which

AREA
274,200 sq km
[105,869 sq mi]
POPULATION
12,272,000
CAPITAL (POPULATION)
Ouagadougou
(690,000)
GOVERNMENT
Multiparty republic

ETHNIC GROUPS
Mossi 48%, Gurunsi, Senufo,
Lobi, Bobo, Mande, Fulani
LANGUAGES
French (official), Mossi, Fulani
RELIGIONS
Islam 50%, traditional beliefs
40%, Christianity 10%
CURRENCY
CFA franc = 100 centimes

BURMA (MYANMAR)

The colours on Burma's flag were adopted in 1948 when the country became independent from Britain. The socialist symbol, added in 1974, includes a ring of 14 stars representing the country's 14 states. The gearwheel represents industry and the rice plant symbolizes agriculture.

Geography and Climate

The Union of Burma is now alternatively known as the Union of Myanmar; its name was changed in 1989. Mountains border the country in the east and west, with the highest mountains in the north. Burma's highest mountain is Hkakabo Razi, which is 5,881 m [19,294 ft] high. Between these ranges is central Burma, which contains the fertile valleys of the Irrawaddy and Sittang rivers. The Irrawaddy delta on the Bay of Bengal is one of the world's leading rice-growing areas. Burma also includes the long Tenasserim coast in the south-east.

Burma has a tropical monsoon climate. There are three seasons. The rainy season runs from late May to mid-October. A cool, dry season follows, between late October and the middle part of February. The hot season lasts from late February to mid-May, though temperatures remain high during the humid rainy season.

History and Politics

Many groups settled in Burma in ancient times. Some, called the hill peoples, live in remote mountain areas where they have retained their own cultures. The ancestors of the country's main ethnic group today, the Burmese, arrived in the 9th century AD.

Britain conquered Burma during the 19th century and made the country a province of British India. In 1937, the British granted Burma limited self-government. Japan conquered Burma in 1942, but the Japanese were driven out in 1945. Burma became fully independent in 1948.

Revolts by Communists and various hill people led to instability in the 1950s. In 1962, Burma became a military dictatorship and, in 1974, a one-party state. Attempts to control minority liberation movements and the opium trade led to repressive rule. The National League for Democracy led by Aung San Suu Kyi won the elections in 1990, but the military ignored the result and continued their repressive rule. They earned Burma the reputation for having one of the world's worst records on human rights. Burma's internal political problems helped to make it one of the world's poorest countries. Its admission to ASEAN (Association of South-east Asian Nations) in 1997 may have implied regional recognition of the regime, but the European Union continued to voice its concern over human rights abuses.

Economy

Agriculture is the main activity, employing 64% of the people. The chief crop is rice. Groundnuts, maize, plantains, pulses, seed cotton, sesame seeds and sugar cane are other farm products. Forestry is important and teak is a major product. Fish and shellfish are also produced. Burma's varied natural resources are mostly underdeveloped, but the country is famous for its precious stones, especially rubies. The country also has sufficient oil and natural gas to meet most of its needs. Manufacturing is small-scale and mainly geared to supplying the home market. Major products include fertilizers, processed food and textiles.

Until 1964, Burma was the world's leading rice producer, but it had slipped to seventh place by 1995. Rice, however, remains a leading export, together with such products as teak, pulses and beans, and rubber. Despite the country's repressive reputation, the number of tourists visiting Burma began to increase in the late 1990s.

AREA	Mon 2%, Kachin 1%
676,577 sq km	**LANGUAGES**
[261,228 sq mi]	Burmese (official),
POPULATION	Shan, Karen,
41,995,000	Rakhine, Mon,
CAPITAL (POPULATION)	Kachin, English,
Rangoon	Chin
(2,513,000)	**RELIGIONS**
GOVERNMENT	Buddhism 89%,
Military regime	Christianity,
ETHNIC GROUPS	Islam
Burman 69%, Shan 9%,	**CURRENCY**
Karen 6%, Rakhine 5%,	Kyat = 100 pyas

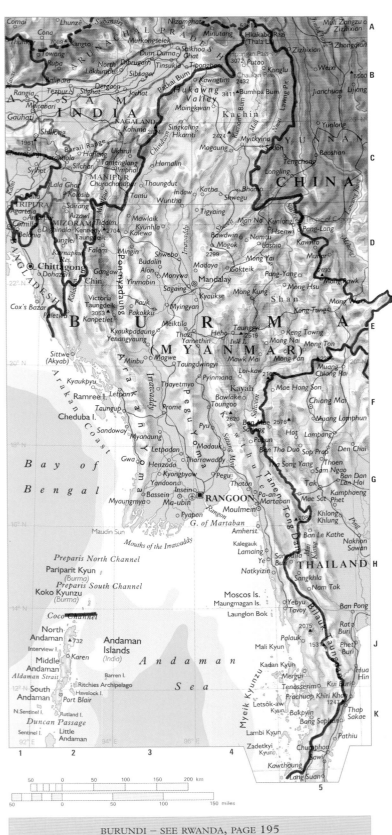

BURUNDI – SEE RWANDA, PAGE 195

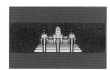

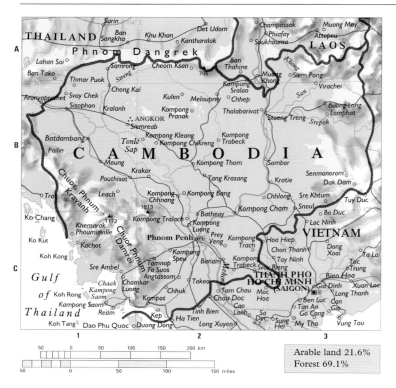

Arable land 21.6%
Forest 69.1%

Geography

The Kingdom of Cambodia is a country in South-east Asia. Low mountains border the country except in the south-east. But most of Cambodia consists of plains drained by the River Mekong, which enters Cambodia from Laos in the north and exits through Vietnam in the south-east. The north-west contains Tonlé Sap (or Great Lake). In the dry season, this lake drains into the River Mekong. But in the wet season, the level of the Mekong rises and water flows in the opposite direction from the river into Tonlé Sap – the lake then becomes the largest freshwater lake in Asia.

Climate

Cambodia has a tropical monsoon climate, with high temperatures all through the year. The dry season, when winds blow from the north or north-east, runs from November to April. During the rainy season, from May to October, moist winds blow from the south or south-east. The high humidity and heat often make conditions unpleasant. The rainfall is heaviest near the coast, and rather lower inland.

CAMBODIA (PHNOM PENH)

Phnom Penh is situated in the southern region of Cambodia. It experiences a tropical climate with uniformly high temperatures throughout the year. The average temperature in January is about 26°C [79°F], while that recorded in July is 29°C [84°F]. Rainfall is slightly lower here than on the coast with most falling between May and November. The average annual amount has been recorded at 1,398 mm [55 in].

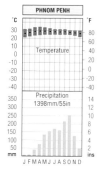

History

Early civilizations in what is now Cambodia included the kingdom of Funan, which developed in the south around AD 100. Another kingdom, called Chenla, had developed north of Funan by around 600, but it broke up in the 8th century. The Tonlé Sap lowlands in the north-west were the cradle of the Hindu-Buddhist Khmer empire, which lasted from 802 to 1431. Its zenith came in the reign of

Suryavarman II (1113–50), who built the great funerary temple of Angkor Wat. Together with Angkor Thom, the Angkor site contains the world's largest group of religious buildings. The wealth of the kingdom rested on fish from the lake and rice from the flooded lowlands, for which an extensive system of irrigation channels and strong reservoirs was developed. Thai forces captured Angkor in 1431 and forests covered the site. Following its rediscovery in 1860, it has been gradually restored and is now a major tourist attraction.

Cambodia was under French rule from 1863 as part of Indo-China until it achieved independence in 1954. In a short period of stability during the late 1950s and 1960s, the country developed its small-scale agricultural resources and rubber plantations. It remained predominantly rural, but achieved self-sufficiency in food, with some exports.

Politics

Despite its claims of neutrality in the struggles between Communist and non-Communist groups in South-east Asia, South Vietnam and the United States argued that North Vietnam had bases in Cambodia during the Vietnam War. In 1969, US planes bombed North Vietnamese targets in Cambodia. In 1970, King Norodom Sihanouk was overthrown and Cambodia became a republic. Under assault from South Vietnamese troops, the Communist Vietnamese withdrew deep into Cambodia. US raids ended in 1973, but fighting continued as Cambodia's Communists in the Khmer Rouge fought against the government. The Khmer Rouge, led by Pol Pot, were victorious in 1975. They began a reign of terror, murdering government officials and educated people. Up to 2 million people were estimated to have been killed. After the overthrow of Pol Pot by Vietnamese forces in 1979, civil war raged between the puppet government of the People's Republic of Kampuchea (Cambodia) and the US-backed government of Democratic Kampuchea, a coalition of Prince Sihanouk, the Khmer Liberation Front, and the Khmer Rouge, who, from 1982, claimed to have abandoned their Communist ideology.

Devastated by war and denied almost any aid, Cambodia continued to decline. It was only the withdrawal of Vietnamese troops in 1989, sparking fear of a Khmer Rouge revival, that forced a settlement. In October 1991, a UN-brokered peace plan for elections in 1993 was accepted by all parties. A new constitution was adopted in September 1993, restoring democracy and the monarchy. Sihanouk again became king. However, the Khmer Rouge continued hostilities and were banned in 1994. In 1997, Hu Sen, the second prime minister, engineered a coup against Prince Norodom Ranariddh (Sihanouk's son), the first prime minister Ranariddh went into exile but returned in 1998. Elections in 1998 resulted in victory for Hu Sen, but Ranariddh alleged electoral fraud. A coalition government was formed in December 1998, with Hu Sen as prime minister. In 2001, the government set up a court to try leaders of the Khmer Rouge.

Economy

Cambodia is a poor country. Until the 1970s, farmers produced most of the food needed by the people. By 1986, it was only able to supply 80% of its needs. Farming is the main activity and rice, rubber and maize are major products. Manufacturing is almost non-existent.

AREA	ETHNIC GROUPS
181,040 sq km [69,900 sq mi]	Khmer 90%, Vietnamese 5%, Chinese 1%, other 5%
POPULATION	**LANGUAGES**
12,492,000	Khmer (official)
CAPITAL (POPULATION)	**RELIGIONS**
Phnom Penh (570,000)	Buddhism 95%, other 5%
GOVERNMENT	**CURRENCY**
Constitutional monarchy	Riel = 100 sen

Cameroon uses the colours that appear on the flag of Ethiopia, Africa's oldest independent nation. These colours symbolize African unity. The flag is based on the tricolour adopted in 1957. The design with the yellow liberty star dates from 1975.

Geography and Climate

The Republic of Cameroon in West Africa got its name from the Portuguese word *camarões*, or prawns. This name was used by Portuguese explorers who fished for prawns along the coast. Behind the narrow coastal plains on the Gulf of Guinea, the land rises to a series of plateaux. In the north, the land slopes down towards the Lake Chad (Tchad) basin. The mountain region in the south-west of the country includes Mount Cameroon, a volcano which erupts from time to time. The vegetation varies greatly from north to south. The deserts in the north merge into dry and moist savanna in central Cameroon, with dense tropical rainforests in the humid south.

The rainfall is heavy, especially in the highlands. The rainiest months near the coast are from June to September. The rainfall decreases to the north and the far north has a hot, dry climate. Temperatures are high on the coast, whereas the inland plateaux are cooler.

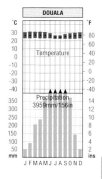

CAMEROON (DOUALA)

Rainfall at Douala is at its heaviest during the months of July, August and September when the south-west monsoon is at its strongest and steadiest, and temperatures hardly vary. Sunshine levels are relatively low, averaging only 3 hours per day. Rainfall on the seaward slopes of Cameroon Peak is even heavier and often exceeds 9,000 mm [350 in] in places.

History

Among the early inhabitants of Cameroon were groups of Bantu-speaking people. (There are now more than 160 ethnic groups, each with their own language.) In the late 15th century, Portuguese explorers, who were seeking a sea route to Asia around Africa, reached the Cameroon coast. From the 17th century, southern Cameroon was a centre of the slave trade, but slavery was ended in the early 19th century. In 1884, the area became a German protectorate.

Politics

Germany lost Cameroon during World War I (1914–18). The country was then divided into two parts, one ruled by Britain and the other by France. In 1960, French Cameroon became the independent Cameroon Republic. In 1961, after a vote in British Cameroon, part of the territory joined the Cameroon Republic to become the Federal Republic of Cameroon. The other part joined Nigeria. In 1972, Cameroon became a unitary state called the United Republic of Cameroon. It adopted the name Republic of Cameroon in 1984, but the country had two official languages. Opposition parties were legalized in 1992, and Paul Biya was elected president in 1993 and 1997. In 1995, partly to placate the English-speaking people, Cameroon became the 52nd member of the Commonwealth.

Economy

Like most countries in tropical Africa, Cameroon's economy is based on agriculture, which employs 73% of the people. The chief food crops include cassava, maize, millet, sweet potatoes and yams. The country also produces such crops as cocoa and coffee for export.

Cameroon is fortunate in having some oil, the country's chief export, and bauxite. Although Cameroon has few manufacturing and processing industries, its mineral exports and its self-sufficiency in

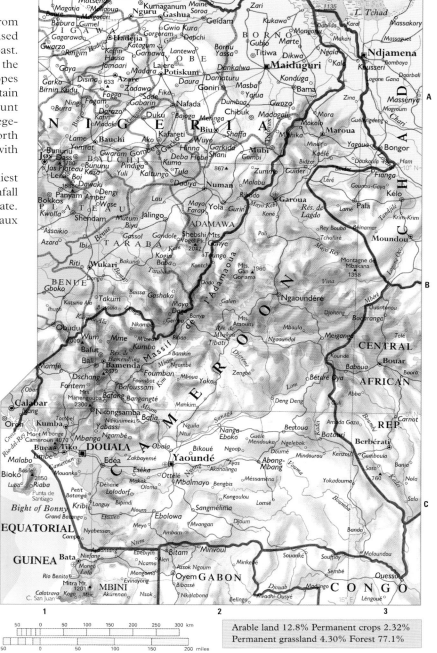

Arable land 12.8% Permanent crops 2.32%
Permanent grassland 4.30% Forest 77.1%

food production make it one of the wealthier countries in tropical Africa. Another important industry is forestry, ranking second among the exports, after oil. Other exports, in order of importance, are cocoa, coffee, aluminium and cotton.

AREA	Bamum 19%,Duala,
475,440 sq km	Luanda and Basa 15%,
[183,567 sq mi]	Fulani 10%
POPULATION	**LANGUAGES**
15,803,000	French and English (both official),
CAPITAL (POPULATION)	many others
Yaoundé (800,000)	**RELIGIONS**
GOVERNMENT	Christianity 40%, traditional
Multiparty republic	beliefs 40%, Islam 20%
ETHNIC GROUPS	**CURRENCY**
Fang 20%, Bamileke and	CFA franc = 100 centimes

Canada's flag, with its simple 11-pointed maple leaf emblem, was adopted in 1965 after many attempts to find an acceptable design. The old flag, used from 1892, was the British Red Ensign, but this flag became unpopular with Canada's French community.

CANADA

NORTHERN CANADA
Continuation northwards on same scale as main map

Arable land 4.93%   Permanent crops 0.01%
Permanent grassland 3.03%   Forest 53.6%

Geography

A vast confederation of ten provinces and three territories, Canada is the world's second largest country after Russia, with an even longer coastline – about 250,000 km [155,000 mi]. It is sparsely populated because it contains vast areas of virtually unoccupied mountains, cold forests, tundra and polar desert in the north and west. About 80% of the population of Canada lives within about 300 km [186 mi] of the southern border. Yet Canada is a land of great beauty and variety.

Western Canada includes the Pacific Ranges and coastlands. This region includes much of British Columbia, the Queen Charlotte Islands, Vancouver Island, and the south-western part of Yukon Territory. In the Yukon Territory stands Canada's highest peak, Mount Logan, which reaches 5,959 m [19,551 ft] in the St Elias Mountains, near the Alaskan border. Glaciers cover many mountains in the St Elias Mountains and glaciation has left its mark along the coast, where it has carved deep fiords.

East of the Pacific Ranges lie the Rocky Mountains. These two highland regions form part of the huge cordillera that stretches from Alaska to Mexico. The magnificent scenery in the Rockies is crowned by Mount Robson, which reaches 3,954 m [12,972 ft] in eastern British Columbia. East of the Rocky Mountains lie vast interior plains extending north to the Arctic Ocean. The southern part of the interior plains are grassy prairies, though the land has been largely transformed by farming. The interior plains are rich in minerals and fossil fuels.

East of the interior plains lies a region called the Canadian Shield, a horseshoe-shaped area curving from the Arctic Ocean, around Hudson Bay to the coast of Labrador. It is a region of ancient rocks that formed the ancient core of North America. North of the Canadian Shield, almost entirely within the Arctic Circle, lie Canada's Arctic Islands.

South of the Canadian Shield are Canada's most populous regions: the lowlands north of lakes Erie and Ontario, and the St Lawrence River lowlands, where more than half of the nation's people live. The far south-east of Canada contains part of the Appalachian Mountains, which extend through the eastern United States.

CANADA – QUÉBEC

The effect of the Great Lakes is felt in the Ontario Peninsula, resulting in slightly warmer winters than in Québec. But the temperatures in northern Canada are extreme: along the Arctic Circle, the mean monthly temperatures are below freezing for much of the year. In Québec, rainfall is moderate all year with no marked peak, and with a reasonable amount of snow. Québec has an average of about 1,053 mm [41 in] of rain each year.

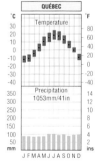

VANCOUVER

West of the Rockies, and to a lesser extent on the eastern coast, the nearby ocean changes the expected climate. At Vancouver, rainfall is high with a maximum occurring between October and March. There is little snow, with just over 50 frost days. Summers are cool, with no mean temperatures above 18°C [64°F], the record being 34°C [93°F] in August. Temperatures in winter decline a little to the north along this coastal fringe.

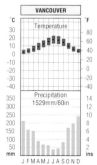

EDMONTON

The July temperature is about 17°C [63°F], but that of December is nearly −14°C [6°F], an annual range of over 30°C [54°F]. But high summer temperatures are recorded in these areas, over 30°C [86°F] having been recorded in all months, April to September. Rainfall is low with a maximum from June to August, and there is little snowfall. On average there are over 210 frost days. Westwards into the Rockies, the snow can reach great depths.

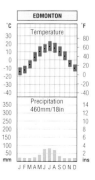

Climate

Canada has a cold climate. In winter, temperatures fall below freezing point throughout most of Canada. But the south-western coast has a relatively mild climate. Along the Arctic Circle, mean temperatures are below freezing for seven months a year. By contrast, hot winds from the Gulf of Mexico warm southern Ontario and the St Lawrence River lowlands in summer. As a result, southern Ontario has a frost-free season of nearly six months.

The coasts of British Columbia are wet, with an average annual rainfall of more than 2,500 mm [98 in] in places. By contrast, the prairies are arid or semi-arid, with an average annual rainfall of 250 mm to 500 mm [10–20 in]. The rainfall in south-eastern Canada ranges from around 800 mm [31 in] in southern Ontario to about 1,500 mm [59 in] on the coasts of Newfoundland and Nova Scotia. Heavy snow falls in eastern Canada in winter.

Vegetation

Forests of cedars, hemlocks and other trees grow on the western mountains, with firs and spruces at the higher levels. The mountain forests provide habitats for bears, deer and mountain lions, while the sure-footed Rocky Mountain goats and bighorn sheep roam above the tree line (the upper limit of tree growth).

The interior plains were once grassy prairies. While the drier areas are still used for grazing cattle, the wetter areas are used largely for growing wheat and other cereals. North of the prairies are the boreal forests which, in turn merge into the treeless tundra and Arctic wastelands in the far north. The lowlands in south-eastern Canada contain forests of deciduous trees, such as beech, hickory, oak and walnut.

The Tundra

Beyond their habitable southern rims, northern Canada and Alaska are thinly populated and bleak. The subarctic zone contains the vast boreal (northern) forests, which are also called the taiga. Winters are long, cold and snowy, while summers are cool. The dominant trees are needleleaf evergreens, including such trees as fir, pine and spruce, which are specially adapted to the climate. For example, their conical shapes prevent overloading by snow, their thick trunks protect them against the cold, and their shallow roots absorb moisture from the soil, even when the subsoil is frozen solid. Many small mammals, such as beavers, mice and hares, live in the forests, while larger mammals include bears, caribou, foxes, moose and wolves. But the number of species is small compared with the mild deciduous forests.

To the north, conditions become more severe and the boreal forest dies out, replaced by tundra. Only 11,000 years ago, the tundra was covered by ice sheets. Glaciation has scoured the surface bare in many areas and new soils have not yet had time to form. In other places, only the top 60 cm [24 in] of soil thaws in summer, while the subsoil (permafrost) is permanently frozen. Winters are long and bitterly cold. Summers are brief and cool. Even in the southern parts of the tundra, the season of plant growth is only 70 to 80 days. Precipitation is light – usually less than 250 mm [10 in] a year, and much falls as snow. Except in areas of snow drifts, snow is seldom deep, but it provides cover for vegetation and burrowing animals.

The treeless tundra supports low grasses, lichens, mosses and spindly shrubs, providing food for migrating reindeer and resident animals, such as hares, lemmings, voles and other small browsers and grazers. Their numbers are augmented each summer by hosts of migrant birds, including ducks, geese, swans, waders and others that fly in from temperate latitudes to feed on the vegetation and on the swarms of insects that fill the air over vast swampy areas. Beyond the Canadian tundra lie Arctic lands, some of which are permanently covered by glaciers and small ice caps. In the seas around the northernmost islands, such animals as polar bears and seals feed on fish, spending much of their lives on the sea ice.

History

Canada's first people, ancestors of the Native Americans, or the Indians, arrived in North America from Asia around 40,000 years ago. Later arrivals were the Inuit (Eskimos), who also came from Asia. Norse voyagers and fishermen were probably the first to visit Canada, but John Cabot's later discovery of North America in 1497 led to the race to annex lands and wealth, with France and Britain the main contenders. Jacques Cartier's discovery of the St Lawrence River in 1534 gave France a head start. From their settlements near Québec, explorers, trappers and missionaries pioneered routes, penetrating into northern North America. With the hope of finding a North-west Passage to China and South-east Asia, the French followed the St Lawrence and Niagara rivers deep into the heartland of the continent.

Discovering the Great Lakes, they then moved north, west and south in their search for trade. From the fertile valley of the upper St Lawrence, French influence spread north through the boreal forests and over the tundra. To the west and south, they reached the prairies, exploring further into the Rocky Mountains and down the Ohio and Mississippi rivers. In 1763, after a series of wars that gave Britain brief control of the whole of North America, French-speaking communities were already scattered widely across the interior. Many of the southern settlements became American after 1776, when the United States declared independence from Britain, while the northern ones became part of a British colony.

British settlers had long been established on the Atlantic coast in fishing communities, farming the land where possible. In the 1780s, a new wave of English-speaking settlers – the United Empire Loyalists – moved north into Nova Scotia, New Brunswick and Lower Canada. With further waves of immigration from Britain, English speakers soon dominated fertile land between lakes Huron and Erie. From there, they spread westwards. Restricted to the north by the boreal forests and tundra and to the south by the United States, they spread through Québec into Upper Canada (now Ontario), the only province on the Canadian shores of the Great Lakes. Mostly English-speaking settlers continued westwards to establish settlements on the prairies, finally crossing the Rocky Mountains to link with embryo settlements along the Pacific coast. Hence, the St Lawrence lowlands and pockets of settlement on the Canadian Shield remained French in language and culture. The bulk of Canada, to the east and west, became predominantly English.

Canada's topography and immense scale inhibited the development of a single nation. The union of British Upper Canada and French Lower Canada was sealed by the confederation of 1867, when, as the newly named provinces of Ontario and Québec, they were united with the maritime core of Nova Scotia and New Brunswick. Three years later, the settlement on the Red River entered the confederation as Manitoba and, in the following year, the Pacific colonies of Vancouver Island and British Columbia, now united as a single province, completed the link from sea to sea. Prince Edward Island joined in 1873, the prairie provinces of Alberta and Saskatchewan in 1905, and Newfoundland in 1949.

Though self-governing in most respects from the time of confederation, Canada remained technically subject to the British Imperial parliament until 1931.

Provinces of Canada

The creation of the British Commonwealth in 1931 made Canada a sovereign nation under the crown. Canada is now a constitutional monarchy. Under the Constitution Act of 1982, Queen Elizabeth II is head of state and a symbol of the close ties between Canada and Britain. The British monarch is represented by an appointed governor-general, but the country is ruled by a prime minister, and an elected, two-chamber parliament.

Canada combines the cabinet system with a federal form of government, with each province having its own government. The federal government can reject any law passed by a provincial legislature, though this seldom happens in practice. The territories are self-governing, but the federal government plays a large part in their administration.

Politics

The promotion of Canadian unity across so wide a continent has been the aim of successive governments for more than 200 years. Yet with the population spread out along a southern ribbon of settlement, about 4,000 km [2,500 mi] long but rarely more than 300 km [186 mi] wide, Canada has made this objective difficult to achieve.

Transcontinental communications have played a critical role. From the eastern provinces, the Canadian Pacific Railway crossed the Rockies to reach Vancouver in 1885. Later, a second route, Canadian National, was pieced together, and the Trans-Canada Highway links the extreme east and west of the country. Transcontinental air routes link the major centres, and local air traffic is especially important in the boreal forests, mountains and tundra. Modern telecommunications have enabled all parts of the confederation – even the most remote parts of the Arctic territories – to be linked. Even so, the vastness is intimidating. The country spans six time zones – at noon in Vancouver, it is 3:00 PM in Toronto and 4:30 PM in St John's, Newfoundland.

A constant hazard to Canadian nationhood is the proximity of the United States. Though benign, with shared British traditions, the prosperous giant to the south has often seemed to threaten the survival of Canada through economic dominance and cultural annexation. The two countries have the largest bilateral trade flow in the world. Economic co-operation was further enhanced in 1993 when Canada, the United States and Mexico set up NAFTA (North American Free Trade Agreement).

A constant problem facing those who want to maintain the unity of Canada is the persistence of French culture in Québec, which has fuelled a separatist movement seeking to turn the province into an independent French-speaking republic. More than 5 million of the 7.5 million Québeckers are French speakers. In 1994, Québeckers voted the separatist Parti Québécois into provincial office. The incoming prime minister announced that the independence for Québec would be the subject of a referendum in 1995. In that referendum, 49.4% voted 'Yes' (for separation) while 50.5% voted 'No'.

Provincial elections in 1998 resulted in another victory for the Parti Québécois. But while the separatist party won 75 out of the 125 seats in the provincial assembly, it won only 43% of the popular vote, compared with 44% for the anti-secessionist Liberal Party and 12% for the floating Action Démocratique de Québec. Also significant was a ruling by Canada's highest court that, under Canadian law, Québec does not have the right to secede unilaterally. The court ruled that, should a clear majority of the people in the province vote by 'a clear majority' to a 'clear question' in favour of independence, the federal government and the other provinces would have to negotiate Québec's secession.

Other problems involve the rights of the aboriginal Native Americans and the Inuit, who together numbered about 470,000 in 1991. In 1999, a new Inuit territory was created. Called Nunavut, it is made up of 64% of the former North-west Territories, and covers 2,201,400 sq km [649,965 sq mi]. The population in 1991 was about 25,000, 85% of whom were Inuit. Nunavut, whose capital is Iqaluit (formerly Frobisher Bay), will depend on future aid, but its mineral reserves and the prospects of an ecotourist industry hold out promise for the future.

Economy

Canada is a highly developed and prosperous country. Rich in natural resources, including oil and natural gas, a wide range of minerals, forests and rich farmland, its economy has traditionally been based on selling commodities – raw materials and farm produce. Up to 78% of the population now live in cities and towns, and manufacturing and service industries play a major role in the economy. Resource-based industries now employ only 5% of the workforce, as compared with 16% in manufacturing and nearly three-quarters in service industries.

Although farmland covers only 8% of the country, Canadian farms are highly mechanized and productive. The leading farm products are beef cattle, milk, pigs and wheat. Also important are barley, chickens and eggs, maize and canola, which is used to make cooking oil. More than three-quarters of Canada's farmland is situated in the prairie provinces of Alberta, Manitoba and Saskatchewan. These provinces produce most of the country's grains, while beef cattle ranching is also important. The other main farming region is the St Lawrence lowlands in the east. Québec is the leading milk-producing province, while Ontario ranks second. The Atlantic provinces are known for their potatoes and dairy farming, while British Columbia produces eggs and poultry, fruits, livestock and milk. The fishing industry dates back to the early days of European settlement, but overfishing now threatens production in the Grand Banks, one of the world's finest fishing areas, off the coast of Newfoundland.

Forestry is a major industry. British Columbia, Québec and Ontario are the leading timber-producing provinces. Cheap hydroelectric power, coupled with improved transmission technology, has encouraged the further development of wood pulp and paper industries, even in the remote parts of the northern forests of Québec and Ontario. It has also stimulated industry and commerce in the south.

Canada is one of the world's leading exporters of minerals. Petroleum and natural gas are the most important products taken from the ground, with Alberta being the leading producer. The country is also the world's top exporter of asbestos, potash, uranium and zinc, and a major producer of copper, gold, iron ore and nickel. Ontario is the leading province for producing metal ores. British Columbia produces copper and is the leading coal producer, while Québec is a major producer of iron ore and gold.

The processing of fuels, minerals and other produce for export form the basis of Canada's manufacturing industries. Other industries include food processing, chemicals and pharmaceuticals, the manufacturing of transport equipment, including cars, trucks and aircraft, and paper products. Other products include metal products, electrical equipment, wood products, and computers and software.

Service industries account for 70% of the country's gross domestic product. They include community, business and personal services, followed by finance, insurance and real estate. Tourism is also important and Canada attracts visitors from all over the world.

Canada's economy is based on foreign trade, and leading exports are machinery and transport equipment, mineral fuels, food (especially wheat), timber, newsprint and paper products, and wood pulp. The share of commodities has fallen from nearly 60% in 1980 to 35% in the late 1990s, while the share of manufacturing has increased. Canada's leading trading partner is the United States. Canada's exports to the United States rose from 15% of the gross domestic product in 1989 to 30% in 1998. Manufacturing accounted for half of the increase.

St-Pierre et Miquelon

The last fragment of the once-extensive French possessions in North America outside the Caribbean, St-Pierre et Miquelon comprises two main islands and some small rocky islets, about 16 km [10 mi] off the south coast of Newfoundland. The total area of the islands is 242 sq km [93 sq mi]. The population is 6,390, almost 90% of whom live on St-Pierre and the rest on Miquelon. The administrative and commercial centre is St-Pierre (see map on page 67).

The islands contain areas of marshes, peat bogs, small lakes and bare hills (called Mornes) that rise to the highest point on the archipelago. This is the Morne de la Grande Montagne, which reaches 240 m [787 ft]. The coast is very scenic. Temperatures vary from about –10°C [–14°F] in winter to 20°C [68°F] in summer, while the average annual rainfall is about 1,500 mm [59 in]. The forests that once covered the islands have been largely cleared, giving them a bare appearance.

The islands were originally settled by seafarers from western France in the early 17th century. After being exchanged several times between France and Britain, St-Pierre et Miquelon finally became a French colony in 1816. Today the people speak French and most are Roman Catholics. The territory became a French overseas department in 1976 and, like Martinique, Guadeloupe, French Guiana and Réunion, it enjoyed the same status as the departments in Metropolitan France. In 1985, however, it became a 'territorial collectivity', a status already held by Mayotte, an island which formerly belonged to the Comoros in the Indian Ocean. Like Mayotte, it sends one deputy to the National Assembly in Paris and one senator to the Senate. A Prefect represents the French government in the territory.

The majority of people depend on fishing. Frozen and dried fish are the main exports. Other economic activities include fox and mink farming and tourism. Much land is barren rock but some vegetables are grown and animals are raised. But the economy of the islands depends on subsidies from France.

AREA	Native American
9,976,140 sq km	(Amerindian/Inuit) 2%,
[3,851,788 sq mi]	other 32%
POPULATION	**LANGUAGES**
31,593,000	English and French
CAPITAL (POPULATION)	(both official)
Ottawa	**RELIGIONS**
(1,107,000)	Roman Catholic 42%,
GOVERNMENT	Protestant 40%,
Federal multiparty	Judaism, Islam,
constitutional monarchy	Hinduism
ETHNIC GROUPS	**CURRENCY**
British 28%, French 23%,	Canadian dollar
other European 15%,	= 100 cents

CANARY ISLANDS – SEE ATLANTIC OCEAN, PAGES 41–43;
CAPE VERDE – SEE ATLANTIC OCEAN, PAGES 41–43

CARIBBEAN SEA

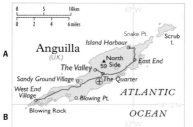

ANGUILLA

AREA	CAPITAL
96 sq km	The Valley
[37 sq mi]	CURRENCY
POPULATION	East Caribbean
12,000	dollar

Formerly part of St Kitts and Nevis, Anguilla, the most northerly of the Leeward Islands, officially became a British dependency (now a British overseas territory) in 1980. A new constitution was adopted in 1982. The main source of revenue is now tourism.

ANTIGUA AND BARBUDA

AREA	CAPITAL
442 sq km	St John's
[170 sq mi]	CURRENCY
POPULATION	East Caribbean
67,000	dollar

A former British dependency, Antigua and Barbuda became independent in 1981. Tourism is the main industry. Antigua contains 98% of the people and Barbuda 2%. A third uninhabited island, Redonda, 40 km [25 mi] to the south-west, is not shown on the map.

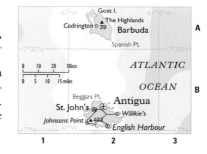

BAHAMAS

The Bahamas is a coral-limestone archipelago comprising 29 inhabited islands, plus more than 3,000 cays, reefs and rocks, centred on the Grand Bahama Bank off eastern Florida and Cuba. The Bahamas has developed close ties with the United States.

More than 90% of the 3.6 million visitors a year are Americans. Tourism now accounts for 70% of the gross domestic product and involves about 40% of the workforce. Off-shore banking, financial services and a large 'open registry' merchant fleet also offset imports (including most foodstuffs), providing the country with a relatively high standard of living.

The remainder of the non-administrative population works mainly in the traditional areas of fishing and agriculture, notably citrus fruit production.

The Bahamas has been a democracy since 1973 when it became independent from Britain. Relations with the United States were strained when it was used as a tax haven for drug traffickers in the 1980s, with government ministers implicated in drug-related corruption.

AREA	CAPITAL
13,940 sq km	Nassau
[5,380 sq mi]	CURRENCY
POPULATION	Bahamian dollar
298,000	= 100 cents

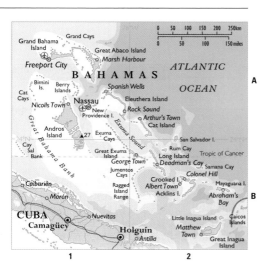

CARIBBEAN SEA

BARBADOS

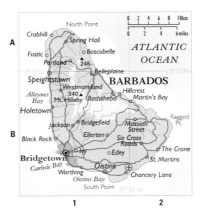

The most eastern Caribbean nation, and first in line for the seasonal hurricanes that batter the region, Barbados is underlain by limestone and capped with coral. Mt Hillaby, which reaches 340 m [1,115 ft], the highest point, is fringed by marine terraces marking stages in the island's emergence from the sea.

AREA	CAPITAL
430 sq km	Bridgetown
[166 sq mi]	CURRENCY
POPULATION	Barbados dollar
275,000	= 100 cents

Barbados became British in 1627, and it became independent as a constitutional monarchy in 1960. However, in 2000, the government announced that it planned to hold a referendum on a proposal to turn Barbados into a republic.

The economy was based on sugar production, using African slave labour. Cane plantations take up most of the cropped land, but sugar now contributes 13% of domestic exports – far less than previously. Manufactures make up the leading exports, but tourism is the growth sector and the most valuable activity for this relatively prosperous, but very overcrowded, island. Despite political stability and advanced welfare and education services, emigration is high, notably to the United States and United Kingdom.

CAYMAN ISLANDS

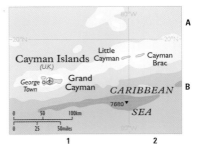

The Cayman Islands are an overseas territory of the UK, consisting of three low-lying islands. Financial services are the main economic activity, and the islands offer a secret tax haven to many companies and banks. The flourishing tourist industry is the second most important activity.

AREA	CAPITAL
259 sq km	George Town
[100 sq mi]	CURRENCY
POPULATION	Cayman Island
36,000	dollar = 100 cents

DOMINICAN REPUBLIC

Second largest of the Caribbean nations in both area and population, the Dominican Republic shares with Haiti the island of Hispaniola, with the Dominican Republic occupying the eastern two-thirds. Of the steep-sided mountains that dominate the island, the country includes the northern Cordillera Septentrional, the huge Cordillera Central, which rises to Pico Duarte, at 3,175 m [10,414 ft] the highest peak in the Caribbean, and the southern Sierra de Baoruco. Between them and to the east lie fertile valleys and lowlands, including the Vega Real and the coastal plains where the main sugar plantations are found.

Typical of the Caribbean region, the climate is hot and humid throughout the year close to sea level, while cooler conditions prevail in the mountains. Rainfall is heavy, especially in the north-east.

Christopher Columbus 'discovered' the island and its Amerindian population, soon to be decimated, on 5 December 1492. The city of Santo Domingo, now the capital and chief port, was founded by Columbus' brother Bartholomew four years later and is the oldest in the Americas. For long a Spanish colony, Hispaniola was initially the centrepiece of their empire, but was later to become a poor relation. In 1795, it became French, then Spanish again in 1809. But in 1821, when it was called Santo Domingo, it won its independence. Haiti held the territory from 1822 until 1844 when, on restoring sovereignty, it became the Dominican Republic. Growing American influence culminated in occupation between 1916 and 1924. This was followed by a period of corrupt dictatorship. From 1930 until his assassination in 1961, the country was ruled by Rafael Trujillo, one of Latin America's best-known dictators, who imprisoned or killed many of his opponents.

A power struggle developed between the military, the upper class, those who wanted the country to become a democracy and others who favoured making it a Communist regime. Juan Bosch became president in 1962, but was ousted in 1963. Bosch supporters tried to seize power in 1965, but were met with strong military opposition. This led to US military intervention in 1965. Since 1966, a young democracy has survived violent elections under the watchful eye of the Americans.

The World Bank describes the Dominican Republic as a 'lower-middle-income' developing country. In the 1990s, industrial growth that exploited the country's huge hydroelectric potential, mining and tourism has augmented the traditional agricultural economy, though the country is far from being politically stable. Agriculture is a major activity. Leading crops include avocados, bananas, beans, mangoes, oranges, plantains, rice, sugar cane and tobacco. Gold and nickel are mined. Sugar refining is a major industry, with the bulk of the production exported to the United States. Leading exports are ferronickel, sugar, coffee, cocoa and gold. The island's main trading partner is the United States.

AREA	ETHNIC GROUPS
48,730 sq km	Mulatto 73%,
[18,815 sq mi]	White 16%,
POPULATION	Black 11%
8,581,000	LANGUAGES
CAPITAL (POPULATION)	Spanish (official)
Santo Domingo	RELIGIONS
(2,135,000)	Roman Catholic 95%
GOVERNMENT	CURRENCY
Multiparty republic	Peso = 100 centavos

DOMINICA

The Commonwealth of Dominica, a former British colony, became independent in 1978. The island has a mountainous spine and less than 10% of the land is cultivated. However, agriculture employs over 60% of the people. The manufacturing of coconut-based soap is important, but much food has to be imported.

The future of Dominica depends a good deal on the development of luxury tourism.

AREA	CAPITAL
751 sq km [290 sq mi]	Roseau
POPULATION	**CURRENCY**
71,000	Franc, pound, E. Car. dollar

GRENADA

The most southerly of the Windward Islands in the Caribbean Sea, Grenada became independent from the UK in 1974. A military group seized power in 1983, when the prime minister was killed. US troops intervened and restored order and constitutional government.

Since the invasion, the island has been reliant on aid. Grenada is the world's leading producer of nutmeg.

AREA	CAPITAL
340 sq km [131 sq mi]	St George's
POPULATION	**CURRENCY**
89,000	Eastern Caribbean dollar

GUADELOUPE

Guadeloupe is a French overseas department which includes seven Caribbean islands, the largest of which is Basse-Terre. French aid has helped to maintain a reasonable standard of living for the people.

Food is the biggest import, much of it coming from France, while bananas are the chief export. Despite French aid and thriving tourism, unemployment remains high.

AREA	CAPITAL
1,706 sq km [658 sq mi]	Basse-Terre
POPULATION	**CURRENCY**
431,000	Euro = 100 cents

HAITI

The Republic of Haiti occupies the western third of Hispaniola, the Caribbean's second largest island. The land is mainly mountainous, with a long, indented coast. Most of the country is centred around the Massif du Nord, with the narrow Massif de la Hotte forming the southern peninsula. The climate is hot and humid. The northern highlands have an average annual rainfall of about 2,000 mm [79 in], more than twice as much as on the southern coast.

Ceded to France in 1697, Haiti developed as a sugar-producing colony. For nearly two centuries, since a slave revolt made it the world's first independent black state in 1804, it has been bedevilled by military coups, government corruption, ethnic violence and political instability, including a period of US control from 1915 to 1934.

The violent regime of François Duvalier ('Papa Doc'), president from 1957, was especially brutal, but that of his son, Jean Claude ('Baby Doc'), president from 1971, was little better – both used their murderous private militia, the Tontons Macoutes, to conduct a reign of terror. In 1986, popular unrest finally forced Duvalier to flee the country, and the military took over. After another period of political chaos, the country's first multiparty elections were held in December 1990. A radical Roman Catholic priest, Father Jean-Bertrand Aristide, won the election, promising sweeping reforms. The army seized power in 1991, but Aristide returned as president in 1994. After Aristide stood down in 1995, René Préval became president, but violence and poverty still prevailed. In 1999, Préval dissolved parliament and announced that he would rule by decree. But Aristide was elected president in 2000 and he survived an attempted coup in 2001.

Coffee is the only significant cash crop. Two-thirds of the population lives at or below the poverty line, subsisting on agriculture and fishing. The country has few industries.

AREA	ETHNIC GROUPS
27,750 sq km	Black 95%, Mulatto 5%
[10,714 sq mi]	**LANGUAGES**
POPULATION	French & Creole (both official)
6,965,000	**RELIGIONS**
CAPITAL (POPULATION)	Roman Catholic 80%,
Port-au-Prince (885,000)	Voodoo
GOVERNMENT	**CURRENCY**
Multiparty republic	Gourde = 100 centimes

CARIBBEAN SEA

JAMAICA

Third largest of the Caribbean islands, half of Jamaica lies above 300 m [1,000 ft]. The country has a central range culminating in Blue Mountain Peak, at 2,256 m [7,402 ft], from which it slopes westwards. The 'cockpit' country in the north-west of the island is an inaccessible limestone area. The climate is hot and humid, with moist south-east trade winds bringing rain to the mountains.

Britain took over Jamaica in 1655 and, with sugar as its staple product, the colony became a prized imperial possession. The African slaves imported to work on the plantations were the forefathers of much of the present population. But the plantations disappeared and the sugar market collapsed in the 19th century. Jamaica became independent in 1962 and economic problems arose under Michael Manley's socialist government in the 1970s. Some progress was made in the 1980s under the pragmatic leadership of Edward Seaga. Manley returned as prime minister in 1989, but he was succeeded in 1992 by Percival Patterson. Jamaica's problems include drug trafficking, violent crime and economic difficulties. Riots in 1999 were caused by price and tax increases, while gun battles occurred in 2001 when the police searched for drugs in a poor district of Kingston.

Jamaica's chief resource is bauxite, most of which is exported as ore. Tourism and bauxite production are the two main industries.

AREA	Mixed 7%,
10,990 sq km [4,243 sq mi]	East Indian 1%
POPULATION	**LANGUAGES**
2,666,000	English (official),
CAPITAL (POPULATION)	Creole
Kingston (644,000)	**RELIGIONS**
GOVERNMENT	Protestant 61%,
Constitutional monarchy	Roman Catholic 4%
ETHNIC GROUPS	**CURRENCY**
Black 91%,	Dollar = 100 cents

MARTINIQUE

Martinique comprises three groups of volcanic islands and the intervening lowlands. The highest peak is Mount Pelée, notorious for its violent eruption in 1902 when, in minutes, it killed all the inhabitants of St Pierre (estimated at 28,000) except one – a prisoner saved by the thickness of his cell. The climate is hot and humid. The heaviest rains often occur in the hurricane season (July–November).

Colonized by France from 1635, Martinique has been French ever since, apart from brief British interludes. It became an overseas department in 1946 and, like Guadeloupe, it was made an administrative region in 1974.

Tourism is the chief industry. Sugar cane is the chief crop although the main farm exports are bananas, rum and pineapples. Manufactures include cement, food processing and oil refining. The crude oil comes from Venezuela, and refined oil is the second most valuable export after bananas. French aid is very important. Making up about 70% of the GDP, it helps to provide jobs and maintain a higher standard of living than on Guadeloupe.

AREA	**CAPITAL**
1,100 sq km	Fort-de-
[425 sq mi]	France
POPULATION	**CURRENCY**
418,000	Euro

MONTSERRAT

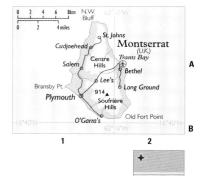

Montserrat is a British overseas territory in the Caribbean. The climate is tropical and hurricanes often cause damage. Intermittent eruptions of the Soufrière Hills volcano between 1995 and 1998 led to the emigration of many inhabitants and the virtual destruction of the capital, Plymouth.

AREA	**CAPITAL**
102 sq km	Plymouth
[39 sq mi]	**CURRENCY**
POPULATION	Eastern
12,000	Caribbean dollar

NETHERLANDS ANTILLES ARUBA

The Netherlands Antilles consists of two different island groups: one off the coast of Venezuela, and the other at the northern end of the Leeward Islands, some 800 km [500 mi] away. With Aruba, they formed part of the Dutch East Indies, attaining internal self-government in 1954. Curaçao is politically dominant in the federation, accounting for nearly 45% of the area and 80% of the population. By Caribbean standards, most people are well off. They enjoy the benefits of an economy buoyed by tourism, offshore banking and oil refining (from Venezuela), mostly for export to the Netherlands and more important than the traditional orange liqueur.

Aruba is a flat limestone island, the most western of the Lesser Antilles, some 68 km [42 mi] west of Curaçao. It was incorporated into the Netherlands Antilles in 1845, but, in 1977, the people voted in a referendum for autonomy. With Dutch agreement in 1981, Aruba separated from the Netherlands Antilles in 1986.

NETHERLANDS ANTILLES	**ARUBA**
AREA	**AREA**
993 sq km [383 sq mi]	193 sq km [75 sq mi]
POPULATION	**POPULATION**
212,000	70,000
CAPITAL	**CAPITAL**
Willemstad	Oranjestad

PUERTO RICO

The Commonwealth of Puerto Rico is the easternmost of the islands in the Greater Antilles. The land is mountainous, with a narrow coastal plain. Cerro de Punta, at 1,338 m [4,389 ft], is the highest peak. The climate is hot and wet, though rainstorms are short in many places.

Ceded by Spain to the United States in 1898, Puerto Rico became a self-governing commonwealth in free association with the United States after a referendum in 1952. Puerto Ricans are US citizens, but they pay no federal taxes, nor do they vote in US congressional or presidential elections. In 1991, Puerto Ricans narrowly rejected a proposal to guarantee 'the island's distinct cultural identity', a result interpreted as a move towards statehood. But in 1998, 50.2% of the people voted for maintaining the status quo, rather than asking for statehood.

Flat land for agriculture is scarce. It is mainly devoted to cash crops, such as bananas, coffee, sugar, tobacco, tropical fruits, vegetables and various spices. However, the island is now the most industrialized and urbanized in the Caribbean – nearly half the population lives in the San Juan area. Manufacturing and tourism are growing industries. The rising standard of living, while low in US terms, is the highest in Latin America outside the tax havens. The chief exports are chemicals and chemical products, machinery and food.

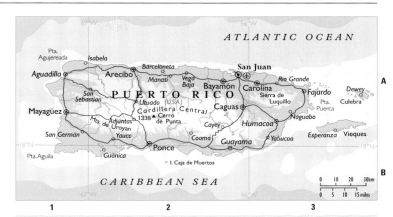

AREA	ETHNIC GROUPS
8,900 sq km [3,436 sq mi]	Spanish 99%, African American
POPULATION	**LANGUAGES**
3,939,000	Spanish and English (both official)
CAPITAL	**CURRENCY**
San Juan	US dollar = 100 cents

ST KITTS AND NEVIS

The Federation of St Kitts and Nevis comprises two well-watered volcanic islands, with mountains rising to around

AREA	CAPITAL
360 sq km [139 sq mi]	Basseterre
POPULATION	**CURRENCY**
39,000	East Caribbean dollar

1,000 m [3,300 ft]. The islands were the first in the Caribbean to be colonized by Britain (1623 and 1628), and they became an independent country in 1983. In 1998, a vote for the secession of Nevis fell short of the two-thirds required. Tourism has replaced sugar as the main earner.

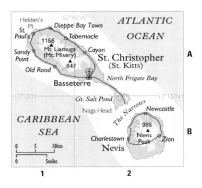

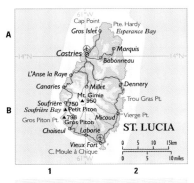

ST LUCIA

St Lucia is a mountainous forested island of extinct volcanoes, graphically represented on its flag. To the south of its highest point of Mt Gimie, at 950 m [3,116 ft] above sea level, lies Qualibou, an area containing 18 volcanic domes and seven craters. In the west are the Pitons, rising from the sea to more than 750 m [2,460 ft]. Temperatures in St Lucia are high, and the rainfall is heavy. The rainiest months are likely to occur during the hurricane season, which runs from July to November. St Lucia boasts a huge variety of plant and animal life.

First settled by the British in 1605, St Lucia changed hands between Britain and France 14 times before being formally ceded to Britain in 1814. Self-governing as an 'Associated State of the UK' from 1967, it gained independence as a member of the Commonwealth in 1979.

Though not poor, St Lucia is still over-dependent on bananas, which are vulnerable to hurricanes and disease. Other agricultural products are coconuts and cocoa, but clothing makes up the second largest export, and the free port of Vieux Fort has attracted modern industries. Cruise liners deliver tourists to Castries, and the Grande Cul de Sac Bay to the south is one of the deepest tanker ports in the Americas. It is used mainly for trans-shipment of oil.

AREA	CAPITAL
610 sq km	Castries
[236 sq mi]	**CURRENCY**
POPULATION	E. Caribbean
158,000	dollar

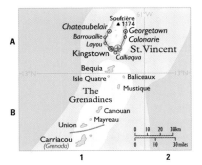

ST VINCENT AND THE GRENADINES

St Vincent and the Grenadines comprises the main island, which makes up 89% of the area and contains 95% of the population, and the northern Grenadines, of which the largest are Bequia, Mustique and Canouan. St Vincent is a mountainous, volcanic island which receives heavy rainfall. Soufrière, at 1,174 m [3,851 ft], is an active volcano.

'Discovered' in 1498, St Vincent was settled in the 16th century and became a British colony in 1783, after a century of conflict with France, often supported by the Caribs – the last of whom were deported to Honduras after the Indian War of 1795–7. The colony became self-governing in 1969 and independent in 1979. Less prosperous than its Commonwealth neighbours, it has wealthy pockets, notably Mustique and Bequia, whose beautiful clean waters have fostered tourism.

AREA	CAPITAL
388 sq km [150 sq mi]	Kingstown
POPULATION	**CURRENCY**
116,000	East Caribbean dollar

CARIBBEAN SEA

TRINIDAD AND TOBAGO

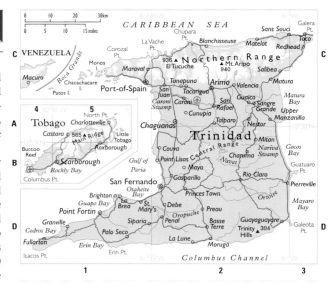

The Republic of Trinidad and Tobago contains Trinidad, a rectangular island situated just 16 km [10 mi] off Venezuela's Orinoco delta, and Tobago, a detached extension of its Northern Range of hills, lying 34 km [21 mi] to the northeast. Trinidad's highest point is Mount Aripo, at 940 m [3,085 ft] in the rugged, forested Northern Range. Temperatures are high throughout the year and the rainfall is heavy, with the wettest months from June to November.

'Discovered' by Christopher Columbus in 1498, Trinidad was later planted by Spanish and French settlers before becoming British in 1797. Black slaves worked the plantations until emancipation in 1834, when Indian and Chinese indentured labourers were brought in. Indian influence is strong in some villages, while African culture dominates in others. Spain, the Netherlands and France competed for Tobago before it came under British control in 1814. It joined Trinidad to become a single colony in 1899. Independence came in 1962, and a republic was established in 1976. Trinidad experienced a sharp change in 1986 when, after 30 years, the People's National Movement was defeated and the National Alliance for Reconstruction coalition took office. In 1994, Baseo Panday, leader of the United National Congress (UNC), became prime minister, leading a new coalition. The UNC won the 2000 elections and Panday continued in office.

Oil was the lifeblood of the nation's economy throughout the 20th century, giving the island a relatively high standard of living. Falling prices in the 1980s had a severe effect, only partly offset by the growth of tourism and continued revenues from asphalt – the other main natural resource – and gas. The country's chief exports in 1995 included refined petroleum, crude petroleum, anhydrous ammonia, iron and steel and methanol.

AREA
5,130 sq km [1,981 sq mi]
POPULATION
1,170,000
CAPITAL
Port-of-Spain
ETHNIC GROUPS
Black 40%, East Indian 40%, Mixed 18%,
White 1%, Chinese 1%
LANGUAGES
English (official)
RELIGIONS
Christianity 40%,
Hinduism 24%, Islam 6%
CURRENCY
Trinidad and Tobago
dollar = 100 cents

TURKS AND CAICOS ISLANDS

The Turks and Caicos Islands are a group of 30 islands, eight of them inhabited, lying at the eastern end of the Grand Bahama, north of Haiti. They are composed of low, flat limestone terrain, with scrub, marsh and swamp providing little space for agriculture.

Previously claimed by France and Spain, the islands have been British since 1766. They were administered from Jamaica until 1959 when they became a separate Crown Colony (though since 1998, they have been described, in common with other former colonies, as a British overseas territory). Tourism and finance have recently overtaken fishing as the main economic activities. More than 70,000 tourists visited the islands in 1994. Over half of the people live in rural areas, but farming is mainly at subsistence level. Dried, frozen and processed fish remain the chief exports. Offshore banking facilities are also expanding.

AREA
430 sq km [166 sq mi]
POPULATION
18,000
CAPITAL
Cockburn Harbour
CURRENCY
US dollar = 100 cents

VIRGIN ISLANDS, BRITISH

VIRGIN ISLANDS, US

The British Virgin Islands comprise four low-lying islands and 36 islets and cays. The largest island, Tortola, contains more than three-quarters of the total population, around a third of whom live in the capital Road Town on the south-east side of Tortola. The climate is pleasant. Road Town has an average annual rainfall of 1,090 mm [43 in].

The islands were 'discovered' by Christopher Columbus in 1493. Dutch from 1648 but British since 1666, they are now a British overseas territory, enjoying, since 1977, a strong measure of self-government. Tourism is the chief source of income. It accounts for 75% of all economic activity.

AREA
153 sq km
[59 sq mi]
POPULATION
21,000
CAPITAL
Road
Town
CURRENCY
US dollar

The US Virgin Islands comprise 68 islands, the three largest being St Thomas, St Croix and St John. The islands, excluding St Croix, are rugged and hilly. The highest point, Crown Mountain on St Thomas, reaches 474 m [1,556 ft].

The United States purchased the islands from Denmark in 1917 for the sum of US $25 million. From 1973, the citizens have elected a delegate to the House of Representatives.

Tourism is the main industry and airborne day-trippers from the US are attracted by the duty-free shops of St Thomas. The islands have the highest density of hotels and condominiums in the Caribbean.

AREA
340 sq km
[130 sq mi]
POPULATION
122,000
CAPITAL
Charlotte
Amalie
CURRENCY
US dollar

CENTRAL AFRICAN REPUBLIC

The red, yellow and green colours on this flag were originally used by Ethiopia, Africa's oldest independent nation. They symbolize African unity. The blue, white and red recall the flag of France, the country's colonial ruler. This flag was adopted in 1958.

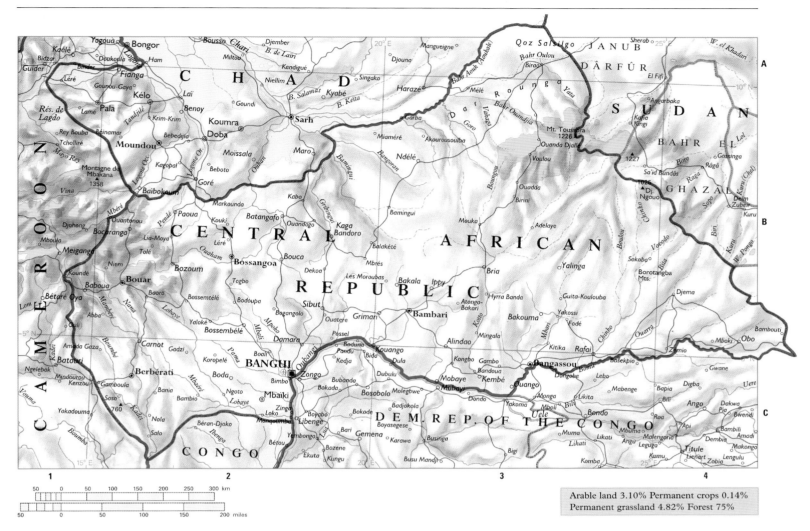

Arable land 3.10% Permanent crops 0.14%
Permanent grassland 4.82% Forest 75%

Geography

The Central African Republic is a landlocked country in central Africa. It consists mostly of a plateau lying between 600 m and 800 m [1,970 ft to 2,620 ft] above sea level. The Oubangi drains the south, while the Chari (or Shari) River flows from the north to the Lake Chad basin.

Climate

The climate is warm throughout the year, with an average yearly rainfall totalling 1,574 mm [62 in]. The north is drier, with an average yearly rainfall total of about 800 mm [31 in].

History and Politics

Little is known of the early history of the area. Between the 16th and 19th centuries, the population was greatly reduced by the slave trade. The country is still thinly populated. Although it is larger than France in area, France has 18 times as many people.

France set up an outpost at Bangui in 1899 and ruled the country as a colony from 1894. Known as Ubangi-Shari, the country was ruled by France as part of French Equatorial Africa until it gained independence in 1960.

The Central African Republic became a one-party state in 1962, but army officers seized power in 1966. The head of the army, Jean-Bedel Bokassa, made himself emperor in 1976. The country was renamed the Central African Empire, but after a brutal and tyrannical reign, Bokassa was overthrown by a military group in 1979. As a result, the monarchy was abolished and the country again became a republic.

The country adopted a new, multiparty constitution during 1991. Elections were held in 1993. An army rebellion in 1996 was finally put down in 1997 with the assistance of French troops. An attempted coup in 2001 was put down, with Libyan help, by President Ange-Félix Patassé, who had served as president since 1993.

Economy

The World Bank classifies the Central African Republic as a 'low-income' developing country. Over 80% of the people are farmers – most of them producing little more than they need to feed their families. The main crops are bananas, maize, manioc, millet and yams. Coffee, cotton, timber and tobacco are also produced for export.

Diamonds, the only major mineral resource, are the most valuable single export. Manufacturing is on a very small scale. Products include beer, cotton fabrics, footwear, leather, soap and sawn timber. The Central African Republic's development has been greatly impeded by its remote position, its poor transport system and its untrained workforce. The country is heavily dependent on aid.

AREA	Mandjia 21%, Sara 10%,
622,980 sq km [240,533 sq mi]	Mbaka 4%, Mboum 4%
POPULATION	**LANGUAGES**
3,577,000	French (official), Sangho
CAPITAL (POPULATION)	**RELIGIONS**
Bangui (553,000)	Traditional beliefs 57%,
GOVERNMENT	Christianity 35%,
Multiparty republic	Islam 8%
ETHNIC GROUPS	**CURRENCY**
Baya 34%, Banda 27%,	CFA franc = 100 centimes

Chad's flag was adopted in 1959 as the country prepared for independence in 1960. The blue represents the sky, the streams in southern Chad, and hope. The yellow symbolizes the sun and the Sahara in the north. The red represents national sacrifice.

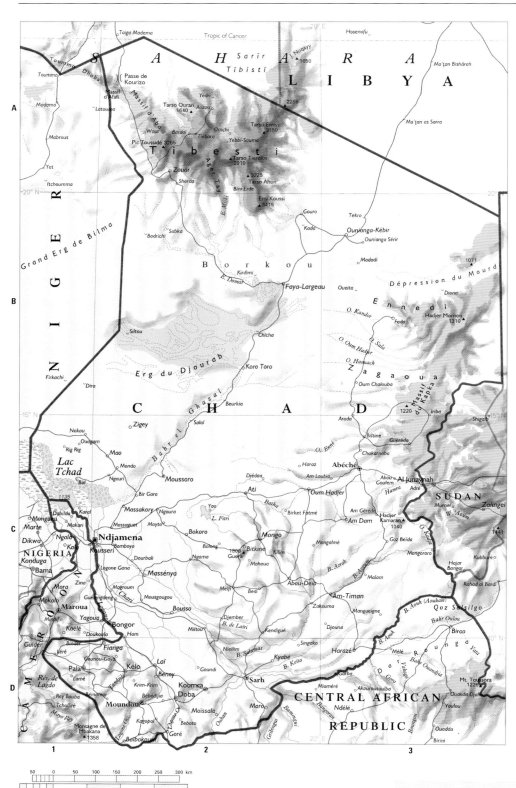

of the Sahara Desert. The mountains contain Chad's highest peak, Emi Koussi, at 3,415 m [11,204 ft] above sea level.

Chad has a hot, tropical climate, with a marked dry season from between November and April. The south of the country is wetter, with an average yearly rainfall of around 1,000 mm [39 in]. The burning-hot desert in the north has an average yearly rainfall of less than 130 mm [5 in].

History and Politics

Chad straddles two worlds. The north is populated by Muslim Arab and Berber peoples, while black Africans, who follow traditional beliefs or who have converted to Christianity, live in the south.

Southern Chad was part of the Kanem empire, which was founded in about AD 700. Other smaller kingdoms developed around Kanem. French explorers were active in the area in the late 19th century. France finally made Chad a colony in 1902.

Since becoming independent in 1960, Chad has been hit by ethnic conflict. In the 1970s, civil war, frequent coups and intervention in the north by Libya, retarded the country's economic development. Chad and Libya agreed a truce in 1987 and, in 1994, the International Court of Justice ruled that Libya had no claim on the Aozou Strip in the far north.

A rebel group, named the Patriotic Salvation Movement, seized power in 1990 and its leader, Idriss Déby, became head of state. In 1991, a law was made permitting political parties, provided they are not based on regionalism, tribalism or intolerance. Following presidential elections in 1996, in which Déby was re-elected, a new constitution was approved in a referendum in 1997.

Economy

Hit by drought and civil war, Chad is one of the world's poorest countries. Farming, fishing and livestock raising employ 83% of the people. Groundnuts, millet, rice and sorghum are major food crops in the wetter south, but the most valuable crop in export terms is cotton. Other exports include live animals, including cattle. The country has few natural resources and few manufacturing industries.

Geography and Climate

The Republic of Chad is a landlocked country in north-central Africa. It is Africa's fifth largest country and is more than twice the size of France, which once ruled it as a colony. The land consists largely of desert and rocky plateaux and most people live in the fertile south.

Southern Chad is crossed by rivers that flow into Lake Chad, on the western border. Beyond a large depression, north-east of Lake Chad, are the Tibesti Mountains which rise steeply from the sands

AREA
1,284,000 sq km [495,752 sq mi]
POPULATION
8,707,000
CAPITAL (POPULATION)
Ndjamena (530,000)
GOVERNMENT
Multiparty republic
ETHNIC GROUPS
Bagirmi, Kreish and Sara 31%,

Sudanic Arab 26%,
Teda 7%, Mbum 6%
LANGUAGES
French and Arabic
(both official), many others
RELIGIONS
Islam 50%, Christianity 25%,
traditional beliefs 25%
CURRENCY
CFA franc = 100 centimes

CHILE

Chile's flag was adopted in 1817. It was designed in that year by an American serving in the Chilean army who was inspired by the US Stars and Stripes. The white represents the snow-capped Andes, the blue the sky, and the red the blood of the nation's patriots.

Geography

The Republic of Chile stretches about 4,260 km [2,650 mi] from north to south, although the maximum east–west distance is only about 430 km [267 mi]. The high Andes Mountains form Chile's eastern borders with Argentina and Bolivia. To the west are basins and valleys, with coastal uplands overlooking the shore. In the south, the land has been worn by glaciers and the coastal uplands are islands, while the inland valleys are arms of the sea. Most people live in the central valley, which contains the capital, Santiago.

Climate

Chile is divided into three main climate zones. The north has an arid climate, but temperatures are moderated by the cold Peru Current. Central Chile has a Mediterranean climate. The south is cool and stormy.

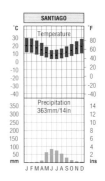

CHILE (SANTIAGO)

Chile has a great variety of climates because of its latitudinal extent and the high Andes in the east. Rainfall increases southwards from the deserts in the north. For example, Antofagasta has an annual average rainfall of 14 mm [0.6 in]. Central Chile has a Mediterranean-type climate, with hot, dry summers and mild, moist winters. The climate of Chile's capital, Santiago, is typical of central Chile, with average temperatures of 21°C [69°F] in January and 9°C [48°F] in July. The average annual rainfall is 360 mm [14 in], of which 280 mm [11 in] falls between May and August. By contrast, southern Chile has a cool, changeable and often stormy, wet climate.

History

Amerindian people reached the southern tip of South America at least 8,000 years ago. In 1520, the Portuguese navigator Ferdinand Magellan became the first European to sight Chile, but the country became a Spanish colony in the 1540s. Under Spain, the economy in the north was based on mining, while huge ranches, or *haciendas*, were set up in central Chile. After Chile became independent in 1818, mining continued to flourish in the north, while Valparaiso developed as a port exporting produce from central Chile to California and Australia. Industrial growth, fuelled by revenue from nitrate exports, began in the early 20th century.

Politics

After World War II, Chile faced economic problems, partly caused by falls in world copper prices. A Christian Democrat was elected president in 1964, but was replaced by Salvador Allende Gossens in 1970. Allende's administration, the world's first democratically elected Marxist government, was overthrown in a CIA-backed coup in 1973. General Augusto Pinochet Ugarte took power as a dictator, banning all political activity in a repressive regime. A new constitution took effect from 1981, allowing for an eventual return to democracy. Elections took place in 1989. President Patrico Aylwin took office in 1990, but Pinochet secured continued office as commander-in-chief of the armed forces. Eduardo Frei was elected president in 1993 and he was succeeded by a socialist, Ricardo Lagos, who narrowly defeated a conservative candidate in January 2000. In 1999, General Pinochet, who was visiting Britain for medical treatment, was faced with extradition to Spain to answer charges that he had presided over acts of torture when he was Chile's dictator. In 2000, he was allowed to return to Chile where, in 2001, he was found to be too ill to stand trial.

Economy

The World Bank classifies Chile as a 'lower-middle-income' developing country. Mining is important. Minerals dominate Chile's exports. But the most valuable activity is manufacturing; products include processed foods, metals, iron and steel, wood products and textiles.

Agriculture employs 18% of the people. The chief crop is wheat, while beans, fruits, maize and livestock products are also important. Chile's fishing industry is one of the world's largest.

AREA	**ETHNIC GROUPS**
756,950 sq km [292,258 sq mi]	Mestizo 95%, Amerindian 3%
POPULATION	**LANGUAGES**
15,328,000	Spanish (official)
CAPITAL (POPULATION)	**RELIGIONS**
Santiago (4,691,000)	Roman Catholic 89%, Protestant 11%
GOVERNMENT	**CURRENCY**
Multiparty republic	Peso = 100 centavos

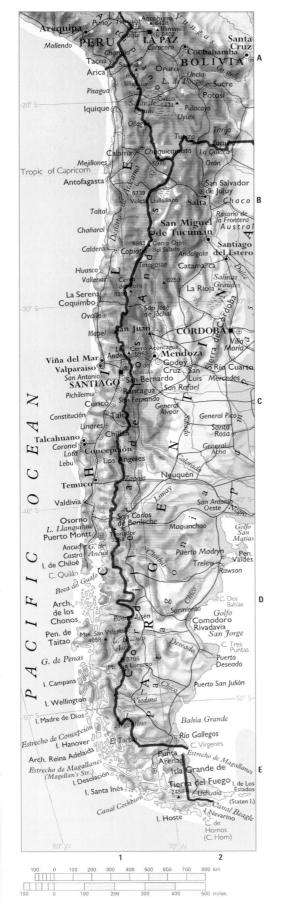

China's flag was adopted in 1949, when the country became a Communist People's Republic. Red is the traditional colour of both China and Communism. The large star represents the Communist Party programme. The smaller stars symbolize the four main social classes.

Geography

By far the most populous country in the world, though India is steadily closing the gap, the People's Republic of China is the world's third largest country after Russia and Canada. Before the development of modern transport systems, the vast size of China often hampered communications between the country's centre and the peripheries. Distances between the major cities are huge. By rail, the distance from Beijing to Guangzhou, for example, is 2,324 km [1,450 mi].

Mountains and plateaux alternate with basins and alluvial plains across China. Soil erosion, caused mainly by deforestation, has devastated many mountain areas. Most of the people live in the eastern lowlands. Manchuria, in the north, comprises a wide area of gently undulating country, originally grassland, but now an important agricultural area. The loess lands of the north-west occupy a broad belt from the great loop of the Huang He into the Shanxi and Henan Provinces. Here, valley sides, hills and mountains are blanketed in loess – a fine-grained, unstratified soil deposited by the wind during the last Ice Age. Within this region, the loess plateaux are deeply incised by gorges and ravines.

By contrast with the loess lands, the landscape of the North China Plain is very flat. Further south, the Chang Jiang (Yangtze) Delta is a region of large lakes. Here, low-lying land is traversed by a large network of canals and other, often ancient, man-made works. Far inland in the Chang Jiang Basin, and separated from the middle Chang Jiang Basin by gorges, lies the Red Basin of Sichuan Province. High mountains surround the basin to the north, west and south. The mountains of the Qin Ling ranges, in particular, protect the basin from cold winter winds.

The Qin Ling ranges are an important boundary between the relatively harsh environments of the north and the more productive lands of the south. A second major line, which follows the Da Hingaan Ling mountains and the eastern edge of the high Tibetan Plateau, divides the intensively cultivated lands of eastern China from the mountains and arid steppes of the interior. In the north, this boundary is marked by the Great Wall of China. Western China includes the Junggar Pendi (Dzungarian Basin), the Turpan (or Turfan) Depression, the Takla Makan (Taklimakan) Desert, and the high, windswept plateau of Tibet edged by the Himalayas.

China's two major rivers are the Chang Jiang and Huang He, the world's third and seventh longest, respectively. The Chang Jiang has a catchment basin almost twice as large as that of the Huang He and it is a major transport artery. The Huang He, or Yellow River, has been called 'China's

Sorrow' because it has, throughout history, been responsible for frequent and disastrous floods. However, since 1949, the introduction of flood prevention schemes has greatly reduced the incidence of flooding.

Climate

The climate of China is influenced by the air masses of Asia, the Pacific Ocean and the mountains in the west. During the winter, the cold, dry Siberian air flows southwards, while during the summer, tropical Pacific air brings relatively high temperatures and rain. Summer temperatures within eastern China are high, with very little difference between the north and the south. The average annual rainfall ranges from more than 2,000 mm [80 in] in the south to desert conditions in the north-west. Tibet has extremely cold winters and low precipitation.

CHINA (BEIJING)

Beijing has a climate representative of much of north-eastern China. Winters are bitterly cold and average temperatures are below freezing from December to February. Precipitation in winter is small, but light snow and frost are common, while strong winds sometimes bring unpleasant dust storms. Summers are warm and wet, though droughts may occur. The average annual rainfall in Beijing is 620 mm [24 in]. In July and August, rainfall totals around 380 mm [15 in].

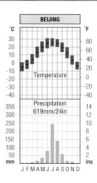

Vegetation

Because of its huge size and varied altitudes, China contains almost every type of vegetation, ranging from deserts and grasslands to boreal forests (or taiga – an extension of the forests of Siberia) near the north-eastern border with Russia, temperate forests with deciduous trees in east-central China, tropical forests in the far south-east, including Yunnan Province and the island of Hainan, together with mangrove swamps along the shores of the South China Sea. Broadly, China can be divided into two main vegetation regions: the dry north-west and the humid south-east.

History

China has one of the world's oldest civilizations, going back more than 3,500 years. Early Chinese civilization arose along the inland margins of the North China Plain, in a markedly harsher – especially in terms of winter temperatures – environment than that of other great civilizations of the Old World. The Shang Dynasty, noted for its fine craftsmanship in bronze, flourished in northern China from 1630–1122 BC. The Shang civilization was followed by many centuries of political fragmentation, and it was not until the 3rd century BC that China was unified into a centrally administered empire. Under the Qin (Ch'in) Dynasty (221–206 BC), the Great Wall of China was completed, while Chinese armies pushed southwards beyond the Chang Jiang (Yangtze River), reaching the southern Chinese coast in the vicinity of Canton (now Guangzhou). Under the Han Dynasty (206 BC–AD 220), the Chinese empire covered a vast area.

In succeeding centuries, there was a gradual movement of people from the north to the warmer, more productive lands of the south. This slow migration was greatly accelerated by incursions of barbarian nomads into northern China, especially during the Song (or Sung) Dynasty (AD 960–1279). By the late 13th century, the southern lands, including the Chiang Jiang Valley, probably contained between 70% and 80% of the Chinese population.

During the Han, T'ang and Song Dynasties, a remarkably stable political and social order evolved within China. Major distinguishing features of Chinese civilization came to include Confucianism, whereby the individual was subordinated to family obligations and to state service, the state bureaucracy, members of which were recruited by public examinations, and the benign rule of the emperor – the 'Son of Heaven'. Great advances were made in the production of porcelain, silk, metals and lacquerware, while gunpowder, the compass and printing were among several Chinese inventions which reached the West in medieval times. But the economy of pre-modern China was overwhelmingly agricultural, and the peasant class accounted for most of the population.

Despite the geographical diversity and size of the territory, China, during pre-modern times, experienced long periods of unity and cohesion rarely disturbed by invasion. Two important dynasties, the Yuan (1279–1368) and

Arable land 9.92% Permanent crops 0.35%
Permanent grassland 42.9% Forest 14%

81

the Qing (or Ch'ing, 1644–1912), were established by the Mongols and Manchus, respectively. But almost invariably, alien rulers found it necessary to adopt Chinese methods of government, and the Chinese cultural tradition was preserved intact.

In the 18th century, China experienced rapid population growth and living standards began to fall. By the early 19th century, the government was weak and corrupt, and the country suffered famines and political unrest. British victory in the Opium War (1839–42) was followed by the division of China into spheres of influence for the major imperialist powers, and by the establishment of treaty ports, controlled by Western countries, along the Chinese coast and the Chang Jiang.

Meanwhile, the disintegration of imperial China was hastened by peasant uprisings, such as the Taiping rebellion (1850–64), and by the defeat of China in the Sino-Japanese War of 1894–5. Belated attempts were made to arrest the decline of the Chinese Empire, but, in 1912, following an uprising in Wuhan, the last of the Chinese emperors abdicated and a republic was proclaimed.

Although the republican administration in Peking (Beijing) was regarded as the legitimate government, real power rested with army generals and provincial governors. Rival generals, or warlords, raised private armies and plunged China into a long period of internal disorder. Alternative solutions were offered by two political parties. One was the Kuomintang (or Chinese Nationalist Party) formed by Sun Yatsen, a Western-educated physician, and later led by the Kuomintang's military leader Chiang Kai-Shek. The other was the Communist Party, which had been founded in 1921 by Mao Zedong (Mao Tse-tung) and 11 others. In 1931, Japan seized Manchuria and, in 1937, full-scale warfare broke out between the countries. In the bitter fighting which followed, the Communists under Mao Zedong, gained the support of the peasantry and proved adept practitioners of guerrilla warfare.

The defeat of Japan in 1945 was followed by a civil war which cost 12 million lives. The Communists routed the Nationalist armies, forcing them to take refuge on the island of Taiwan, where they established a government under Chiang Kai-Shek. On the mainland, the Chinese People's Republic was established on 1 October 1949.

Politics

Under Communist rule, the instability that afflicted China before World War II was virtually eliminated and living standards for the people greatly improved, especially in rural areas where land was seized from private landowners and redistributed among the peasants. By 1957, virtually all economic activities were under government control. However, many of the subsequent changes in Chinese society brought great suffering. In 1958, the government launched the country's Second Five-Year Plan, which was called the 'Great Leap Forward'. Based on Mao's belief that human effort could overcome all obstacles, the plan aimed to speed economic development by increasing the workforce and the number of hours worked.

One of the salient features of Communist society was the organization of the rural population into about 50,000 communes – self-sufficient units of varying sizes which were intended to increase the efficiency of agriculture. The communes also ran rural industries and were responsible for the administration of schools and clinics. Labour was organized on a vast scale to tackle public works, such as water conservation, flood control and land reclamation. In manufacturing, machinery was operated continuously, without any time for maintenance, and people were encouraged to increase steel production by using backyard furnaces. The end products were often useless. The Great Leap Forward proved to be an economic disaster, causing food shortages and a real fall in industrial production. Famine and disease caused the deaths of an estimated 20 million people. A split developed between the revolutionaries who wanted to build a classless society in which everyone worked for the common good, and the moderates who believed that China's future depended on real economic development.

In 1966, Mao gave his support to the radicals, triggering off a period called the Cultural Revolution. The radicals attacked party and government officials who were deemed to be counter-revolutionary. Universities were closed between 1966 and 1970, and students were

organized into groups called Red Guards. The Red Guards rampaged through the country destroying property, demonstrating and seizing control of many provincial and city governments. The Cultural Revolution caused such upheaval that, in 1967, Mao had to use the army to restore order. By 1969, things were returning to normal, though deep political differences between the radicals and the moderates remained.

In international affairs, China began to fall out with the Soviet Union in 1956, criticizing its policy of co-existence with the West. In 1960, the Soviet Union stopped all technical aid to China and, in 1963, all relations between the countries were broken off when the Soviet Union signed a nuclear-test ban treaty with the United Kingdom and the United States. It was only in 1989, shortly before the abandonment of Communism in the Soviet Union, that relations began to improve. By contrast, relations with Western nations improved from the 1970s. In 1971, the United Nations agreed to admit the People's Republic of China instead of Taiwan (the Republic of China). Relations with the United States also improved following a visit to China by President Richard M. Nixon in 1972.

Mao Zedong, chairman of the Communist Party, and Zhou Enlai, the prime minister, both died in 1976. A struggle for power then ensued between the moderates led by Hua Guofeng, and the radicals led by Mao's widow, Jiang Qing. Hua prevailed and became prime minister and chairman of the Communist Party. Jiang Qing and her three main supporters, who were known as the 'Gang of Four', were imprisoned. In 1977, Deng Xiaoping, a moderate who had been removed from office during the Cultural Revolution, became deputy prime minister and vice-chairman of the Communist Party. In 1980, Hua resigned as prime minister and, in 1981, he resigned as chairman of the Communist Party. Deng then became the most powerful leader in China. He set about reforming the economy, reducing government control over business, abolishing the commune system and permitting private ownership of the land. China also encouraged foreign investment and free enterprise in developing new industries in 'special economic zones' in eastern coastlands of China. People began to migrate to these zones in search of jobs.

However, economic reforms were not matched by political changes. In 1986, students began to call for political reforms and more freedom

Tibet

With an average elevation of 4,500 m [14,750 ft] and an area of 1.2 million sq km [460,000 sq mi], Tibet is the highest and most extensive plateau in the world. It is a harsh, hostile place, and most of its population of just over 2 million people live in the relatively sheltered south of the country.

For much of its history, Tibet has been ruled by Buddhist priests – *lamas* – as a theocracy. The Dalai Lama, a title passed on in successive incarnations from a dying elder to a newborn junior, usually dominated from Lhasa. Between 1720 and 1911 Tibet was under Chinese control, and was reabsorbed by Chinese forces in 1950, after the establishment of the People's Republic of China the previous year. At first, Tibet retained the right to regional self-government and was guaranteed freedom of worship. But from 1956, China tightened its control and the Dalai Lama fled to India in 1959. He was followed by more than 100,000 refugees. A brutal process of Chinese acculturation began and, in 1961, a report of the International Commission of Jurists accused China of genocide. An 'Autonomous Region of Tibet', called Xizang in Chinese, was proclaimed in 1965, but during the Cultural Revolution (1966–76) many Tibetan shrines and monasteries were destroyed.

After Mao's death in 1976, liberalization policies led to monasteries being rebuilt. Reforms led to a massive influx of Chinese immigrants. This influx, and China's control over religious life further threatened Tibetan culture. For example, in 1995, when the Dalai Lama, who had been awarded the Nobel Peace Prize in 1989, selected the new incarnation of the Panchen Lama, the second-ranking leader of his sect, China arrested the boy and enthroned another in his place.

of speech. In 1987, the secretary of the Communist Party, Hu Yaobang, who had liberal views on freedom of speech and political reform, was removed from office. When he died in April 1989, students held demonstrations to honour him. Large crowds collected in Tiananmen Square in central Beijing, where military parades were held, and also in some other cities. The students called for more democracy, but they were crushed by the armed forces who killed hundreds of protesters. After the suppression of the demonstrations, many students were arrested and Zhao Ziyang, the prime minister, was dismissed from office because of his support for the pro-democracy movement. A hard line faction within the Communist Party *Politburo* appointed Jiang Zemin as secretary-general, who became Deng's favoured successor. From the late 1980s, Deng gradually withdrew from politics. He finally died in 1997 at the age of 92.

Other important developments in the 1990s included the return to China of the former British territory of Hong Kong in 1997, and also the formerly Portuguese territory of Macau in 1999. Hong Kong, a small territory but one of the economic success stories of eastern Asia after World War II, seemed bound to contribute substantially to the continuing economic development of south-eastern China. China would also like to restore Taiwan to its status as a Chinese province, but, in 1999, the Taiwanese President Lee Teng-hui angered President Jiang Zemin by declaring that relations between Taiwan and China should be on a 'special state-to-state' basis. This was at odds with China's 'one nation' policy, whereby China and Taiwan should be regarded as one country with two equal governments. With the United States prepared to defend the island in the event of Chinese aggression, it seemed unlikely that Taiwan would be prepared to reunite with mainland China in the near future.

Against all the optimism surrounding the country's economic prospects at the start of the 21st century, China remains a developing country, and it needs high economic growth rates in order to provide employment for its already huge and growing population. However, its policies aimed at limiting population growth have achieved much success – in 1999, the Chinese government claimed that its birth control policies had reduced the number of births by 338 million between 1978 and 1998. As a result, at the turn of the century, the government seemed prepared for a gradual relaxation of its one-child policy, easing the penalties for having a bigger family. China's admission to the World Trade Organization (WTO) in 2001 seemed likely to increase the country's share of world trade. Economic relations with Taiwan also seemed likely to improve after Taiwan was admitted to the WTO on 1 January 2002.

So far the benefits of economic growth have been unevenly felt – it has been confined mainly to the east, while much of the vast interior remains untouched. However, evidence for China's commitment to continuing economic reform was provided in 1998 by the appointment of Zhu Rongji as prime minister, replacing the conservative Li Peng. Zhu, an economist and protégé of Deng Xiaoping, had, as deputy prime minister, already been in overall charge of the economy. He was also associated with programmes of modernizing the economy, ensuring gradual growth in the prosperity of the Chinese people, though he had shown little interest in political reform. However, providing that the country's leaders continue to follow their pragmatic path, many experts predict a major economic and also, eventually, a political blossoming for China in the 21st century.

Economy

Since the 1970s, economic reforms have allowed market forces to operate alongside public ownership. Technocrats, who solve problems and push forward the economic reforms, have become increasingly important in government. These new leaders have encouraged foreign investment, especially in special economic zones in eastern China, and the promotion of the country's potential for tourism. The reforms have led to rapid economic growth. Between 1978 and 1997, economic growth rates reached 8% to 10% per annum. The economy continued to expand in the late 1990s, when other countries in eastern Asia suffered economic setbacks. China's total gross national product (GNP) of US $979,894 in 1999 placed it seventh among the world's largest economies, after the United States, Japan, Germany, France, the

---

Hong Kong and Macau

Hong Kong and Macau are Special Administrative Regions of China, which were formerly ruled by Britain and Portugal respectively. The island of Hong Kong, off the coast of south-eastern China, became British under the Treaty of Nanjing (1842). The Kowloon Peninsula on the mainland was added in 1860 and another mainland area called the 'New Territories' was added in 1898. On 1 July 1997, Hong Kong was returned to China, which agreed to allow it to enjoy full economic autonomy and to pursue its capitalist path for at least 50 years. Hong Kong is a small territory covering only 1,071 sq km [413 sq mi], with a population of about 6 million. However, in 1997, it was the world's biggest container port, the world's biggest exporter of clothes and the tenth biggest trader. Its economy had been so successful since the end of World War II that its huge neighbour stood to increase its export earnings by more than 25%, when the handover occurred. The fortunes of this dynamic, densely populated community have been based on manufacturing, banking and commerce, with the sheltered waters between Kowloon and Hong Kong island providing one of the world's finest natural deep-water harbours. Yet Hong Kong has few natural resources and its prosperity has rested on the ingenuity and hard work of its people.

Nearby Macau was a Portuguese colony from 1557 until December 1999, when it, too, became a Special Administrative Region of China. From the 16th to the 18th centuries, it was a trading centre for silk, gold, spices and opium, but was overtaken in importance by Hong Kong in the 19th century. With an area of 16 sq km [6 sq mi] and a population of about 490,000, Macau lies on a peninsula at the head of the Canton (Pearl) River, 64 km [40 mi] west of Hong Kong and connected to China by a narrow isthmus. The main industries are textiles and tourism, and the territory is heavily reliant on the Chinese mainland for food, water and raw materials.

United Kingdom and Italy. However, with its population of more than 1.2 billion, its per capita GNP was only $780, which placed it among the world's poorer developing countries.

In the mid-1990s, despite moves towards industrialization, agriculture still employed 53% of the population, while mining and manufacturing employed another 17%. The collectivization of agriculture through the creation of communes was replaced from 1978 by household enterprises, numbering more than 230 million in 1996, together with town and village enterprises, co-operatives and some state farms, where workers are paid wages. These changes led to a rise in national production, and agricultural output doubled in the 1980s.

While less than 3% of the country can be cultivated, China has practised intensive farming for thousands of years and, as a result, the country is largely self-sufficient in food. However, the threat of floods and drought remain, despite government initiatives in soil conservancy, afforestation, together with irrigation and drainage projects. The crops grown vary according to the climate. The warm south-east has a long growing season and two to three crops can be grown on the same plot of land in a single year. Major crops in the area include rice, tea and sweet potatoes. In the north, with its cooler climate and shorter growing season, wheat is the chief crop, together with maize and sorghum. Western China is largely arid and barren and crops are grown only around isolated oases. However, nomadic pastoralists, such as the Uighurs in Xinjiang, raise goats, horses and sheep.

China leads the world in the production of rice, sweet potatoes and wheat. It also ranks among the top five producers of bananas, barley, natural rubber, sesame seed, sorghum, soya beans, sugar cane and tea. Livestock are also important. China leads the world in producing eggs, goats, horses and mules. It also ranks among the top five producers of beef and veal, cattle, poultry meat, sheep and wool.

Forestry remains important. China's total roundwood production in 1996 made it the world's second largest producer after the United States.

Regions of China

R U S S I A

KAZAKSTAN

M O N G O L I A

HEILONGJIANG

KYRGYZSTAN

JILIN

XINJIANG
UYGUR
ZIZHIQU
(SINKIANG A.R.)

LIAONING

NEI MONGGOL ZIZHIQU
(INNER MONGOLIA A.R.)

NORTH
KOREA

BEIJING SHI

TIANJIN SHI

HEBEI

SHANXI

SHANDONG

SOUTH
KOREA

QINGHAI

NINGXIA
HUIZA
ZIZHIQU
(A.R.)

SHAANXI

HENAN

JIANGSU

JAPAN

XIZANG
ZIZHIQU
(TIBET A.R.)

ANHUI

SHANGHAI SHI

SICHUAN

HUBEI

CHONGQING
SHI

ZHEJIANG

NEPAL

BHUTAN

HUNAN

JIANGXI

GUIZHOU

FUJIAN

INDIA

BANGLADESH

YUNNAN

GUANGXI
ZHUANGZU
ZIZHIQU
(A.R.)

GUANGDONG

TAIWAN

HONG KONG (S.A.R.)
MACAU

BURMA
(MYANMAR)

VIETNAM

- - - - - Disputed international boundary
(A.R.) = Autonomous Region
(S.A.R.) = Special Administrative Region

THAILAND

LAOS

HAINAN

PHILIPPINES

China has massive natural resources. Coal is found in most of the country's provinces, and China leads the world in coal production. In the 1950s, coal accounted for more than 90% of the country's total energy supply. However, China is now a major producer of oil. Oil and gas contribute 19% of the energy supply, as compared with coal, 75%, and hydroelectric power, 6%. China has other large mineral deposits. It leads the world in producing antimony, iron ore, tin and tungsten, and ranks among the top five producers of bauxite, copper, lead, manganese ore, molybdenum, phosphates, salt and zinc ore.

With its massive reserves of coal and iron ore, China is a major producer of steel, ranking second only in the world to Japan. Manufacturing now plays a major part in China's economy. Besides steel, China also manufactures tools and machinery for new factories, cement, chemicals and fertilizers, military equipment and transport equipment, including locomotives, trucks and tractors. The leading consumer goods include processed food and textiles, bicycles, radios and sewing machines. China still has many cottage industries in rural areas. Many of them produce such items as silk and cotton textiles.

The rapid growth of the manufacturing sector since 1978 has not been without problems, including the clash between market forces and the rigid political controls of the Communist Party, such as the collapse of some out-of-date, government-owned enterprises that can no longer compete with new, technologically advanced factories. However, inefficient state enterprises still survive, together with corruption, bureaucracy and environmental pollution, including the use of coal which causes severe air pollution, while water supplies are polluted by industrial effluents and untreated sewage. But the march

of industrialization in the east seems irresistible and foreign investment and trade are increasing. Another major change that has resulted from the economic reforms is the increase in the internal migrant population, which was estimated at 21 million in 1990. Many of the migrants were looking for seasonal work or jobs in the new industries being established in the special economic zones. Under Communism, everyone had a job. However, in the new China, unemployment, especially in urban areas, had reached 5.1% by mid-2000, though many believed that the real figure was much higher.

Prior to 1997, when Britain returned Hong Kong to China, the country's overseas trade accounted for less than 3% of the world total. In 1995, the leading exports were manufactures, including machinery and transport equipment, metal products, rubber and textiles. Other important items include food and live animals, chemicals and chemical products, and mineral fuels and lubricants. Leading trading partners include Japan, the United States, Taiwan and South Korea.

AREA	**ETHNIC GROUPS**
9,596,960 sq km	Han Chinese 92%,
[3,705,386 sq mi]	55 minority groups
POPULATION	**LANGUAGES**
1,273,111,000	Mandarin Chinese
CAPITAL (POPULATION)	(official)
Beijing	**RELIGIONS**
(Peking, 12,362,000)	Atheist (official)
GOVERNMENT	**CURRENCY**
Single-party	Renminbi yuan = 10 jiao =
Communist republic	100 fen

COLOMBIA

The yellow on Colombia's flag depicts the land, which is separated from the tyranny of Spain by the blue, symbolizing the Atlantic Ocean. The red symbolizes the blood of the people who fought to make the country independent. The flag has been used since 1806.

Geography

The Republic of Colombia, in north-western South America, is the only country in the continent to have coastlines on both the Pacific and the Caribbean Sea. Colombia also contains the northernmost ranges of the Andes Mountains.

Climate

There is a tropical climate in the lowlands. But the altitude greatly affects the climate of the Andes. The capital, Bogotá, which stands on a plateau in the eastern Andes at about 2,800 m [9,200 ft] above sea level, has mild temperatures throughout the year. The rainfall is heavy, especially on the Pacific coast.

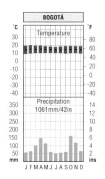

COLOMBIA (BOGOTÁ)

Colombia is split by the northern Andes. The altitude of these mountains changes the tropical climate of the country, lowering temperatures and increasing the amount of rainfall, with permanent snow at the higher levels. Elsewhere, temperatures are high with very little annual variation. Rainfall is high on the Pacific coast, but it is drier on the Caribbean coast and in the Magdalena Valley, which both experience dry seasons.

History

Amerindian people have lived in Colombia for thousands of years. Today, however, only a small proportion of the people are of unmixed Amerindian ancestry. Mestizos (people of mixed white and Amerindian ancestry) form the largest group, followed by whites and mulattos (people of mixed European and African ancestry).

Spaniards opened up the area in the early 16th century and they set up a territory known as the Viceroyalty of the New Kingdom of Granada, which included Colombia, Ecuador, Panama and Venezuela. In 1819, the area became independent, but Ecuador and Venezuela soon split away, followed by Panama in 1903.

The Drugs Trade

Colombia is notorious for its illegal export of cocaine, and reliable estimates class the drug as the country's most lucrative source of foreign exchange as kilo after kilo feeds the insatiable demand from the USA and, to a lesser extent, Western Europe. In addition to the indigenous crop, far larger amounts of leaf are smuggled in from Bolivia and Peru for refining, processing and 're-export'. US agencies estimated that in 1987 retail sales of South American cocaine totalled US $22 billion.

Violence, though focused on the drug capitals of Medellín and Cali, is endemic, with warfare between rival gangs and between producers and the authorities on an almost daily basis. Assassinations of civil servants, judicial officials, police officers or anyone attempting to investigate, control or end the rule of the multimillionaire drug barons are commonplace.

In 1990, as part of US President George Bush's US $10.6 billion 'war on drugs', the governments of three Andean states – Colombia, Bolivia and Peru – joined forces with the US Drug Enforcement Agency in an attempt to clamp down on the production and distribution of cocaine. But while early results from Bolivia were encouraging, the situation in Colombia hardened, despite the brave attempts of politicians, administrators and police to break the socio-economic stranglehold of the drug cartels. Throughout the 1990s, the country was faced with terrorism caused by rival drug-producing groups and also by the activities of two left-wing guerrilla groups.

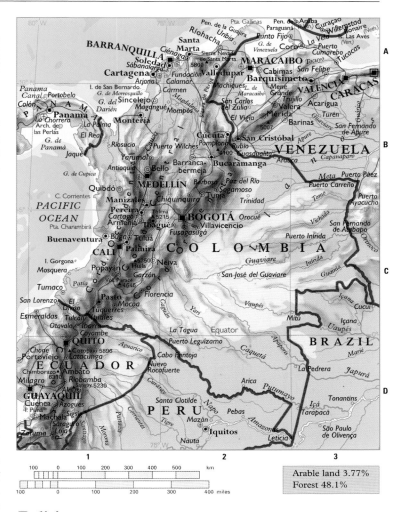

Arable land 3.77%
Forest 48.1%

Politics

Colombia's recent history has been very unstable. Rivalries between political parties led to civil wars in 1899–1902 and 1949–57, when the parties formed a coalition. Coalition government ended in 1986. Colombia's problems include the illicit drugs industry and violent guerrilla activity. Between 1999 and 2001, Andrés Pastrana, who was elected president in 1998, worked to end the guerrilla war, but peace talks finally collapsed in 2002, when full-scale fighting was resumed.

Economy

The World Bank classifies Colombia as a 'lower-middle-income' developing country. Agriculture is important and coffee is the leading export crop. Other crops include bananas, cocoa, maize and tobacco. Colombia exports coal and oil, and it produces emeralds and gold. Manufacturing is based mainly in Bogotá, Cali and Medellín.

AREA	ETHNIC GROUPS
1,138,910 sq km	Mestizo 58%,
[439,733 sq mi]	White 20%,
POPULATION	Mulatto 14%, Black 4%
40,349,000	**LANGUAGES**
CAPITAL (POPULATION)	Spanish (official)
Bogotá	**RELIGIONS**
(6,005,000)	Roman Catholic 90%
GOVERNMENT	**CURRENCY**
Multiparty republic	Peso = 100 centavos

COMOROS – SEE INDIAN OCEAN, PAGES 122–123

Congo's red flag, with the national emblem of a crossed hoe and mattock (a kind of pick-axe), was dropped in 1990, when the country officially abandoned the Communist policies it had followed since 1970. This new flag was adopted in its place.

Congo: Arable land 0.42% Permanent crops 0.07% Forest 58.3%
Congo (Dem. Rep. of the): Arable land 3.21% Permanent crops 0.27% Forest 76.7%

Geography and Climate

The Republic of Congo lies on the River Congo in Africa. The Equator runs through the centre of the country. Congo has a narrow coastal plain on which its main port, Pointe Noire, stands. Behind the plain are uplands through which the River Niari has carved a valley. To the east lies Malebo (formerly Stanley) Pool, a large lake where the River Congo widens. Central Congo consists of high plains, while the north has large swampy areas in the valleys of rivers that flow into the River Congo and its tributary, the Oubangi.

Most of the country has a humid, equatorial climate, with rain all through the year. The coastal plain is drier and cooler than the rest of the country, because the cold Benguela current flows northwards along the coast.

History and Politics

Between the 15th and 18th centuries, part of Congo probably belonged to the huge Kongo kingdom, whose centre lay to the south. Portuguese explorers reached the coast of Congo in the 15th century and the area soon became a trading region, the main commodities being slaves and ivory. The slave trade continued until the 19th century. European exploration of the interior did not occur until the late 19th century. The area came under French protection in 1880. It became known as Middle Congo, a country within French Equatorial Africa, which also included Chad, Gabon, and Ubangi-Shari (now called Central African Republic). Congo remained under French control until 1960.

Congo became a one-party state in 1964 and a military group took over the government in 1968. In 1970, Congo declared itself a Communist country, though it continued to seek aid from Western countries. The government officially abandoned its Communist policies in 1990. Multiparty elections were held in 1992 and the former military leader, Denis Sassou-Nguesso, was defeated by Pascal Lissouba. However, in 1997, Sassou-Nguesso, assisted by his personal militia and also by troops from Angola, launched an uprising which overthrew Lissouba, who fled the country, taking refuge in Burkina Faso. But forces loyal to Lissouba fought back, starting a civil war. Cease-fires were agreed in 1999 and, in 2002, Sassou-Nguesso was elected president, winning 89% of the vote.

Economy

The World Bank classifies Congo as a 'lower-middle-income' developing country. Agriculture employs about 60% of the people, though many farmers produce little more than they need to feed their families. The chief food crops include bananas, cassava, maize, plantains, rice and yams. Cash crops include cocoa, coffee and sugar cane.

Congo's main exports are oil and oil products, which account for over 80% of the exports. The industrial sector is small but growing.

AREA	Teke 17%,
342,000 sq km	M'bochi 12%
[132,046 sq mi]	**LANGUAGES**
POPULATION	French (official),
2,894,000	many others
CAPITAL (POPULATION)	**RELIGIONS**
Brazzaville (938,000)	Christianity 50%,
GOVERNMENT	Animist 48%,
Military regime	Islam 2%
ETHNIC GROUPS	**CURRENCY**
Kongo 48%, Sangha 20%,	CFA franc = 100 centimes

CONGO (DEMOCRATIC REPUBLIC OF THE)

The Democratic Republic of the Congo adopted a new flag in 1997 after Laurent Kabila rose to power. The blue represents the UN's role in securing independence for the country, and the six small stars represent the original provinces of the independent state.

Geography

The Democratic Republic of the Congo, formerly known as Zaïre, is the world's 12th largest country. Much of the country lies within the drainage basin of the huge River Congo. The river reaches the sea along the country's coastline, which is 40 km [25 mi] long. Mountains rise in the east, where the country's borders run through lakes Tanganyika, Kivu, Edward and Albert. These lakes lie on the floor of an arm of the Great Rift Valley.

Climate

The equatorial region has high temperatures and heavy rainfall throughout the year. In the subtropical south, where the town of Lubumbashi is situated, there is a marked wet and dry season.

History

Pygmies, who lived by hunting and gathering, were the first inhabitants of what is now the Democratic Republic of the Congo. But around 2,000 years ago the area was gradually settled by the technologically far more advanced Bantu-speaking people, who used iron tools and farmed the land. The pygmies, unable to compete, gradually moved into remote parts of the northern rainforests, while such Bantu-speaking peoples as the Kongo, Kuba, Luba and Lunda later founded large, powerful kingdoms.

The Portuguese reached the coast in the late 15th century and, soon afterwards, the slave trade began when Europeans bought slaves from coastal chiefs. The slave trade weakened the African kingdoms which lay in the interior. European exploration of the interior began in the late 19th century and, in 1908, the country, then called Congo Free State, became the personal property of King Leopold II of Belgium. The king's agents treated the local people badly, employing forced labour, and, in 1908, the Congo Free State became a Belgian colony, which was renamed Belgian Congo.

Politics

The Belgian Congo became independent in 1960 and was renamed Zaïre in 1971. Ethnic rivalries caused instability until 1965, when the country became a one-party state, ruled by President Mobutu. The government allowed the formation of political parties in 1990, but elections were repeatedly postponed. In 1996, fighting broke out in eastern Zaïre, as the Tutsi-Hutu conflict in Burundi and Rwanda spilled over. Laurent Kabila, an outspoken opponent of Mobutu, led an uprising spearheaded by Tutsis who lived in Zaïre and eventually took power in Kinshasa in 1997. A rebellion against Kabila broke out in 1998. Rwanda and Uganda supported the rebels, while Angola, Chad, Namibia and Zimbabwe sent troops to assist Kabila. A cease-fire was signed in 1999 by six African heads of state, including Kabila, and later by rebel leaders. In January 2001, Kabila was assassinated and his son, Major-General Joseph Kabila, became president. Hopes of a peace deal were raised, but the conflict continued.

Economy

The World Bank classifies the Democratic Republic of the Congo as a 'low-income' developing country, despite its abundant mineral reserves. The country is the world's leading producer and exporter of diamonds. It also has offshore oil deposits, and petroleum ranks as the second most valuable export, followed by copper. Coffee is also exported, while other cash crops include cocoa, cotton, palm products, rubber and tea. Agriculture employs 65% of the people, although many farmers live at subsistence level. Food crops include bananas, cassava, groundnuts, maize, plantains, rice, sugar cane and yams. Manufactures include beer and other beverages, bicycles, cement, leather, metals, processed food, rubber, tobacco, textiles, vehicles and wood products.

AREA	Mongo, Luba,
2,344,885 sq km	Kongo,
[905,365 sq mi]	Mangbetu-Azande
POPULATION	**LANGUAGES**
53,625,000	French (official),
CAPITAL (POPULATION)	tribal languages
Kinshasa	**RELIGIONS**
(2,664,000)	Roman Catholic 50%,
GOVERNMENT	Protestant 20%,
Single-party	Islam 10%,
republic	others 20%
ETHNIC GROUPS	**CURRENCY**
Over 200; the largest are	Congolese franc

Costa Rica's flag is based on the blue-white-blue pattern used by the Central American Federation (1823–39). This Federation consisted of Costa Rica, El Salvador, Guatemala, Honduras and Nicaragua. The red stripe, which was adopted in 1848, reflects the colours of France.

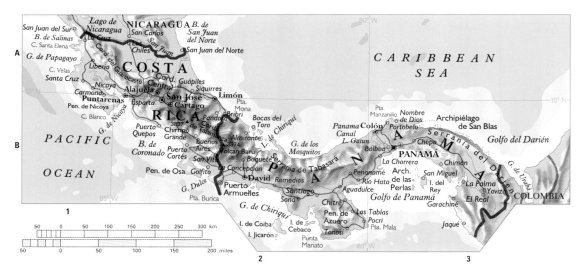

American states broke with Mexico and set up the Central American Federation. Later, this large union broke up and Costa Rica became fully independent in 1838. From the late 19th century, Costa Rica experienced a number of revolutions, with both periods of dictatorship and democracy. In 1948, following a revolt, the armed forces were abolished. Since 1948, Costa Rica has enjoyed a long period of stable democracy, which many in Latin America admire and envy.

Geography and Climate

The Republic of Costa Rica in Central America has coastlines on both the Pacific Ocean and also on the Caribbean Sea. Central Costa Rica consists of mountain ranges and plateaux with many volcanoes. The Meseta Central, where the capital, San José is situated, and the Valle del General in the south-east, have rich, volcanic soils and are the most thickly populated parts of Costa Rica. The highlands descend to the Caribbean lowlands and the Pacific Coast region, with its low mountain ranges.

The coolest months are December and January. The north-east trade winds bring heavy rain to the Caribbean coast. There is less rainfall in the highlands and on the Pacific coastlands.

History and Politics

Christopher Columbus reached the Caribbean coast in 1502 and rumours of treasure attracted many Spaniards to settle in the country. Spain ruled the country until 1821, when Spain's Central American colonies broke away to join Mexico in 1822. In 1823, the Central

Economy

Costa Rica is classified by the World Bank as a 'lower-middle-income' developing country and one of the most prosperous countries in Central America. There are high educational standards, and a high life expectancy of 73.5 years.

The country's resources include its forests, but it lacks minerals apart from some bauxite and manganese. Manufacturing is increasing. The United States is Costa Rica's chief trading partner. Tourism is a fast-growing industry.

AREA	Black and Mulatto 3%,
51,100 sq km [19,730 sq mi]	East Asian (mostly
POPULATION	Chinese) 1%
3,773,000	**LANGUAGES**
CAPITAL (POPULATION)	Spanish (official)
San José (1,220,000)	**RELIGIONS**
GOVERNMENT	Roman Catholic 76%,
Multiparty republic	Evangelical 14%
ETHNIC GROUPS	**CURRENCY**
White 85%, Mestizo 8%,	Colón = 100 céntimos

PANAMA

Geography and Climate

The Republic of Panama forms an isthmus linking Central America to South America. The Panama Canal, which is 81.6 km [50.7 mi] long, cuts across the isthmus. Panama has a tropical climate, with high temperatures, though the highlands are cooler than the coastal plains. The main rainy season is between May and September.

History and Politics

Christopher Columbus landed in Panama in 1502 and Spain took control of the area. In 1821, Panama became a province of Colombia.

In 1903, Colombia refused a request by the United States to build a canal. Panama revolted against Colombia, and became independent. The United States began to build the canal, which opened in 1914, and they administered the Panama Canal Zone, a strip of land along the canal. But many Panamanians resented US influence and, in 1979, the Canal Zone was returned to Panama. Control of the Canal itself was handed over by the USA to Panama on 31 December 1999.

Panama's government has changed many times since independence, and there have been periods of military dictatorships. In 1983, General Manuel Antonio Noriega became Panama's leader. In 1988, two US grand juries in Florida indicted Noriega on charges of drug trafficking. In 1989, Noriega was apparently defeated in a presidential election, but the government declared the election invalid. After the killing of a US

marine, US troops entered Panama and arrested Noriega, who was convicted by a Miami court of drug offences in 1992. In 1999, Mireya Moscoso became Panama's first woman president. In the early 21st century, revenues from the Canal rose, but, overall, the economy slowed, causing social discontent and problems for the government.

Economy

The World Bank classifies Panama as a 'lower-middle-income' developing country. The Panama Canal is an important source of revenue, generating jobs in commerce, trade, manufacturing and transport. The main activity is agriculture, which employs 27% of the people.

AREA	Black and Mulatto 14%,
77,080 sq km [29,761 sq mi]	White 10%, Amerindian 6%
POPULATION	**LANGUAGES**
2,846,000	Spanish (official)
CAPITAL (POPULATION)	**RELIGIONS**
Panama City (452,000)	Roman Catholic 84%,
GOVERNMENT	Protestant 5%
Multiparty republic	**CURRENCY**
ETHNIC GROUPS	US dollar; Balboa =
Mestizo 70%,	100 centésimos

CROATIA

Croatia adopted a red, white and blue flag in 1848. Under Communist rule, a red star appeared at the centre. In 1990, the red star was replaced by the present coat of arms, which symbolizes the various parts of the country.

Geography

The Republic of Croatia was one of six republics making up the former Communist country of Yugoslavia until it became independent in 1991. The region bordering the Adriatic Sea is called Dalmatia. It includes the coastal ranges, which contain large areas of bare limestone, reaching 1,913 m [6,276 ft] at Mount Troglav. Other highlands lie in the north-east. Most of the rest of the country consists of the fertile Pannonian Plains, which are drained by Croatia's two main rivers, the Drava and the Sava.

Climate

The coastal area has a typical Mediterranean climate, with hot, dry summers and mild, moist winters. Inland, the climate becomes more continental. Winters are cold, while temperatures often soar to 38°C [100°F] in the summer months.

History

Slav people settled in the area around 1,400 years ago. In 803, Croatia became part of the Holy Roman Empire and the Croats soon adopted Christianity. Croatia was an independent kingdom in the 10th and 11th centuries. In 1102, the king of Hungary also became king of Croatia, creating a union that lasted 800 years. In 1526, much of Croatia and Hungary came under the Ottoman Turks following Hungary's defeat in the Battle of Mohács. At about the same time, the Austrian Habsburgs gained control of the rest of Croatia. In 1699, the Habsburgs drove out the Turks and Croatia again came under Hungarian rule. In 1809, Croatia became part of the Illyrian provinces of Napoleon I of France, but the Habsburgs took over in 1815.

In 1867, Croatia became part of the dual monarchy of Austria-Hungary and in 1868 Croatia signed an agreement with Hungary guaranteeing Croatia some of its historic rights. During World War I, Austria-Hungary fought on the side of the defeated Axis powers, and, in 1918, the empire was broken up. Croatia declared its independence and joined with neighbouring states to form the Kingdom of the Serbs, Croats and Slovenes. The Croats hoped to achieve regional autonomy, but the Serbs enforced a centralized system based on Belgrade. Serbian domination provoked Croatian opposition. In 1929, the king changed the country's name to Yugoslavia and began to rule as a dictator. He was assassinated in 1934 by a Bulgarian employed by a Croatian terrorist group, provoking more hostility between Croats and Serbs.

Germany occupied Croatia in World War II. Croatia was declared an independent state, though, in reality, it was ruled by the invaders. After the war, Communists took power in Yugoslavia, with Josip Broz Tito as its leader. After Tito's death in 1980, economic and ethnic rivalries threatened stability. In the early 1990s, Yugoslavia split into five nations. One of them, Croatia, declared itself independent in 1991.

Politics

After Serbia supplied arms to Serbs living in Croatia, war broke out between the two republics, causing great damage, large-scale movements of refugees and disruption of the economy, including the vital tourist industry. Rivalry between the Croats and Serbs goes back centuries – Croatia was politically linked with Hungary and, therefore, to Western Europe and the Roman Catholic church, from 1102 to 1918. The rivalry was fuelled in World War II by the setting up in Croatia and much of Bosnia-Herzegovina of a puppet Fascist regime by Germany, with the support of Croatian Catholics.

In 1992, the United Nations sent a peace-keeping force to Croatia, effectively ending the war with Serbia. However, in 1992, war broke out

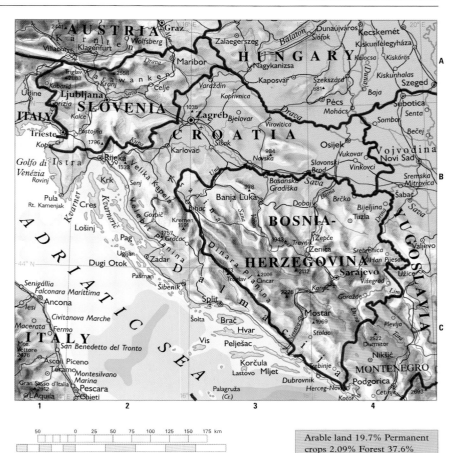

Arable land 19.7% Permanent crops 2.09% Forest 37.6%

in Bosnia-Herzegovina and Bosnian Croats occupied parts of that country. But in 1994, Croatia helped to end the Croat-Muslim conflict in Bosnia-Herzegovina and, in 1995, after retaking some areas occupied by Serbs, it contributed to the drawing up of the Dayton Peace Accord, which ended the civil war. Croatia's arch-nationalist president, Franco Tudjman, died in December 1999. In January 2000, Tudjman's Croatian Democratic Union was defeated in a general election by a more liberal, westward-leaning alliance of Social Democrats and Social Liberals. Stipe Mesic, the last head of state of the former Yugoslavia before it disintegrated in 1991, was elected president. In 2000, the government announced that it would prosecute suspected war criminals and co-operate with the war crimes tribunal in The Hague.

Economy

The wars of the early 1990s disrupted Croatia's economy, which had been quite prosperous before the disturbances. Tourism on the Dalmatian coast had been a major industry. Croatia also had major manufacturing industries, and manufactures remain the chief exports. Manufactures include cement, chemicals, refined oil and oil products, ships, steel and wood products. Major farm products include fruits, livestock, maize, soya beans, sugar beet and wheat.

AREA	Serb 12%,
56,538 sq km [21,824 sq mi]	Bosnian
POPULATION	**LANGUAGES**
4,334,000	Serbo-Croatian
CAPITAL (POPULATION)	**RELIGIONS**
Zagreb (868,000)	Roman Catholic 77%,
GOVERNMENT	Eastern Orthodox 11%,
Multiparty republic	Islam 1%
ETHNIC GROUPS	**CURRENCY**
Croat 78%,	Kuna = 100 lipas

Cuba's flag, the 'Lone Star' banner, was designed in 1849, but it was not adopted as the national flag until 1901, after Spain had withdrawn from the country. The red triangle represents the Cuban people's bloody struggle for independence.

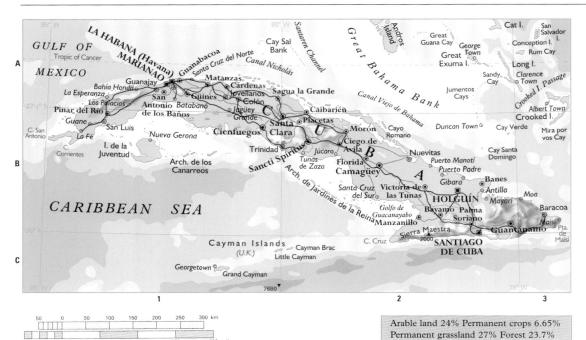

Arable land 24% Permanent crops 6.65%
Permanent grassland 27% Forest 23.7%

Geography

The Republic of Cuba is the largest island country in the Caribbean Sea. It consists of one large island, Cuba, the Isle of Youth (Isla de la Juventud) and about 1,600 small islets. Mountains and hills cover about a quarter of Cuba. The highest mountain range, the Sierra Maestra in the south-east, reaches 2,000 m [6,562 ft] above sea level. The rest of the land consists of gently rolling country or coastal plains, crossed by fertile valleys carved by the short, mostly shallow and narrow rivers.

Climate

Cuba lies in the tropics. But sea breezes moderate the temperature, warming the land in winter and cooling it in summer.

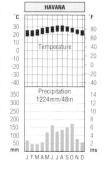

CUBA (HAVANA)

Cuba experiences uniformly high temperatures throughout the year: 22°C [72°F] in January, and 28°C [82°F] during August. The highest temperature ever recorded in Cuba is 36°C [97°F], with the lowest at 10°C [50°F]. Rainfall is heavier on the northern side of the island and falls in a marked wet season which runs from May to October – this season may also experience hurricanes, which often cause widespread devastation.

History

Christopher Columbus discovered the island in 1492 and Spaniards began to settle there from 1511. Spanish rule ended in 1898, when the United States defeated Spain in the Spanish-American War. The United States ruled Cuba from 1898 until 1902, when the people elected Tomás Estrada Palma as president of the independent Republic of Cuba, though American influence remained strong. In 1933, an army sergeant named Fulgencio Batista seized power and ruled as dictator. However, under a new constitution, he was elected president in 1940, serving until 1944. He again seized power in 1952 and became dictator, but, on 1 January 1959, he fled Cuba following the overthrow of his regime by a revolutionary force led by a young lawyer, Fidel Castro. Many Cubans who were opposed to Castro left the country, settling in the United States. Groups of exiles mounted anti-Castro campaigns.

Politics

The United States opposed Castro's policies, so he turned to the Soviet Union for assistance. In 1961, Cuban exiles attempting an invasion were defeated. In 1962, the US learned that nuclear missile bases armed by the Soviet Union had been established in Cuba. The US ordered the Soviet Union to remove the missiles and bases. After a few days, during which many people feared that a world war might break out, the Soviet Union agreed to American demands.

Cuba's relations with the Soviet Union remained strong until 1991, when the Soviet Union was broken up. The loss of Soviet aid greatly damaged Cuba's economy. Castro continued the country's left-wing policies, despite the isolation of his Marxist regime and the disruption of trade, which severely affected the economy of a country that had been highly dependent on oil and aid from the Soviet Union. The new situation undermined Castro's considerable social achievements, but, in February 1993, elections showed a high level of support for his left-wing policies. In 1998, hopes of a thaw in relations with the United States were raised when the US government announced that it was lifting the ban on flights to Cuba. The Pope, making his first visit to Cuba, criticized the 'unjust and ethically unacceptable' US blockade on Cuba.

Economy

Sugar cane remains Cuba's outstandingly important cash crop, accounting for more than 60% of the country's exports. It is grown on more than half of the island's cultivated land and Cuba is one of the world's top ten producers of the product. Before 1959, the sugar cane was grown on large estates, many of them owned by US companies. Following the Revolution, they were nationalized and the Soviet Union and Eastern European countries replaced the United States as the main market. The other main crop is tobacco, which is grown in the northwest. Cattle raising, milk production and rice cultivation have also been encouraged to help diversify the economy, and the Castro regime has devoted considerable efforts to improving the quality of rural life, making standards of living more homogeneous throughout the island.

Minerals and concentrates rank second to sugar among Cuba's exports, followed by fish products, tobacco and tobacco products, including the famous cigars, and citrus fruits. In the 1990s, Cuba sought to increase its trade with Latin America and China. Tourism is a major source of income, but the industry was badly hit following the terrorist attack on the United States on 11 September 2001.

AREA	ETHNIC GROUPS
110,860 sq km [42,803 sq mi]	Mulatto 51%, White 37%, Black 11%
POPULATION	**LANGUAGES**
11,184,000	Spanish (official)
CAPITAL (POPULATION)	**RELIGIONS**
Havana (La Habana, 2,204,000)	Roman Catholic 40%, Protestant 3%
GOVERNMENT	**CURRENCY**
Socialist republic	Cuban peso = 100 centavos

CYPRUS

This flag became the official flag when the country became independent from Britain in 1960. It shows an outline map of the island, with two olive branches. Since Cyprus was divided, the separate communities have flown the Greek and Turkish flags.

Geography

The Republic of Cyprus is an island nation which lies in the north-eastern Mediterranean Sea. Cyprus has scenic mountain ranges, including the Kyrenia Range in the north and the Troodos Mountains in the south, which rise to 1,951 m [6,401 ft] at Mount Olympus. The island also contains fertile lowlands, including the broad Mesaoria Plain.

Climate

Cyprus experiences hot, dry summers and mild, wet winters. Summers are hotter than those in the western Mediterranean since Cyprus lies close to the hot mainland of south-western Asia.

History and Politics

Greeks settled on Cyprus 3,200 years ago. In the 1570s, the island became part of the Turkish Ottoman Empire. In 1878, it was leased to Britain, who annexed it in 1914 and made it a colony in 1925. In the 1950s, Greek Cypriots, led by Archbishop Makarios, began a campaign for union with Greece. A guerrilla force called EOKA attacked the British who exiled Makarios. Cyprus became independent in 1960, but Britain retained two military bases.

The constitution of Cyprus provided for power-sharing between the Greek and Turkish Cypriots. When this proved unworkable, fighting broke out. In 1974, Makarios was overthrown and Turkey invaded northern Cyprus. Many Greek Cypriots fled from the north, which, in 1983, was proclaimed an independent state called the Turkish Republic of Northern Cyprus. In 2002, with negotiations for Cyprus's entry into the European Union at an advanced stage, the Greek and Turkish leaders began new talks aimed at resolving the conflict.

Economy

The chief minerals are asbestos and chromium. However, the most valuable activity is tourism. Industry employs 37% of the workforce and manufactures include cement, clothes, footwear, tiles and wine. In the early 1990s, the United Nations reclassified Cyprus as a developed country, though the economy of the Turkish-Cypriot north lags behind that of the Greek-Cypriot south.

AREA	CAPITAL (POPULATION)
9,250 sq km [3,571 sq mi]	Nicosia (189,000)
POPULATION	**CURRENCY**
763,000	Cyprus pound = 100 cents

MALTA

The Republic of Malta comprises two main islands, Malta and Gozo, a smaller island, Comino and two tiny islets.

Malta has hot, dry summers and mild, wet winters. The sirocco, a hot wind from North Africa, may raise temperatures in the spring.

During World War I (1914–18), Malta was an important naval base. In World War II (1939–45), Italian and German aircraft bombed the islands. In recognition of the bravery of the Maltese, the British King George VI awarded the George Cross to Malta in 1942. In 1953, Malta became a base for NATO (North Atlantic Treaty Organization). The country became independent in 1964, and a republic in 1974. In 1979, Britain's military agreement with Malta expired, and Malta ceased to be a military base. In the 1980s, the people declared Malta a neutral country. Malta applied to join the European Union in the 1990s, but the application was scrapped when the Labour Party won the elections in 1996. But, following its election defeat in 1998, the bid for EU membership was renewed.

The World Bank has classified Malta as an 'upper-middle income' developing country. It lacks natural resources, but most of the people work in commercial shipbuilding, manufacturing and the tourist industry.

Manufactures include chemicals and processed food. Farming is extremely difficult, due to rocky soils. Crops include barley, fruits, potatoes and wheat.

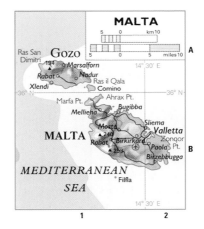

AREA	CAPITAL (POPULATION)
316 sq km [122 sq mi]	Valletta (102,000)
POPULATION	**CURRENCY**
395,000	Maltese lira = 100 cents

After independence, on 1 January 1993, the Czech Republic adopted the former flag of Czechoslovakia. It features the red and white of Bohemia in the west, together with the blue of Moravia and Slovakia. Red, white and blue are the colours of Pan-Slavic liberation.

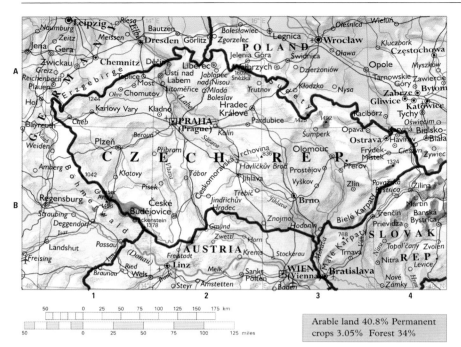

Arable land 40.8% Permanent crops 3.05% Forest 34%

German culture was dominant until the late 18th century. However, although Austria continued to rule Bohemia and Moravia, Czech nationalism continued to grow throughout the 19th century. During World War I, Czech nationalists advocated the creation of an independent nation. At the end of the war, when Austria-Hungary collapsed, the new republic of Czechoslovakia was founded. The 1920s and 1930s were generally a period of stability and economic progress, but problems arose concerning the country's minority groups. Many Slovaks wanted a greater degree of self-government, while Germans living in Sudetenland, in western Czechoslovakia, were unhappy under Czech rule.

In 1938, Sudetenland was turned over to Germany and, in March 1939, Germany occupied the rest of the country. By 1945, following the Nazi defeat, a coalition government, including Czech Communists, was formed to rule the country. In 1948, Communist leaders seized control and made the country an ally of the Soviet Union in the Cold War. In 1968, the Communist government introduced reforms, which were known as the 'Prague spring'. However, Russian and other East European troops invaded and suppressed the reform group.

Geography

The Czech Republic is the western three-fifths of the former country of Czechoslovakia. It contains two regions: Bohemia in the west and Moravia in the east. Mountains border much of the country in the west. The Bohemian basin in the north-centre is a fertile lowland region, with Prague, the capital city, as its main centre. Highlands cover much of the centre of the country, with lowlands in the south-east. Some rivers, such as the Elbe (Labe) and Oder (Odra) flow north into Germany and Poland. In the south, rivers flow into the Danube Basin.

Climate

The climate of the Czech Republic is influenced by its landlocked position in east-central Europe. The country experiences a humid continental climate, with warm summers and cold winters. Rainfall is generally higher in summer, with occasional thunderstorms.

CZECH REPUBLIC (PRAGUE)

Prague has a climate that is transitional between the severe continental conditions experienced in Russia, and the mild and wet conditions of Western Europe. The weather is often changeable. Summers are warm and sunny, although hot spells frequently end in thunderstorms. Spring and summer are the wettest seasons, while the precipitation in winter is low. Bitterly cold spells occur during winter when easterly winds blow.

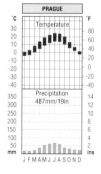

History

The ancestors of the Czech people began to settle in what is now the Czech Republic around 1,500 years ago. Bohemia, in the west, became important in the 10th century as a kingdom within the Holy Roman Empire. In the 13th century, craftworkers and merchants from Germany settled there, adding to the region's prosperity. By the 14th century, Prague was one of Europe's major cultural cities. Religious wars in the first half of the 15th century led many Czech people to become Protestants. From 1526, the Roman Catholic Habsburgs from Austria began to rule the area, but, in 1618, a Czech Protestant rebellion started the Thirty Years' War. From 1620, most Czechs were made to convert to Catholicism and adopt German as their language.

Politics

When democratic reforms were introduced in the Soviet Union in the 1980s, the Czechs also demanded change. In 1989, the Federal Assembly elected Václav Havel, a noted playwright and dissident, as the country's president and, in 1990, free elections were held. The smooth transition from Communism to democracy was called the 'Velvet Revolution'. The road to a free-market economy was not easy, with resulting inflation, falling production, strikes and unemployment, though tourism has partly made up for some of the economic decline. Political problems also arose when Slovaks began to demand independence. Finally, on 1 January 1993, the more statist Slovakia broke away from the free-market Czech Republic. However, the split was generally amicable and border adjustments were negligible. The Czechs and Slovaks maintained a customs union and other economic ties.

Economy

Under Communist rule the Czech Republic became one of the most industrialized parts of Eastern Europe. The country has deposits of coal, uranium, iron ore, magnesite, tin and zinc. Manufactures include such products as chemicals, iron and steel and machinery, but the country also has light industries making such things as glassware and textiles for export. Manufacturing employs about 40% of the Czech Republic's entire workforce.

Farming is important. The main crops include barley, fruit, hops for beer-making, maize, potatoes, sugar beet, vegetables and wheat. Cattle and other livestock are raised. Under Communist rule, the land was owned by the government. But the private ownership of the land is now being restored. The country was admitted into the Organization for Economic Co-operation and Development (OECD) in 1995.

AREA	Slovak 3%, Polish,
78,864 sq km [30,449 sq mi]	German, Silesian, Gypsy,
POPULATION	Hungarian, Ukrainian
10,264,000	**LANGUAGES**
CAPITAL (POPULATION)	Czech (official)
Prague (Praha, 1,203,000)	**RELIGIONS**
GOVERNMENT	Atheist 40%, Roman Catholic 39%,
Multiparty republic	Protestant 4%
ETHNIC GROUPS	**CURRENCY**
Czech 81%, Moravian 13%,	Czech koruna = 100 haler

DENMARK

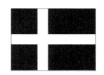

Denmark's flag is called the Dannebrog, or 'the spirit of Denmark'. It may be the oldest national flag in continuous use. It represents a vision thought to have been seen by the Danish King Waldemar II before the Battle of Lyndanisse, which took place in Estonia in 1219.

Geography

The Kingdom of Denmark is the smallest country in Scandinavia. It consists of a peninsula, called Jutland (or Jylland), which is joined to Germany, and more than 400 islands, 89 of which are inhabited.

The land is flat and mostly covered by rocks dropped there by huge ice sheets during the last Ice Age. The highest point in Denmark is on Jutland and is only 173 m [568 ft] above sea level.

Climate

Denmark has a cool but pleasant climate, except during cold spells in the winter when The Sound between Sjælland and Sweden may freeze over. Summers are warm. Rainfall occurs throughout the year.

History

Danish Vikings terrorized much of Western Europe for about 300 years after AD 800. Danish kings ruled England in the 11th century. Control of the entrances to the Baltic Sea contributed to the power of Denmark in the Middle Ages, when the kingdom dominated its neighbours and expanded its territories to include Norway, Iceland, Greenland and the Faroe Islands. The link with Norway was broken in 1814, and with Iceland in 1944. But Greenland and the Faroes retained connections with Denmark. The granite island of Bornholm, off the southern tip of Sweden, also remains a Danish possession. This island was occupied by Germany in World War II, but it was liberated by the Soviet Union and returned to Denmark in 1946. Denmark was also occupied by Germany in 1940, but it was liberated in 1945. The Danes then set about rebuilding their industries and restoring their economy.

Politics

Denmark is a generally comfortable mixture of striking political opposites. The Lutheran tradition and the cradle of Hans Christian Andersen's fairy tales co-exist with open attitudes to pornography and one of the highest illegitimacy rates in the West. A reputation for caring and welfare services, which necessitates high taxation, is somewhat dented by the high suicide rate.

The country is also one of the 'greenest' of the developed nations, with a pioneering Ministry of Pollution that has real power to act – in 1991, it became the first government anywhere to fine industries for emissions of carbon dioxide, the primary 'greenhouse' gas. At the same time, Denmark has Europe's highest rate of deaths from cancer.

Denmark gets on well with its neighbours. It joined the North Atlantic Treaty Organization in 1949, and in 1973 it joined the European Economic Community (now the European Union). However, it remains one of the European Union's least enthusiastic members and was one of the four countries that did not adopt the euro, the single EU currency, when it was introduced on 1 January 1999. In 1972, in order to join the EEC, Denmark had become the first Scandinavian country to break away from the other major economic grouping in Europe, the European Free Trade Association (EFTA), but it continued to co-operate with its five Scandinavian partners through the consultative Nordic Council which was set up in 1953.

Denmark granted home rule to the Faroe Islands in 1948, although in 1998, the government of the Faroes announced plans for independence. In 1979, home rule was also granted to Greenland, which demonstrated its new-found independence by withdrawing from the European Union in 1985. Denmark is a constitutional monarchy, with a hereditary monarch, and its constitution was amended in 1953 to allow female succession to the throne.

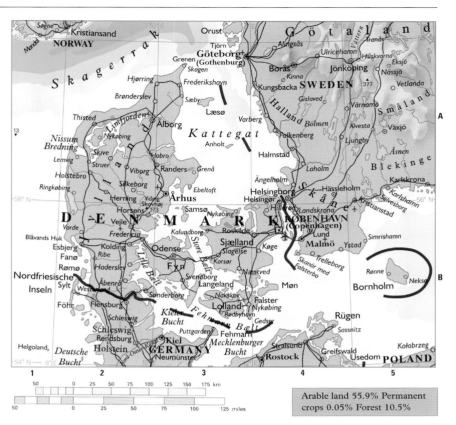

Arable land 55.9% Permanent crops 0.05% Forest 10.5%

Economy

Denmark has few mineral resources and no coal, though there is now some oil and natural gas from the North Sea. A century ago, Denmark was a poor farming and fishing country, but it has been transformed into one of Europe's wealthiest industrial nations. The first steps were taken in the late 19th century, with the introduction of co-operative methods of processing and distributing farm produce, and the development of modern methods of dairy farming and pig and poultry breeding. Farming now employs only 4% of workers, but it is highly scientific and productive.

From a firm agricultural base, Denmark has developed a wide range of industries. Some, including brewing, meat canning, fish processing, pottery, textiles and furniture making, use Danish products, but others, such as shipbuilding, oil refining, engineering and metal-working, depend on imported raw materials. Copenhagen is the chief industrial centre and draws more than a million tourists each year. At the other end of the scale is Legoland, the famous miniature town of plastic bricks, built at Billand, north-west of Vejle in eastern Jutland. It was here that Lego was created before it became the world's best-selling construction toy and a prominent Danish export. The country's main exports are machinery, meat, pharmaceuticals, furniture and textiles.

AREA	ETHNIC GROUPS
43,070 sq km [16,629 sq mi]	Danish 97%
POPULATION	**LANGUAGES**
5,353,000	Danish (official)
CAPITAL (POPULATION)	**RELIGIONS**
Copenhagen	Lutheran 95%,
(København, 1,362,000)	Roman Catholic 1%
GOVERNMENT	**CURRENCY**
Parliamentary monarchy	Krone = 100 øre

DJIBOUTI – SEE SOMALIA, PAGE 202;
DOMINICA – SEE CARIBBEAN SEA, PAGES 71–76;
DOMINICAN REPUBLIC – SEE CARIBBEAN SEA, PAGES 71–76;
EAST TIMOR – SEE INDONESIA, PAGES 124–125

Ecuador's flag was created by a patriot, Francisco de Miranda, in 1806. The armies of Simón Bolívar, the South American general, won victories over Spain, and flew this flag. At the centre is Ecuador's coat of arms, showing a condor over Mount Chimborazo.

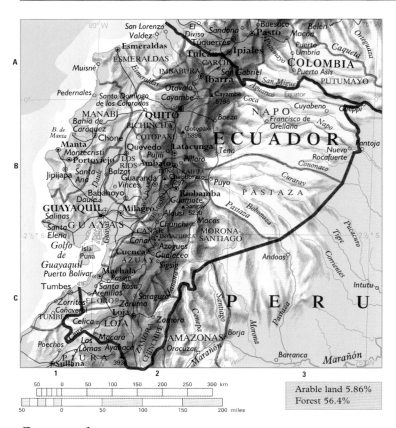

Arable land 5.86%
Forest 56.4%

Geography

The Republic of Ecuador straddles the Equator on the west coast of South America. Three ranges of the high Andes Mountains form the backbone of the country. Between the towering, snow-capped peaks of the mountains, some of which are volcanoes, lie a series of high plateaux, or basins. Nearly half of Ecuador's population lives on these plateaux.

West of the Andes lie the flat coastal lowlands, which border the Pacific Ocean and average 100 km [60 mi] in width. The eastern alluvial lowlands, often called the Oriente, are drained by headwaters of the River Amazon.

Climate

The climate in Ecuador is greatly influenced by the altitude. The coastal lowlands are hot, despite the cooling effect of the cold offshore Peru Current. The Andes have spring-like temperatures throughout the year, while the eastern lowlands are hot and humid. The rainfall is heaviest in the eastern lowlands and the northern coastal lowlands.

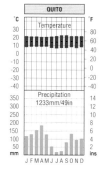

ECUADOR (QUITO)

Ecuador lies on the Equator but is bisected by the Andes, where temperatures are moderated by the altitude. Temperatures on the coastal lowlands range from 23–25°C [73–77°F]. But in Quito, which stands at 2,500 m [8,200 ft] above sea level, average temperatures are around 14–15°C [57–59°F], though days are warm and nights are often chilly. Permanent snowfields and glaciers lie not far from Quito in the high Andes.

History

The Inca people of Peru conquered much of what is now Ecuador in the late 15th century. They introduced their language, Quechua, which is widely spoken today. In 1532 a colony was founded by the Spaniards

in the territory, which was then called Quito. The country became independent in 1822, following the defeat of a Spanish force by an army led by General Antonio Jose de Sucre in a battle near Quito. Ecuador became part of Gran Colombia, a confederation which also included Colombia and Venezuela. Ecuador became a separate nation in 1830. The 19th century was very unstable and presidents and dictators came and went. This instability continued into the 20th century.

In 1832, Ecuador annexed the volcanic Galapagos Islands, which lie 970 km [610 mi] west of Ecuador, of which they form a province. The archipelago, which contains six main islands and more than 50 smaller ones, later became world-famous through the writings of Charles Darwin, who visited the islands in 1835. His descriptions of the unique endemic flora and fauna gave him crucial evidence for his theory of natural selection.

Politics

The failure of successive governments to tackle the country's many social and economic problems caused great instability in Ecuador throughout the 20th century. A war with Peru in 1941 led to loss of territory and border disputes flared up again in 1995, though the two countries eventually signed a peace treaty in January 1998.

Military regimes ruled the country between 1963 and 1966 and again from 1976 to 1979. However, under a new constitution introduced by the second of these military juntas and approved by a national referendum, civilian government was restored. Civilian governments have ruled Ecuador since multiparty elections in 1979. But the volatile character of politics here was evident throughout the 1980s and 1990s. For example, a state of emergency, albeit of short duration, was declared in 1986 and, in 1995, the vice-president was forced to leave the country after accusations that he had bribed opposition deputies.

In 1996, the president was deposed on the grounds of mental incompetence and, in 1998, accusations of fraud marred the victory of President Jamil Mahaud of the centre-right Popular Democracy Party. In January 2000, Mahaud was toppled from power by huge demonstrations against his economic policies and a military coup. Vice-President Gustavo Noboa then became head of state. In 2000, the government made the US dollar Ecuador's sole unit of currency.

Economy

The World Bank classifies Ecuador as a 'lower-middle-income' developing country. Agriculture employs 30% of the people. Bananas, cocoa and coffee are all important export crops. Other products in the hot coastal lowlands include citrus fruits, rice and sugar cane, while beans, maize and wheat are important in the highlands. Cattle are raised for dairy products and meat, while fishing is important in the coastal waters. Forestry is a major activity. Ecuador produces balsa wood and such hardwoods as mahogany. Mining is important and oil and oil products now play a major part in the economy. Ecuador started to export oil in the early 1970s and is a member of the Organization of Petroleum Exporting Countries. Manufactures include cement, Panama hats, paper products, processed food and textiles. Major exports are food and live animals, and mineral fuels. Ecuador's main trading partners are the United States and Colombia.

AREA	and Amerindian) 40%,
283,560 sq km [109,483 sq mi]	Amerindian 40%,
POPULATION	White 15%, Black 5%
13,184,000	**LANGUAGES**
CAPITAL (POPULATION)	Spanish (official),
Quito (1,574,000)	Quechua
GOVERNMENT	**RELIGIONS**
Multiparty republic	Roman Catholic 92%
ETHNIC GROUPS	**CURRENCY**
Mestizo (mixed White	US dollar = 100 cents

A flag consisting of three bands of red, white and black, the colours of the Pan-Arab movement, was adopted in 1958. The present design has a gold eagle in the centre. This symbolizes Saladin, the warrior who led the Arabs in the 12th century.

Geography

The Arab Republic of Egypt is Africa's second largest country by population after Nigeria, though it ranks 13th in area. Most of Egypt is desert. Almost all the people live either in the Nile Valley and its fertile delta or along the Suez Canal, the artificial waterway between the Mediterranean and Red seas. This canal shortens the sea journey between the United Kingdom and India by 9,700 km [6,027 mi]. Recent attempts have been made to irrigate parts of the Western Desert and thus redistribute the rapidly growing Egyptian population into previously uninhabited regions.

If not for the valley of the River Nile, Egypt would be sparsely populated. Egypt's other main regions are the Western and Eastern Deserts, which are parts of the vast Sahara, and the Sinai Peninsula in the north-east.

The Western Desert includes almost three-quarters of Egypt and consists of low vales and scarps, mainly of limestone. A number of depressions are below sea level and in some of them the prospect of tapping artesian water holds out hope for future development.

The Eastern Desert between the Nile and the Red Sea, is a much dissected area, and parts of the Red Sea Hills rise to more than 2,000 m [6,560 ft] above sea level. Beyond the Gulf of Suez and the Suez Canal, the Sinai Peninsula is largely mountainous and rugged. It contains the highest of Egypt's mountains – Gebel Katherîna, which reaches 2,637 m [8,650 ft] – and is almost entirely uninhabited.

Climate

Egypt, one of the world's hottest and sunniest countries, has a desert climate. The northern Mediterranean region, which extends south from the coast for about 80 km [50 mi], has the highest rainfall, with between 100 mm and 200 mm [4–8 in] a year. The rainfall occurs in winter and is brought by depressions coming from the west. Summers are hot, though sea breezes bring relief in the daytime. In winter, the weather is mostly warm and sunny, though northerly winds sometimes lower temperatures.

South of Cairo (El Qâhira), average annual rainfall is 25 mm to 50 mm [1–2 in], though, in reality, years may pass without significant rainfall until a freak storm occurs, sometimes causing local flooding. Winter days are warm and sunny, though nights are sometimes chilly. In the Nile Valley, because of the high humidity, mists and fog sometimes occur in the early morning but they soon clear as the sun rises in the sky. The heat in the summer is intense, though the low humidity makes conditions more bearable. In parts of the Sinai Peninsula, snow sometimes falls in winter but it seldom lasts more than a day or two.

Arable land 3.12% Permanent crops 0.39%
Permanent grassland 0% Forest 0.03%

EGYPT (CAIRO)

Cairo experiences a desert climate with sparse rainfall that occurs mostly between November and March. Winters are warm, with average temperatures of around 13°C [55°F] in January. Summers may be extremely hot. Between March and June, the Nile Valley, including Cairo, is often affected by a hot, dry and dusty wind that blows from the Sahara. Called the *khamsin*, it often raises dust and sand that reduce visibility.

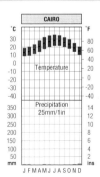

Vegetation

The Nile Valley forms a long, green ribbon of farmland, dotted with date palm trees, the most characteristic plant in northern Africa and south-western Asia. Bamboo and reeds also grow in the Nile Valley and the northern Mediterranean strip is rich in plants in spring.

But, dry landscapes, with sand dunes (called *erg* in Arabic), plains of loose gravel (*reg*) and areas of bare rock (*hammada*) cover most of the country. The Western Desert is devoid of plant life except around oases, the most important of which are Khârga, Dakhla, Farâfra, Bahariya and Siwa. Thorny shrubs and acacia trees grow in the Eastern Desert. The number of shrubs and trees increases in the Red Sea Hills.

History

The Nile Valley was one of the cradles of civilization. The dependable annual flooding of the great river each summer and the discovery of the art of cultivating wheat and barley fostered simple irrigation techniques and favoured co-operation between the farmers. City life began, and the foundations of writing, arithmetic, geometry and astronomy were laid. Great temples, magnificent statuary and pyramid tombs preserved in the dry climate in the valley remain as memorials to this early civilization.

Ancient Egypt was founded 5,000 years ago and thrived for about 2,000 years. The Egyptian civilization began in 3100 BC, when King Menes of Upper Egypt conquered Lower Egypt, creating a united nation under a central government. Menes established the first of more than 30 dynasties that ruled Ancient Egypt. The Old Kingdom, which began in 2686 BC, is known as the Pyramid Age. The first Step Pyramid was built at Saqqarah in about 2650 BC, followed by the great pyramids at El Giza which were built between 2600 and 2500 BC. The Middle Kingdom began in 1991 BC and continued until 1786 BC. It was a time of territorial expansion, trade and a flowering of the arts. Towards the end of the Middle Kingdom, settlers from Asia spread into the Nile Delta and, in 1670 BC, they seized power. In the New Kingdom, which began in 1554 BC, the Egyptians drove out the immigrants and founded a major empire extending into south-western Asia.

Ancient Egypt began to decline around 1070 BC. It lost its overseas territories and succumbed to a series of invaders, including Nubians, Assyrians and Persians. In 332 BC, Egypt became part of the empire of Alexander the Great, who founded the city of Alexandria, which later became Egypt's capital and one of the great cultural centres of the ancient world. In 30 BC, Egypt became part of the Roman Empire. Muslim Arabs invaded Egypt between AD 639 and 642. They introduced their language, Arabic, and their religion, Islam, which gradually began to replace Coptic Christianity. Their influence was so great that most Egyptians now regard themselves as Arabs.

Egypt became an important part of the Islamic Empire. At first, it was ruled from Damascus by caliphs of the Ummayad Dynasty and later from Baghdad by the Abbasid caliphs. Between 969 and 1171, Egypt was ruled by the Fatimid Dynasty. They claimed descent from Fatima, daughter of the Prophet Muhammad, and they were members of the Shiite minority of Muslims. However, in 1171, Saladin, the general who led Muslim armies against the Crusaders, overthrew the Fatimids and restored the Sunni form of Islam to Egypt. His descendants formed the Ayyubid Dynasty which ruled Egypt until 1250.

In 1250, the Mamelukes, who had served as the sultan's guards, revolted and Mameluke rule continued until 1517, when the Ottoman Turks invaded Egypt from Syria. However, the Mamelukes retained power as regional governors, or *beys*.

In 1798, Napoleon Bonaparte's French army invaded Egypt, but the Ottomans, with British assistance, drove them out in 1801. By 1805, Muhammad Ali, a Turkish officer sent to drive the French out of Egypt, became the country's ruler. His period in power was marked by reforms aimed at modernizing the country. After Muhammad Ali's death in 1849, his son gave the French a contract to build the Suez Canal, which opened in 1869. Britain became increasingly involved in Egypt after buying Egypt's shares in the Canal in 1875. In 1882, British troops intervened and defeated the Egyptian army in the battle of At Tall al-Kabir.

In the late 19th century, Britain effectively ruled Egypt. During World War I the Ottoman Turks, to whose empire Egypt nominally belonged, were allies of Germany. In 1914, Britain declared Egypt a protectorate. In 1919, Egyptian nationalists called for independence which was achieved in 1922 when Egypt became a constitutional monarchy. But Britain retained the right to keep troops in the country.

In World War II, German and Italian armies invaded Egypt in an attempt to capture the strategic Suez Canal, but they were halted at the Battle of El Alamein and subsequently driven out of North Africa. After World War II, Egyptian leaders tried unsuccessfully to remove British troops from their country. In 1948, when the State of Israel was established, Egyptian and other forces launched an attack on the Israelis, but the Israelis were victorious, and the United Nations finally brought the war to an end in 1949.

Politics

In 1952, following a military revolution led by General Muhammad Naguib, the monarchy was abolished and Egypt became a republic. Naguib became president, but he was overthrown in 1954 by Colonel Gamal Abdel Nasser. President Nasser sought to develop Egypt's economy, and he announced a major project to build a new dam at Aswan to provide electricity and water for irrigation. When Britain and the United States failed to provide finance for building the dam, Nasser seized the Suez Canal Company in July 1956. In retaliation, Israel, backed by British and French troops, invaded the Sinai Peninsula and the Suez Canal region. However, under international pressure, they were forced to withdraw. Construction of the Aswan High Dam began in 1960 and it was fully operational by 1968.

In 1967, Egypt lost territory to Israel in the Six-Day War and Nasser tendered his resignation, but the people refused to accept it. After his death in 1970, Nasser was succeeded by his vice-president, Anwar el-Sadat. In 1973, Egypt launched a surprise attack in the Sinai Peninsula, but its troops were finally forced back to the Suez Canal. In 1977, Sadat began a peace process when he visited Israel and addressed the Knesset (Israel's parliament). Finally, in 1979, Egypt and Israel signed a peace treaty under which Egypt regained the Sinai Peninsula. However, extremists opposed contacts with Israel and, in 1981, Sadat was assassinated. He was succeeded as president by Hosni Mubarak.

While Egypt has played an important role in foreign affairs, it has continued to face several problems at home. Despite economic progress, most people remain poor, while some groups dislike what they see as increasing Western influence and would like to return to the fundamental values of Islam. In the 1990s, attacks on foreign visitors severely damaged tourism, despite efforts to curb the activities of Islamic extremists. In 1997, terrorists killed 58 foreign tourists near Luxor, while, in 1999, Mubarak was attacked, though he only suffered a small wound. Tourism was again hit following the terrorist attacks on the United States on 11 September 2001. In 2002, the Americans placed several Egyptians on its 'most wanted' list of terrorists.

Economy

Egypt is Africa's second most industrialized country after South Africa, but it remains a developing country. The majority of the people are poor. Farming employs 34% of the workers. Most *fellahin* (peasants) grow such food crops as beans, maize, rice, sugar cane and wheat, but cotton is the chief cash crop. Egypt depends increasingly on the Nile. Its waters are seasonal, and control and storage have become essential in the last 100 years. The Aswan High Dam is the greatest of the Nile dams, and the water behind it in Lake Nasser is making desert reclamation possible. The electricity produced at the dam has also been important in the development of industry.

Most industrial development has come about since World War II. Textiles, including the spinning, weaving, dyeing and printing of cotton, wool, silk and artificial fibres, form the largest industry. Other products derive from local agricultural and mineral raw materials and include sugar refining, milling, oil-seed pressing, and the manufacture of chemicals, glass and cement. Egypt also has iron and steel, oil refining and car assembly industries, while many consumer goods, such as radios, TV sets and refrigerators, are also made. The chief exports are oil and oil products, followed by cotton yarn, textiles and clothing.

AREA	**ETHNIC GROUPS**
1,001,450 sq km	Egyptian 99%
[386,660 sq mi]	**LANGUAGES**
POPULATION	Arabic (official), French, English
69,537,000	**RELIGIONS**
CAPITAL (POPULATION)	Islam (Sunni Muslim 94%),
Cairo	Christianity (mainly Coptic
(El Qâhira, 6,800,000)	Christian 6%)
GOVERNMENT	**CURRENCY**
Republic	Pound = 100 piastres

EL SALVADOR – SEE GUATEMALA, PAGES 110–111;
EQUATORIAL GUINEA – SEE GABON, PAGE 103;
ERITREA – SEE ETHIOPIA, PAGE 98

ESTONIA

Estonia's flag was used between 1918 and 1940, when the country was an independent republic. It was readopted in June 1988. The blue is said to symbolize the sky, the black Estonia's black soil, and the white the snow that blankets the land in winter.

Geography

The Republic of Estonia is the smallest of the three states on the Baltic Sea, which were formerly part of the Soviet Union, but became independent in the early 1990s. Estonia consists of a generally flat plain which was covered by ice sheets during the Ice Age. The land is strewn with moraine (rocks deposited by the ice).

The country is dotted with more than 1,500 small lakes. Water, including the large Lake Peipus (Ozero Chudskoye) and the River Narva, makes up much of Estonia's eastern border with Russia. Estonia has more than 800 islands, which together comprise about a tenth of the country. The largest island is Saaremaa (Sarema).

Climate

Despite its northerly position, Estonia has a fairly mild climate due to its proximity to the sea. This is because sea winds tend to warm the land during winter and cool it in summer. Winters are cold, with temperatures in January ranging from –7°C to –2°C [19–28°F]. In July, temperatures range from 16°C to 18°C [61–64°F]. The precipitation ranges from about 500 mm to 700 mm [20–28 in].

History

The ancestors of the Estonians, who are related to the Finns, settled in the area several thousand years ago. Divided into several separate states, they were vulnerable to Viking attacks, but in the early 13th century, German crusaders, known as the Teutonic Knights, introduced Christianity. Germany took control of the southern part of Estonia and Denmark took control of the north. The Danes sold the north to the Germans in 1324 and Estonia became part of the Holy Roman Empire. By the 17th century, much of Estonia consisted of large estates owned by German noblemen. However, in 1561, Sweden took over northern Estonia and Poland ruled the south. Sweden controlled the entire country from 1625 until 1721 but, following the victory of Peter the Great over Sweden in 1721, the area became part of the Russian Empire. German nobles still had estates there until 1919, though the Estonian serfs who worked for them were freed in 1816. The serfs were granted the right to own land in 1868 and some of them became successful landowners. A national revival in the 19th century culminated on 24 February 1918, when Estonia declared its independence. A democratic form of government was established in 1919. However, a fascist coup in 1934 ended democratic rule.

Politics

In 1939, Germany and the Soviet Union agreed to take over large areas of eastern Europe, and it was agreed that the Soviet Union would take over Estonia. The Soviet Union forcibly annexed the country in 1940. Germany invaded Estonia in 1941, but the Soviet Union regained control in 1944 when the country became the Estonian Soviet Socialist Republic. Many Estonians opposed Soviet rule and were deported to Siberia. About 100,000 Estonians settled in the West.

Resistance to Soviet rule was fuelled in the 1980s when the Soviet leader Mikhail Gorbachev began to introduce reforms and many Estonians called for independence. In 1990, the Estonian parliament declared Soviet rule invalid and called for a gradual transition to full independence. The Soviet Union regarded this action as illegal, but finally the Soviet State Council recognized the Estonian parliament's proclamation of independence in September 1991, shortly before the Soviet Union itself was dissolved in December 1991.

Since independence, the Estonians have sought to increase their links with Europe. It was admitted to the Council of Europe in 1993; it is also a member of the NATO Partnership for Peace, an associate member of the European Union since 1995, and, since 1999, a member of the World Trade Organization. But despite the fact that it had the highest standard of living among the 15 former Soviet republics, Estonia has found the change to a free-market economy hard-going.

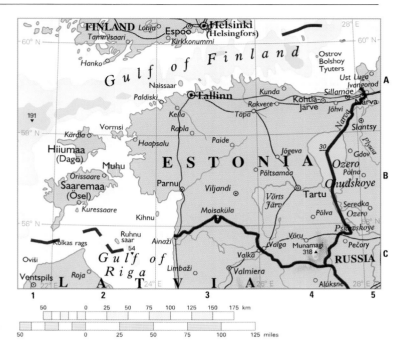

In January 1992, the combination of food shortages and an energy crisis forced the resignation of prime minister Edgar Savissar, who enjoyed wide popular and parliamentary support. A co-founder of the Popular Front, the country's pro-democracy movement, he was held responsible for a recession which appeared to have hit Estonia far harder than the other two Baltic states to the south.

Other problems facing Estonia include crime, rural underdevelopment and the status of its non-Estonian citizens, including Russians who make up about 30% of the population. In the country's first free elections in 1992, only Estonians were permitted to vote and all Russians were excluded. Tension on this issue continued through the 1990s as dual citizenship was outlawed, while restrictions were placed on Russians applying for Estonian citizenship. In the mid-1990s, Russia described Estonia's citizenship policies as discriminatory against ethnic Russians. In 1996, Estonia dropped the requirement that candidates for local office pass an Estonian language test.

Economy

Manufacturing is the most valuable activity. The timber industry is among the most important industries, alongside metal-working, shipbuilding, clothing, textiles, chemicals and food processing. Food processing is based primarily on extremely efficient dairy farming and pig breeding, but oats, barley and potatoes are suited to the cool climate and the average soils. Like the other two Baltic states, Estonia is not rich in natural resources, though its oil shale is an important mineral deposit; enough gas is extracted to supply St Petersburg, Russia's second largest city. The leading exports are mineral fuels and chemical products, followed by food, textiles and cloth, and wood and paper products. Finland and Russia are the leading trading partners.

AREA	Russian 28%, Ukrainian 3%,
44,700 sq km [17,300 sq mi]	Belarussian 2%, Finnish 1%
POPULATION	**LANGUAGES**
1,423,000	Estonian (official), Russian
CAPITAL (POPULATION)	**RELIGIONS**
Tallinn (435,000)	Lutheran, Russian and Estonian
GOVERNMENT	Orthodox, Methodist, Baptist,
Multiparty republic	Roman Catholic
ETHNIC GROUPS	**CURRENCY**
Estonian 65%,	Kroon = 100 sents

ETHIOPIA

The tricolour flag of Ethiopia first appeared in 1897. The central pentangle was introduced in 1996, and represents the common will of the country's 68 ethnic groups, and the present sequence was adopted in 1914.

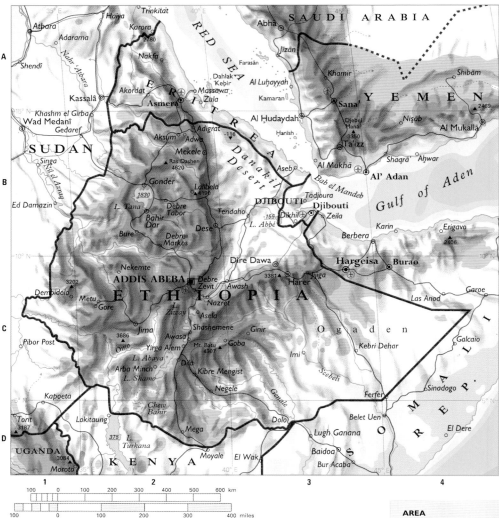

20°C [68°F]. The rainfall is generally more than 1,000 mm [39 in]. But the lowlands bordering the Eritrean coast are hot.

History

Ethiopia was the home of an ancient monarchy, which became Christian in the 4th century. In the 7th century, Muslims gained control of the lowlands, but Christianity survived in the highlands. In the 19th century, Ethiopia resisted attempts to colonize it. Italy invaded in 1935, but Ethiopian and British troops defeated the Italians in 1941.

Politics

In 1952, Eritrea, on the Red Sea coast, was federated with Ethiopia. But in 1961, Eritrean nationalists launched a struggle that ended in their independence in 1993. Border clashes with Eritrea occurred in 1998 and 1999, but a peace treaty was agreed in 2000. Ethnic diversity in Ethiopia has led to demands by minorities for self-government. As a result, in 1995, Ethiopia was divided into nine provinces, each with its own regional assembly.

Economy

Having been afflicted by drought and civil war in the 1970s and 1980s, Ethiopia is now one of the world's poorest countries. Agriculture is the main activity. Coffee is the leading cash crop and export, followed by hides, skins and pulses.

Geography and Climate

Ethiopia is a landlocked country in north-eastern Africa. The land is mainly mountainous, though there are extensive plains in the east and south. The highlands are divided into two blocks by an arm of the Great Rift Valley. North of the Rift Valley, the land is especially rugged, rising to 4,620 m [15,157 ft] at Ras Dashen. South-east of Ras Dashen is Lake Tana, source of the River Abay (Blue Nile).

The climate in Ethiopia is greatly affected by the altitude. Addis Abeba, at 2,450 m [8,000 ft], has an average yearly temperature of

AREA	Sidamo 9%, Shankella 6%,
1,128,000 sq km	Somali 6%
[435,521 sq mi]	**LANGUAGES**
POPULATION	Amharic (official),
65,892,000	280 others
CAPITAL (POPULATION)	**RELIGIONS**
Addis Abeba (2,316,000)	Islam 47%,
GOVERNMENT	Ethiopian Orthodox 40%,
Federation of nine provinces	traditional beliefs 11%
ETHNIC GROUPS	**CURRENCY**
Oromo 40%, Amharic 32%,	Birr = 100 cents

ERITREA

Geography

The State of Eritrea consists of a hot, dry coastal plain, with a mountainous central area. Most people live in the cooler highland area.

Politics and Economy

Eritrea, an Italian colony from the 1880s, was part of Ethiopia from 1952–93, when it became a fully independent nation. National reconstruction was hampered by conflict with Yemen over three islands in the Red Sea, while border disputes led to clashes with Ethiopia in the late 1990s. However, Eritrea and Ethiopia signed a peace treaty in 2000.

Farming and nomadic livestock rearing are the main activities in this poor, war-ravaged country. Eritrea has a few manufacturing industries, based mainly in Asmera.

AREA	**ETHNIC GROUPS**
94,000 sq km	Tigrinya 49%, Tigre 32%,
[36,293 sq mi]	Afar 4%, Beja 3%, Saho 3%,
POPULATION	Kunama 3%, Nara 2%
4,298,000	**LANGUAGES**
CAPITAL (POPULATION)	Afar, Amharic, Arabic, Tigrinya
Asmera	**RELIGIONS**
(367,500)	Coptic Christian 50%, Islam 50%
GOVERNMENT	**CURRENCY**
Transitional government	Nakfa

FALKLAND ISLANDS – SEE ATLANTIC OCEAN, PAGES 41–43;
FIJI – SEE PACIFIC OCEAN, PAGES 174–178

FINLAND

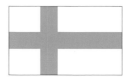

The flag of Finland was adopted in 1918, after the country had become an independent republic in 1917, following a century of Russian rule. The blue represents Finland's many lakes. The white symbolizes the blanket of snow which masks the land in winter.

Geography and Climate

The Republic of Finland is a beautiful country in northern Europe. Part of the country lies north of the Arctic Circle, in the 'Land of the Midnight Sun'. Here the sun shines for 24 hours a day for extended periods of time in summer, especially in June.

In the south, behind the coastal lowlands where most Finns live, lies the Lake District, a region of sparkling lakes worn out by ice sheets in the Ice Age. The thinly populated northern uplands cover about two-fifths of the country.

Helsinki has warm summers, but the average temperatures between the months of December and March are below freezing point. Snow covers the land in winter. The north has less precipitation than the south, but is much colder.

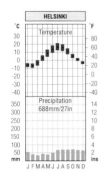

FINLAND (HELSINKI)

Finland's winters are long and harsh. A third of the country is north of the Arctic Circle where temperatures can reach −30°C [−22°F]. Snow may lie for up to six months, never clearing from north-facing slopes. Helsinki has four or five months below 0°C [32°F]. The seas and lakes nearly always freeze in winter. Summers can be hot. Rainfall is low, decreasing northwards and falling from late summer to winter, often as snow.

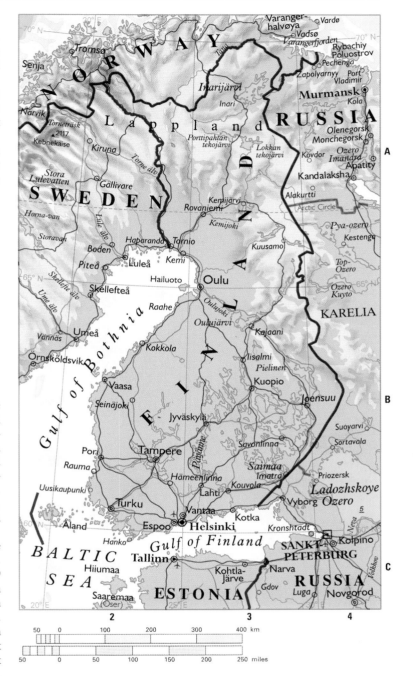

History and Politics

Between 1150 and 1809, Finland was under Swedish rule. The close links between the countries continue today. Swedish remains an official language in Finland and one of the legacies of this period is a Swedish-speaking minority of 6% of the total population. In some localities on the south and west coasts, Swedish speakers are in the majority and Åland, an island closer to the Swedish coast than to Finland, is a self-governing province. Many towns use both Finnish and Swedish names. For example, Helsinki is Helsingfors, and Turku is Åbo in Swedish. Finnish bears little relation to the Swedish or any other Scandinavian language. It is closest to Magyar, the language of Hungary.

In 1809, Finland became an independent grand duchy of the Russian Empire, though the Russian tsar was its grand duke. Nationalist feelings developed during the 19th century, but in 1899 Russia sought to enforce its culture on the Finns. In 1903, the Russian governor suspended the constitution and became dictator, though following much resistance, self-government was restored in 1906. Finland proclaimed its independence in 1917, after the Russian Revolution and the collapse of the Russian Empire and, in 1919, it adopted a republican constitution. During World War I, the Soviet Union declared war on Finland and took the southern part of Karelia, where 12% of the Finnish people lived. Finland allied itself to Germany and Finnish troops regained southern Karelia. But at the end of the war, Russia regained southern Karelia and other parts of Finland. It also had to pay massive reparations to the Soviet Union.

After World War II, Finland pursued a policy of neutralism acceptable to the Soviet Union and this continued into the 1990s until the collapse of the Soviet Union. Finland also strengthened its links with other north European countries and became an associate member of the European Free Trade Association (EFTA) in 1961. Finland became a full member of EFTA in 1986, in a decade when its economy was growing at a faster rate than that of Japan.

In 1992, along with most of its fellow EFTA members, Finland, which had no longer any need to be neutral, applied for membership of the European Union (EU). In 1994, the Finnish people voted in favour of joining the EU and the country officially joined on 1 January 1995. In 2000, Finland elected Tarja Halonen, candidate of the Social Democratic Party, as its first woman president.

Economy

Forests are Finland's most valuable resource, and forestry accounts for about 35% of the country's exports. The chief manufactures are wood products, pulp and paper. Since World War II, Finland has set up many other industries, producing such things as machinery and transport equipment. Its economy has expanded rapidly, but there has been a large increase in the number of unemployed people.

AREA	ETHNIC GROUPS
338,130 sq km	Finnish 93%, Swedish 6%
[130,552 sq mi]	**LANGUAGES**
POPULATION	Finnish and Swedish
5,176,000	(both official)
CAPITAL (POPULATION)	**RELIGIONS**
Helsinki (532,000)	Evangelical Lutheran 88%
GOVERNMENT	**CURRENCY**
Multiparty republic	Euro = 100 cents

Geography

The Republic of France is the largest country in Western Europe. The scenery is extremely varied. The Vosges Mountains overlook the Rhine Valley in the north-east, the Jura Mountains and the Alps form the borders with Switzerland and Italy in the south-east, while the Pyrenees straddle France's border with Spain. The only large highland area entirely within France is the Massif Central between the Rhône-Saône Valley and the basin of Aquitaine. This dramatic area, covering one-sixth of the country, has peaks rising to more than 1,800 m [5,900 ft]. Volcanic activity dating back 10 to 30 million years ago appears in the form of steep-sided volcanic plugs. Older rocks, such as limestone, provide soil for agriculture, while coal measures have been mined for centuries at St-Etienne and Le Creusot.

Brittany (Bretagne) and Normandy (Normande) form a scenic hill region. Fertile lowlands cover most of northern France, including the densely populated Paris Basin. Another major lowland area, the Aquitanian Basin, is in the south-west, while the Rhône-Saône Valley and the Mediterranean lowlands are in the south-east.

Climate

The climate of France varies from west to east and from north to south. The west comes under the moderating influence of the Atlantic Ocean, giving generally mild weather. To the east, summers are warmer and winters colder. The climate also becomes warmer as one travels from north to south. The Mediterranean Sea coast experiences hot, dry summers and mild, moist winters. The Alps, Jura and Pyrenees mountains have snowy winters. Winter sports centres are found in all three areas. Large glaciers occupy high valleys in the Alps.

FRANCE – PARIS

The climate is influenced by the Atlantic, the Mediterranean and the continent. With no mountain barriers, the Atlantic regime extends far inland, giving mild weather with much wind and rain, but little snow. To the east the climate gets warmer, but with colder winters. Towards the mountains and to the south, rainfall increases, with permanent snow above 3,000 m [12,000 ft]. At Paris, low rainfall is distributed evenly all year.

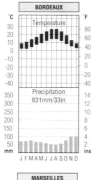

BORDEAUX

Winters are mild and summers warm; the average temperature for January is 5°C [41°F], and for June to September 18–21°C [64–70°F]. Rain falls fairly evenly all year, with a slight maximum in November and December. Rain falls on over 160 days in the year. Snow is common and there may be 20–35 days with frost each year. The annual amount of sunshine exceeds 2,000 hours, with over seven hours daily from April to October.

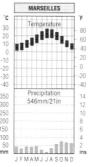

MARSEILLES

The Mediterranean climate extends over the south-east, pushing northwards into the Rhône Valley, mountain foothills, and over Corsica. The winters are very mild. Summers are dry and the rain falls mainly from September to March but on only around 75 days per year. One feature of the area is its peculiar winds, notably the Mistral, a cold, dry and strong wind which blows southwards during winter and spring, causing crop damage.

History

The Romans conquered France (then called Gaul) in the 50s BC. Roman rule began to decline in the fifth century AD and, in 486, the Frankish realm (as France was called) became independent under a

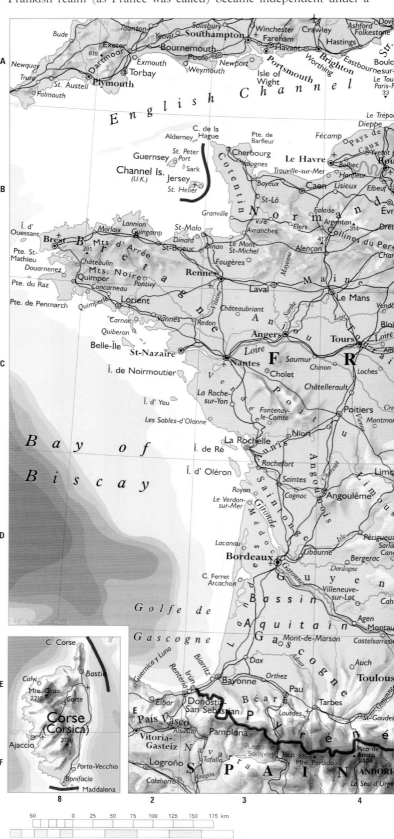

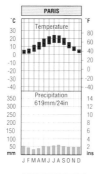

Christian king, Clovis. In 800, Charlemagne, who had been king of the Franks since 768, became emperor of the Romans. Through conquest, his empire extended from central Italy to Denmark, and from eastern Germany to the Atlantic Ocean. However, in 843, the empire was divided into three parts and the area of France contracted.

After the Norman invasion of England in 1066, large areas of France came under English rule. By 1453, after the Hundred Years' War, France drove most of the English out. In this war, the French kings lost much power to French nobles, but Louis XI, who reigned from 1461 to 1483, laid the foundations for absolute rule by French kings.

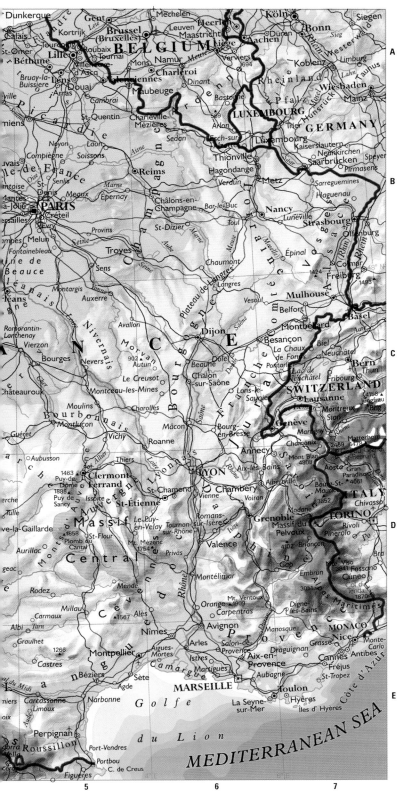

France developed into a powerful monarchy between the 16th and 18th centuries. The monarchy was supported by a large bureaucracy, which maintained a standing army and collected taxes. In 1786, a new land tax was proposed and opposition to this and other measures was a major factor that triggered off the French Revolution (1789–99). In 1792, France was declared a republic. However, in 1799, an army officer and military genius, Napoleon Bonaparte, took power and founded the First Empire in 1804. He fought a series of brilliant military campaigns, building up a vast French empire. But, to maintain control over the empire, France's resources became overstretched and Napoleon's armies were finally defeated at the Battle of Waterloo in 1815. The monarchy was restored after Napoleon's downfall, but revolutionaries founded the Second Republic in 1848.

A nephew of Napoleon, Louis Napoleon Bonaparte, was elected president in 1848, but he seized power in 1851 and established the Second Empire. In 1852, he took the title of Napoleon III. In 1870, France, concerned at the growing power of Prussia, declared war, but it met with defeat the following year. At the end of the war, France was forced to give up most of Alsace and part of Lorraine to the new German Empire, an issue that remained a bone of contention between the two countries. Following the defeats in the Franco-Prussian War, the French revolted and the Third Republic was established.

France grew in strength in the later 19th century, founding a major overseas empire in Africa and Asia. But its growing economy was shattered during World War I, when millions of French military personnel were slaughtered in a series of major battles. The rise of Hitler in Germany in the 1930s led to serious unrest in France. Finally, in September 1939, France and Britain declared war on Germany, following Germany's invasion of Poland. In 1945, at the end of the war, Charles De Gaulle, leader of the Free French, formed a provisional government, but he resigned as president in 1946 when the National Assembly supported a new constitution, creating the Fourth Republic. De Gaulle opposed the constitution because it did not provide strong executive powers.

Politics

France faced many problems in the 1940s and 1950s. With aid from the United States, it began to revive its economy, but Communist-led strikes often crippled production. France also faced growing support for independence movements in its overseas empire. After a bitter war, France withdrew from French Indo-China in 1954 and then faced a long and costly struggle in Algeria, which finally ended when Algeria became independent in 1962. The threat to French power in Algeria caused considerable unrest in France in the 1950s and, in 1958, De Gaulle was recalled to power as prime minister. His government prepared a new constitution, establishing the Fifth Republic. It gave the president greater executive powers and reduced the power of parliament. The Electoral College elected De Gaulle as president for a seven-year term.

De Gaulle set about giving independence to many of its overseas territories and worked to make France a major player in an alliance of western European nations. In 1957, France had become a founder member of the European Economic Alliance (EEC) and, in 1963, De Gaulle opposed British membership, considering that Britain's links with the United States would give it too much influence in Europe's economy. However, De Gaulle's popularity waned in the late 1960s when huge student demonstrations and workers' strikes paralyzed the country. De Gaulle resigned as president in 1969. His successor, Georges Pompidou, changed course in foreign affairs by re-establishing closer contacts with the United States and supporting the entry of Britain into the EEC. After the death of Pompidou in 1974, the Gaullist Party, which had backed both De Gaulle and Pompidou, was weakened by internal divisions. But France continued, under a variety of governments, of the right and the left, to become a prosperous and dynamic country.

French life is still focused on Paris, where the traditional luxury industries, such as perfumes, thrive alongside commerce, light and heavy industry and services of all kinds. Virtually all the major French enterprises have their headquarters in Paris, whose metropolitan area contains about a sixth of the country's population. Modern economic

Arable land 33.3%	Permanent crops 2.13%
Permanent grassland 19.3%	Forest 27.3%

planning has been pursued and consumer industries have prospered. However, some critics say that there is still an inadequate provision for social services, including housing. Since 1945, many people have argued about the poor standard of housing, both rural and urban, much of which is obsolete and without basic amenities. Rapid urban growth has resulted in overcrowding and even the growth of poorly built new districts to house immigrants, especially those from Spain and North Africa. The 4 million underprivileged workers from the Maghreb became a major political issue in the 1990s, leading to political successes in some areas for the extreme right. In France, as in most other countries, there also remains a disparity between the richer and the poorer regions. Other problems faced by France included unemployment, pollution and the growing number of elderly people.

A socialist government under Lionel Jospin was elected in 1997. He increased the minimum wage, shortened the working week, and took France into the European single currency on 1 January 1999. The high social security taxes and inflexible labour laws seem likely to continue, but, in the early 21st century, the economy was continuing to grow and inflation rates were low.

Economy

France is one of the world's most developed countries. It has the world's fourth largest economy, after the United States, Japan and Germany, and it had a high per capita gross national product of US $24,170 in 1999. Before World War II, agriculture was the mainstay of the economy, although it now contributes only 2.6% of the gross domestic product, as compared with a 22% contribution by manufacturing.

However, France remains the largest producer of farm products in Western Europe. It produces most of the food it needs and is a leading food exporter. Wheat is the single most important crop. Apples, barley, grapes, maize, oats and

rapeseed are other leading crops. Livestock, including beef and dairy cattle, sheep, pigs and poultry are also important. Fishing and forestry are also significant activities.

Besides its fertile soils, France's other natural resources include large deposits of iron ore and bauxite, together with coal, some petroleum and natural gas, and potash, but it has to import petroleum and petroleum products. In 1997, about 73% of the country's electricity supply came from nuclear power stations, while hydroelectric plants contributed another 20%. France was the European Union's biggest exporter of electricity in 1997.

France is one of the world's leading manufacturing nations. While Paris is the leading manufacturing centre, many other cities and towns throughout the country have factories. France ranks fourth among the world's producers of cars and eighth among the producers of commercial vehicles. The country is also known for its aircraft, both military and commercial. It also produces aerospace equipment, many kinds of weapons and electronic goods, including computers, radios and television sets. Other products include chemicals, industrial machinery, iron and steel, machine tools, medicines, textiles and timber, wood pulp and paper. The food-processing industry is well known, especially for its cheeses, such as Brie and Camembert, and its top-quality wines from such areas as Alsace, Bordeaux, Burgundy, Champagne and the Loire valley.

The leading exports of France are machinery and transport equipment, followed by agricultural products, chemical products and plastics. The country's leading trading partners are Germany, Italy and Belgium-Luxembourg, all of which are fellow members of the European Union.

Regions of France

Corsica

Annexed by France from Genoa in 1768 – months before the birth of Napoleon Bonaparte – Corsica (or Corse) lies 168 km [105 mi] from France and 11 km [7 mi] from Sardinia. Corsica is divided into two departments of France, with its administrative centre at Ajaccio on the west coast. Roughly oval in shape, it is 190 km [118 mi] long and half as wide, with a population of 240,178.

Most of the island is formed of rugged mountains, some reaching to over 2,710 m [8,890 ft]. Only about a quarter of Corsica provides rough grazing for sheep and goats; another quarter is in forests with evergreen oak and cork oak to 650 m [2,000 ft], then chestnuts with beech followed by pines to the tree line, between 1,600 m and 2,000 m [5,000–6,000 ft]. During winter there is heavy snow on the mountains. Only 2% of the island is cultivated, mainly in the valleys, on terraced hillsides or on the narrow coastal lowlands. Fishing is important and industries include tunny and lobster canning, chiefly at Ajaccio and Bastia – though tourism is now the main earner. In 2001, France enhanced the powers of Corsica's regional government in an attempt to end nationalist violence.

AREA
551,500 sq km
[212,934 sq mi]
POPULATION
59,551,000
CAPITAL
(POPULATION)
Paris (11,175,000)
GOVERNMENT
Multiparty
republic
ETHNIC GROUPS
Celtic, Latin,
Arab, Teutonic,
Slavic
LANGUAGES
French (official),
Breton,
Occitan
RELIGIONS
Roman Catholic
90%, Islam 3%
CURRENCY
Euro = 100 cents

MONACO

The tiny Principality of Monaco consists of a narrow strip of coastline and a rocky peninsula on the French Riviera. Like the rest of the Riviera, it has mild, moist winters and dry, sunny summers. Average temperatures range from 10°C [50°F] in January to 24°C [75°F] in July. The average annual rainfall is about 800 mm [31 in].

The Genoese from northern Italy gained control of Monaco in the 12th century and, from 1297, it has been ruled for most of the time by the Genoese Grimaldi family. Monaco attracted little attention until the late 19th century when it developed into a major tourist resort. World attention was focused on Monaco in 1956 when Prince Rainier III of Monaco married the actress Grace Kelly. Their son, Prince Albert, is the heir apparent. The country's wealth comes mainly from banking, finance, gambling and tourism. Monaco has three casinos, a marine

museum, a zoo and botanical gardens. It also stages such sporting events as the Monte Carlo Rally and the Monaco Grand Prix. Manufactures include chemicals, electronic goods and plastics. In 2001, France threatened to break its ties with Monaco unless it revised its legal system and prevented money laundering.

AREA	CAPITAL
1.5 sq km [0.6 sq mi]	Monaco
POPULATION	CURRENCY
32,000	Euro = 100 cents

FRENCH GUIANA – SEE GUYANA, PAGE 115;
FRENCH POLYNESIA – SEE PACIFIC OCEAN, PAGES 174–178

GABON

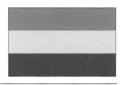

Gabon's flag was adopted in 1960 when the country became independent from France. The central yellow stripe symbolizes the Equator which runs through Gabon. The green stands for the country's forests. The blue symbolizes the sea.

Geography

The Gabonese Republic lies on the Equator in west-central Africa. In area, it is a little larger than the United Kingdom, with a coastline 800 km [500 mi] long. Behind the narrow, partly lagoon-lined coastal plain, the land rises to hills, plateaux and mountains divided by deep valleys carved by the River Ogooué and its tributaries.

Climate

Most of Gabon has an equatorial climate, with high temperatures and humidity throughout the year. The rainfall is heavy and the skies are often cloudy.

History and Politics

Gabon became a French colony in the 1880s, but it achieved full independence in 1960. In 1964, an attempted coup was put down when French troops intervened and crushed the revolt. In 1967, following the death of the first president, Léon Mba, Bernard-Albert Bongo, who later renamed himself El Hadj Omar Bongo, became president. He made Gabon a one-party state in 1968, but opposition parties were legalized in 1991. Bongo was re-elected in 1993 and 1998.

Economy

Gabon's abundant natural resources include its forests, oil and gas deposits near Port Gentil, together with manganese and uranium. These mineral deposits make Gabon one of Africa's wealthier countries. But agriculture still employs about 75% of the population, most farmers producing little more than they need to support their families.

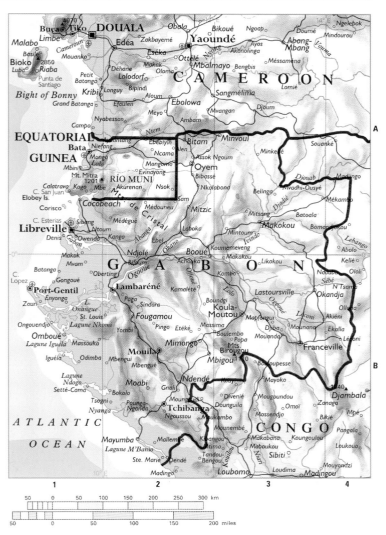

AREA	Eshira, Bapounou and Bateke
267,670 sq km [103,347 sq mi]	**LANGUAGES**
POPULATION	French (official), Bantu languages
1,221,000	**RELIGIONS**
CAPITAL (POPULATION)	Roman Catholic 65%,
Libreville (418,000)	Protestant 19%,
GOVERNMENT	African churches 12%,
Multiparty republic	traditional beliefs 3%, Islam 2%
ETHNIC GROUPS	**CURRENCY**
Four major Bantu tribes: Fang,	CFA franc = 100 centimes

EQUATORIAL GUINEA

Geography and Climate

The Republic of Equatorial Guinea is a republic in west-central Africa. It consists of a mainland territory which makes up 90% of the land area, called Rio Muni. This area includes coastal plains, hills and plateaux. The country also includes five islands, the largest of which is Bioko. The other islands, including Annobón, 560 km [350 mi] south-west of the mainland, do not appear on the map.

The climate is hot and humid with significant rainfall which diminishes inland. There is a dry season between December and February.

History and Politics

Portuguese navigators reached the area in 1471. In 1778, Portugal granted Bioko, together with rights over Rio Muni, to Spain.

In 1959, Spain made Bioko and Rio Muni provinces of overseas Spain. In 1963, it gave the provinces a degree of self-government. Equatorial Guinea became independent in 1968. The first president, Francisco Macias Nguema, proved to be a tyrant. He was overthrown in 1979 and a group of officers, led by Lt.-Col. Teodoro Obiang Nguema Mbasogo, set up a Supreme Military Council to rule the country. Elections were held in the 1990s, though the president continued to rule in a semi-dictatorial manner despite protests by opposition parties.

Economy

Equatorial Guinea is a poor country. Agriculture employs around 60% of the people, though many farmers live at subsistence level, making little contribution to the economy. The main food crops are bananas, cassava and sweet potatoes, but the chief cash crop is cocoa, grown on Bioko. Oil and gas are produced off Bioko. In the mid-1990s, oil and wood products were the leading exports, followed by cocoa.

AREA	ETHNIC GROUPS
28,050 sq km	Fang 83%, Bubi 10%,
[10,830 sq mi]	Ndowe 4%
POPULATION	**LANGUAGES**
486,000	Spanish and French
CAPITAL (POPULATION)	(both official)
Malabo (35,000)	**RELIGIONS**
GOVERNMENT	Roman Catholic 89%
Multiparty republic	**CURRENCY**
(transitional)	CFA franc = 100 centimes

GAMBIA, THE – SEE SENEGAL, PAGE 198

Georgia's flag was first used between 1917 and 1921. It was readopted when Georgia became independent. The wine-red colour represents the good times of the past and the future. The black symbolizes Russian rule and the white represents hope for peace.

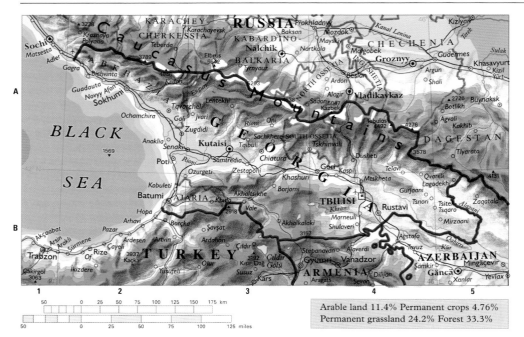

Arable land 11.4% Permanent crops 4.76%
Permanent grassland 24.2% Forest 33.3%

Geography

Georgia is a country on the borders of Europe and Asia, facing the Black Sea. The land is rugged with the Caucasus Mountains forming its northern border. The highest mountain in this range, Mount Elbrus (5,642 m [18,506 ft]), lies over the border in Russia.

Lower ranges run through southern Georgia, through which pass the borders with Turkey and Armenia. The Black Sea coastal plains are in the west. In the east a low plateau extends into Azerbaijan. The main river in the east is the River Kura, on which the capital Tbilisi stands.

Climate

The Black Sea plains have hot summers and mild winters, when the temperatures seldom drop below freezing point. The rainfall is heavy, but inland Tbilisi has moderate rainfall, with the heaviest rains in the spring and early summer.

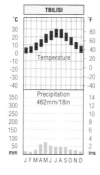

GEORGIA (TBILISI)

Nestling between the Caucasus and the mountains of Armenia, Tbilisi is sheltered from the winter cold of central Asia and the heavy rain of the Black Sea coast. The sparse rainfall is effective in spring but evaporates quickly in the summer heat. Rain falls on about 70 days per year. The winters are less severe than expected in a continental location; temperatures rarely fall below freezing in December and January.

History

The first Georgian state was set up nearly 2,000 years ago and, by the 3rd century BC, most of what is now Georgia was united as a single kingdom. For much of its history, Georgia was ruled by various conquerors. For example, between about 60 BC and the 11th century, the area was ruled successively by Romans, Persians, Byzantines, Arabs and Seljuk Turks. Christianity was introduced in AD 330 and most Georgians are now members of the Georgian Orthodox Church. Georgia freed itself from foreign rule in the 11th and 12th centuries, but Mongol armies invaded in the 13th century. From the 16th to the 18th centuries, Iran and the Turkish Ottoman Empire struggled for control of the area.

In the late 18th century, Georgia sought the protection of Russia and, by the early 19th century, became part of the Russian Empire. After the Russian Revolution of 1917, Georgia declared itself independent and was recognized by the League of Nations. However, Russian troops invaded in 1921, making Georgia a Communist republic. From 1922, Georgia, Armenia and Azerbaijan were linked, forming the Transcaucasian Republic. But, in 1936, the territories became separate republics within the Soviet Union. Renowned for their longevity, the people of Georgia are famous for producing Josef Stalin, who was born in Gori, 65 km [40 mi] north-west of the capital Tbilisi. Stalin ruled the Soviet Union from 1929 until his death in 1953.

Politics

A maverick among the Soviet republics, Georgia was the first to declare its independence after the Baltic states (April 1991) and deferred joining the Commonwealth of Independent States (CIS) until 1993.

In 1991, Zviad Gamsakhurdia, a non-Communist who had been democratically elected president of Georgia in 1990, found himself holed up in Tbilisi's KGB headquarters, under siege from rebel forces. They represented widespread opposition to his government's policies, ranging from the economy to the imprisonment of his opponents. Gamsakhurdia had also been in conflict with the minority in South Ossetia, in north-central Georgia, one of the country's three regions where nationalists had demanded the right to set up their own governments. The others are Abkhazia in the north-west, which proclaimed its sovereignty in 1994, and Adjaria (or Adzharia) in the south-west. In January 1992, following the break-up of the Soviet Union, Gamsakhurdia fled the country and a military council took power.

In March, Eduard Shevardnadze, former Soviet Foreign Minister, was named head of state and was elected, unopposed, later that year. Shevardnadze was re-elected in 1995 and 2000, but Georgia faced mounting problems, which threatened its stability. In 2002, Russia stated that Chechen rebels were taking refuge in part of eastern Georgia. US officials also believed that Taliban fighters from Afghanistan and other terrorists had also moved into this region.

Economy

Georgia is a developing country. Agriculture is important – major products include barley, citrus fruits, grapes for wine-making, maize, tea, tobacco and vegetables. Food processing, and silk- and perfume-making are other important activities. Sheep and cattle are reared.

Barite (barium ore), coal, copper and manganese are mined, and tourism is a major industry on the Black Sea coast. Georgia's mountains have huge potential for generating hydroelectric power, but most of Georgia's electricity is generated in Russia or Ukraine.

AREA	Ossetian 3%, Greek 2%,
69,700 sq km [26,910 sq mi]	Abkhaz 2%, others 3%
POPULATION	**LANGUAGES**
4,989,000	Georgian (official), Russian
CAPITAL (POPULATION)	**RELIGIONS**
Tbilisi (1,253,000)	Georgian Orthodox 65%,
GOVERNMENT	Islam 11%,
Multiparty republic	Russian Orthodox 10%,
ETHNIC GROUPS	Armenian Apostolic 8%
Georgian 70%, Armenian 8%,	**CURRENCY**
Russian 6%, Azeri 6%,	Lari = 100 tetri

This flag, adopted by the Federal Republic of Germany (West Germany) in 1949, became the flag of the reunified Germany in 1990. The red, black and gold colours date back to the Holy Roman Empire. They are associated with the struggle for a united Germany from the 1830s.

Geography

The Federal Republic of Germany is the fourth largest country in Western Europe, after France, Spain and Sweden. The North German Plain borders the North Sea in the north-west and the Baltic Sea in the north-east. Rivers draining the plain include the Weser, Elbe and Oder.

The central highlands contain plateaux and highlands, including the Harz Mountains, the Thuringian Forest (Thüringer Wald), the Ore Mountains (Erzgebirge), and the Bohemian Forest (Böhmerwald) on the Czech border. South Germany is hilly, but the land rises in the south to the Bavarian Alps, which contain Germany's highest peak, Zugspitze, at 2,963 m [9,721 ft] above sea level. The Black Forest (Scharzwald) overlooks the River Rhine to the west. The Black Forest contains the source of the Danube.

A third kind of country is provided by the downfaulted basins filled with softer deposits, notably the Upper Rhine Plain between Basel and Mainz. Earth movements and eruptions produced another element, such as volcanic mountains at Vogelsberg and hot mineral springs that gave rise to famous spas. Here is Germany at its most picturesque, with castles on wooded heights, looking down over vineyards to clustered villages of half-timbered houses.

Climate

North-west Germany has a mild climate, but the Baltic coastlands are cooler. To the south, the climate becomes more continental, especially in the highlands. The precipitation is greatest on the uplands, many of which are snow-capped in winter.

Arable land 33.8% Permanent crops 0.60%
Permanent grassland 15.1% Forest 30.6%

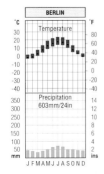

GERMANY – BERLIN

The climate of northern Germany is affected by weather from the Atlantic. January and February are the only months with mean temperatures just below 0°C [32°F], and summers are warm. Rainfall is moderate, 500–750 mm [20–30 in], falling in all months. Humidity is high with fog in the autumn. Winter can be overcast. Snow lies for long spells inland and in the hills. When the winds blow from Scandinavia, very cold weather follows.

HAMBURG

Average temperatures, from December to March, are low and frost is usual on over 50 days in this period. Summers are pleasantly warm, the highest recorded temperatures being 34–35°C [93–95°F] in July and August, the averages being 16–17°C [61–62°F]. Moderate rainfall is evenly distributed all year with a slight peak in July and August. Rain falls on nearly 200 days in the year. Fog is frequent and winter sunshine totals are low.

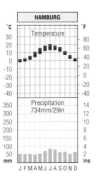

MUNICH

In the south it is a little warmer in the summer and slightly colder in winter. It is also wetter, Munich receiving nearly twice as much rain as Berlin. Further south it is even wetter with more snow. Rainfall is heavier in the summer months. The coming of spring is much earlier in the Rhine Valley and the south. The Föhn wind gets its name from this area. It is a dry warm wind that blows northwards from the Alps, mainly in the summer.

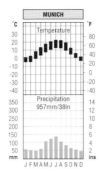

Vegetation

The North German Plain contains large areas of heathland, with such plants as grasses, heather, mosses and lichens. The most common trees in the forests of central and southern Germany are pine, beech (on the higher mountain slopes) and oak. The common oak grows throughout the country, while the Durmast oak is found mainly in the east. The western oak forests also contain hornbeam. Plantations of spruce are important commercially. More tolerant to extreme cold than beech, spruce are found up to the tree line in the southern mountains. Alder grows in river valleys, often with poplar and willow. Industrial pollution is the cause of acid rain, which has damaged many trees.

History

Around 3,000 years ago, various tribes from northern Europe began to settle in what is now Germany, occupying the valleys of the Rhine and the Danube. The Romans called this region Germania after the

The Reunification of Germany

In 1945, a devastated Germany was divided into four zones, each occupied by one of the victorious powers: Britain, France, the USA and the Soviet Union. The division was originally a temporary expedient (the Allies had formally agreed to maintain German unity), but the Russians published a constitution for the German Democratic Republic in 1946. The split solidified when the Russians rejected a currency reform common to all three Western zones. The German Federal Republic – 'West Germany' – was created in 1949.

Throughout the years of the Cold War, as NATO troops faced Warsaw Pact tanks across the barbed wire and minefields of the new frontier, the partition seemed irrevocable. Although both German constitutions maintained hopes of reunification, it appeared that nothing short of total war could bring it about. The West, with three-quarters of the population, rebuilt war damage and prospered. The East was hailed as the industrial jewel of the Soviet European empire, though some of its people were prepared to risk being shot to escape westwards.

By the late 1980s, it was clear that the Soviet Empire was crumbling. In the autumn of 1989, thousands of East Germans migrated illegally to the West across the newly open Hungarian border and mass demonstrations in East German cities followed. At first, the government issued a stream of threats, but when it became clear that there would be no Soviet tanks to enforce its rule, it simply packed up. With the frontiers open, the 'successful' East German economy was a catastrophic shambles, a scrapyard poisoned by uncontrolled pollution, with bankruptcy imminent. The choice facing German leaders in 1990 was starkly simple: either unite East and West, or accept virtually the entire Eastern population as penniless refugees.

The West German government, led by Chancellor Helmut Kohl, acted quickly, often bullying the weaker Easterners. The Western Deutschmark became the common currency, and on 3 October 1990 – more than 45 years after Germany had lost the war – the country was formally reunited. However, the costs of restructuring the economy of the East are high, and the German people will be paying for many years.

Germani, the name of one of the tribes. Other tribes included the Franks, Goths and Vandals. The Romans attempted to conquer the tribes in AD 9, but they were defeated in a battle in the Teutoburg Forest. In the 5th century, the Germanic tribes attacked the Roman Empire and plundered Rome. The western part of the Roman Empire split up into several kingdoms, the largest of which was the Kingdom of the Franks.

In 486, Clovis, a Frankish king, extended his rule to include Gaul (now France) and western Germany, introducing Christianity and other Roman practices. A later Frankish ruler, Charlemagne, came to power in 768 and established his capital at Aachen. He expanded the territory, uniting many tribes into his empire. He became emperor of the Romans in 800 but, in 843, his empire was split into three, the eastern part being what is now Germany. From 962, much of the German Empire became part of what was later known as the Holy Roman Empire under King Otto II of Germany. The Holy Roman Empire was never entirely German. Some Germans lived outside its boundaries, while many non-German areas, such as Italy and parts of eastern Europe, lay within it.

In 1517, a German monk, Martin Luther, began to criticize many of the practices and teachings of the Roman Catholic Church. A Protestant movement called the Reformation soon attracted much support in Germany. By the early 17th century, the people of Germany were deeply divided by political and religious rivalries. The Thirty Years' War, which began in 1618 and lasted for 30 years, ravaged much of the country. The conflict was partly a struggle between Protestants and Roman Catholics, but it was also a battle between certain princes and the emperor, a member of the royal Austrian Habsburg family. At the end of the war, Germany had lost territory to France and Sweden, while Germany itself was split into hundreds of states and free cities. It took almost 200 years for Germany to recover from this disastrous war.

In the 17th century, the Hohenzollern family began to assume importance in eastern Germany. Its rise to power began with Frederick William, who became ruler of Brandenburg in 1648. His son, Frederick I, became the king of Prussia. The Hohenzollerns gradually extended their power and built up a professional civil service and army. Between 1740 and 1768, Frederick II (the Great) made Prussia a great power.

During the Napoleonic wars, some German states allied themselves with France, and Prussia stayed out of the wars until 1806. Following defeats by Napoleon, Prussia lost its territories west of the Elbe, but Prussia helped to defeat Napoleon's armies at the battles of Leipzig (1813) and Waterloo (1815). Following the Napoleonic wars, Prussia gained the Rhineland, Westphalia and much of Saxony.

German nationalism increased during the 19th century. In the early 1860s, the Prussian king, Wilhelm I, appointed Otto von Bismarck as prime minister in order to resolve a constitutional crisis about army reforms. Bismarck set about strengthening Prussian power through three short wars that led to the annexation of territory. One conflict led to the acquisition of Schleswig-Holstein from Denmark, while another led to the annexation of territory from Austria. The third was the Franco-Prussian War (1870–1), following which victorious Germany was granted Alsace and part of Lorraine. In 1871, Wilhelm I was crowned the first Kaiser of the new German Empire and Bismarck became the chancellor and head of government. Bismarck sought to consolidate German power and avoid conflict with Austria-Hungary and Russia, but he was forced to resign in 1890 when Frederick III's son, Wilhelm II, wanted to establish his own authority and extend Germany's influence in the world. Wilhelm's ambitions led Britain and France to establish the Entente Cordiale in 1904, while Britain and Russia signed a similar agreement in 1907. This left Europe divided, with Germany, Austria-Hungary and Italy forming the Triple Alliance.

Germany and its allies were defeated in World War I, which ended on 11 November 1918. Germany became a republic and lost territories, including Alsace, the German part of Lorraine, Poland, some of Silesia and part of West Prussia. Overseas, it lost its colonies. Germany's humiliation under the terms of the Versailles Treaty caused much resentment, which was made worse by an economic collapse in 1922 and 1923. Support grew for the Nazi Party and its leader Adolf

Berlin

Like defeated Germany itself, Berlin was formally divided between the four victorious powers – despite the fact that it was located in Prussia, 160 km [100 mi] inside Soviet-occupied eastern Germany. In June 1948, in an attempt to bring the whole city under their control, the Soviets closed all road and rail links with the West. The Western Allies supplied the city by a massive airlift; in October 1949 the blockade was abandoned, but Berlin's anomalous situation remained a potential flashpoint, and provoked a series of diplomatic crises – mainly because it offered an easy escape route to the West for discontented East Germans.

In August 1961, alarmed at the steady drain of some of its best-trained people, the East German authorities built a dividing wall across the city. Over the years, the original improvised structure – it was thrown up overnight – became a substantial barrier of concrete and barbed wire, with machine-gun towers and minefields; despite the hazards, many still risked the perilous crossing, and hundreds of would-be refugees – often youngsters – died in the attempt.

The Berlin Wall, with its few heavily guarded crossing points, became the most indelible symbol of the Cold War. When the East German government collapsed in 1989, the Wall's demolition became the most unambiguous sign of the Cold War's ending. When East Germany joined the West, it was agreed that Berlin would become the formal capital of the unified state in the year 2000 – until that time, both Berlin and the quiet Rhineland city of Bonn were to be joint capitals. The renovated Reichstag with its spectacular glass dome, the work of the British architect Sir Norman Foster, was officially opened in April 1999.

Federal structure of Germany

Hitler, who became chancellor in 1933. Hitler's order to invade Poland in 1939 triggered off World War II. Hitler's armies were finally defeated in 1945 and the country was left in ruins. Germany was obliged to transfer to Poland and the Soviet Union 114,500 sq km [44,200 sq mi], situated east of the Oder and Neisse rivers, nearly a quarter of the country's pre-war area. The German-speaking inhabitants were expelled – as were most German-speaking minorities in the countries of Eastern Europe – and the remainder of Germany was occupied by the four victorious Allied powers. In 1948, West Germany, consisting of the American, British and French zones, was proclaimed the Federal Republic of Germany with its provisional capital at Bonn, while the Soviet zone became the German Democratic Republic with its capital in East Berlin.

Politics

The post-war partition of Germany into the democratic West Germany and a Communist East Germany, together with its geographical position, made it a central hub of the Cold War which ended in the collapse of Communism in the late 1980s and early 1990s. In Germany, it ended with the reunification of Germany on 3 October 1990. West Germany, initially under constraints imposed by the Allies, had become a showpiece of the West through its phenomenal recovery and sustained growth – the so-called *Wirtschaftswunder* ('economic miracle'). It also played a major part, together with France, in the revival of Western Europe through the development of the European Community (now the European Union). By contrast, although East Germany had achieved the highest standard of living in the Soviet bloc, it was short of the levels of the European Union members.

Following reunification, when the new country adopted West Germany's official name, the Federal Republic of Germany, massive investment was needed to rebuild the East's industrial base and transport system. This meant increased taxation. In addition, the new nation found itself funnelling aid into Eastern Europe – Germany led the European Union in recognizing the independence of Slovenia and Croatia and then the former Soviet republics. All this took place against the background of a continued downturn of world trade. There were also social effects. While Germans in the West resented added taxes and the burden imposed by the East, easterners resented what many saw as the overbearing attitudes of westerners. Others feared a revival of the far right, with neo-Nazis and other right-wingers protesting against the increasing numbers of immigrant workers.

Reunification appeared in the late 1990s to be the beginning rather than the end of a chapter in German history. The creation of a unified state proved to be a much more complicated, expensive and lengthy undertaking than anyone had envisaged when the Berlin Wall came down. In 1998, the centre-right government of Helmut Kohl, who had presided over reunification, was defeated by the left-of-centre Social Democratic Party (SPD) which was led by Gerhard Schröder. Schröder led an SPD-Green Party coalition which set about tackling Germany's high unemployment and a sluggish economy. Following the attacks on the United States on 11 September 2001, Schröder announced Germany's support for the campaign against terrorism, despite the opposition of most Green Party members to the military action in Afghanistan.

Economy

Despite the problems associated with reunification, Germany has the world's third largest economy after the United States and Japan. The foundation of the 'economic miracle' that led to Germany's astonishing post-war recovery was manufacturing.

Germany's industrial strength was based on its coal reserves, though oil-burning and nuclear generating plants have become increasingly important since the 1970s. Lower Saxony has oilfields, while southern Germany also obtains power from hydroelectric plants. The country has supplies of potash and rock salt, together with smaller quantities of copper, lead, tin, uranium and zinc. The leading industrial region is the Ruhr, which produces iron and steel, together with major chemical and textiles industries. Germany is the world's third largest producer of cars, while other manufactures include cameras, electronic equipment, fertilizers, processed food, plastics, scientific instruments, ships, tools, and wood and pulp products.

Agriculture employs 2.4% of the workforce, but Germany imports about a third of its food. Products include barley, fruits, grapes, oats, potatoes, rye, sugar beet, vegetables and wheat. Beef and dairy cattle are raised, together with pigs, poultry and sheep. Chief exports are machinery and transport equipment, and chemicals and chemical products. Germany's major trading partners include France, the Netherlands, Italy, the United States and the United Kingdom.

AREA	Serbo-Croat 1%, Italian 1%,
356,910 sq km	Greek, Polish, Spanish
[137,803 sq mi]	**LANGUAGES**
POPULATION	German (official)
83,030,000	**RELIGIONS**
CAPITAL (POPULATION)	Protestant (mainly
Berlin (3,426,000)	Lutheran) 38%,
GOVERNMENT	Roman Catholic 34%,
Federal multiparty republic	Islam 2%
ETHNIC GROUPS	**CURRENCY**
German 93%, Turkish 2%,	Euro = 100 cents

GHANA

Ghana's flag has red, green and yellow bands like the flag of Ethiopia, Africa's oldest independent nation. These colours symbolize African unity. The black star is a symbol of African freedom. Ghana's flag was adopted when the country became independent in 1957.

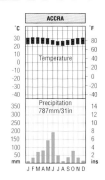

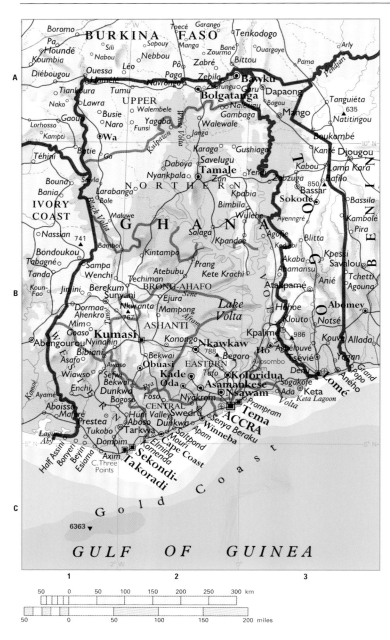

GHANA (ACCRA)

The climate of coastal regions is similar to much of the Guinea coast, with high temperatures, high humidity and a double maximum of rainfall associated with two passages of the intertropical rainbelt. However, the total rainfall is less than that of coastal regions to the east and west of Ghana, a feature attributed to the presence of a local upwell of cooler water offshore. The total yearly rainfall can be as low as 300 mm [12 in].

History

Portuguese explorers reached the area in 1471 and named it the Gold Coast. The area became a centre of the slave trade in the 17th century. The slave trade was ended in the 1860s and the British gradually took control of the area. The country became independent in 1957, when it was renamed Ghana. Ghana was a great African empire which flourished to the north-west of present-day Ghana between the AD 300s and 1000s. Modern Ghana was the first country in the Commonwealth to be ruled by black Africans.

Politics

After independence in 1957, attempts were made to develop the economy by creating large state-owned manufacturing industries. But debt and corruption, together with falls in the price of cocoa, the chief export, caused economic problems. This led to instability and frequent coups. In 1981, power was invested in a Provisional National Defence Council, led by Flight-Lieutenant Jerry Rawlings.

The government steadied the economy and introduced several new policies, including the relaxation of government controls. In 1992, a new constitution was introduced which allowed for multiparty elections. Rawlings was re-elected later that year, and again in 1996. The economy expanded in the 1990s, largely because the government followed World Bank policies. When Rawlings retired in 2000, the opposition leader, John Agyekum Kufuor, leader of the New Patriotic Party, was elected president, defeating Rawlings' vice-president.

Economy

The World Bank classifies Ghana as a 'low-income' developing country. Most people are poor and farming employs 59% of the population. Food crops include cassava, groundnuts, maize, millet, plantains, rice and yams. But cocoa is the most valuable export crop. Timber and gold are also exported. Other valuable crops include tobacco, coffee, coconuts and palm kernels.

Many small factories produce goods, such as beverages, cement and clothing, for local consumption.

The aluminium smelter at Tema, a port near Accra, is the country's largest factory. Electricity for southern Ghana is produced from a hydroelectric station at the Akosombo Dam. There are plans to construct around 600 km [378 mi] of pipeline which will form part of the West African Gas Pipeline Project. It is hoped that this will lessen the dependence of electricity production on hydroelectric stations.

Geography

The Republic of Ghana faces the Gulf of Guinea in West Africa. This hot country, just north of the Equator, was formerly called the Gold Coast. Behind the thickly populated southern coastal plains, which are lined with lagoons, lies a plateau region in the south-west.

Northern Ghana is drained by the Black and White Volta Rivers, which flow into Lake Volta. This lake, which has formed behind the Akosombo Dam, is one of the world's largest artificially created lakes.

Climate

Ghana has a tropical climate. A cool offshore current reduces temperatures on the coast, and the north is hotter. The heaviest rains occur in the south-west. Northern and eastern Ghana have marked dry seasons.

Vegetation

Rainforests grow in the south-west. To the north, the forests merge into savanna (tropical grassland with some woodland). More open grasslands dominate in the far north.

AREA	
238,540 sq km [92,100 sq mi]	Moshi-Dagombe 16%, Ewe 12%, Ga 8%
POPULATION	**LANGUAGES**
19,894,000	English (official), Akan, Moshi-Dagombe
CAPITAL (POPULATION)	
Accra (1,781,000)	**RELIGIONS**
GOVERNMENT	Traditional beliefs 38%,
Republic	Islam 30%, Christianity 24%
ETHNIC GROUPS	**CURRENCY**
Akan 44%,	Cedi = 100 pesewas

GREECE

Blue and white became Greece's national colours during the war of independence (1821–9). The nine horizontal stripes on the flag, which was finally adopted in 1970, represent the nine syllables of the battle cry 'Eleutheria i thanatos' ('Freedom or Death').

Geography

The Hellenic Republic, as Greece is officially called, lies at the southern end of the Balkan Peninsula. Olympus (Ólimbos), at 2,917 m [9,570 ft], is the highest peak. Nearly a fifth of the land area is made up of around 2,000 islands, mainly in the Aegean Sea, east of the main peninsula, but also in the Ionian Sea to the west. Only 154 are inhabited. The island of Crete is structurally related to the main Alpine fold mountain system to which the mainland Pindos Range belongs.

Climate

Low-lying areas in Greece have mild, moist winters and hot, dry summers. The east coast has more than 2,700 hours of sunshine a year and only about half of the rainfall of the west. The mountains have a more severe climate, with snow on the higher slopes in winter.

History and Politics

Crete was the centre of the Minoan civilization, an early Greek culture, between about 3000 and 1450 BC. The Minoans were followed by the Mycenian culture which prospered on the mainland until about 1100 BC.

In about 750 BC, the Greeks began to colonize the Mediterranean, creating wealth through trade. The city-state of Athens reached its peak in the 400s BC, but in 338 BC Macedonia became the dominant power. In 334–331 BC, Alexander the Great conquered south-western Asia. Greece became a Roman province in 146 BC and, in AD 365, part of the Byzantine Empire. In 1453, the Turks defeated the Byzantine Empire. But between 1821 and 1829, the Greeks defeated the Turks. The country became an independent monarchy in 1830.

After World War II (1939–45), when Germany had occupied Greece, a civil war broke out between Communist and nationalist forces. This war ended in 1949. A military dictatorship took power in 1967. The monarchy was abolished in 1973 and democratic government was restored in 1974. Greece joined the European Community in 1981. But despite efforts to develop the economy, Greece remains one of the poorest countries in the European Union. Greece adopted the euro on 1 January 2001. Relations with Turkey have long been difficult. In 1999, the two countries helped each other when both were hit by major earthquakes. In 2000, Greece and Turkey signed agreements aimed at improving relations between them.

Economy

Manufacturing is important. Products include processed food, cement, chemicals, metal products, textiles and tobacco. Greece also mines lignite (brown coal), bauxite and chromite.

Arable land 18.8% Permanent crops 8.39%
Permanent grassland 40.7% Forest 20.3%

Farmland covers about a third of the country, and grazing land another 40%. Major crops include barley, grapes for wine-making, dried fruits, olives, potatoes, sugar beet and wheat. Poultry, sheep, goats, pigs and cattle are raised. The vital tourist industry is based on the warm climate, the beautiful scenery, especially on the islands, and the historical sites dating back to the days of classical Greece.

AREA	ETHNIC GROUPS
131,990 sq km	Greek 98%
[50,961 sq mi]	**LANGUAGES**
POPULATION	Greek (official), English,
10,624,000	French
CAPITAL (POPULATION)	**RELIGIONS**
Athens	Greek Orthodox 98%,
(Athínai, 3,097,000)	Islam 1%
GOVERNMENT	**CURRENCY**
Multiparty republic	Euro = 100 cents

GREENLAND – SEE ATLANTIC OCEAN, PAGES 41–43;
GRENADA – SEE CARIBBEAN SEA, PAGES 71–76;
GUADELOUPE – SEE CARIBBEAN SEA, PAGES 71–76;
GUAM – SEE PACIFIC OCEAN, PAGES 174–178

Guatemala's flag was adopted in 1871, but its origins go back to the days of the Central American Federation (1823–39), which was set up after the break from Spain in 1821. The Federation included Costa Rica, El Salvador, Guatemala, Honduras and Nicaragua.

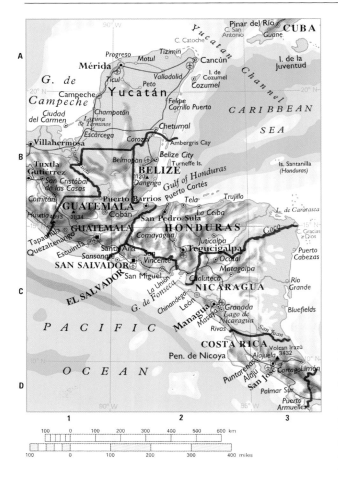

Geography and Climate

The Republic of Guatemala in Central America contains a thickly populated, fertile, mountain region. The mountains run in an east–west direction and contain many volcanoes, some of which are active. Volcanic eruptions and earthquakes are common. South of the mountains lie the thinly-populated Pacific coastlands.

Guatemala lies in the tropics. The lowlands are hot and wet, but the central mountain region is cooler and drier.

History and Politics

In 1823, Guatemala joined the Central American Federation. It became fully independent in 1839 but has since been plagued by instability and periodic violence.

Guatemala has a long-standing claim over Belize, but this was reduced in 1983 to the southern fifth of the country. Violence became widespread in Guatemala from the early 1960s, because of conflict between left-wing groups, including many Amerindians, and government forces. A peace accord was signed in December 1996, ending a war that had lasted 36 years and claimed around 200,000 lives.

Economy

The World Bank classifies Guatemala as a 'lower-middle-income' developing country. Agriculture employs nearly half of the population and coffee, sugar, bananas and beef are the leading exports.

AREA	Amerindian) 55%, Amerindian 43%,
108,890 sq km [42,042 sq mi]	other 2%
POPULATION	**LANGUAGES**
12,974,000	Spanish (official), Amerindian
CAPITAL (POPULATION)	languages
Guatemala City (1,167,000)	**RELIGIONS**
GOVERNMENT	Roman Catholic 75%, Protestant 25%
Republic	**CURRENCY**
ETHNIC GROUPS	US dollar;
Ladino (mixed Hispanic and	Guatemalan quetzal = 100 centavos

BELIZE

Geography and Climate

Behind the swampy coastal plain in the south, the land rises to the low Maya Mountains, which reach a height of 1,120 m [3,674 ft] at Victoria Peak. The north is mostly low-lying and swampy.

Belize has a tropical, humid climate. Temperatures are high all year and the average yearly rainfall ranges from 1,300 mm [51 in] in the north to over 3,800 mm [150 in] in the south.

History and Politics

From 1862, Belize (then called British Honduras) was a British colony. Full independence was achieved in 1981, but Guatemala, which had claimed the area since the early 19th century, opposed Belize's independence and British troops remained to prevent a possible invasion. In 1983, Guatemala reduced its claim to the southern fifth of Belize. Improved relations in the early 1990s led Guatemala to recognize Belize's independence and, in 1992, Britain agreed to withdraw its troops from the country.

Economy

The World Bank classifies Belize as a 'lower-middle-income' developing country. Its economy is based on agriculture. Sugar cane is the chief commercial crop and export. Other crops include bananas, beans, maize and rice. Forestry and tourism are other important activities.

AREA	American) 30%,
22,960 sq km [8,865 sq mi]	Mayan Indian 11%,
POPULATION	Garifuna (Black-Carib Indian) 7%,
256,000	other 8%
CAPITAL (POPULATION)	**LANGUAGES**
Belmopan (4,000)	English (official), Creole, Spanish
GOVERNMENT	**RELIGIONS**
Constitutional monarchy	Roman Catholic 62%,
ETHNIC GROUPS	Protestant 30%
Mestizo (Spanish-Indian) 44%,	**CURRENCY**
Creole (mainly African	Belize dollar = 100 cents

EL SALVADOR

Geography and Climate

The Republic of El Salvador is the only country in Central America without a coast on the Caribbean Sea. The country has a narrow coastal plain along the Pacific Ocean. Behind the coastal plain, the coastal range is a zone of rugged mountains, including volcanoes, overlooking a densely populated inland plateau. Beyond the plateau, the land rises to the sparsely populated interior highlands.

The coast has a hot, tropical climate. Inland, the climate is moderated by altitude. Rain falls nearly every day between May and October.

GUATEMALA / EL SALVADOR

History and Politics

Amerindians have lived in El Salvador for thousands of years. The ruins of Mayan pyramids built between AD 100 and 1000 are still found in the western part of the country. Spanish soldiers conquered the area in 1524 and 1525, and Spain ruled until 1821. In 1823, all the Central American countries, except for Panama, set up a Central American Federation. But El Salvador withdrew in 1840 and declared its independence in 1841. El Salvador suffered from instability throughout the 19th century. The 20th century saw a more stable government, but from 1931 military dictatorships alternated with elected governments and the country remained poor.

In the 1970s, El Salvador was plagued by conflict as protesters demanded that the government introduce reforms to help the poor. Kidnappings and murders committed by left- and right-wing groups caused instability. A civil war broke out in 1979 between the US-backed, right-wing government forces and left-wing guerrillas in the FMLN (Farabundo Marti National Liberation Front). In 12 years, more than 750,000 people died. A cease-fire was agreed in 1992 and presidential elections were held in 1993 and 1999. An earthquake in 2001 made about one-sixth of El Salvador's population homeless.

Economy

El Salvador is classified as a 'lower-middle-income' economy. Coffee is the main export, followed by sugar and cotton. Fishing is important.

AREA	and Amerindian) 89%,
21,040 sq km [8,124 sq mi]	White 10%,
POPULATION	Amerindian 1%
6,238,000	**LANGUAGES**
CAPITAL (POPULATION)	Spanish (official)
San Salvador (1,522,000)	**RELIGIONS**
GOVERNMENT	Roman Catholic 86%
Republic	**CURRENCY**
ETHNIC GROUPS	US dollar;
Mestizo (mixed White	Colón = 100 centavos

HONDURAS

Geography and Climate

Honduras is a republic in Central America. The northern coast extends for more than 600 km [373 mi]. The Pacific coast in the south-east is only about 80 km [50 mi] long.

The climate is tropical, though the uplands are cooler than the coastal plains. The rainiest months are November to May. In October 1998, Honduras and Nicaragua were hit by Hurricane Mitch, which caused floods and mudslides. The death toll was about 7,000.

History and Politics

In the 1890s, American companies developed plantations in Honduras to grow bananas. The companies exerted great political influence and the country became known as a 'banana republic'. Instability continued to mar the country's progress and American aid was crucial. During the 1980s, Honduras allowed US-backed 'Contra' rebels from Nicaragua to operate in Honduras against Nicaragua's left-wing Sandinista government. A cease-fire was signed in Nicaragua in 1988, after which the 'Contra' bases were closed down. Since 1980, civilian governments have ruled Honduras, but the military retains much influence.

Economy

Honduras is a developing country – one of the poorest in the Americas. It has few resources besides some silver, lead and zinc. Agriculture dominates the economy. Bananas and coffee are the leading exports, and maize is the main food crop.

Honduras is the least industrialized country in Central America. Manufactures include processed food, textiles, and a wide variety of wood products.

AREA	Amerindian 7%, Black
112,090 sq km [43,278 sq mi]	(including Black Carib) 2%,
POPULATION	White 1%
6,406,000	**LANGUAGES**
CAPITAL (POPULATION)	Spanish (official)
Tegucigalpa (813,000)	**RELIGIONS**
GOVERNMENT	Roman Catholic 85%
Republic	**CURRENCY**
ETHNIC GROUPS	Honduran lempira =
Mestizo 90%,	100 centavos

NICARAGUA

Geography and Climate

The Republic of Nicaragua is the second largest country in Central America. In the east is a broad plain which is drained by rivers that flow from the Central Highlands. The fertile western Pacific region contains volcanoes, many of which are active, and earthquakes are common.

Nicaragua has a tropical climate and there is a marked wet season from May to October. In October 1998, Hurricane Mitch caused great devastation in Nicaragua, causing at least 1,800 deaths.

History and Politics

In 1502, Christopher Columbus claimed the area for Spain, which ruled Nicaragua until 1821. By the early 20th century, the United States had considerable influence in the country and, in 1912, US forces entered Nicaragua to protect US interests. From 1927 to 1933, rebels under General Augusto César Sandino tried to drive US forces out of the country. In 1933, US marines set up a Nicaraguan army, the National Guard, to help defeat the rebels. Its leader, Anastasio Somoza Garcia, had Sandino murdered in 1934. From 1937, Somoza ruled as a dictator.

In the mid-1970s, people began to protest against Somoza's rule. Many joined a guerrilla force, called the Sandinista National Liberation Front, named after General Sandino. The rebels defeated the Somoza regime in 1979. In the 1980s, the US-supported forces, called the 'Contras', launched a campaign against the Sandinista government. The US government opposed the Sandinista regime, under Daniel José Ortega Saavedra, claiming it was a Communist dictatorship. The National Opposition Union, a coalition, defeated the Sandinistas in elections in 1990. The Sandinista presidential candidate, Daniel Ortega, was again defeated in elections in 1996 and 2001.

Economy

Agriculture is the main activity, employing nearly half of the people. Coffee, cotton, sugar and bananas are grown for export, while rice is the main food crop.

AREA	Black 9%,
130,000 sq km [50,193 sq mi]	Amerindian 5%
POPULATION	**LANGUAGES**
4,918,000	Spanish (official),
CAPITAL (POPULATION)	Misumalpan
Managua (864,000)	**RELIGIONS**
GOVERNMENT	Roman Catholic 85%
Multiparty republic	**CURRENCY**
ETHNIC GROUPS	Córdoba oro (gold córdoba) =
Mestizo 69%, White 17%,	100 centavos

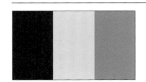

Guinea's flag was adopted when the country became independent from France in 1958. It uses the colours of the flag of Ethiopia, Africa's oldest nation, which symbolize African unity. The red represents work, the yellow justice and the green solidarity.

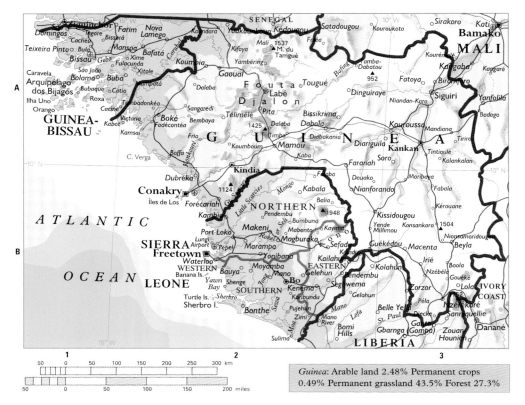

Guinea: Arable land 2.48% Permanent crops 0.49% Permanent grassland 43.5% Forest 27.3%

History and Politics

Portuguese explorers arrived in the mid-15th century and the slave trade began soon afterwards. From the 17th century, other European slave traders became active in Guinea. France became involved in the area in the mid-19th century and, in 1891, it made Guinea a French colony.

Guinea became independent in 1958. The first president, Sékou Touré, followed socialist policies, but he had to use repressive measures to hold on to power. After his death in 1984, military leaders took over and Colonel Lansana Conté became president. His government adopted free enterprise policies.

In 2000, fighting broke out between government and dissident forces as Guinea was drawn into the civil conflicts in neighbouring Liberia and Sierra Leone.

Economy

The World Bank classifies Guinea as a 'low-income' developing country. It has several natural resources, including bauxite (aluminium ore), uranium, diamonds, gold and iron ore. Bauxite and alumina (processed bauxite) account for 90% of the value of the exports.

Geography and Climate

The Republic of Guinea faces the Atlantic Ocean in West Africa. A flat, swampy plain borders the coast. Behind this plain, the land rises to a plateau region called Fouta Djalon. The Upper Niger Plains, named after one of Africa's longest rivers, the Niger, which rises there, are in the north-east. Guinea has a tropical climate. Conakry on the coast has heavy rains during its relatively cool season between May and November. Hot, dry harmattan winds blow south-westwards from the Sahara in the dry season. The Fouta Djalon is cooler than the coast. The driest region is in the north-east. This region and the south-eastern highlands have greater temperature variations than on the coast.

AREA	Soussou 20%,
245,860 sq km [94,927 sq mi]	other 10%
POPULATION	**LANGUAGES**
7,614,000	French (official)
CAPITAL (POPULATION)	**RELIGIONS**
Conakry (1,508,000)	Islam 85%,
GOVERNMENT	Christianity 8%,
Multiparty republic	traditional beliefs 7%
ETHNIC GROUPS	**CURRENCY**
Peuml 40%, Malinke 30%,	Guinean franc = 100 cauris

GUINEA-BISSAU

Geography and Climate

The Republic of Guinea-Bissau is a small country in West Africa. The land is mostly low-lying, with a broad, swampy, coastal plain and many flat offshore islands, including the Bijagós Archipelago.

The country has a tropical climate, with one dry season from December to May and a rainy season from June to November.

History, Politics and Economy

Portugal appointed a governor to administer Guinea-Bissau and the Cape Verde Islands in 1836, but in 1879 the territories separated and Guinea-Bissau became a colony, then called Portuguese Guinea. Development was slow, partly because the territory did not attract settlers on the same scale as the African colonies of Angola and Mozambique.

In 1956, African nationalists in Portuguese Guinea and Cape Verde founded the African Party for the Independence of Guinea and Cape Verde (PAIGC). Because Portugal seemed determined to hang on to its overseas territories, the PAIGC began a guerrilla war in 1963. By 1968, it held two-thirds of the country. In 1972, a rebel National Assembly, elected by the people in the PAIGC-controlled areas, voted to make the country independent as Guinea-Bissau.

Following independence in 1975, Guinea-Bissau's leaders favoured union with Cape Verde. This objective was abandoned in 1980, following a military coup. The country ceased to be a one-party state in 1991 and elections were held in 1994. In 1998 an army rebellion sparked a civil war. The army rebels took power in 1999, but elections were held in 1999–2000. Kumba Ialá became president.

Guinea-Bissau is a poor country. Most farming is at subsistence level. Major crops include beans, coconuts, groundnuts and maize.

AREA	Manjaca 14%, Mandinga 13%,
36,120 sq km [13,946 sq mi]	Papel 7%
POPULATION	**LANGUAGES**
1,316,000	Portuguese (official),
CAPITAL (POPULATION)	Crioulo
Bissau (145,000)	**RELIGIONS**
GOVERNMENT	Traditional beliefs 50%,
'Interim' government	Islam 45%, Christianity 5%
ETHNIC GROUPS	**CURRENCY**
Balanta 30%, Fula 20%,	CFA franc = 100 centimes

BAHRAIN

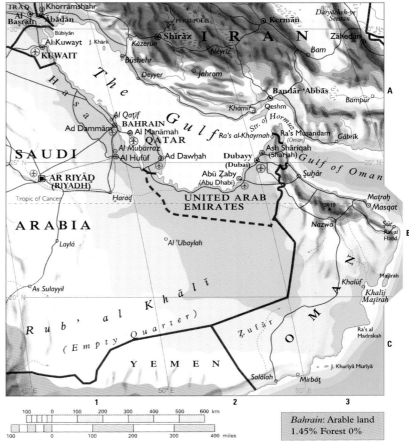

The Emirate of Bahrain, whose flag dates from about 1932, consists of the island of Bahrain and 34 smaller islands. A causeway links the island of Bahrain to the Saudi Arabian mainland. Most of the land is desert, but there are freshwater springs on the north coast of Bahrain island. Summers are hot and humid, with average temperatures of 33°C [91°F] in July, while winters are mild, with average January temperatures of about 17°C [63°F].

Bahrain has long been a centre of trade, but was largely undeveloped until the discovery of oil in 1932. The Al Khalifa Arabs took over Bahrain from Persia in 1728, and have ruled ever since. Bahrain became a British protectorate in 1861. Britain withdrew from the Gulf region in 1971 and Bahrain became independent.

In 1973, Bahrain adopted a new constitution, creating a National Assembly with 30 elected members. However, relations between the Al Khalifa family and the National Assembly proved unsuccessful and the National Assembly was dissolved in 1975. Since then, the country has been ruled by the Emir and a cabinet, headed by a prime minister, whom he appoints. Bahrain faces several problems. Tension between the Sunni and the majority Shiite population, who favour the establishment of an Islamic republic, has been apparent since before independence. During the First Gulf War, Iran responded to Bahrain's support for Iraq by reiterating claims to the territory. In 1996, relations with Iran again deteriorated when Bahrain accused Iran of supporting an underground Shiite organization. In 2001, the people of Bahrain voted in favour of a liberal national charter, calling for a constitutional monarchy, a partly elected parliament and an independent judiciary. In 2002, the Emir declared Bahrain to be a democratic constitutional monarchy, in which women would be allowed to vote and stand for office.

The people of Bahrain enjoy one of the highest standards of living in the Gulf region. The adult literacy rate is 85%, while free medical care is available. The country's prosperity is based on oil, which accounted for 60% of the exports in 1995. However, when production waned in the 1970s, Bahrain diversified into other sectors: its aluminium-smelting plant is the Gulf's largest non-oil industrial complex, while banking, communications and leisure are also important. Bahrain is now a major banking and financial centre, serving the Gulf region. Construction, fishing, manufacturing and transport have all been developed in recent years.

Bahrain: Arable land 1.45% Forest 0%

AREA	other Arab 10%,
678 sq km [262 sq mi]	Iranian 8%
POPULATION	**LANGUAGES**
645,000	Arabic (official),
CAPITAL (POPULATION)	English, Farsi, Urdu
Manama (Al Manámah, 143,000)	**RELIGIONS**
GOVERNMENT	Islam (Shi'a Muslim 70%,
Monarchy (emirate) with a	Sunni Muslim 30%)
cabinet appointed by the Emir	**CURRENCY**
ETHNIC GROUPS	Bahrain dinar =
Bahraini 63%, Asian 19%,	1,000 fils

KUWAIT

The State of Kuwait, whose flag dates from 1961, consists of a mainland area and several offshore islands at the head of the Gulf. Kuwait City lies on a fine natural harbour called Kuwait Bay. Kuwait is a low-lying country covered mostly by desert scrub. Average annual rainfall is around 125 mm [5 in] and most rain occurs between November and March. Winters are mild, but summers are hot, with average temperatures of 33°C to 35°C [91–95°F] between June and September. Inland, the high humidity makes conditions extremely uncomfortable.

The area was thinly populated until about 1710, when people from Arabia arrived. They built the port that later became Kuwait City and elected the head of the Al Sabah family as their ruler. The family rules the country today. British interest in the area began in the late 18th century. In 1899, Britain became responsible for the territory's defence and, in 1914, it became a British protectorate. Drilling for oil began in 1936 and oil was produced commercially in 1946. Kuwait soon became a prosperous oil exporter and became independent in 1961.

In August 1990, Iraq invaded Kuwait, claiming that it was legally part of Iraq. When Iraq refused to withdraw, a US-led multinational force invaded on 17 January 1991, expelling the Iraqis, but not before they had set fire to more than 500 oil wells, causing massive pollution, and destroying almost all industrial and commercial installations. Kuwait's revenge was directed mainly at the huge contingent of Palestinian,

Jordanian and Yemeni immigrant workers, who were seen as pro-Iraq. In 1994, Iraq recognized Kuwait's independence and boundaries. A partly elected National Council was established in 1990, and, in 1999, proposals were made to give women the vote, but a bill advocating this change was later rejected by parliament.

The economy is based on oil, which accounted for 95% of the exports in 1995. Kuwait has about 10% of the world's known reserves. The country has a small fishing fleet but, otherwise, most food is imported. The shortage of water has inhibited the development of industries. About three-quarters of Kuwait's drinking water is either imported or produced from sea water in desalination plants.

AREA	other Arab 35%,
17,820 sq km [6,880 sq mi]	South Asian 9%,
POPULATION	Iranian 4%, other 7%
2,042,000	**LANGUAGES**
CAPITAL (POPULATION)	Arabic (official), English
Kuwait City (Al Kuwayt, 189,000)	**RELIGIONS**
GOVERNMENT	Islam 85%,
Constitutional monarchy	Christianity, Hinduism
ETHNIC GROUPS	**CURRENCY**
Kuwaiti 45%,	Kuwaiti dinar = 1,000 fils

OMAN

The Sultanate of Oman occupies the south-eastern corner of the Arabian Peninsula. It also includes the tip of the Musandam Peninsula, overlooking the Strait of Hormuz. The fertile coastal plain along the Gulf of Oman, called Al Battinah, is backed by mountains. Inland are deserts, including part of the Rub' al Khali (Empty Quarter). While most of the coast along the Arabian Sea is barren, the south-east province of Zufar (also called Dhofar) has tropical vegetation. The south-east has an average annual rainfall of up to 630 mm [25 in], but most of Oman has less than 150 mm [6 in]. In summer, temperatures may reach 54°C [129°F], but winters are mild to warm.

Oman was an important trading area in ancient times. The Portuguese conquered its ports in the early 16th century, but local Arabs forced them out in 1650. The Al Bu Said family came to power in the 1740s and has ruled the country ever since. British influence dates back to the end of the 18th century, when the two countries entered into the first of several treaties. The country became independent in 1971.

Until 1970, Oman was a backward country compared to its oil-rich Gulf neighbours. However, when, with British collusion, Sultan Said bin Taimur was deposed by his son, Qaboos, Oman made substantial strides. It saw an end to the civil war against Yemen-backed separatist guerrillas in the province of Zufar and enjoyed an expanding economy based on oil reserves far larger than expected when production began in 1967. An absolute ruler, Qaboos forewent the prestigious projects favoured by Arab leaders to concentrate on social programmes. In 2000, Oman held its first direct elections for its consultative parliament. Unusual for the Gulf region, two women were elected.

The World Bank classifies Oman as an 'upper-middle-income' developing country. Oil accounts for over 90% of Oman's export revenues. Huge natural gas deposits were discovered in 1991 that were equal to all the finds of the previous 20 years. Although less than 1% of the land is cultivated, agriculture provides a living for half of the people. Major crops include alfalfa, bananas, coconuts, dates, tobacco and wheat.

AREA	ETHNIC GROUPS
212,460 sq km [82,031 sq mi]	Omani Arab 74%, Pakistani 21%
POPULATION	**LANGUAGES**
2,622,000	Arabic (official), Baluchi, English
CAPITAL (POPULATION)	**RELIGIONS**
Muscat (Masqat, 350,000)	Islam (Ibadiyah),
GOVERNMENT	Hinduism
Monarchy with consultative	**CURRENCY**
council	Omani rial = 100 baizas

QATAR

The State of Qatar occupies a low, barren peninsula which juts out from the Arabian peninsula into the Gulf. The land is mostly stony desert, with some barren salt flats. There is a lack of freshwater supplies and much of the drinking water is distilled sea water, produced in desalination plants.

From May to September it is very hot, with temperatures soaring to 49°C [120°F], but winters are mild to warm. Average annual rainfall total seldom exceeds 100 mm [4 in]. Most rain falls in winter.

During the mid-19th century, members of the Al-Thani family became the leaders of Qatar and this remains the ruling family today. The Ottoman Turks took over in the late 19th century, but the peninsula became a British protectorate. Oil was struck in 1939, though commercial exploitation did not begin until 1949.

Qatar became independent in 1971 when it chose not to unite with the United Arab Emirates. In 1982, Qatar, Bahrain, Kuwait, Oman, Saudi Arabia and the United Arab Emirates united to form the Gulf Co-operation Council, which is concerned with such matters as defence and economic development. In 1995, Qatar signed a security pact with the United States. A bloodless coup also occurred in 1995, when the heir apparent, Sheikh Hamad, deposed his father, Sheikh Khalifa bin Hamad Al-Thani, while Khalifa was abroad. An attempted counter-coup failed in 1996.

The high standard of living in Qatar derives from oil revenue, which accounts for more than 80% of the country's export revenues. Money from oil sales has been used to diversify the economy. Industries have been set up, while wells have been dug to develop agriculture. The economy is heavily dependent on an immigrant workforce, notably from the Indian subcontinent and poor states in south-western Asia.

AREA	ETHNIC GROUPS
11,000 sq km [4,247 sq mi]	Arab 40%, Pakistani 18%, Indian
POPULATION	18%, Iranian 10%, other 14%
769,000	**LANGUAGES**
CAPITAL (POPULATION)	Arabic (official), English
Doha (Ad Dawhah, 243,000)	**RELIGIONS**
GOVERNMENT	Islam 95%
Constitutional absolute	**CURRENCY**
monarchy	Qatar riyal = 100 dirhams

UNITED ARAB EMIRATES

The United Arab Emirates (UAE) is largely flat, stony or sandy desert, with occasional oases. Average annual rainfall is less than 130 mm [5 in]. In summer (May to September), temperatures may soar to 49°C [120°F] with high humidity on the coast. Winters are warm to mild.

European contact began in the 16th century when trading posts were set up along the coast. The Arab states which now form the UAE began to develop in the 18th century. In 1820, conflict between the states led Britain to force the states to sign the first of a series of truces. This led the region to become known as the Trucial States. Oil was discovered in 1958. The Trucial States became independent in 1971 when six of the seven Trucial States – Abu Dhabi, Ajman, Dubai, Fujairah, Sharjah and Umm-al-Qaiwain – opted to form a single country called the United Arab Emirates, with Ras al-Khaimah joining in 1972. Instead of joining to form nine states, Bahrain and Qatar chose independence.

The economy is based on oil production, and oil makes up more than 90% of the country's exports. Because of its mineral wealth, the UAE has one of the highest per capita GNPs in Asia. However, many of the people are immigrants from southern Asia, south-western Asia and northern Africa, including Egypt. Less than 1% of the land is farmed, but such crops as dates are grown at oases. Some desert nomads herd camels, goats and sheep. Fishing is important along the coast. The country has four international airports.

AREA	ETHNIC GROUPS
83,600 sq km [32,278 sq mi]	Arab 87%, Indo-Pakistani 9%,
POPULATION	Iranian 2%
2,407,000	**LANGUAGES**
CAPITAL (POPULATION)	Arabic (official), English
Abu Dhabi (Abū Zāby, 928,000)	**RELIGIONS**
GOVERNMENT	Islam 95%, Christianity 4%
Federation of seven emirates,	**CURRENCY**
each with its own government	Dirham = 100 fils

GUYANA

Guyana's flag was adopted in 1966 when the country became independent from Britain. The colours symbolize the people's energy in building a new nation (red), their perseverance (black), minerals (yellow), rivers (white), and agriculture and forests (green).

Geography and Climate

Guyana faces the Atlantic Ocean in north-eastern South America. The coastal plain is flat and mainly below sea level. Dykes (sea walls) prevent flooding. Inland is a hilly region which rises to the Pakaraima Mountains, part of the Guiana Highlands, in the west. Other highlands are in the south. Guyana has several grand waterfalls, including the King George VI Falls (488 m [1,601 ft]).

The climate is hot and humid, although temperatures are lower in the highlands in the west and south. The rainfall is heavy, occurring on more than 200 days a year.

Politics and Economy

British Guiana became independent in 1966. A black lawyer, Forbes Burnham, became the first prime minister. Burnham died in 1985 and was succeeded by Hugh Desmond Hoyte. The East Indian Cheddi Jagan served as president from 1993 until 1997, when his wife Janet succeeded him. She retired in 1999 and, in elections in 2001, Jagdeo Bharrat was elected president.

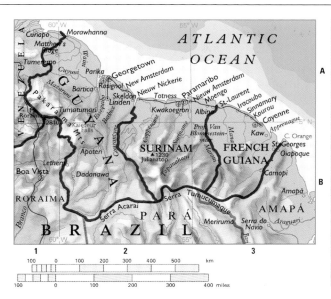

AREA
214,970 sq km [83,000 sq mi]
POPULATION
697,000
CAPITAL (POPULATION)
Georgetown (200,000)
GOVERNMENT
Multiparty republic
ETHNIC GROUPS
East Indian 49%, Black 32%,
Mixed 12%, Amerindian 6%,
Portuguese, Chinese
LANGUAGES
English (official), Creole,
Hindi, Urdu
RELIGIONS
Protestant 34%, Roman Catholic
18%, Hinduism 34%, Islam 9%
CURRENCY
Guyana dollar = 100 cents

Guyana is a developing country. Its resources include gold, bauxite, forests and fertile soils. Agriculture employs 27% of the people. Sugar cane and rice are the leading crops.

FRENCH GUIANA

Geography and Climate

French Guiana is the smallest country in mainland South America. The coastal plain is swampy in places, but dry areas are cultivated. Inland lies a plateau, with the low Serra Tumucumaque in the south. Most of the rivers run north towards the Atlantic Ocean.

French Guiana has high temperatures throughout the year. Rainfall is heavy, especially between December and June, but it is dry between August and October.

History, Politics and Economy

The area became a French colony in the late 17th century, and in the 1790s was used by France as a penal settlement for political prisoners. In 1946, French Guiana became an overseas department of France, and in 1974 also became an administrative region. An independence movement developed in the 1980s, but most of the people want to retain links with France and continue to obtain financial aid for development.

AREA	Chinese and
90,000 sq km	Amerindian 12%,
[34,749 sq mi]	White 10%
POPULATION	**LANGUAGES**
178,000	French (official)
CAPITAL	**RELIGIONS**
(POPULATION)	Roman
Cayenne (42,000)	Catholic 80%,
GOVERNMENT	Protestant 4%
Overseas department	**CURRENCY**
of France	Euro;
ETHNIC GROUPS	French franc =
Mulatto 66%,	100 centimes

SURINAM

Geography and Climate

The Republic of Surinam lies between French Guiana and Guyana in north-eastern South America. The once swampy coastal plain has been drained and now consists of farmland.

Surinam has a humid climate. Temperatures are high all year round.

History, Politics and Economy

In 1667, Britain handed Surinam to the Dutch in return for New Amsterdam (now the state of New York). Slave revolts hampered development and in the early 19th century Britain and the Netherlands disputed the ownership of the area. The British gave up their claims in 1813. Slavery was abolished in 1863, and Indian and Indonesian labourers were introduced to work on plantations. Surinam became independent in 1975, but the economy was weakened when thousands of skilled people emigrated to the Netherlands. In 1992, the government negotiated a peace agreement with the *boschneger*, descendants of African slaves, who had launched a struggle against the government. In 1992, a peace agreement was reached with the rebels and elections

were held in 1996 and again in 2000. From 1996, the president was Ronald Venetiaan, of the National Party of Surinam.

AREA	Indonesian 14%, Black 9%,
163,270 sq km [63,039 sq mi]	Amerindian 3%, Chinese 3%,
POPULATION	Dutch 1%
434,000	**LANGUAGES**
CAPITAL (POPULATION)	Dutch (official), Sranantonga
Paramaribo (201,000)	**RELIGIONS**
GOVERNMENT	Hinduism 27%,
Multiparty republic	Roman Catholic 23%,
ETHNIC GROUPS	Islam 20%, Protestant 19%
Asian Indian 37%, Creole	**CURRENCY**
(mixed White and Black) 31%,	Surinam guilder = 100 cents

HAITI – SEE CARIBBEAN SEA, PAGES 71–76;
HONDURAS – SEE GUATEMALA, PAGES 110–111

Hungary's flag was adopted in 1919. A state emblem was added in 1949 and removed in 1957. The colours of red, white and green had been used in the Hungarian arms since the 15th century. The tricolour design became popular during the 1848 rebellion against Habsburg rule.

Arable 51.4% Permanent crops 2.44% Forest 19.1%

Geography

The Hungarian Republic is a landlocked country in central Europe. The land is mostly low-lying and drained by the Danube (Duna) and its tributary, the Tisza. Most of the land east of the Danube belongs to a region called the Great Plain (Nagyalföld), which covers about half of Hungary.

West of the Danube is a hilly region, with some low mountains, called Transdanubia. This region contains the country's largest lake, Balaton. In the north-west is a small, fertile and mostly flat region called the Little Plain (Kisalföld).

Climate

Hungary lies far from the moderating influence of the sea. As a result, summers are warmer and sunnier, and the winters colder than in Western Europe.

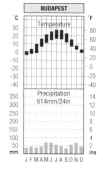

HUNGARY (BUDAPEST)

The plains of Hungary have warm summers and cold winters with snow between 30 and 40 days. At Budapest, maximum temperatures exceed 20°C [68°F] from May to September, with the minimum below freezing from December to February. A double maximum of rainfall occurs. The first is in summer when convectional storms are most active. The second in November is a feature of the climate to the south-west.

History

Magyars first arrived in the area from the east in the 9th century. In the 11th century, Hungary's first king, Stephen I, made Roman Catholicism the official religion. Hungary became a powerful kingdom, but in 1526 it was defeated by Turkish forces, who later occupied much of Hungary. In the late 17th century, the Austrian Habsburgs conquered Hungary. In 1867, Austria granted Hungary equal status in a 'dual monarchy', called Austria-Hungary. In 1914, a Bosnian student killed the heir to the Austria-Hungary throne. This led to World War I, when Austria-Hungary fought alongside Germany. Defeat in 1918

led to nearly 70% of its territory being apportioned by the Treaty of Versailles to Czechoslovakia, Yugoslavia and Romania. Some 2.6 million Hungarians live in these countries today. The government hoped to regain these territories by siding with Hitler's Germany in World War II, but the result was the occupation of the Red Army in late 1944. Elections were held in 1945 and, in 1946, the country was declared a republic. Although the small-holders had won a clear majority of the votes in the 1945 elections, the Communists gradually took control even after failing to win a majority of the votes cast in new elections in 1947.

Politics

Hungary became a Communist state in 1949, with a constitution based on that of the Soviet Union. The first leader of the Communist government was Mathias Rákosi, who was replaced in 1953 by Imre Nagy. Nagy sought to relax Communist policies and was forced from office in 1955. He was replaced by Rákosi in 1956 and this led to a major uprising in which many Hungarians were killed or imprisoned. Nagy and his co-workers were executed for treason in 1958.

Janos Kádár came to power in the wake of the suppression, but his was a relatively progressive leadership, including an element of political reform and a measure of economic liberalism. However, in the late 1970s, the economic situation worsened and new political parties started to appear.

Kádár resigned in 1989 and the central Committee of the Socialist Workers' Party (the Communist Party) agreed to sweeping reforms, including the introduction of a pluralist system and a democratic parliament, which had formally been little more than a rubber-stamp assembly. The trial of Imre Nagy and his co-workers was declared unlawful and their bodies were reburied with honour in June 1989.

In 1990, Hungarians voted into office a centre-right coalition headed by the Democratic Forum. In 1994, the Hungarian Socialist Party (made up of ex-Communists) won a majority and governed in coalition with the Alliance of Free Democrats. However, in elections in 1998, Victor Orbán, leader of the Fidesz-Hungarian Civic Party, became prime minister. In 2002, the Socialists and the Free Democrat coalition, led by Peter Medgyessy, won a majority in parliament. In 1999, Hungary joined NATO.

Economy

Before World War II, Hungary's economy was based mainly on agriculture. But the Communists set up many manufacturing industries. The new factories were owned by the government, as also was most of the land. However, from the late 1980s, the government has worked to increase private ownership. This change of policy caused many problems, including inflation and high rates of unemployment.

Manufacturing is the most valuable activity. The major products include aluminium made from local bauxite, chemicals, electrical and electronic goods, processed food, iron and steel, and vehicles.

AREA	Gypsy, German, Croat,
93,030 sq km [35,919 sq mi]	Romanian, Slovak
POPULATION	**LANGUAGES**
10,106,000	Hungarian (official)
CAPITAL (POPULATION)	**RELIGIONS**
Budapest (1,885,000)	Roman Catholic 64%,
GOVERNMENT	Protestant 23%,
Multiparty republic	Orthodox 1%, Judaism 1%
ETHNIC GROUPS	**CURRENCY**
Magyar 90%,	Forint = 100 fillér

ICELAND

Iceland's flag dates from 1915. It became the official flag in 1944, when Iceland became fully independent. The flag, which uses Iceland's traditional colours, blue and white, is the same as Norway's flag, except that the blue and red colours are reversed.

Geography

The Republic of Iceland, in the North Atlantic Ocean, is closer to Greenland than Scotland. Iceland sits astride the Mid-Atlantic Ridge, the geological boundary between Europe and North America. The island is slowly getting wider as the ocean is stretched apart by the forces of plate tectonics.

Iceland has around 200 volcanoes and eruptions are frequent. An eruption under the Vatnajökull ice cap in 1996 created a subglacial lake which subsequently burst, causing severe flooding. Geysers and hot springs are other volcanic features. During the thousand years that Iceland has been settled, between 150 and 200 volcanic eruptions have occurred. Ice caps and glaciers cover about one-eighth of the land. The only habitable regions are the coastal lowlands.

Climate

Although it lies far to the north, Iceland's climate is moderated by the warm waters of the Gulf Stream. The port of Reykjavik is ice-free all the year round.

ICELAND (REYKJAVIK)

Due to the influence of the Gulf Stream, Iceland is relatively warm. The coldest month at Reykjavik, January, is normally 0°C [32°F], while the warmest month is July at 12°C [54°F]. Precipitation falls on 200 days a year, 65 of them as snow. There is very high rainfall on the south coast, exceeding 800 mm [32 in], with half of this in the north. Sunshine levels are low, being 5–6 hours from May to August. Gales are frequent.

History

Norwegian Vikings colonized Iceland in the AD 870s and the population grew as more settlers arrived from Norway, and from the Viking colonies in the British Isles. In 930, the settlers founded the oldest, and what is thought to be the world's first, parliament (the *Althing*). One early settler was Eric the Red, a Viking who sailed to Greenland in about 982 and founded another colony there in about 985.

Iceland was an independent country until 1262 when, following a series of civil wars, the Althing recognized the rule of the king of Norway. When Norway united with Denmark in 1380, Iceland came under the rule of Danish kingdoms. Life on Iceland was never easy. The Black Death, which swept the island in 1402, claimed two-thirds of the population, while, in the late 18th century, volcanic eruptions destroyed crops, farmland and livestock, causing a famine. Then, during the Napoleonic Wars in the early 19th century, food supplies from Europe failed to reach the island and many people starved.

When Norway was separated from Denmark in 1814, Iceland remained under Danish rule. In the late 19th century, the invention of motorized craft, which changed the fishing industry, led to mounting demands for self-government. In 1918, Iceland was acknowledged as a sovereign state, but remained united with Denmark through a common monarch. During World War II, when Germany occupied Denmark, British and American troops landed in Iceland to protect it from invasion by the Germans. Finally, following a referendum in which 97% of the people voted to cut all ties with Denmark, Iceland became a fully independent republic on 17 June 1944.

Politics

Fishing, on which Iceland's economy is based, is a major political issue. From 1975, Iceland extended its territorial waters to 200 nautical miles, causing skirmishes between Icelandic and British vessels. The issue was resolved in 1977 when Britain agreed not to fish in the disputed waters. Another problem developed in the late 1980s when Iceland reduced the allowable catches in its waters, because overfishing was causing the depletion of fishing stocks, especially of cod. The reduction of the fish catch led to a slowdown in the economy and, eventually, to a recession, though the economy recovered in the mid-1990s when the conservation measures appeared to have been successful. In the late 1990s, Iceland had outstanding disputes over fishing rights with Norway, Russia, the Faroe Islands and Canada.

Iceland has no armed forces of its own. However, it joined the North Atlantic Treaty Organization (NATO) in 1949 and, under a NATO agreement, the United States maintains a base on the island.

Economy

Iceland has few resources besides the fishing grounds which surround it. Fishing and fish processing are major industries which dominate Iceland's overseas trade. Barely 1% of the land is used to grow crops, mainly root vegetables and fodder for livestock. However, 23% of the country is used for grazing sheep and cattle. Iceland is self-sufficient in meat and dairy products. Vegetables and fruits are grown in greenhouses heated by water from hot springs. Manufacturing is important. Products include aluminium, cement, clothing, electrical equipment, fertilizers and processed foods.

AREA	Danish 1%
103,000 sq km [39,768 sq mi]	**LANGUAGES**
POPULATION	Icelandic (official)
278,000	**RELIGIONS**
CAPITAL (POPULATION)	Evangelical
Reykjavik (103,000)	Lutheran 92%,
GOVERNMENT	other Lutheran 3%,
Multiparty republic	Roman Catholic 1%
ETHNIC GROUPS	**CURRENCY**
Icelandic 97%,	Króna = 100 aurar

Arable land 0.06% Permanent crops 0%
Permanent grassland 22.7% Forest 1.20%

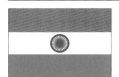

The Indian flag was adopted shortly after the country gained independence from Britain in 1947. The saffron (orange) represents renunciation, the white represents truth, and the green symbolizes mankind's relationship with nature. The central wheel represents dynamism and change.

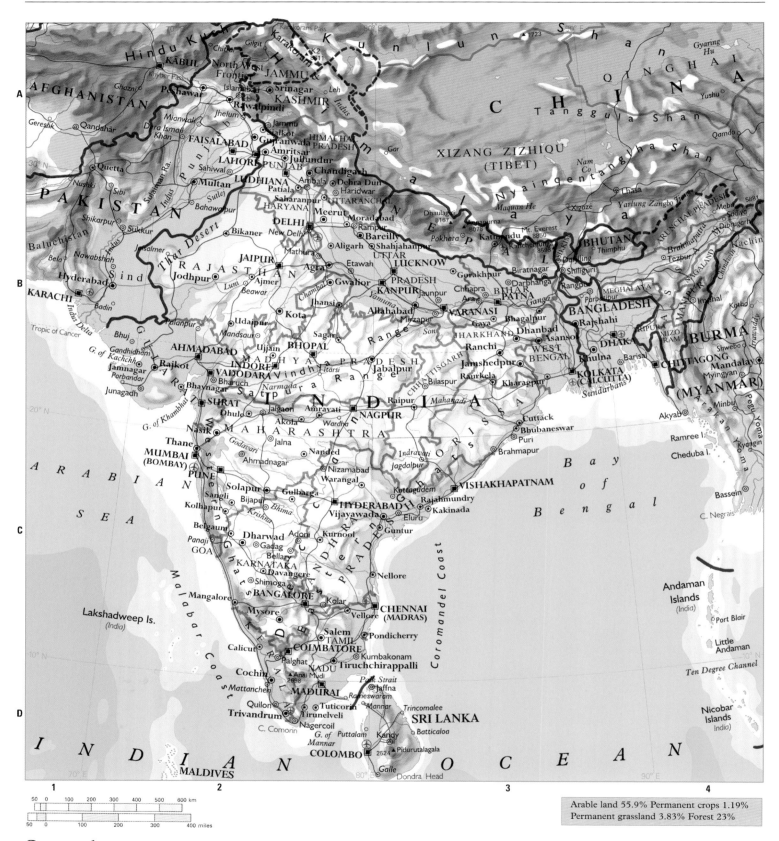

Arable land 55.9% Permanent crops 1.19%
Permanent grassland 3.83% Forest 23%

Geography

The Republic of India, the world's seventh largest country, extends from high in the Himalayas, through the Tropic of Cancer, to the warm waters of the Indian Ocean at Cape Comorin. In 2000, the population was reported to have topped the 1 billion mark. India is the world's second most populous nation after China, and the largest democracy.

The foothills of the Himalayas, the world's youngest and highest mountain range, form a stunning backdrop for northern India, rising abruptly from the plains in towering ranks. The Himalayas include Kanchenjunga, India's highest peak at 8,598 m [28,208 ft] above sea level on the Sikkim-Nepal border. In the north-west, harsh dry highlands, sparsely occupied by herders, stretch northwards to the everlasting snows of the Karakoram Range in Kashmir. Beyond lie alpine meadows, lakes and woodlands, often grazed in summer by seasonally migrant flocks from lower villages. The Vale of Kashmir is a fertile land, claimed by both India and Pakistan. In the east lies the high plateau of Meghalaya ('abode of the clouds'), Assam, where the slopes of the Himalayas are ablaze with rhododendrons and magnolias, and the forested ridges of Nagaland, Manipur and Nizoram.

The great plains form a continuous strip from the Punjab eastwards. The fertile soils of the Punjab have provided prosperity for the Sikh farmers of the Punjab and Haryana states. Somewhat similar landscapes extend east to the plains surrounding Delhi, the third largest city which stands on the banks of the Jumna (Yamuna) River. The vast and fertile northern plains, India's most densely populated and developed region, are drained by the Indus, Ganges (Ganga) and Brahmaputra rivers, all of which rise in the snowy highlands to the north. To the east again lie the lowlands of Uttar Pradesh, which are crisscrossed by the Ganges and Jumna rivers and their many tributaries. Along the border with Nepal lie the *terai*, or foothill plains.

Near the Bangladesh border, the Ganges begins to divide into distributary streams, while still receiving tributaries from the north and west. West Bengal consists largely of rice- and jute-growing lands flanking the distributary streams that flow south to become the Hoogly, on which Calcutta, India's largest city, is situated. The Sundarbans, a World Heritage site of mangrove and swamp forests at the seaward margin of the Ganges Delta, extend eastwards into Bangladesh.

South-west of the Punjab Plains lies the Great Indian, or Thar, Desert. Its western fringes are in Pakistan, but it contains a broad tract of dunes in the north-western lowlands of Rajasthan, India's largest state. The desert ranges from perennially dry wastelands of shifting sands to areas capable of cultivation in wet years. Rajasthan rises in a series of steps to the jagged, bare range of brightly coloured sandstone ridges, the Aravallis, that extend north-eastwards and end at Delhi.

South and west of the Aravallis lie the cotton-growing lands of tropical Gujerat, where Ahmadabad is the chief city. Between the gulfs of Khambat and Kachchh is the low peninsular plateau of Kathiawar. Between this plateau and the Pakistan border stretches the desert salt marsh of the Rann of Kachchh. Formerly an arm of the Arabian Sea, this region is still occasionally flooded by exceptionally heavy rains. South-east of the Aravallis is an area of transition between the great plains of the north and the uplands and plateaux of southern India. First come the Chambal badlands – wastelands south of Agra which have been partly reclaimed – and then rough hill country extending south-eastwards to Rewa. The Son River provides a lowland corridor through the hills south of Rewa. Eastwards again the hills are forested around Ambikapur and Lohardaga. Industrial development becomes important around the coalfields of the Damodar Valley, centred on Asanol.

South of the Chambal River and of Indore, the sandy plateau of the north gives way to forested hills, split by the broad corridors of the Narmada and Tapi rivers. Tribal lands persist in the Satpura Range, and the Ajanta Range to the south is noted for primitive cave paintings near Aurangabad. From here to the south, the soils are mainly volcanic. Mumbai (formerly Bombay), India's second largest city, lies on the coastal lowlands by a broad estuary, among rice fields dotted with low lava ridges. Fishing villages line the shore, while inland rise the stepped, forested slopes and pinnacles of peninsular India's longest mountain range, the Western Ghats (Sahyadri). South of Goa, formerly a Portuguese enclave which retains a Portuguese atmosphere, to Trivandrum in the south, the coast is a kaleidoscope of farms, orchards and fishing villages. Here the Ghats are edged with granite, gneiss, sandstone and schist, and clad in dense rainforest.

To the east, the peninsula is drier, with rolling plateaux given over to such dry crops as millet and pulses. The central plateau, called the Deccan, is bordered in the east by the Eastern Ghats, which meet the Western Ghats in the southern Nilgiri Hills. The longest rivers in southern India, including the Godavari, Krishna and Cauvery, drain eastwards from the Western Ghats and empty into the Bay of Bengal. Shorter rivers flow westwards down the slopes of the Western Ghats into the Arabian Sea.

Climate

India has three seasons. The weather during the cool season, which extends from October to February, is mild in the northern plains, but southern India remains hot, though temperatures are a little lower than for the rest of the year. Temperatures on the northern plains sometimes soar to 49°C [120°F] during the hot season from March to the end of June. The monsoon season starts in the middle of June and continues into September. At this time, moist south-easterly winds from the Indian Ocean bring heavy rains to India. Darjeeling in the north-east has an average annual rainfall of 3,040 mm [120 in], but parts of the Great Indian Desert in the north-west have only 50 mm [2 in] of rain a year. The monsoon rains are essential for India's farmers. If they arrive late, crops may be ruined. If the rainfall is considerably higher than average, floods may cause great destruction.

INDIA (DELHI)

The summer rains, typical of the Indian monsoon, arrive later and are less intense at Delhi than in lower parts of the Ganges Valley. From November to May, it is sunny and temperatures increase rapidly until the arrival of the rains in June. During the rainy season the temperature is uniformly hot. The latter part of the year is sunny, dry and cooler. Night temperatures from December to February are usually below 10°C [50°F].

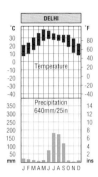

Vegetation

India has a wide range of vegetation types. Palm trees abound on the southern Deccan Plateau, with bamboo, rosewood, ironwood and teak in the Western Ghats. By contrast, the vegetation in the Great Indian Desert is very limited. In uncultivated parts of the northern plains, there are forests of many kinds of trees, of which the sal (*Shorea robusta*) is typical. The north-east, including Assam, has luxuriant plant life, with broadleaved forests and bamboo. The Himalayan foothills have an equally varied vegetation, with such trees as alders, birches, junipers, laurels, maples, rhododendrons and dwarf willows. The mountains have a range of vegetation zones depending on the altitude.

The Himalayas

The Earth's highest mountain range, with an average height of 6,100 m [20,000 ft], the Himalayas are structurally part of the high plateau of Central Asia. The range stretches over 2,400 km [1,500 mi] from the Pamirs in the north-west to the Chinese border in the east. There are three main ranges: Outer, Middle and Inner; in Kashmir, the Inner Himalayas divide into five more ranges, including the Ladakh Range and the Karakorams. The world's highest mountain, Mt Everest (8,850 m [29,035 ft]), is on the Tibet-Nepal border; next highest is K2 (8,611 m [28,251 ft]) in the Karakorams, and there are a further six peaks over 8,000 m [26,250 ft].

The name comes from the Nepalese words *him* ('snows') and *alya* ('home of'), and the mountains are very much revered in Hindu mythology as the abode of gods. Recently, the hydroelectric potential of the range has inspired more secular reverence: enormous quantities of energy could be tapped, although certainly at some cost to one of the world's most pristine environments.

The Himalayas began to rise over 50 million years ago, as two continental plates, the Indian and the Eurasian, collided. As the Indian plate moved northwards, it tended to underride the Eurasian plate, squeezing up the intervening sediments on the floor of the now vanished Tethys Sea into a fold mountain range. The northwards movement of the Indian plate continues, which accounts for the frequent earthquakes in the region. The process is further thickening what is already about the thickest part of the Earth's crust. In parts of the Himalayas, the crust is 90 km [56 mi] deep, as compared to an average continental thickness of 35 km to 40 km [22–25 mi].

History

India's early settlers were scattered across the subcontinent in Stone Age times. The first of its many civilizations began to flourish in the Indus Valley in what is now Pakistan and western India around 4,500 years ago, and in the Ganges Valley from about 1500 BC, when Aryan people arrived in India from central Asia. The earlier, darker-skinned people, the Dravidians, moved southwards, ahead of the Aryans, and their descendants are now the main people in southern India.

In 326 BC, the armies of Alexander the Great conquered north-western India, but the area was soon reconquered by Indians. In 321 BC, after Alexander's death, the Maurya Empire, named after its first leader, Chandragupta Maurya, was founded in India. Its most famous ruler was Emperor Asoka, who built up a huge, though loosely held empire with its centre at Pataliputra (modern Patna). However, military conquest ceased after Asoka, a Hindu, converted to Buddhism. After the death of Asoka in 232 BC, the empire broke up into smaller areas. Buddhism became the common religion of India, but Hinduism finally became the majority religion by around AD 800.

In about AD 120, the Scythians occupied northern India and founded the Kushan Dynasty, but from 320 to about 500, northern India was ruled by the native Indian Gupta Dynasty. This period saw a great revival in the arts, learning and science. Another Hindu-Buddhist civilization developed in southern India at the same time. The southern Indians were a sea-faring people and they spread their culture into South-east Asia. From about 450, India was conquered by many invaders who introduced their cultures. Important among these was the arrival of Muslim armies from Arabia in the 8th century, and other armies from Persia and Afghanistan in the 11th century. Islam became an important religion in the north-west. A Muslim sultanate established in Delhi in 1206 continued until 1526. The Tartar armies of Tamerlane, a Muslim conqueror from central Asia, raided India in 1398 and briefly occupied Delhi. Another central Asian leader, Babar, a descendant of Tamerlane and Genghis Khan, invaded India in 1526 and founded the Mogul Dynasty. A new religion, Sikhism, which combined elements of Hinduism and Islam, emerged during Mogul rule and it became especially strong in Punjab.

The Mogul Empire began to decline in the 18th century as the British East India Company was gradually taking control of India.

Vasco da Gama had reached Calicut in southern India in 1498 and, for a period, the Portuguese were in control of the ports along the west coast of India. The Portuguese were followed by traders from the Netherlands, France and England. The British East India Company was formed in 1600 and, by 1757, following the victory by one of the company's military leaders, Robert Clive, in the Battle of Plassey, it became the leading power in India. In the first half of the 19th century, the Company extended its rule into Afghanistan, Burma and Nepal, together with Punjab and Kashmir. But, under the India Act of 1858, the British government took over the territories occupied by the East India Company, which then became known as British India.

An independence movement began in India after the Sepoy Rebellion (1857–9) and, in 1885, the Indian National Congress was founded. It was initially a debating society but it developed into a political movement advocating self-government. In 1906, Indian Muslims, concerned that Hindus formed the majority of the members of the Indian National Congress, founded the Muslim League. In 1920, Mohandas K. Gandhi, a former lawyer, became leader of the Indian National Congress which soon became a mass movement. Gandhi's policy of non-violent disobedience proved highly effective, and in response Britain began to introduce political reforms. In the 1930s, the Muslim League, led by Muhammad Ali Jinnah, called for the establishment of a Muslim state, called Pakistan.

Politics

In 1946, after the end of World War II, Britain offered independence to India providing that it could agree on a form of government. But differences between the religious groups delayed progress until, in 1947, it was agreed that British India be partitioned into the mainly Hindu India and the Muslim Pakistan. Both countries became independent in August 1947, but the events were marred by mass slaughter as Hindus and Sikhs fled from Pakistan, and Muslims flocked to Pakistan from India. In the boundary disputes and reshuffling of minority populations that followed, some 1 million lives were lost. Since 1947–8, events have done little to promote good relations between the countries.

India's first prime minister was Jawaharlal Nehru, a close associate of Gandhi, who was assassinated in 1948 by a Hindu extremist who hated him for his tolerant attitude towards Muslims. The country adopted a new constitution in 1948 making the country a democratic republic within the Commonwealth, and elections were held in 1951 and 1952. The government sought to develop the economy and raise living standards at home, while, on the international stage, Nehru won great respect for his policy of non-alignment and neutrality. But he was criticized in 1961 when India invaded three small Portuguese colonies – Damao (now Daman), Diu and Goa – and integrated them into India. In mid-1987, Goa was made India's 25th state, while Daman and Diu remained a territory.

India also came into conflict with China during armed border disputes in 1959 and 1962, when a cease-fire was agreed. This conflict shattered the people's confidence in neutrality, though it was the disputed status of Kashmir that became India's thorniest security problem. The border disputes led to an increase in defence spending and this, in turn, slowed down India's economic development.

Following Nehru's death in 1964, Lal Bahadur Shastri, a cabinet member under Nehru, became prime minister. He led India during a dispute with Pakistan that led to border fighting. After Shastri's death in 1966, Nehru's daughter, Mrs Indira Gandhi, took office. Her Congress Party lost support because of food shortages, unemployment and other problems. In 1971, India helped the people of East Pakistan achieve their independence from West Pakistan to become Bangladesh. India tested its first atomic bomb in 1974, but it pledged to use nuclear power for peaceful purposes only. In 1975, Mrs Gandhi was found guilty of using illegal methods during the parliamentary elections in 1971. Mrs Gandhi refused to resign and governed by emergency rule, imposing censorship on the press. The government passed measures that made Mrs Gandhi's actions in 1971 legal and the Supreme Court overthrew her conviction.

In 1977, Mrs Gandhi lost her seat in parliament and her Congress Party was defeated by the Janata Party, a coalition led by Morarji R.

Kashmir

Until Indian independence in August 1947, Kashmir's mainly Muslim population was ruled, under British supervision, by a Hindu maharaja. Independence obliged the maharaja to choose between Pakistan or India; hoping to preserve his own independence, he refused to make a decision. In October, a ragtag army of Pathan tribesmen invaded from newly created Pakistan. Looting industriously, the Pathans advanced slowly, and India had time to rush troops to the region. The first Indo-Pakistan war resulted in a partition that satisfied neither side, with Pakistan holding one-third and India the remainder, with a 60% Muslim population. Despite promises, India has refused to allow a plebiscite to decide the province's fate. Two wars in 1965 and 1972 failed to alter greatly the 1948 cease-fire lines.

During the late 1980s, Kashmiri nationalists in the Indian-controlled area began a violent campaign in favour of either secession to Pakistan, or local independence. India responded by flooding Kashmir with troops and accusing Pakistan of intervention. During the 1990s, Pakistani-backed guerrillas attempted to break India's hold on the Srinagar Valley, Kashmir's most populous region, and tension increased following the testing of nuclear devices by India and Pakistan in 1998.

In 1999, armed troops occupied strategic positions on the Indian side of the cease-fire line. India said that the troops were Pakistani soldiers, while Pakistan claimed that they were Muslim rebels with local support in Kashmir. Fighting ensued, arousing fears of a war between India and Pakistan. From 2000 to 2002, attempts were made to achieve a lasting cease-fire, but the fighting continued as the leaders of the two countries, both nuclear powers, failed to reach an agreement.

Desai. Disputes in the Janata Party led to Desai's resignation in 1979 and, in 1980, Congress-I (the I standing for Indira) won the elections. Mrs Gandhi again became prime minister, but her government faced many problems, especially those arising from communal conflict. One problem was that many Sikhs wanted more control over the Punjab, and Sikh radicals began to commit acts of violence to draw attention to their cause. In 1984, armed Sikhs occupied the sacred Golden Temple, in Amritsar. In response, Indian troops attacked the temple, causing much damage and deaths. This led to further violent acts and, in October, 1984, two of Mrs Gandhi's Sikh guards assassinated her.

Mrs Gandhi's son, Rajiv, was chosen to succeed his mother as prime minister, but, in 1989, Congress lost its majority in parliament and Rajiv resigned as prime minister. He was succeeded by Vishwanath Pratap Singh, of the National Front, a coalition of opposition parties. Singh resigned in 1990 and was succeeded by Chandra Shekhar of the socialist Janata Party. During elections in 1991, Rajiv Gandhi was assassinated by Tamil extremists. But Congress went on to win the elections and P. J. Narasimha Rao became prime minister. Congress was defeated at elections in 1996 and a series of short-lived coalition governments ruled until fresh elections were held in 1998 and 1999. Atal Behari Vajpayee of the Bharatiya Janata Party (Hindu nationalists) became prime minister, leading a 24-party coalition called the National Democratic Alliance.

India is a vast country with an enormous diversity of cultures and problems of organization. It has more than a dozen major languages, each with a rich literature, and many minor languages. Hindi, the national language, and the Dravidian languages of the south (Kannada, Tamil, Telugu and Malayam) are Indo-European. Sino-Tibetan languages are spoken in the north and east, while smaller groups speak residual languages in forested hill refuges. Ethnic origins also differ and the mosaic of religions adds variety – and potential conflict.

Hinduism is all-pervasive, though the country is officially secular and Buddhism is slowly reviving in the country of its origin – the Buddha was born on the borders of India and Nepal. Jainism is strong in the merchant towns around Mt Abu in the Aravallis hills north of Ahmadabad. Islam has contributed many mosques and monuments, the Taj Mahal being the best known. The forts of Delhi, Agra and many other northern cities, together with the ghost city of Fatehpur Sikri, near Agra, are Islamic relics of the Mogul period. Despite the formation of Pakistan, India retains a large Muslim minority. Now it is the turn of the Punjab's militant Sikhs who seek separation. Christian influences include elaborate Roman Catholic churches and many schools and colleges set up by various denominations. The British also left their mark. Mumbai (Bombay) and Kolkata (Calcutta) have some notable Victoriana, while New Delhi is a planned Edwardian city.

Cultural differences are further complicated by huge gaps in the standards of living between labourers, prosperous farmers, the educated urban middle classes and slum dwellers. India's complex society always appears on the verge of collapse into chaos. But despite its size, population and potential for division, it manages to remain intact.

Economy

According to the World Bank, India is a 'low-income' developing country. While it ranked 11th in total gross national product in 1999, its per capita GNP of US $440 placed it among the world's poorer countries. Despite initiatives, including the Green Revolution, its socialist policies have failed to raise the living standards of the poor. In the 1990s, the government introduced private enterprise policies to stimulate growth.

India ranks fifth in the world in total farm area, and agriculture employs about 60% of the people. About 80% of farmland is devoted to growing grains, such as rice, wheat, millet and sorghum, and pulses, such as beans and chickpeas. India ranks second only to China in rice and wheat production, it leads the world in millet production, and it ranks second in producing sorghum. India also leads the world in producing bananas, hemp, jute, lemons and limes, mangoes and tea. India has more cattle and buffaloes than any other country. But, because they are sacred to Hindus, these animals are not killed for meat except by Muslims and Christians. Water buffaloes are important as sources of milk, while the hides of dead animals are used

Administrative regions of India

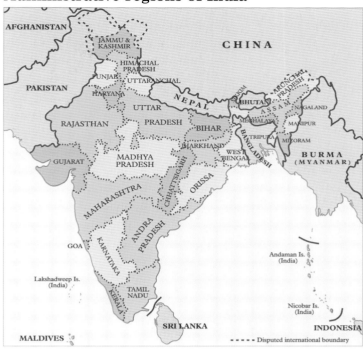

to make leather. India is also a major sheep and poultry producer.

India's mineral resources include coal and petroleum. It also has large deposits of bauxite, chromite, iron ore, manganese, and many smaller deposits of other minerals. Many of its minerals are used in domestic industries. In 1947, India was already a partially industrialized country and it has made great strides during a succession of five-year plans that provided explicitly for both nationalized and private industry. The Damodar coalfield around Asanol has been developed and several new fields opened. The Tata family's steel city of Jamshedpur, itself now diversified by other industries, has been complemented by new state plants and planned towns in Durgapur and other places, in collaboration with Britain, Germany and the former Soviet Union. Major engineering factories have been built at Bangalore, Vishakhapatnam and elsewhere, including the ill-fated Bhopal, where a major industrial accident occurred in 1984. Oil refineries have been set up at Barauni in the north-east and also near Mumbai, for new fields developed in the north-west. Several nuclear power stations are now in operation and the country's massive hydro-electric potential is being developed, but not without controversy about the effect of new dams on the environment. Small-scale and high-tech electronic industries are also important.

Clothing and textile industries employ more workers than any other industries. Other industries produce cement, chemicals, dyes, medicines, fertilizers, food products, paper, sugar, sewing machines, tractors, transport equipment and wood products. India also imports rough diamonds and exports jewellery. Major exports include agricultural and allied products, cut and polished diamonds, garments, machinery, transport equipment, metal products, iron and steel, and electronic components. Leading trading partners include the United States, Germany and Japan.

AREA	**LANGUAGES**
3,287,590 sq km	Hindi, English, Telugu,
[1,269,338 sq mi]	Bengali, Marati, Urdu, Gujarati,
POPULATION	Malayalam, Kannada, Oriya,
1,029,991,000	Punjabi, Assamese, Kashmiri,
CAPITAL (POPULATION)	Sindhi and Sanskrit are all
New Delhi (7,207,000)	official languages
GOVERNMENT	**RELIGIONS**
Multiparty federal republic	Hinduism 83%, Islam (Sunni
ETHNIC GROUPS	Muslim) 11%, Christianity 2%,
Indo-Aryan (Caucasoid) 72%,	Sikhism 2%, Buddhism 1%
Dravidian (Aboriginal) 25%,	**CURRENCY**
other (mainly Mongoloid) 3%	Rupee = 100 paisa

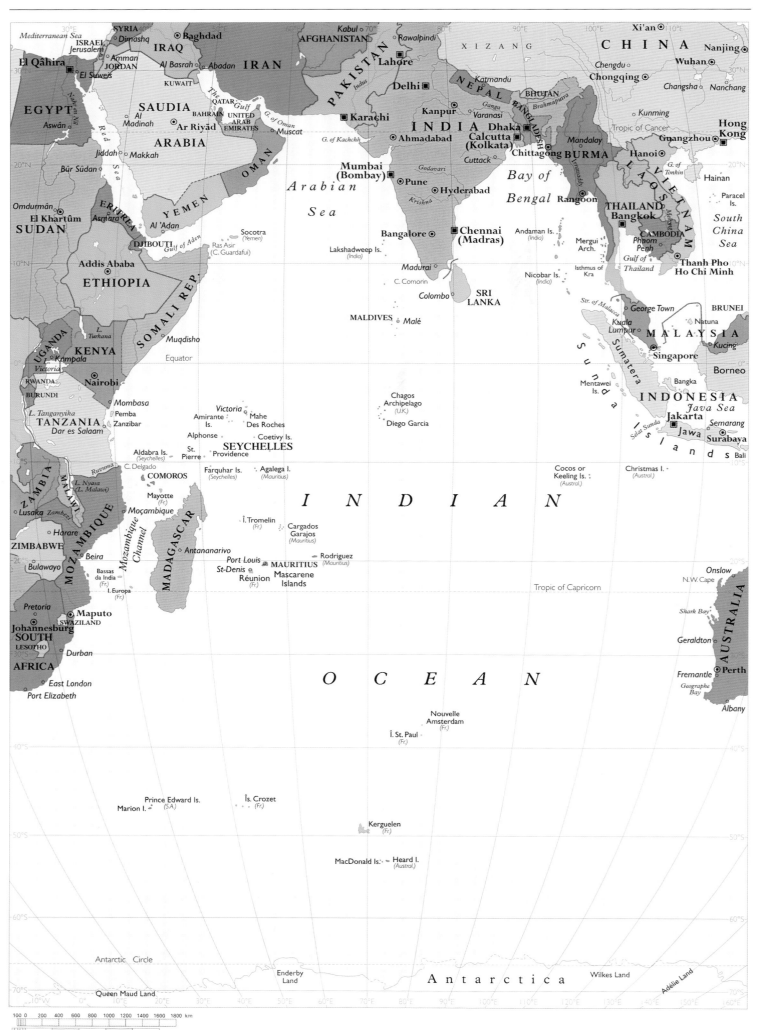

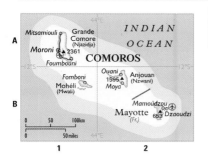

COMOROS

The Federal Islamic Republic of the Comoros is an island nation at the northern end of the Mozambique Channel. Formerly French, the territory became independent in 1974, but Mayotte, the fourth and easternmost of the large islands, seceded and became a French Territorial Collectivity. In 1997, two other islands, Anjouan and Mohéli, announced their secession, but the government refused to accept these acts and tried to negotiate greater autonomy for the islands. In 1999, the military overthrew the elected president. Comoros is poor and depends on subsistence agriculture.

AREA	CAPITAL
2,230 sq km [861 sq mi]	Moroni
POPULATION	CURRENCY
596,000	Com. franc = 100 centimes

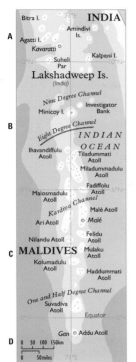

MALDIVES

The Republic of the Maldives comprises some 1,900 small, low-lying islands and atolls, 202 of which are inhabited. They are scattered along a broad north–south line, starting about 650 km [400 mi] west-south-west of the southern tip of India.

Sri Lanka settled the islands in about 500 BC. For a time under Portuguese and, later, Dutch rule, they became a British protectorate in 1887. They achieved independence in 1965. The country became a republic when the sultan was deposed in 1968. The chief crops are bananas, coconuts, mangoes, sweet potatoes and spices, but much food is imported. Fishing is important, but tourism has displaced it as the mainstay of the economy.

AREA	CAPITAL
298 sq km [115 sq mi]	Malé
POPULATION	CURRENCY
311,000	Rufiyaa = 100 laari

MAURITIUS

The Republic of Mauritius consists of the main island situated 800 km [500 mi] east of Madagascar, Rodrigues and several small islands. The main island, fringed with coral reefs, rises to a high lava plateau. The climate is tropical with heavy rains in winter. French from 1715, and British from 1810, the territory gained independence as a constitutional monarch, in 1992. The islands suffer tensions between the Indian majority, who are descended from contract workers brought in after the end of slavery in 1834, and the Creole minority.

Sugar-cane plantations cover extensive areas of Mauritius and, although the sugar industry has declined, sugar is still exported. Tea and tobacco are also grown. The expansion of textiles and clothing, together with growth in tourism, have to some extent offset the decline in sugar, although Mauritius remains heavily in debt.

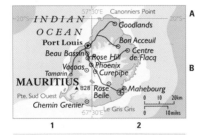

AREA	CAPITAL
1,860 sq km	Port Louis
[718 sq mi]	CURRENCY
POPULATION	Maur. rupee
1,190,000	= 100 cents

RÉUNION

Réunion, which lies south-west of Mauritius, has a mountainous, wooded centre, which is surrounded by a fertile coastal plain. The climate is similar to Mauritius. French since 1638, it became a French Department in 1946, though there is increasing pressure on France for independence.

Sugar cane dominates the economy, though vanilla, perfume oils and tea also produce revenue. Tourism is the big hope for the future, but unemployment is high and the island relies on French aid.

AREA
2,510 sq km
[969 sq mi]
POPULATION
733,000
CAPITAL
St-Denis

SEYCHELLES

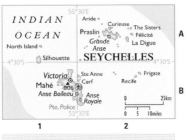

The Republic of Seychelles includes a group of four large and 36 small granitic islands, plus a wide scattering of coralline islands, 14 of them inhabited, lying to the south and west. French from 1756 and British from 1814, the islands gained their independence in 1976. A year later, a coup resulted in the setting up of a one-party socialist state that several attempts failed to remove. Multiparty elections were held in 1992 and France-Albert René, who had been elected president unopposed in 1979 and 1984, was re-elected president under a new constitution adopted in 1993. René was again re-elected president in 1998.

Experiencing a tropical oceanic climate, the Seychelles produces copra, cinnamon and tea, although rice is imported. Fishing and luxury tourism are the two main industries.

Formerly part of the British Indian Ocean Territory, Farquhar, Des Roches and Aldabra (famous for its unique wildlife) were returned to the Seychelles in 1976. The British Indian Ocean Territory now consists only of the Chagos Archipelago, with Diego Garcia, the largest island, supporting a US Navy base.

AREA	CAPITAL
455 sq km	Victoria
[176 sq mi]	CURRENCY
POPULATION	Seych. rupee
80,000	= 100 cents

This flag was adopted in 1945, when Indonesia proclaimed itself independent from the Netherlands. The colours, which date back to the Middle Ages, were adopted in the 1920s by political groups in their struggle against Dutch rule.

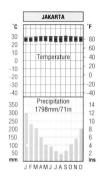

Geography

The Republic of Indonesia, in South-east Asia, consists of about 13,600 islands, less than 6,000 of which are inhabited. The island of Java covers only 7% of the country's area but it contains more than half of Indonesia's population. The islands are mountainous and many have extensive coastal lowlands. Indonesia contains more than 200 volcanoes, but the highest peak is Puncak Jaya, which reaches 5,030 m [16,503 ft] above sea level, is in West Papua (Irian Jaya).

Climate

Indonesia has a hot and humid monsoon climate. Only Java and the Sunda Islands have a relatively dry season. From December to March, moist prevailing winds blow from mainland Asia. Between mid-June and October, dry prevailing winds blow from Australia.

History

From the 8th century, the empire of Sri Vijaya, which was centred on Palembang, held sway until it was replaced in the 14th century by the kingdom of Madjapahit, whose centre was east-central Java. European influences began in the 16th century and the area came under the domination the Dutch East India Company. The Dutch government took over the islands in 1799. Japan occupied the islands in World War II and Indonesia declared its independence in 1945. The Dutch finally recognized Indonesia's independence in 1949.

INDONESIA (JAKARTA)

Temperatures in Jakarta are almost constantly high all year round. Daytime temperatures reach 29°C to 31°C [84–88°F], only cooling to around 23°C [73°F] at night. This is due to its location on the shores of the hot Java Sea, the uniform intensity of the midday sun and the duration of daylight, with an average of more than 6 hours of sunshine a day. Rainfall is heaviest in summer, most falling in thunderstorms.

Politics

Indonesia's first president, the anti-Western Achmed Sukarno, plunged his country into chaos, while military adventures drained the treasury. In 1962, Indonesia invaded Dutch New Guinea (now West Papua), and between 1963 and 1966 Sukarno sought to destabilize the Federation of Malaysia through incursions into northern Borneo. In 1967, Sukarno was toppled by General Suharto, following Sukarno's suppression of an alleged Communist-inspired uprising that cost 80,000 lives. Suharto's military regime, with US help, achieved significant economic growth, though corruption was rife. In 1975, Indonesian troops invaded East (formerly Portuguese) Timor against the opposition of the local people. A depression in 1997 hit the economies of most nations in

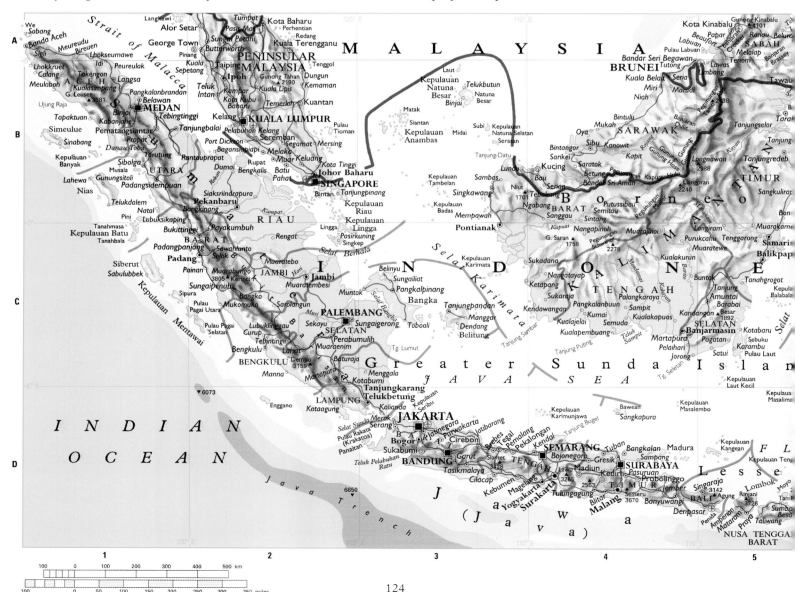

INDONESIA

eastern Asia, including Indonesia. In 1998, Suharto was forced to stand down and his deputy, Bacharuddin Jusuf Habibie, succeeded him. In June 1999, Habibie's ruling Golkar Party was defeated in elections and, in October, the parliament elected Abdurrahman Wahid as president. However, Wahid, charged with corruption and general incompetence, was dismissed in 2001. He was succeeded by the vice-president, Megawati Sukarnoputri (daughter of President Sukarno).

In the early 21st century, Indonesia faced many problems. East Timor seceded in 2002, while secessionist groups in Aceh province, northern Sumatra, and the Free Papua Movement in West Papua also demanded independence. To add to Indonesia's problems, Muslim-Christian clashes broke out in the Moluccas at the end of 1999, while indigenous Dyaks in Kalimantan clashed with immigrants from Madura, an overcrowded island off Java.

Economy

The World Bank describes Indonesia as a 'lower-middle-income' developing country. Agriculture employs more than 40% of the people and rice is the main food crop. Bananas, cassava, coconuts, groundnuts, maize, spices and sweet potatoes are also grown. Major cash crops include coffee, palm oil, rubber, sugar cane, tea and tobacco. Fishing and forestry are also important activities.

Indonesia has important mineral reserves, including oil and natural gas. Bauxite, coal, iron ore, nickel and tin are also mined. Manufacturing has increased greatly since the 1970s, especially on Java. Industries include the refining of oil and natural gas, together with the manufacture of steel, aluminium, cement, fertilizers, paper and textiles.

AREA	Madurese 7%,
1,889,700 sq km [729,613 sq mi]	Coastal Malays 7%,
POPULATION	more than 300 others
227,701,000	**LANGUAGES**
CAPITAL (POPULATION)	Bahasa Indonesian (official)
Jakarta (11,500,000)	**RELIGIONS**
GOVERNMENT	Islam 88%, Roman Catholic 3%,
Multiparty republic	Hinduism 2%, Buddhism 1%
ETHNIC GROUPS	**CURRENCY**
Javanese 45%, Sundanese 14%,	Indonesian rupiah = 100 sen

EAST TIMOR

The Republic of East Timor became fully independent on 20 May 2002. The land is mainly rugged, rising to 2,960 m [9,711 ft]. Temperatures are high, but the rainfall is moderate. East Timor came under Portuguese rule by treaties in 1859 and 1893. When Portugal withdrew in 1975, Indonesia seized the area. Indonesian rule proved oppressive and guerrilla resistance increased. Finally, in 1999, the people voted for independence, although pro-Indonesian militias caused massive destruction and killed hundreds of people. East Timor is heavily dependent on foreign aid, but offshore deposits of oil and natural gas, due to be exploited in 2004, hold out hopes for the future. Agriculture is the main activity.

AREA
14,870 sq km
[5,731 sq mi]
POPULATION
737,000
CAPITAL Dili

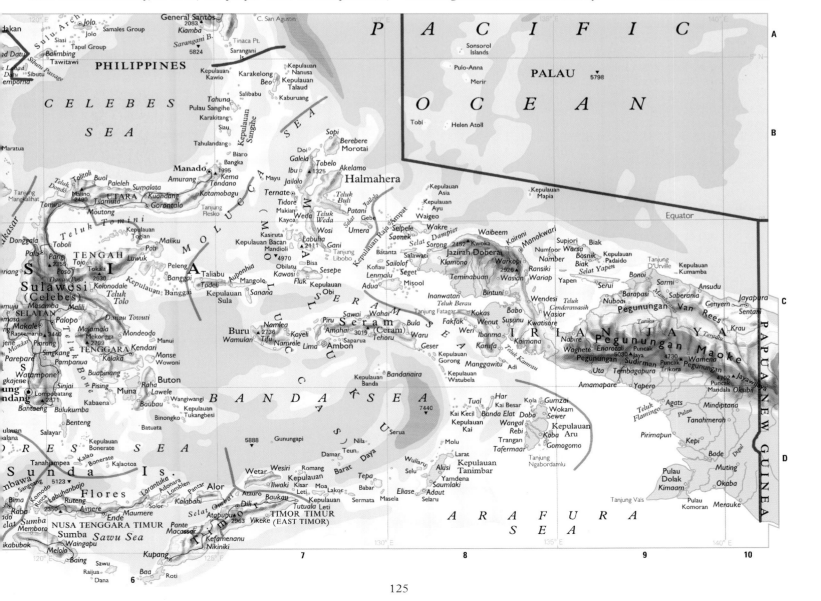

IRAN

Iran's flag was adopted in 1980 by the country's Islamic government. The white stripe contains the national emblem, which is the word for Allah (God) in formal Arabic script. The words Allah Akbar (God is Great) is repeated 11 times on both the green and red stripes.

Geography and Climate

The Republic of Iran contains a barren central plateau which covers about half of the country. It includes the Great Salt Desert (Dasht-e-Kavir) and the Great Sand Desert (Dasht-e-Lut). The Elburz Mountains (Alborz), which border the plateau to the north, contain Iran's highest peak, Damavand, which reaches 5,604 m [18,386 ft]. North of the Elburz Mountains are the fertile, densely populated lowlands around the Caspian Sea, which have a mild climate with abundant rainfall. Bordering the plateau to the west are the Zagros Mountains, whose high plateaux are the summer retreats of the Bakhtiars and Kurds.

The Zagros Mountains separate the central plateau from the Khuzistan Plain, a region of sugar plantations and oil fields, which extend to the Iraqi border. The Khuzistan Plain has Iran's most important petroleum deposits and it was the target of the Iraqi invasion in 1980.

Much of Iran experiences a severe, dry climate, with hot summers and cold winters. In Tehran, rain falls on only about 30 days in the year and the annual temperature range is more than 25°C [45°F]. The climate in the lowlands, however, is generally milder.

History and Politics

Iran was called Persia until 1935. Ancient Persia was a powerful empire. It flourished from 550 BC, when its king, Cyrus the Great, conquered the Medes, to 331 BC, when the empire was then conquered by Alexander the Great.

Arab armies introduced Islam in AD 641 and they made Iran a great centre of learning. But the area split up into a number of small kingdoms in the 10th century. Seljuk Turks conquered Iran in the 11th century, but, in 1220, Mongol armies seized the region. Mongol power declined in the 15th century and Iran was ruled by the Turkish Safavid Dynasty from 1501 to 1722 and by the Qajars, a Turkoman group, from 1794 until 1925.

Britain and Russia competed for influence in the area in the 19th century, and in the early 20th century the British began to develop the country's oil resources. In 1925, the Pahlavi family took power. Reza Khan became shah (king) and worked to modernize Iran. The Pahlavi Dynasty ended in 1979 when a religious leader, Ayatollah Ruhollah Khomeini, made Iran an Islamic republic. In 1980–8, Iran and Iraq fought over disputed borders. Khomeini died in 1989 but his views and anti-Western attitudes continued to exert influence around the world. Arab leaders in the Gulf saw his revolution as a threat to their oil-rich governments, but other Arab states were less hostile.

The 1980–8 war led to a great reduction in Iran's vital oil production, but output returned to its mid-1970s levels by 1994. In 1997, the election of a liberal, Mohammad Khatami, as president appeared to herald a move away from strict Islamic fundamentalist policies, though the spiritual leader, Ayatollah Al Khameini, retained much power. Khatami was re-elected president in 2001, but the clerical establishment and such institutions as the judiciary and the Expediency Council, which rules on disputed legislation passed by parliament, still blocked most of his reformist plans.

Economy

Iran's prosperity is based on its oil production and oil accounts for 75% of the country's exports. However, the economy was severely damaged by the Iran–Iraq war in the 1980s. Oil revenues have been used to develop a growing manufacturing sector, but agriculture still accounts for about 25% of the gross domestic product, even though farms cover only a tenth of the land. The main crops are wheat and barley. Livestock farming and fishing are other important activities.

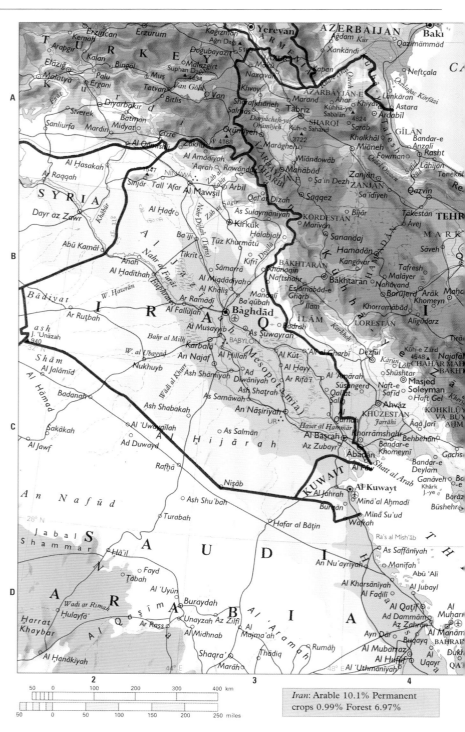

Iran: Arable 10.1% Permanent crops 0.99% Forest 6.97%

AREA	Gilaki and Mazandarani 8%,
1,648,000 sq km [636,293 sq mi]	Kurd 7%, Arab 3%, Lur 2%,
POPULATION	Baluchi 2%, Turkmen 2%
66,129,000	**LANGUAGES**
CAPITAL (POPULATION)	Persian 58%, Turkic 26%,
Tehran (6,759,000)	Kurdish
GOVERNMENT	**RELIGIONS**
Islamic republic	Islam 99%
ETHNIC GROUPS	**CURRENCY**
Persian 51%, Azeri 24%,	Rial = 100 dinars

Iraq's flag was adopted in 1963, when the country was planning to federate with Egypt and Syria. It uses the four Pan-Arab colours. The three green stars symbolize the three countries. Iraq retained these stars even though the union failed to come into being.

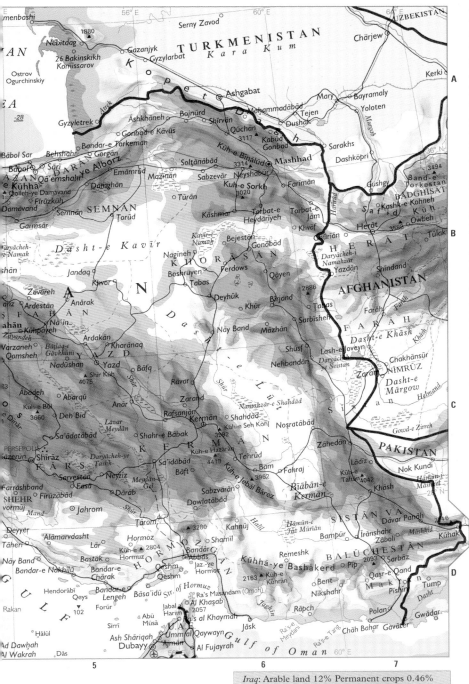

Iraq: Arable land 12% Permanent crops 0.46%
Permanent grassland 9.15% Forest 4.28%

History and Politics

Mesopotamia was the home of several great civilizations, including Sumer, Babylon and Assyria. It later became part of the Persian Empire. Islam was introduced in AD 637 and Baghdad became the brilliant capital of the powerful Arab Empire. However, Mesopotamia declined after the Mongols invaded it in 1258. From 1534, Mesopotamia became part of the Turkish Ottoman Empire. Britain invaded the area in 1916. In 1921, Britain renamed the country Iraq and set up an Arab monarchy. Iraq finally became independent in 1932.

By the 1950s, oil dominated Iraq's economy. In 1952, Iraq agreed to take 50% of the profits of the foreign oil companies. This revenue enabled the government to pay for welfare services and development projects. But many Iraqis felt that they should benefit more from their oil.

Since 1958, when army officers killed the king and made Iraq a republic, the country has undergone turbulent times. In the 1960s, the Kurds, who live in northern Iraq, Iran, Turkey, Syria and Armenia, asked for self-rule. The government rejected their demands and war broke out. A peace treaty was signed in 1975, but conflict continued.

In 1979, Saddam Hussein became Iraq's president. Under his leadership, Iraq invaded Iran in 1980, starting an eight-year war. During this war, Iraqi Kurds supported Iran and the Iraqi government attacked Kurdish villages with poison gas.

In 1990, Iraqi troops occupied Kuwait, but an international force drove them out in 1991. Since 1991, Iraqi troops have attacked Shiite Marsh Arabs and Kurds. In 1996, the government aided the forces of the Kurdish Democratic Party in an offensive against the Patriotic Union of Kurdistan, a rival Kurdish faction. In 1998, Iraq's failure to permit UNSCOM, the UN body charged with disposing of Iraq's deadliest weapons, access to all suspect sites led to Western bombardment of military sites. Periodic bombardment and economic sanctions continued, but Iraq was allowed to export a limited amount of oil in exchange for food and medicines. The threat of war mounted after the terrorist attacks on the United States in 2001 and the rejection by Iraq in 2002 of the return of UN weapons inspectors.

Economy

Civil war, Gulf War damage, UN sanctions and economic mismanagement have all contributed to economic chaos in the 1990s. Oil remains Iraq's main resource, but a UN trade embargo in 1990 halted oil exports. Farmland, including pasture, covers around a fifth of the land. Products include barley, cotton, dates, fruit, livestock, wheat and wool, but Iraq still has to import food. Industries include oil refining and the manufacture of petrochemicals and consumer goods.

Geography and Climate

The Republic of Iraq is a south-west Asian country at the head of The Gulf. Deserts cover western and south-western Iraq, with part of the Zagros Mountains in the north-east, where farming can be practised without irrigation. Western Iraq contains a large slice of the Hamad, or Syrian, Desert, but essentially comprises lower valleys of the rivers Euphrates (Nahr al Furat) and Tigris (Nahr Dijlah). The region is arid, but has fertile alluvial soils. The Euphrates and Tigris join south of Al Qurnah, to form the Shatt al Arab. The Shatt al Arab's delta is an area of irrigated farmland and marshes. This waterway is shared with Iran; it was the alleged cause of the First Gulf War.

The climate of Iraq varies from temperate in the north to subtropical in the south and east. Baghdad, in central Iraq, has cool winters, with occasional frosts, and hot summers. Rainfall is generally low.

AREA	Turkmen, Persian, Assyrian
438,320 sq km [169,235 sq mi]	**LANGUAGES**
POPULATION	Arabic (official),
23,332,000	Kurdish (official in
CAPITAL (POPULATION)	Kurdish areas)
Baghdad (3,841,000)	**RELIGIONS**
GOVERNMENT	Islam 96%, Christianity 4%
Republic	**CURRENCY**
ETHNIC GROUPS	Iraqi dinar = 20 dirhams
Arab 77%, Kurdish 19%,	= 1,000 fils

Ireland's flag was adopted in 1922 after the country had become independent from Britain, though nationalists had used it as early as 1848. Green represents Ireland's Roman Catholics, orange the Protestants, and the white a desire for peace between the two.

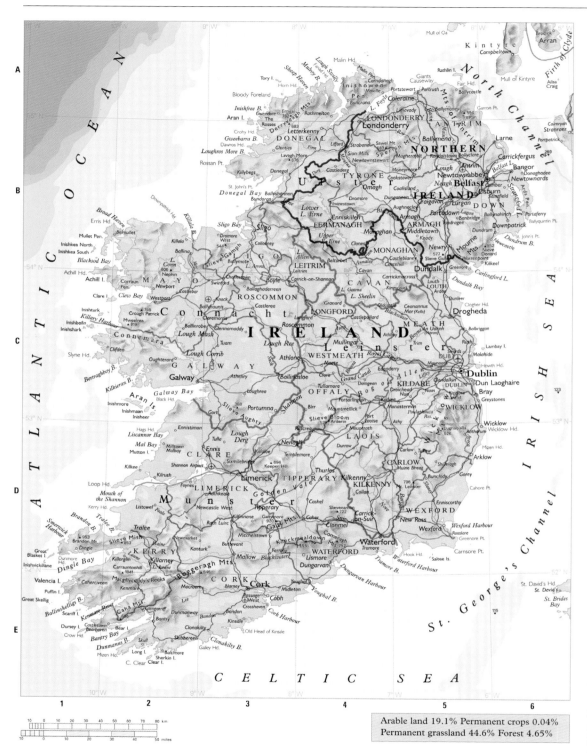

| Arable land 19.1% | Permanent crops 0.04% |
| Permanent grassland 44.6% | Forest 4.65% |

Vegetation

Forests cover approximately 5% of Ireland. Much of the land is under pasture and a very small percentage of land is set aside for crops.

History

Most Irish people are descendants of waves of immigrants who settled on the island over a long period. Celts settled in Ireland from about 400 BC. They were followed later by the Vikings, Normans and the English.

Vikings raided Ireland from the 790s and in the 8th century they established settlements. But Norse domination was ended in 1014 when they were defeated by Ireland's king, Brian Boru. The Normans arrived in 1169 and, gradually, Ireland came under English influence. Much of Ireland's history after that time was concerned with the struggle against British rule and, from the 1530s, the preservation of Roman Catholicism.

In 1801, the Act of Union created the United Kingdom of Great Britain and Ireland. But Irish discontent intensified in the 1840s when a potato blight caused a famine in which a million people died and nearly a million emigrated. Britain was blamed for not having done enough to help but, as the years went by, it introduced a number of reforms, improving the lot of the rural community. In the late 19th century, demands were made for home rule, but the British parliament defeated home rule bills in 1886 and 1892. In 1905, Arthur Griffith, a journalist, founded a movement advocating self-government for Ireland. It was called *Sinn Féin*, a name meaning 'We Ourselves'.

Geography and Climate

The Republic of Ireland occupies five-sixths of the island of Ireland. The country consists of a large lowland region surrounded by a broken rim of low mountains. The lowlands include peat bogs, where the peat (formed of partly decayed plants) is dug up and used as fuel. The uplands include the Mountains of Kerry where Carrauntoohill, Ireland's highest peak at 1,041 m [3,415 ft], is situated. The River Shannon is the longest in the British Isles. It flows through three large lakes, loughs Allen, Ree and Derg.

Ireland has a mild, damp climate influenced by the warm Gulf Stream current. The effects of this are greatest in the west. Dublin in the east is cooler than places on the west coast. Rain occurs all year.

Another organization which operated in secret, the Irish Republican Brotherhood, was also active in the early 20th century and its supporters became known as republicans. In 1914, the British parliament passed a home rule bill, but it was agreed to postpone its implementation until the end of World War I. In 1916, republicans launched what was called the Easter Rebellion in Dublin, but the uprising was crushed. In 1918, the republicans took over the Sinn Féin movement. They won a majority of Ireland's seats in the British parliament, but instead of going to London, they set up the *Dáil Éireann* (House of Representatives) in Dublin and declared Ireland an independent republic in January 1919.

In 1920, the British parliament passed the Government of Ireland

The Troubles

The Anglo-Irish Treaty of 1921 established southern Ireland – Eire – as an independent state, with the six northern Irish counties, and their Protestant majority, remaining part of the United Kingdom (though Eire's constitution claimed authority over the whole island). Northern Ireland (Ulster) was granted local self-government from the Stormont parliament in Belfast. However, the Protestant majority (roughly two-thirds of the population) systematically excluded the Catholic minority from power and often from employment, despite occasional attacks from the near-moribund IRA – the Irish Republican Army, which had done most of the fighting that led to Eire's independence.

In 1968, inspired by the Civil Rights movement in the southern states of the USA, northern Catholics launched a civil rights movement of their own. But Protestant hostility threatened a bloodbath, and in August 1969 British Prime Minister Harold Wilson deployed army units to protect Catholics from attack.

Within a short period, the welcome given by Catholics to British troops turned to bitterness; the IRA and many of the Catholic minority came to see them as a hostile occupying force, and there were deaths on both sides. Protestant extremists were quick to form terrorist organizations of their own. In 1971, the British introduced internment without trial for suspected IRA terrorists, removing some of the main security risks from the streets but provoking violent protest demonstrations. In 1972, British troops killed 13 demonstrators in Londonderry, claiming to have been fired upon: the claims were vigorously denied by the demonstrators.

In an attempt to end the alienation of the Catholics, Britain negotiated an agreement with Protestant politicians to share power in an executive composed of both communities, but the plan collapsed after dissatisfied Protestants staged a general strike. The British government responded by suspending the Stormont parliament and ruling Northern Ireland direct from Westminster. The failure of power-sharing encapsulated the British policy dilemma in Ulster: the Catholics, or most of them, wanted to join the Irish Republic; the Protestants, virtually without exception, did not. Each side bitterly distrusted the other, and long years of sectarian killing only increased the distrust.

The violence continued throughout the 1970s and 1980s, despite a series of political initiatives that included an Anglo-Irish agreement giving the Republic a modest say in Ulster's affairs. Among the conflict's victims were several British politicians, as well as soldiers, policemen, and thousands of ordinary men and women. Armed troops patrolling the streets and almost daily reports of sectarian murders became a way of life. But with the increasing war-weariness of the people, a joint declaration on Northern Ireland was agreed between Britain and Ireland in 1993. Further proposals for a settlement in 1995 led to a resumption of terrorism by the IRA, but talks later resumed to produce a framework for power-sharing which was subsequently approved by referenda in 1998.

Act, partitioning Ireland. The six Ulster countries accepted the Act, but fighting broke out in southern Ireland. The Irish Republican Army attacked British army and government buildings, while Britain replied with repressive measures. In 1921, a treaty was agreed allowing southern Ireland to become a self-governing dominion, called the Irish Free State, within the British Commonwealth. One Irish group, led by Michael Collins and later by William T. Cosgrave, accepted the treaty and the Irish Free State came into being in 1921. But another group, led by Eamon de Valera, wanted complete independence. Civil war occurred between 1922 and 1923. Cosgrave, leader of the Cumann na nGaedheal Party, served as president of the Executive Council that governed the Irish Free State between 1922 and 1932, when it was defeated by Fianna Fáil, a party set up by de Valera who had left Sinn Féin. De Valera cut most ties between the Irish Free State and Britain.

Politics

The Irish Free State was neutral during World War II. In 1949, John A. Costello, leader of Finna Gael (formerly the Cumann na nGaedheal Party) cut all remaining ties with Britain and declared southern Ireland to be an independent republic. Ireland has subsequently played an independent role in Europe. It joined the European Economic Community (now the European Union) in 1973 and, unlike Britain, it adopted the euro, the single currency of the EU, in 1999.

However, the government of Ireland has worked with British governments in attempts to solve the problems of Northern Ireland. In 1998, it supported the creation of a Northern Ireland Assembly, the setting up of north–south political structures and the amendment of the 1937 constitution by removing from it the republic's claim to Northern Ireland. A referendum showed strong support for the proposals and the amendments to the constitution. The 1998 Good Friday Agreement in Northern Ireland, which aimed to end the long-standing conflict, met with much support but it ran into difficulties when the underground Irish Republican Army (IRA) refused to disarm. However, when the IRA agreed to dispose of some of its weapons in October 2001, the peace process appeared to be back on track.

Economy

Agriculture was the traditional mainstay of the economy, although fishing, home crafts and local labouring were also important extra sources of income in the poorer western areas. A marked contrast exists between the richest and poorest rural areas. The eastern central lowland and the south-east, particularly the lowland areas of Wicklow and Wexford, contain splendid large farms, with pastures supporting fine-quality cattle, sheep and, in some areas, racehorses. From Wexford, too, rich farmland extends through the valleys and lowlands westwards to the counties of Tipperary and Limerick, and from Waterford to Cork and Killarney. North of the Shannon, in Clare and east Galway, there is intensive sheep and some cattle production. To the north, farming is mixed – with dairying, meat production and, in some areas, specialization in such crops as potatoes and barley. Little wheat is grown – oats are better suited to the damp summer climate.

Aided by EU grants, farming is now relatively prosperous. The number of people working on the land continues to decline, because of the introduction of machinery, the union of small farms into larger ones, and the increased number of jobs in the towns. Industrialization was confined, until recent years, to the north-east, especially Belfast. This meant that southern Ireland had an essentially agrarian economy, with industries mainly confined to food processing and beverage-making. Manufacturing is now the leading activity, with high-tech industries producing such products as chemicals and pharmaceuticals, electronic equipment, machinery, paper and textiles. The leading exports include machinery and transport equipment, chemical products and food products. Ireland's main trading partners are the United Kingdom, Germany and France. Prosperity during the 1960s was followed by a slowdown, caused partly by high government spending. However, a new spirit of co-operation in the 1980s and 1990s brought strong growth.

AREA	**ETHNIC GROUPS**
70,280 sq km	Irish 94%
[27,135 sq mi]	**LANGUAGES**
POPULATION	Irish and English
3,841,000	(both official)
CAPITAL (POPULATION)	**RELIGIONS**
Dublin	Roman Catholic 93%,
(1,024,000)	Protestant 3%
GOVERNMENT	**CURRENCY**
Multiparty republic	Euro = 100 cents

Israel's flag was adopted when the Jewish state declared itself independent in 1948. The blue and white stripes are based on the tallit, a Hebrew prayer shawl. The ancient, six-pointed Star of David is in the centre. The flag was designed in America in 1891.

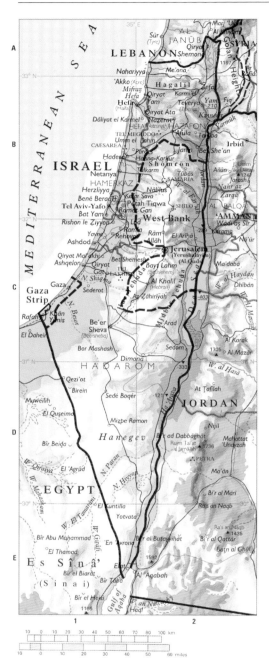

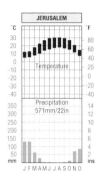

AREA
20,600 sq km [7,960 sq mi]
POPULATION
5,938,000
CAPITAL (POPULATION)
Jerusalem (591,000)
GOVERNMENT
Multiparty republic
ETHNIC GROUPS
Jewish 82%, Arab and others 18%
LANGUAGES
Hebrew and Arabic
(both official)
RELIGIONS
Judaism 80%, Islam (mostly Sunni) 14%,
Christianity 2%, Druze and others 2%
CURRENCY
New Israeli sheqel = 100 agorat

Geography

The State of Israel is a small country in the eastern Mediterranean. It includes a fertile coastal plain, where Israel's main industrial cities, Haifa (Hefa) and Tel Aviv-Jafo are situated. Inland lie the Judaeo-Galilean highlands, which run from northern Israel to the northern tip of the Negev Desert in the south. To the east lies part of the Great Rift Valley which runs through East Africa into Asia. In Israel, the Rift Valley contains the River Jordan, the Sea of Galilee (Yam Kinneret) and the Dead Sea, whose shoreline is 403 m [1,322 ft] below sea level, the world's lowest point on land.

Climate

Israel has hot, dry, sunny summers. Winters are mild and moist on the coast, but the total annual rainfall decreases from west to east and also from north to south, where the Dead Sea region has only 70 mm [2.5 in] a year.

ISRAEL (JERUSALEM)

East of the Mediterranean Sea, the annual rainfall amount decreases inland and the length of the summer dry season increases to more than five months, which last from May through to September. At over 700 m [2,250 ft], Jerusalem has lower temperatures and a greater range of temperatures than the coastal regions of Israel. The average temperature in January is 13°C [55°F], while in July an average of 29°C [84°F] is experienced. To the south, the rainfall decreases rapidly in the rocky desert around the Dead Sea. Sunshine levels are high. In Jerusalem there is an average daily sunshine total of over 9 hours, ranging from 6–12 hours.

History

Israel is part of a region called Palestine. Some Jews have always lived in the area, though most modern Israelis are descendants of immigrants who began to settle there from the 1880s. Britain ruled Palestine from 1917. Large numbers of Jews escaping Nazi persecution arrived in the 1930s, provoking an Arab uprising against British rule. In 1947, the UN agreed to partition Palestine into an Arab and a Jewish state. Fighting broke out after Arabs rejected the plan. The State of Israel came into being in May 1948, but fighting continued into 1949. Other Arab-Israeli wars were fought in 1956, 1967 and 1973. The Six Day War in 1967 led to the acquisition by Israel of the West Bank, which had been formerly under Jordanian administration, along with East Jerusalem. At the same time, Israel also occupied the Gaza Strip and the Sinai Peninsula from Egypt and the Golan Heights from Syria. In 1982, Israel invaded Lebanon to destroy the stronghold of the PLO (Palestine Liberation Organization), but they left in 1985.

Politics

Hopes of a Middle Eastern peace settlement were first raised in 1978, when Israel signed a treaty with Egypt which led to the return of the Sinai Peninsula to Egypt in 1979. However, conflict continued between Israel and the PLO. In 1993, the PLO and Israel agreed to establish Palestinian self-rule in two areas: the Gaza Strip and the town of Jericho on the West Bank. The agreement was extended in 1995 to include more than 30% of the West Bank. Israel's prime minister, Yitzhak Rabin, who had been seeking a 'land for peace' settlement, was assassinated in 1995 and his successor, Simon Peres, was narrowly defeated in elections in 1996. Peres was succeeded as prime minister by the right-wing Binyamin Netanyahu, who favoured a more hardline policy towards the Palestinians. As a result, the peace process stalled.

In May 1999, Netanyahu was defeated in national elections by his challenger, the left-wing Ehud Barak, who promised to resume the peace process. But many problems remained, including the extension of Jewish settlements in the occupied areas and attacks on Israel by the militant Islamic group, the Hezbollah, based in southern Lebanon. These attacks caused an escalation of the conflict in southern Lebanon in early 2000.

In 2001, Ariel Sharon, leader of the right-wing Likud Party and former general, was elected prime minister. Sharon adopted a hardline policy against the Palestinians and, in December 2001, severed all contacts with Yasir Arafat, the Palestinian leader. The violence mounted and the killing of Israeli citizens by suicide bombers brought the region close to war.

Economy

Since 1948, the State of Israel has developed rapidly and its citizens now enjoy a high standard of living. The leading activity is manufacturing, and products include chemicals, electronic equipment, fertilizers, military equipment, plastics, processed food, scientific instruments and textiles. Israel produces potash, while cotton, fruits, grain, poultry and vegetables are major farm products. Machinery and transport equipment, cut diamonds and chemicals are exported.

The Italian flag is based on the military standard carried by the French Republican National Guard when Napoleon invaded Italy in 1796, causing great changes in Italy's map. It was finally adopted as the national flag after Italy was unified in 1861.

Geography

The Republic of Italy is famous for its history and traditions, its art and culture, and beautiful scenery. Northern Italy is bordered in the north by the Alps, with their many climbing and skiing resorts. The Alps overlook the northern plains – Italy's most fertile and densely populated region – drained by the River Po. Generally lower than the Alps, the Apennines (Appennini), which form the backbone of southern Italy, reach their highest peaks – almost 3,000 m [9,800 ft] – in the Gran Sasso Range overlooking the the central Adriatic Sea, near Pescara. Limestones are the most common rocks. Between the mountains, however, are long, narrow basins, some with lakes, others as farms.

Southern Italy contains a string of volcanoes, stretching from Vesuvius, near Naples (Nápoli), through the Lipari Islands, to Mount Etna on Sicily. Traces of volcanic activity are found throughout Italy. Ancient lava flows cover large areas and, where they have weathered, they produce fertile soils. Italy is still subject to earthquakes and volcanic eruptions. Sicily is the largest island in the Mediterranean. Sardinia, also part of Italy, is more isolated from the mainland and its rugged, windswept terrain and lack of resources have set it apart.

Climate

Milan (Milano), in the north, has cold, often snowy winters. But the summer months are warm and sunny. Rainfall is plentiful, with brief but powerful thunderstorms in summer. Southern Italy has mild, moist winters and warm, dry summers.

ITALY (ROME)

Summers are warm with June to September averages of over 20°C [68°F], but the winters can be cold, with very low averages, and sub-zero temperatures having been recorded from November to March. There are over 2,500 hours of sunshine per year, ranging from only 3 hours in December, to 8–10 hours from May to September. Rain falls mainly in the winter and, in all, on only about 65 days per year.

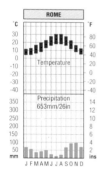

History and Politics

Magnificent ruins throughout Italy testify to the glories of the ancient Roman Empire, which was founded, according to legend, in 753 BC. It reached its peak in the AD 100s. It finally collapsed in the 400s, although the Eastern Roman Empire, also called the Byzantine Empire, survived for another 1,000 years.

In the Middle Ages, Italy was split into many tiny states. They made a huge contribution to the revival of art and learning, called the Renaissance. Cities, such as Florence (Firenze) and Venice (Venézia), testify to the artistic achievements of this period.

In 1800, present-day Italy was made up of several political units including the Papal States (a large area in central Italy ruled by the Roman Catholic Church), while a substantial part of the north-east was occupied by Austria. The struggle for unification – the *Risorgimento* – began early in the 19th century, but little progress was made until an alliance between France and Piedmont (then part of the Kingdom of Sardinia) drove Austria from Lombardy in 1859. Tuscany, Parma and Modena joined Piedmont-Lombardy in 1860, and the Papal States, Sicily, Naples – including most of the southern peninsula – and Romagna were brought into the alliance. King Victor Emmanuel II was proclaimed ruler of a united Italy the following year. Venetia was acquired from Austria in 1866 and Rome was finally annexed in 1871. Since then, Italy has been a unified state, though the pope and his successors disputed the takeover of the Papal States. This dispute was not resolved until 1929, when Vatican City was established as a fully independent state.

Since unification, the population has doubled, and though the rate of increase is notoriously slow today, the rapid growth of population, in a poor country attempting to develop its resources, forced millions of Italians to emigrate during the first quarter of the 20th century. Italy's short-lived African Empire enabled some Italians to settle overseas, but it did not substantially relieve the population pressure. Now there are immigrant Italians to be found on all the inhabited continents. Especially large numbers settled in the United States, South America and Australia, and more recently, large numbers of Italians have moved for similar reasons into northern Europe.

In 1915, during World War I, Italy entered the war alongside the Allies. After the war, Italy was given nearly 23,000 sq km [9,000 sq mi] of territory that had belonged to Austria-Hungary, including Trentino and Trieste, but it was far less than Italy had hoped to gain. In 1922, Benito Mussolini became prime minister of Italy and, from 1925, he ruled as a dictator, with the title *Il Duce*. Many of his internal policies proved successful, but he pursued an aggressive foreign policy, aimed at increasing Italy's status in the world. In 1936, Italian forces invaded Ethiopia, while military personnel were sent to support the rebellion of General Francisco Franco in Spain. In 1939, Italy agreed to fight alongside Germany in the event of war, though it did not enter the war in June 1940. During the war, Italy lost much of its colonial empire to the Allies and, in late 1943, Italy declared war on Germany. German forces then took control and installed Mussolini as head of a puppet government. Mussolini was captured and shot by partisans in 1945, when he tried to escape to Switzerland.

Italy became a republic in 1946 following a referendum, and Allied troops left the country in 1947. Since then, the Christian Democrats resisted the opposition of the Communist Party to pursue a strongly pro-Western and European policy. However, no single government

Regions of Italy

was able to face up to the country's many social problems, including corruption at high levels of society, and changes of the mostly weak coalition governments were frequent, leading to instability.

Italy became a founder member of the North Atlantic Treaty Organization in 1949, and of the European Economic Community (EEC, now the European Union) in 1957. After the establishment of the EEC, Italy's economy began to expand. However, much of the economic development took place in the great triangular plain of Lombardy, between the Alps and the Apennines, which has long been Italy's most productive region, both agriculturally and industrially. By contrast, central Italy between the Po Valley and the Tiber, is less developed. It represents a transition zone between the developed north and the poor agrarian south, which is known as the Mezzogiorno.

The Mezzogiorno displays, albeit in a less severe form, many of the characteristics of the developing world, with its heavy dependence on its peasant farms, which are too small to lend themselves to modern techniques, although there are some large estates. The eight regions of the Mezzogiorno cover some 40% of Italy's land area (including Sicily and Sardinia), but they contribute only about a quarter of the gross domestic product. The birth rate is also much higher in the south and overpopulation is always a threat. But, the situation is eased because many poor southerners are forced to migrate to northern cities or to other parts of the European Union. But migration tends to take away the younger and more active members of the population, leaving the older people behind. Italy also faces urban problems, caused by the rapid growth of such cities as Naples when young people leave rural areas and settle in city slums. The problems of the Mezzogiorno are no longer a problem only for Italy, because the stability and prosperity of the country is now a matter for the entire European Union.

Overall, however, Italy has made enormous progress since World War II. By the late 1990s, it had the world's sixth largest economy and, on 1 January 1999, it adopted the euro, the single unit of currency of the European Union. In 1992, the old political establishment was driven from office and several prominent leaders were accused of links to organized crime and some were imprisoned. In 1996, the left-wing Olive Tree alliance led by Romano Prodi took office, but Prodi was forced to resign in 1998 following his rejection of demands made by his Communist allies. He was replaced by Massimo D'Alemo, the first former Communist to become prime minister. His attempts to create a two-party system in Italy failed in 1999.

In 2001, Italy moved towards the political right when a coalition of centre-right parties won 368 seats in the 630-seat Chamber of Deputies. Silvio Berlusconi, who had briefly served as prime minister in 1994 and who had spent several years fighting criminal prosecution on charges of tax evasion, became prime minister.

Economy

Only 50 years ago, Italy was a mainly agricultural society. Today it is a major industrial power. Apart from natural gas in the Po Valley, it lacks mineral resources, and has to import most of the fuels and other materials used in its industries. Manufactures include cars, chemicals, food products, machinery, steel, televisions, textiles and clothing, and wine. Major crops include grapes for wine-making, and olives, which are used to make olive oil. Other crops include citrus fruits, maize, rice, sugar beet and wheat. Cattle, pigs, poultry and sheep are raised, but Italy imports meat. Leading exports include machinery and transport equipment, chemicals, textiles and clothing. Italy's main trading partners are Germany, France, the United Kingdom and the United States.

AREA
301,270 sq km [116,320 sq mi]
POPULATION
57,680,000
CAPITAL (POPULATION)
Rome (Roma, 2,654,000)
GOVERNMENT
Multiparty republic
ETHNIC GROUPS
Italian 94%, German,

French, Albanian,
Ladino, Slovene,
Greek
LANGUAGES
Italian 94% (official),
German, French, Slovene
RELIGIONS
Roman Catholic 83%
CURRENCY
Euro = 100 cents

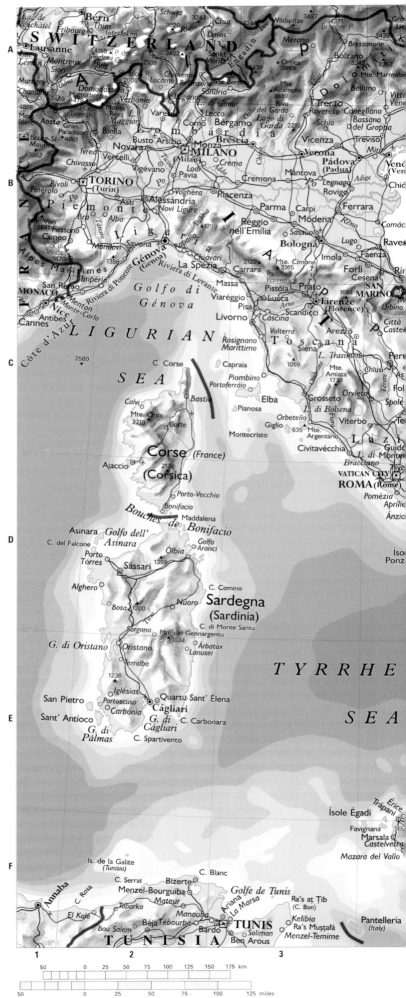

SAN MARINO

Surrounded by Italy, the 'Most Serene Republic of San Marino' – the world's smallest republic – lies 20 km [12 mi] south-west of the Adriatic port of Rimini. It consists largely of the limestone mass of Monte Titano, which reaches a height of 725 m [2,382 ft]. Around this are clustered wooded mountains, pastures, fortresses and medieval villages. San Marino has pleasant, mild summers and cool winters.

The republic was named after St Marinus, the stonemason saint who is said to have first established a community here in the 4th century AD. San Marino has been independent since 1885 and a republic since the 14th century. It has a friendship and co-operation treaty with Italy dating back to 1862. It uses Italian currency, but issues its own stamps, which are an important source of revenue. The state is governed by an elected council and has its own legal system. It has no armed forces and the police are 'hired' from the Italian constabulary. Most of the people live in the medieval city of San Marino, which receives more than 3 million tourists a year. The chief occupations are tourism, limestone quarrying and the making of ceramics, textiles and wine. The *de facto* customs union with Italy makes San Marino an easy conduit for the illegal export of lira and certain kinds of tax evasion for Italians.

AREA	GOVERNMENT
61 sq km	Republic
[24 sq mi]	**ETHNIC GROUPS**
POPULATION	San Marinese, Italian
27,000	**LANGUAGES**
CAPITAL	Italian (official)
San Marino	**CURRENCY**
(2,395)	Euro = 100 cents

VATICAN CITY

Vatican City State, the world's smallest independent nation, is an enclave on the west bank of the River Tiber in Rome. It forms an independent base for the Holy See, the governing body of the Roman Catholic Church. It consists of 44 hectares [109 acres] and includes St Peter's Square, St Peter's Basilica and Vatican Palace. Summers are warm, but winters can be cold. The average annual rainfall is about 650 mm [26 in] and most of the rain occurs in winter. Vatican City has more than 2,500 hours of sunshine a year.

The popes have been prominent patrons of the arts, and the treasures of the Vatican, including Michelangelo's frescoes in the Sistine Chapel, attract tourists from all over the world. Similarly, the Vatican Library contains a priceless collection of manuscripts from both pre-Christian and Christian times. The popes have lived in the Vatican since the 5th century, apart from a brief period at Avignon, France, in the 14th century. Sustained by investment income and voluntary contributions, it is all that remains of the Papal States which, until 1870, occupied most of central Italy. In 1929, Benito Mussolini recognized the independence of the Vatican City, in return for papal recognition of the kingdom of Italy. Since the 1960s, the Vatican has played an important role in some areas of international diplomacy.

The population, which includes the country's only armed force of 100 Swiss Guards, is made up entirely of unmarried males. The Commission appointed by the Pope to administer the affairs of the Vatican also has control over a radio station, the Pope's summer palace at Castel Gandolfo, and several churches in Rome. Vatican City has its own newspaper, police and railway station, and it issues its own stamps and coins.

AREA	POPULATION
0.44 sq km [0.17 sq mi]	890

Italy: Arable land 28.3% Permanent crops 9.57% Permanent grassland 15.4% Forest 23%

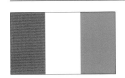

This flag was adopted in 1960 when the country became independent from France. It combines elements from the French tricolour and the Pan-African colours. The orange represents the northern savanna, the white peace and unity, and the green the forests in the south.

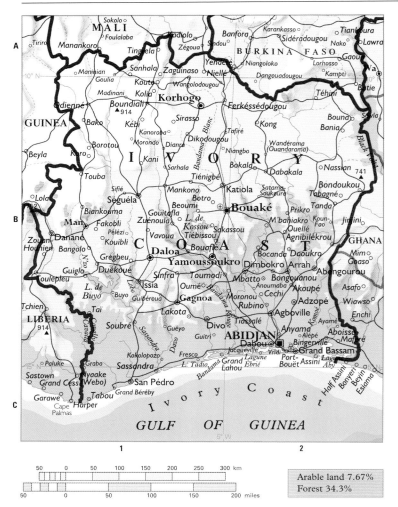

Arable land 7.67%
Forest 34.3%

Geography

The Republic of the Ivory Coast, in West Africa, is officially known as Côte d'Ivoire. The south-east coast is bordered by sand bars that enclose lagoons, on one of which the former capital and chief port of Abidjan is situated. But the south-western coast is lined by rocky cliffs. Behind the coast is a coastal plain, but the land rises inland to high plains. The highest land is an extension of the Guinea Highlands in the north-west, along the borders with Liberia and Guinea. The rivers run generally north–south.

Climate

Ivory Coast has a hot and humid tropical climate, with high temperatures throughout the year. The south of the country has two distinct rainy seasons: between May and July, and from October to November. Inland, the rainfall decreases. Northern Ivory Coast has a dry season and only one rainy season. As a result, the forests in central Ivory Coast thin out to the north, giving way to savanna.

IVORY COAST (ABIDJAN)

The uniform high temperature and humidity and the double rainfall maxima are features of the climate of the West African coast as far west as Liberia. The total rainfall amount increases steadily westwards as the south-west summer monsoon winds have a longer sea track. Heavier, more prolonged rainfall occurs in May and June, when the intertropical rainbelt moves northwards ahead of the monsoon.

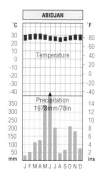

History

The region that is now Ivory Coast came under successive black African rulers until the late 15th century, when Europeans, attracted by the chance to trade in slaves and such local products as ivory, began to establish contacts along the coast. French missionaries reached the area in 1637 and, by the end of the 17th century, the French had set up trading posts on the coast. In 1842, France brought the Grand-Bassam area under its protection and Ivory Coast became a French colony in 1893. From 1895, it was ruled as part of French West Africa, a massive union which also included Benin, Burkina Faso, Guinea, Mali, Mauritania, Niger and Senegal. In 1946, Ivory Coast became a territory in the French Union. The port of Abidjan was built in the early 1950s, but the country achieved autonomy in 1958.

Politics

Ivory Coast became fully independent in 1960. Its first president, Félix Houphouët-Boigny, became the longest serving head of state in Africa with an uninterrupted period in office that ended with his death in 1993. Houphouët-Boigny was a paternalistic, pro-Western leader, who made his country a one-party state. In 1983, the National Assembly agreed to move the capital from Abidjan to Yamoussoukro, Houphouët-Boigny's birthplace. Visitors to Abidjan, where most of the country's Europeans live, are usually impressed by the city's general air of prosperity, but the cost of living for local people is high and there are great social and regional inequalities. Despite its political stability since independence, the country faces such economic problems as variations in the price of its export commodities, unemployment and high foreign debt.

Following the death of Houphouët-Boigny in 1993, the Speaker of the National Assembly, Henri Konan Bédié, proclaimed himself president. He was re-elected president in 1995. However, in December 1999, Bédié was overthrown during an army mutiny and a new administration was set up by General Robert Guei. Presidential elections, held after a new constitution was adopted in 2000, resulted in defeat for Guei by a veteran politician, Laurent Gbago.

Economy

In terms of such indices as gross national product and international trade figures, Ivory Coast is one of Africa's more prosperous countries. Its free-market economy has proved attractive to foreign investors, especially French firms, while France has given much aid, especially for basic services and education. Its economy is based on agriculture, which employs about three-fifths of the people. The chief farm products are cocoa, coffee, cotton and cotton cloth, which together make up nearly half of the value of the total exports. Other exports include bananas, palm oil, pineapples and tropical woods. Food crops include cassava, maize, plantains, rice, vegetables and yams.

The country has few worked minerals, but manufacturing is growing. Manufactures include processed farm products, timber and textiles. Ivory Coast imports crude petroleum for its refineries.

AREA	Northern Mande 16%,
322,460 sq km [124,502 sq mi]	Kru 11%, Southern Mande 10%
POPULATION	**LANGUAGES**
16,393,000	French (official), Akan,
CAPITAL (POPULATION)	Voltaic
Yamoussoukro (120,000)	**RELIGIONS**
GOVERNMENT	Christianity 34%, Islam 27%,
Multiparty republic	traditional beliefs 17%
ETHNIC GROUPS	**CURRENCY**
Akan 42%, Voltaic 18%,	CFA franc = 100 centimes

JAMAICA – SEE CARIBBEAN SEA, PAGES 71–76

JAPAN

Japan's flag was officially adopted in 1870, though Japanese emperors had used this simple design for many centuries. The flag shows a red sun on a white background. The geographical position of Japan is also expressed in its name 'Nippon' or 'Nihon', meaning 'source of the Sun'.

Geography

Japan is an island nation in north-eastern Asia. It is a constitutional monarchy, with an emperor as its head of state.

Japan contains four large islands. In order of size, they are Honshu, Hokkaido, Kyushu and Shikoku. These islands make up more than 98% of the country. But Japan also has thousands of small islands, including the Ryukyu island chain which extends south of Kyushu towards the island of Taiwan.

The four main islands are mainly mountainous, while many of the small islands are the tips of volcanoes rising from the sea bed. Japan has more than 150 volcanoes, about 60 of which are active. Volcanic eruptions, earthquakes and tsunamis (destructive sea waves triggered by underwater eruptions and earthquakes) often occur. For example, an earthquake in 1995 killed over 5,000 people in Kobe. This is because the islands lie on an unstable part of the Earth where the land is constantly moving.

Throughout Japan, complex folding and faulting has produced an intricate mosaic of landforms. Mountains and forested hills alternate with small basins and coastal lowlands, covered by alluvium which has been deposited there by the short rivers that rise in the uplands. Most of the people live on the coastal plains. One densely populated zone stretches from the Kanto Plain, where Tokyo is situated, along the narrow plains that border the southern coasts of Honshu, to northern Kyushu.

The pattern of landforms is further complicated by the presence of volcanic cones and calderas. The highest mountain in Japan, the majestic cone of Fuji-san (3,776 m [12,388 ft]), is a long dormant volcano which last erupted in 1707. It is considered sacred, and is visited by thousands of pilgrims every year.

Climate

The climate of Japan varies greatly. Hokkaido in the north has cold, snowy winters. At Sapporo, temperatures below –20°C [4°F] have been recorded from between December and March. Summers are warm, with temperatures often exceeding 30°C [86°F]. Rain falls all year.

Tokyo has higher rainfall and temperatures than the rest of the country. The southern islands of Shikoku and Kyushu in the south have warm temperate climates. Summers are hot. Winters are mild.

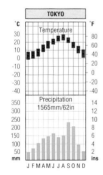

JAPAN – TOKYO

Despite its maritime location, Tokyo has a large annual range of temperature (23°C [41°F]) due to the seasonal reversal of wind, blowing from the cold heart of Asia in winter and from the warm Pacific in summer. Winter is usually sunny, but cold, dry, north-westerly winds often blow, and frosts may occur as late as April. Summer in Tokyo is wet, hot and humid. In August it is usually over 30°C [86°F] during the day.

History

The Ainu may have been the first people to have settled in Japan. Scientists do not agree about their origins, some suggesting that they are related to European or Asian groups, and others suggesting they are related to Australian Aborigines. Today the Ainu, who are ethnically and culturally different from the Japanese, number only about 15,000, most of whom live in Hokkaido. Many have intermarried with Japanese. But, most modern Japanese are descendants of early immigrants who arrived in successive waves from the Korean Peninsula and other parts of the Asian mainland, though some may also have come from the islands to the south. Anthropologists have found evidence that people with a hunting and gathering culture had reached the islands around 6,500 years ago. This culture is named *Jomon*, or 'cord pattern',

after the ropelike patterns on their pottery. A new agricultural society, called the *Yayoi*, replaced the Jomon in the 3rd century BC. Under this new society, most people lived in farming villages.

The earliest zone of settlement included the northern part of Kyushu Island and the coastlands of Setonaikai (Inland Sea). By the 5th century AD, Japan was divided among numerous clans, of which the largest and most powerful was the Yamato. The Yamato ruled from the area which now contains the city of Nara. They controlled most of central Japan, together with parts of southern Korea. Shinto, a polytheistic religion based on nature worship, was already practised, and the Japanese imperial dynasty already established. The chiefs of the Yamato clan are regarded as the ancestors of the Japanese imperial family.

The 5th century AD was also a time when new ideas and technology reached Japan from China. The Japanese adopted the Chinese system of writing and Chinese methods of calculating the calendar. Confucianism was also introduced from China and, in about 552, Buddhism reached Japan from Korea and China. In 646, the imperial court introduced a programme to adopt Chinese methods of government and administration. Under the so-called Taika Reform, Japan was divided into provinces, districts and villages. Also introduced was a central system of taxation and a land distribution programme. Early cities, modelled on the capital of T'ang-dynasty China, were built at Nara in 710 and, in 794, at Heian, which was later known as Kyoto. Kyoto remained the seat of Japan's imperial court until 1868.

The adoption of the Chinese system of centralized, bureaucratic government was relatively short-lived and, in the 9th century, the emperor and his court fell under the control of a powerful noble family called the Fujiwaras. The Fujiwara family ruled Japan for about 300 years. During this period, the emperors lost real power although they remained the official rulers, while the *daimyo*, the feudal lords who ruled great estates, became more and more powerful.

From the early 12th century onwards, political power passed increasingly to military aristocrats. Government was conducted in the name of the emperor by warrior leaders called *shoguns*. Civil warfare between rival groups of feudal lords was endemic over long periods, but, under the rule of the Tokugawa shoguns, between 1603 and 1867, Japan enjoyed a great period of peace and prosperity. Society was rigidly stratified, with military families (the feudal lords and their retainers, or *samurai*) forming a powerful elite. During the shogun era, a code of conduct was developed for the samurai. Called *bushido* ('the way of the warrior'), it stressed military skills and fearlessness, as well as frugality, kindness, honesty and filial piety. But, above all, the samurai's supreme obligation was to his feudal lord.

Japan's isolated position afforded the country some security. But they were threatened by the Mongol emperor Kublai Khan in 1274. His armies landed on Kyushu but withdrew because of an approaching typhoon. Kublai Khan attacked again in 1281, but this time his fleet was destroyed by a typhoon. The Japanese called this typhoon *kamikaze* ('divine wind'), the name used for the suicide pilots of World War II. European contact began when Portuguese sailors reached Japan in 1543. In 1549, a Spanish priest arrived and began to convert the Japanese to Christianity. His work was continued by other Spanish and Portuguese missionaries. Besides missionaries, Dutch and English traders arrived in the early 17th century. In the 1630s, the Japanese, fearing European conquest, ordered all Christian missionaries to leave the country, and forced Japanese converts to give up their faith. This led Japan to embark on a lengthy period of enforced isolation from the rest of the world. Japanese who lived abroad were not allowed to return, while no Japanese person was allowed to leave the country. The only Europeans allowed to stay were Dutch traders, who had not been involved in Christian missionary work. The Japanese allowed the Dutch to maintain a single trading station based on a small island in Nagasaki harbour. They permitted one Dutch ship to visit this station every year.

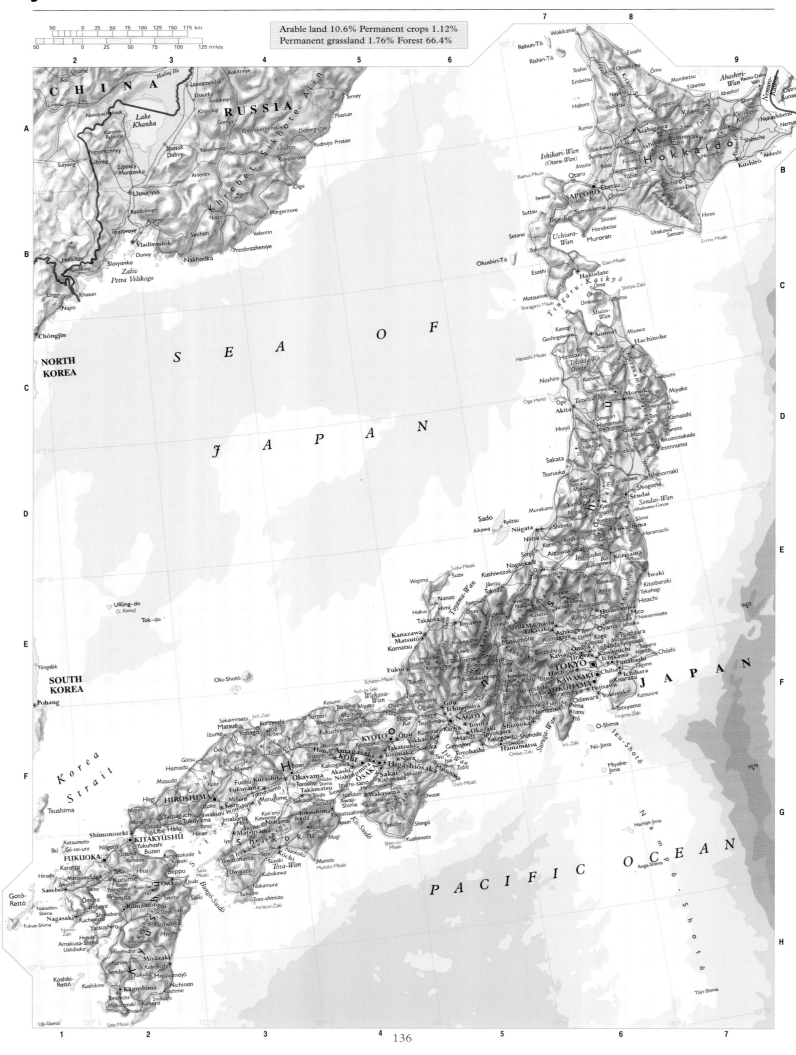

Arable land 10.6% Permanent crops 1.12%
Permanent grassland 1.76% Forest 66.4%

The policy of seclusion could not be maintained indefinitely. In the early 19th century, the United States became concerned about the mistreatment of American sailors who had been shipwrecked in Japan. In 1853, a mission led by Commodore Matthew C. Perry of the US Navy arrived at Edo (now Tokyo) with four warships. He demanded that diplomatic relations be restored, that all ports be opened to Western trade, and that shipwrecked Americans should be well treated. In 1854, Perry returned to Edo Bay and the government agreed to sign a treaty with the United States. The treaty provided for a US diplomat to reside in Japan and for the United States to have trading rights in two Japanese ports, Hakodate and Shimoda. Britain, the Netherlands and Russia soon signed similar agreements.

Most treaties gave foreigners the right of extra-territoriality, whereby foreigners were allowed to live in Japan, where they were subject to the laws of their own countries, not to the laws of Japan. They were called 'unequal treaties', because they gave foreigners powers that were not granted to the Japanese in return. The capitulation of the shogun to Perry's demands prepared the way for the overthrow of the now weak Tokugawa shogunate in 1867. In 1868, the Meiji Restoration restored the emperor's traditional powers.

That same year, the capital of Japan was moved from Kyoto to Edo (Tokyo). Emperor Mutsuhito, who adopted the title *Meiji*, a title meaning 'enlightened rule', reigned from 1867 to 1912. The Meiji period was marked by the adoption of Western ideas and technology. The Japanese set up an educational system and a telegraph network. They began to build railways and introduced modern systems of banking and taxation. They also abolished the samurai and established a modern army and navy.

In 1889, Japan introduced its first constitution under which the emperor became head of state and supreme commander of the army and navy. The emperor appointed government ministers, who were responsible to him. The constitution also allowed for a parliament, called the Diet, with two houses. The 1890s saw the revision of the unequal treaties and Westerners gave up the right to extra-territoriality.

From the 1890s, Japan also began to build up an overseas empire. In 1894–5, Japan fought China over the control of Korea, which had been under Chinese control for centuries. Japan was victorious and, under the Treaty of Shimonoseki (1895), Japan took Taiwan. Korea was made an independent territory, thus leaving it open to Japanese influence. Rivalry with Russia led to the Russo-Japanese War (1904–5). The causes of the war included the conflicting interests of both countries in Korea and Manchuria. With the help of President Theodore Roosevelt, peace was negotiated after a year of heavy fighting. Under the Treaty of Portsmouth (named after Portsmouth, New Hampshire, where it was signed), Japan gained the Liaodong peninsula, which Russia had leased from China, while Russia recognized the supremacy of Japan's interests in Korea. The Treaty of Portsmouth established Japan as a world power. It also demonstrated for all the world that an Asian power could take on and defeat a European power.

In World War I, Japan supported the Allies and it seized German holdings in the Shandong peninsula, as well as taking Micronesian islands in the western Pacific Ocean, namely the Caroline, Mariana and Marshall groups. After the war, Japan's foreign policy strongly supported the maintenance of world peace, and Japan became a founding member of the League of Nations in 1920. However, many problems arose in the 1920s, including the earthquake that struck Tokyo and Yokohama in 1923, and the world depression in the late 1920s. The growing strength of the Japanese military was demonstrated by the army's seizure of Manchuria in 1931. They made Manchuria a puppet state called Manchukuo, and extended their influence into other parts of northern China. In Japan, nationalists threatened those civilian politicians who opposed the military. In 1932, Japanese nationalists assassinated the prime minister. Japan left the League of Nations in 1933 after that institution had condemned its actions in Manchuria.

During the 1930s, and especially after the outbreak of war between Japan and China in 1937, militarist control of Japan's government grew steadily. By the end of 1938, when Japan controlled most of eastern China, militarists began to talk of bringing all of eastern Asia under Japanese control. In September 1939, Japan occupied the northern part of French Indo-China and, later that month, signed an agreement

The Japanese Boom

In 1945 Japan lay in ruins, with its major cities in ashes – two of them dangerously radioactive. Its smouldering ports were choked with the sunken remnants of its merchant marine fleet, and its people were demoralized. Less than two generations later, the Japanese economy was second only to that of the USA. Its high-technology products dominated world markets, while Japanese banks and private investors owned huge slices of industry and real estate on every continent.

The far-sighted American Occupation authorities deserve some of the credit. Realizing that industrial recovery could go hand in hand only with political development, they wrote a new constitution for Japan. As a link with the past, the Emperor kept his place, but as a constitutional monarch answerable to a democratically elected Diet, with women given full voting rights for the first time. Trade unions, with the right to strike, were established, and land reform eliminated politically subservient tenants. By 1950, 90% of farmland was owner-cultivated. Great industrial conglomerates were broken into smaller units, and education was enormously expanded. Most ordinary Japanese accepted the reforms; they remembered the pain the old ways had brought.

The Korean War in 1950 gave the slowly recovering Japanese economy a tremendous boost. Japanese factories, well paid in American dollars, provided much of the steel, vehicles and other equipment the war demanded. When the Occupation formally ended in 1952, Japan was clearly on the way up. The American military presence, guaranteed by treaty, continued, but caused no resentment; on the contrary, safe beneath the US defence umbrella, Japan could devote its resources to productive industry, not armaments.

The Japanese owed the first stage of their transformation to the Americans; the rest, they did themselves. Carefully planned economic policies, directed by the Ministry of Trade and Industry (MITI) – nicknamed 'Japan Inc.'s Corporate Head-quarters' – directed investment to key industries. First, the metal, engineering and chemical industries were rationalized and modernized. With the education system producing a steady stream of graduates, already trained in the industrial disciplines their future employers required, results were soon appearing. In the 1950s and 1960s efficient Japanese steel-makers consistently undersold European and American rivals, while producing better-quality steel. 'Made in Japan', once a sneering joke to describe shoddy goods, was taking on an entirely new commercial meaning.

Japan's major weakness was its near-total lack of natural resources; but foresight and planning made up for them. After the 1970s oil crisis, it was clear that the costs of heavy industry were going to rise unprofitably high; besides, the pollution they had brought was reaching dangerous levels. MITI switched resources to automobiles and electronics. Soon, Japan began to capture and dominate these markets, too.

By the 1980s, Japan's trading partners were becoming alarmed. Noting that trade with Japan was largely a one-way street – Japan's home market is still hard to penetrate – they built protective walls of tariffs and duties. Japan responded with its usual flexibility: it bought factories within its rivals' walls, and traded from there. The Tokyo stock market survived a serious 'crash' in the spring of 1992 – testament to the strength of the national economy. Even so, Japan's colossal trade surpluses in the early 1990s were causing resentment and danger to the world economic system. In 1997, Japan, and much of eastern Asia, entered into a period of economic recession. Drastic measures were taken to restore confidence and, by the turn of the century, the economy was reported to be slowly growing again. However, Japan faces several long-term problems, including the squeezing of the economy by an ageing population needing expensive social services, and also by competition with other dynamic developing countries.

with Italy and Germany, which assured their co-operation in building a 'new world order', while acknowledging Japan's leadership in Asia.

In 1941, Japanese troops entered southern Indo-China, causing mounting tension with the United States. Then, in December 1941, it launched a surprise attack on the American naval base of Pearl Harbor, in Hawaii. This action drew the United States into World War II. The Japanese soon conquered large areas in South-east Asia and the South Pacific, but after their defeat in the naval Battle of Midway in 1942, their power began to decline.

In 1945, American bombers attacked Japan and, on 6 August, the first atomic bomb was dropped on Hiroshima. The USSR declared war on Japan and invaded Manchuria and Korea. On 9 August, the Americans dropped a second atomic bomb on Nagasaki. On 2 September, World War II ended when Japan officially surrendered.

Politics

At the end of the war, Japan lost all the territories it had gained in mainland Asia, together with most of the islands it had governed in the Pacific, including the Bonin Islands, Iwo Jima, the Kuril Islands, southern Sakhalin, the Ryukyu Islands and Taiwan. This reduced Japan to its four main islands, plus a few small nearby islands. However, the United States returned the northern Ryukyu Islands to Japan in 1958, the Bonin Islands and Iwo Jima in 1968, and the southern Ryukyu Islands in 1972. Russia still occupies southern Sakhalin. It has also refused to give up the four small islands at the southern end of the Kuril Islands, which were historically ruled by Japan. These islands have become a matter of dispute between Japan and Russia.

The Allies occupied Japan in August 1945. Most of the occupation forces were Americans, led by General Douglas MacArthur, who, with his advisers, drafted a new democratic constitution in 1946. Under the constitution, power was transferred from the emperor to the people. The army and navy were abolished and the country renounced war as a political weapon. The emperor, who had been regarded as divine ruler, became a constitutional monarch. MacArthur also introduced many economic reforms that laid the foundations for Japan's remarkable post-war recovery, which transformed it into the world's second largest economic power.

From 1949, the Americans began to ease their control over Japan. In 1951, Japan signed a Treaty of Peace with 48 nations, not including the Soviet Union, together with a peace treaty with the United States that permitted the US to have military bases in Japan until Japan was able to undertake its own defence. The peace treaty went into effect on 28 April 1952 and the Allied occupation ended on that day. Japan became a member of the UN in 1956, when the Soviet Union and Japan agreed to end the state of war between them.

In 1955, members of rival Japanese parties came together to form the conservative Liberal-Democratic Party. This party controlled Japan's government until the 1990s, when a series of coalition governments were formed. A true opposition party emerged in the late 1990s, when the Democratic Party of Japan united with several small parties. The economy began to slow down in the early 1990s and, in 1997, the country underwent a serious economic crisis. Its banking system was saddled with large loans. Bankruptcies and unemployment were rising, while stock prices and the exchange rates for the yen were falling. The crisis caused fears that Japan's deteriorating economy threatened financial markets around the world. The government was forced to take drastic steps, including massive increases in public spending and income tax cuts and reforms of the banking system, to restore consumer and investor confidence. In the 1998 elections, the Liberal-Democratic Party (LDP) lost seats and was forced to govern in a coalition. In 2001, the LDP chose Junichiro Koizumi as prime minister. Koizumi promised drastic reforms to revive the economy.

Economy

Japan's natural resources are limited and the country has to import many of the materials, including fuels, that it requires for manufacturing. Yet the country has the world's second largest economy after the United States. Japan's gross national product is about twice as large as the GNP of Germany and more than four times that of China. The most important sector of the economy is manufacturing which

has grown enormously in the last 50 years. Japan's success is owed to several factors, including its use of the latest technology, its skilled and hard-working labour force, its vigorous export policies and the comparatively small governing expenditure on defence. About 77% of the population lives in cities and towns where most of the manufacturing industries are situated. Increasing urbanization has created housing shortages and the cities inevitably suffer from pollution. Another problem is the growing number of people of pensionable age. As a result, the retirement age is being progressively raised from 60 years to 65 by 2013. Unemployment in 2000 stood at 4.9%, the highest rate since records began in 1953.

Japan has reserves of a variety of minerals, but most deposits are too small to be mined economically. Minerals include coal, copper, lead, manganese, silver, tin and zinc. Some petroleum is produced off Honshu, but it accounts for less than 1% of the country's needs. Such minerals as bauxite, copper and petroleum, together with the coking coal and iron ore needed to make steel, are imported for use in manufacturing. Imported petroleum and natural gas are the most important fuels used in generating electricity. Coal and hydroelectric power are also used and nuclear power stations have become increasingly important. Nuclear power stations account for about 32% of the country's electricity in 2000. However, parliament passed new legislation to tighten inspections of nuclear facilities after a major accident in a uranium processing plant at Tokaimura, north-east of Tokyo, in September 1999. Experts described this accident as the second worst after the one at Chernobyl (Chornobyl) in the Ukraine, in 1986.

Manufacturing accounts for 25% of Japan's gross domestic product. The leading manufacturing sector involves the production of transport equipment. Japan is a one of the world's leading producers of ships, though it has been overtaken by South Korea. Its annual production of about 11 million motor vehicles makes it the world's second largest producer after the United States. Japan also manufactures machinery, electrical appliances, electronic equipment and chemicals. Japan is the world's leading producer of steel, much of which is exported.

Agriculture accounts for 2% of the gross domestic product and employs about 5% of the workforce. Because so much of the land is rugged, only a small percentage is cultivated. But through intensive farming and the use of terracing and irrigation, Japan produces nearly three-quarters of the food it needs. Rice is the leading staple crop, though its consumption is declining. Japan ranks eighth in the world in the production of rice. It is grown on about half of the country's farmland. Other major crops include fruits, soya beans, sugar beet, tea, tobacco and wheat. Mulberry bushes are cultivated to produce food for silkworms. Before 1945, Japan lacked animal proteins. However, in the last 50 years, livestock farming has become increasingly important. Today, dairy products, eggs and meat are consumed in increasingly large quantities. Traditionally, fish were the main source of protein.

Japan has a highly developed and modern transport system, with a modern road, rail and air system, together with coastal shipping. Japan's high-speed electric trains are famous and the undersea Seikan Tunnel, which was opened to traffic in 1988 connecting Honshu and Hokkaido, is one of the world's longest. The world's longest undersea road tunnel, spanning Tokyo Bay, was opened in 1997.

The United States accounts for about 27% of Japan's total trade and Japan is the second most important trading partner of the United States after Canada. Japan's other major trading partners include China, South Korea and Taiwan.

AREA	Chinese, Korean,
377,800 sq km	Ainu
[145,869 sq mi]	**LANGUAGES**
POPULATION	Japanese (official)
126,772,000	**RELIGIONS**
CAPITAL (POPULATION)	Shintoism and Buddhism 84%
Tokyo (17,950,000)	(most Japanese consider
GOVERNMENT	themselves to be both
Constitutional monarchy	Shinto and Buddhist)
ETHNIC GROUPS	**CURRENCY**
Japanese 99%,	Yen = 100 sen

JORDAN

The green, white and black on this flag are the colours of the three tribes who led the Arab Revolt against the Turks in 1917. Red is the colour of the Hussein Dynasty. The star was added in 1928. Its seven points represent the first seven verses of the sacred book, the Koran.

Geography and Climate

The Hashemite Kingdom of Jordan is an Arab country in south-western Asia. The Great Rift Valley in the west contains the River Jordan and the Dead Sea, which Jordan shares with Israel. The Great Rift Valley is part of a huge gash in the Earth's crust, which runs south through East Africa to Mozambique. East of the Rift Valley is the Transjordan Plateau, where most Jordanians live. To the east and south lie vast areas of desert. Jordan has a short coastline on an arm of the Red Sea, the Gulf of Aqaba. The country's highest peak, Jabal Ramm, reaches 1,754 m [5,755 ft] in the south.

About 90% of Jordan has a desert climate, with an average annual rainfall of less than 200 mm [8 in]. Summers are hot, but winters may be cold, with snow on higher areas. The north-west is the wettest area, with an average annual rainfall of 800 mm [31 in] in higher areas.

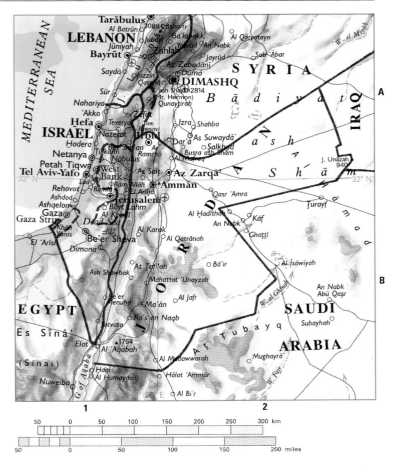

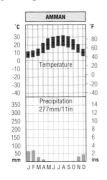

JORDAN (AMMAN)

The Jordan Valley marks the eastern limit of the true Mediterranean region, and although Amman lies only a short distance east of Jerusalem, it has a much lower rainfall and a longer dry season. Rain is almost unknown from May to September. Amman's semi-arid climate is transitional between the Mediterranean type and the true desert to the east. Temperatures are similar on average to those of Jerusalem, but summer days are hotter.

History

Jordan's early history is closely linked with that of Israel. It was first settled by Semitic peoples about 4,000 years ago, and was later conquered by Egyptian, Assyrian, Chaldean, Persian and Roman forces. The area fell to the Muslim Arabs in AD 636 and the Arab culture they introduced survives to this day.

By the end of the 12th century, Christian crusaders controlled parts of western Jordan, but they were driven out by the great Muslim warrior Saladin in 1187. The Egyptian Mamelukes overthrew Saladin's successors in 1250. The Mamelukes ruled until 1517, when the area was conquered by the Ottoman Turks. Jordan stagnated under the rule of the Ottoman Turks, but the opening of a railway in 1908 stimulated the economy. Arab and British forces defeated the Turks during World War I and, after the war, the area east of the River Jordan was awarded to Britain by the League of Nations.

Politics

In 1921, Britain created a territory called Transjordan, east of the River Jordan. In 1923, Transjordan became self-governing, but Britain retained control of its defences, finances and foreign affairs. This territory became fully independent as Jordan in 1946.

Jordan has suffered from instability arising from the Arab-Israeli conflict since the creation of the State of Israel in 1948. After the first Arab-Israeli War (1948–9), Jordan acquired the fertile West Bank, which was officially incorporated into the state in 1950. This crucial area, which included East Jerusalem, was lost to Israel in the 1967 war and Jordan subsequently carried the burden of Palestinian refugees on its own territory. In the 1970s, Palestinian guerrillas using Jordan as a base became a challenge to the authority of the government of King Hussein, who had become king in 1953. After a short civil war, the Palestinian leadership fled the country.

In 1988, King Hussein suddenly renounced all responsibility for the West Bank – a recognition that the Palestine Liberation Organization, and not the long-suffering Jordan, was the legitimate representative of the Palestinian people. Nevertheless, Palestinians still formed a majority of the population. The refugees, numbering around 900,000, placed a huge burden on an already weak economy. Jordan

was further undermined by the 1991 Gulf War when, despite its official neutrality, the pro-Iraq, anti-Western stance of the Palestinians in Jordan did nothing to improve prospects of trade and aid deals with Europe and the United States, while Jordan's vital economic links with Israel had already been severed. The ban on political parties was removed in 1991, and martial law was lifted after 21 years. Multiparty elections were held in 1993 and, in 1994, Jordan and Israel signed a peace treaty, ending a state of war which had been going on for more than 40 years. The treaty restored some land in the south to Jordan.

Jordan's King Hussein, who had commanded great respect for playing an important role in Middle Eastern affairs, died in 1999. He was succeeded by his eldest son who became King Abdullah II.

Economy

Jordan lacks natural resources, apart from phosphates and potash, and the country's economy depends substantially on aid. The World Bank classifies Jordan as a 'lower-middle-income' developing country. Because of the dry climate, under 6% of the land is farmed or used as pasture. Major crops include barley, citrus fruits, grapes, olives, vegetables and wheat.

Jordan has an oil refinery and manufactures include cement, pharmaceuticals, processed food, fertilizers and textiles. The main exports are phosphates, fertilizers, potash, fruits and vegetables.

AREA	ETHNIC GROUPS
89,210 sq km [34,444 sq mi]	Arab 99% (50% are Palestinians)
POPULATION	**LANGUAGES**
5,153,000	Arabic (official)
CAPITAL (POPULATION)	**RELIGIONS**
Amman (1,752,000)	Islam 93%, Christianity 5%
GOVERNMENT	**CURRENCY**
Constitutional monarchy	Jordan dinar = 1,000 fils

Kazakstan's flag was adopted on 4 June 1992, about six months after it had become independent. The blue represents cloudless skies, while the golden sun and the soaring eagle represent love of freedom. A vertical strip of gold ornamentation is on the left.

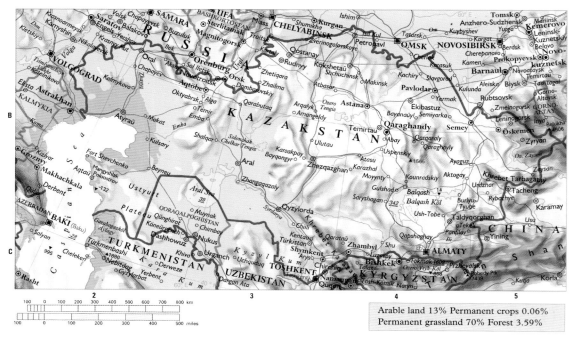

Arable land 13% Permanent crops 0.06%
Permanent grassland 70% Forest 3.59%

Geography

Kazakstan is a large country in west-central Asia. In the west, the Caspian Sea lowlands include the Karagiye Depression, which reaches 132 m [433 ft] below sea level. The lowlands extend eastwards through the Aral Sea area. The north contains high plains, but the highest land is along the eastern and southern borders. These areas include parts of the Altai and Tian Shan mountain ranges.

Eastern Kazakstan contains several freshwater lakes, the largest of which is Lake Balkhash (Balqash Köl). The water in the rivers has been used for irrigation, causing ecological problems. For example, the Aral Sea, deprived of water, shrank from 66,900 sq km [25,830 sq mi] in 1960, to 33,642 sq km [12,989 sq mi] in 1993. Areas which once provided fish have dried up and are now barren desert.

Climate

The climate reflects Kazakstan's position in the heart of Asia, far from the influence of the oceans. Winters are cold and snow covers the land for about 100 days, on average, at Alma Ata (Almaty). Rainfall is generally quite low.

KAZAKSTAN (ALMA ATA)

Kazakstan is a large country in the centre of Asia and its climate is markedly continental. The summers are warm and the winters cold, the annual temperature range being 30°C [54°F]. Half the year will experience frost (at Alma Ata) and snow lies for about 100 days. Rainfall is low with only around 250 mm [10 in] in the north and twice this amount in the south, with desert and semi-desert conditions covering large areas.

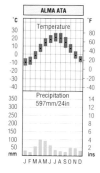

ALMA ATA
Temperature
Precipitation
597mm/24in

History

From the late 15th century, the Kazaks built up a large nomadic empire ruled by khans. But Kazak power declined in the 17th century. In the early 18th century, Russia became influential in the area. In 1731, the Kazaks in the west accepted Russian rule to gain protection from attack from neighbouring peoples. By the mid-1740s, Russia ruled most of the region and, in the early 19th century, Russia abolished the khanates. They also encouraged Russians and Ukrainians to settle in Kazakstan.

After the Russian Revolution of 1917, many Kazaks wanted to make their country independent. But the Communists prevailed and in 1936 Kazakstan became a republic of the Soviet Union, called the Kazak Soviet Socialist Republic. During World War II, and also after the war, the Soviet government moved many people from the west into Kazakstan. From the 1950s, people were encouraged to work on a 'Virgin Lands' project, which involved bringing large areas of grassland under cultivation.

Politics

Reforms in the Soviet Union in the 1980s led to the break-up of the country in December 1991. Kazakstan kept contacts with Russia and most of the other republics in the former Soviet Union by joining the Commonwealth of Independent States (CIS), and in 1995 Kazakstan announced that its army would unite with that of Russia. In December 1997, the government moved the capital from Alma Ata to Aqmola (later renamed Astana), a town in the Russian-dominated north. It was hoped that this move would bring some Kazak identity to the area.

Under Soviet rule, Kazakstan was a dumping ground and test bed – the Soviet missile- and rocket-launching site at Baykonur (Bayqongyr) suffered great environmental damage, including the shrinking of the Aral Sea by 70%. But Kazakstan has emerged as a powerful entity, wealthier and more diversified than other Asian republics. It could provide the 'new order' between East and West. It is the only former Soviet republic whose ethnic population is almost outnumbered by another group (the Russians), and its Muslim revival is relatively muted. Its first elected president, Nursultan Nazarbayev, a former Communist leader, introduced many reforms, including a multiparty system.

Economy

The World Bank classifies Kazakstan as a 'lower-middle-income' developing country. Livestock farming, especially sheep and cattle, is important, and major crops include barley, cotton, rice and wheat. The country is rich in mineral resources, including coal and oil reserves, together with bauxite, copper, lead, tungsten and zinc. Manufactures include chemicals, food products, machinery and textiles. Oil is exported via a pipeline through Russia. However, to reduce dependence on Russia, Kazakstan signed an agreement in 1997 to build a new pipeline to China. Other exports include metals, chemicals, grain, wool and meat.

AREA
2,717,300 sq km
[1,049,150 sq mi]
POPULATION
16,731,000
CAPITAL (POPULATION)
Astana (280,000)
GOVERNMENT
Multiparty republic
ETHNIC GROUPS
Kazak 53%, Russian 30%,
Ukrainian 4%, German 2%,
Uzbek 2%
LANGUAGES
Kazak (official); Russian,
the former official language,
is widely spoken
RELIGIONS
Islam 47%,
Russian Orthodox 44%
CURRENCY
Tenge

KENYA

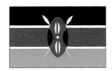

Kenya's flag dates from 1963, when the country became independent. It is based on the flag of KANU (Kenya African National Union), the political party which led the nationalist struggle. The Masai warrior's shield and crossed spears represent the defence of freedom.

Geography

The Republic of Kenya is a country in East Africa which straddles the Equator. It is slightly larger in area than France. Behind the narrow coastal plain on the Indian Ocean, the land rises to high plains and highlands, broken by volcanic mountains, including Mount Kenya, the country's highest peak at 5,199 m [17,057 ft].

Crossing the country is an arm of the Great Rift Valley. On the floor of this steep-sided valley are several lakes, including Baringo, Magadi, Naivasha, Nakuru and, on the northern frontier, Lake Turkana (formerly Lake Rudolf).

Climate

The Equator passes through Kenya just north of the snow-capped Mount Kenya. While the climate is tropical, it is very much affected by altitude, especially in the south-western highlands. This region is distinctly cooler than the hot and humid coast.

The average annual rainfall is between 1,000 mm and 1,300 mm [39–51 in]. However, the rainfall is variable. Only about 15% of Kenya has a reliable annual rainfall of 800 mm [31 in].

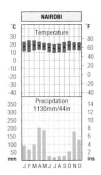

KENYA (NAIROBI)

Nairobi lies in the south-western highlands, at a height of 1,820 m [5,971 ft] above sea level. Temperatures here have been recorded at about 10°C [18°F] lower than those in Mombasa. The main rains occur during April and May, with a lesser rainy season in November and December.

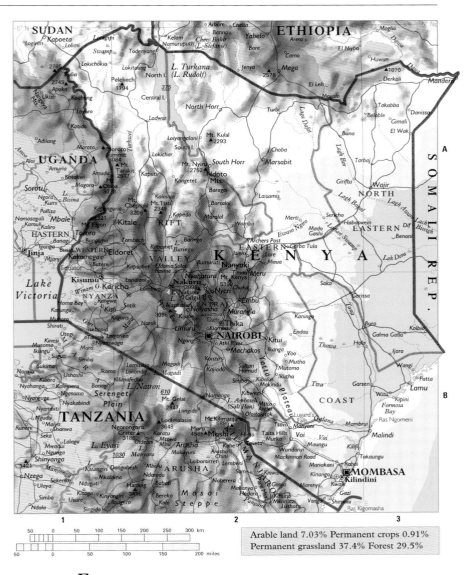

Arable land 7.03% Permanent crops 0.91%
Permanent grassland 37.4% Forest 29.5%

History

The Kenyan coast has been an important trading centre for more than 2,000 years. Early Arab traders carried goods from eastern Asia and exchanged them for items from the local people. The Portuguese explorer Vasco da Gama reached the coast in 1498. Later, the Portuguese competed with the Arabs for control of the coast.

The British took control of the coast in 1895 and soon extended their influence inland. Many Britons set up large farms in Kenya. However, opposition to British rule mounted in the 1940s, and, in 1953, a secret movement called Mau Mau launched an armed struggle. Mau Mau was defeated, but Kenya gained its independence in 1963.

Politics

Many Kenyan leaders felt that the division of the population into 40 ethnic groups might lead to instability. They argued that Kenya should have a strong central government and, as a result, Kenya has been a one-party state for much of the time since independence. Multiparty democracy was restored in the early 1990s and elections were held in 1992 and 1997, each resulting in a victory for the ruling president Daniel Arap Moi.

In the 1960s, attempts by Kenya, Tanzania and Uganda to collaborate collapsed because of the deep differences between the political and economic policies of the countries. However, hopes were revived in 1999, when a new East African Community was created. It aims to establish a customs union, a common market, a monetary union, and, ultimately, a political union.

Economy

According to the United Nations, Kenya is a 'low-income' developing country. Agriculture employs about 80% of the people, but many Kenyans are subsistence farmers, growing little more than they need to support their families. The chief food crop is maize. Bananas, beans, cassava and sweet potatoes are also grown. The main cash crops and leading exports are coffee and tea. Manufactures include chemicals, leather and footwear, processed food, petroleum products and textiles.

By the standards of tropical Africa, Kenya has a stable economy, even allowing for a thriving black market and the usual reliance on aid.

AREA
580,370 sq km [224,081 sq mi]
POPULATION
30,766,000
CAPITAL (POPULATION)
Nairobi (2,000,000)
GOVERNMENT
Multiparty republic
ETHNIC GROUPS
Kikuyu 21%, Luhya 14%,
Luo 13%, Kalenjin 12%,
Kamba 11%
LANGUAGES
Kiswahili and English (both official)
RELIGIONS
Protestant 38%, Roman Catholic 28%, other Christian 27%, traditional beliefs 26%, Islam 7%
CURRENCY
Kenya shilling = 100 cents

KIRIBATI – SEE PACIFIC OCEAN, PAGES 174–178

KOREA, NORTH

The flag of the Democratic People's Republic of Korea (North Korea) has been flown since Korea was split into two states in 1948. The colours are traditional ones in Korea. The design, with the red star, indicates that North Korea is a Communist country.

Geography

The Democratic People's Republic of Korea occupies the northern part of the Korean Peninsula which extends south from north-eastern China. Mountains form the heart of the country, with the highest peak, Paektu-san, reaching 2,744 m [9,003 ft] on the northern border.

Climate

North Korea has a fairly severe climate, with bitterly cold winters when winds blow from across central Asia, bringing snow and freezing conditions. In summer, moist winds from the oceans bring rain.

History

The early history of the Korean peninsula is covered in the article on South Korea on page 143. North Korea came into being in 1945 when the peninsula, which had been a Japanese colony since 1910, was partitioned. Soviet forces occupied the north, while US troops controlled the south.

Politics

Soviet occupation led to a Communist government being established in 1948 under the leadership of Kim Il Sung. He initiated a Stalinist regime in which he assumed role of dictator, and a personality cult developed around him. He became the world's most durable Communist leader.

The Korean War began in June 1950 when North Korean troops invaded the south. North Korea, aided by China and the Soviet Union, fought with South Korea, which was supported by troops from the United States and other UN members. The war ended in July 1953. An armistice was signed but no permanent peace treaty was agreed upon. After the war, North Korea adopted a hostile policy towards South Korea in pursuit of its policy of reunification. At times, the situation grew so tense that it became a matter of international concern.

The ending of the Cold War in the late 1980s eased the situation and both countries joined the United Nations in 1991. However, as Communism collapsed in the Soviet Union, North Korea remained isolated and self-reliant.

In 1993, North Korea began a new international crisis by announcing that it was withdrawing from the Nuclear Non-Proliferation Treaty. This led to suspicions that North Korea, which had signed the Treaty in 1985, was developing its own nuclear weapons. Kim Il Sung, who had ruled as a virtual dictator from 1948 until his death in 1994, was succeeded by his son, Kim Jong Il. In the early 2000s, uncertainty surrounding North Korea's nuclear capabilities cast unease across the entire region. In 2001, the United States accused North Korea of supporting international terrorism, while, at the same time, talks between North and South Korea continued in an attempt to normalize relations between them.

Economy

North Korea has considerable resources, including coal, copper, iron ore, lead, tin, tungsten and zinc. Under Communism, North Korea has concentrated on developing heavy, state-owned industries. Manufactures include chemicals, iron and steel, machinery, processed food and textiles. Agriculture employs about a third of the people and rice is the leading crop. Economic decline and mismanagement, aggravated by three successive crop failures caused by floods in 1995 and 1996, and a drought in 1997, led to famine on a large scale.

AREA	ETHNIC GROUPS
120,540 sq km [46,540 sq mi]	Korean 99%
POPULATION	**LANGUAGES**
21,968,000	Korean (official)
CAPITAL (POPULATION)	**RELIGIONS**
P'yŏngyang (2,741,000)	Buddhism and Confucianism
GOVERNMENT	**CURRENCY**
Single-party people's republic	North Korean won = 100 chon

KOREA, SOUTH

South Korea's flag, adopted in 1950, is white, the traditional symbol for peace. The central 'yin-yang' symbol signifies the opposing forces of nature. The four black symbols stand for the four seasons, the points of the compass, and the Sun, Moon, Earth and Heaven.

Geography

The Republic of Korea, as South Korea is officially known, occupies the southern part of the Korean Peninsula. Mountains cover much of the country. The southern and western coasts are major farming regions. Many islands are found along the west and south coasts, the largest of which is Cheju-do, which contains South Korea's highest peak, Halla-san, which rises to 1,950 m [6,398 ft].

Climate

Like North Korea, South Korea is chilled in winter by cold, dry winds blowing from central Asia. Snow often covers the mountains in the east. The summers are hot and wet, especially in July and August.

SOUTH KOREA (SEOUL)

North-westerly winds from central Asia give cold, dry weather in winter, and night temperatures from December to March are usually below freezing. Snow lies on western mountain slopes east of Seoul. Summer is hot and wet, causing coastal sea fog in spring as warmer air from the south moves over the cold water surface. In July and August it rains on average every other day. During winter it rains less than 5 days a month.

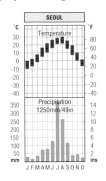

History

In the last 2,000 years, China has had a great influence on the people of Korea. The Chinese conquered the north in 108 BC and ruled until they were thrown out in AD 313. Mongol armies attacked Korea in the 13th century, but in 1388, a general, Yi Songgye, founded a dynasty of rulers which lasted until 1910.

From the 17th century, Korea prevented foreigners from entering the country. Korea was often called the 'Hermit Kingdom' until 1876, when Japan forced it to open some of its ports. Soon, the United States, Russia and some European countries were trading with Korea. In 1910, Korea became a Japanese colony.

After Japan's defeat in World War II (1939–45), North Korea was occupied by troops from the Soviet Union, while South Korea was occupied by United States forces. Attempts to reunify Korea failed and, in 1948, a National Assembly was elected in South Korea. This Assembly created the Republic of Korea, while North Korea became a Communist state. North Korean troops invaded the South in June 1950, sparking off the Korean War (1950–3).

Politics

The story of South Korea after the civil war was a very different one from that of the North, though the South was hardly a Far Eastern oasis of liberalism. While land reform based on smallholdings worked well enough to produce some of the world's highest rice yields (and self-sufficiency in food grains), the real economic miracle came in industrial expansion which started in the early 1960s. Initiated by a military government – one of several bouts of army rule since the inauguration of the republic – and based on slender natural resources, the country utilized its cheap, plentiful but well-educated labour force to transform the economy. The original manufacturing base of textiles remained important, but South Korea became a world leader in footwear, shipbuilding, consumer electronics, toys and vehicles.

The country's dynamism had to be linked to more liberal policies and, in 1988, a new constitution came into force, enabling presidential elections to be held every five years. Evidence of the new spirit of democracy came in 1997 when, in presidential elections, Kim Dae-jung, leader of past pro-democracy campaigns, narrowly defeated Hoi-chang, the governing party's candidate. In foreign affairs, a major breakthrough had occurred in 1991 when both North Korea and

South Korea were admitted as full members of the United Nations. The two countries signed several agreements, including one in which they agreed not to use force against each other, but tensions between them continued. In 2000, South Korea's President Dae-jung met with North Korea's Kim Jong Il in talks aimed at establishing better relations between the countries. But the prospect of reunification seemed as distant as ever.

Economy

The World Bank classifies South Korea as an 'upper-middle-income' developing country. It is also one of the world's fastest growing industrial economies. Resources include coal and tungsten. South Korea's main manufactures are processed food and textiles. Since partition, heavy industries have been built up, making chemicals, fertilizers, iron and steel, and ships. South Korea has also developed the production of computers, cars and televisions. In late 1997, however, dramatic expansion of the economy was halted by a market crash which affected many of the booming economies of Asia. In an effort to negate the economic and social turmoil that resulted, tough reforms were demanded by the International Monetary Fund. An agreement was reached to restructure much of the short-term debt faced by the government.

Farming remains important in South Korea. Rice is the chief crop, together with fruit, grains and vegetables. Fishing is also important.

The Korean War

Hastily divided in 1945 between a Soviet-occupied North and an American-occupied South, Korea was considered by most Western strategists an irrelevance to the developing Cold War. But when the heavily armed North invaded the South in June 1950, US President Truman decided to make a stand against what he saw (mistakenly) as Moscow-organized aggression. A Soviet boycott of the UN allowed US troops – assisted by contingents from Britain, Canada, France and other allies – to fight under the UN flag, and under General Douglas MacArthur they went on the offensive. American seapower permitted a landing far behind North Korean lines, and soon the Northerners were in retreat.

With some misgivings, Truman ordered his forces north of the 38th parallel, the former partition line. But as US troops neared the Chinese frontier in November 1950, hundreds of thousands of Chinese 'volunteers' surged across the Yalu River and threatened to overwhelm them. The UN troops retreated far southwards in disarray, until a 1951 counterattack slowly pushed back up the country, and the combatants became entrenched along the 38th parallel in a bitter war of attrition that endured until an armistice was negotiated in 1953. Not until 1991, almost 40 years later, were North and South able to agree to a tentative non-aggression pact.

AREA	**ETHNIC GROUPS**
99,020 sq km	Korean 99%
[38,232 sq mi]	**LANGUAGES**
POPULATION	Korean (official)
47,904,000	**RELIGIONS**
CAPITAL (POPULATION)	Christianity 49%, Buddhism 47%,
Seoul (Soul, 10,231,000)	Confucianism 3%
GOVERNMENT	**CURRENCY**
Multiparty republic	South Korean won = 100 chon

KUWAIT – SEE GULF STATES, PAGES 113–114

Kyrgyzstan's flag was adopted in March 1992. The flag depicts a bird's-eye view of a 'yurt' (circular tent) within a radiant sun. The 'yurt' recalls the traditional nomadic way of life. The 40 rays of the sun stand for the 40 traditional tribes.

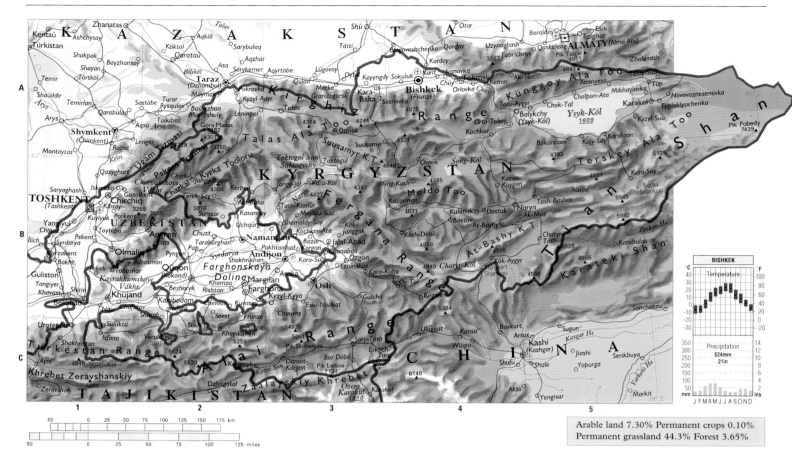

Arable land 7.30% Permanent crops 0.10%
Permanent grassland 44.3% Forest 3.65%

Geography and Climate

The Republic of Kyrgyzstan, or Kirghizia as it is also known, is a landlocked country between China, Tajikistan, Uzbekistan and Kazakstan. The country is mountainous, with spectacular scenery. The highest mountain, Pik Pobedy in the Tian Shan Range, reaches 7,439 m [24,406 ft] above sea level in the east. Less than a sixth of the country is below 900 m [2,950 ft]. The largest of the country's many lakes is Lake Issyk Kul (Ysyk-Köl) in the north-east.

The lowlands of Kyrgyzstan have warm summers and cold winters. But the altitude influences the climate in the mountains, where the January temperatures plummet to –28°C [–18°F]. Far from any sea, Kyrgyzstan has a low annual rainfall.

History

The area that is now Kyrgyzstan was populated in ancient times by nomadic herders. Mongol armies conquered the region in the early 13th century. They set up areas called khanates, ruled by chieftains, or khans. Islam was introduced in the 17th century.

China gained control of the area in the mid-18th century, but, in 1876, Kyrgyzstan became a province of Russia, and Russian settlement in the area began.

Politics

In 1916, Russia crushed a rebellion among the Kyrgyz, and many subsequently fled to China. In 1922, the area became an autonomous *oblast* (self-governing region) of the newly formed Soviet Union but, in 1936, it became one of the Soviet Socialist Republics. Under Communist rule, nomads were forced to work on government-run farms, while local customs and religious worship were suppressed. However, there were improvements in education and health.

In 1991, Kyrgyzstan became an independent country following the break-up of the Soviet Union. The Communist Party was dissolved, but the country retained ties with Russia through the Commonwealth of Independent States. Kyrgyzstan adopted a new constitution in 1994 and elections were held in 1995. However, in the late 1990s, Akayev introduced constitutional changes and other measures which gave him greater powers and limited press freedom. In 2000, Akayev was elected to a third five-year term as president.

Kyrgyzstan has the potential for an ethnic tinderbox, with its large Russian minority (who held positions of power in the days of the Soviet Union), disenchanted Uzbeks, and an influx of Chinese Muslim immigrants. In the early 2000s, many people were alarmed when Islamic guerrillas staged border raids on Kyrgyzstan as they sought to set up an Islamic state in the Fergana valley, where Kyrgyzstan borders Uzbekistan and Tajikistan.

Economy

In the early 1990s, when Kyrgyzstan was working to reform its economy, the World Bank classified it as a 'lower-middle-income' developing country. Agriculture, especially livestock rearing, is the chief activity. The chief products include cotton, eggs, fruits, grain, tobacco, vegetables and wool. However, food is imported. Manufactures include machinery, processed food, metals and textiles. Exports include wool, chemicals, cotton and metals.

AREA	Uzbek 13%,
198,500 sq km [76,640 sq mi]	Ukrainian 3%,
POPULATION	German, Tatar
4,753,000	**LANGUAGES**
CAPITAL (POPULATION)	Kyrgyz and Russian
Bishkek (589,000)	(both official), Uzbek
GOVERNMENT	**RELIGIONS**
Multiparty republic	Islam
ETHNIC GROUPS	**CURRENCY**
Kyrgyz 52%, Russian 18%,	Som = 100 tyiyn

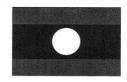

Since 1975, Laos has flown the flag of the Pathet Lao, the Communist movement which won control of the country after a long struggle. The blue stands for the River Mekong, the white disc for the Moon, and the red for the unity and purpose of the people.

Geography

The Lao People's Democratic Republic is a landlocked country in South-east Asia. Mountains and plateaux cover much of the country. The highest point is Mount Bia, which reaches 2,819 m [9,249 ft] in central Laos.

Most people live on the plains bordering the River Mekong and its tributaries. This river, one of Asia's longest, forms much of the country's north-western and south-western borders. A range of mountains called the Annam Cordillera (Chaîne Annamatique) runs along the eastern border with Vietnam.

Climate

Laos has a tropical monsoon climate. Winters are dry and sunny, with winds blowing in from the north-east. The temperatures rise until April, when the wind directions are reversed and moist south-westerly winds reach Laos, heralding the start of the wet monsoon season.

History

From the 9th century AD, Lao and Tai people set up a number of small states ruled by princes. But the area that is now Laos was united in 1353 in a kingdom called Lan Xang ('land of a million elephants'). Apart from a period of Burmese rule between 1574 and 1637, the Lan Xang ruled Laos until the early 18th century. In 1713, the region was divided into three separate kingdoms – Champasak, Vientiane and Louangphrabang – which became vassals of Siam (now Thailand).

In the 19th century, Chao Anou, the king of Vientiane, united his kingdom with Vietnam in an attempt to break Siamese domination, but he was defeated and Vientiane became a Siamese province. In the late 19th century, however, France gradually gained control of all Siamese territory east of the River Mekong.

Arable land 3.79% Permanent crops 0.11%
Permanent grassland 3.47% Forest 54.4%

Politics

France made Laos a protectorate in the late 19th century and ruled it as part of French Indo-China, a region which also included Cambodia and Vietnam. After France's surrender to Germany in 1945, Japanese forces moved into Indo-China. They allowed the French to continue as puppet rulers until 1945, when they interned all French authorities and military units. A Free Laos movement set up a government, but it collapsed when the French returned in 1946.

Under a new constitution, Laos became a monarchy in 1947 and, in 1949, the country became a self-governing state within the French Union. After full independence in 1954, Laos suffered from instability caused by a power struggle between royalist government forces and a pro-Communist group called the Pathet Lao. The Pathet Lao took power in 1975 after two decades of chaotic civil war in which the royalist forces were supported by American bombing and Thai mercenaries, while the Patriotic Front Pathet Lao was assisted by North Vietnam. The king, Savang Vatthana, abdicated in 1975, and the People's Democratic Republic of Laos was proclaimed. Over 300,000 Laotians, including technicians and other experts, as well as farmers, and members of ethnic minorities, fled the country. Many opponents of the government who remained were sent to re-education camps.

Communist policies brought isolation and stagnation under the domination of the Vietnamese government in Hanoi, who had used Laos as a great supply line in their war against the United States. In 1986, the Laotian Politburo embarked on its own version of *perestroika*, opening up its doors to tourists and also opening up trade links with its neighbours, notably China and Japan. In 1997, Laos became a member of the Association of South-east Asian Nations (ASEAN).

Also important was the development of the hydroelectric power potential from the River Mekong and the export of electricity to Thailand, earning Laos the title of the 'battery of South-east Asia'.

Most enterprises are now outside state control while the government works to develop alternative crops to opium. But political reform towards a multiparty democracy seems a forlorn hope.

Economy

Laos is one of the world's poorest countries. Agriculture employs about 76% of the people, as compared with 7% in industry and 17% in services. Rice is the main crop, and timber and coffee are both exported. But the most valuable export is electricity, which is produced at hydroelectric power stations on the River Mekong and is exported to Thailand. Laos also produces opium. In the early 1990s, Laos was thought to be the world's third biggest source of this illegal drug.

AREA	Lao Theung 22%, Lao Soung 9%
236,800 sq km [91,428 sq mi]	**LANGUAGES**
POPULATION	Lao (official), Khmer,
5,636,000	Tai, Miao
CAPITAL (POPULATION)	**RELIGIONS**
Vientiane (532,000)	Buddhism 58%,
GOVERNMENT	traditional beliefs 34%,
Single-party republic	Christianity 2%, Islam 1%
ETHNIC GROUPS	**CURRENCY**
Lao Loum 68%,	Kip = 100 at

The burgundy and white Latvian flag, which dates back to at least 1280, was revived after Latvia achieved its independence in 1991. According to one legend, the flag was first made from a white sheet which had been stained with the blood of a Latvian hero.

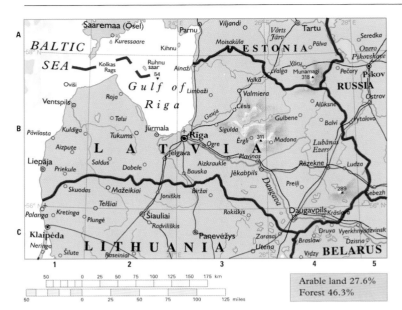

Arable land 27.6%
Forest 46.3%

Geography

The Republic of Latvia is one of three states on the south-eastern corner of the Baltic Sea which were ruled as parts of the Soviet Union between 1940 and 1991. Latvia consists mainly of flat plains separated by low hills, composed of moraine (ice-worn rocks). The moraine was dumped there by ice sheets during the Ice Age. The country's highest point is only 311 m [1,020 ft] above sea level. Small lakes and peat bogs are common. The country's main river, the Daugava, is also known as the Western Dvina.

Climate

Air masses from the Atlantic influence the climate of Latvia, bringing warm and rainy conditions in summer. Winters are cold. The average temperature range is 16°C to 18°C [61–64°F] in July, and –7°C to –3°C [19–27°F] in January.

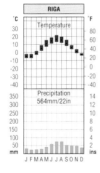

LATVIA (RIGA)

Riga has warm summers and cold winters, with rain or snow in all months. June to August are the warmest months with temperatures over 15°C [59°F], and sub-zero averages from December to March. Temperature extremes are just over 34°C [93°F] and –29°C [–20°F]. On average, rain falls on a third of the days in the second half of the year, but the total is relatively light. It can be overcast for long periods.

History

The ancestors of most modern Latvians settled in the area about 2,000 years ago. Between the 9th and 11th centuries, the region was attacked by Vikings from the west and Russians from the east. In the 13th century, German invaders took over, naming the country Livland, or Livonia in Latin.

In 1561, Latvia was partitioned and most of the land came under Polish or Lithuanian rule. A Germany duchy was also established there. In 1621, the Swedish king Gustavus II Adolphus took over Riga. In 1629, the greater part of the country north of the Daugava (Western Dvina) River was ceded to Sweden, though the south-east remained under Lithuanian rule. But, in 1710, Peter the Great took control of Riga and, by the end of the 18th century, all of Latvia was under Russian control, although the German landowners and merchants continued to exercise considerable power. The 19th century saw the

rise of Latvian nationalism and calls for independence became increasingly frequent in the early 20th century, as German and Russian power declined.

After the Russian Revolution of March 1917, the Latvian National Political Conference demanded independence, but Germany occupied Riga in September. However, after the November Revolution, the Latvian National Political Conference proclaimed the country's independence on 18 November 1918. Russia and Germany, which had both tried to maintain control, finally recognized Latvia's independence in 1920. In 1922, Latvia adopted a democratic constitution and the elected government introduced land reforms. However, a coup in May 1934 ended this period of democratic rule. In 1939, Germany and the Soviet Union agreed to divide up much of eastern Europe. Soviet troops invaded Latvia in June 1940 and Latvia was made a part of the Soviet Union. But German forces invaded the area in 1941 and held it until 1944, when Soviet troops reoccupied the country. Many Latvians opposed to Russian rule were either killed or deported.

Politics

Under Soviet rule, many Russians settled in Latvia and many Latvians feared that the Russians would become the dominant ethnic group. From the mid-1980s, when Mikhail Gorbachev was introducing reforms in the Soviet Union, Latvian nationalists campaigned against Soviet rule. In the late 1980s, the Latvian government ended absolute Communist rule and voted to restore the banned national flag and anthem. It also proclaimed Latvian the country's official language.

In 1990, Latvia established a multiparty political system. In elections in March, candidates in favour of separation from the Soviet Union won two-thirds of parliamentary seats. The parliament declared Latvia independent on 4 May 1990, though the Soviet Union declared this act illegal. However, the Soviet government recognized Latvia's independence in September 1991, shortly before the Soviet Union itself was dissolved. Latvia held its first free elections to its parliament (the Saeima) in 1993. Voting was limited only to people who were citizens on 17 June 1940 and their descendants. This meant that about 34% of Latvian residents were unable to vote. In 1994, Latvia restricted the naturalization of non-Latvians, including many Russian settlers, who were not allowed to vote or own land. However, in 1998, the government agreed that all children born since independence should have automatic citizenship, regardless of the status of their parents.

Economy

The World Bank classifies Latvia as a 'lower-middle-income' country. In the 1990s, it faced problems in transforming its government-run economy into a free-market one. The country lacks natural resources apart from land and forests, and has to import many raw materials.

Its industries cover a wide range, with products including electronic goods, farm machinery, fertilizers, processed food, plastics, radios, washing machines and vehicles. But Latvia produces only about a tenth of the electricity it needs. The rest has to be imported from Belarus, Russia and Ukraine. Farm products include barley, dairy products, beef, oats, potatoes and rye.

AREA	Belarussian 4%, Ukrainian 3%,
64,589 sq km [24,938 sq mi]	Polish 2%, Lithuanian,
POPULATION	Jewish
2,385,000	**LANGUAGES**
CAPITAL (POPULATION)	Latvian (official), Russian
Riga (811,000)	**RELIGIONS**
GOVERNMENT	Lutheran, Russian Orthodox
Multiparty republic	and Roman Catholic
ETHNIC GROUPS	**CURRENCY**
Latvian 56%, Russian 30%,	Lats = 10 santimi

LEBANON

Geography and Climate

The Republic of Lebanon is a country on the eastern shores of the Mediterranean Sea. Behind the coastal plain are the rugged Lebanon Mountains (Jabal Lubnán), which rise to 3,088 m [10,131 ft]. Another range, the Anti-Lebanon Mountains (Al Jabal ash Sharqi), form the eastern border with Syria. Between the two ranges is the Bekaa Valley, a fertile farming region.

The Lebanese coast has hot, dry summers and mild, wet winters. Inland, onshore winds bring heavy rain to the western slopes of the mountains in the winter months, with snow at the higher altitudes.

History and Politics

The Phoenicians, who probably settled in the area that is now Lebanon around 5,000 years ago, were traders and explorers who founded city-states along the coast. From about 800 BC the area came under waves of invaders – Egyptians, Hittites, Assyrians, Babylonians and Persians. The armies of the Macedonian general Alexander the Great seized the area in 332 BC and the Romans took control in 64 BC, leaving behind them many structures that still stand today. Christianity was introduced in AD 325. In 395, the area became part of the Byzantine Empire. However, Muslim Arabs occupied the area in the early 7th century, converting many people to Islam, although Christian worship continued in the mountains.

European Crusaders arrived in Lebanon in about 1100 and the area became a battlefield between Christian and Muslim armies. Around 1300, the Muslim Mamelukes of Egypt drove the last of the Crusaders out of the area. In 1516, Lebanon was taken over by the Turkish Ottoman Empire, whose capital was Istanbul, in western Turkey. Turkish rule continued until World War I, when British and French forces defeated the Ottoman Turks, whose empire collapsed. France took over Lebanon's political affairs from 1922.

France ruled Lebanon until 1944 and, for three decades, the country was relatively peaceful and prosperous by Middle Eastern standards. Its association with France had bequeathed a distinct Gallic flavour, though with so many racial and religious groups, the population was truly cosmopolitan. Beirut, the dominant city, was both the centre of international commerce (the Lebanese are, after all, descendants of the Phoenicians) and a playground of the wealthy.

All that changed after March 1975, when this beautiful country saw sporadic conflict spiral into fierce civil war between Christians, Muslims and Druzes, who practise a secret religion related to Islam. The complex politics of the ensuing years proved almost as unfathomable as Lebanon sank into a seemingly permanent state of chaos. Assassinations, bombings and kidnappings became routine as numerous factions – Maronite Christians, Druzes, Sunni and Shiite Muslims, including fundamentalists backed by Iran – fought for control.

The situation was complicated by a succession of interventions by Palestinian refugees, the Syrian army, Western and then UN forces as the country became a patchwork of occupied zones and 'no-go areas'. The core religious confrontation has deep roots. In 1860, thousands of Maronites, who are aligned to the Roman Catholic Church, were murdered by Druzes, who are so tangential to other Islamic sects that they are not now regarded as Muslims, and Muslim tolerance to Christian power after independence lasted only until 1958.

Although it was not directly involved, Lebanon was destabilized by the Arab-Israel War of 1967 and by the exile of the PLO leadership to Beirut in 1970. By 1990, the Syrian army had crushed the two-year revolt of Christian rebels against the Lebanese government, but peace proved fragile and a solution elusive. In 1996, Israeli forces launched

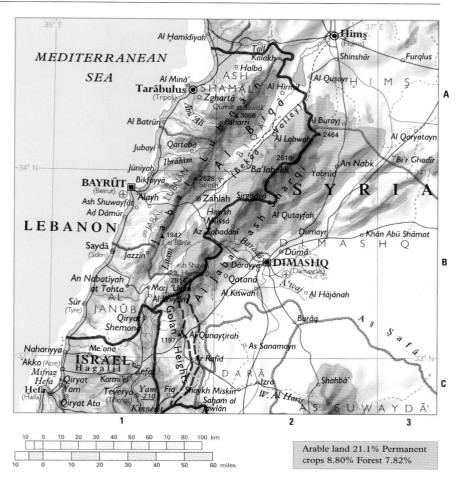

Arable land 21.1% Permanent crops 8.80% Forest 7.82%

a sustained attack on the pro-Iranian Hezbollah positions in southern Lebanon, resulting in heavy civilian casualties. Sporadic fighting continued in southern Lebanon in 1997 and it again flared up in early 2000. In 2001, following the terrorist attacks on the United States, US officials demanded that the government prosecute or extradite alleged terrorists in Lebanon who were on their most-wanted list.

Economy

Civil war almost destroyed valuable trade and financial services which, together with tourism, had been Lebanon's chief source of income. Manufacturing was also hit and many factories were damaged.

Manufactures include chemicals, electrical goods, processed food and textiles. Farm products include fruits, vegetables and sugar beet. The relative stability of the economy in the 1990s led to an annual growth rate of the gross national product of 4.9% between 1990 and 1997. By 1997, Lebanon's per capita GNP of US $3,350 placed it among the 'upper-middle-income' developing countries.

AREA	Palestinian 12%, Armenian 5%,
10,400 sq km [4,015 sq mi]	Syrian, Kurdish
POPULATION	**LANGUAGES**
3,628,000	Arabic (official)
CAPITAL (POPULATION)	**RELIGIONS**
Beirut (Bayrūt, 1,500,000)	Islam 70%,
GOVERNMENT	Christianity 30%
Multiparty republic	
ETHNIC GROUPS	**CURRENCY**
Lebanese 80%,	Lebanese pound = 100 piastres

LESOTHO – SEE SOUTH AFRICA, PAGES 203–205

147

LIBERIA

Liberia was founded in the early 19th century as an American colony for freed slaves who wanted to return to Africa. Its flag was adopted in 1847, when Liberia became independent. The 11 red and white stripes represent the 11 men who signed Liberia's Declaration of Independence.

Geography

The Republic of Liberia is a country in West Africa. Behind the coastline lies a narrow coastal plain. Beyond, the land rises to a plateau region, with the highest land along the border with Guinea.

Climate

Liberia has a tropical climate with high temperatures and humidity throughout the year. The rainfall is abundant all year, but there is a particularly wet period from June to November.

History and Politics

In the late 18th century, some white Americans in the United States wanted to help freed black slaves to return to Africa. They set up the American Colonization Society in 1816, which bought land in what is now Liberia.

In 1822, the Society landed former slaves at a settlement on the coast which they named Monrovia. In 1847, Liberia became a fully independent republic with a constitution much like that of the United States. For many years, the Americo-Liberians controlled the government and US influence was strong. In 1980, a military force composed of locals killed the Americo-Liberian president, and an army sergeant, Samuel K. Doe, became president. Civil war between various ethnic groups erupted in 1989. Peace-keeping forces from other West African countries intervened and a cease-fire was agreed in 1995, when a Council of State, composed of former warlords, was set up. In 1997, one of the warlords, Charles Taylor, was elected president. But fighting continued and Taylor declared a state of emergency in 2002.

Economy

Agriculture employs 70% of the people, but many families live at subsistence level. Food crops include cassava, fruits, rice and sugar cane. Rubber is grown on plantations and cash crops include cocoa and coffee. Liberia's natural resources include its forests and iron ore, while gold and diamonds are also mined. Liberia has an oil refinery, but manufacturing is small-scale. Exports include rubber, timber, diamonds, gold and coffee.

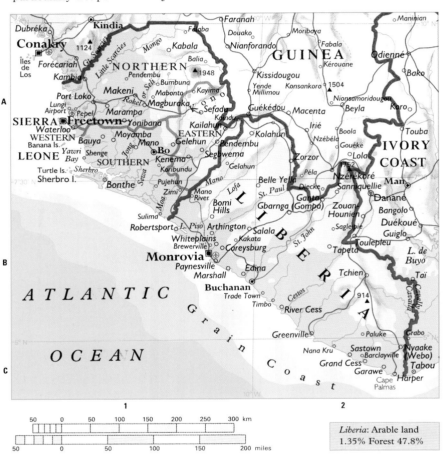

Liberia: Arable land 1.35% Forest 47.8%

AREA	Grebo 9%, Gio 8%,
111,370 sq km	Kru 7%, Mano 7%
[43,000 sq mi]	**LANGUAGES**
POPULATION	English (official), Mande,
3,226,000	Mel, Kwa
CAPITAL (POPULATION)	**RELIGIONS**
Monrovia (962,000)	Christianity 40%,
GOVERNMENT	Islam 20%, traditional
Multiparty republic	beliefs and others 40%
ETHNIC GROUPS	**CURRENCY**
Kpelle 19%, Bassa 14%,	Liberian dollar = 100 cents

SIERRA LEONE

Geography and Climate

The Republic of Sierra Leone contains broad, largely swampy coastal plains, with plateaux and uplands in the north-east. The climate is tropical, with heavy rainfall. In the north, it is dry between December and March. In the south, it is dry in January and February.

History and Politics

A former British territory, Sierra Leone became independent in 1961 and a republic in 1971. It became a one-party state in 1978, but in 1991 people voted for the restoration of democracy. A military group seized power in 1992 and a civil war caused destruction in 1994–5. Elections in 1996 were followed by another military coup. In 1998, the West African Peace Force restored the deposed President Ahmed Tejan Kabbah, but further conflict in 1999 forced Kabbah to enter into a peace agreement with rebel leaders. The peace accord collapsed, but in late 2000 another cease-fire was signed. Disarmament continued throughout 2001 through a UN-brokered peace plan and, in 2002, the war, which had left about 50,000 people dead, appeared to be over.

Economy

The World Bank classifies Sierra Leone among the 'low-income' economies. Agriculture provides a living for 70% of the people, though farming is mostly at subsistence level. Food crops include cassava, maize and rice, the staple food. The most valuable exports include diamonds, bauxite and rutile. The country has few manufacturing industries.

AREA	Temne 30%, Creole
71,740 sq km [27,699 sq mi]	**LANGUAGES**
POPULATION	English (official), Mende,
5,427,000	Temne, Krio
CAPITAL (POPULATION)	**RELIGIONS**
Freetown (505,000)	Islam 60%,
GOVERNMENT	traditional beliefs 30%,
Single-party republic	Christianity 10%
ETHNIC GROUPS	**CURRENCY**
Mende 35%,	Leone = 100 cents

LIBYA

Libya's flag was adopted in 1977. It replaced the flag of the Federation of Arab Republics which Libya left in that year. Libya's flag is the simplest of all world flags. It represents the country's quest for a green revolution in agriculture.

Geography

The Socialist People's Libyan Arab Jamahiriya, as Libya is officially called, is a large country in North Africa. Most people live on the Mediterranean coastal plains in the north-east and north-west. The Sahara, the world's largest desert, occupying 95% of Libya, reaches the Mediterranean coast along the Gulf of Sidra (Khalij Surt). The Sahara is virtually uninhabited except around scattered oases. The land rises towards the south, reaching 2,286 m [7,500 ft] at Bitti Peak (Bikku Bitti) on the border with Chad.

Climate

The coastal plains in the north-west and north-east of Libya experience hot summers. Winters are mild with some rain. Inland, the average yearly rainfall drops to around 100 mm [4 in] or less. Daytime temperatures are high but nights are cool.

Vegetation

Shrubs and grasses grow on northern coasts, with some trees in wetter areas. Few plants grow in the desert, except at oases where date palms provide protection from the hot sun.

History

Libya's first known inhabitants were the Berbers. From the 7th century BC to the 5th century AD, Libya came under the Carthaginians, Greeks and Romans. The Romans left superb ruins, but the Arabs, who invaded the area in AD 642, imposed their culture, including their religion, Islam. From 1551, Libya was part of the Ottoman empire. Italy took control in 1911, but lost the territory in World War II. Libya became an independent kingdom in 1951.

Politics

In 1969, a military group headed by Colonel Muammar Gaddafi deposed the king and set up a military government. Under Gaddafi, the government took control of the economy and used money from oil exports to finance welfare services and development projects. However, although Libya appears to be democratic, political parties are not permitted. Gaddafi has attracted international criticism for his support for radical movements, such as the PLO (Palestine Liberation Organization) and various terrorist groups. In 1986, his policies led the United States to bomb installations in the capital and in Benghazi. Libya has disputes with its neighbours, including Chad, where it sent troops to intervene in a civil war. In 1994, the International Court of Justice ruled against Libya's claim to an area in northern Chad.

In 1999, Gaddafi sought to restore good relations with the outside world by surrendering for trial two Libyans suspected of planting a bomb on a PanAm plane, which exploded over the Scottish town of Lockerbie in 1988. He also accepted Libya's responsibility for the shooting of a British policewoman in London in 1984. Diplomatic relations with Britain were restored, but, in 2002, Libya remained one of the countries blacklisted by the US for supporting terrorism.

Economy

The discovery of oil and natural gas in 1959 led to the transformation of Libya's economy. Formerly one of the world's poorest countries, it has become Africa's richest in terms of its per capita income. However, it remains a developing country because of its dependence on oil, which accounts for nearly all of its export revenues.

Agriculture is important, although Libya has to import food. Crops include barley, citrus fruits, dates, olives, potatoes and wheat. Cattle, sheep and poultry are raised. Libya has oil refineries and petrochemical plants. Other manufactures include cement, processed food and steel. The government has invested money from its oil revenues in developing the economy, providing services for the people, and improving farmland. One of its most ambitious projects is the 'Great Man-Made River' which involves tapping subterranean water from rocks beneath the Sahara and piping it to the dry, populated areas in the north. However, the water in the aquifers is non-renewable and will eventually run dry.

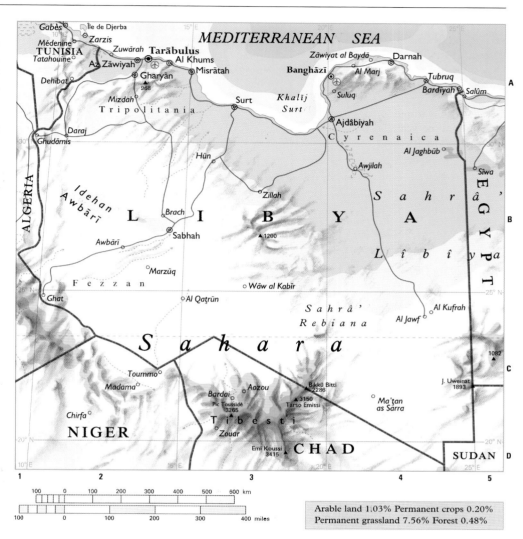

Arable land 1.03% Permanent crops 0.20%
Permanent grassland 7.56% Forest 0.48%

AREA	ETHNIC GROUPS
1,759,540 sq km	Libyan Arab and
[679,358 sq mi]	Berber 97%
POPULATION	**LANGUAGES**
5,241,000	Arabic (official), Berber
CAPITAL (POPULATION)	**RELIGIONS**
Tripoli (Tarābulus, 960,000)	Islam (Sunni)
GOVERNMENT	**CURRENCY**
Single-party socialist state	Libyan dinar = 1,000 dirhams

LIECHTENSTEIN – SEE SWITZERLAND, PAGE 213

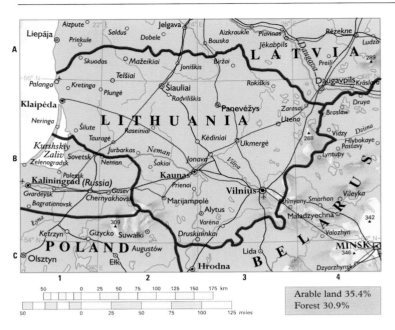

Arable land 35.4%
Forest 30.9%

Geography

The Republic of Lithuania is the southernmost of the three Baltic states which were ruled as part of the Soviet Union between 1940 and 1991. Much of the land is flat or gently rolling. The highest point is a hill, north-east of Vilnius, which reaches 288 m [945 ft] above sea level. From the south-east, the land slopes down to the fertile central lowland, which is used primarily for raising cattle, pigs and poultry. In the west is an area of forested sandy ridges, dotted with lakes. South of Klaipeda, sand dunes separate a large lagoon from the Baltic Sea.

Most of the land is covered by moraine (ice-worn rocks) which was deposited there by ice sheets during the Ice Age. Hollows in the moraine contain about 3,000 lakes. The longest of the many rivers is the Neman, which rises in Belarus and flows through Lithuania to the Baltic Sea.

Climate

Winters are cold. January's temperatures average –3°C [27°F] in the west and –6°C [21°F] in the east. Summers are warm, with average temperatures in July of 17°C [63°F]. The average rainfall in the west is about 630 mm [25 in]. Inland areas are drier.

History

The Lithuanian people were united into a single nation in the 12th century and developed into a powerful kingdom. Its first great ruler was Mindaugas who became king in 1251. In the 13th century, the region was attacked by German crusaders called the Teutonic Knights, but by the 14th century, Lithuania ruled a territory which extended nearly as far as Moscow in the east and the Black Sea in the south. In 1386, Lithuania united with Poland and the two countries became a single state in 1569. This state collapsed in the 18th century and, by 1795, Lithuania came under the control of Russia. Despite rebellions in 1833 and 1863, Lithuania failed to regain its independence.

Nationalism became a major issue in the late 19th century. In 1905, a conference of elected representatives called for self-government, which Russia refused to grant. German troops occupied Lithuania during World War I and, in February 1918, Lithuania declared its independence from Germany and Russia. Although fighting with Russia continued after the end of World War I, Lithuania established a democratic form of government, and in 1920, Russia and Lithuania signed a peace treaty. However, Poland occupied Vilnius from 1920 until 1939, having incorporated it into Poland in 1923. In 1926, a coup overthrew the democratic regime in Lithuania.

In 1939, Germany and the Soviet Union agreed to divide up much of eastern Europe. Lithuania and Vilnius were ceded to the Soviet Union in 1940 and a government acceptable to the Soviet Union was set up. But German forces invaded the area in 1941 and held it until 1944, when Soviet troops reoccupied the country. Many Lithuanian guerrillas fought against Soviet rule between 1944 and 1952. Thousands of Lithuanians were killed and many sent to labour camps.

Politics

From the mid-1980s, while Mikhail Gorbachev was introducing reforms in the Soviet Union, several non-Communist movements developed, calling for independence for Lithuania. From 1988, Lithuania led the way among the three Baltic states in the drive to shed Communism and regain nationhood. In 1989, the parliament in Lithuania declared that Soviet laws were invalid unless they had been approved by the Lithuanian parliament and that Lithuanian should be the official language. It also restored religious freedom and the freedom of the press, abolishing the monopoly of power held by the Communist Party and establishing a multiparty system.

Following elections to parliament in February 1990, in which pro-independence candidates won more than 90% of the seats, Lithuania declared itself independent on 11 March 1990, a declaration that was rejected by the Soviet leaders. This resulted in the occupation of most of the capital by Soviet troops and a crippling economic blockade. After negotiations to end the sanctions failed, Soviet troops moved into Lithuania in January 1990 and 14 people were killed when the troops fired on demonstrators. Finally, on 6 September 1991, the Soviet government recognized Lithuania's independence.

Parliamentary elections in 1992 were, surprisingly, won by the Lithuanian Democratic Labour Party (which was made up of former Communists). Russian troops withdrew from the country in 1993, but the government faced mounting problems as it sought to privatize the economy. In 1996, following new parliamentary elections, a coalition government was set up by the conservative Homeland Union and the Christian Democratic Party. In 1998, an independent, Valdas Adamkus, a Lithuanian-American who had fled the country in 1944, was elected president. By the turn of the century, the government was seeking closer ties with the West. Lithuania also had better relations with Russia than the other two Baltic states, partly because ethnic Russians make up a lower proportion of the population than in Estonia and Latvia.

Economy

The World Bank classifies Lithuania as a 'lower-middle-income' developing country. Lithuania lacks natural resources, but manufacturing, based on imported materials, is the most valuable activity. Products include chemicals, electronic goods, processed food and machine tools. Dairy and meat farming are important, as also is fishing. The main exports are textiles, chemicals, mineral products and machinery. Russia and Germany are Lithuania's leading trading partners.

AREA	Russian 9%,
65,200 sq km [25,200 sq mi]	Polish 7%,
POPULATION	Belarussian 2%
3,611,000	**LANGUAGES**
CAPITAL (POPULATION)	Lithuanian (official),
Vilnius (580,000)	Russian, Polish
GOVERNMENT	**RELIGIONS**
Multiparty republic	Mainly Roman Catholic
ETHNIC GROUPS	**CURRENCY**
Lithuanian 80%,	Litas = 100 centai

LUXEMBOURG – SEE BELGIUM, PAGES 52–53

MACEDONIA (FYROM)

Macedonia's flag was introduced in August 1992. The emblem in the centre of the flag was the device from the war-chest of Philip of Macedon; however, the Greeks claimed this symbol as their own. In 1995, Macedonia agreed to redesign their flag, as shown here.

Geography

The Republic of Macedonia is a country in south-eastern Europe, which was once one of the six republics that made up the former Federal People's Republic of Yugoslavia. This landlocked country is largely mountainous or hilly. The highest point is Mount Korab, which reaches 2,764 m [9,068 ft] above sea level on the border with Albania. Most of the country is drained by the River Vardar and its many tributaries. In the south-west, Macedonia shares two large lakes – Ohrid and Prespa – with Albania and Greece. Forests of beech, oak and pine cover large areas, especially in the west.

Climate

Macedonia has hot summers, though highland areas are cooler. Winters are cold and snowfalls are often heavy. The climate is fairly continental in character and precipitation occurs throughout the year. Average temperatures in Skopje range from 1°C [34°F] in January to 24°C [75°F] in July. The average annual precipitation in the city is 550 mm [21 in].

History

Until the 20th century, Macedonia's history was closely tied to that of a larger area, also called Macedonia, which included parts of northern Greece and south-western Bulgaria. The region reached its peak in power at the time of Philip II (382–336 BC) and his son Alexander the Great (336–323 BC), who conquered an empire that stretched from Greece to India. After Alexander's death, the empire was split up by Macedonian generals and it gradually declined. The area became a Roman province in the 140s BC and part of the Byzantine Empire from AD 395. In the 6th century, Slavs from eastern Europe attacked and settled in the area, followed by Bulgars from central Asia in the late 9th century. The Byzantine Empire regained control in 1018, but Serbs took Macedonia in the early 14th century.

However, in 1371, the area was conquered by the Ottoman Turks who ruled for more than 500 years. The Ottoman Empire began to collapse in the late 19th century. In 1913, at the end of the Balkan Wars, the area was divided between Bulgaria, Greece and Serbia.

Politics

As a result of the division of the area known as Macedonia, Serbia took the north and centre of the region, Bulgaria took a small area in the south-east, and Greece gained the south. At the end of World War I, Serbian Macedonia became part of the Kingdom of the Serbs, Croats and Slovenes, which was renamed Yugoslavia in 1929. Yugoslavia was conquered by Germany during World War II, but when the war ended in 1945 the Communist partisan leader Josip Broz Tito set up a Communist government. Tito maintained unity among the diverse peoples of Yugoslavia but, after his death in 1980, the ethnic and religious differences began to reassert themselves. In the early 1990s, Yugoslavia broke apart into five sovereign republics. Macedonia declared its independence on 18 September 1991 and it subsequently avoided the civil war that shattered other parts of the former Yugoslavia.

However, Macedonia ran into problems concerning recognition. Greece, worried by the consequences for its own Macedonian region, vetoed any acknowledgement of an independent Macedonia on its borders. It considered Macedonia to be a Greek name. It also objected to a symbol on Macedonia's flag, which was associated with Philip of Macedon, and a reference in the country's constitution to the desire to reunite the three parts of the old Macedonia.

Macedonia adopted a new clause in its constitution rejecting all claims on Greek territory and, in 1993, it joined the United Nations under the name of The Former Yugoslav Republic of Macedonia (FYROM). In late 1993, all EU countries, except for Greece, were establishing diplomatic relations with the FYROM. Greece barred

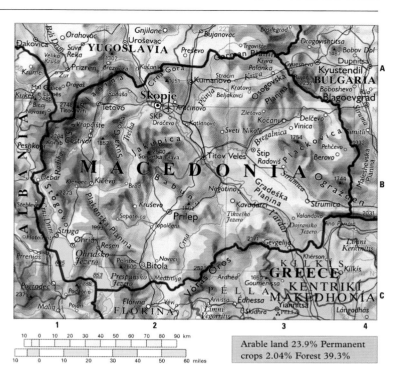

Arable land 23.9% Permanent crops 2.04% Forest 39.3%

Macedonian trade in 1994, but lifted the ban in 1995. In 1999, Macedonia's stability was threatened when Albanian-speaking refugees flooded into Macedonia from Kosovo, Yugoslavia. In 2001, Albanian-speaking Macedonians in northern Macedonia launched an armed struggle. The uprising ended when the government introduced changes that gave Albanian-speakers increased rights, including the recognition of Albanian as an official language.

Economy

According to the World Bank, Macedonia ranks as a 'lower-middle-income' developing country. Manufactures dominate the country's exports. Macedonia mines coal, but has to import all its oil and natural gas. Chromium, copper, iron ore, lead, manganese, uranium and zinc are also mined. Manufactures include cement, chemicals, cigarettes, cotton fabric, footwear, iron and steel, refrigerators, sulphuric acid, tobacco products and wool yarn.

Agriculture employs 9% of the population, as compared with 23% in manufacturing and mining. Most other people work in service industries, including government and defence. About a quarter of the land is farmed and major crops include cotton, fruits, including grapes, maize, potatoes, tobacco, vegetables and wheat. Cattle, pigs, poultry and sheep are also raised, and the country produces most of its basic food needs. Forestry is another important activity in some areas.

The country's main exports are manufactures, machinery and transport equipment, food products, raw materials and chemicals. The leading trading partners include Germany, Russia and Italy.

AREA	Albanian 23%,
25,710 sq km	Turkish 4%,
[9,927 sq mi]	Romanian 2%,
POPULATION	Serb 2%
2,046,000	**LANGUAGES**
CAPITAL (POPULATION)	Macedonian and Albanian
Skopje	(both official)
(541,000)	**RELIGIONS**
GOVERNMENT	Macedonian Orthodox,
Multiparty republic	Islam
ETHNIC GROUPS	**CURRENCY**
Macedonian 67%,	Dinar = 100 paras

The colours on this flag are those used on historic flags in South-east Asia. It was from this region that the ancestors of many Madagascans came around 2,000 years ago. This flag was adopted in 1958, when Madagascar became a self-governing republic under French rule.

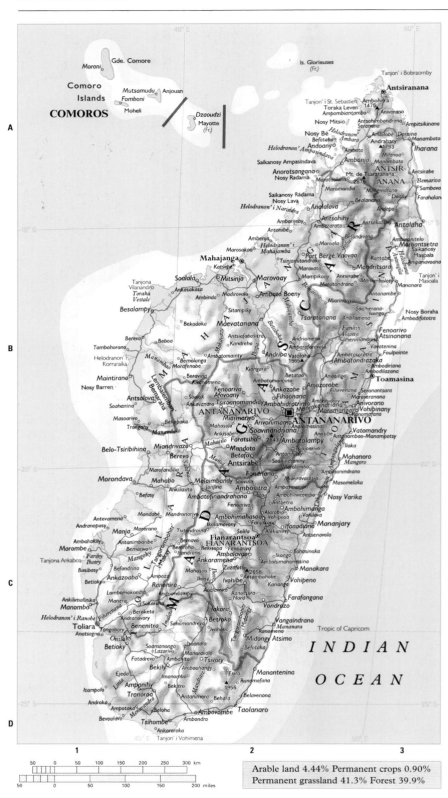

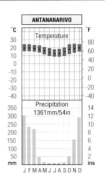

MADAGASCAR (ANTANANARIVO)

Apart from the east coast, which has rain at all seasons, Madagascar has a summer rainy season and a winter dry season. Antananarivo's high altitude moderates temperatures. In February tropical cyclones may affect the island. On a few occasions temperatures have exceeded 30°C [86°F].

History and Politics

People from South-east Asia began to settle on Madagascar around 2,000 years ago. Other immigrants from Africa and Arabia settled on the coasts. The Malagasy language is of South-east Asian origin, though it included words from Arabic, Bantu languages and European languages. The first Europeans to reach Madagascar were Portuguese. Later, the island, which was ruled by powerful monarchs, became a haven for pirates. France made contacts with the island in the 1860s. Finally, French troops defeated a Malagasy army in 1895 and Madagascar became a French colony. In 1960, it achieved full independence as the Malagasy Republic.

In 1972, army officers seized control and, in 1975, under the leadership of Lt-Commander Didier Ratsiraka, the country was renamed Madagascar. Parliamentary elections were held in 1977, but Ratsiraka remained president of a one-party socialist state. The government resigned in 1991 following large demonstrations. In 1992–3, Ratsiraka was defeated by the opposition leader, Albert Zafy, but Ratsiraka returned to power following presidential elections in 1996. In 2002, Madagascar came to the brink of civil war when Ratsiraka and his opponent, Marc Ravalomanana, both claimed victory in presidential elections.

Economy

Madagascar is one of the world's poorest countries. The land has been badly eroded because of the cutting down of the forests and overgrazing of the grasslands. Farming, fishing and forestry employ about 80% of the people.

The country's food crops include bananas, cassava, rice and sweet potatoes. Coffee is the leading export. Other exports include cloves, sisal, sugar and vanilla. There are few manufacturing industries and mining is unimportant at present.

Arable land 4.44% Permanent crops 0.90%
Permanent grassland 41.3% Forest 39.9%

AREA	Betsileo 11%, Tsimihety
587,040 sq km	7%, Sakalava 6%
[226,656 sq mi]	**LANGUAGES**
POPULATION	Malagasy and French
15,983,000	(both official)
CAPITAL (POPULATION)	**RELIGIONS**
Antananarivo (1,053,000)	Traditional beliefs 52%,
GOVERNMENT	Christianity 41%,
Republic	Islam 7%
ETHNIC GROUPS	**CURRENCY**
Merina 27%,	Malagasy franc
Betsimisaraka 15%,	= 100 centimes

Geography and Climate

The Democratic Republic of Madagascar, in south-eastern Africa, is an island nation, which has a larger area than France. Behind the narrow eastern coastal plains is a highland zone, mostly between 610 m and 1,220 m [2,000–4,000 ft] above sea level. Some volcanic peaks, such as Tsaratanana in the north, rise above this level. Broad plains border the Mozambique Channel in the west. The altitude moderates temperatures in the highlands. Winters (April–September) are dry, but heavy rains occur in summer. The eastern coastlands are warm and humid. The west is drier, and the south and south-west are hot and dry.

MADEIRA – SEE ATLANTIC OCEAN, PAGES 41–43

MALAWI

The colours in Malawi's flag come from the flag of the Malawi Congress Party, which was adopted in 1953. The symbol of the rising sun was added when Malawi became independent from Britain in 1964. It represents the beginning of a new era for Malawi and Africa.

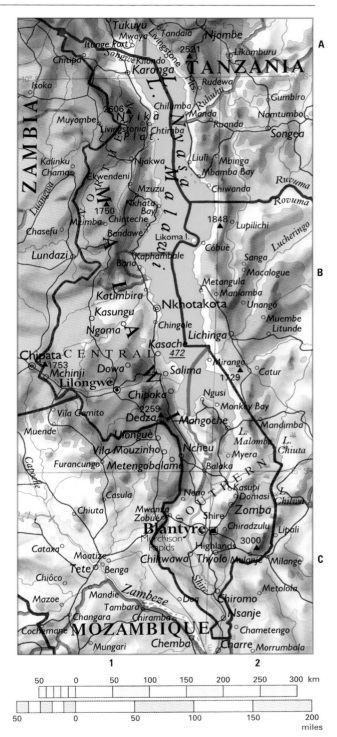

Geography and Climate

The Republic of Malawi in southern Africa is a small, landlocked and oddly shaped country, which is nowhere more than 160 km [100 mi] wide. Its dominant physical feature is Lake Malawi, which is drained in the south by the River Shire, a tributary of the Zambezi. The highest point is Mulanje, which reaches 3,000 m [9,843 ft] in the south-east.

While the low-lying areas of Malawi are hot and humid all year round, the uplands have a pleasant climate. Lilongwe, at about 1,100 m [3,609 ft] above sea level, has a warm and sunny climate. Frosts sometimes occur in July and August, in the middle of the long dry season. The wet season extends from November to May. Wooded savanna and tropical grasslands cover much of the country, with swampy vegetation in many river valleys.

History and Politics

The Bantu-speaking ancestors of the people of Malawi, who first reached the area around 2,000 years ago, introducing an iron age culture, developed kingdoms in the region. In the first half of the 19th century, two other Bantu-speaking groups, the Ngoni (or Angoni) and the Yao invaded the area. The Yao took slaves and sold them to Arabs who traded along the coast. In 1859, the British missionary-explorer David Livingstone reached the area and was horrified by the cruelty of the slave trade. In 1875, the Free Church of Scotland established a mission in the area, while Scottish businessmen worked to found businesses to replace the slave trade. The British made treaties with local chiefs on the western banks of what was then called Lake Nyasa and, in 1889, the area was made the British Protectorate of Nyasaland.

In 1953, Britain made the protectorate part of the Federation of Rhodesia and Nyasaland. This included Northern Rhodesia (now Zambia) and Southern Rhodesia (Zimbabwe). The people of Nyasaland opposed the creation of the federation, fearing domination by the white minority community in Southern Rhodesia. In 1958, Dr Hastings Kamuzu Banda, a doctor educated in the United States, took over the leadership of the opposition to the federation and also to the continuance of British rule. Faced with mounting protests, especially in Nyasaland and Northern Rhodesia, Britain dissolved the federation in 1963. During 1964, Nyasaland became fully independent as Malawi, the name of a kingdom that existed in the area in the 16th century. Banda became the country's first prime minister and, in 1966, after the country adopted a new constitution, making the country a republic, Banda became the first president.

Malawi's recent history was largely dominated by Banda who declared Malawi a one-party republic in 1966 and himself president for life in 1971. However, his autocratic regime differed from most of black Africa in being conservative and pragmatic – hostile to its socialist neighbours, but friendly with South Africa. At first, his austerity programme and agricultural policies seemed to have wrought an economic miracle, but a swift decline in the 1980s, combined with the problems arising from the arrival of a million refugees from war-torn Mozambique, led to a return to poverty, despite massive aid packages. Another immediate and ongoing problem was the high incidence of AIDS, which put pressure on the country's limited welfare services. Mounting political dissent led to the restoration of a multiparty system in 1993. In national elections in 1994, Banda and his party were defeated and Bakili Muluzi became president. Banda was arrested and charged with murder, but he died in 1997.

Economy

The overthrow of Banda led to a restoration of political freedoms, and the abolition of school fees and school uniforms has nearly doubled school enrolment. However, Malawi remains one of the world's poorest countries. Reforms in the 1990s included the encouragement of small farmers to diversify their production, but free enterprise and privatization have angered some farmers who have suffered from the ending of subsidies. The country lacks mineral resources, and manufacturing and tourism are on a small scale. The country's game reserves, with their limited wildlife, do not compare with those of its neighbours.

Although fertile farmland is limited, agriculture dominates the economy employing more than 80% of the labour force. Tobacco is the leading export, followed by tea, sugar and cotton. The main food crops include cassava, groundnuts, maize, rice and sorghum. Many farmers raise cattle, goats and other livestock.

AREA
118,480 sq km
[45,745 sq mi]
POPULATION
10,548,000
CAPITAL (POPULATION)
Lilongwe (395,000)
GOVERNMENT
Multiparty republic
ETHNIC GROUPS
Maravi (Chewa,
Nyanja, Tonga,
Tumbuka) 58%,
Lomwe 18%,
Yao 13%,
Ngoni 7%
LANGUAGES
Chichewa and English
(both official)
RELIGIONS
Protestant 55%,
Roman Catholic 20%,
Islam 20%
CURRENCY
Kwacha =
100 tambala

This flag was adopted when the Federation of Malaysia was set up in 1963. The red and white bands date back to a revolt in the 13th century. The star and crescent are symbols of Islam. The blue represents Malaysia's role in the Commonwealth.

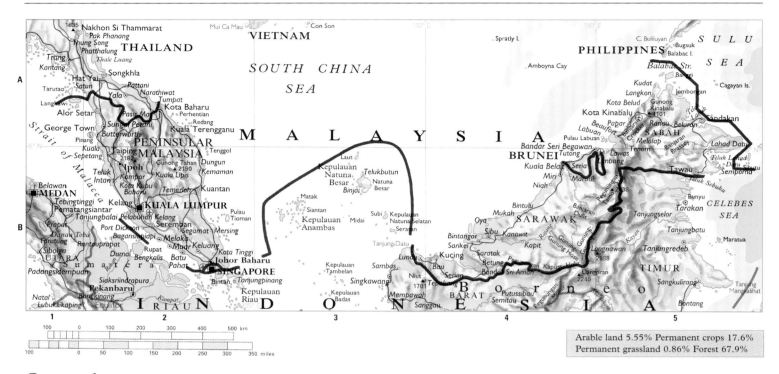

Arable land 5.55% Permanent crops 17.6%
Permanent grassland 0.86% Forest 67.9%

Geography

The Federation of Malaysia consists of two main parts. Peninsular Malaysia consists of 11 states and a federal territory (Kuala Lumpur), with two states (Sabah and Sarawak) and a federal territory (Labuan) in northern Borneo. The Malay peninsula is dominated by fold mountains with a north–south axis. The most important is the Main Range, which runs from the Thai border to the south-east of Kuala Lumpur, reaching 2,182 m [7,159 ft] at its highest point, Gunong Kerbau. South of the Main Range lies the flat, poorly drained lowlands of Johor. The short rivers have built up a margin of lowlands around the coast.

Northern Borneo has a mangrove-fringed coastal plain, backed by hill country, with east–west fold mountains in the interior. The most striking mountain, and Malaysia's highest point, is the granite peak of Mount Kinabalu, in Sabah, which reaches 4,101 m [13,455 ft].

Climate

Malaysia has a hot equatorial climate. Temperatures are high all year, though the mountains are much cooler than lowland areas. Rainfall is heavy throughout the year.

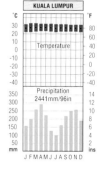

MALAYSIA (KUALA LUMPUR)

Kuala Lumpur experiences uniform temperature throughout the year. The length of daylight and the intensity of the noonday sun varies little from season to season and the sea is always very warm. The daytime temperature is about 32°C [90°F]. Rainfall is high at all seasons, but with a double maximum around the equinoxes, when the tropical rainbelt lies close to the Equator. Rain falls on over 200 days in the year.

History

The ancestors of the Malays probably reached the Malay peninsula from China around 4,000 years ago. The peninsula later became a crossroads for sea traders from China and India. Hinduism and Buddhism were introduced from India in the 9th century AD. An early golden age of Malay political power came in the 15th century with the rise of the Kingdom of Malacca (now Melaka), on the south-western

coast of the Malay peninsula. Malacca controlled the important sea routes and attracted traders from all parts of Asia. Arab traders introduced Islam and, in 1414, Malacca's ruler became a Muslim. Many of the people on the peninsula soon embraced Islam, which remains the official religion of Malaysia today.

The first Europeans to reach the area were the Portuguese and Malacca became a Portuguese possession in 1511. The Dutch, who had been trading in the area during the early 17th century, took Malacca in 1641, and many people from the Dutch-controlled Sulawesi and Sumatra settled in the peninsula, adding to the region's complex ethnic mix. The British, who had been seeking a suitable trading post in South-east Asia, took over Malacca in 1794 and, though Malacca was returned to the Dutch in 1814, it became British in 1824. Through the activities of Stamford Raffles, an agent for the British-owned East India Company, the British occupied Singapore in 1819 and made it a British territory in 1824. In 1826, the British founded the Straits Settlement, which consisted of Penang (now Pinang), Malacca and Singapore. In 1867, the Straits Settlement became a British colony. British rule was gradually extended, with Sabah and Sarawak becoming a British protectorate in 1888. In 1896, Negeri Sembilan, Penang, Perak and Selangor became the Federated Malay States. Under British rule, the economy developed and thousands of Chinese and Indian workers came to work on the rubber plantations.

Japan occupied what is now Malaysia and Singapore during World War II, but British rule was restored in 1945 following Japan's defeat. In the late 1940s and the 1950s, Communists, inspired by the Chinese revolution, fought the British, but guerrilla warfare ended with the independence of the Federation of Malaya in 1957. In 1963, Malaya joined with Singapore, and what is now Sabah and Sarawak, to form the nation of Malaysia, with Tunku Abdul Rahman of the Alliance Party as prime minister. Brunei was invited to join, but no agreement was achieved on entry terms. But, from the start, arguments between Singapore and the Malaysian government occurred, causing Singapore to withdraw in 1965, and become an independent sovereign state.

Politics

One of the problems faced by the new nation was its great ethnic and religious diversity, with Malays of Chinese and Indian origin, many brought in by the British to work the tin mines and rubber plantations. There are also a number of Eurasians, Europeans and aboriginal peoples, notably in Sabah and Sarawak. This patchwork has caused tensions, especially between the Muslim Malays and the politically dominant, mainly Buddhist, Chinese. But while riots did break out in 1969, it never escalated into serious armed conflict, nor did it prevent economic development.

In foreign affairs, Malaysia faced attacks by Indonesia, which objected to Sabah and Sarawak joining Malaysia. Indonesia's policy of 'confrontation' forced Malaysia to increase its defence expenditure. Malaysia was also reluctant to have dealings with Communist countries, but at the same time it was keen to remain independent of the Western bloc and was aware of the need for South-east Asian nations to work together. From 1967, it was playing a major part in regional affairs, especially through its membership of ASEAN (Association of South-east Asian Nations), together with Indonesia, the Philippines, Singapore and Thailand. (Later members of ASEAN include Brunei in 1984, Vietnam in 1995, Laos and Burma (Myanmar) in 1997, and Cambodia in 1999.)

From the 1970s, Malaysia achieved rapid economic progress, especially under the leadership of Dr Mahathir Mohamad, who became prime minister in 1981. Mahathir encouraged the development of industry in order to diversify the economy and reduce the country's reliance on agriculture and mining. For example, the first Malaysian car, the *Proton Saga*, went into production in 1985. In the early 1990s, manufacturing accounted for about 20% of the gross domestic product. By 1996, its share of the GDP had risen to nearly 35%. However, together with most of the 'economic tigers' in Asia's eastern rim, Malaysia was hit by an economic recession in 1997–8. In response to the crisis, the government ordered the repatriation of many temporary foreign workers and initiated a series of austerity measures aimed at restoring confidence and avoiding the chronic debt problems affecting some other Asian countries. In 1998, the economy shrank by about 5%.

During the economic crisis, differences developed between Mahathir Mohamad and his deputy prime minister and finance minister, Anwar Ibrahim. Anwar wanted Malaysia to work closely with the International Monetary Fund (IMF) to promote domestic reforms and strict monetary and fiscal policies. By the summer of 1998, he had gone further, attacking corruption and nepotism in government. Mahathir, who was suspicious of international 'plots' to undermine Malaysia's economy, put much of the blame for the crisis on foreign speculators. He sacked Ibrahim from the government and also from the ruling United Malays National Organization (UMNO). Anwar was later convicted of conspiracy and charged with sexual misconduct. He was jailed for six years.

In late 1999, Mahathir called a snap election to consolidate his power and strengthen his mandate to deal with the economy. With the economy appearing to be rebounding from recession, Mahathir's coalition retained its two-thirds majority in parliament. But many Malays voted for the conservative Muslim Parti Islam. This meant that Mahathir had to rely more on the Chinese and Indian parties in his coalition. The opposition also gained strength by forming a united front at the 1999 elections. In 2000, Mahathir announced that he was serving his last term as prime minister.

Economy

The World Bank classifies Malaysia as an 'upper-middle-income' developing country. Its per capita gross national product of US $3,390 in 1999 was second only to that of Singapore among the members of ASEAN. Manufacturing is the most important sector of the economy and it accounts for a sizeable proportion of the exports. During the 1970s, the economy was stimulated by the arrival of electronics companies from Japan and the United States, whose managements were attracted by Malaysia's social and political stability, its efficient workforce and favourable economic climate. The manufacture of electronic equipment is now a major industry, and, by 1994, Malaysia ranked second in the world in producing radios and fifth in television receivers. Other electronic products include clocks, semiconductors for computers, stereo equipment, tape recorders and telephones. Other major industrial products include chemicals, petroleum products, plastics, processed food, textiles and clothing, rubber and wood products. Partly because of industrialization, Malaysia is becoming increasingly urbanized. By 2000, about 57% of the population lived in cities and towns.

In 1996, manufacturing employed 26% of the workforce, as compared with agriculture which employed 16%. Malaysia leads the world in the production of palm oil, and, in the mid-1990s, it ranked third in producing natural rubber. Malaysia also ranked fifth in the production of cocoa beans, the commercial cultivation of which began only in the 1950s. Other important crops include apples, bananas, coconuts, pepper, pineapples and many other tropical fruits, rice (Malaysia's chief food crop), sugar cane, tea and tobacco. Some farmers raise livestock, including cattle, pigs and poultry. The country's rainforests contain large reserves of timber, and wood and wood products, including plywood and furniture, play an important part in the economy.

The mining of tin originally laid the foundations of industry in Malaysia, but its relative importance has declined and, by the mid-1990s, the country had slipped to eighth place in the world among tin ore producers. Malaysia also has some bauxite, copper, gold, iron ore and ilmenite (an ore from which titanium is obtained). Since the 1970s, the production of oil and natural gas has steadily increased.

The expansion of Malaysia's economy has depended on its ability to expand its export markets. By the mid-1990s, the country's leading exports were machinery and transport equipment, which accounted for about 55% of the value of the exports. Other exports included manufactures, mineral fuels, animal and vegetable oils, inedible raw materials and food.

AREA	groups 58%, Chinese 27%,
329,750 sq km	Indian 8%
[127,316 sq mi]	**LANGUAGES**
POPULATION	Malay (official), Chinese, English
22,229,000	**RELIGIONS**
CAPITAL (POPULATION)	Islam 53%, Buddhism 17%,
Kuala Lumpur (1,145,000)	Chinese folk religionist 12%,
GOVERNMENT	Hinduism 7%, Christianity 6%
Federal constitutional monarchy	**CURRENCY**
ETHNIC GROUPS	Ringgit (Malaysian dollar)
Malay and other indigenous	= 100 cents

BRUNEI

The Negara Brunei Darussalem (or State of Brunei, Abode of Peace, as it is officially known) was a British protectorate until its independence in 1984. Lying on the north coast of Borneo, most of the land is flat and covered by dense rainforest. Temperatures are high all through the year. The average annual rainfall on the coast is 2,500 mm [98 in].

Britain took Brunei in the 19th century in order to protect the shipping lanes between India and China. In 1888, the territory became a British protectorate. Oil and natural gas found in offshore waters have made Brunei a prosperous state and the Sultan is said to be among the world's richest men. Oil, natural gas and oil products make up around 90% of the country's exports. Japan is Brunei's leading export market, but ASEAN nations account for nearly half of the country's imports.

AREA	CAPITAL
5,770 sq km [2,228 sq mi]	Bandar Seri Begawan
POPULATION	**CURRENCY**
344,000	Brunei dollar (BND) = 100 cents

MALDIVES – SEE INDIAN OCEAN, PAGES 122–123

The colours on Mali's flag are those used on the flag of Ethiopia, Africa's oldest independent nation. They symbolize African unity. This flag was used by Mali's African Democratic Rally prior to the country becoming independent from France in 1960.

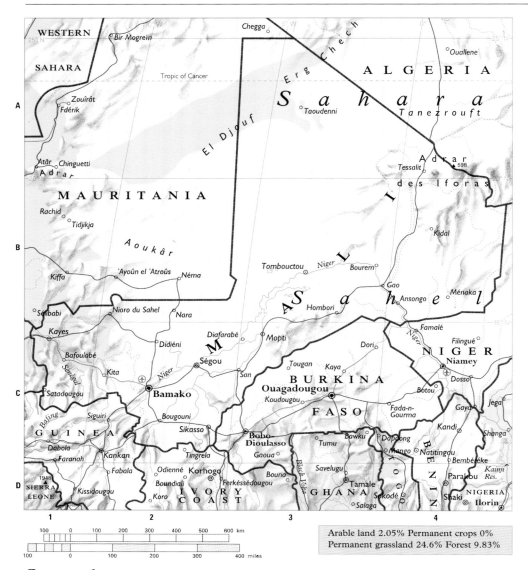

Arable land 2.05% Permanent crops 0%
Permanent grassland 24.6% Forest 9.83%

History

From the 4th to the 16th centuries, Mali was part of three major black African cultures – ancient Ghana, Mali and Songhai. Reports on these empires were made by Arab scholars who crossed the Sahara to visit them. One major centre was Timbuktu (Tombouctou), in central Mali. In the 14th century, this town was a great centre of learning in history, law and the Muslim religion. It was also a trading centre and stopping point for Arabs and their camel caravans. At its height, the Mali Empire was West Africa's richest and most powerful state. France ruled the area, which was then known as French Sudan, from 1893. The country became independent as Mali in 1960, after attempts to create a union with Senegal had failed.

Politics

The first socialist government was overthrown in 1968 by an army group led by Moussa Traoré. But his repressive military, single-party regime did little for the country, despite pressure from the aid donor nations to liberalize the economy. Moussa Traoré was finally ousted by a military group in 1991. Multiparty democracy was restored in 1992 and Alpha Oumar Konaré was elected president. The new government agreed a pact providing for a special administration for the Tuareg minority in the north.

Economy

Mali is one of the world's poorest countries and 70% of the land is desert or semi-desert. Only about 2% of the land is used for growing crops, while 25% is used for grazing animals. Despite this, agriculture employs more than 80% of the people, many of whom still subsist by nomadic livestock rearing. Farming is hampered by water shortages, and the severe droughts in the 1970s and 1980s led to a great loss of animals and much human suffering. The farmers in the south grow millet, rice, sorghum and other food crops to feed their families. The chief cash crops are cotton (the main export), groundnuts and sugar cane. Many of these crops are grown on land which is irrigated with river water. Only a few small areas in the south are worked without irrigation, while the barren deserts in the north are populated only by a few poor nomads.

Geography

The Republic of Mali is a landlocked country in northern Africa. The land is generally flat, with the highest land in the Adrar des Iforas on the border with Algeria. Today, the only permanent rivers are in the south. The main rivers are the Sénégal, which flows westwards to the Atlantic Ocean to the north of Kayes, and the Niger, which makes a large turn, called the Niger Bend, in south-central Mali.

Climate

Northern Mali is part of the Sahara, with a hot, practically rainless climate. But the south has enough rain for farming. In the south-west of the country, unpleasant weather is experienced when dry and dusty harmattan winds blow from the Sahara Desert.

MALI (BAMAKO)

Bamako, situated in the south-west region of the country, experiences a tropical climate. There is a distinct rainy season that occurs between May and October. The average annual rainfall amount has been recorded at around 1,120 mm [45 in]. Temperatures are very constant and relatively high throughout the year, ranging from an average of 24°C [75°F] in January to 27°C [81°F] in July.

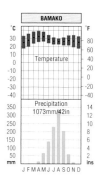

AREA	14%, Senufo 12%, Soninke 9%,
1,240,190 sq km [478,837 sq mi]	Tuareg 7%, Songhai 7%, Malinke
POPULATION	(Mandingo or Mandinke) 7%
11,009,000	**LANGUAGES**
CAPITAL (POPULATION)	French (official), Voltaic languages
Bamako (810,000)	**RELIGIONS**
GOVERNMENT	Islam 90%, traditional beliefs 9%,
Multiparty republic	Christianity 1%
ETHNIC GROUPS	**CURRENCY**
Bambara 32%, Fulani (or Peul)	CFA franc = 100 centimes

MALTA – SEE CYPRUS, PAGE 91;
MARSHALL ISLANDS – SEE PACIFIC OCEAN, PAGES 174–178;
MARTINIQUE – SEE CARIBBEAN SEA, PAGES 71–76

MAURITANIA

The Islamic Republic of Mauritania adopted its flag in 1959, the year before it became fully independent from France. It features a yellow star and crescent. These are traditional symbols of the national religion, Islam, as also is the colour green.

Geography

The Islamic Republic of Mauritania in north-western Africa is nearly twice the size of France, though France has more than 21 times as many people. Over two-thirds of the land is barren, most of it being part of the Sahara, the world's largest desert. Apart from a few nomads, most Mauritanians live in the south, either on the plains bordering the Senegal River in the south-west or on the tropical savanna in the south-east. The highest point, Kediet Ijill, reaches 915 m [3,002 ft] above sea level. It is an area rich in haematite (high-quality iron ore).

Climate

The amount of rainfall and the length of the rainy season increase from north to south. Much of the land is desert, with dry north-east and easterly winds all year. But south-westerly winds bring summer rain to the south.

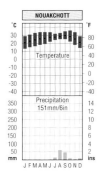

MAURITANIA
(NOUAKCHOTT)

Nouakchott is situated in the south of the country, where south-westerlies bring rain in summer. Sunshine hours and temperatures are very high, every month having recorded over 40°C [104°F]. The monthly temperature ranges from 30°C [86°F], from August to October, to 20°C [68°F] in January.

History

From the 4th to the 16th centuries, parts of Mauritania belonged to two great African empires – ancient Ghana and Mali. Portuguese explorers arrived in the 1440s. But European contact did not begin in the area until the 17th century when trade in gum arabic, a substance obtained from an acacia tree, became important. Britain, France and the Netherlands were all interested in this trade.

France set up a protectorate in Mauritania in 1903, attempting to exploit the trade in gum arabic. The country became a territory of French West Africa and a French colony in 1920. French West Africa was a huge territory, which included present-day Benin, Burkina Faso, Guinea, Ivory Coast, Mali, Niger and Senegal, as well as Mauritania. In 1958, Mauritania became a self-governing territory in the French Union and it became fully independent in 1960.

Politics

In 1961, Mauritania's political parties were merged into one by the president, Mokhtar Ould Daddah, who made the country a one-party state. In 1976, Spain withdrew from Spanish (now Western) Sahara, a territory bordering Mauritania to the north. Morocco occupied the northern two-thirds of this territory, while Mauritania took the rest. But Saharan guerrillas belonging to POLISARIO (the Popular Front for the Liberation of Saharan Territories) began an armed struggle for independence. In 1979, Mauritania withdrew from the southern part of Western Sahara, which was then occupied by Morocco.

Following independence, Mauritania became a one-party state in 1965 and, from 1978, it was ruled by a series of military regimes. In 1991, the country adopted a new constitution when the people voted to create a multiparty democracy. In 1992, an army colonel, Maaouiya Ould Sidi Ahmed Taya, who had served as leader of a military administration since December 1984, was elected president. However, subsequent legislative elections in 1992 were boycotted by opposition parties who alleged fraud. Taya was re-elected in 1997.

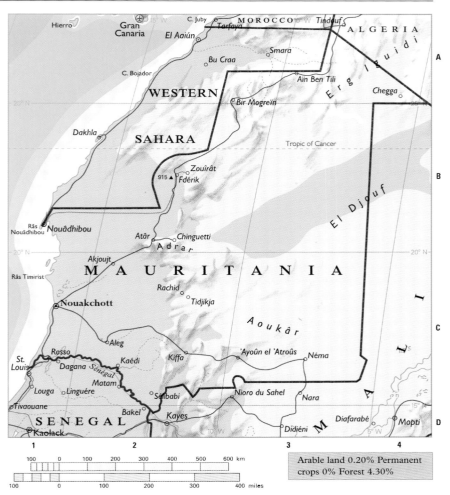

Arable land 0.20% Permanent crops 0% Forest 4.30%

Economy

The World Bank classifies Mauritania as a 'low-income' developing country. Agriculture employs 69% of the people, though the majority live at subsistence level. Many are still cattle herders who drive their herds from the Senegal River through the Sahelian steppelands, coinciding with the seasonal rains. However, droughts in the 1980s greatly reduced the domestic animal populations, forcing many nomadic farmers to seek help in urban areas. Farmers in the south-east grow such crops as beans, dates, millet, rice and sorghum. Rich fishing grounds lie off the coast. However, in the early 2000s, a deal with the EU enabling 250 EU boats to operate in the area was depleting fish stocks and threatening the local fishing industry.

The country's chief natural resource is iron ore and the vast reserves around Fderik provide a major source of revenue. Besides iron ore, Mauritania's other leading exports include fish and cephalopods. Other exports include animal products, dates and gum arabic.

AREA	Wolof 7%, Tukulor 5%,
1,030,700 sq km [397,953 sq mi]	Soninke 3%, Fulani 1%
POPULATION	**LANGUAGES**
2,747,000	Arabic and Wolof
CAPITAL (POPULATION)	(both official),
Nouakchott (735,000)	French
GOVERNMENT	**RELIGIONS**
Multiparty Islamic republic	Islam 99%
ETHNIC GROUPS	**CURRENCY**
Moor (Arab-Berber) 70%,	Ouguiya = 5 khoums

MAURITIUS – SEE INDIAN OCEAN, PAGES 122–123

Mexico's flag dates from 1821. The stripes were inspired by the French tricolour. The emblem in the centre contains an eagle, a snake and a cactus. It is based on an ancient Aztec legend about the founding of their capital, Tenochtitlán (now Mexico City).

Arable land 12.1% Permanent crops 0.83%
Permanent grassland 39% Forest 25.5%

Geography

The United Mexican States, as Mexico is officially named, is the world's most populous Spanish-speaking country. Mountain ranges and plateaux cover about two-thirds of the land, with extensive coastal plains, especially along the Gulf of Mexico. The chief natural region is the Plateau of Mexico, which is bordered by two ranges: the Sierra Madre Occidental and the Sierra Madre Oriental. The southern part of the Plateau of Mexico is dotted with volcanoes, many of which are active. The volcanoes include the snow-capped Orizaba (also called Citlaltépetl), which reaches 5,700 m [18,701 ft], and Popocatépetl, which stands close to Mexico City.

Besides frequent volcanic activity, this region is also prone to many earthquakes. Earthquakes occur as a relatively small plate, underlying the Pacific Ocean west of south-western Mexico and Central America, sinks down in occasional jerky movements beneath the south-western tip of the North American plate. Such a plate movement, with its epicentre 400 km [250 mi] west of Mexico City, triggered the 1985 earthquake, measured at 8.1 on the Richter scale, that led to about 10,000 deaths in the capital. The massive damage was attributed to the fact that Mexico City stands on thick silt deposits formed on an old

lake floor. Regions between Mexico City and the epicentre were relatively undamaged.

Mexico also contains two large peninsulas: the isolated Baja (Lower) California in the north-west with its mountainous core, and the Yucatan Peninsula, a low, flat limestone plateau in the south-east. Southern Mexico contains two highland regions broken only by the low, narrow isthmus of Tehuantepec: the Southern Uplands, which include the Sierra Madre del Sur, and the Chiapas Highlands which extend to the border with Guatemala in Central America.

Climate

The climate is especially affected by the altitude. There are three main altitudinal climatic zones. The *tierra caliente* (hot land) includes regions up to 910 m [3,000 ft], the *tierra templada* (temperate land) extends from 910 m to 1,800 m [3,000–6,000 ft], while the *tierra fria* (cold land) lies above 1,800 m [6,000 ft]. The highest peaks in the *tierra fria* are always snow-capped. The effects of altitude are evident by comparing the dry, sunny climate of the resort of Acapulco with the much cooler Mexico City, which lies at about 2,300 m [7,546 ft] above sea level. Most rainfall occurs in summer. More than 70% of the country is arid. Northern Mexico contains deserts and semi-deserts, where many kinds of cactus plants are found, though mountains with higher rainfall are forested.

MEXICO – MEXICO CITY

The tropical climate at Mexico City lacks a winter season. The weather is cool and dry, except during the rainy season, which runs from May through to September. The annual median temperature is 18°C [64°F]. The warmer months are July and August, when temperatures average around 21°C [70°F]. Night frosts occur during December, and sudden temperature changes are usual.

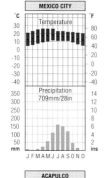

ACAPULCO

Acapulco, on the Pacific coast, has high rainfall in the form of storms. Around 1,500 mm [59 in] falls in a year but on only 70 days – 50 of them between June and September. Practically no rain falls from February to April. On average there are over 7 hours of sunshine each day with over 9 hours in the rainless months. The climate is hot, every day recording over 30°C [86°F], but this falls towards 20°C [68°F] at night.

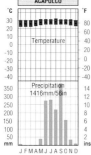

Vegetation

The vegetation of Mexico ranges from deserts in the north to rainforests in the south. The country also has areas of tropical grassland. The high mountains contain zones of vegetation which vary according to the altitude.

History

The Pre-Colombian civilizations that flourished for centuries before the Spanish conquest still play a strong role in fostering Mexican national identity. The Olmecs, the classical cultures of Teotihuacán, the Zapotecs and the Toltecs all left remarkable architectural monuments, though the most outstanding culture in Mexico and Central America was that of the Maya. The Maya civilization flourished from the 3rd to the 10th centuries and extended from the Yucatán Peninsula to Honduras. The magnificent ruins left by the Maya and other cultures in Mexico and Central America now attract visitors from all over the world.

However, the culture that was at its height when Mexico succumbed to the Spanish *conquistadores* was that of the Aztecs. The Aztecs invaded central Mexico during the 13th century and founded their island-city of Tenochtitlán in Lake Texcoco in 1325. During the 15th century, they conquered neighbouring states and drew tribute from an empire that extended from the Pacific to the Gulf of Mexico and into northern Central America. Spain conquered the Aztecs in 1519–21. In the early 17th century, the Spaniards drained Lake Texcoco in order to expand the new capital of Mexico City.

Spain ruled Mexico until the country gained its independence in 1821. In the 1830s and 1840s, Mexico lost land to the United States. The mid-19th century was a time of upheaval and, in 1862, British, French and Spanish troops arrived in Mexico after the government stopped payments on its national debts. The British and Spanish troops soon left, but the French invaded Mexico City in 1863. In 1864, Maximilian, brother of the emperor of Austria, was proclaimed emperor. But Mexican forces regained power in 1867, and Maximilian was shot. Between 1876 and 1880, and also from 1884 to 1911, Mexico was ruled as a dictatorship by Porfirio Diaz, a mestizo general. This time of relative stability led to an expansion of Mexico's economy. However, the peasants received few of the benefits, while the big landowners, businessmen and foreign investors prospered.

Politics

Between 1910 and 1921, violent revolutions caused chaos. Reforms were introduced in the 1920s and, in 1929, the Institutional Revolutionary Party (PRI) was formed. The PRI won every election from 1929 until 1997, when opposition parties gained a majority in the Chamber of Deputies. However, the PRI leader, Ernesto Zedillo Ponce de Leon, who had been sworn in as the country's president in 1994, remained in office. The 71-year-long dominance of the PRI in Mexican politics was finally ended in 2000 when Vicente Fox Quesada of the centre-right National Action Party defeated the PRI candidate, Francisco Labastida, in presidential elections.

Mexico faces many problems, including unemployment, poverty and rapid urbanization. The country's recent history has been marked by massive migrations of people. Many have moved from rural areas to cities, especially the capital, which has become one of the world's largest urban areas. Others have emigrated illegally to the United States, where they hope to enjoy higher living standards. Other problems faced by Mexico in the 1990s were demands by Native American groups in the south, such as the Zapatista National Liberation Army and the Popular Revolutionary Army, for increased rights for the indigenous peoples and greater democracy in the country. In 2001, President Fox began talks with the Zapatista rebels, who mounted demonstrations in Mexico City to explain their demands. However, despite concessions to Mexican Indians, the problem of their rights remained unresolved.

Economy

The World Bank classifies Mexico as an 'upper-middle-income' developing country. Until the mid-20th century, agriculture and mining dominated the economy, but manufacturing is now the leading activity. Mexico has also been a major oil exporter since the 1970s. Oil revenues have brought many benefits, but Mexico has found it hard to repay its loans whenever the world prices of oil have fallen.

In the 1990s, despite its growing economy, Mexico suffered from severe financial crises. Hope for the future lies in increasing co-operation with the United States and Canada through NAFTA (North American Free Trade Association), which came into being on 1 January 1994. Many believe that, through NAFTA, Mexico will have the chance to attract more foreign investment, reduce the national debt, raise living standards, and enable it to tackle the problem of illegal emigration to the United States.

Agriculture employs about 24% of the workforce. Crops are grown on 12% of the land area, with the best farmland being on the fertile volcanic soils on the southern part of the Plateau of Mexico. The main food crops include beans, maize and rice, while major cash crops include coffee, cotton, fruits and vegetables. Farm animals are raised throughout the country.

Mexico is the world's leading silver producer. It also mines copper, gold, lead, zinc and other minerals. Mexico City is the main industrial centre, but new factories, called *maquiladoras*, have been built near the United States border. Many of them assemble goods, such as car parts and electrical goods, for US companies. Craft products, including silver jewellery, glassware, pottery and textiles, are important, especially for sale to tourists. Tourism is a major activity in Mexico, with visitors attracted by both the ancient ruins and the seaside resorts.

AREA	Amerindian 30%,
1,958,200 sq km [756,061 sq mi]	White 9%
POPULATION	**LANGUAGES**
101,879,000	Spanish (official)
CAPITAL (POPULATION)	**RELIGIONS**
Mexico City (15,643,000)	Roman Catholic 90%,
GOVERNMENT	Protestant 5%
Federal republic	**CURRENCY**
ETHNIC GROUPS	New peso =
Mestizo 60%,	100 centavos

MICRONESIA, FED. STATES OF – SEE PACIFIC OCEAN, PAGES 174–178;
MOLDOVA – SEE ROMANIA, PAGES 188–189;
MONACO – SEE FRANCE, PAGES 100–102

Mongolia's flag contains blue, the national colour, together with red for Communism. The traditional Mongolian golden 'soyonbo' symbol represents freedom. Within this, the flame is seen as a promise of prosperity and progress.

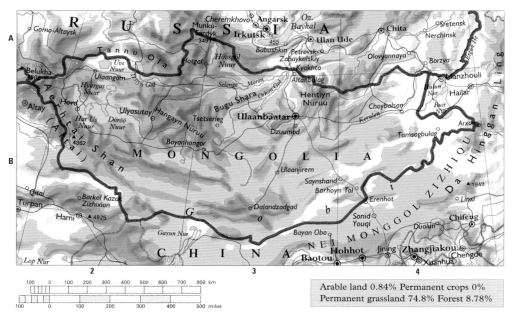

Arable land 0.84% Permanent crops 0%
Permanent grassland 74.8% Forest 8.78%

Geography

The State of Mongolia, which is sandwiched between China and Russia, is the world's largest landlocked country. High plateaux cover most of Mongolia. The highest plateaux are in the west, between the Altai Mountains (or Aerhtai Shan) and the Hangayn Mountains (or Hangayn Nuruu).

The Altai Mountains contain the country's highest peaks, which reach 4,362 m [14,311 ft] above sea level. The land descends towards the east and south, where part of the huge Gobi Desert is situated.

Climate

Because of its remote position, Mongolia has an extreme continental climate, with long, bitterly cold winters and short, warm summers. The average annual rainfall ranges from no more than 500 mm [20 in] in the highlands to 125 mm [5 in] in lowland areas.

MONGOLIA (ULAN BATOR)

Ulan Bator lies on the northern edge of a vast desert plateau in the heart of Asia. Winters are bitterly cold and dry. During the summer, the temperatures are moderated by the height of the land above sea level. A large diurnal temperature range of over 15°C [27°F] occurs all year. Rain falls almost entirely in summer, the amount varying greatly from year to year, and decreasing to the south.

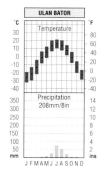

History

In the 13th century, the great Mongol conqueror Genghis Khan united the Mongol people, created a ruthless army, and founded the largest land empire in history. Under his grandson, Kublai Khan, the Mongol empire stretched from Korea and China, across Asia into what is now Iraq. In the north-west, Mongol rule extended beyond the Black Sea into eastern Europe. Learning flourished under Kublai Khan, but, after his death in 1294, the empire broke up into several parts. It was not until the late 16th century that Mongol princes reunited Mongolia. During their rule, they introduced Lamaism (a form of Buddhism).

In the early 17th century, the Manchu leaders of Manchuria took over Inner Mongolia. They later conquered China in 1644 and Outer Mongolia some 40 years later. Present-day Mongolia then became a remote Chinese province with little contact with the outside world.

Outer Mongolia broke away from China following the collapse of the Qing (or Ch'ing) Dynasty in 1911, and the Mongols appointed a priest, called the Living Buddha, as their king. Legally, Outer Mongolia remained Chinese territory, although China and Russia agreed to grant it control over its own affairs in 1913. Russian influence increased and, in 1921, Mongolian and Russian Communists took control of Outer Mongolia. In 1924, they proclaimed the Mongolian People's Republic.

Politics

Mongolia became an ally of the Soviet Union which was set up in 1922. Its support was particularly significant from the 1950s, when the Soviet Union was in dispute with Mongolia's neighbour, China. The Soviet Union helped to develop Mongolia's mineral reserves so that, by the late 1980s, minerals had overtaken agriculture as the country's main source of revenue.

In 1990, the people, influenced by reforms taking place in the Soviet Union, held demonstrations, demanding more freedom. Free elections in June 1990 resulted in victory for the Communist Mongolian People's Revolutionary Party (MPRP). But the new government began to move away from Communist policies, launching into privatization and developing a free-market economy. The 'People's Democracy' was abolished in 1992 and democratic institutions were introduced.

However, the MPRP was defeated in elections in 1996 by the opposition Mongolian Democratic Union coalition. In office, the Democratic Union ran into economic problems and, in the presidential elections of 1997, the MPRP candidate, Natasagiyn Babagandi, defeated the Democratic Union nominee. This achievement was followed by the parliamentary elections in July 2000, which resulted in a landslide victory for the MPRP, who gained 72 out of the 76 available seats in the Great Hural (parliament). The MPRP chairman, Nambaryn Enhbayar, became prime minister.

Economy

The World Bank classifies Mongolia as a 'lower-middle-income' developing country. Many people were once nomads, moving around with their herds of animals. Under Communist rule, most people were moved into permanent homes on government-owned farms. Livestock and animal products remain important, but the Communists developed mining and manufacturing. By 1996, mineral products accounted for nearly 60% of the country's exports. Minerals produced in Mongolia include coal, copper, fluorspar, gold, molybdenum, tin and tungsten. The leading manufactures are textiles and metal products. Chemicals, clothing, food and wood products are also important.

AREA	**ETHNIC GROUPS**
1,566,500 sq km	Khalkha Mongol 85%,
[604,826 sq mi]	Kazak 6%
POPULATION	**LANGUAGES**
2,655,000	Khalkha Mongolian (official),
CAPITAL (POPULATION)	Turkic, Russian
Ulan Bator	**RELIGIONS**
(Ulaanbaatar, 673,000)	Tibetan Buddhist (Lamaist)
GOVERNMENT	**CURRENCY**
Multiparty republic	Tugrik = 100 möngös

MONTSERRAT– SEE CARIBBEAN SEA, PAGES 71–76

MOROCCO

Morocco has flown a red flag since the 16th century. The green pentagram (five-pointed star), called the Seal of Solomon, was added in 1915. This design was retained when Morocco gained its independence from French and Spanish rule in 1956.

Geography

The Kingdom of Morocco lies in north-western Africa. Its name comes from the Arabic Maghreb-el-Aksa, meaning 'the furthest west'. Behind the western coastal plain the land rises to a broad plateau and the ranges of the Atlas Mountains. The High (Haut) Atlas contains the highest peak, Djebel Toubkal, at 4,165 m [13,665 ft]. Other ranges include the Anti Atlas in the south, the Middle (*Moyen*) Atlas and the Rif Atlas (or Er Rif) in the far north.

Climate

The Atlantic coast of Morocco is cooled by the Canaries Current. Inland, summers are very hot and dry and winters are mild. Between the months of October and April, south-westerly winds from the Atlantic Ocean bring rainfall, and snow frequently falls on the High Atlas Mountains.

History

The original people of Morocco were the Berbers. But in the 680s, Arab invaders introduced Islam and the Arabic language. By the early 20th century, France and Spain controlled Morocco, but the country became an independent kingdom in 1956.

Politics

Although Morocco is a constitutional monarchy, King Hassan II ruled the country in a generally authoritarian way between coming to the throne in 1961 and his death in 1999. His successor, King Mohamed VI, faced a number of problems, including finding a solution to the future of Western Sahara.

Economy

Morocco is classified as a 'lower-middle-income' developing country. It is the world's third largest producer of phosphate rock, which is used to make fertilizer. One of the reasons why Morocco wants to keep Western Sahara is that it, too, has large phosphate reserves. Farming employs 44% of Moroccans. Chief crops include barley, beans, citrus fruits, maize, olives, sugar beet and wheat. Processed phosphates are exported, but most of Morocco's manufactures are for home consumption. Fishing and tourism are important.

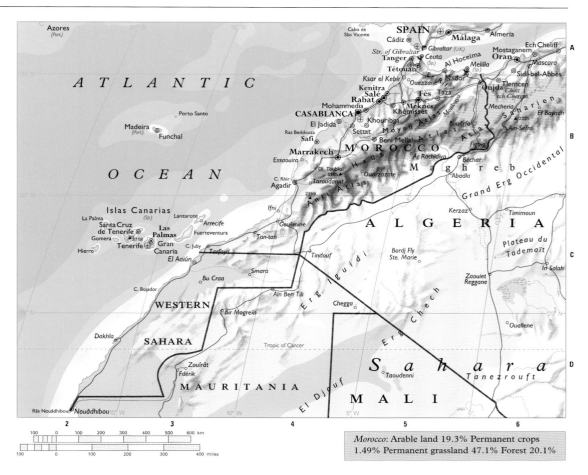

Morocco: Arable land 19.3% Permanent crops 1.49% Permanent grassland 47.1% Forest 20.1%

AREA	ETHNIC GROUPS
446,550 sq km	Arab 70%, Berber 30%
[172,413 sq mi]	LANGUAGES
POPULATION	Arabic (official), Berber,
30,645,000	French
CAPITAL (POPULATION)	RELIGIONS
Rabat (1,220,000)	Islam 99%, Christianity 1%
GOVERNMENT	CURRENCY
Constitutional monarchy	Moroccan dirham = 100 centimes

WESTERN SAHARA

Western Sahara is a disputed territory in north-western Africa. It is mostly barren, though it contains large reserves of phosphates. Spain claimed the area in the early 16th century, though it was under Moroccan control until 1860, when Spain took over.

In 1958, it became a Spanish province called the Province of Spanish Sahara.

In 1976, Spain withdrew. Morocco took the northern two-thirds of the territory, which became known as Western Sahara, while Mauritania took the rest. However, local Saharans in POLISARIO (Popular Front for the Liberation of Saharan Territories) formed a government in exile and called for the establishment of an independent Sahrawi Arab Democratic Republic. POLISARIO also launched a guerrilla war against Moroccan and Mauritanian forces. Hit by the conflict, Mauritania withdrew in 1979, and Morocco took over the entire territory. A cease-fire was declared in 1991, but a proposed referendum on the territory's future was repeatedly delayed owing to the lack of agreement between Morocco and POLISARIO on an electoral register.

AREA	CAPITAL
266,000 sq km [102,700 sq mi]	El Aaiún
POPULATION	CURRENCY
251,000	Moroccan dirham = 100 centimes

Mozambique's flag was adopted when the country became independent from Portugal in 1975. The green stripe represents fertile land, the black stands for Africa and the yellow for mineral wealth. The badge on the red triangle contains a rifle, a hoe, a cogwheel and a book.

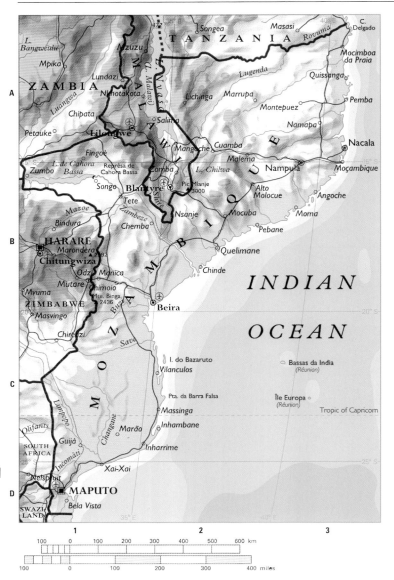

Geography

The Republic of Mozambique borders the Indian Ocean in south-eastern Africa. The coastal plains are narrow in the north but broaden in the south and they make up nearly half of the country. Inland lie plateaux and hills, which make up another two-fifths of Mozambique, with highlands along the borders with Zimbabwe, Zambia, Malawi and Tanzania.

Climate

Most of Mozambique has a tropical maritime climate, with two main seasons. The hot, wet season runs from November to March, with a dry, milder season between April and October. The rainfall varies,

being greatest on the north-western highlands and lowest on the south-eastern lowlands. Temperatures in the lowlands vary from between 20°C and 30°C [79–86°F] in January, and between 11°C and 15°C [52–59°F] in January. The interior highlands are much cooler and generally less humid.

History

Arab traders began to operate in the area in the 9th century AD, and Portuguese explorers arrived in 1497. The Portuguese set up trading stations in the early 16th century and the area became a source of slaves. In 1885, when the European powers divided Africa, Mozambique was recognized as a Portuguese colony. But black African opposition to European rule gradually increased. In 1961, the Front for the Liberation of Mozambique (FRELIMO) was founded to oppose Portuguese rule. In 1964, FRELIMO launched a guerrilla war, which continued for ten years. Mozambique became independent in 1975, when FRELIMO, which followed Marxist-Leninist policies, took over the government.

Politics

After independence, Mozambique became a one-party state. Its government aided African nationalists in Rhodesia (now Zimbabwe) and South Africa. But the white governments of these countries helped an opposition group, the Mozambique National Resistance Movement (RENAMO), to lead an armed struggle against Mozambique's government. The civil war, combined with severe droughts, caused much human suffering in the 1980s. In 1989, FRELIMO declared that it had dropped its Communist policies and ended one-party rule. The war officially ended in 1992 and multiparty elections in 1994 were won by FRELIMO, whose leader, Joaquim A. Chissano, became president. RENAMO's leader, Afonso Dhlakama, accepted the election results and stated that the civil war would not be resumed. This led to a period of relative stability. In 1995, Mozambique became the 53rd member of the Commonwealth, joining its English-speaking allies in southern Africa.

Economy

By the early 1990s, Mozambique was one of the world's poorest countries. Battered by civil war, which had killed around a million people and had driven 5 million from their homes, combined with devastating droughts and floods, the economy collapsed. However, by the end of the century, economists were praising Mozambique for its economic recovery. Although 80% of the people are poor, support from the World Bank and other international institutions, privatization and rescheduling of the country's foreign debts, led to an expansion of the economy and the bringing down of inflation to less than 10% by 1999. However, massive floods at the start of 2000 killed and made thousands homeless, devastating the economy for many years to come.

Agriculture is important. Crops include cassava, cotton, cashew nuts, fruits, maize, rice, sugar cane and tea. Fishing is important and shrimps, cashew nuts, sugar and copra are exported. Despite its large hydroelectric plant at the Cahora Bassa Dam on the River Zambezi, manufacturing is small-scale. Electricity is exported to South Africa.

MOZAMBIQUE (MAPUTO)

Maputo is located on the coast of Mozambique, and lies south of the Tropic of Capricorn. The winters here are dry with average temperatures of around 18°C [64°F] recorded in June and July. The south is drier than the rest of the country and Maputo has an average annual rainfall total of 760 mm [30 in]. This compares with 1,520 mm [60 in] at Sofala, which is situated in central Mozambique.

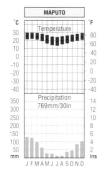

AREA	(Shangaan, Chokwe, Manyika,
801,590 sq km [309,494 sq mi]	Sena, Makua, others) 99%
POPULATION	**LANGUAGES**
19,371,000	Portuguese (official), many others
CAPITAL (POPULATION)	**RELIGIONS**
Maputo (2,000,000)	Traditional beliefs 48%,
GOVERNMENT	Roman Catholic 31%,
Multiparty republic	Islam 20%
ETHNIC GROUPS	**CURRENCY**
Indigenous tribal groups	Metical = 100 centavos

NAMIBIA

Namibia adopted this flag in 1990 when it gained its independence from South Africa. The red diagonal stripe and white borders are symbols of Namibia's human resources. The green and blue triangles and the gold sun represent the country's resources.

Geography

The Republic of Namibia was formerly ruled by South Africa, which called it South West Africa. The country became independent in 1990. The coastal region contains the arid Namib Desert, mostly between 900 m and 2,000 m [2,950–6,560 ft] above sea level, which is virtually uninhabited. Inland is a central plateau, bordered by a rugged spine of mountains stretching north–south.

Eastern Namibia contains part of the Kalahari, a semi-desert area which extends into Botswana. The Orange River forms Namibia's southern border, while the Cunene and Cubango rivers form parts of the northern borders.

Climate

Namibia has a warm and largely arid climate. Average daily temperatures range from about 24°C [75°F] in January to 20°C [68°F] in July. The average annual rainfall ranges from about 500 mm [20 in] in the north to between 25 mm and 150 mm [1–6 in] in the south. Most of the rain falls in summer.

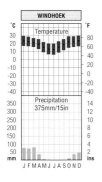

NAMIBIA (WINDHOEK)

Windhoek stands at a height of around 1,700 m [5,500 ft] above sea level on the Namibian Plateau and it is very well isolated from the effects of the cold Benguela Current. Windhoek has an average annual rainfall total of 360 mm [14 in], often occurring during thunderstorms in the hot summer months. However, the rainfall can be unreliable. The climate here is warm and sunny, but frosts may occur during the winter.

History

The earliest people in Namibia were the San (also called Bushmen) and the Damara (Hottentots). Later arrivals were people who spoke Bantu languages. They migrated into Namibia from the north and included the Ovambo, Kavango and Herero. From 1868, Germans began to operate along the coast and, in 1884, Germany annexed the entire territory which they called German South West Africa. In the 1890s, the Germans forcibly removed the Damara and Herero from the Windhoek area. About 65,000 Herero were killed when they revolted against their eviction.

In 1915, South African troops took over the territory. In 1920, the League of Nations gave South Africa a mandate to govern the country. But South Africa ruled it as though it were a South African province.

Politics

After World War II, many people challenged South Africa's right to govern the territory. A civil war began during the 1960s between African guerrillas and South African troops. A cease-fire in Namibia's long-running civil war was agreed in 1989 and the country became independent in 1990. After independence, the government pursued a policy of 'national reconciliation'. An area on Namibia's coast, called Walvis Bay (Walvisbaai), remained part of South Africa until 1994, when South Africa transferred it to Namibia. Elections in 1994 resulted in victory for the ruling South West African People's Organization (SWAPO) and Sam Nujoma was re-elected president.

Namibia's Caprivi Strip, a geographical oddity which European powers gave to Germany in the late 19th century so it would have access to the River Zambezi, became the scene of a rebellion in 1999. A small band of rebels tried, unsuccessfully, to seize the regional capital, Kutima Mulilo, as part of an attempt to make the Caprivi Strip independent. The Strip is populated mainly by Lozi people, who resent SWAPO rule. Lozi separatists also live in Botswana and Zambia.

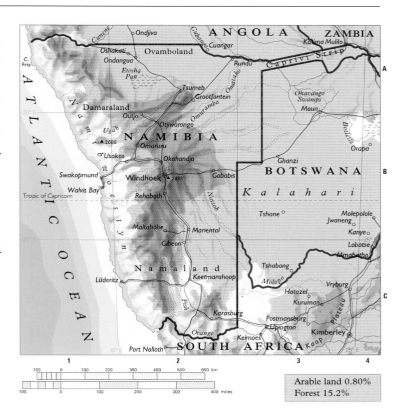

Arable land 0.80%
Forest 15.2%

Economy

Namibia has important mineral reserves, including diamonds, zinc, uranium, copper, lead and tin. Mining is the most valuable economic activity and, by the mid-1990s, minerals accounted for as much as 90% of the exports, with diamonds making up over half the total revenue from minerals.

Farming employs around two out of every five Namibians, although many farmers live at subsistence level, making little or no contribution to the economy. Because most of the land in Namibia has too little rainfall for arable farming, the principal agricultural activities are cattle and sheep raising. However, livestock raising has been hit in the last 20 years by extended droughts that have depleted the number of farm animals. The chief crops are maize, millet and vegetables.

Fishing in the Atlantic Ocean is also important, though overfishing has reduced the yields of Namibia's fishing fleet. The country has few manufacturing industries apart from jewellery-making, some metal smelting, the processing of farm products, such as karakul pelts (sheepskins that are used to make fur coats), and textiles. Tourism is developing, especially in the Etosha National Park in northern Namibia, which is rich in wildlife.

AREA	ETHNIC GROUPS
825,414 sq km [318,434 sq mi], including Walvis Bay, a former South African territory	Ovambo 50%, Kavango 9%, Herero 7%, Damara 7%, White 6%, Nama 5%
POPULATION	**LANGUAGES**
1,798,000	English (official), Ovambo, Akrikaans, German
CAPITAL (POPULATION)	
Windhoek (126,000)	**RELIGIONS**
	Christianity 90% (Lutheran 51%)
GOVERNMENT	**CURRENCY**
Multiparty republic	Namibian dollar = 100 cents

NAURU – SEE PACIFIC OCEAN, PAGES 174–178

This Himalayan kingdom's uniquely shaped flag was adopted in 1962. It came about in the 19th century when two triangular pennants – the royal family's crescent moon symbol and the powerful Rana family's sun symbol – were joined together.

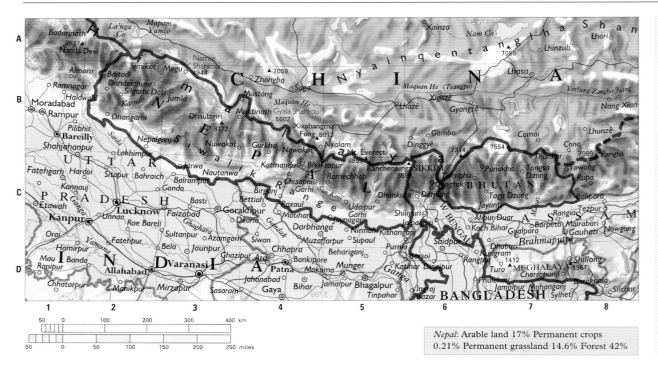

Nepal: Arable land 17% Permanent crops 0.21% Permanent grassland 14.6% Forest 42%

AREA
140,800 sq km
[54,363 sq mi]

POPULATION
25,284,000

CAPITAL
(POPULATION)
Katmandu
(535,000)

GOVERNMENT
Constitutional
monarchy

ETHNIC GROUPS
Nepalese 53%,
Bihari 18%, Tharu
5%, Tamang 5%,
Newar 3%

LANGUAGES
Nepali (official)

RELIGIONS
Hinduism 86%,
Buddhism 8%,
Islam 4%

CURRENCY
Nepalese rupee
= 100 paisa

Geography and Climate

More than three-quarters of the Kingdom of Nepal lies in the Himalayan mountain heartland, culminating in Mount Everest (or Chomolongma in Nepali), at 8,850 m [29,035 ft]. The far lower Siwalik Range overlooks the Ganges plain. The huge differences in altitude give Nepal a wide variety of climatic and vegetation regions.

History, Politics and Economy

Nepal was united by the Gurkhas in the late 18th century, but until 1951, when it was opened up to foreigners, it was a patchwork of feudal valley kingdoms where local leaders displayed more allegiance to their clans than to the state. However, in 1951, the monarchy was re-established. A brief period of democracy ended with the return of autocratic royal rule in 1960 under King Mahendra.

Mass demonstrations followed the return of autocratic rule, and King Mahendra's son, Birendra, was forced in 1990 to concede a new constitution incorporating pluralism and basic human rights. In May 1991, the first democratic elections for 32 years took place and were won by the centrist Nepali Congress Party. In 2001, King Birendra, his queen and six other members of his family were shot dead by his heir, Crown Prince Dipendra. This event was unconnected with the ongoing conflict with anti-royalist Maoist guerrillas in rural areas.

Nepal is one of the world's poorest countries, with a per capita gross national product of US $220 in 1999. Agriculture employed over 80% of the workforce, accounting for two-fifths of the gross domestic product. Export crops include herbs, jute, rice, spices and wheat. Tourism, which is centred around the high Himalaya, has grown in importance since 1951, when the country first opened to foreigners. The government is highly dependent on aid to develop the infrastructure and set up small businesses. There are also plans to exploit the hydroelectric potential offered by the Himalayan rivers.

BHUTAN

Geography and Climate

The Kingdom of Bhutan is a mountainous, isolated country located between India and Tibet.

The climate is similar to that of Nepal, being dependent on altitude and affected by monsoon winds.

History

Bhutan became a separate state in the early 17th century when a Tibetan lama became its spiritual and temporal ruler. In 1907, Bhutan became a monarchy when Ugyen Wangchuk, a powerful local governor, made himself king and set up the country's first effective central government.

Politics

In 1910, Britain took control of Bhutan's foreign affairs, but it did not interfere with internal affairs. The monarch of Bhutan, King Jigme Singye Wangchuk, who came to the throne in 1972, is both head of state and government. However, under a 1949 treaty, India took responsibility for Bhutan's foreign affairs and, later, took control of its defence.

Economy

Bhutan is a low-income developing country. Agriculture employs 90% of the workforce and barley, rice and wheat are the chief crops. People living in the mountains raise cattle and yaks. Economic development depends largely on harnessing the country's hydroelectric potential.

AREA 47,000 sq km [18,147 sq mi]	**ETHNIC GROUPS** Bhutanese 50%, Nepali 35%
POPULATION 2,049,000	**LANGUAGES** Dzongkha (official)
CAPITAL (POPULATION) Thimphu (30,000)	**RELIGIONS** Buddhism 75%, Hinduism
GOVERNMENT Constitutional monarchy	**CURRENCY** Ngultrum = 100 chetrum

NETHERLANDS

The flag of the Netherlands, one of Europe's oldest, dates from 1630, during the long struggle for independence from Spain which began in 1568. The tricolour became a symbol of liberty which inspired many other revolutionary flags around the world.

Geography

The Kingdom of the Netherlands is one of the 'Low Countries'. The others are Belgium and Luxembourg. The Netherlands lies at the western end of the North European Plain, which extends to the Ural Mountains in Russia. Except for the far south-eastern corner, the Netherlands is flat, and about 40% lies below sea level at high tide. To prevent flooding, the Dutch have built dykes (sea walls) to hold back the waves. Large areas which were once under the sea, but which have been reclaimed, are called polders.

The Netherlands is often inaccurately called Holland. This name refers only to the two north-western provinces, where less than 40% of the population lives. The Netherlands is Europe's most crowded country, yet the east and south are relatively sparsely populated. The figure for Zuid-Holland province is about 1,080 per sq km [2,800 per sq mi].

The greatest density of population is in the urban area of Randstad Holland, a horseshoe-shaped region, 50 km [31 mi] in diameter, with Dordrecht at the centre of the loop. This area includes many major cities, such as Hilversum, Utrecht, Dordrecht, Rotterdam, The Hague ('s-Gravenhage), Leiden, Haarlem and Amsterdam. Nearly all this crucial area lies well below sea level.

Climate

Because of its position on the North Sea, the Netherlands has a temperate climate. Winters are mild, with rain coming from the Atlantic depressions which pass over the country. North Sea storms often batter the coasts. Storm waves have periodically breached the dykes, causing flooding and sometimes loss of life.

NETHERLANDS (AMSTERDAM)

Amsterdam has a climate typical of the coastal margins of north-west Europe. Daily and annual temperature range is small. Winters are mild with wind and rain from Atlantic depressions. No monthly minimum temperature is below freezing. The prevailing westerly winds keep summers cool. Rainfall increases from a spring minimum to a maximum in late summer and autumn, falling on about 130 days per year.

Vegetation

Plant and animal life in this densely populated country have been highly modified by human activity. Seen from the air, most of the Netherlands is made up of richly cultivated fields, mainly rectangular in shape, with water-filled ditches between them, along which farmers travel by boat. Control of water to prevent flooding is a major problem. Without the protection of dykes and sand dunes, around two-fifths of the land would be flooded. To prevent soil erosion, the sand dunes that line much of the coast are planted with marram grass and, where possible, trees. Salt-resistant plants also grow along the coast, while woodland covers about a fifth of the land area.

Arable land 27.1% Permanent crops 0.83%
Permanent grassland 31% Forest 10.3%

History

Roman armies led by Julius Caesar conquered the Low Countries in 58 BC. Roman rule continued until the 5th century AD when the area came under the Franks, but when the Frankish Empire was divided in the 9th century, the Low Countries became part of the East Frankish Kingdom.

From the 12th century, the region became increasingly prosperous and this led to the growth of trading towns, which attracted the interest of the rulers of France and Germany. Despite the efforts of nobles to maintain the independence of the Low Countries, the region came under the French dukes of Burgundy in the 14th century. In 1516, Charles V, who inherited the Low Countries from the dukes of Burgundy in 1506, became king of Spain and the area came under Spanish control. In the 16th century, the Protestant Reformation movement gained influence in the Low Countries. The Roman Catholic monarchy tried to suppress Protestantism and conflict broke out in 1568 when William I of Orange, outraged at Spain's behaviour towards Protestants, led a revolt against the rule of Philip II of Spain. The revolt began to falter in 1579, when nobles in what is now Belgium returned to Spanish control, but the Protestants in the northern provinces continued their revolt. The Dutch declared themselves independent in 1581, though the struggle continued until the end of the Thirty Years' War in 1648, when Spain finally recognized Dutch independence.

The 17th century saw a great expansion of Dutch sea power. Dutch explorers, such as Abel Janszoon Tasman, were active in opening up new lands, and expanding trade. The rapid growth of the East India Company made the Netherlands the leading power in what is now Indonesia, while other traders operated in other parts of Asia, including Sri Lanka and Japan. In addition, the Dutch West India Company was active in western Africa and the Americas. For a time, the huge expansion of trade developed by these companies made Amsterdam the world's leading commercial centre.

Between 1652 and 1674, the Netherlands maintained its superiority at sea after fighting three naval wars with England. However, the situation was reversed between 1701 and 1714 when the Dutch lost control of the seas to Britain, a setback which curtailed Dutch trade. During the American Revolutionary War (1775–84), the Dutch supported the Americans, but the Dutch were again defeated by Britain in a naval war between 1780 and 1784. The weakened Netherlands was conquered by France in 1795, while Britain occupied much of the country's overseas territories. In 1806, the brother of Napoleon I, Louis, became king of the country which became the Kingdom of Holland. However, the French were driven out in 1813.

After the Napoleonic Wars, the Congress of Vienna reorganized the countries of Europe. Belgium, Luxembourg and the Netherlands were united to form the Kingdom of the Netherlands. William VI, prince of Orange, became William I of the Netherlands and Grand Duke of Luxembourg. Internal differences caused the break-up of the kingdom. Belgium broke away in 1830, and in 1839 Belgium and the Netherlands were recognized as separate monarchies. When Queen Wilhelmina ascended to the throne in 1890, Luxembourg ended its ties with the Dutch royal family because its laws did not permit a female ruler.

The Netherlands was neutral in World War I, but German troops invaded the country on 10 May 1940. Much of the Dutch fleet escaped and served with the Allies. The people suffered greatly during the occupation and around three-quarters of the country's Jews were murdered, while many other people were forced to work in German factories. By the end of the war, about 270,000 Netherlanders had been killed or had died of starvation.

Politics

After World War II, the Netherlands began to play a major part in European affairs. In 1948, it joined with Belgium and Luxembourg to form an economic union called Benelux and, in 1949, it abandoned its traditional neutrality when it became a member of the North Atlantic Treaty Organization. The country's economic recovery was rapid, and the economy received a further stimulus when it became a founder member of the European Economic Community (EEC) in 1957. The Maastricht Treaty, which transformed the EEC into the European Union, was signed in the Dutch city of Maastricht in 1991. On 1 January 2001, the Netherlands officially adopted the euro, the single currency of the European Union, as its sole currency, replacing the guilder.

Because of ill health, Queen Wilhelmina abdicated in favour of her daughter, Juliana, in 1948. Juliana reigned until 1980 when she, in turn, abdicated in favour of her daughter, Beatrix. The Netherlands is a constitutional monarchy with a parliament which consists of two chambers. The 75 members of the First Chamber are elected by members of the Provincial States, the representative bodies of the 12 provinces, while the 150-member Second Chamber is directly elected. The Hague is the seat of the government, the parliament and the High Court, but Amsterdam is the national capital.

In 1949, after much fighting, the Dutch recognized the independence of its largest overseas possession, Indonesia. In 1954, Surinam and the Netherlands Antilles were granted self-government. In 1962, the Dutch handed over Netherlands New Guinea to the United Nations, which handed it over, as Irian Jaya, to Indonesia in 1963. Surinam became fully independent in 1975, leaving the Netherlands with only two remaining overseas territories, Netherlands Antilles and Aruba, which had been part of Netherlands Antilles until it broke away in 1986.

Partly because of its policies of economic co-operation with other European nations, the Netherlands is now one of Europe's most prosperous countries, with well-developed social services and government-funded health care. However, its high standard of living also owes much to its domestic policies and the determination of its people.

The truth of the old saying that 'God created the world but the Dutch created Holland' was again demonstrated after the North Sea storm of January 1953. During this storm, waves penetrated the coastal defences in the south-western delta region, flooding about 4.3% of the country, destroying or damaging more than 30,000 houses and killing 1,800 people. The Dutch response to the disaster was typical. Within three weeks, a commission of enquiry had recommended the Delta Plan, a huge project to protect the delta region. Completed in 1986, it involved the construction of massive dams and floodgates, which can be closed during severe storms. However, global warming, with its predicted rise in sea levels and increasing frequency of storms, may provide the Netherlands with its greatest challenge of how it can hang on to the land it has so laboriously wrested from the sea.

Economy

The Dutch economy is one of the strongest economies in Europe. Despite its comparatively small size, its economy is the world's 14th largest, with a total gross national product in 1999 of US $397,384 million. The Netherlands is a highly industrialized country and manufacturing and commerce are the most valuable activities. Mineral resources include china clay, which is abundant, natural gas from the North Sea, and coal, though commercial mining ceased in 1965. However, the country has to import many of the materials needed by its manufacturers. The emphasis of modern industry is on oil, steel, chemicals and electrical engineering. The products are wide-ranging, including aircraft, chemical products, electronic equipment, machinery, textiles and vehicles. In the area south of Rotterdam, the Dutch have constructed a vast port and industrial area, Europoort. Together with Rotterdam's own facilities, the complex is the largest and busiest in the world.

Agriculture employs only 3% of the workforce, but, through the use of scientific techniques, yields are high. The use of the land varies. In the west, the concentration on bulb farming is marked near Haarlem in soils of clay mixed with sand. There, too, glasshouse cultivation, combined on a number of holdings with the growing of flowers and vegetables out-of-doors, is widespread. The Dutch cut and sell more than 3 billion flowers a year. Much of the produce is exported, some of it by air to London and other north European cities.

Some soils are better suited to pastoral farming and dairy farming is the leading farming activity, with milk, cheese and butter production. Gouda has a famous cheese market and the well-known red-coated, round Edam cheeses come from northern areas. In the areas above sea level, farming is varied, with a combination of cattle and crops. Major food crops include barley, potatoes, sugar beet and wheat.

The Netherlands is one of the world's leading trading nations. Its chief exports include machinery and transport equipment, food, chemicals and chemical products, petroleum products, iron and steel, and clothing. The main trading partners are Germany, Belgium-Luxembourg, France and the United Kingdom.

AREA	ETHNIC GROUPS
41,526 sq km	Dutch 95%, Indonesian,
[16,033 sq mi]	Turkish, Moroccan
POPULATION	**LANGUAGES**
15,981,000	Dutch (official), Frisian
CAPITAL (POPULATION)	**RELIGIONS**
Amsterdam (1,115,000);	Roman Catholic 34%,
The Hague (seat of government,	Protestant 21%,
700,000)	Islam 4%
GOVERNMENT	**CURRENCY**
Constitutional monarchy	Euro = 100 cents

NETHERLANDS ANTILLES – SEE CARIBBEAN SEA, PAGES 71–76;
NEW CALEDONIA – SEE PACIFIC OCEAN, PAGES 174–178

New Zealand's flag was designed in 1869 and adopted as the national flag in 1907 when New Zealand became an independent dominion. The flag includes the British Blue Ensign and four of the five stars in the Southern Cross constellation.

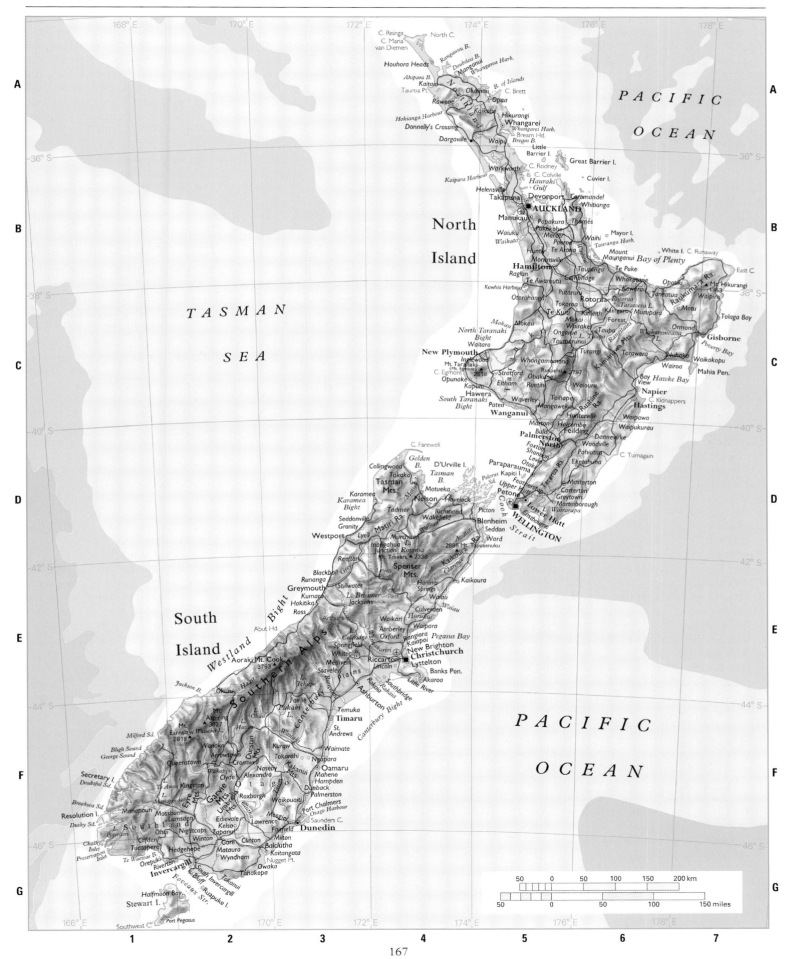

167

Geography

New Zealand lies about 1,600 km [994 mi] south-east of Australia. It consists of two main islands and several other small ones. Geologically part of the Circum-Pacific Mobile Belt of tectonic activity (the 'Pacific ring of fire'), New Zealand is mountainous and partly volcanic. Many of the highest mountains, including the Southern Alps, which contain the country's highest peak, Mount Cook (Aoraki) at 3,753 m [12,313 ft], were thrust up from the seabed in the past 10 to 15 million years. Much of North Island was formed by volcanic activity even more recently, mainly in the past 4 million years. Minor earthquakes are common and there are several areas of volcanic and geothermal activity, especially on North Island.

About 75% of New Zealand lies above the 200 m [650 ft] contour, but in the south-east, rivers have cut broad, fertile valleys between low ranges. New Zealand's only extensive lowland area is the Canterbury Plains.

Climate

Auckland in the north has a warm, humid climate throughout the year. Wellington has cooler summers, while in Dunedin, in the south-east, temperatures sometimes dip below freezing in winter. The rainfall is heaviest on the western highlands.

Vegetation

Because of New Zealand's isolation, almost 90% of the country's indigenous plants are peculiar to the country.

However, much of the original vegetation has been destroyed and only small areas of the kauri forests have survived. Mixed evergreen forest grows on the west side of South Island. Along the Southern Alps, the false beech is the chief forest tree. New Zealand also has large plantations of introduced species, including the radiata pine, which covers large areas on the Volcanic Plateau on North Island, together with willows and poplars which have been planted in areas suffering from soil erosion.

History

Evidence suggests that early Maori settlers who came from islands to the north arrived in New Zealand, which they called Aotearoa, more than 1,000 years ago. The Dutch navigator Abel Janszoon Tasman reached the area in 1642, but, after several of his men were killed by Maoris, he made no further attempt to land. His discovery was not followed up until 1769, when the British Captain James Cook rediscovered the islands and thoroughly charted them. Cook like Tasman recorded the presence of Maoris, who were Polynesians, and hunted and farmed from well-defended coastal settlements.

Sealing gangs, whalers and traders, mainly from Australia, were New Zealand's first European inhabitants, closely followed by missionaries and farmers from Britain and Australia. By the early 1830s, about 2,000 Europeans had settled there. New Zealand remained a lawless frontier territory with no legal government until 1840 when the Treaty of Waitangi signed by Maori chiefs and Captain William Hobson of the British Navy (who became New Zealand's first governor) made New Zealand a British colony. In return, the Treaty gave rights and privileges of British subjects to the Maori people. The following decades saw the arrival of thousands of new settlers from Britain and, by the mid-century, there were more than 30,000 of them. New Zealand set up its first elected House of Representatives in 1852.

Though their relationships with the Maoris, who at this stage outnumbered them by two to one, were generally good, difficulties over land ownership led to conflict between 1845 and 1872. Thereafter, the Maori population declined, partly as a result of contracting European diseases, while the numbers of Europeans continued to increase. British settlers found a climate slightly warmer than their own, with longer growing seasons but variable rainfall – crippling droughts sometimes occurred in dry areas.

From 1884, when the first Merino sheep were introduced from Australia, New Zealand became predominantly a land of sheep, the grassy lowlands, especially on South Island, providing year-round forage. Huge flocks were built up, mainly for wool and tallow

production. From the lowlands, they spread into the hills – the 'high country' – which was cleared of native bush and sown with European grasses for pasture. North Island proved more difficult to turn into farmland, later proving its value for dairying.

New Zealand's early prosperity was finally established when the export of frozen mutton and lamb carcasses began in 1882. Soon, a steady stream of chilled meat and dairy products, and later of fruit, was crossing the oceans to established markets in Britain – New Zealand is still the world's second largest producer of lamb. Wheat and other cereals were also grown. High productivity was maintained by applications of fertilizers, mainly based on phosphate mined on Nauru.

Politics

In 1893, New Zealand became the first country in the world to give women the vote. In 1907, New Zealand became a self-governing dominion in the British Empire (now the British Commonwealth) and New Zealanders fought alongside the Allies against Germany, Italy and Japan in both World Wars. In 1952, New Zealand signed the ANZUS treaty, a mutual defence pact with Australia and the United States. Troops from New Zealand served in the Korean War (1950–3) and a few units later served in the war in Vietnam.

After World War II, New Zealand diversified its economy. Though agricultural products remain the chief exports, fishing and forestry were developed, along with geothermal energy and hydroelectricity. The timber and forest products found valuable overseas markets. The country also began to develop its tourist potential.

However, after Britain joined the European Economic Community (now the European Union) in 1973, New Zealand's exports to Britain shrank from 70% to 10%. Along with its re-evaluation of its defence position through ANZUS, it also had to reassess its economic strategy. This has involved seeking new markets in Asia, cutting subsidies to farmers, privatization and cutting back on its extensive welfare programmes in the 1990s. The rights of Maoris and the preservation of their culture are other major political issues in New Zealand. In 1998, New Zealand completed a NZ $170 million settlement with the Ngai Tahu group on South Island in compensation for forced land purchases in the 19th century. The government expressed its profound regret for past suffering and for injustices that had impaired the development of the Ngai Tahu.

Economy

New Zealand's economy has traditionally depended on agriculture, although manufacturing now employs twice as many people as agriculture. Meat and dairy products are the most valuable agricultural products. In 1995, New Zealand ranked seventh among the world's leading butter producers. In 1999, New Zealand had about 44.5 million sheep, 4.3 million dairy cattle, and 4.6 million beef cattle. Major crops include barley, fruits, potatoes and other vegetables, and wheat. Fishing is also important. The chief manufactures are processed food products, including butter, cheese, frozen meat and woollen products. Food and live animals make up 45% of New Zealand's exports. The country's chief trading partners are Australia, Japan and the United States.

AREA	New Zealand Maori 10%,
268,680 sq km	Polynesian 4%
[103,737 sq mi]	**LANGUAGES**
POPULATION	English and Maori
3,864,000	(both official)
CAPITAL (POPULATION)	**RELIGIONS**
Wellington (329,000)	Anglican 24%,
GOVERNMENT	Presbyterian 18%,
Constitutional monarchy	Roman Catholic 15%
ETHNIC GROUPS	**CURRENCY**
New Zealand European 74%,	New Zealand dollar = 100 cents

NICARAGUA – SEE GUATEMALA, PAGES 110–111

NIGER

This flag was adopted shortly before Niger became independent from France in 1960. The orange stripe represents the Sahara in the north and the green represents the grasslands in the south. Between them, the white stripe represents the River Niger, with a circle for the sun.

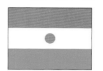

Geography

The Republic of Niger is a landlocked nation in north-central Africa. The northern plateaux lie in the Sahara, while north-central Niger contains the rugged Aïr Mountains, which reach a height of 2,022 m [6,632 ft] above sea level. The rainfall in the mountains – averaging around 175 mm [7 in] per year – is sufficient in places to permit the growth of thorny shrub. However, severe droughts since the 1970s have crippled the traditional lifestyle of the nomads in northern and central Niger as the Sahara has slowly advanced south. The southern region has also been hit by droughts.

The south consists of broad plains. The Lake Chad Basin lies in south-eastern Niger on the borders with Chad and Nigeria. The only permanent rivers are the Niger and its tributaries in the south-west. The narrow Niger Valley is the country's most fertile and densely populated region. Yet Niger, a title which comes from a Tuareg word meaning 'flowing water', seems scarcely appropriate for a country which consists mainly of hot, arid, sandy, and stony basins.

Climate

Niger has a tropical climate and the south has a rainy season between June and September. The rainfall decreases in both quantity and reliability from south to north.

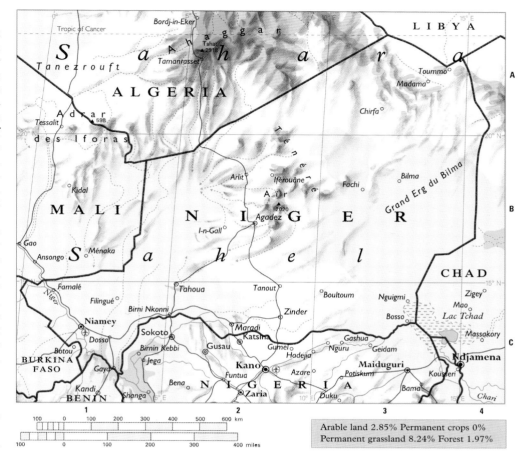

Arable land 2.85% Permanent crops 0%
Permanent grassland 8.24% Forest 1.97%

NIGER (NIAMEY)

The climate of southern Niger is similar to other places within the vast tropical grassland belt of northern Africa – the Sahel. From November to April, the hot, dry harmattan wind blows from the Sahara, the skies are clear and there is no rain. Between March and May the intensity of the sun increases rapidly. But in June, the intertropical rainbelt reaches the region, and the increasing cloud and rain give rise to cooler conditions.

NIAMEY
Temperature
Precipitation
614mm/24in

History

Nomadic Tuaregs settled in the Aïr Mountains around 1,000 years ago. By the 15th century they had built an empire based on Agadez. At around that time, the Zerma-Songhai people founded the Songhai Empire along the River Niger and conquered the Tuaregs, but in the late 16th century Songhai was defeated by a Moroccan army.

Later on, the Hausa and then the Fulani set up kingdoms in the region. European explorers reached Niger in the early 19th century. France became involved in West Africa in the late 19th century and it gained control of Niger in 1900. In 1906, France put down a Tuareg uprising and, between 1922 and 1958, it ruled Niger as part of a huge territory called French West Africa. In 1958, Niger became an autonomous republic and, in 1960, it finally became fully independent.

Politics

Since independence, Niger has been badly hit by severe droughts which have caused extensive damage and suffering. Food shortages and the collapse of the traditional nomadic way of life of some of

Niger's people have caused political instability. In 1974, a group of army officers, led by Lt.-Col. Seyni Kountché, overthrew the country's first president, Hamani Diori, and seized control of the government, suspending the constitution. Kountché died in 1987, and in 1989 civilian rule was restored. A multiparty constitution was adopted in 1992, but the military once again seized power in 1996. The coup leader, Col. Ibrahim Barre Mainassara, was elected president later that year, but he was assassinated in 1999 and replaced briefly by Major Daouda Malam Wanke. Parliamentary rule was restored and, later that year, Tandjou Mamadou was elected president.

Economy

Niger's chief resource is uranium and it is the fourth largest producer in the world. Some tin and tungsten are also mined, although other mineral resources are largely untouched. Despite its resources, Niger is one of the world's poorest countries. Farming employs 85% of the population, though only a small percentage of the total land area can be used for crops and for grazing. Food crops include beans, cassava, millet, rice and sorghum. Groundnuts and cotton are major cash crops.

AREA	Djerma 22%,
1,267,000 sq km [489,189 sq mi]	Tuareg 8%,
POPULATION	Fula 8%
10,355,000	**LANGUAGES**
CAPITAL (POPULATION)	French (official),
Niamey	Hausa, Djerma
(398,000)	**RELIGIONS**
GOVERNMENT	Islam 98%
Multiparty republic	**CURRENCY**
ETHNIC GROUPS	CFA franc =
Hausa 56%,	100 centimes

Nigeria's flag was adopted in 1960 when Nigeria became independent from Britain. It was selected after a competition to find a suitable design. The green represents Nigeria's forests. The white in the centre stands for peace.

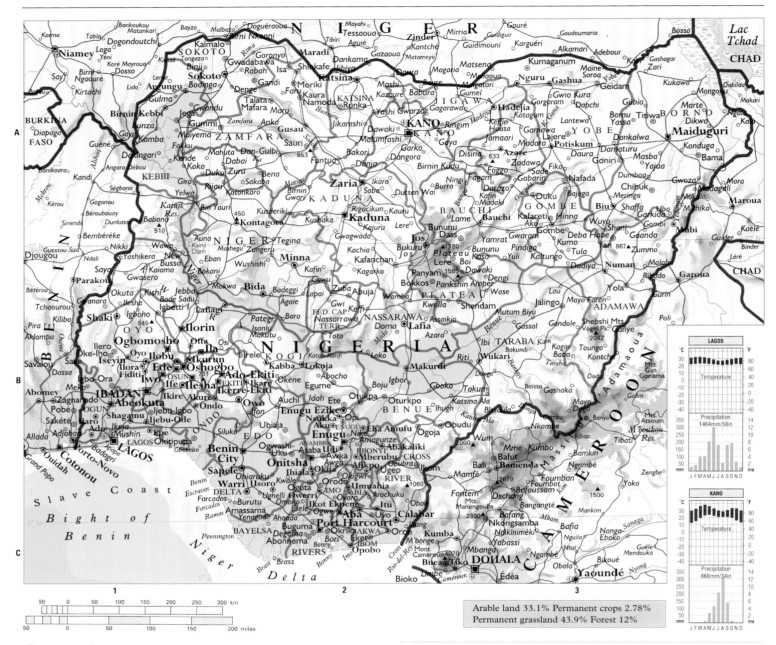

Arable land 33.1% Permanent crops 2.78%
Permanent grassland 43.9% Forest 12%

Geography

The Federal Republic of Nigeria is the most populous nation in Africa. The country's main rivers are the Niger and Benue, which meet in central Nigeria. North of the two river valleys are high plains and plateaux. The Lake Chad Basin is in the north-east, with the Sokoto plains in the north-west. Southern Nigeria contains hilly uplands and broad coastal plains, including the swampy Niger Delta. Highlands form the border with Cameroon.

Climate

The south of the country has high temperatures and rain all year. Parts of the coast have an average annual rainfall of 3,800 mm [150 in]. The north has a marked dry season and higher temperatures than the south.

Vegetation

Behind the mangrove swamps along the coast are rainforests, though extensive areas have been cleared by farmers. The north contains large areas of savanna (tropical grassland with scattered trees) with forests along the rivers. Open grassland and semi-desert occur in drier areas.

NIGERIA – LAGOS

The coastal belt of Nigeria experiences uniformly high temperatures and humidity throughout most of the year. The coolest months of the year are July and August, when the monsoon brings oceanic air from beyond the Equator. Even then the lowest recorded temperature is 16°C [61°F]. There are two periods of heavy rain: the long rains with a maximum during June, and the short rains with a maximum during October, with rain falling on every other day during the month. Humidity in Lagos remains high and sunshine levels are relatively low.

KANO

The north of Nigeria also experiences high temperatures and humidity most of the year. Average annual rainfall is generally less than 1,000 mm [39 in]. For example, Kano, in north-central Nigeria, has an average annual rainfall of 870 mm [34 in]. But during the marked dry season, from October to April, the average rainfall totals only 26 mm [1 in]. Heaviest rains occur from July to September. The hottest period of the year is from March to June; the coolest from December to January.

NIGERIA

History

Among the earliest civilizations that grew up in Nigeria was the Nok (500 BC to AD 200). The Nok civilization, which flourished in a valley near the confluence of the Benue and Niger rivers, was named after a village where black Africa's oldest sculptures, made from terracotta, were first excavated. Northern Nigeria became part of the kingdom of Kanem in the 8th century, while the kingdom of Bornu developed later in what is now north-eastern Nigeria. Powerful Hausa states grew up from AD 1000 and, later, some of them became part of the Songhai Empire which flourished in the region in the 15th and 16th centuries.

Two civilizations in southern Nigeria were known for their superb art. Ife was a major Yoruba culture, which developed around 1,000 years ago. It produced terracotta and bronze sculptures. The other was Benin, which flourished between Lagos and the Niger delta in the 15th and 17th centuries. Benin sculptures, including its famous brasses, were discovered by the Portuguese, who used Benin as a slave trading centre in the late 15th century. Benin declined when it fought wars with other African states that traded slaves with Europeans on the coast.

Britain outlawed slavery in 1807 and, soon afterwards, the British began to trade in agricultural products. In 1851, Britain made Lagos a base from which they could continue their efforts to stop the slave trade. During the second half of the 19th century, Britain gradually extended its influence over Nigeria. By 1914 it ruled the entire country.

Politics

Nigeria became independent in 1960 and a federal republic in 1963. A federal constitution dividing the country into regions was necessary because Nigeria contains more than 250 ethnic and linguistic groups, as well as several religious ones. Local rivalries have long been a threat to national unity. In 1967, in an attempt to meet the demands of more ethnic groups, the country's four regions were replaced by 12 states. The division of the Eastern Region provoked an uprising. In May 1967, the governor of the Eastern Region, Colonel Odumegwu Ojukwu, proclaimed it an independent republic called Biafra. Civil war continued until Biafra's surrender in January 1970.

After the end of the war, the country's revenues were enhanced by its oil exports. But oil did not bring stability. Instead, political problems continued and the country had only nine years of civilian government between independence in 1960 and 1998. In 1998, Nigeria's military dictator, General Sani Abacha, died. He was succeeded by General Abdulsalam Abubakar, who pushed ahead with a timetable to hold state and national elections, culminating in the election of a president in 1999. The successful candidate was a former military leader, Olusegun Obasanjo, who set about tackling corruption. However, ethnic and religious differences are a threat to national unity. In the late 1990s and early 2000s, ethnic riots broke out between Yorubas and Hausas in the south-west, while the introduction of *sharia* (Islamic law) in northern states has caused friction between Muslims and Christians. In 2002, Nigeria was divided into 30 states and the federal territory of Abuja.

Economy

Although blessed with many natural resources, including oil reserves, metals, forests and fertile farmland, Nigeria has a low per capita GNP of US $260 (1997) which makes it a 'low-income' developing economy.

Agriculture employs 43% of the people and Nigeria is one of the world's leading producers of cocoa beans, groundnuts (peanuts), palm oil and kernels, and natural rubber. The leading food crops include beans, cassava, maize, millet, plantains, rice in river valleys or on irrigated land, sorghum and yams. Goats, poultry and sheep are raised throughout the country, but most of the cattle are concentrated in the northern tropical savanna region. Besides oil and tin, Nigeria produces some coal, gold, iron ore, lead, natural gas and zinc. Industry is increasing and manufactures include cement, chemicals, fertilizers, processed food, metal products, textiles and timber. The country also has oil refineries, as well as motor car assembly plants and steel mills. In the mid-1990s, crude petroleum accounted for about 98% of the total value of Nigeria's exports. Other exports include cocoa, rubber, urea and ammonia, and fish. Manufactures, including machinery and transport equipment, are leading imports.

Democracy and Africa's future

In the early 1950s, most of Africa was under colonial rule. The great flush of optimism that followed decolonization in the 1950s and 1960s did not bring the rewards of peace, unity and prosperity that many African leaders had envisaged. Instead, ancient divisions between ethnic and religious groups caused civil conflict, the collapse of elected democracies, and their replacement by corrupt and incompetent dictatorships.

Nigeria, whose large oil reserves appeared to assure it a prosperous future, is a case in point. Nigerians are divided into more than 250 ethnic groups, and the people are further divided by religion. Strong but mostly corrupt and inefficient military administrations have sought to maintain the unity of the country, at the expense of human rights.

In such countries as Burundi and Rwanda, the ancient rivalries between the Hutu majority and the Tutsi overlords expressed itself in blood-letting on an appalling scale. Elsewhere, rival groups were backed by Western or Soviet aid, and civil wars became bloody reflections of the Cold War. The collapse of the Soviet Union in the early 1990s led many to hope for an end to the civil war in Angola, which had long been a scene of proxy West/East conflict. But the war continued.

Yet, from the late 1980s, there were promising signs that new hope had reached the world's poorest continent. In many countries, dictators were succumbing quite peacefully to popular demands for multiparty elections. Instead of the *coup d'etat* being the only way to change governments, politicians were again being chosen through the ballot box. The transition to democracy was not always smooth. For example, Sierra Leone's President Ahmed Tejan Kabbah was elected in 1996 and deposed in 1997. He returned to office in 1998 only after a Nigerian-led intervention force mounted an offensive against the military junta.

Democracy does not provide all the answers for Africa's problems, including its poverty, high debts and the periodic collapses in the prices for many African commodities. In this context, Western powers in 1999 made moves to cancel debts, providing African leaders ensured that the money would be spent on such matters as education and health. Many African leaders were also conscious of the need for a fresh start. In 2001, a top-level meeting in Nigeria endorsed a New African Initiative which called for clean, accountable and open government, an end to human rights abuses, and efforts to end wars. In return, Western countries were asked for more aid for infrastructure, development and education, more investment, and the lifting of trade barriers that impede African exports.

Yet, even as new initiatives provide reason for hope, so too new dangers threaten. In eastern and southern Africa, health workers are faced with a major challenge – the control of AIDS. For example, in Botswana, Namibia, Swaziland and Zimbabwe, between a fifth and a quarter of people aged 15–49 are afflicted by HIV or AIDS. In Botswana, children born in the early 21st century will have a life expectancy of 40 years. Without AIDS, it would have been around 70 years.

AREA	Ibo (or Igbo) 18%,
923,770 sq km [356,668 sq mi]	Ijaw 10%, Kanuri 4%
POPULATION	**LANGUAGES**
126,636,000	English (official),
CAPITAL (POPULATION)	Hausa, Yoruba, Ibo
Abuja (339,000)	**RELIGIONS**
GOVERNMENT	Islam 50%,
Federal multiparty republic	Christianity 40%,
ETHNIC GROUPS	traditional beliefs 10%
Hausa and Fulani 29%,	**CURRENCY**
Yoruba 21%,	Naira = 100 kobo

NORTHERN MARIANA ISLANDS – SEE PACIFIC OCEAN, PAGES 174–178

This flag became the national flag of Norway in 1898, although merchant ships had used it since 1821. The design is based on the Dannebrog, the flag of Denmark, the country which ruled Norway from the 14th century until the early 19th century.

Arable land 2.94% Permanent crops 0%
Permanent grassland 0.42% Forest 27.1%

The configuration of Norway's jagged coastline, which is the longest in Europe, helps to explain the ease with which the Norwegians took to the sea in early times and why they have remained a seafaring nation. The *vidda* are cut by long, narrow, steep-sided fjords on the west coast, whose spectacular scenery attracts a large number of cruise liners. The largest of the fjords, which were worn out by the great northern ice sheet, is Sognefjord, which is 203 km [127 mi] long and less than 5 km [3 mi] wide. It is the longest inlet in Europe and is the best known of Norway's fjords. Inland, the moving ice eroded deep valleys which now contain ribbon lakes.

About 150,000 islands, some of which are no more than rocky reefs, lie along the coast. The largest group, the Lofoten Islands, lie above the Arctic Circle. These islands, known as the skerryguard, protect the mainland shore of Norway from the battering of Atlantic breakers and provide sheltered leads of water for ferries and fishing boats.

Communications along the country's coast were until recently much easier by boat than by land. The two island groups, the Svalbard and the Jan Mayen Islands, are possessions of Norway in the Arctic Ocean.

Climate

The warm North Atlantic Drift, the northern extension of the Gulf Stream, which flows off the coast of Norway, moderates the country's climate, with milder winters and cooler summers. Nearly all the country's ports remain ice-free throughout the year. However, inland, away from the moderating effects of the sea, the climate becomes more severe. Winters are bitterly cold and snow covers the land for at least three months a year.

Geography

The Kingdom of Norway forms the western part of the mountainous Scandinavian Peninsula. It is a rugged country in which communication is difficult. The landscape is dominated by rolling plateaux, the *vidda*, which are generally between 300 m and 900 m [1,000–3,000 ft] high, but some peaks rise from 1,500 m to 2,500 m [5,000–8,000 ft] in the area between Oslo, Bergen and Trondheim. In the far north, the summits are around 1,000 m [3,000 ft] lower. The highest areas retain permanent icefields, as in the Jotunheimen Mountains above Sognefjord. The mountains were uplifted during three mountain-building periods over the last 400 million years. Intrusions of volcanic material accompanied uplifting and folding and there are great masses of granites and gneisses – the source of Norway's mineral wealth.

Norway has few large areas of flat land, but in the east the *vidda* are broken by the deep valleys of rivers flowing to the lowlands of southern Norway, focused on Oslo. During the last Ice Age, the land was covered by the great northern ice sheet. When it melted about 10,000 years ago, it left behind large deposits of glacial moraine, well represented around Oslo in the Raa moraine.

NORWAY (OSLO)

The warm waters and cyclones of the North Atlantic give the western coastlands of Norway a warm maritime climate of mild winters and cool, wet summers. Rain is heavy on the coast but lighter inland and northwards. Inland winters are more severe and summers warmer. At Oslo, snow begins in November, lying until late March. Sunshine from November to January is only about one hour, but from April to August it is 6–8 hours.

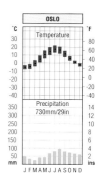

Vegetation

Landscapes dominated by bare rock exist in places where ice stripped away the soil during the Ice Age. Icefields still occur in some higher areas, but Norway also has large forests of pine and spruce, which flourish in the broad, glaciated valleys. Pines and spruce grow up to 850 m [2,800 ft] in the east and up to 700 m [2,300 ft] in the area around Trondheim. Birch forest extends from about 900 m to 1,900 m [3,000–3,900 ft]. Higher up, dwarf birches occur in the willow zone. Wild berries, including blueberries and cranberries, grow in all regions.

History

The sea has always been a major influence in Norwegian life. From about AD 800, Vikings from Norway roamed the northern seas, raiding and founding colonies around the coasts of Britain, Iceland and even North America. In about 900, Norway was united under Harold I, the country's first king, and Christianity was introduced under Olav II in the late 10th century. Viking power ended in the late 11th century. In 1380, Norway was united with Denmark, when Margaret, wife of Norway's King Haakon VI and daughter of the king of Denmark, began to rule Denmark as its regent. In 1388, Swedish noblemen chose Margaret to rule Sweden and, in 1397, the three countries were united. Sweden broke away from the union in 1523 and, in 1526, Denmark, which had become increasingly powerful, made Norway a Danish province.

In 1813, towards the end of the Napoleonic Wars, Sweden defeated Denmark, an ally of France. In 1814, Denmark ceded Norway to Sweden, though Denmark retained Norway's island colonies of Greenland, Iceland and the Faroe Islands. Norway wanted independence, but Sweden defeated the Norwegians and made them accept Charles XIII of Sweden as their ruler in November 1814. Norway finally ended its union with Sweden in 1905. The Norwegians then chose as their king a Danish prince, who took the title Haakon VII. At the time of independence, Norway had one of the world's largest merchant fleets, and its industries, powered mainly by hydroelectricity, were increasing.

Norway was neutral in World War I, but it lost about half of its merchant fleet, which was used for carrying cargo for the Allies. Norway sought to maintain its neutrality in World War II, but German troops invaded the country in 1940. In 1945, however, the Germans surrendered and Haakon VII returned to Norway in triumph.

Scandinavia

There are several possible definitions of the term Scandinavia. In the narrow geographical sense it refers to the peninsula shared by Norway and Sweden; in a broader cultural and political sense it includes the five countries of the Nordic Council – Norway, Sweden, Denmark, Finland and Iceland. These five countries are sometimes collectively known as Norden. Two other terms are also in use: Fennoscandia refers to Finland and the Scandinavian peninsula, while Balto-scandia refers to the regions that surround the Baltic Sea. Of the five countries of Norden, all, except Finland, have related languages, and all have a tradition of parliamentary democracy. Finland and Iceland are republics, while Denmark, Norway and Sweden are constitutional monarchies.

There are also strong historical links between the countries, beginning in the 8th century when their ancestors, the Norsemen, colonized large parts of northern Europe. All have at different times been governed together, Sweden and Finland separating in 1809, Norway and Sweden in 1905, and Denmark and Iceland as recently as 1944.

Because of their northerly position and exposure to Atlantic weather systems, Scandinavia has a cool, wet climate, not favourable to crops. But, due to long hours of daylight in the northern summer, crops are grown north of the Arctic Circle.

Scandinavians were once among the poorest peoples of Europe, but during the last century they have become among the richest, making use of limited natural resources, and seizing opportunities provided by their maritime position to become major shipping and fishing nations.

Of Norway's Arctic territories, Svalbard, an archipelago half as big as Denmark and situated halfway between the North Pole and the Arctic Circle, is the largest. It was claimed at various times by Norway, Britain and the Netherlands. However, in 1920, a treaty signed in Paris recognized Norwegian sovereignty and, in 1925, the islands were officially incorporated into the kingdom of Norway.

The volcanic Jan Mayen Island, which lies north-north-east of Iceland, was named after the Dutch whaling captain Jan Jacobsz May. Though uninhabited, it was used by seal trappers and other hunters, and, in 1921, Norway established a meteorological and radio station there. It was officially incorporated into Norway in 1929, but its only residents today are the 30 or so staff at a weather station.

Politics

After World War II, Norwegians worked to rebuild their economy and their merchant fleet. The economy was boosted in the 1970s, when Norway began producing petroleum and natural gas from wells in the North Sea. Rapid economic growth has ensured that Norwegians are among the most prosperous people in Europe. Few people are wealthy, because taxation is high, but few are very poor, and an advanced welfare system provides good services even to the most isolated communities. The majority of the people now own their homes and many families have second homes on the shores of fjords or lakes. Norway is by far Europe's biggest donor of foreign aid per capita, with a figure of 1.1% of the gross national product, as compared with the Organization for Economic Co-operation and Development (OECD) target of 0.7%.

Norway has played an important role in Europe. In 1949, it became a member of the North Atlantic Treaty Organization, though it did not allow NATO bases or nuclear weapons on its soil for fear of provoking its neighbour, the Soviet Union. During 1960, Norway and six other countries formed an economic union called the European Free Trade Association (EFTA). Norway refused to join the European Economic Community (EEC) when Britain, Denmark and Ireland decided to join on 1 January 1973. However, it continued to work with its Scandinavian neighbours through the Nordic Council, even after Sweden and Finland left EFTA to join the European Union in 1995.

In 1994, Norwegians again voted against membership of the European Union, with 52.4% voting against joining. Some Norwegians feared that membership would involve a loss of their hard-won sovereignty, while people working in agriculture and fishing anticipated massive cuts in government subsidies. There were also fears that Norway might lose control over its natural resources, including fish, oil, natural gas and metals, while others believed that EU membership might undermine Norway's cradle-to-grave welfare system.

Economy

Norway's chief resources and exports are oil and natural gas which come from wells under the North Sea. Farmland covers only 3% of the land. Dairy farming and meat production are the chief activities, though Norway has to import food. Using cheap hydroelectric power, Norway has set up many industries. Manufactures include petroleum products, chemicals, aluminium, wood pulp and paper, machinery, clothing and furniture. Fuel and fuel products make up more than half of the total value of exports, followed by machinery and transport equipment, metals and metal products, and food products.

AREA	ETHNIC GROUPS
323,900 sq km	Norwegian 97%
[125,050 sq mi]	**LANGUAGES**
POPULATION	Norwegian
4,503,000	(official)
CAPITAL (POPULATION)	**RELIGIONS**
Oslo (502,000)	Lutheran 88%
GOVERNMENT	**CURRENCY**
Constitutional monarchy	Krone = 100 ore

OMAN – SEE GULF STATES, PAGES 113–114

PACIFIC OCEAN

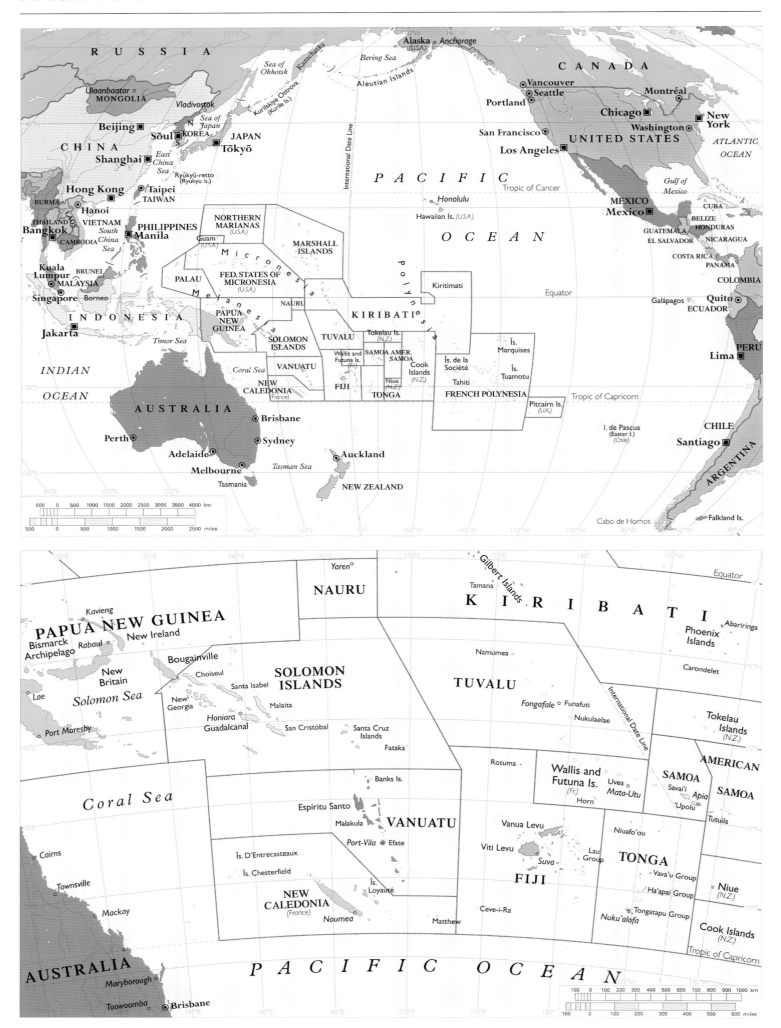

AMERICAN SAMOA

A self-governing 'unincorporated territory' of the United States, American Samoa, in the south-central Pacific Ocean, consists of two volcanic islands and two atolls. Assistance by the United States has given its people a standard of living ten times that of Samoa.

AREA	CAPITAL
200 sq km [77 sq mi]	Pago Pago
POPULATION	**CURRENCY**
67,000	US dollar = 100 cents

FEDERATED STATES OF MICRONESIA

The Federated States of Micronesia, a former US territory in the western Pacific, became fully independent in 1991. Most people are subsistence farmers, but some cash crops are grown and the main export is copra. Fishing and tourism are also important.

AREA	CAPITAL
705 sq km [272 sq mi]	Palikir
POPULATION	**CURRENCY**
135,000	US dollar = 100 cents

FIJI

The Republic of the Fiji Islands (Fiji's official name since 1998) comprises more than 800 Melanesian islands. The larger ones are volcanic and mountainous and surrounded by coral reefs. The rest are low coral atolls. Easily the biggest are Viti Levu, with the capital of Suva on its south coast, and Vanua Levu, which is just over half the size of the larger island. The climate is tropical, with south-east trade winds blowing throughout the year. Heavy rains occur, especially between November and May. Tropical forests cover much of the land.

The Dutch navigator, Abel Janszoon Tasman reached the islands in 1643, while Captain James Cook visited one of the southern islands in 1774. Following conflict between various Fijian tribes in the 19th century, a local chief named Cacobau asked Britain to make Fiji a colony. Fiji became a colony in 1874 and remained so until 1970.

Fiji suffers today from its colonial past. Until the late 1980s, Indian workers brought in by the British to work on the sugar plantations outnumbered the native Fijians, but were second-class citizens in terms of electoral representation, economic opportunity and land ownership. However, they played an important part in the economy. The constitution adopted on independence was intended to ease racial tension, but military coups in 1987 overthrew the recently elected (and first) Indian-majority government, suspended the constitution and set up a Fijian-dominated republic outside the Commonwealth. The country returned to civilian rule in 1990 and Fiji rejoined the Commonwealth in 1997. However, with a new constitution guaranteeing Melanesian

political supremacy, many Indians had already emigrated before the 1992 elections, taking their valuable skills with them. A new constitution was introduced in 1998. Elections in 1999 led to victory for the Fiji Labour Party, whose leader, an ethnic Indian, Mahendra Chaudhry, became prime minister. In 2000, ethnic Fijian gunmen seized parliament. They were eventually disarmed and arrested, but Chaudhry was dismissed. The army appointed an ethnic Fijian, Laisenia Qarase, as prime minister.

Agriculture is the mainstay of the economy. Sugar cane, copra and ginger are the main cash crops, and fish and timber are also exported. Manufactures include beer, cement and cigarettes. The leading markets for Fiji's exports are Australia, the United Kingdom, the United States and Japan. Imports come from Australia, New Zealand, the United States and Japan. Tourism is also important.

AREA	
18,270 sq km	
[7,054 sq mi]	
POPULATION	
844,000	
CAPITAL	
Suva	
CURRENCY	
Fiji doll. = 100 cents	

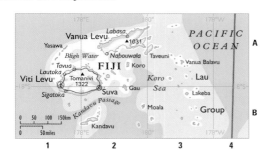

FRENCH POLYNESIA

French Polynesia consists of 130 islands, scattered over 4 million sq km [1.5 million sq mi]. Tahiti is the largest island. The territory became a French protectorate in 1843 and an Overseas Territory in 1958. In 1984, the islands gained increased autonomy and a territorial assembly. The high standard of living comes largely from links with France, including a substantial military presence. France began stationing personnel there in 1962, and started nuclear testing at Mururoa –

recent underground tests took place there in 1995–6. Tourism has also improved the original subsistence agriculture and fishing economy.

AREA	CAPITAL
3,941 sq km [1,520 sq mi]	Papeete
POPULATION	**CURRENCY**
254,000	Euro = 100 cents

GUAM

Guam, a strategically important 'unincorporated territory' of the USA, is the largest of the Mariana Islands in the Pacific Ocean. It is composed of a coralline plateau. Populated for more than 3,000 years, it was charted by Ferdinand Magellan in 1521, colonized by Spain from 1688, but ceded to the United States after the 1896–8 war, and occupied by the Japanese in 1941–4. It is now of great strategic importance to the United States. Exports include textiles, beverages,

tobacco and copra, but most food is imported. Guam is also a major tourist destination, and enjoys a relatively high standard of living.

AREA	CAPITAL
549 sq km [212 sq mi]	Agana
POPULATION	**CURRENCY**
158,000	US dollar = 100 cents

PACIFIC OCEAN

KIRIBATI

The Republic of Kiribati (pronounced Kiri-bass, the closest that the Gilbertese language can get to Gilberts) comprises three groups of coral atolls – 16 islands which used to form the Gilbert Islands, 8 Phoenix Islands, and 11 of the Line Islands – plus the higher and volcanic Banaba (formerly Ocean Island). The largest island, Kiritimati Atoll (formerly Christmas Island), in the east, covers more than half of the area of the country. (Kiritimati, which was used for British and US nuclear tests from 1957 until 1962, is the Gilbertese version of the word 'Christmas'.) Though the land area is relatively small, the islands are scattered over 5 million sq km [2 million sq mi] of the Pacific, straddling the Equator. Temperatures are high and the rainfall is generally abundant.

Together with the Ellice Islands, which broke away as Tuvalu in 1975, becoming independent in 1978, the (mainly Micronesian) Gilbert and the Polynesian Ellice Islands were a British protectorate from 1892, and a colony from 1916. Some of the Line and Phoenix Islands were added later. The islands were occupied by Japan during World War II, but were recaptured after the battle of Tarawa in 1943. In 1976, the Gilbert and Ellice Islands separated into two. The Gilbert Islands became fully independent in 1979 as the Republic of Kiribati.

Few of the coral islands rise more than 4 m [13 ft] above sea level, though bananas, breadfruits, coconuts and papayas are harvested, with taro (babai) cultivated in deep pits to provide the staple vegetable.

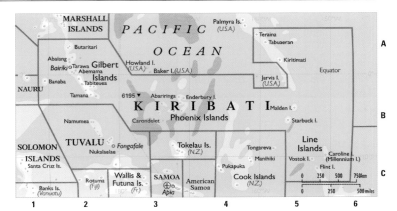

Following the exhaustion of Banaba's phosphate deposits in 1980, the leading exports are copra, and fish and fish preparations – fishing and the making of canoes are an important part of life in Kiribati.

Kiribati remains heavily dependent on foreign aid and its future, both medium-term economic, and long-term environmental (due to possible rising sea levels caused by global warming), is bleak. Kiribati's difficulties are compounded by an overcrowding problem that forced the resettlement of some 4,200 people in the 1990s.

AREA	CAPITAL
728 sq km [281 sq mi]	Tarawa
POPULATION	**CURRENCY**
94,000	Australian dollar = 100 cents

MARSHALL ISLANDS

The Republic of the Marshall Islands comprises an archipelago of 31 coral atolls, 5 single islands and about 1,150 islets in two chains – the eastern and western. The capital is situated on Majuro Atoll in the eastern chain. The chief atoll in the western chain is Kwajalein. The islands also include the former US nuclear testing sites of Bikini and Enewatak. The climate is hot and humid, with the rainy season between May and November.

A German protectorate from 1886, the Marshall Islands were occupied by Japan in World War I and, after the war, Japan was granted a League of Nations mandate to rule the islands. Occupied by Allied forces in 1944, the islands became part of the UN Territory of the Pacific Islands in 1947, administered by the United States. In 1986, the islands became a republic 'in free association' with the United States.

The United Nations recognized the termination of the Trusteeship in 1990 and the new country became a member of the United Nations in 1991. The republic then became a sovereign state, with responsibility for its foreign affairs, although not for its defence and security until 2001. The economy, based on agriculture and tourism, is heavily supported by aid from the United States, which still retains a missile site on the island of Kwajalein. A plan to produce high-quality black pearls, employing thousands of workers, was announced in 1999.

AREA	CAPITAL
181 sq km [70 sq mi]	Dalap-Uliga-Darrit
POPULATION	**CURRENCY**
71,000	US dollar = 100 cents

NAURU

Nauru is the world's smallest republic, located in the western Pacific Ocean, close to the Equator. Formerly ruled by Australia, Nauru became independent in 1968. Its prosperity is based on phosphate mining, but the reserves are running out.

AREA	CAPITAL
21 sq km [8 sq mi]	Yaren
POPULATION	**CURRENCY**
12,000	Australian dollar = 100 cents

NEW CALEDONIA

New Caledonia is the most southerly of the Melanesian countries in the Pacific. It comprises the main island of Grande Terre and the dependencies of the Loyalty Islands (Îsles Loyauté, Îsle des Pins and the Bélep archipelago). The remaining islands, many of them coral atolls, are small and uninhabited.

A French possession since 1853 and a French Overseas Territory from 1958, New Caledonia split with France on the question of independence. The Kanaks, the indigenous Melanesian people but numbering under half of the population, support independence, while the less numerous French settlers, many of whom fled Algeria after it gained independence, are against it. In the 1990s, an agreement for increased autonomy helped to ease the tension. But, in 1998 France announced an agreement with local Melanesians that a vote on independence should be postponed for 15 years. New Caledonia is rich in minerals.

AREA	CAPITAL
18,580 sq km [7,174 sq mi]	Nouméa
POPULATION	**CURRENCY**
205,000	Euro = 100 cents

NORTHERN MARIANA ISLANDS

The Commonwealth of the Northern Mariana Islands comprise all 17 Mariana Islands except for Guam, the most southerly. Part of the US Trust Territory of the Pacific from 1947, its people voted in the United Nations plebiscite for Commonwealth status in union with the United States. The US approved the change in 1976, and internal self-government followed in 1978. In 1986, the islanders, most of whom live on Saipan, were granted US citizenship. Fishing is important but tourism, which is growing rapidly, seems to be the key to the future. The number of tourists rose from 130,000 in 1984 to 481,000 in 1998.

AREA	CAPITAL
477 sq km [184 sq mi]	Saipan
POPULATION	**CURRENCY**
75,000	US dollar = 100 cents

PALAU (BELAU)

The Republic of Palau comprises an archipelago of six Caroline groups in the Caroline Islands, totalling 26 islands and more than 300 islets, varying in terrain from mountain to reef. Palau was part of the US Trust Territory of the Pacific Ocean, which was established in 1947. In 1978, it voted to break away from the Federated States of Micronesia and a new, self-governing constitution became effective in 1981. The territory then entered into 'free association with the United States', providing sovereign-state status. However, in 1983, the proposal was rejected in a referendum, because the US refused to accede to a 92% vote in a 1979 referendum that would have made it a nuclear-free zone. On 1 October 1994, Palau finally became an independent republic and, in December 1994, it joined the United Nations. Palau relies heavily on US aid. Other activities include tourism and subsistence agriculture.

AREA	CAPITAL
458 sq km [177 sq mi]	Koror
POPULATION	**CURRENCY**
19,000	US dollar = 100 cents

PITCAIRN

Pitcairn Island is a British overseas territory in the Pacific Ocean about halfway between New Zealand and Panama. This isolated island rises steeply from the sea to an elevation of about 250 m [820 ft] and the climate is mild and wet. The Pitcairn Island Group also includes the uninhabited islands of Henderson, Ducie and Oeno. Uninhabited until 1790, it was occupied by nine mutineers from HMS *Bounty*, together with some men and women from Tahiti. The present population lives in Adamstown on Pitcairn, which comes under the administration of the British High Commissioner in Wellington, New Zealand.

AREA	CAPITAL
48 sq km [19 sq mi]	Adamstown
POPULATION	**CURRENCY**
47	New Zealand dollar = 100 cents

SAMOA

The Independent State of Samoa, which was known as Western Samoa until its name was officially changed in July 1997, comprises two large volcanic islands, seven small islands and a number of islets. The main islands of Upolu and Savai'i both have central mountainous regions, surrounded by coastal lowlands and coral reefs. Upolu contains two-thirds of the country's population. Samoa has a tropical climate, but the south-east trade winds moderate the climate. Temperatures seldom fall below 24°C [75°F], or rise above 29°C [85°F]. The coolest months are May to November, while the rainy season extends from December to April. The south and east coasts receive the most rainfall.

The first European contacts occurred in the 18th century but, following the establishment of a Christian mission on Savai'i in the 1830s, missionaries, as well as whaling and trading ships, began to visit the islands. In 1899, Germany and the United States took control, with Germany taking Western Samoa. Ruled by New Zealand from 1920 – first under a League of Nations mandate and later a United Nations trusteeship – the islands achieved independence as a parliamentary democracy in 1962. Before 1991, when the first elections under universal suffrage were held, the 49-member Legislative Assembly was elected exclusively by *matai* (heads of Samoan family groups).

Agriculture employs more than 60% of the workforce. The chief food crops are bananas, breadfruit, coconuts, mangoes, papayas, pineapples and taro, while some farmers raise cattle, chickens and pigs. Besides its fertile soils, Samoa's other resources are its forests and fish. With aid from the United Nations, fishing has become an important activity. The few industries are powered mainly by hydroelectricity. Samoa's exports include coconut oil, coconut cream and copra, which together made up 52% of the value of the exports in 1997.

Other important sources of revenue are remittances from Samoans working overseas, together with foreign aid. Tourism is growing. More than 78,000 foreign tourists visited the country in 1998. Many come to see the home of the writer Robert Louis Stevenson, which is now the official home of Samoa's head of state.

AREA	CAPITAL
2,840 sq km [1,097 sq mi]	Apia
POPULATION	**CURRENCY**
179,000	Tala = 100 sene

SOLOMON ISLANDS

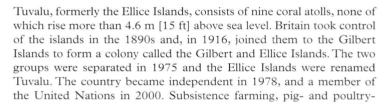

The Solomon Islands represent part of the drowned outermost crustal fold of the ancient Australian continent. New Caledonia lies on an inner fold, nearer the mainland. The main islands in the Solomon Islands are volcanic in origin and the mountains are covered by dense forests. The northern islands have a tropical marine climate, but the south is cooler.

The southern Solomons became British in 1893, while Germany ceded islands in the north in 1900. During World War II, Japan occupied the islands, which became the scene of fierce fighting, notably the battle of Guadalcanal. Known as the British Solomons, the islands won independence in 1978. Since then, the Solomons have faced many economic problems, while ethnic violence occurred in 1999–2000.

The coastal plains are used for subsistence farming. While coconut products and cocoa are exported, forestry and fishing are the main industries, accounting for four-fifths of the exports.

AREA	CAPITAL
28,370 sq km [10,954 sq mi]	Honiara
POPULATION	**CURRENCY**
480,000	Solomon Island dollar = 100 cents

TONGA

The Kingdom of Tonga comprises more than 170 islands, 36 of which are inhabited. They are a mixture of coralline outcrops and higher volcanic outcrops. The largest island, Tongatapu, contains nearly two-thirds of the population.

Dutch navigators visited the islands in the early 17th century, and British missionaries converted most people to Christianity in the early 19th century. Tonga became a British protectorate in 1900. Tonga is a monarchy and the king rules with a prime minister and cabinet. From 1965, the ruler has been King Taufa'ahau Tupou IV, whose line goes back a thousand years. He presided over the islands' transition from British protectorate to independent Commonwealth country in 1970. Tonga became a member of the United Nations in 1999.

Most Tongans live off their own produce, which includes fish, tapioca and yams. While the government owns all the land, men are entitled to rent areas to grow food – a policy that is now under pressure with Tonga's young population. The main exports include squash, fish and vanilla beans. Tourism is developing – Tonga received 27,000 foreign visitors in 1998.

AREA	CAPITAL
750 sq km [290 sq mi]	Nuku'alofa
POPULATION	**CURRENCY**
104,000	Pa'anga = 100 seniti

TUVALU

Tuvalu, formerly the Ellice Islands, consists of nine coral atolls, none of which rise more than 4.6 m [15 ft] above sea level. Britain took control of the islands in the 1890s and, in 1916, joined them to the Gilbert Islands to form a colony called the Gilbert and Ellice Islands. The two groups were separated in 1975 and the Ellice Islands were renamed Tuvalu. The country became independent in 1978, and a member of the United Nations in 2000. Subsistence farming, pig- and poultry-raising, and fishing are the main activities. Exports include clothing and footwear, copra and fruits.

AREA	CAPITAL
24 sq km [9 sq mi]	Fongafale
POPULATION	**CURRENCY**
11,000	Australian dollar = 100 cents

VANUATU

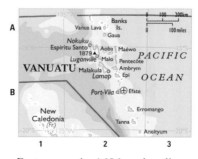

The Republic of Vanuatu is an archipelago of 30 large islands and 70 islets, the majority of which are mountainous and volcanic, with coral beaches, reefs, forests and limited coastal cultivation. The climate is tropical, but moderated by the influence of the oceans and the trade winds.

The islands were visited by the Portuguese in 1696 and rediscovered by the French in 1768. They were charted by Captain James Cook in 1774, who named the islands New Hebrides. In 1888, France and Britain agreed on joint supervision and, from 1906, the islands were ruled as an Anglo-French condominium. The islands became independent as Vanuatu in 1980. The Francophone Espiritu Santo, the largest island, attempted to secede from Vanuatu, whose government was anglophone, and politics have remained unstable. Agriculture is the main activity and Vanuatu exports copra, beef and veal, timber and cocoa.

AREA	CAPITAL
12,190 sq km [4,707 sq mi]	Port-Vila
POPULATION	**CURRENCY**
193,000	Vatu (VUV)

WALLIS AND FUTUNA

The Wallis and Futuna Islands comprise three main islands and many islets. In a 1959 referendum, the Polynesian islanders voted in favour of a change from a dependency to a French Overseas Territory. French aid remains vital to an economy based on subsistence agriculture.

AREA	CAPITAL
200 sq km [77 sq mi]	Mata-Utu
POPULATION	**CURRENCY**
15,000	Euro = 100 cents

PAKISTAN

Pakistan's flag was adopted in 1947, when the country became independent from Britain. The colour green, the crescent Moon and the five-pointed star are all traditional symbols of Islam. The white stripe represents the other religions in Pakistan.

Geography

The Republic of Pakistan contains mountains, fertile plains and rocky deserts. The Karakoram range, which contains K2, the world's second highest mountain at 8,611 m [28,251 ft], lies on the border with China in northern Jammu and Kashmir – disputed areas, occupied by Pakistan but claimed by India. Other mountains rise in the west. The Thar (or Great Indian) Desert straddles the border with India in the south-east. The arid Baluchistan Plateau lies in the south-west.

Like Egypt, most of the terrain in Pakistan is inhospitable, and, just as Egypt is the gift of the Nile, so Pakistan is the gift of the River Indus and its tributaries. Irrigation is vital both in the Punjab in eastern Pakistan, 'the land of five rivers' (the Indus, Jhelum, Beas, Ravi and Sutlej), and on the dry plains that flank the Indus between Khairpur and Hyderabad. The stations at Tarbela, on the Indus, and Mangla, on the Jhelum, are among the world's biggest earth- and rock-filled dams.

Climate

The mountains have cold, snowy winters. But most of Pakistan has hot summers and cool winters. Rainfall is sparse over much of the country.

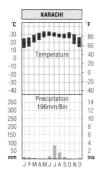

PAKISTAN (KARACHI)

The summer monsoon rains decrease in intensity from the Indian peninsula westwards into Pakistan, leaving much of the Indus lowland arid. Rain falls on approximately 20 days in the year, half of these in July and August. Karachi is hot all year but, being on the coast, has a smaller temperature range than inland. Summer rains are thundery. Small amounts of winter rain are brought by low-pressure systems from the west.

Vegetation

Forests grow on mountain slopes, but most of Pakistan is covered by dry grassland and low bushes, with only occasional trees, apart from forest plantations and the many fruit orchards in farming areas. Plants that are adapted to surviving in dry conditions grow in semi-arid areas. Wild animals found in the northern mountains include bears, leopards and wild sheep. Crocodiles and wild boars are found in the delta region.

History

Pakistan was the site of the Indus Valley civilization which developed about 4,500 years ago. Two major archaeological sites, at Harappa, in the Ravi valley south of Faisalabad, and at Mohenjo-Daro, south-west of Sukkur, are the remains of large, well-planned cities. The Indus Valley civilization, which developed a system of weights and measures and a type of writing using pictographs, broke up into smaller cultures around 1700 BC. Historians believe that its break-up may have been caused by changes in the courses of the rivers.

The region that is now Pakistan was subsequently conquered by successive waves of people from south-western and central Asia. The Aryans reached the area by about 1500 BC and, in time, they settled across northern India. From the 6th century BC, the area was conquered by the Persians, and then, in 326 BC, it was occupied by the armies of Alexander the Great. Soon afterwards it became part of the Maurya Empire until that empire began to break up around 230 BC. It was then invaded successively by Bactrians, Scythians, Afghans and Parthians, until it became part of the Kushan Empire between about AD 50 and the mid-3rd century.

Islam was introduced in AD 711 by Muslims who had sailed across the Arabian Sea. In about AD 1000, Turkish Muslims invaded from the north and founded a kingdom that included the entire Indus Valley, with its capital at Lahore. Between 1206 and 1526, the area was part of the Delhi Sultanate, which included northern India. In 1526, it became part of the Mogul Empire which was founded by Babar, a Muslim ruler from Afghanistan. Under the Mogul Empire, a new religion emerged, which became especially strong in Punjab. This religion, called Sikhism, combined elements of Hinduism and Islam. The Mogul Empire began to decline in the 18th century as the British East India Company was taking control of India. In the 1840s, the Company gained areas in Punjab and Sind. In 1858, when the British government took over from the British East India Company, the region, which became known as British India, included all of what is now Pakistan.

Politics

From the early 20th century, the Muslim League and the Indian National Congress sought greater self-government for British India. In the 1930s, the Muslim League, led by Muhammad Ali Jinnah, called for the creation of a Muslim state called Pakistan, a name that means 'land of the pure' in Urdu. On 14 August 1947, Pakistan became an independent nation, with India gaining independence the following day. The partition of British India was accompanied by slaughter as Hindus and Sikhs fled from Pakistan and Muslims fled from India.

In 1948, India and Pakistan went to war over Kashmir (officially the Indian state of Jammu and Kashmir). At the end of the war, Pakistan was left in control of the area to the west of the 1949 cease-fire line, with India in control to the east. The Kashmir problem was partly religious – with a mainly Muslim population ruled by a Hindu maharaja who had acceded to India. But there was also a strategic issue, namely that the five rivers that rise in or pass across Kashmir or the neighbouring state of Himachal Pradesh are vital to Pakistan's economy. This region has remained a disputed zone, with fighting breaking out periodically. The present boundary is a truce line established in 1972, following further conflict in 1971.

When Pakistan became independent, it consisted of two parts: West and East Pakistan. Following a bitter civil war and Indian military intervention, East Pakistan broke away from the western wing in 1971 to become Bangladesh. However, neither nation has enjoyed stability or sound government since the civil war. The nation that is now Pakistan has been subject to military rule and martial law, interspersed with periods of fragile democracy, generally resting on army consent.

Following the resignation of President Mohammad Yahya Khan, after the civil war in 1971, Zulfiquar Ali Bhutto became president. Under a new constitution in 1973, which provided for a head of state and a prime minister as the head of the government, Bhutto resigned as president to become prime minister. But the military thought him to be too pro-Western in his policies and, in 1977, following his party's victory in elections, he was overthrown by an army coup. The coup was led by General Mohammad Zia ul-Haq, who became president in 1978. Bhutto was convicted of the murder of a political opponent while he was serving as prime minister and he was executed in 1979.

Elections were held in February 1985 and martial law was ended in December 1985. Zia ul-Haq dismissed the prime minister, the cabinet and the parliament in 1988, but in August that year he was killed in a plane crash. Ghulam Ishaq Khan, leader of the Senate, became the acting president. In November 1988, elections brought Benazir Bhutto, daughter of the former prime minister and leader of the Pakistan People's Party (PPP), to power as prime minister. In August 1990, President Ishaq Khan dismissed Benazir Bhutto and her cabinet, accusing the government of corruption. He dissolved the National Assembly and declared a state of emergency.

Elections in 1990 resulted in victory for a coalition group, the Islamic Democratic Alliance. The leader of the chief party in the coalition, Nawaz Sharif of the Pakistan Muslim League, became prime minister. In further elections in 1993, following the resignations of the president and prime minister, the PPP won the most seats and Benazir Bhutto

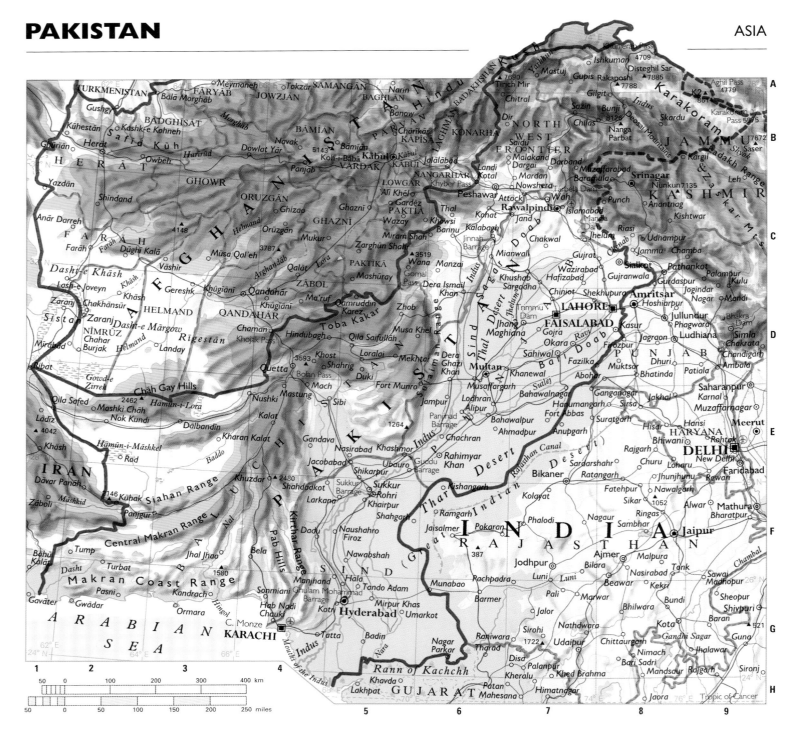

again became prime minister. History repeated itself in the late 1990s. In 1996, President Farooq Leghari dismissed Benazir Bhutto and her cabinet. Further elections in 1997 restored Nawaz Sharif as prime minister. But in October 1999, a military coup occurred. Martial law was declared, Nawaz Sharif was arrested and charged with kidnapping, attempted murder, hijacking and terrorism, and General Pervez Musharraf proclaimed himself the country's 'chief executive'.

In May 1998, nuclear tests carried out first by India and then by Pakistan created fears of a nuclear war in Kashmir. However, clashes in Kashmir continued into the 21st century without the use of nuclear weapons. In 2001, Pakistan supported the West in its military strikes against the Taliban in Afghanistan. The United States lifted sanctions and promised new aid to Pakistan. Musharraf adopted the title of president.

Economy

According to the World Bank, Pakistan is a 'low-income' developing country, with a per capita gross national product of US $470 in 1999. Agriculture employs about 44% of the workforce. Major crops, grown mostly on irrigated land, include cotton, fruits, rice, sugar cane, vegetables and wheat. Livestock include goats and sheep, while cattle and buffaloes are mainly important as beasts of burden. Fishing is important in the Arabian Sea.

Some chromite, gypsum, iron ore, limestone and rock salt are mined, and manufacturing industries employ approximately 9% of the workforce. Manufacturing has increased substantially since Pakistan became independent in 1947. Leading manufactures include bicycles, car tyres, cement, industrial chemicals, cotton yarn, fertilizers, processed food products, especially flour and sugar, and jute and cotton textiles. Textiles and ready-made garments are major exports. Pakistan's major trading partners include the United States, Japan and Germany.

AREA
796,100 sq km
[307,374 sq mi]

POPULATION
144,617,000

CAPITAL (POPULATION)
Islamabad
(525,000)

GOVERNMENT
Military regime

ETHNIC GROUPS
Punjabi 60%, Sindhi 12%,
Pashtun 13%, Baluch, Muhajir

LANGUAGES
Urdu (official), many others

RELIGIONS
Islam 97%, Christianity,
Hinduism

CURRENCY
Pakistan rupee = 100 paisa

PALAU – SEE PACIFIC OCEAN, PAGES 174–178;
PANAMA – SEE COSTA RICA, PAGE 88

PAPUA NEW GUINEA

Papua New Guinea's flag was first adopted in 1971, four years before the country became independent from Australia. It includes a local bird of paradise, the 'kumul', in flight, together with the stars of the Southern Cross. The colours are those often used by local artists.

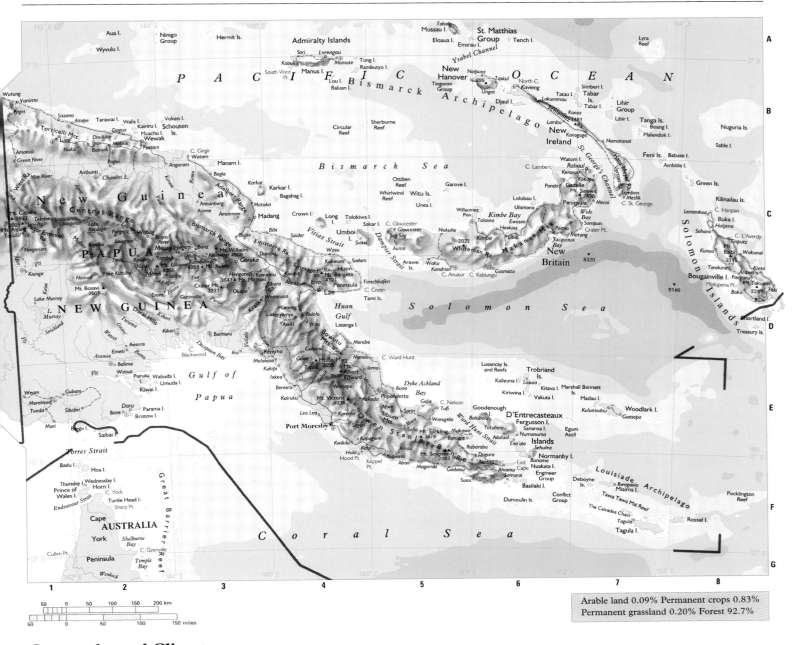

Arable land 0.09% Permanent crops 0.83%
Permanent grassland 0.20% Forest 92.7%

Geography and Climate

Papua New Guinea is part of a Pacific island region called Melanesia. It includes the eastern part of New Guinea, the Bismarck Archipelago, the northern Solomon Islands, the D'Entrecasteaux Islands and the Louisiade Archipelago. The land is largely mountainous.

The climate is tropical. It is hot all year with most rain occurring during the monsoon season (December–April), when north-westerly winds blow. Winds blow from the south-east during the dry season.

History, Politics and Economy

The Dutch took western New Guinea (now part of Indonesia) in 1828. In 1884, Germany took north-eastern New Guinea and Britain took the south-east. In 1906, Britain handed the south-east over to Australia. It then became known as the Territory of Papua. When World War I broke out in 1914, Australia took German New Guinea. In 1921, the League of Nations gave Australia a mandate to rule the area, which was named the Territory of New Guinea.

Japan invaded New Guinea in 1942, but the Allies reconquered in 1944. In 1949, Papua and New Guinea combined into the Territory of Papua and New Guinea. The country became independent in 1975.

Since independence, the government has worked to develop mineral reserves. At one of the most valuable mines on Bougainville, in the northern Solomon Islands, people demanded a larger share in profits, causing conflict. The mine was closed and the Bougainville rebels proclaimed the island independent. But this secession was not recognized internationally. An agreement to end the conflict was signed in 1998. Local autonomy was granted to Bougainville in 2000.

The World Bank classifies Papua New Guinea as a 'lower-middle-income' developing country. Agriculture employs most of the people.

AREA
462,840 sq km
[178,703 sq mi]
POPULATION
5,049,000
CAPITAL (POPULATION)
Port Moresby (174,000)
GOVERNMENT
Constitutional monarchy

ETHNIC GROUPS
Papuan, Melanesian
LANGUAGES
English (official), about 800 others
RELIGIONS
Traditional beliefs 34%, Roman Catholic 22%, Lutheran 16%
CURRENCY
Kina = 100 toea

The front (obverse) side of Paraguay's tricolour flag, which evolved in the early 19th century, contains the state emblem, which displays the May Star, commemorating liberation from Spain in 1811. The reverse side shows the treasury seal – a lion and staff.

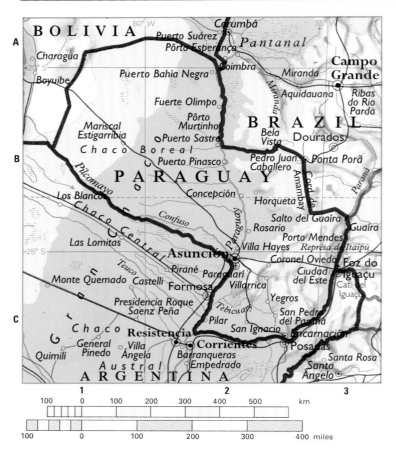

Geography and Climate

The Republic of Paraguay is a landlocked country in South America. Rivers form most of its borders. They include the Paraná in the south and the east, the Pilcomayo (Brazo Sur) in the south-west, and the Paraguay in the north-east. West of the River Paraguay is a region known as the Chaco, which extends into Bolivia and Argentina. The Chaco is mostly flat, but the land rises to the north-west. East of the Paraguay is a region of plains, hills and, in the east, the Paraná Plateau region.

Northern Paraguay lies in the tropics, while the south is subtropical. Most of the country has a warm, humid climate. The Chaco is the driest and hottest part of the country. Rainfall increases to the Paraná Plateau in the south-east.

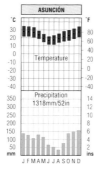

PARAGUAY (ASUNCIÓN)

In South America, between 20°S and 30°S, there is a prominent summer wet season. Rain is often heavy, yielding as much as 20 mm [0.8 in] a day in Asunción. Summers throughout the plains of Paraguay are very hot and humid, but winters are mild and relatively dry. Much of the winter rain is associated with surges of cold air from the Southern Ocean, which can give surprisingly low temperatures, especially in the south.

History

The Guarani, an Amerindian people, were the indigenous people of what is now Paraguay. Spanish and Portuguese explorers reached the area in the early 16th century and, in 1537, a Spanish expedition built a fort at Asunción, which later became the capital of Spain's colonies in south-eastern South America. The Spaniards were attracted by the potential labour supply of the Guarani and the chance to find a short cut to the silver mines of Peru. From the late 16th century, Jesuit missionaries arrived to convert the Guarani to Christianity and to protect them against those who wanted to exploit them as cheap labour. Complaints against the Jesuits' power led to their expulsion in 1767.

From 1766, Paraguay formed part of the Rio de la Plata Viceroyalty, with its capital at Buenos Aires. However, this proved unpopular and Paraguay broke free in 1811, achieving its independence from Buenos Aires in 1813. For more than a century, the country struggled for nationhood and was torn by destructive internal strife and conflict with neighbouring states: between 1865 and 1870, war against Brazil, Argentina and Uruguay cost the country more than half of its 600,000 people and much of its territory. Some territory was regained after the Chaco Wars against Bolivia between 1920 and 1935, and, in 1947, a period of civil war was followed by a spell of political and economic stability. At a time when most other South American countries were attracting European settlers and foreign capital for development, Paraguay remained isolated and forbidding.

Politics

In 1954, General Alfredo Stroessner seized power and assumed the presidency. During his dictatorship, there was considerable economic growth, particularly in the 1970s, with an emphasis on developing hydroelectricity. By 1976, Paraguay was self-sufficient in electrical energy since the completion of the Aracay complex. A second hydroelectric project, the world's largest, started production in 1984, at Itaipu. This was a joint US $20 billion venture with Brazil to harness the Paraná. Paraguay was then generating 99.9% of its electricity from water power. However, demand slackened and income declined, making it difficult for Paraguay to repay foreign debts incurred on the projects. High inflation and balance of payments problems followed.

Stroessner's regime was an unpleasant variety of nepotism. He ruled with an increasing disregard for human rights during nearly 35 years of fear and fraud until his supporters deposed him in 1989. Three elections were held in the 1990s, but the fragility of democracy was demonstrated in 1998, when the newly elected president, Raul Cubas Grau, was threatened with impeachment after issuing a decree freeing his former running mate, General Lino Oviedo, who had been imprisoned for attempting a coup against the previous president, Juan Carlos Wasmosy. In March 1999, Paraguay's vice-president, an opponent of Cubas, was assassinated and the Congress impeached Cubas, who resigned and fled to Argentina. The head of the Senate, Luis Gonzalez, then assumed the presidency.

Economy

The World Bank classifies Paraguay as a 'lower-middle-income' developing country. Agriculture and forestry are the leading activities, employing 48% of the population. The country has very large cattle ranches, while crops are grown in the fertile soils of eastern Paraguay. Major exports include cotton, soya beans, timber, vegetable oils, coffee, tannin and meat products.

The country has abundant hydroelectricity and it exports power to Argentina and Brazil. Its factories produce cement, processed food, leather goods and textiles. Paraguay has no major mineral or fossil fuel resources.

AREA	**ETHNIC GROUPS**
406,750 sq km	Mestizo 90%, Amerindian 3%
[157,046 sq mi]	**LANGUAGES**
POPULATION	Spanish and Guaraní (both official)
5,734,000	**RELIGIONS**
CAPITAL (POPULATION)	Roman Catholic 96%,
Asunción (945,000)	Protestant 2%
GOVERNMENT	**CURRENCY**
Multiparty republic	Guaraní = 100 céntimos

Peru's flag was adopted in 1825. The colours are said to have been inspired by a flock of red and white flamingos which the Argentine patriot General José de San Martín saw flying over his marching army when he arrived in 1820 to liberate Peru from Spain.

Geography

The Republic of Peru lies in the tropics in western South America. A narrow coastal plain borders the Pacific Ocean in the west. Inland are ranges of the Andes Mountains, which rise to 6,768 m [22,205 ft] at Mount Huascarán, an extinct volcano. The Andes also contain active volcanoes, windswept plateaux, broad valleys and, in the far south, part of Lake Titicaca, the world's highest navigable lake. To the east the Andes descend to a hilly region and a huge plain. Eastern Peru is part of the Amazon basin.

Climate

The coastal region is arid and chilled by the cold offshore Peru Current. In the Andes, temperatures are moderated by the altitude. The eastern lowlands are hot and humid.

PERU (LIMA)

Lima lies a short distance inland, but its climate is typical of the coastal plain. Midday temperatures are a little higher than those on the coast, which is affected by the cold Peru Current. Most of the Peruvian coast, has a desert climate. However, the northern coast often has very heavy rainfall which is caused when the cold Peru Current retreats during a climatic phenomenon known as El Niño.

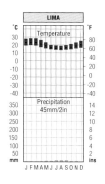

History

Amerindian people probably reached the area about 12,000 years ago. Several civilizations developed in the Andes region. By about AD 1200, the Inca were established in southern Peru. In 1500, their empire extended from Ecuador to Chile. The Spanish adventurer Francisco Pizarro visited Peru in the 1520s. Hearing of Inca riches, he returned in 1532. By 1533, he had conquered most of Peru.

In 1820, the Argentinian José de San Martín led an army into Peru and declared the country to be independent. However, Spain still held large areas. In 1823, the Venezuelan Simón Bolívar led another army into Peru and, in 1824, one of his generals defeated the Spaniards at Ayacucho. The Spaniards surrendered in 1826. Peru suffered much instability throughout the 19th century.

Politics

Instability continued into the 20th century. When civilian rule was restored in 1980, a left-wing group called the Sendero Luminoso, or the 'Shining Path', began guerrilla warfare against the government. In 1990, Alberto Fujimori, son of Japanese immigrants, became president. In 1992, he suspended the constitution and dismissed the legislature. The guerrilla leader, Abimael Guzmán, was arrested in 1992, but instability continued. In 1996, Tupac Amaru (MRTA) rebels seized the Japanese ambassador's residence, taking hostages and demanding the release of guerrilla prisoners. The stalemate ended in April 1997, when Peruvian troops attacked and freed the remaining 72 hostages.

A new constitution was introduced in 1993, giving increased power to President Albert Fujimori, who had been elected in 1990. Peru faced many problems in the 1990s, including a cholera outbreak, the worst El Niño in the 20th century, and a border dispute with Ecuador which was finally settled in 1998. Fujimori began his third term as president in 2000, but, in November, the Congress declared him 'morally unfit' to govern. In 2001, Alejandro Toledo became the first Peruvian of Amerindian descent to hold the office of president.

Economy

The World Bank classifies Peru as a 'lower-middle-income' developing country. Agriculture employs 35% of the people and major food crops include beans, maize, potatoes and rice. Coffee, cotton and sugar are the chief cash crops. Many farms are small and the farmers live at subsistence level. Other farms are co-operatives, where farmers own and operate the farm as a group. Fishing is important, except in years when El Niño wrecks the industry.

Peru is one of the world's main producers of copper, silver and zinc. Iron ore, lead and oil are also produced, while gold is mined in the highlands. Most manufacturing is small-scale. Larger plants produce such things as chemicals, clothing and textiles, paper products, processed food and steel. The country's leading exports are copper and copper products, fish meal, zinc products, coffee, oil and lead products.

Arable land 2.93%
Forest 66.3%

AREA	ETHNIC GROUPS
1,285,220 sq km	Quechua 45%,
[496,223 sq mi]	Mestizo 37%, White 15%
POPULATION	**LANGUAGES**
27,484,000	Spanish and Quechua
CAPITAL (POPULATION)	(both official), Aymara
Lima (Lima-Callao,	**RELIGIONS**
6,601,000)	Roman Catholic 90%
GOVERNMENT	**CURRENCY**
Transitional republic	New sol = 100 centavos

This flag was adopted in 1946, when the country won its independence from the United States. The eight rays of the large sun represent the eight provinces which led the revolt against Spanish rule in 1898. The three smaller stars stand for the three main island groups.

Geography

The Republic of the Philippines is an island country in southeastern Asia. It includes about 7,100 islands, of which 2,770 are named and about 1,000 are inhabited. Luzon and Mindanao, the two largest islands, make up more than two-thirds of the country. The land is mainly mountainous and lacks large lowlands. The country lies in an unstable region and earthquakes are common. The islands also have several active volcanoes, one of which is the highest peak, Mount Apo, at 2,954 m [9,692 ft] above sea level.

Climate

The country has a tropical climate, with high temperatures throughout the year. The dry season runs from December to April. The rest of the year is wet. The high rainfall is associated with typhoons which periodically strike the east coast.

PHILIPPINES (MANILA)

The islands in the southern Philippines have an equatorial climate, but the northern and central islands have a tropical monsoon climate, with a marked dry season. Manila has a typical monsoon climate. Of the average annual rainfall of 2,085 mm [82 in], around 1,930 mm [76 in] occurs between May and November. December to April is the dry season. Between August and October, much of the rain comes from typhoons (hurricanes).

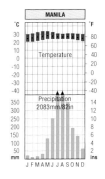

History

The earliest people to settle in the Philippines were probably Negritos, small groups of whom are still found in remote mountain areas. But most modern Filipinos are descendants of people who probably came from the Asian mainland more than 30,000 years ago. Little is known about the early history of the islands. However, most people were probably hunters and gatherers, except in the interior of northern Luzon, where the Igorot people built spectacular irrigated rice terraces contouring the mountain slopes. Most people practised animism, a mixture of monotheism and polytheism, and contacts with traders from China and Indonesia never led to the adoption of Buddhism or Hinduism. However, things changed from the 15th century, with the introduction of Islam to the southern islands.

The first European to reach the Philippines was Ferdinand Magellan in 1521. He was killed in a battle with local warriors and his round-the-world voyage was completed without him. Spanish explorers claimed the region in 1565 when they established their first permanent settlement on Cebu. Manila was founded in 1571. The Spaniards regarded their new territory as a stepping stone to the Spice Islands to the south, but their motives for colonization were not entirely commercial. Soon after the conquest of the islands, they converted most people (except for the Muslims on Mindanao and Sulu) to Roman Catholicism.

The economy grew from the late 18th century when the islands were opened up to foreign trade. Public education began in the 1860s, but in 1892 a secret revolutionary society was formed. Called Katipunan, it launched a revolt against Spanish rule in 1896. The revolt was put down and the rebel leader Emilio Aguinaldo left the country.

In April 1898, the United States declared war on Spain and the first major engagement was the destruction of all the Spanish ships in Manila Bay. Aguinaldo returned to the Philippines and formed an army which fought alongside the Americans. On 12 June, Aguinaldo proclaimed the Philippines an independent nation. A peace treaty between Spain and the United States was signed in December 1898 and the United States took over the government of the Philippines. However, Aguinaldo still wanted independence and fighting took place between 1899 and 1901, when Aguinaldo was captured.

Politics

The Philippines became a self-governing US Commonwealth in 1935 and the Act guaranteed the territory full independence after a ten-year transitional period. However, Japanese troops occupied the islands between 1942 and 1945, and the Philippines finally achieved independence on 4 July 1946 though ties with the United States remained strong. The new country faced many problems, both economic and political. For example, the army had to put down a Communist rebellion between 1949 and 1954.

From 1946 until 1971, the country was governed under a constitution that was similar to that of the United States, with the president serving one four-year term in office. In 1971, constitutional changes were proposed, but before the new constitution had been ratified, President Ferdinand Marcos declared martial law in 1972. In 1977, the main opposition leader, Benigno Aquino, Jr, was sentenced to death. He was allowed a stay of execution and went to the United States for medical treatment. Martial law was lifted in 1981, but Aquino was shot dead on his return to the Philippines in 1983.

Following presidential elections in 1986, Marcos was proclaimed president by the parliament, but the elections were proved to be fraudulent and his opponent, Corazon Aquino, Benigno Aquino's widow, became president. Having lost the support of the public and important figures in the church and armed forces, and charged with corruption, Marcos fled the country and a new constitution was introduced in 1987, restricting the president to one six-year term in office.

Attempts to overthrow Corazon Aquino failed, but she decided not to run for re-election in 1992 and was succeeded by Fidel Ramos, who had been her defence minister. Ramos was succeeded in 1998 by Joseph Estrada, a film star. In 2000, Estrada was accused of corruption and he was forced to resign. He was succeeded in January 2001 by his vice-president, Mrs Gloria Macapagal-Arroyo, who tried to find peace in the southern Philippines. A cease-fire was agreed with the Moro Islamic Liberation Front, but the small Abu Sayyaf terrorist group continued its activities. The economy remains weak, with high levels of emigration and unemployment, though the country escaped the worst of the recession in eastern Asia in the late 1990s.

Economy

The Philippines is a developing country with a 'lower-middle-income' economy. Agriculture employs 40% of the workforce. Rice and maize are the main food crops, while bananas, cassava, coconuts, coffee, cocoa, fruits, sugar cane, sweet potatoes and tobacco are also important. Farm animals include water buffaloes, goats and pigs. Forests cover nearly half of the land and forestry is a valuable industry. Sea fishing is also important and shellfish are obtained from inshore waters.

While agriculture accounted for 22% of the gross domestic product in 1995, manufacturing accounted for 23% of the GDP. Manufactures include chemicals, clothing and footwear, food products, petroleum and coal products. The chief exports include electronics, garments and coconut oil. Some coal, copper, gold, nickel and silver are mined. The leading trading partners are the United States, Japan and Singapore.

AREA	Ilocano 10%,
300,000 sq km	Hiligaynon Ilongo 9%,
[115,300 sq mi]	Bicol 6%
POPULATION	**LANGUAGES**
82,842,000	Pilipino (Tagalog) and English
CAPITAL (POPULATION)	(both official), Spanish,
Manila (8,594,000)	many others
GOVERNMENT	**RELIGIONS**
Multiparty republic	Roman Catholic 83%,
ETHNIC GROUPS	Protestant 9%, Islam 4%
Tagalog 30%,	**CURRENCY**
Cebuano 24%,	Philippine peso = 100 centavos

PHILIPPINES

Arable land 18.5% Permanent crops 12.3%
Permanent grassland 4.29% Forest 45.6%

PITCAIRN – SEE PACIFIC OCEAN, PAGES 174–178

Poland's flag was adopted when the country became a republic in 1919. Its colours were taken from the 13th-century coat of arms of a white eagle on a red field. This coat of arms still appears on Poland's merchant flag.

Arable land 47% Permanent crops 1.12%
Permanent grassland 13.3% Forest 28.9%

Geography

The Republic of Poland faces the Baltic Sea in north-central Europe. Behind the lagoon-fringed coast is a broad plain. Much of the soil is infertile, being made up of stony moraine (rock deposited by ice sheets during the Ice Age). The plains of central Poland are more fertile.

The land rises to a plateau region in the south-east of the country. The Sudetey Highlands straddle the border with the Czech Republic. Part of the Carpathian Range lies on the south-eastern border with the Slovak Republic.

Climate

Poland's climate is influenced by its position in Europe. Warm, moist air masses come from the west, while cold air masses come from the north and east. Summers are warm, but winters are cold and snowy.

History

Poland's boundaries have changed several times in the last 200 years, partly as a result of its geographical location between the powers of Germany and Russia. It disappeared from the map in the late 18th century, when a Polish state called the Grand Duchy of Warsaw was set up. But in 1815, the country was partitioned, between Austria, Prussia and Russia. Poland became independent in 1918, but in 1939 it was divided between Germany and the Soviet Union. The country again became independent in 1945, when around 6 million people, or a massive 17% of its total population were lost, when Poland gave up territory to the Soviet Union and, in compensation, gained parts of Germany as far as the River Oder. As a result, Poland lost poor agricultural land in the east and gained an important industrial region in the west, including in the south-west Silesia and the former German city of Breslau (now called Wroclaw), in the north-west the Baltic port of Stettin (now Szczecin), and in the north the other port of Danzig (now Gdańsk).

Acquisition of a length of Baltic coastline gave Poland an opportunity to develop maritime interests. Today the Polish fleets operate worldwide.

Politics

Communists took power in 1948, but opposition mounted and became focused through an organization called Solidarity.

Solidarity was led by a trade unionist, Lech Walesa. A coalition government was formed between Solidarity and the Communists in 1989. In 1990, the Communist Party was dissolved and Walesa became president. But Walesa faced many problems in turning Poland towards a market economy. Solidarity dividing in 1990 over personality and the speed of reform, and the adoption of its reforms was interrupted in 1993, when the former Communists won the parliamentary elections.

In 1995, the ex-Communist Aleksander Krasniewski defeated Walesa in presidential elections, but he continued to follow westward-looking policies. Parliamentary elections in 1997 resulted in defeat for the reformed Communist government and the return of a right-wing coalition. In 1999, Poland joined NATO and appeared likely to be on the fast track to becoming a member of the European Union. Krasniewski was re-elected president in 2000, while parliamentary elections in 2001 resulted in the establishment of a coalition government formed by the left-wing Democratic Left Alliance and the Polish Peasants Party.

Economy

Poland has large reserves of coal and deposits of various minerals which are used in its factories. Manufactures include chemicals, processed food, machinery, ships, steel and textiles. Major crops include barley, potatoes, rye, sugar beet and wheat. Machinery, metals, chemicals and fuels are the country's leading exports.

AREA	**ETHNIC GROUPS**
312,680 sq km	Polish 98%, Ukrainian 1%,
[120,726 sq mi]	German 1%
POPULATION	**LANGUAGES**
38,634,000	Polish (official)
CAPITAL (POPULATION)	**RELIGIONS**
Warsaw (Warszawa,	Roman Catholic 94%,
1,626,000)	Orthodox 2%
GOVERNMENT	**CURRENCY**
Multiparty republic	Zloty = 100 groszy

PORTUGAL

Portugal's colours, which were adopted in 1910 when the country became a republic, represent the soldiers who died in the war (red), and hope (green). The armillary sphere – an early navigational instrument – reflects Portugal's leading role in world exploration.

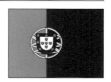

Geography

The Republic of Portugal shares the Iberian Peninsula with Spain. It is the most westerly of Europe's mainland countries. The land rises from the coastal plains on the Atlantic Ocean to the western edge of the huge plateau, or *Meseta*, which occupies most of the Iberian Peninsula. In central Portugal, the Sera da Estrela contains Portugal's highest point, at 1,993 m [6,537 ft]. Portugal also contains two autonomous regions, the Azores and Madeira Island groups.

Climate

The climate is moderated by winds blowing from the Atlantic Ocean. Summers are cooler and winters are milder than in other Mediterranean lands.

PORTUGAL (LISBON)

The west coast of the Iberian Peninsula has the oceanic variety of a Mediterranean climate with cooler summers, milder winters and a smaller temperature range than in true Mediterranean lands. Sunshine at Lisbon is abundant, averaging 7.5 hours a day all year. Frosts are rare, and temperatures over 30°C [86°F] have been recorded from March to September, and over 40°C [104°F] in July and August. Most rain falls in the winter half of the year, with July and August being virtually rainless. The severity of the summer drought decreases from south to north.

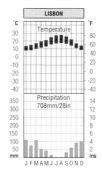

History

The Romans completed their conquest of the Iberian Peninsula, including Portugal, around 2,000 years ago and Christianity was introduced in the 4th century AD. The Romans called Portugal *Lusitania*. Following the collapse of the Roman Empire in the 5th century, Portugal was conquered by the Visigoths, who were Christians, but in the early 8th century, the Iberian Peninsula was conquered by Muslim Moors. The Christians strove to drive out the Muslims and, by the mid-13th century, they had retaken Portugal and most of Spain.

In 1143, Portugal became a separate country, independent from Spain. In the 15th century, the Portuguese, who were skilled navigators, led the 'Age of Exploration', pioneering routes around Africa onwards to Asia. Portugal set up colonies in Africa and Asia, though the biggest prize was Brazil in South America. Portugal became wealthy through trade and the exploitation of its colonies, but its power began to decline in the 16th century, when it could no longer defend its far-flung empire. Spain ruled Portugal from 1580 to 1640, when Portugal's independence was restored by John, Duke of Braganza, who took the title of John IV. England supported Portuguese independence and several times defended it from invasion or threats by Spain and its allies. However, in 1822, Portugal suffered a major blow when it lost Brazil. Portugal became a republic in 1910, but its first attempts at democracy led to great instability. Portugal fought alongside the Allies in World War I.

Politics

A coup in 1926 brought an army group to power. They abolished the parliament and set up a dictatorial regime. In 1928, they selected António de Oliveira Salazar, an economist, as minister of finance. He became prime minister in 1932 and ruled as a dictator from 1933. After World War II, when other European powers began to grant independence to their colonies, Salazar was determined to maintain his country's empire. Colonial wars flared up and weakened Portugal's economy. Salazar suffered a stroke in 1968 and died two years later. His successor, Marcello Caetano, was overthrown by another military coup in 1974 and the new military leaders set about granting independence to Portugal's colonies. Free elections were held in 1978 and full democracy was restored in 1982, when a new constitution abolished the military Council of the Revolution and reduced the powers of the president.

Portugal joined the European Community (now the European Union) in 1986, and on 1 January 1999 it became one of the 12 EU countries to adopt the euro, the single currency of the EU. However, although its economy was growing strongly in the late 1990s, Portugal remains one of the EU's poorer members, with the comparatively low per capita gross national product of US $11,030 in 1999.

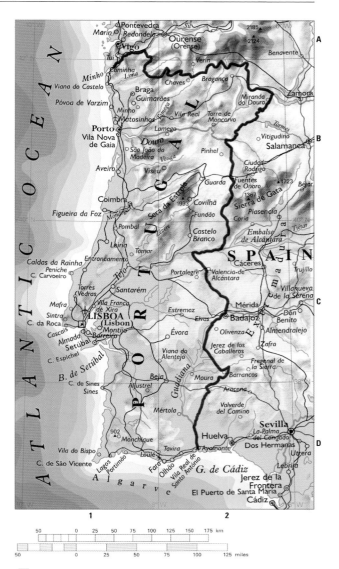

Economy

Agriculture and fishing were the mainstays of the economy until the mid-20th century. But manufacturing is now the most valuable sector. Textiles, processed food, paper products and machinery are important manufactures. Major crops include grapes for wine-making, olives, potatoes, rice, maize and wheat. Cattle and other livestock are raised and fishing catches include cod, sardines and tuna.

AREA	Cape Verdean,
92,390 sq km	Brazilian, Spanish,
[35,670 sq mi]	British
POPULATION	**LANGUAGES**
9,444,000	Portuguese
CAPITAL (POPULATION)	(official)
Lisbon (Lisboa, 2,561,000)	**RELIGIONS**
GOVERNMENT	Roman Catholic 95%,
Multiparty republic	other Christians 2%
ETHNIC GROUPS	**CURRENCY**
Portuguese 99%,	Euro = 100 cents

PUERTO RICO – SEE CARIBBEAN SEA, PAGES 71–76;
QATAR – SEE GULF STATES, PAGES 113–114;
RÉUNION – SEE INDIAN OCEAN, PAGES 122–123

ROMANIA

Romania's flag, adopted in 1948, uses colours from the arms of the provinces, which united in 1861 to form Romania. A central coat of arms, added in 1965, was deleted in 1990 after the fall of the Communist regime under the dictator Nicolae Ceaucescu.

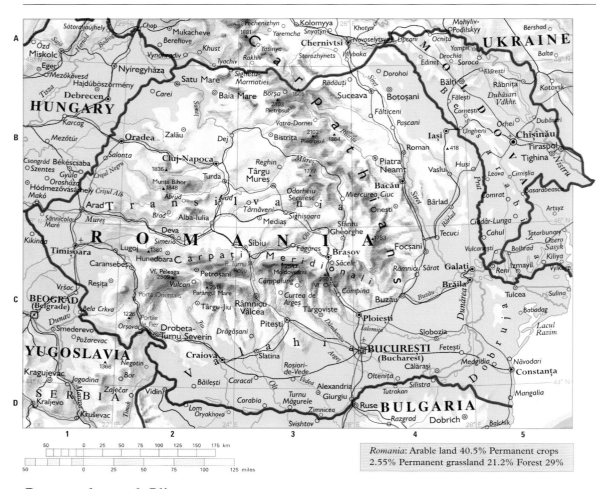

Romania: Arable land 40.5% Permanent crops 2.55% Permanent grassland 21.2% Forest 29%

lands and the plateaux. In the mountains, the vegetation changes with the altitude. Oaks are the dominant trees up to about 800 m [2,600 ft] above sea level, while beeches predominate between 800 m and 1,400 m [2,600–4,600 ft]. Conifers grow from between 1,400 m and 1,800 m [4,600–5,900 ft]. At the highest levels there are alpine and subalpine pastures. By contrast, the Danube Delta, a massive marshland region, contains large regions of reeds, which form floating or fixed islands of decaying vegetation, while feather grass and other steppe species grow on sandy areas.

History

Around 2,300 years ago, Romania was called Dacia, after the local Dacian people. But after the Romans conquered the area in AD 106, the Dacians embraced Roman culture and the Latin language so completely that the region then became known as Romania. After the fall of the Roman Empire, Romania was invaded many times. The first step towards the creation of the modern state occurred in the 14th century when two principalities (states ruled by princes) were formed: Walachia (or Valachi) in the south and Moldavia in the east. But they were conquered by the Ottoman Turks around 1500.

From the late 18th century, the Turkish Empire began to break up. The modern history of Romania began in 1861 when Walachia and Moldavia united. After World War I (1914–18), Romania, which had fought on the side of the victorious Allies, obtained large areas, including Transylvania, where most people were Romanians. This almost doubled the country's size and population. In 1939, Romania lost territory to Bulgaria, Hungary and the Soviet Union. Romania fought alongside Germany in World War II, and Soviet troops occupied the country in 1944. Hungary returned northern Transylvania to Romania in 1945, but Bulgaria and the Soviet Union kept former Romanian territory when King Michael was forcibly removed from the throne. During the 1950s, the Soviet Union maintained a tight control over their satellite. But in the 1960s, Romania's Communist Party, led by Gheorghe Gheorghiu-Dej, began to oppose Soviet control. This policy was carried on by Nicolae Ceaucescu, who became the Communist Party chief after the death of Gheorghiu-Dej in 1965.

Under Ceaucescu, Romania began to develop industries based on the oil and natural gas reserves on the flanks of the Transylvanian Alps. However, Ceaucescu's rule was one of the most odious in the Communist world. Corrupt and self-seeking, he nevertheless won plaudits from the West for his independent stance against Soviet control – including a knighthood from Queen Elizabeth II. But while he distanced Romania from Soviet foreign aims, he pursued a strict Stalinist approach on the domestic front. The remorseless industrialization and urbanization programmes of the 1970s caused a severe debt problem and, in the 1980s, he modified his policies, cutting imports and diverting output to exports. But while Romania achieved the

Geography and Climate

Romania is a country on the Black Sea in eastern Europe. Eastern and southern Romania form part of the Danube River Basin. The delta region, near the mouths of the Danube, where the river flows into the Black Sea, is one of Europe's finest wetlands. The southern part of the coast contains several resorts.

The country is dominated by a great arc of fold mountains, the Carpathians, which curve around the plateaux of Transylvania in central Romania. The southern arm of the mountains, which rise to 2,543 m [8,341 ft] at Mount Moldoveanu, is known as the Transylvanian Alps. On the Yugoslav border, the River Danube (Dunav/Dunărea) has cut a gorge – the Iron Gate (Portile de Fier) – whose rapids are tamed by the building of a huge dam.

Romania has hot summers and cold winters. The rainfall is heaviest in spring and early summer, when thundery showers are common.

ROMANIA (BUCHAREST)

In general, central Europe has a large seasonal range of temperature and a summer rainfall maximum. Winter depressions, which bring much rain to north-west Europe, are mostly prevented from reaching the east by high pressure. At Bucharest, the heaviest rains fall as thundery showers in spring and early summer, when the air warms rapidly. Romania is one of the sunniest parts of Europe.

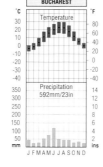

Vegetation

Forests cover large areas, creating fairy-tale landscapes in Transylvania and the Carpathians, while farmland dominates in the Danubian low-

enviable status of a net creditor, its people – brainwashed by incessant propaganda – were reduced from self-sufficiency to subsistence and shortages, with food and energy both savagely rationed.

Meanwhile, with many of his relations in positions of power, Ceaucescu built ghetto-like 'agro-industrial' housing complexes, desecrating some of the country's finest architecture and demolishing thousands of villages in the process. In December 1989, mass anti-government demonstrations were held in Timisoara and protests spread across Romania. Security forces fired on crowds, causing many deaths. But after army units joined the protests, Nicolae Ceaucescu and his wife Elena fled from Bucharest on 22 December. Both were executed on Christmas Day on charges of genocide and corruption.

Politics

A provisional government of the National Salvation Front (NSF), which had been founded only on 22 December 1989, took control of the government. Much of the old administrative apparatus was dismantled, the Communist Party was dissolved, and religion was re-legalized. In May 1990, under Ion Iliescu, the NSF won Romania's first free elections since World War II by a huge majority – a result that international observers judged flawed but not fraudulent.

A new constitution enshrining pluralist democracy, human rights and a market economy was passed by parliament in November 1991. Though not special by contemporary eastern European standards, it was a far cry from the despotic rule of Nicolae Ceaucescu. However, the NSF contained many old-guard Communists and its credibility sank further when Iliescu used miners to curb anti-government demonstrations. Strikes and protests continued, not only against the new authorities, but also against the effects of a gradual but nevertheless marked switch to a market economy, which had caused food shortages, rampant inflation and increasing unemployment. In addition, foreign investment was sluggish, deterred by the political instability. Presidential elections in 1996 led to defeat for Iliescu and victory for the centre-right Emil Constantinescu. His party also emerged as the largest in parliament. This made Romania the last

country in eastern Europe, apart from the rump Yugoslavia, to replace a regime closely associated with Communism with a democratic regime. However, in 2000, Iliescu was re-elected president, though the government continued its privatization policies.

One problem faced by Romania concerns the independent nation of Moldova on the country's eastern border. Two-thirds of Moldovans speak Romanian, the country's official language. Some people on both sides of the border favour reunification. This led to conflict after the break-up of the Soviet Union in 1991. Another problem facing Romania concerns the status of the Hungarian ethnic minority in the west.

Economy

According to the World Bank, Romania is a 'lower-middle-income' economy. Under Communist rule, industry, including mining and manufacturing, became more important than agriculture. Oil and natural gas are the chief mineral resources, but the aluminium, copper, lead and zinc industries use domestic supplies, and the iron and steel industry relies on imported ores. Besides metals, Romania also manufactures cement, processed food, petroleum products, textiles and wood products. Agriculture employs nearly a third of the workforce. Crops include fruits, maize, potatoes, sugar beet and wheat. Sheep are the chief livestock. Romania's leading exports include textiles, mineral products, chemicals, machinery and footwear. The country's chief trading partners include Germany, Italy, Russia and France.

AREA	Hungarian 7%, Roma 2%
237,500 sq km [91,699 sq mi]	**LANGUAGES**
POPULATION	Romanian (official),
22,364,000	Hungarian, German
CAPITAL (POPULATION)	**RELIGIONS**
Bucharest (Bucuresti, 2,028,000)	Romanian Orthodox 70%,
GOVERNMENT	Protestant 6%,
Multiparty republic	Roman Catholic 3%
ETHNIC GROUPS	**CURRENCY**
Romanian 89%,	Romanian leu = 100 bani

Geography and Climate

The Republic of Moldova is a small country sandwiched between Ukraine and Romania. It was formerly one of the 15 republics that made up the Soviet Union. Much of the land is hilly and the highest areas are near the centre of the country.

Moldova has a moderately continental climate, with warm summers and fairly cold winters when temperatures dip below freezing point. Most of the rain falls in the warmer months.

History

In the 14th century, the Moldavians formed a state called Moldavia. It included part of Romania and Bessarabia (now the modern country of Moldova). The Ottoman Turks took the area in the 16th century, but in 1812 Russia took over Bessarabia. In 1861, Moldavia and Walachia united to form Romania. Russia retook southern Bessarabia in 1878.

After World War I (1914–18), all of Bessarabia was returned to Romania, but the Soviet Union did not recognize this act. From 1944, the Moldovan Soviet Socialist Republic was part of the Soviet Union.

Politics

In 1989, the Moldovans asserted their independence and ethnicity by making Romanian the official language and, at the end of 1991, Moldova became independent. Moldova is ethnically complex. It combines the Moldavian part of Ukraine with the larger Bessarabia – the section of Romania between the Prut and Nistru (Dnister) rivers. Its majority Moldovan population is ethnically Romanian, and there are people on both sides who favour reunification. This is opposed by Russians, Ukrainians and, in the south, by the Gagauz, the Christian Orthodox Turks. In 1992, fighting occurred between Moldovans and

Russians in Trans-Dnestr, the mainly Russian-speaking area east of the River Dnestr, and a joint Moldovan-Russian peace-keeping force was established to restore order.

In 1994, Moldova adopted a new constitution making the country a democratic republic. On 1 January 1997, a former Communist, Petru Lucinschi, became president. In 1998 and 2001, the Party of the Moldovan Communists (PCRM) won the highest share of the votes. In 2000, the constitution was changed, turning Moldova from a semi-presidential republic to a parliamentary republic. In 2001, the Communist leader Vladimir Voronin was elected president.

Economy

Moldova is a fertile country in which agriculture remains central to the economy. Major products include fruits, maize, tobacco and wine.

There are few natural resources within Moldova, and the government imports materials and fuels for its industries. Light industries, such as food processing and the manufacturing of household appliances, are gradually expanding.

AREA	**ETHNIC GROUPS**
33,700 sq km	Moldovan 65%, Ukrainian 14%,
[13,010 sq mi]	Russian 13%, Gagauz 4%,
POPULATION	Jewish 2%, Bulgarian
4,432,000	**LANGUAGES**
CAPITAL (POPULATION)	Moldovan/Romanian (official)
Chişinău	**RELIGIONS**
(658,000)	Eastern Orthodox
GOVERNMENT	**CURRENCY**
Multiparty republic	Leu = 100 bani

In August 1991, Russia's traditional flag, which had first been used in 1699, was restored as Russia's national flag. It uses colours from the flag of the Netherlands. This flag was suppressed when Russia was part of the Soviet Union.

Geography and Climate

Russia is the world's largest country. About 25% lies west of the Ural Mountains (Uralskie Gory) in European Russia, where 80% of the population lives. It is an indication of the size of the former Soviet Union that, having shed nearly a quarter of its area with the departure of the 14 republics in 1991, the remaining Russian Federation (as the country is also officially called) remains by far the largest country in the world.

Diversity certainly characterizes Russia's landforms. Within its borders are rugged peaks and salt flats, glaciers and deserts, marshes and rolling hills, as well as broad level plains. In the west, the North European Plain occupies the greater part of European Russia, as well as much of Ukraine, all of Belarus and the three Baltic states. On the eastern side of the plain are the Ural Mountains, an ancient, heavy eroded range that forms the geographical divide between Europe and

SMALL ADMINISTRATIVE
SUB-DIVISIONS
WITHIN RUSSIA

1 Adygea
2 Karachey-Cherkessia
3 Kabardino-Balkana
4 North Ossetia
5 Ingushetia
6 Chechenia
7 Dagestan
8 Mordvinia
9 Chuvashia
10 Mari El
11 Tatarstan
12 Udmurtia
13 Khakassia

Asia. The Urals have few peaks rising above 1,600 m [5,248 ft]. The eastern slopes of the Ural Mountains merge into the West Siberian lowland, the largest plain in the world, with extensive low-lying marshes. The plains of Russia are surrounded on the south and east by mountain ranges. In the south, the Caucasus Mountains on the borders of Azerbaijan and Georgia contain Russia's highest peak, Mount Elbrus, which rises 5,642 m [18,506 ft] above sea level. In the east, the Altai (Altay) and Sayan ranges extend into Mongolia, while beyond Lake Baykal, the world's deepest lake, and the River Lena are the East Siberian ranges in the eastern extremity of the Asian landmass. The Kamchatka Peninsula is geologically unstable – being part of the

'Pacific ring of fire' – and earthquakes and volcanic eruptions are very common.

Much of Russia's landscape bears the imprint of the last Ice Age in the form of chaotic drainage systems, extensive marshlands, lakes and moraines in lowland areas, and cirques and U-shaped valleys in the mountains. Over half of the total area has permafrost – permanently frozen ground which may extend hundreds of metres in depth. The rivers that flow across the Russian plains are among the longest and most languid in the world. Drainage in European Russia forms a radial pattern, with the hub in the Central Uplands west of Moscow. The Volga, Europe's longest river at 3,700 km [2,300 mi], flows from

Arable land 7.72% Permanent crops 0.12%
Permanent grassland 5.17% Forest 45.4%

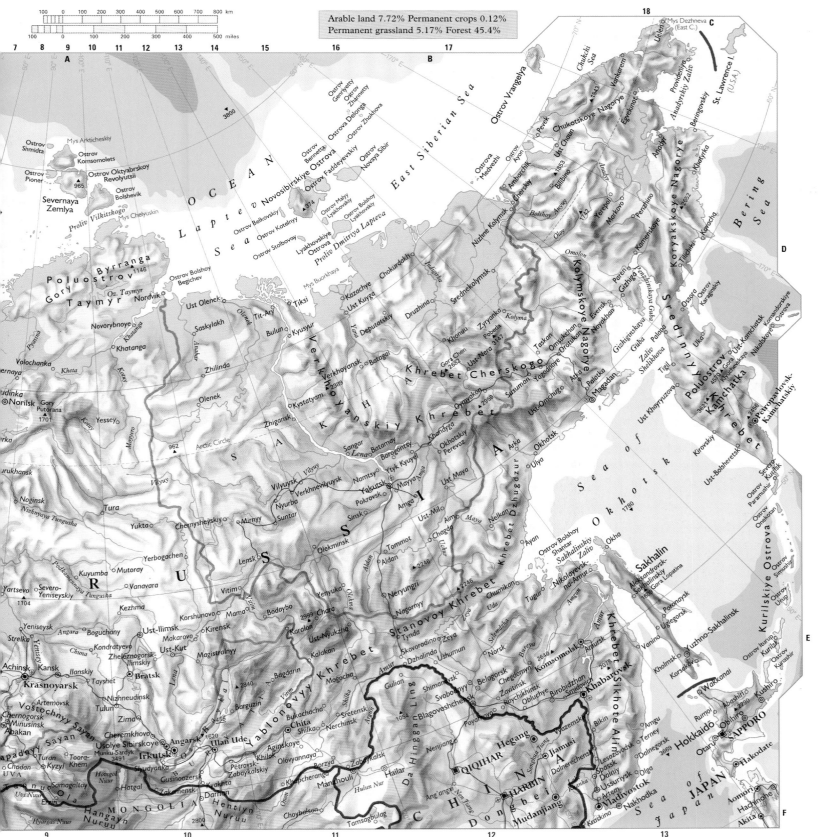

this area south to the landlocked Caspian Sea, the world's largest inland body of water. The main rivers in Siberia flow north to the Arctic. They include the Yenisey-Angara, the Ob-Irtysh and the Lena, which are, respectively, the fifth, sixth and 11th longest in the world. Another major river in eastern Siberia, the Amur, is formed by the joining of the Argun and Shilka rivers. The Amur forms much of Russia's border with China before turning north and emptying into the Tatar Strait, a stretch of water separating Siberia from Sakhalin Island.

Moscow has a continental climate with cold and snowy winters and warm summers. Krasnoyarsk in south-central Siberia has a harsher, drier climate, but it is not as severe as parts of northern Siberia.

RUSSIA – MOSCOW

Despite a large temperature range and cold winters, Moscow has a less extreme continental climate than more easterly regions. Prevailing westerly winds and an absence of mountains allow the Atlantic Ocean to extend its influence deep into the continent. Rainfall is uniform, with a slight summer maximum. Winters are cloudy with frequent snow and a very small daily variation in temperature.

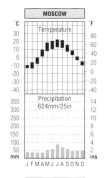

KRASNOYARSK

The climate of Krasnoyarsk is harsh. There are sub-zero temperature averages for seven months, October to April, with low records exceeding –30°C [–22°F]. Summers are not too warm, though a temperature of over 40°C [104°F] has been measured in July. The annual range of temperature is 36°C [65°F]. Snow lies on the ground for over six months of the year, but the amounts are not great. The rainfall total is low.

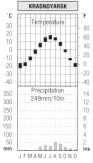

VLADIVOSTOK

The prevailing winds in winter from the north-west give low temperatures to Vladivostok. Temperatures below –20°C [–4°F] have been recorded from November to March. Snow usually lies from mid-December to mid-February. There are many foggy days in May to July, making the sunshine totals lower in summer than winter. Rainfall is low, with the monthly total exceeding 100 mm [4 in] from July to September.

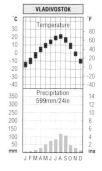

Vegetation

Extending latitudinally across Russia, and corresponding to the major climatic belts, are a series of sharply differentiated natural zones. These zones can also be seen as vertical bands on high mountains. The first of these zones is the tundra, which stretches north of the Arctic Circle from the Norwegian border to the Kamchatka Peninsula. Climatic conditions here restrict plant growth and soil formation, so that the region well deserves its name 'bald mountain top', the meaning of the term tundra in the Sami (Lapp) language. Stunted shrubs, mosses, lichens and berry-bearing bushes growing in thin, infertile soils form the vegetation cover, supporting the herds of reindeer which, for hundreds of years, have formed the basis of the local people's economy.

Extending south of the tundra, and occupying about 60% of the country, are the coniferous forests of fir, pine, silver fir, cedar and Siberian larch, that make up a region called the taiga. This is the world's largest forest covering an area more than three times that of the Amazonian rainforest. Marshes are common in the taiga, especially in western Siberia. The wildlife of the taiga includes fur-bearing animals, such as ermine, sable and beaver.

In the west and east, the coniferous forests merge into zones of mixed forests, the third main vegetation zone. These forests contain coniferous trees together with such broadleaved trees as beech,

hornbeam, maple and oak. Much of this mixed forest has been cleared for farming.

The fourth main vegetation zone is the steppe, which is sandwiched between the forests to the north, and the semi-deserts and deserts of the central Asian republics to the south. Hardly any of the natural grassland vegetation of the steppes has survived, since vast expanses have been brought under the plough. The soils of the steppe are chernozems, or black earths. They are the most fertile in the world.

History

The present size of Russia is a product of a long period of evolution. In the 9th century AD, a state called Kievan Rus was formed at the junction of the forest and the steppe in what is now Ukraine. As time went by, other states were formed further to the north. All were eventually united under the principality of Muscovy. In the 13th century, Mongol armies from the east penetrated the forests and held sway over the Slavic peoples there. It was only in the 16th century that the Mongol yoke was thrown off as the Slavs, under Ivan the Terrible (1530–84), began to advance across the steppes.

This signalled the beginning of a period of expansion from the core area of Slavic settlement to the south, east and west. Expansion across Siberia was rapid and the first Russian settlement on the Pacific, Okhotsk, was established in 1649. Progress across the open steppe was slower but, by 1696, Azov, the key to the Black Sea, was secured. A series of struggles in the 17th and 18th centuries against the Swedes and the Poles resulted in the addition of the Gulf of Finland, the Baltic coast and part of Poland to the growing Russian Empire, while, in the 19th century, the Caucasus, Central Asia and new territories in the Far East were added.

Russia had been a centralized state throughout its history, although many Russians began to demand reforms in the 19th century. A major historic landmark, and indeed a major event in world history, took place towards the end of World War I. This was the 1917 Russian Revolution, when Tsar Nicholas II was forced to abdicate and a Bolshevik (Communist) government was established under Vladimir Lenin (1870–1924). The years following the Revolution witnessed many changes, including the establishment of the Union of Soviet Socialist Republics (also called the USSR or the Soviet Union) in 1922. The most dramatic and far-reaching changes took place from the 1930s, when Joseph Stalin (1879–1953) instituted central planning of the economy, collectivized agriculture and began a period of rapid industrialization. After Stalin's death, the Soviet leaders modified some

Lake Baykal

With a lowest point of 1,620 m [5,315 ft], Lake (Oz) Baykal in southern Siberia is the world's deepest. Also the largest in Eurasia – at 636 km [395 mi] long by an average width of 48 km [30 mi] – it measures some 31,500 sq km [12,160 sq mi] more than the area of Belgium. It is so deep that it is the world's largest body of fresh water and indeed contains no less than a fifth of the fresh water contained in all the world's lakes. Its volume of 23,000 cu km [5,520 cu mi] is as much as the five Great Lakes of North America combined.

Situated in a deep tectonic basin, and fed by 336 rivers and streams, it acts as a reservoir for only one river, the Angara, which flows north to join the Yenisey. Though renowned for its purity and endemic lifeforms (65% of its 1,500 animal species and 35% of its plant species are unique to Lake Baykal), industrial plants have caused increasing pollution since the 1960s.

The graben fault that hosts the arc-shaped lake was caused by gigantic upheavals in the Earth's crust some 80 million years ago. When the climate turned wetter, about 25 million years ago, the lake began to fill – and it is still getting larger. When the *sarma* wind blows from the north-west, it generates waves over 5 m [16.5 ft] high. Located 80 km [50 mi] from the Mongolian border, Baykal drains an area of 540,000 sq km [208,500 sq mi] – 13% more than the area drained by all five of North America's Great Lakes.

policies, but they remained true to the principles of Communism until Mikhail Gorbachev changed the face of Russia in the 1980s.

The state that the Communists inherited in 1917 was not merely large, but was also made up of peoples of very diverse ethnic, religious and cultural backgrounds. Among the varied peoples – speaking more than 100 languages – the Slavs, consisting of the Russians, Ukrainians and Belarussians, were the most numerous. Other groups include the Turkic and Persian peoples of Central Asia, Finno-Ugrians, Mongols and many others. Under Soviet rule, the ethnic diversity of the nation was recognized by the existence of federal republics (of very disparate size), autonomous republics and regions set up to recognize smaller ethnic groups. Although Russia is inhabited throughout, the greatest concentration of people has, traditionally, been in the European part. It was here that the first Russian towns, with their fortresses (kremlins) and onion-domed churches, were founded. Outside this settled core, there were towns and cities which the Russians acquired during their expansion, or themselves established on the frontiers.

After the Revolution, changes took place in the distribution of the population so that the former pattern of a small highly populated core and 'empty' periphery began to break down. Today, the settled area extends into southern Siberia and, in a narrow band, across to the Pacific Ocean. As a result, a far higher proportion of the Russian population is to be found east of the Ural Mountains than before the Revolution, and even before World War II. The redistribution was actively encouraged by a regime committed to a policy of developing the east. Migration to the towns and cities has also been marked since 1917, so that, by 1997, some 73% of the population lived in cities and towns. The capital Moscow, like the other cities of the North European Plain, is a mixture of old and new, but Moscow is also a blend of European and Asian styles and cultures.

Under Communism, the country was transformed from an underdeveloped nation into a powerful industrial one. In 1917, most industrial development was concentrated in a few centres in the European part of the country, including Moscow, St Petersburg and the Donbas region of the Ukraine. As in many other parts of the world, industrialization was initially based on the iron and steel industry. In the 1930s, heavy national investment went into expanding production in the already existing industrial areas of European Russia, and establishing industry in central and eastern Russia. For example, new, large integrated steel mills were built in the southern Urals and on the Kuzbas coalfield in western Siberia. The shift away from coal as a basis for industrial development to alternative energy sources took place later in the Soviet Union than in many other countries. From the 1960s, however, petroleum and natural gas industries began to develop rapidly and the same was true of industries based on hydroelectric power. Hydroelectric power was especially important in building up industry in eastern Siberia, where massive installations on the River Angara provided energy for aluminium production. Although the introduction of large-scale industry into formerly backward areas helped to even out levels of development, regional imbalances remained large. The pre-revolutionary foci of development continued to attract a large proportion of available investment and this has meant that, of the regions developed since the Revolution, only western Siberia can be said today to have a well-developed, mature industrial structure.

While overall industrial production forged ahead, agriculture was the 'Achilles' heel' of the Soviet economy and, in several years from the mid-1960s, foreign grain had to be imported. Soviet farms were of two types: collective (kolkhozi) and state (sovkhozi). The former were, according to the definition, democratically run producers' co-operatives which, in return for a grant of land, delivered some of their produce to the state. In theory free to run their affairs, they were always subject to government interference. The state farms were state-owned and state-managed. While the greater part of the total Soviet agricultural output came from collective and state farms, a large share of market garden produce and some livestock products originated on the so-called personal plots.

In the drive for economic development, the Soviet government neglected the consumer sector. For example, growth rates in textiles, food industries and wood processing lagged behind those for iron and steel production. The paucity of consumer goods, often compounded by gross inefficiencies in the state distribution system, was obvious in the size of queues that formed whenever any scarce product came on sale. Another indication was the existence of a flourishing black market.

During Stalin's rule, a conscious policy to restrict foreign trade and maximize self-sufficiency was pursued. With the formation of COMECON (the eastern trading bloc) and the realization that much of Western technology would be useful to its own continued development, the Soviet Union revised its policy. By the 1980s, the Soviet Union had begun to trade with most countries of the world, though its share of the total turnover of world trade was small.

Politics

The 1980s was a time of change when Mikhail Gorbachev sought to introduce economic and political reforms necessitated by the failures of Communist economic policies. Two Russian words, which seemed to sum up Gorbachev's efforts at reform, became well known internationally. They were glasnost, meaning 'openness', and perestroika, meaning 'restructuring'. When the Soviet Union broke up in December 1991, the consequence of growing unrest, mounting nationalism and acute economic problems were experienced and Russia maintained contact with 11 of the 15 former Soviet republics through a loose confederation called the Commonwealth of Independent States (CIS).

Despite Gorbachev's brave efforts at reform, his successor Boris Yeltsin inherited an economy in crisis, bogged down by lumbering and often obstructive bureaucracy, inept use of resources and an inefficient transport system. After the abolition of price controls sent the cost of basic commodities rocketing, the early 1990s saw food shortages worsen and unemployment rise. However, despite these many difficulties, which also included a rise in corruption and crime, the people backed the government's programme of reforms in a referendum in 1993 and returned Yeltsin as president in July 1996, defeating his Communist opponent Gennady Zyuganov in the second round of voting.

The Kuril Islands (Kurilskiye Ostrova)

A chain of 56 windswept, volcanically active islands extending 1,200 km [750 mi] between the end of Russia's Kamchatka Peninsula and the tip of Japan's northern island of Hokkaido, the Kurils separate the Sea of Okhotsk from the Pacific Ocean. With a total area of 15,600 sq km [6,000 sq mi], the islands have a stormy, foggy climate – the consequence of a cold offshore current, which comes from the Arctic.

When they were first visited by the Dutch in 1634, the islands were sparsely populated by a people called the Ainu, who are related to the Ainu of Hokkaido, Japan. Russian fur traders founded a station on the islands in 1795 and Russia claimed the northern islands in 1830. The Kurils were ceded to Japan in 1875 when Japan traded the Russians the southern half of Sakhalin Island for the Kurils. At the end of World War II, Soviet forces seized the islands, giving the Soviet Union ice-free northern access to the Pacific Ocean. However, the Japanese still regard the southern section, consisting of Etorofu, Kunashir, Shikotan and the Habomai islets, as theirs, referring to them as the 'northern territories' and allotting 7 February as a national day in their honour.

Although there are rich fishing grounds in the territorial waters and the possibility of mineral wealth, it is indeed a matter of honour rather than economics for Tokyo. The Soviets offered to return Shikotan and the Habomai islands in 1956, but the Japanese held out for all four, and the offer was withdrawn. While the advent of Gorbachev and glasnost made little difference, the deconstruction of the Soviet Union has: Boris Yeltsin's Russia, desperate for substantial Japanese aid and co-operation, found the islands a stumbling block to assistance. However, more than half of the population who have moved there since 1945 are Russian, and in a 1991 poll the islanders voted 4–1 to remain under Moscow's control.

Republics of Russia

1 KABARDINO-BALKARIA
2 NORTH OSSETIA
3 INGUSHETIA
4 CHECHENIA
5 ADYGEA
6 KARACHEY-CHERKESSIA
- - - Republic boundary
...... Autonomous okrug boundary

However, Yeltsin, who was known to be in poor health, resigned on 31 December 1999 and appointed the prime minister Vladimir Putin as the acting president. Putin, who was elected president by a landslide in March 2000, faced many problems. Besides finding solutions to the country's profound economic problems, Putin also has to maintain national unity in a country consisting of 21 republics, six territories and 49 provinces. Fighting began in the secessionist Chechen Republic during the 1990s and flared up into full-scale war in 1999. The conflict slowed in 2000, but Russia faced a new threat, namely bombings of its cities by Chechen terrorists. After the attacks on the United States on 11 September 2001, Putin and President George W. Bush found common cause in the campaign against international terrorism and the assault on the Taliban in Afghanistan.

Economy

In the early 1990s, the break-up of the Soviet Union and the ongoing government policies to privatize agriculture and industry threw Russia's economy into disarray and, according to World Bank data, the country was ranked as a 'middle-income' economy. Russia was admitted to the Council of Europe in 1997, essentially to discourage instability in the Caucasus region. More significantly still, Boris Yeltsin was invited to attend the G7 summit in Denver in 1997. The summit

became known as the 'Summit of Eight', and it appeared that Russia would thereafter be included in future meetings of the world's most powerful economies.

Industry is the most valuable activity and manufacturing and mining account for 35% of the gross national product, as compared with about 7% from agriculture. Under Communism, manufacturing in the Soviet Union was much less efficient than in the West and the emphasis was firmly on heavy industry. But today, light industry, producing a wide range of consumer goods, is becoming increasingly important. Mining remains important and the country's massive resources include oil and natural gas. Russia ranks first in natural gas production and third in oil. It also ranks among the world's top ten producers of chromite, coal, copper, diamonds, gold, phosphate rock, iron ore, molybdenum, nickel, potash, silver, tin ore, tungsten and uranium. Other natural resources include vast forests, which supply coniferous wood and wood pulp, and it has great hydroelectrical potential.

Agriculture employs about 11% of the workforce. Grains are very important and Russia remains one of the world's top producers of barley, oats, rye and wheat. The country is also a major producer of butter, cattle, cheese, eggs, milk, pigs, potatoes and other vegetables, sheep, sunflower seeds and wool. However, Russia periodically has to import the food that it needs. Fishing is also very important and Russia ranks sixth among the world's leading fishing nations.

In 1999, Russia had the world's 16th largest economy. The leading exports include fuels and lubricants, metals, machinery and transport equipment, chemicals, precious metals and wood products. Before the break-up of the Soviet Union, much of the country's foreign trade was with its satellite countries in eastern Europe, but, although these countries, especially Poland, remain important, the leading trading partners in 1998 included Germany, Belarus, Ukraine, the United States, Italy and Kazakstan.

The Trans-Siberian Railway

The world's longest line, the Trans-Siberian Railway (formerly called the Great Siberian Railway), runs for 9,310 km [5,785 mi] from Moscow to Vladivostok and Nakhodka on the Sea of Japan. Construction began as part of a new development programme for Siberia. The Siberian section, starting at Chelyabinsk in the southern Urals, was built between 1881 and 1905, with an extension to Lake Baykal in 1917. The railway has played a crucial role in the settlement and industrialization of Siberia and it was used in both World Wars to transport troops and supplies. Since the 1920s, the Trans-Siberian Railway has been linked to other railways in the region.

Today, the complete journey from the capital to the Pacific coast, involving 92 stops in eight time zones, takes more than seven days. It has become a route much used by the adventurous tourists, some of whom do not complete the entire trip and, instead, change on to other lines. One route takes tourists from the Trans-Siberian Railway through Mongolia and into China.

AREA	Ukrainian 3%, Chuvash 1%,
17,075,000 sq km	more than 100 other
[6,592,800 sq mi]	nationalities
POPULATION	**LANGUAGES**
145,470,000	Russian (official),
CAPITAL (POPULATION)	many others
Moscow (Moskva, 8,405,000)	**RELIGIONS**
GOVERNMENT	Mainly Russian Orthodox,
Federal multiparty republic	Islam, Judaism
ETHNIC GROUPS	**CURRENCY**
Russian 82%, Tatar 4%,	Russian rouble = 100 kopeks

RWANDA

Rwanda's new flag was adopted in 2002. The colour blue is used to symbolize peace and tranquillity. Yellow represents wealth as the country works to achieve sustainable economic growth, while green denotes prosperity, work and productivity. The 24-ray golden sun symbolizes new hope.

Geography and Climate

The Republic of Rwanda is a small, landlocked country in east-central Africa. Lake Kivu (Lac Kivu) and the River Ruzizi in the Great African Rift Valley form the country's western border.

Kigali, the capital, stands on the central plateau of Rwanda. Here, temperatures are moderated by the altitude. The rainfall is abundant, but much heavier rain falls on the western mountains. The floor of the Great Rift Valley is warmer and drier than the rest of the country.

History and Politics

The Twa, a pygmy people, were the first known people to live in Rwanda. About 1,000 years ago, a farming people, the Hutu, settled in the area, gradually displacing the Twa.

From the 15th century, a cattle-owning people from the north, the Tutsi, began to dominate the Hutu, who had to serve the Tutsi overlords.

Germany conquered the area, called Ruanda-Urundi, in the 1890s. But Belgium occupied the region during World War I (1914–18) and ruled it until 1961, when the people of Ruanda voted for their country to become a republic, called Rwanda. This decision followed a rebellion by the majority of Hutu people against the Tutsi monarchy. About 150,000 deaths resulted from this conflict. Many Tutsis fled to Uganda, where they formed a rebel army. Burundi became independent as a monarchy, though it became a republic in 1966. Relations between Hutus and Tutsis continued to cause friction. Civil war broke out in 1994, and in 1996 the conflict spilled over into the Democratic Republic of the Congo (then Zaïre), where Tutsis clashed with government troops. The Tutsi uprising in eastern Zaïre eventually led to the overthrow of President Mobutu and his replacement by Laurent Kabila in 1997. In the early 21st century, prosecutions began in both Belgium and Tanzania of people accused of genocide.

Economy

According to the World Bank, Rwanda is a 'low-income' developing country, with a low per capita GNP of only US $210 (1997). Agriculture employs 90% of the people, but many farmers live at subsistence level, contributing little to the economy. The chief food crops include bananas, beans, cassava, plantains, potatoes, sorghum and sweet potatoes, and some farmers raise cattle and other livestock. The chief cash crop is coffee, which is also the leading export, followed by tea and hides and skins. Rwanda also produces pyrethrum, which is used to make insecticide. The country produces some cassiterite (tin ore) and wolframite (tungsten ore), but manufacturing is small-scale. Manufactures include beverages, cement and sugar.

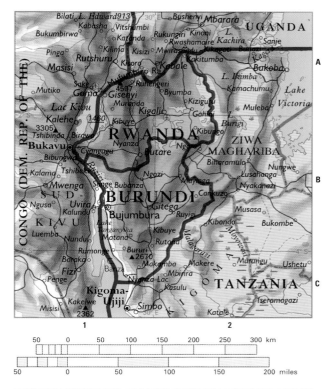

AREA	Tutsi 15%, Twa 1%
26,340 sq km	**LANGUAGES**
[10,170 sq mi]	French, English and
POPULATION	Kinyarwanda
7,313,000	(all official)
CAPITAL (POPULATION)	**RELIGIONS**
Kigali	Roman Catholic 53%,
(235,000)	Protestant 24%,
GOVERNMENT	Adventist 10%
Republic	**CURRENCY**
ETHNIC GROUPS	Rwanda franc
Hutu 84%,	= 100 centimes

BURUNDI

The Republic of Burundi is a small country in mainland Africa. Part of the Great African Rift Valley, which runs throughout eastern Africa into south-western Asia, lies in western Burundi.

Bujumbura, the capital city, lies on the shore of Lake Tanganyika. It has a warm climate. June to September is a dry season, but the rest of the year is fairly rainy. Rainfall gradually decreases to the east.

Germany conquered the area that is now Burundi and Rwanda in the late 1890s. The area was taken by Belgium during World War I (1914–18). In 1961, the people of Urundi voted to become a monarchy, while the people of Ruanda voted to become a republic. The two territories became fully independent as Burundi and Rwanda in 1962, but rivalries between the Hutu and Tutsi led to periodic outbreaks of fighting. The Tutsi monarchy ended in 1966 and Burundi became a republic. Instability continued with coups in 1976, 1987, 1993 and 1996. In 2001, a power-sharing agreement was finally signed and hopes were high that killing might be coming to an end.

Burundi is one of the world's ten poorest countries. About 92% of the people are farmers, who mostly grow little more than they need to feed their own families. The main food crops are beans, cassava, maize and sweet potatoes. Cattle, goats and sheep are raised, while fish are an important supplement to people's diets. However, Burundi has to import food. Coffee is by far the most valuable export, followed by tea, cotton, and hides and skins. Burundi has some peat and nickel deposits, but manufacturing is small-scale.

AREA	ETHNIC GROUPS
27,830 sq km	Hutu 85%, Tutsi 14%, Twa 1%
[10,745 sq mi]	**LANGUAGES**
POPULATION	French and Kirundi (both official)
6,224,000	**RELIGIONS**
CAPITAL (POPULATION)	Roman Catholic 62%, traditional
Bujumbura (300,000)	beliefs 23%, Islam 10%, Protestant
GOVERNMENT	**CURRENCY**
Republic	Burundi franc = 100 centimes

ST HELENA – SEE ATLANTIC OCEAN, PAGES 41–43;
ST KITTS & NEVIS, ST LUCIA, ST VINCENT AND
THE GRENADINES – SEE CARIBBEAN SEA, PAGES 71–76;
SAN MARINO – SEE ITALY, PAGES 131–133;
SÃO TOMÉ & PRÍNCIPE – SEE ATLANTIC OCEAN, PAGES 41–43

SAUDI ARABIA

Saudi Arabia's flag was adopted in 1938. It is the only national flag with an inscription as its main feature. The Arabic inscription above the sword means 'There is no God but Allah, and Muhammad is the Prophet of Allah'.

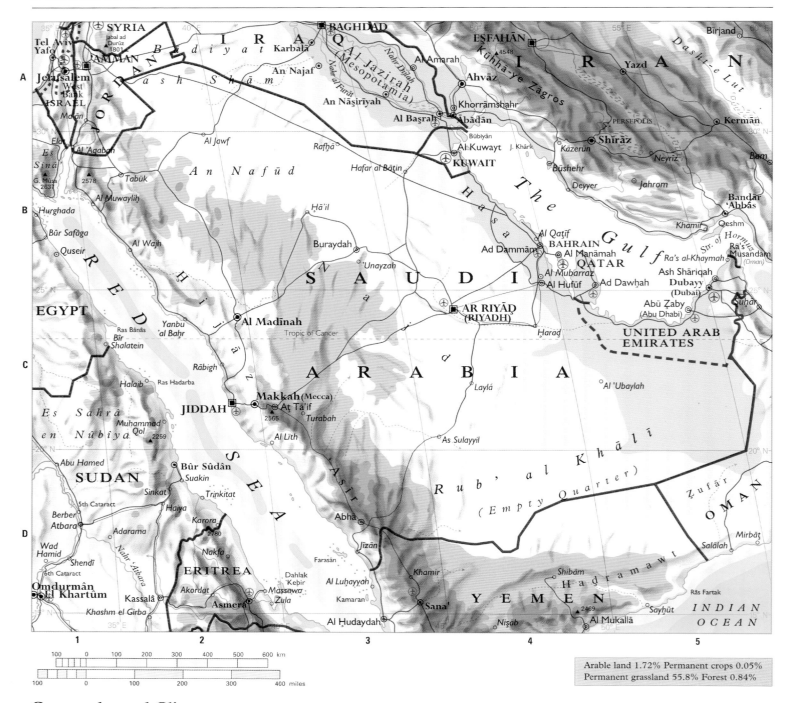

| Arable land 1.72% Permanent crops 0.05% |
| Permanent grassland 55.8% Forest 0.84% |

Geography and Climate

The Kingdom of Saudi Arabia occupies about three-quarters of the Arabian Peninsula. The heart of the state consists of the province of Najd, within which there are three main groups of oases. Najd is enclosed on its east side by an arc of sandy desert, which broadens out into the two great dune seas of Arabia. The An Nafūd lies in the north. To the south, the Rub' al Khāli, or 'Empty Quarter', the largest expanse of sand in the world, covers an area of 647,500 sq km [250,000 sq mi]. Many of the Bedouin nomads are found here, still trading and herding.

To the west, Najd is separated from the border hills along the Red Sea by fields of rough basaltic lava. The northern part of the highland region, called the Hejaz (Hijāz), consists of low rocky mountains rising steeply from the sea. But in the southern section, towards the border with Yemen, the coastal strip is well supplied with water, and a high storage dam has been built inland from Jizan in the far south-west. The hills of Asir in the south-west benefit from the summer monsoon

and are terraced in order to grow grain and fruits in the orchards.

Saudi Arabia has a hot, dry climate. In the summer, the temperatures are extremely high, though the nights are cool.

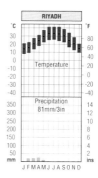

SAUDI ARABIA (RIYADH)

In the interior of Saudi Arabia the diurnal temperature range is much greater than in the coastal regions. During the summer, daytime temperatures frequently exceed 40°C [100°F], but fall sharply at night. Over 400 m [1,300 ft] above sea level, Riyadh has unusually cold winters for its latitude, with no rain between June and October. Most rain falls as short, heavy showers in spring. Frosts have been recorded in January and February.

SAUDI ARABIA

History

Groups of Bedouin nomads have lived in the interior of Arabia for thousands of years. Other groups founded trade centres along the caravan routes, or traded around the margins of the peninsula. They included the Sabaeans, who traded in frankincense, myrrh and spices in the south-west around 2,700 years ago, and the Nabataeans who controlled the north-western trade routes from the 5th century BC to the 2nd century AD.

Saudi Arabia contains the two holiest places in Islam – Mecca (or Makkah), the birthplace of the Prophet Muhammad in AD 570, and Medina (Al Madinah) where Muhammad and his followers went in 622 when Muhammad met with opposition from people in Mecca. Muhammad died in 632 and soon afterwards his successors, called caliphs, conquered a large empire beyond Arabia. The Muslim Empire began to break up in the mid-700s and Arabia was split into small areas ruled by warring groups.

In the mid-15th century, the Saud Dynasty established control over a small area near present-day Riyadh. In the mid-18th century, the Saudi ruler established an alliance with a religious leader, Muhammad Ibn Abd al-Wahhab, who wanted to restore strict observance of Islam. The Wahhabi movement swept across Arabia and the Saud family took over areas converted to the Wahhabi beliefs. By the early 19th century, they had taken Mecca and Medina, and the Ottoman governor of Egypt attacked to halt their expansion. By the late 19th century, most of the Arabian Peninsula was under the rule of Ottoman Turks and tribal chiefs, and leading members of the Saud family fled into exile.

Politics

In 1902, a young member of the Saud family, Abd al-Aziz Ibn Saud, led a force from Kuwait, where he had been living in exile, and captured Riyadh. From 1906, the Saud family gradually won control over the territory held by their ancestors and extended their land following the defeat of the Ottoman Empire in World War I. After further conquests in the 1920s at the expense of the Rashidis and Hashemites, Ibn Saud proclaimed the country the Kingdom of Saudi Arabia in 1932. Frontiers with neighbours to the south and east remained ill-defined, but this mattered little until the discovery of vast reserves of oil.

In 1932, Saudi Arabia was a poor, isolated country, but from 1933 the oil industry began when Ibn Saud's government granted Standard Oil of California the right to explore for oil. Other companies later became involved and the first major discovery was made in 1938, though full-scale production did not begin until after the end of World War II. Saudi Arabia eventually became the world's leading oil exporter and its export revenues brought enormous benefits. Oil revenues were used to finance educational and social programmes, and its five-year development plans have launched colossal industrial and domestic projects and the expansion of a private industrial base. In addition, Saudi Arabia became highly influential in the Arab world where it played a major role in supplying development aid.

Ibn Saud died in 1953 and was succeeded by his son, Saud, while Saud's brother Faisal became prime minister. Saud proved to be a poor manager of the country's economy, although Faisal proved to be an adept politician. In 1962, Saudi Arabia supported the royalist forces in Yemen (Sana), while Egypt supported the Yemeni military who had established a republic. War with Egypt seemed possible, but the tension was defused when Egypt withdrew its forces from Yemen in 1967. Saud, who had been suffering ill health, abdicated in 1964 in favour of his brother Faisal. In 1967, Saudi Arabia supported Egypt, Jordan and Syria in the Six-Day War against Israel. Although it did not send troops, it gave aid to the Arab combatants.

In March 1975, King Faisal was assassinated by one of his nephews. King Khalid, Faisal's half-brother, succeeded him. Khalid served as prime minister and he appointed another half-brother, Prince Fahd, as deputy prime minister. When Khalid died in 1982, Fahd became king. When Fahd suffered a stroke in 1995, he appointed his half-brother, Crown Prince Abdullah Ibn Abdulaziz, to act on his behalf. Although he is assisted by a Consultative Council, the monarch holds executive and legislative powers and is also the imam (supreme religious ruler). Saudi Arabia is an absolute monarchy with no formal constitution.

Progress in Saudi Arabia has not always been smooth. In the mid-1980s, world oil prices slumped dramatically, disrupting many of the projects started in the boom years, though expenditure on arms remained high. The country's position as the West's staunchest Middle Eastern ally has often conflicted with its other role as the guardian of Islam's holy places. While supporting Iraq against the Shiite Iran in the First Gulf War in the 1980s, Saudi Arabia then invited Western forces to protect it against possible Iraqi aggression following the invasion of Kuwait in 1990. In 1991, the country played a significant role in the quick victory of the Allies over Iraq's Saddam Hussein.

Relations between Saudi Arabia and the United States became strained following the terrorist attacks on the US on 11 September 2001. This was partly because Osama bin Laden, the alleged mastermind behind the attacks, was Saudi-born as also were many of his followers. However, Saudi authorities denounced the attacks and severed their relations with Afghanistan's Taliban regime.

Economy

Saudi Arabia has about 25% of the world's known oil reserves, and oil and oil products make up 85% of its exports. Agriculture employs 48% of the people, including nomadic herders who rear various animals. Crops grown in the south-western highlands and at oases include fruits, vegetables and wheat. The rearing of animals by nomads is a leading activity, as also is the production of dairy products, eggs and poultry. Since the mid-20th century, modern irrigation and desalination schemes have greatly increased crop production. The government encourages the development of agriculture and manufacturing as a means of diversifying the economy. Manufactures include cement, glass, industrial chemicals, food products and refined petroleum. Petroleum and petrochemicals dominate exports, while machinery, transport equipment and food products are the chief imports.

Mecca (Makkah)

Mecca, the holiest city of Islam, was a centre of pilgrimage long before the birth of the Prophet Muhammad. Its chief sanctuary, then as now, was the Ka'ba, a building that houses a striking black stone of probable meteoric origin, said to have been given to the patriarch Abraham by the Archangel Gabriel.

In 632, shortly before his death, the Prophet undertook his own final pilgrimage to the city; the pilgrimage to Mecca – the Hajj – remains the fifth of the Five Pillars of Islam, and every Muslim is expected to make it at least once in a lifetime.

Mecca is also part of the Second Pillar, the duty of prayer, for it is towards the Ka'ba (now enclosed by Mecca's Great Mosque) that Muslims face five times daily when they pray.

At the start of the 20th century, Mecca was a provincial town in the Ottoman Empire. Today, with a population of more than 600,000, it is the capital of the Western Province (formerly Hejaz) of Saudi Arabia. Despite development of various industries, its chief business remains the Hajj. Over 1.5 million pilgrims visit it during the month of pilgrimage (the Muslim month of Dhu al-Hijjah). Most of them travel through the port of Jiddah, situated 70 km [43 mi] to the west on the Red Sea coast. Non-Muslims (infidels) are excluded from the city and any intruders face heavy penalties. An early description of the city was written by the explorer Sir Richard Burton, who visited it in 1853 disguised as a Muslim from Afghanistan. Although Burton was not the first non-Muslim to reach the city, his account was the most accurate up to that date.

AREA	**ETHNIC GROUPS**
2,149,690 sq km [829,995 sq mi]	Arab 90%,
POPULATION	Afro-Asian 10%
22,757,000	**LANGUAGES**
CAPITAL (POPULATION)	Arabic (official)
Riyadh (Ar Riyād, 1,800,000)	**RELIGIONS**
GOVERNMENT	Islam 100%
Absolute monarchy with	**CURRENCY**
consultative assembly	Saudi riyal = 100 halalas

This flag was adopted in 1960 when Senegal became independent from France. It uses the three colours that symbolize African unity. It is identical to the flag of Mali, except for the five-pointed green star. This star symbolizes the Muslim faith of most of the people.

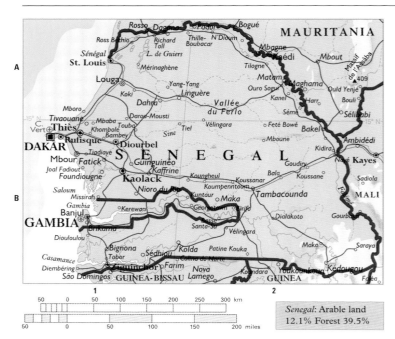

Senegal: Arable land 12.1% Forest 39.5%

Geography and Climate

The Republic of Senegal is situated on the north-west coast of Africa. The volcanic Cape Verde (Cap Vert), on which Dakar stands, is the most westerly point in Africa. Plains cover most of Senegal, though the land rises gently in the south-east.

Dakar has a tropical climate, with a short rainy season between July and October when moist winds blow from the south-west.

History and Politics

In 1882, Senegal became a French colony, and from 1895 it was ruled as part of French West Africa, the capital of which, Dakar, developed as a major port and city.

In 1959, Senegal joined French Sudan (now Mali) to form the Federation of Mali. Senegal withdrew in 1960 to become the separate Republic of Senegal. Its first president, Léopold Sédar Senghor, was a noted African poet. He continued in office until 1981, when he was succeeded by the prime minister, Abdou Diouf. Diouf was re-elected president in 1983, 1988 and 1993. However, in 2000, he was surprisingly beaten in presidential elections by veteran opposition leader Abdoulaye Wade. In 2001, the government signed a peace treaty with the separatist rebels in the southern Casamance province.

Senegal and The Gambia have always enjoyed close relations despite their differing French and British traditions. In 1981, Senegalese troops put down an attempted coup in The Gambia. In 1982, the two countries set up a defence alliance, called the Confederation of Senegambia, but this confederation was dissolved in 1989.

Economy

According to the World Bank, Senegal is a 'lower-middle-income' developing country. It was badly hit in the 1960s and 1970s by droughts, which caused starvation. Agriculture still employs 81% of the population, though many farmers produce little more than they need to feed their families. Food crops include groundnuts, millet and rice. Phosphates are the chief resource, and Senegal also refines oil imported from Gabon and Nigeria. Dakar is an industrial port. Senegal exports fish products, groundnuts, oil products and phosphates.

AREA	Pular 24%, Serer 15%
196,720 sq km [75,954 sq mi]	**LANGUAGES**
POPULATION	French (official),
10,285,000	tribal languages
CAPITAL (POPULATION)	**RELIGIONS**
Dakar (1,905,000)	Islam 92%, traditional beliefs
GOVERNMENT	and others 6%, Christianity
Multiparty republic	(mainly Roman Catholic) 2%
ETHNIC GROUPS	**CURRENCY**
Wolof 44%,	CFA franc = 100 centimes

GAMBIA, THE

Geography and Climate

The Republic of The Gambia is the smallest country in mainland Africa. It consists of a narrow strip of land bordering the River Gambia. The Gambia is almost entirely enclosed by Senegal, except along the short Atlantic coastline.

The Gambia has hot and humid summers, but winter temperatures (from November to May) drop to around 16°C [61°F]. In the summer, moist south-westerlies bring rain, which is heaviest on the coast.

History and Politics

English traders bought rights to trade on the River Gambia in 1588, and in 1664 the English established a settlement on an island in the river estuary. In 1765, the British founded a colony called Senegambia, which included parts of The Gambia and Senegal. In 1783, Britain handed this colony over to France.

During the 1860s and 1870s, Britain and France discussed the exchange of The Gambia for some other French territory. No agreement was reached and Britain made The Gambia a British colony in 1888. It achieved full independence in 1965 and became a republic in 1970. Relations between the French-speaking Senegalese and the English-speaking Gambians form a major political issue. In 1981, an attempted coup in The Gambia was put down with the help of Senegalese troops. In 1982, The Gambia and Senegal set up a defence alliance, called the Confederation of Senegambia, though this alliance was later dissolved in 1989. In July 1994, a military group overthrew the president, Sir Dawda Jawara, who fled into exile. Captain Yahya Jammeh, who took power, was elected president in 1996.

Economy

Agriculture employs more than 80% of the people. The main food crops include cassava, millet and sorghum, but groundnuts and groundnut products are the chief exports. Tourism is a growing industry.

AREA	Fula 18%, Wolof 16%,
11,300 sq km [4,363 sq mi]	Jola 10%, Serahuli 9%
POPULATION	**LANGUAGES**
1,411,000	English (official), Mandinka,
CAPITAL (POPULATION)	Wolof, Fula
Banjul (171,000)	**RELIGIONS**
GOVERNMENT	Islam 90%, Christianity 9%,
Military regime	traditional beliefs 1%
ETHNIC GROUPS	**CURRENCY**
Mandinka 42%,	Dalasi = 100 butut

SEYCHELLES – SEE INDIAN OCEAN, PAGES 122–123;
SIERRA LEONE – SEE LIBERIA, PAGE 148

SINGAPORE

Singapore's flag was adopted in 1959 and it was retained when Singapore became part of the Federation of Malaysia in 1963. The crescent stands for the nation's ascent. The stars stand for Singapore's aims of democracy, peace, progress, justice and equality.

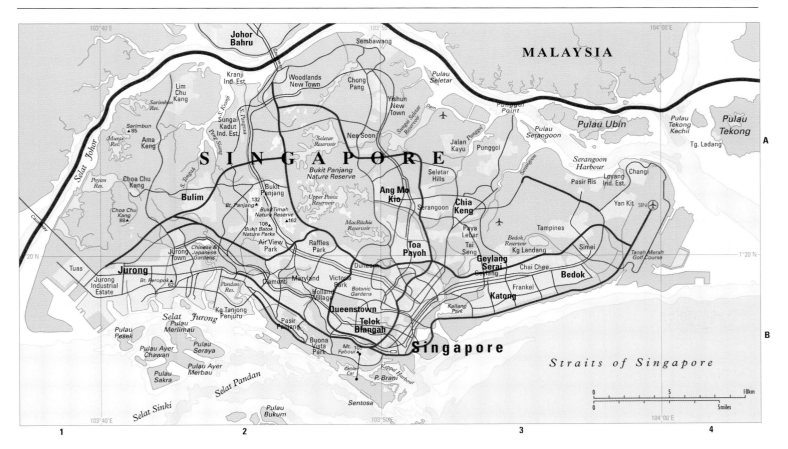

Geography and Climate

The Republic of Singapore is an island country at the southern tip of the Malay Peninsula. It consists of the large Singapore Island and 58 small islands, 20 of which are inhabited.

Singapore has a hot and humid climate, typical of places near the Equator. Temperatures are high and rainfall is heavy through the year.

SINGAPORE (SINGAPORE CITY)

Uniformly high temperatures, averaging 27°C [80°F], high humidity and heavy rain all year are typical of a place situated very close to the Equator and surrounded by water. Daytime temperatures are usually above 30°C [86°F]. Rain is often intense and thunder occurs on average 40 days a year. Rainfall varies greatly from year to year, the highest recorded being more than twice the lowest. Rain falls on over 180 days per year.

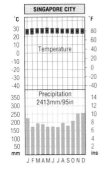

Vegetation

Rainforest once covered Singapore, but forests now grow on only 5% of the land. Today, about 50% of Singapore is built-up. Most of the rest consists of open spaces, including parks, granite quarries and inland waters. Farmland covers 4% of the land and plantations of permanent crops make up 7%.

History

According to legend, Singapore was founded in 1299. It was first called Temasak ('sea town'), but was named Singapura ('city of the lion') when an Indian prince thought he saw a lion there. Singapore soon became a busy trading centre, but Javanese raiders destroyed it in 1377.

In 1819, Sir Thomas Stamford Raffles, agent of the British East India Company, made a treaty with the Sultan of Johor which allowed the British to build a settlement on Singapore Island. Singapore soon became the leading British trading centre in South-east Asia. Japanese forces seized the island in 1942, but British rule was restored in 1945.

Politics

In 1963, Singapore became part of the Federation of Malaysia, which included Malaya and the territories of Sabah and Sarawak on the island of Borneo. But, in 1965, Singapore became an independent country.

The People's Action Party (PAP) has ruled Singapore since 1959. Its leader, Lee Kuan Yew, served as prime minister from 1959 until 1990, when he resigned and was succeeded by Goh Chok Tong. Under the PAP, the economy has expanded rapidly, although some people consider that the PAP's rule has been dictatorial and oversensitive to criticism.

Economy

The World Bank classifies Singapore as a 'high-income' economy. Its highly skilled workforce has created one of the world's fastest growing economies. Trade and finance are leading activities and manufactures include chemicals, electronic products, machinery, metal products, scientific instruments, ships and textiles. Singapore has a large oil refinery, and petroleum products and manufactures are the main exports.

AREA	Malay 14%, Indian 8%
618 sq km [239 sq mi]	**LANGUAGES**
POPULATION	Chinese, Malay, Tamil
4,300,000	and English (all official)
CAPITAL (POPULATION)	**RELIGIONS**
Singapore City (3,866,000)	Buddhism, Islam,
GOVERNMENT	Christianity,
Multiparty republic	Hinduism
ETHNIC GROUPS	**CURRENCY**
Chinese 77%,	Singapore dollar = 100 cents

This flag, using the typical red, white and blue Slavonic colours, dates back to 1848. The Slovak Republic adopted it in September 1992, prior to independence on 1 January 1994. The three blue mounds in the shield represent three mountain ranges.

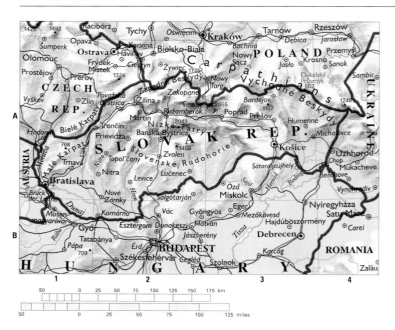

Geography

The Slovak Republic, or Slovakia, is a mainly mountainous country, with part of the Carpathian system that divides the Slovak Republic from Poland in the north. The highest peak is in the scenic Tatra (Tatry) Mountains on the Polish border, where Gerlachovsky Stit reaches 2,655 m [8,711 ft] above sea level. Forests cover much of the mountain slopes and there are also extensive areas of pasture. The south-western Danubian lowlands form a fertile lowland region. The Danube (Dunaj) forms part of the southern border with Hungary. Most of the country's rivers flow south from the northern mountains to the Danube Basin.

Climate

The climate is transitional between the milder conditions of western Europe, which are influenced by air masses from the Atlantic, and the continental conditions of Russia to the east. The conditions in Kosice in the eastern part of the country are fairly typical. Here, average temperatures range from −3°C [27°F] in January to 20°C [68°F] in July. Kosice has an average annual rainfall of 600 mm [24 in], the wettest months being July and August. The mountains have a more extreme climate, and snow or rain occurs throughout the year.

History

Slav peoples settled in the region in the 5th century AD. In the 9th century, the region, together with Bohemia and Moravia in what is now the Cezch Republic, became part of the Greater Moravian Empire. Hungarians conquered this empire in 907 and ruled the area for nearly a thousand years. Religious wars in the 15th century led many Czech nobles to settle in what is now the Slovak Republic. Then, in 1526, Hungary was defeated by the Turkish Ottomans and, soon afterwards, the Ottomans occupied much of eastern and central Hungary. As a result, the centre of Hungarian power shifted into Slovakia.

Slovak nationalism developed from the late 18th century, but it was kept under check by the Hungarians. In 1867, Hungary and Austria were united to form the dual monarchy of Austria-Hungary. Under Hungary, the Slovaks suffered from enforced 'Magyarization'. At the end of World War I, Austria-Hungary collapsed and the Czechs and Slovaks united to form a new nation called Czechoslovakia. However, the dominant status of the Czechs, who largely controlled the economy and government of the new country, led to much Slovak resentment, and support for Slovak nationalism increased. In 1938, Hungary forced Czechoslovakia to give up several areas with large Hungarian populations. These areas included Kosice in the east.

In 1939, fearing that it might be divided up between Germany, Poland and Hungary, Slovakia declared itself independent, but the country was soon conquered by Germany. At the end of World War II, Slovakia again became part of Czechoslovakia. In 1948, Communists seized control of the government. In the late 1960s, many Czechs and Slovaks, led by Alexander Dubcek, tried to reform the Communist system. This movement, known as 'the Prague Spring' or 'socialism with a human face', was put down in 1968 by Soviet and other troops. However, demands for democracy re-emerged in the 1980s, when the Soviet leader Mikhail Gorbachev launched a series of reforms in the USSR.

Politics

At the end of November 1989, Czechoslovakia's parliament abolished the Communist Party's sole right to govern. In December, the Communist Gustáv Hável, who had been head of the party since the removal of Alexander Dubcek, resigned. Non-Communists led by the playwright and dissident Václav Havel formed a new government. Non-Communists won a majority in elections in June 1990.

However, in elections in 1992, the Movement for Democratic Slovakia, led by Vladimir Meciar, campaigned for Slovak independence and won a majority in Slovakia's parliament. In September 1992, the Slovak National Council approved a new constitution for the Slovak Republic, which came into existence on 1 January 1993.

The Slovak Republic, which became a member of the OECD (Organization for Economic Co-operation of Development) in 1997, maintained close contacts with its former partner, although occasional diplomatic spats occurred. However, Slovak independence raised national aspirations among the Magyar-speaking community. Relations with Hungary were not helped in 1996, when the Slovak government initiated eight new administrative regions which the Hungarian minority claimed under-represented them politically. The government also made Slovak the only official language. The government's autocratic rule, human rights record and apparent tolerance of organized crime led to mounting international criticism. In 1998, Meciar's party was defeated in a general election by a four-party coalition and Mikulas Dzurinda, leader of the centre-right Slovak Democratic Coalition, replaced Meciar as prime minister. In April 2000, Meciar was arrested and charged with abuse of power and fraud.

Economy

Before 1948, the Slovak Republic's economy was based on farming, but Communist governments developed manufacturing industries, producing such things as chemicals, machinery, steel and weapons. Since the late 1980s, many state-run businesses have been handed over to private owners.

Farming employs about 12% of the people. Major crops include barley, grapes for wine-making, maize, sugar beet and wheat.

Manufacturing employs around 33% of workers. Bratislava and Kosice are the chief industrial cities. The armaments industry is based at Martin, in the north-west. Products include ceramics, machinery and steel.

AREA	Hungarian 11%,
49,035 sq km	Roma 2%
[18,932 sq mi]	**LANGUAGES**
POPULATION	Slovak (official),
5,415,000	Hungarian
CAPITAL (POPULATION)	**RELIGIONS**
Bratislava (451,000)	Roman Catholic 60%,
GOVERNMENT	Protestant 8%,
Multiparty republic	Orthodox 4%
ETHNIC GROUPS	**CURRENCY**
Slovak 86%,	Koruna = 100 halierov

SLOVENIA

Slovenia's flag, which was based on the flag of Russia, was originally adopted in 1848. Under Communist rule, a red star appeared at the centre. This flag, which was adopted in 1991 when Slovenia proclaimed its independence, has a new emblem, the national coat of arms.

Geography

The Republic of Slovenia was one of the six republics which made up the former Yugoslavia. Much of the land is mountainous and forested. The highest peak is Mount Triglav in the Julian Alps (Julijske Alpe), an extension of the main Alpine ranges in the north-west. Mount Triglav reaches 2,863 m [9,393 ft] above sea level. Ski resorts and impressive mountain scenery make the region a tourist attraction. Much of central and eastern Slovenia is hilly. The River Sava which flows through central Slovenia is a tributary of the Danube, as also is the Drava in the north-east.

The central area also contains a limestone karst region, with numerous underground streams and cave networks. The Postojna Caves, south-west of Ljubljana, are among the largest in Europe. The country has a short coastline on the Adriatic Sea.

Climate

The short coast of Slovenia has a mild Mediterranean climate. Inland, the climate is more continental. The mountains are snow-capped in winter. Eastern Slovenia has cold winters and hot summers. Rain occurs in every month in Ljubljana. Late summer is the rainiest season.

Vegetation

Forests cover about half of Slovenia. Mountain pines grow on higher slopes, with beech, oak and hornbeam at lower levels. The Karst region is largely bare of vegetation because of the lack of surface water. Farmland covers about a third of Slovenia.

History

The ancestors of the Slovenes, the western branch of a group of people called the South Slavs, settled in the area around 1,400 years ago. An independent Slovene state was formed in AD 623, but the area came under Bavarian-Frankish rule in 748. In 1278, the Austrian royal family of the Habsburgs took control of the region which, apart from a short period of French rule between 1809 and 1815 (during the Napoleonic wars), remained under Austrian control until 1918, when the dual monarchy of Austria-Hungary collapsed.

In 1918, at the end of World War I, Slovenia became part of a new country called the Kingdom of the Serbs, Croats and Slovenes, which was renamed Yugoslavia in 1929. Slovenia was invaded by Germany and Italy in 1941 and was partitioned between them and Hungary. At the end of the war, however, Slovenia again became one of the six republics that made up the Federal Republic of Yugoslavia.

In the late 1960s and early 1970s, some Slovenes called for the secession of their federal republic from Yugoslavia, but the dissidents were removed from the Communist Party by President Josip Broz Tito, whose strong rule maintained the unity of his country.

Politics

After Tito's death in 1980, the federal government in Belgrade found it increasingly difficult to maintain the unity of the disparate elements of the population. It was also weakened by the fact that Communism was increasingly seen to have failed in Eastern Europe and the Soviet Union. In 1990, as Communist governments were collapsing in other parts of Eastern Europe, Slovenia held multiparty elections and a non-Communist coalition was formed to rule the country.

In June 1991, Slovenia and neighbouring Croatia proclaimed their independence, but these acts were not accepted by the central government. However, after a few days of fighting between the Slovene militia and Yugoslav forces, Slovenia, the most ethnically homogenous of Yugoslavia's six component parts, found ready support from Italy and Austria (which had Slovene minorities of about 100,000 and 80,000, respectively), as well as Germany, which was an early supporter of Slovene independence. After a three-month moratorium, during which there was a negotiated, peaceful withdrawal, Slovenia

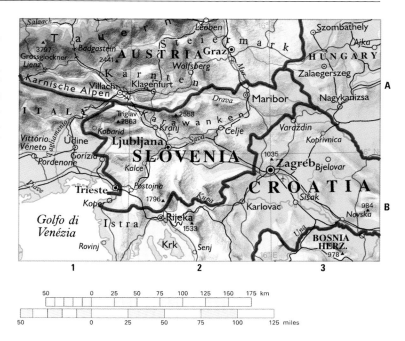

became independent on 8 October 1991. It was fortunate in avoiding the civil conflict that plagued other parts of the former Yugoslavia.

Slovenia's independence was recognized by the European Community in 1992. Multiparty elections were held and Milan Kucan (a former Communist) of the Party of Democratic Reform became president, while Janez Drnovsek, of the centre-left Liberal Democratic Party, became prime minister, heading a coalition government. In 1996, Kucan was re-elected president and, when the Liberal Democrats emerged as the party with the largest number of seats in the National Assembly, Drnovsek continued in office as prime minister and pushed ahead with the development of a market economy. Slovenia became an associate member of the European Union in 1996.

Economy

The reform of the economy, formerly run by the government, and the fighting in areas to the south have caused problems for Slovenia, although it remains one of the fastest growing economies in Europe, with a per capita gross national product of US $10,000 in 1999. At the turn of the century, Slovenia was expected to be among the first countries to join an expanded European Union.

Manufacturing is the principal activity. Manufactures include chemicals, machinery and transport equipment, metal goods and textiles. Slovenia mines some iron ore, lead, lignite and mercury. The leading crops are maize, potatoes and wheat. Slovenia's chief exports include machinery and transport equipment, other manufactures, chemicals, food products and mineral fuels. Slovenia's leading trading partners include Germany, Italy, Croatia, France and Austria.

AREA	ETHNIC GROUPS
20,251 sq km	Slovene 88%, Croat 3%,
[7,817 sq mi]	Serb 2%, Bosnian 1%
POPULATION	**LANGUAGES**
1,930,000	Slovene (official),
CAPITAL (POPULATION)	Serbo-Croat
Ljubljana	**RELIGIONS**
(280,000)	Mainly Roman Catholic
GOVERNMENT	**CURRENCY**
Multiparty republic	Tolar = 100 stotin

SOLOMON ISLANDS – SEE PACIFIC OCEAN, PAGES 174–178

SOMALI REPUBLIC

FRICA

This flag was adopted in 1960, when Italian Somaliland in the south united with British Somaliland in the north to form Somalia. The colours are based on the United Nations flag and the points of the star represent the five regions of East Africa where Somalis live.

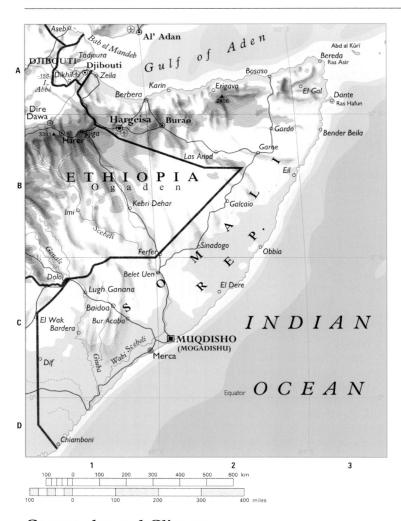

Geography and Climate

The Somali Democratic Republic consists of broad plains with mountains in the north. Rainfall is light. The wettest regions are in the south and the northern mountains, but droughts often occur. Temperatures are high, except in the northern mountains.

History, Politics and Economy

European powers became interested in the Horn of Africa in the 19th century. In 1884, Britain made the northern part of what is now Somalia a protectorate, while Italy took the south in 1905. Somali was thus divided into five areas: the two Somalilands, Djibouti (taken by France in the 1880s), Ethiopia and Kenya. Many Somalis have since longed for reunification in a Greater Somalia.

Italy entered World War II in 1940 and invaded British Somaliland. However, British forces conquered the region in 1941 and ruled both Somalilands until 1950, when the United Nations asked Italy to take over the former Italian Somaliland for ten years. In 1960, both Somalilands became independent and united to become Somalia.

Economic problems since independence led a military group to seize power in 1969. In the 1970s, Somalia supported an uprising of Somali-speaking people in the Ogaden region of Ethiopia. But Ethiopian forces prevailed and, in 1988, Somalia signed a peace treaty with Ethiopia. The fighting weakened Somalia's economy. More problems occurred when people in the north fought to secede from Somalia. In 1991, they set up the 'Somaliland Republic'. The new state was recognized neither internationally nor by Somalia's government. Fighting continued and US troops sent in by the UN in 1993 had to withdraw in 1994. By 1999, Somalia was divided into three regions – the north, north-east (called Puntland) and the south – and had no effective government. In 2001, however, a peace conference held in Djibouti agreed to set up a transitional Assembly based on clan representation in southern Somalia. But the new government had little power.

Somalia is a developing country whose economy has been shattered by drought and war. Catastrophic flooding in 1997 further damaged the infrastrucure, destroying any hope of recovery. Many Somalis are nomads who raise livestock. Live animals and meat are major exports.

AREA	ETHNIC GROUPS
637,660 sq km [246,201 sq mi]	Somali 85%, Arab 1%
POPULATION	**LANGUAGES**
7,489,000	Somali and Arabic (both official),
CAPITAL (POPULATION)	English, Italian
Mogadishu (Muqdisho, 997,000)	**RELIGIONS**
GOVERNMENT	Islam 99%
Single-party republic, military	**CURRENCY**
dominated	Somali shilling = 100 cents

DJIBOUTI

Geography and Climate

The Republic of Djibouti in eastern Africa is situated where the Red Sea meets the Gulf of Aden. Behind the coastal plain on the northern side of the Gulf of Tadjoura is a highland region, the Mabla Mountains.

Djibouti has a very hot climate. Summer temperatures of more than 44°C [112°F] have been recorded. It rains about 26 days every year.

History, Politics and Economy

Islam was introduced into the area which is now Djibouti in the 9th century AD. The conversion of the Afars led to conflict between them and the Christian Ethiopians who lived in the interior. By the 19th century, the Issas, who are Somalis, had moved north and occupied much of the land of the Afars. France gained influence in the second half of the 19th century and, in 1888, set up a territory called French Somaliland. The capital of the territory, Djibouti, became important when the Ethiopian emperor, Menelik II, decided to build a railway to it from Addis Ababa, making it the main port handling Ethiopian trade.

In 1967, the people voted to retain their links with France, though most of the Issas favoured independence. The country was renamed the French Territory of the Afars and Issas, but it was named Djibouti when it became fully independent in 1977.

Djibouti became a one-party state in 1981, but a new constitution was introduced in 1992, permitting four parties that must maintain a balance between the ethnic groups in the country. But in 1992 and 1993, the Afars launched an uprising which was put down by government troops. A peace agreement was signed in 1994.

Djibouti is a poor country. Its economy is based mainly on money it gets for use of its port and the railway that links it to Addis Ababa.

AREA	ETHNIC GROUPS
23,200 sq km [8,958 sq mi]	Somali 60%, Afar 35%
POPULATION	**LANGUAGES**
461,000	Arabic and French (both official)
CAPITAL (POPULATION)	**RELIGIONS**
Djibouti (383,000)	Islam 94%, Christianity 6%
GOVERNMENT	**CURRENCY**
Multiparty republic	Djibouti franc = 100 centimes

SOUTH AFRICA

South Africa's flag was first flown in 1994 when the country adopted a new, non-racial constitution. It incorporates the red, white and blue of former colonial powers, Britain and the Netherlands, together with the green, black and gold of black organizations.

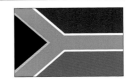

Geography

The Republic of South Africa is geologically very ancient, with few deposits less than 600 million years old. The country can be divided into two main regions – the interior plateau, the southern part of the huge plateau that makes up most of southern Africa, and the coastal fringes. The interior consist of two main parts. Most of Northern Cape Province and Free State are drained by the Orange River and its right-bank tributaries that flow over level plateaux, varying in height from 1,200 m to 2,000 m [4,000–6,000 ft]. The Northern Province is occupied by the Bushveld, an area of granites and igneous intrusions.

The Fringing Escarpment divides the interior from the coastal fringe. This escarpment makes communication within the country very difficult. In the east, the massive basalt-capped rock wall of the Drakensberg, at its most majestic near Mont-aux-Sources and rising to more than 3,000 m [10,000 ft], overlooks KwaZulu-Natal and Eastern Cape coastlands. In the west there is a similar, though less well developed, divide between the interior plateau and the coastlands. The Fringing Escarpment also parallels the south coast, where it is fronted by a series of ranges, including the folded Cape Ranges.

Climate

Most of South Africa has a mild, sunny climate. Much of the coastal strip, including the city of Cape Town, has warm, dry summers and mild, rainy winters, just like the Mediterranean lands in northern Africa. Inland, large areas are arid.

SOUTH AFRICA – JOHANNESBURG

In winter the air is very dry and the sky almost cloudless on the High Veld. The large diurnal range of temperature often exceeds 15°C [59°F]. Summer is the rainy season, when north-easterly winds bring moist air from the Indian Ocean. Rainfall is more abundant and the winter dry season shorter than in western areas at the same latitude. From May to September it usually rains on 1–3 days per month.

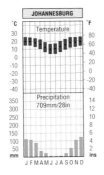

CAPE TOWN

The south-western corner of South Africa has a different climate from the rest of the country. It lies far enough south to be affected by westerly winds which bring rain in winter. The dry summers and wet winters resemble those of the Mediterranean, but it is cooler in summer due to the cold Benguela Current flowing northwards along the coast. From October to February, there are over 10 hours of sunshine per day.

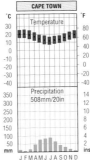

History

Early inhabitants were the Khoisan (also called Hottentots and Bushmen). However, the majority of the people today are Bantu-speakers from the north who entered the country, introducing a cattle-keeping, grain-growing culture. Arriving via the plateaux of the north-east, they continued southwards into the well-watered zones below the Fringing Escarpment of KwaZulu-Natal and Eastern Cape. By the 18th century, these people had reached the south-east. They formed large groups, including the Zulu, Xhosa, Sotho and Tswana.

Simultaneously with this advance, a group of Europeans was establishing a supply base for the Dutch East India Company on the site of present-day Cape Town. The first group was led by Jan van Riebeeck who founded the base in 1652. In 1657, some Company employees set up their own farms and were known as Boers (farmers). After Britain took over the Cape Town settlement in the early 19th century, many Boers, who resented British rule, began to move inland to develop their own Afrikaner culture. Beginning in 1836, this migration was known as the Great Trek. Their advance was channelled in the south by parallel coastal ranges, and eventually black and white met near the Kei River. To the north, once the Fringing Escarpment had been overcome, the level plateau surfaces allowed a rapid spread northwards, with the Boers founding the Transvaal in 1852 and Orange Free State in 1854.

In 1870, diamonds were found near the site where Kimberley now stands. Both the British and the Boers claimed the area, but Britain annexed it in 1871. In 1880, the Boers rebelled and defeated the British in the First Boer War. In 1886, gold was discovered in the Witwaters-rand in what is now Gauteng. Many immigrants, called *uitlanders* (foreigners), flooded to the area. Most of them were British and, to maintain their control, the Boers restricted their freedom. Tension developed, culminating in the Second Boer War (1899–1902). The Boer republics of Orange Free State and Transvaal then surrendered and became British colonies. Meanwhile, British forces had overcome Zulu resistance to European settlement. By 1898, all opposition had been suppressed and the black people had lost their independence.

Politics

In 1906, Transvaal was granted self-rule, followed by Orange Free State in 1907. The other two parts of the country, Cape Colony and Natal, already had self-rule. In 1910, the entire country was united as the Union of South Africa, a self-governing country within the British Empire. During World War I, two Boer generals led South African forces against Germany. In German South West Africa (now Namibia), General Louis Botha conquered the Germans, while General Jan Christiaan Smuts led Allied forces in German East Africa (now Tanzania). In 1920, the League of Nations gave South Africa control over South West Africa, under a trusteeship agreement. In 1931, Britain granted South Africa full independence as a member of the Commonwealth of Nations.

The Rise and Fall of Apartheid

From its 1948 institution, apartheid ('separate development') meant not only racial segregation but also massive racial discrimination. Over the next generation, a whole body of apartheid law was created. Key measures deprived blacks of political rights except in 'homelands' – modest tracts of poor land. Whites were guaranteed exclusive ownership of most of the country's best land, and most blacks, with no right of residence outside homelands few had ever seen, found themselves foreigners in their own country, obliged to carry passes at all times in a police state.

The African National Congress (ANC), the main black political organization, was banned, and black opposition was brutally suppressed. South Africa's racial policies led to increasing isolation from the rest of the world.

Changing demographic patterns (blacks were increasingly outnumbering whites) combined with international sanctions made apartheid unsupportable. The 1989 election of liberal Nationalist President F. W. de Klerk brought dramatic change. Veteran ANC leader Nelson Mandela was released from jail to the negotiating table, and in 1991 de Klerk announced his intention to dismantle the entire structure of apartheid. In 1992, an all-white referendum gave him a mandate to move quickly towards a multiracial democratic system. The first multiracial elections were held in April 1994, after which all internal boundaries were changed and the homelands abolished. A new constitution was adopted in 1996.

The development of minerals and urban complexes in South Africa caused an even greater divergence between black and white. The African farmers gained little from the mineral boom. With taxes to pay, they had little alternative but to seek employment in the mines or on European-owned farms. Migrant labour became the normal way of life for many men, while agriculture in black areas stagnated. Groups of Africans took up urban life, living in communities set apart from the white settlements. These townships, with their rudimentary housing often supplemented by shanty dwellings and without any real services, mushroomed during World War II and left South Africa with a major housing problem in the late 1940s. Nowhere was this problem greater than in Johannesburg, where a vast complex of brick boxes called SOWETO (South-Western Townships) was built. The contrast between the living standards of blacks and whites increased rapidly.

At the start of World War II, opinion was divided as to whether South Africa should remain neutral or support Britain. The pro-British General Smuts triumphed. He became prime minister and South African forces served in Ethiopia, northern Africa and Europe. During the war, Daniel Malan, a supporter of Afrikaner nationalism, reorganized the National Party. The Nationalists came to power in 1948, with Malan as prime minister, and introduced the policy of apartheid. The African National Congress, which had been founded in 1912, became the leading black opposition group. Opposition to South Africa's segregationist policies mounted around the world. Stung by criticism from Britain and other Commonwealth members, South Africa became a republic and withdrew from the Commonwealth in 1961. In 1966, the United Nations voted to end South Africa's control over South West Africa, though it was not until 1990 that the territory finally became independent as Namibia.

In response to continuing opposition, South Africa repealed some apartheid laws and, in 1984, under a new constitution, a new three-house parliament was set up. The three houses were for whites, Coloureds and Asians, but there was still no provision for the black majority. In 1986, the European Community (now the European Union), the Commonwealth and the United States applied sanctions on South Africa, banning trade in certain areas. In 1989, F. W. de Klerk was elected president and in 1990 he released the banned ANC leader Nelson Mandela from prison.

In the early 1990s, more apartheid laws were repealed. The country began to prepare a new constitution giving all non-whites the right to vote, though progress towards majority rule was marred by fighting between the Zulu-dominated Inkatha Freedom Party and the ANC. Elections held in 1994 resulted in victory for the ANC and Nelson Mandela became president. Mandela advocated reconciliation between whites and non-whites, and his government sought to alleviate the poverty of Africans in the townships. The slow rate of progress disappointed many as did other problems, including an increase in crime and the continuing massive gap in living standards between the whites and the blacks. However, in 1999, following the retirement of Nelson Mandela, his successor, Thabo Mbeki, led the African National Congress to an overwhelming electoral victory. Besides poverty, one of the biggest problems facing the government is the estimate given in a government study that one in five South Africans is infected with the HIV virus.

Economy

South Africa is Africa's most developed country. However, most of the black people – rural and urban – are poor with low standards of living. Natural resources include diamonds and gold, which formed the basis of its economy from the late 19th century. Today, South Africa ranks first in the world in gold production and fifth in diamond production. South Africa also produces coal, chromite, copper, iron ore, manganese, platinum, phosphate rock, silver, uranium and vanadium. Mining and manufacturing are the most valuable economic activities and gold, metals and metal products, and gem diamonds are the chief exports.

Manufactures include chemicals, processed food, iron and steel, machinery, motor vehicles and textiles. The main industrial areas lie in and around the cities of Cape Town, Durban, Johannesburg, Port Elizabeth and Pretoria. Investment in South African mining and manufacturing declined in the 1980s, but foreign companies began to invest again following the abolition of apartheid.

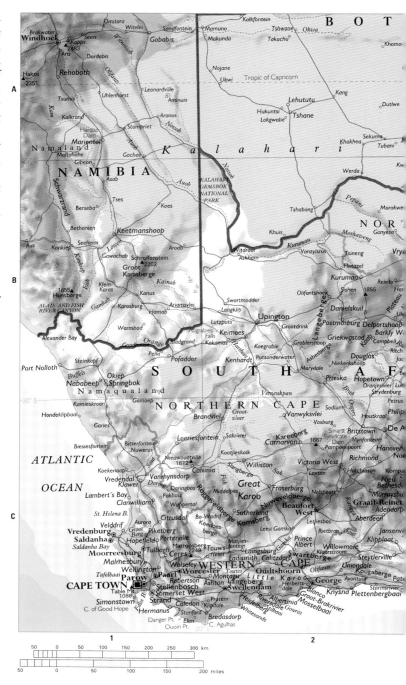

Farmland is limited by the aridity of many areas, but the country produces most of the food it needs and food products make up around 7% of South Africa's exports. Major crops include apples, grapes (for wine-making), maize, oranges, pineapples, sugar cane, tobacco and wheat. Sheep-rearing is important on land which is unfit for arable farming. Other livestock products include beef, dairy products, eggs and milk.

AREA	Coloured 9%,
1,219,916 sq km	Asian 2%
[470,566 sq mi]	**LANGUAGES**
POPULATION	Afrikaans, English,
43,586,000	Ndebele, North Sotho,
CAPITAL (POPULATION)	South Sotho, Swazi,
Cape Town (legislative,	Tsonga, Tswana, Venda, Xhosa
2,350,000); Pretoria	and Zulu (all official)
(administrative, 1,080,000);	**RELIGIONS**
Bloemfontein (judiciary, 300,000)	Christianity 68%,
GOVERNMENT	Islam 2%,
Multiparty republic	Hinduism 1%
ETHNIC GROUPS	**CURRENCY**
Black 76%, White 13%,	Rand = 100 cents

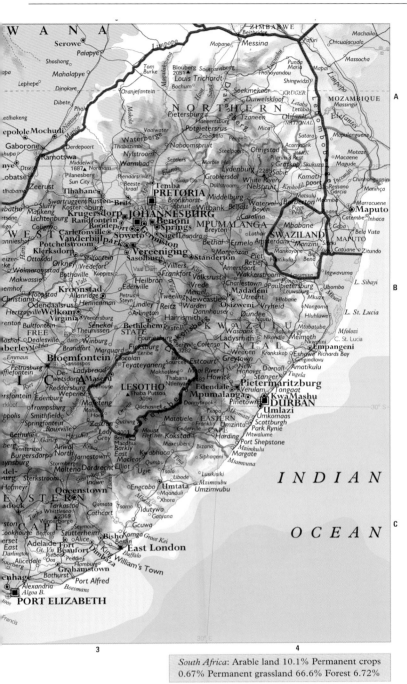

The country finally became independent in 1966 as the Kingdom of Lesotho, with Moshoeshoe II, great-grandson of Moshoeshoe I, as its king. Since independence, Lesotho has suffered instability. The military seized power in 1986 and stripped Moshoeshoe II of his powers in 1990, installing his son, Letsie III, as monarch. After elections in 1993, Moshoeshoe II was restored to office in 1995. But after his death in a car crash in 1996, Letsie III again became king. In 1998, an army revolt, following an election in which the ruling party won 78 out of the 80 seats, caused much damage to the economy, despite the intervention of a South African force intended to maintain order.

Economy

Lesotho is a 'low-income' developing country, which lacks natural resources. Agriculture, light manufacturing and money sent home by Basotho working abroad, mainly in the mines of South Africa, are the main sources of income.

AREA	ETHNIC GROUPS
30,350 sq km	Sotho 99%
[11,718 sq mi]	**LANGUAGES**
POPULATION	Sesotho and English
2,177,000	(both official)
CAPITAL (POPULATION)	**RELIGIONS**
Maseru	Christianity 80%,
(130,000)	traditional beliefs 20%
GOVERNMENT	**CURRENCY**
Constitutional monarchy	Loti = 100 lisente

SWAZILAND

Geography and Climate

The Kingdom of Swaziland is a small, landlocked country in southern Africa. The country has four regions which run north–south. In the west, the Highveld, with an average height of 1,200 m [3,937 ft], makes up 30% of Swaziland. The Middleveld, between 350 m and 1,000 m [1,148–3,281 ft], covers 28% of the country. The Lowveld, with an average height of 270 m [886 ft], covers another 33%. The Lebombo Mountains reach 800 m [2,600 ft] along the eastern border.

The Lowveld is almost tropical, with an average temperature of 22°C [72°F] and low rainfall. The altitude moderates the climate in the west of the country.

History and Politics

In 1894, Britain and the Boers of South Africa placed Swaziland under the control of the South African Republic (the Transvaal). But at the end of the Anglo-Boer War (1899–1902), Britain took control of the country. In 1968, when Swaziland became fully independent as a constitutional monarchy, the head of state was King Sobhuza II, who died in 1982 after a reign of 82 years. In 1983, his son, Prince Makhosetive, was chosen as his heir. In 1986, he became King Mswati III. Elections were held in 1993 and 1998, but political parties were illegal.

Economy

The World Bank classifies Swaziland as a 'lower-middle-income' developing country. Agriculture employs 74% of the people, and farm products and processed foods are the leading exports. Many farmers live at subsistence level. Swaziland is heavily dependent on South Africa and the two countries are linked through a customs union.

AREA	ETHNIC GROUPS
17,360 sq km [6,703 sq mi]	Swazi 84%, Zulu 10%, Tsonga
POPULATION	**LANGUAGES**
1,104,000	Siswati and English (both official)
CAPITAL (POPULATION)	**RELIGIONS**
Mbabane (42,000)	Christianity 60%, Islam 10%
GOVERNMENT	**CURRENCY**
Monarchy	Lilangeni = 100 cents

South Africa: Arable land 10.1% Permanent crops 0.67% Permanent grassland 66.6% Forest 6.72%

LESOTHO

Geography and Climate

The Kingdom of Lesotho is a landlocked country, enclosed by South Africa. The land is very mountainous, rising to 3,096 m [10,115 ft] at Thaba Putsoa. The Drakensberg Range covers most of the country.

The climate is affected by the altitude, because most of the country lies above 1,500 m [4,921 ft]. Maseru experiences warm summers, but the temperatures fall below freezing in the winter. The mountains are colder. Rainfall varies, averaging around 700 mm [28 in].

History and Politics

The Basotho nation was founded in the 1820s by King Moshoeshoe I, who united various groups fleeing from tribal wars in southern Africa. Britain made the area a protectorate in 1868 and, in 1871, placed it under the British Cape Colony in South Africa. However, in 1884, Basutoland, as the area was called, was reconstituted as a British protectorate, where whites were not allowed to own land.

SPAIN

The colours on the Spanish flag date back to those used by the old kingdom of Aragon in the 12th century. The present design, in which the central yellow stripe is twice as wide as each of the red stripes, was adopted in 1938, during the Civil War.

Geography

The Kingdom of Spain is the second largest country in Western Europe after France. It shares the Iberian Peninsula with Portugal. A plateau, called the Meseta, covers most of Spain. Much of the Meseta is flat, but it is crossed by several mountain ranges, called sierras.

The northern highlands include the Cantabrian Mountains (Cordillera Cantabrica) and the high Pyrenees, which form Spain's border with France. But Mulhacén, the highest peak on the Spanish mainland, is in the Sierra Nevada in the south-east. Spain also contains fertile coastal plains. Other lowlands are the Ebro River Basin in the north-east and the Guadalquivir River Basin in the south-west. Spain also includes the Balearic Islands (Islas Baleares) in the Mediterranean Sea and the Canary Islands off the north-west coast of Africa. Tenerife in the Canary Islands contains Pico de Teide, Spain's highest peak at 3,718 m [12,918 ft].

Gibraltar

Local rock carvings demonstrate that Gibraltar has been inhabited since Neolithic times. Greeks and Romans also settled here, but the first sure date for colonization is AD 711 when Tariq ibn Zaid, a Berber chieftain, occupied it. Although taken over by Spaniards for a short while during the 14th century, it remained Moorish until 1462. An Anglo-Dutch naval force captured it in 1704 and it was formally recognized as a British possession at the Treaty of Utrecht in 1713. In spite of long sieges and assaults – not to mention pressure from Spain – it has remained British ever since, becoming a strategically vital naval dockyard and air base.

The Rock, as it is popularly known, guards the north-eastern end of the Strait of Gibraltar. It is 6.5 sq km [2.5 sq mi] in area and occupies a narrow peninsula, consisting largely of a ridge thrusting south along the eastern side of Algeciras Bay, terminating in the 30 m [100 ft] cliffs of Europa Point. The topography prohibits cultivation and the Gibraltarians rely on the port, the ship-repairing yards, the military and air bases, and on tourism for their livelihood.

The 28,051 Gibraltarians are of British, Spanish, Maltese, Portuguese and Genoan descent. Though bilingual in Spanish and English, they remain staunchly pro-British. In 1966, following a long-standing claim, the Spanish government called on Britain to give 'substantial sovereignty' of Gibraltar to Spain and closed the border (1.2 km [0.74 mi]) to all but pedestrian traffic. In a 1967 referendum the residents voted to remain under British control, and in 1969 they were granted the status of a self-governing dependency.

In 2000, Britain and Spain agreed that Gibraltarian identity cards would be recognized throughout the European Union, that police co-operation would be increased, and that Gibraltarian banks and financial institutions would be able to export their services through the EU. Despite these changes, relations with Spain showed no improvement and a proposal, leaked in 2001, that Gibraltar might be placed under shared British and Spanish sovereignty met with much opposition in Gibraltar.

Climate

Spain has perhaps the widest range of climate in Western Europe. One of the most striking contrasts is between the humid north and north-west, where winds from the Atlantic bring mild, wet weather throughout the year, and the mainly arid remainder of the country. Droughts are common in much of Spain, though they are occasionally interrupted by sudden thunderstorms.

The Meseta, removed from the influence of the sea, has a continental climate, with hot summers and cold winters, when frosts often occur and snow blankets the mountain ranges that rise above the plateau surface. By contrast, the Mediterranean coastlands and the Balearic Islands have mild, moist winters. Summers along the

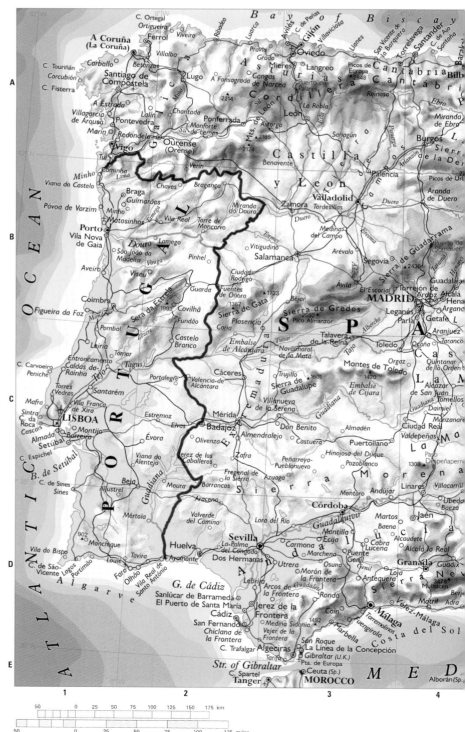

Mediterranean coast are hot and dry – ideal for tourists in search of sun and sea. The Canary Islands, with their mild to warm weather throughout the year, are another popular tourist area.

Vegetation

Spain's vegetation falls into three broad categories: forest, matorral and steppe. The forests are today mainly confined to the rainier north and north-west, with beech and deciduous oak being common. Towards the drier south and east, Mediterranean pines and evergreen oaks take over, and the forests resemble open parkland. Widespread clearance of natural vegetation for fuel and cultivation, together with overgrazing, have turned large areas into matorral, a Mediterranean scrub like the French *maquis*. This low bush growth, often of aromatic evergreen plants, may be dominated over large tracts by one species. Hence, *romillares* consist predominantly of rosemary, *tomillares* of thyme, and *retamales* of broom. Where soils are thin and drought is prevalent, matorral gives way to steppe, mainly of alfalfa and esparto.

History

About 5,000 years ago, Spain was inhabited by farming people called Iberians. Some historians believe the Basques in northern Spain may be descendants of these people. Around 3,000 years ago, Phoenicians from the eastern Mediterranean reached the Iberian Peninsula and began to establish trading colonies, some on the sites of modern cities, such as Cádiz and Málaga. Celtic peoples arrived later from the north, while Greeks reached the east coast of Spain around 600 BC.

In the 5th century BC, Carthaginians conquered much of Spain, but after the Second Punic War (218–201 BC), the Iberian Peninsula gradually came under Roman rule. The Romans made the peninsula a Roman province called *Hispania* and the Spanish name for Spain, *España*, is derived from this Latin word. The Romans left numerous monuments to their rule which can still be seen today.

During the 5th century AD, Germanic forces attacked the Iberian Peninsula, helping to bring about the final collapse of the Roman Empire in 476. By 573, the Visigoths had conquered the entire peninsula, including what is now Portugal, and they ruled until the early 8th century. In 711, Muslim Moors invaded from North Africa and, by 718, they had taken the entire peninsula, apart from some mountain areas in the far north. The Moors introduced their culture and scholarship, which was far ahead of that of Europe at that time. They built superb mosques and palaces, some of which still stand today. However, in the 11th century, the country began to divide into many small Moorish kingdoms, leaving them open to attack by the Christian kingdoms in the north, while Portugal broke away from Spain in the 11th and 12th centuries.

By the late 13th century, Muslim power was confined to the Kingdom of Granada in the south. The rest of Spain was ruled by the Christian kingdoms of Aragon, Navarre and, the most powerful of all, Castile. In 1469, Prince Ferdinand of Aragon married Princess Isabella of Castile. When Ferdinand became king of Aragon in 1479, the kingdoms united. Ferdinand and Isabella started the Spanish Inquisition which persecuted Jews, Muslims and other non-Roman Catholics. In 1492, Ferdinand's forces captured the last Muslim stronghold of Granada and, in 1512, the Kingdom of Navarre was taken by Ferdinand. This completed the union of Spain.

In 1492, Christopher Columbus was sent by Ferdinand and Isabella on an expedition that opened up the Americas. By the mid-16th century, Spain was a great world power. At its peak, Spain controlled much of Central and South America, parts of Africa and the Philippines in Asia, but its power soon began to decline as a series of wars weakened its economy. A major disaster occurred in 1588, when King Philip II sent a fleet, the Armada, to conquer England, but the English navy and bad weather destroyed half of the Spanish ships. In the early 19th century, Spain lost all its American colonies, except for Cuba and Puerto Rico. However, these latter territories, together with the Philippines, were lost in the Spanish-American War of 1898. All that remained of Spain's empire were a few small territories in Africa.

Despite being neutral during World War I, Spain was one of Europe's poorest countries in the 1920s. A military government was established in 1923 and King Alfonso III allowed General Miguel Primo de Rivera, the prime minister, to rule as a dictator. After Primo de Rivera was forced to resign in 1930, Alfonso called for city elections. Republican candidates scored such a major victory in these elections that he left the country, though he did not renounce his claim to the throne. The republicans took over the government and called for parliamentary elections which were held in June 1931. In December, the elected Cortes (parliament) adopted a new democratic constitution. The new government faced many problems, both economic and political.

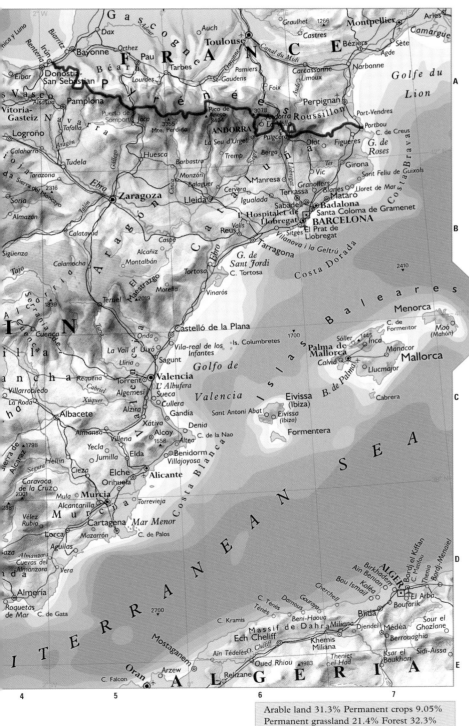

Arable land 31.3% Permanent crops 9.05%
Permanent grassland 21.4% Forest 32.3%

Deep political differences existed between the monarchists and the republicans, and also between the republicans themselves. In a highly charged situation, Spanish forces in Morocco launched a rebellion in 1936. In October of that year, the rebel Nationalists chose General Francisco Franco (1892–1975) as their commander and, supported by the Falange (Spain's fascist party), the Nationalists defeated the government forces in 1939. Franco became the dictator of Spain, ruling much like the Axis dictators, though technically the country was a monarchy. During World War II, Spain was officially neutral.

Politics

The revival of Spain's shattered economy began in the 1950s through the growth of manufacturing industries and tourism. As standards of living rose, people began to demand more freedom, while people in several regions agitated for self-government or full independence. After Franco died in 1975, the monarchy was restored and Juan Carlos, grandson of Alfonso III, became king. In 1976, the ban on political parties was lifted and, in 1977, elections were held. A new constitution making Spain a parliamentary democracy, with the king as head of state, came into effect in December 1978.

From the late 1970s, Spain began to tackle the problem of its regions. In 1980, a regional parliament with a considerable degree of autonomy was set up in the Basque Country (called *Euskadi* in Basque and *Pais Vasco* in Spanish). Similar parliaments were initiated in Catalonia (Cataluña) in the north-east and Galicia in the north-west. All of these regions have their own languages and cultures. While regional devolution was welcomed in Catalonia and Galicia, it did not end the terrorist campaign of the Basque separatist movement, the *Euskadi ta Askatasuna* (ETA). ETA announced an indefinite cease-fire in September 1998, but the truce was ended in December 1999 and the conflict continued.

The return to democracy led to rapid economic growth and, in 1986, Felipe Gonzalez, prime minister and leader of the Socialist Workers' Party, took Spain into the European Community. However, after 13 years in office, the socialist government was defeated in 1996 by the conservative Popular Party. José Maria Aznar López became prime minister, heading a minority government, beholden in parliament to the Catalan nationalists. The Aznar government maintained the socialists' commitment to adopting the euro, the single European currency, on 1 January 1999, and in March 2000 Aznar's Popular Party won a second term by a landslide.

Economy

Since the 1950s, Spain has been transformed from a poor country, dependent on agriculture, into a fairly prosperous industrial nation. It has the fifth largest economy in the European Union, though its per capita gross national product, at US $14,800 in 1999, is relatively modest, exceeding only the per capita GNPs of Greece and Portugal.

By 1997, agriculture employed only 8% of the workforce. About two-thirds of the land is used for farming, including pasture, though productivity is low because of poor soils and the arid climate. Spain has about 20 million sheep, mainly of the native merino type which produces a fine fleece. Areas too steep for sheep are grazed by goats, while cattle are mainly restricted to regions with ample grass and water, as in the north. Pigs are also raised in the northern cattle districts.

Major crops include grapes for wine-making, olives and wheat, while maize is grown in wetter areas, and citrus fruits and vegetables in areas where irrigation is possible. Spain is the world's leading olive oil producer and ranks third among wine producers. In dry areas, barley, oats and rye, grown for fodder, replace wheat. Rice is important – Spain ranks second to Italy among European rice producers. Spain also outstrips other European countries in citrus fruit production, while industrial crops include cotton, hemp, flax and sugar beet.

Spain has some high-grade iron ore in the north, but the country generally lacks mineral resources. Small deposits of oil exist, though Spain is heavily dependent on imported oil. However, Spain is the world's leading producer of mercury, which accounted for 37% of the world production in the mid-1990s.

Manufactures include cars, chemicals, clothing, electronic goods, processed food, metal goods, steel and textiles. The leading manufacturing centres are Barcelona, Bilbao and Madrid. Tourism accounts for a tenth of the gross domestic product – in 1998 around 48 million tourists visited Spain. Also important to the economy are the foreigners who come to stay permanently or for much of the year. Spain's chief exports are transport equipment, farm products and machinery. France, Germany, Italy and the United Kingdom are Spain's major trading partners.

Regions of Spain

AREA	Catalan 16%,
504,780 sq km	Galician 8%, Basque 2%
[194,896 sq mi]	**LANGUAGES**
POPULATION	Castilian Spanish
38,432,000	(official) 74%,
CAPITAL (POPULATION)	Catalan 17%,
Madrid (3,030,000)	Galician 7%, Basque 2%
GOVERNMENT	**RELIGIONS**
Constitutional monarchy	Roman Catholic 99%
ETHNIC GROUPS	**CURRENCY**
Castilian Spanish 72%,	Euro = 100 cents

ANDORRA

Andorra is a tiny mini-state that is sandwiched between France and Spain. It is a co-principality and lies high in the Pyrenees Mountains. Most Andorrans live in the six valleys (the Valls) that drain into the River Valira.

Andorra experiences cold and fairly dry winters. The summers are a little rainier, but they are pleasantly cool.

Tourism remains Andorra's chief activity in both the winter, for winter sports, and in the summer. There is some farming in the valleys and tobacco is the main crop. Cattle and sheep are grazed on the mountain slopes.

AREA	**CAPITAL**
453 sq km [175 sq mi]	Andorra La Vella
POPULATION	**CURRENCY**
68,000	Euro = 100 cents

SRI LANKA

Sri Lanka's unusual flag was adopted in 1951, three years after the country, then called Ceylon, became independent from Britain. The lion banner represents the ancient Buddhist kingdom. The stripes symbolize the minorities – Muslims (green) and Hindus (orange).

Geography

The Democratic Socialist Republic of Sri Lanka is a beautiful island nation. Often called the 'pearl of the Indian Ocean', it was once part of the ancient continent of Gondwanaland. It lies on the same continental shelf as India, being separated from its neighbour by the shallow Palk Strait. Most of the land is low-lying but, in the south-central part of Sri Lanka, the land rises to a mountain massif. The nation's highest peak is Pidurutalagala, which reaches 2,524 m [8,281 ft] above sea level. The nearby Adam's Peak, at 2,243 m [7,359 ft], is a place of pilgrimage. The south-west is also mountainous, with long ridges.

Around the south-central highlands are broad plains, while the Jaffna Peninsula in the far north is made of limestone. The coastline is varied. Cliffs overlook the sea in the south-west, while lagoons line the coast in many other areas.

Climate

The western part of Sri Lanka experiences a wet equatorial climate. Temperatures are high and the rainfall is heavy. The wettest months are May and October, marking the advance and the retreat of the summer monsoon. Eastern Sri Lanka is drier than the west.

Vegetation

Forests cover nearly two-fifths of the land in Sri Lanka, with open grasslands in the eastern highlands. Farmland, including pasture, covers another two-fifths of the country.

History

The ancestors of the Sinhalese people probably came from northern India and settled on the island around 2,400 years ago. They pushed the Veddahs, descendants of the earliest inhabitants, into the interior. The Sinhalese founded the city of Anuradhapura, which was their centre from the 3rd century BC to the 10th century AD.

Tamils arrived around 2,100 years ago and the early history of Ceylon, as the island was known, was concerned with a struggle between the Sinhalese and the Tamils. Victory for the Tamils led the Sinhalese to move south.

Politics

From the early 16th century, Ceylon was ruled successively by the Portuguese, Dutch and British. Independence was achieved in 1948 and the country was renamed Sri Lanka in 1972.

After independence, rivalries between the two main ethnic groups, the Sinhalese and Tamils, marred progress. In the 1950s, the government made Sinhala the official language. Following protests, the prime minister made provisions for Tamil to be used in some areas. In 1959, the prime minister was assassinated by a Sinhalese extremist and he was succeeded by Sirimavo Bandanaraike, who became the world's first woman prime minister.

Conflict between Tamils and Sinhalese continued in the 1970s and 1980s. In 1987, India helped to engineer a cease-fire. Indian troops arrived to enforce the agreement. They withdrew in 1990 after failing to subdue the main guerrilla group, the Tamil Tigers, who wanted to set up an independent Tamil homeland in northern Sri Lanka. In 1993, the country's president, Ranasinghe Premadasa, was assassinated by a suspected Tamil separatist. A cease-fire was signed on 1 May 1993, but fighting soon broke out again. In 1995, government forces captured Jaffna, the stronghold of the 'Liberation Tigers of the Tamil Eelam' (LTTE). But the bombing of the Temple of the Tooth in Kandy in 1998 created great outrage among the Sinhalese Buddhists, who believe that the temple's treasured tooth belonged to the Buddha.

The bombing led to rioting and provoked President Chandrika Kumaratunga to ban the LTTE. These events led to some of the fiercest fighting in the civil war, including several suicide bombings. The government lost most of the gains it had made in the mid-1990s

and, in December 1999, Kumaratunga herself was injured in a suicide bomb attack in her last election rally in Colombo. She went on to be re-elected president for a second term. By 2002, when a long-term cease-fire agreement was signed, an estimated 65,000 people had died in the conflict.

Economy

The World Bank classifies Sri Lanka as a 'low-income' developing country. Agriculture employs around a third of the workforce and coconuts, rubber and tea are the cash crops. Rice is the chief food crop. Cattle, water buffalo and goats are the chief farm animals, while fish provide another source of protein. Manufacturing is concerned mainly with processing agricultural products and producing textiles. The country's leading exports are clothing and accessories, gemstones, tea and natural rubber.

AREA	Sri Lankan Moor 7%
65,610 sq km [25,332 sq mi]	**LANGUAGES**
POPULATION	Sinhala and Tamil
19,409,000	(both official)
CAPITAL (POPULATION)	**RELIGIONS**
Colombo (1,863,000)	Buddhism 69%, Hinduism 16%,
GOVERNMENT	Christianity 8%, Islam 7%
Multiparty republic	**CURRENCY**
ETHNIC GROUPS	Sri Lankan rupee
Sinhalese 74%, Tamil 18%,	= 100 cents

Adopted in 1969, Sudan's flag uses colours associated with the Pan-Arab movement. The Islamic green triangle symbolizes prosperity and spiritual wealth. The flag is based on the one used in the Arab revolt against Turkish rule in World War I (1914–18).

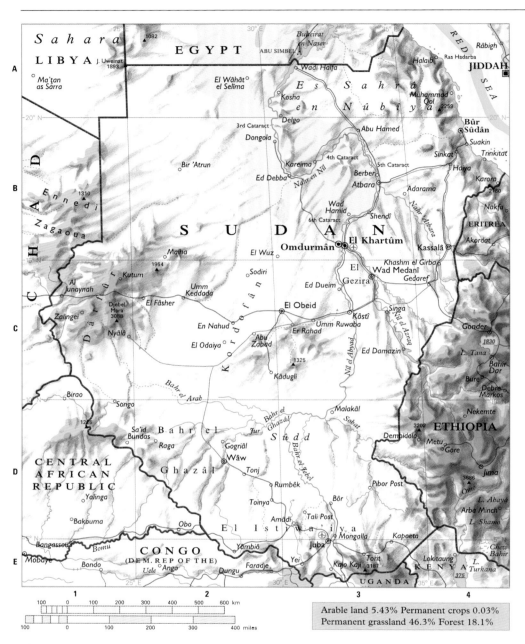

Arable land 5.43% Permanent crops 0.03%
Permanent grassland 46.3% Forest 18.1%

History

One of the earliest civilizations in the Nile region of northern Sudan was Nubia, which came under Ancient Egypt around 4,000 years ago. Another Nubian civilization, called Kush, developed from about 1000 BC, finally collapsing in AD 350. Christianity was introduced to northern Sudan in the 6th century, but Islam later became the dominant religion. In the 19th century, Egypt gradually took over Sudan. In 1881, a Muslim religious teacher, the Mahdi ('divinely appointed guide'), led an uprising. Britain and Egypt put the rebellion down in 1898. In 1899, they agreed to rule Sudan jointly as a condominium.

Politics

After Sudan's independence in 1952, the black Africans in the south, who were either Christians or followers of traditional beliefs, feared domination by the Muslim northerners. For example, they objected to the government declaring that Arabic was the only official language. In 1964, civil war broke out and continued until 1972, when the south was given regional self-government, though executive power was still vested in the military government in Khartoum.

In 1983, the government established Islamic law throughout the country. This sparked further conflict when the Sudan People's Liberation Army in the south launched attacks on government positions. Fighting continued and food shortages and the plight of refugees added to Sudan's difficulties, attracting global attention and humanitarian aid. In 1998, the government announced that it accepted, in principle, the holding of a referendum on the possible secession of the south, though definitions of what constituted the south varied.

Economy

The World Bank classifies Sudan as a 'low-income' economy. Agriculture employs 62% of the population. The leading crop is cotton. Other crops include groundnuts, gum arabic, millet, sesame, sorghum and sugar cane, while many people raise livestock. Minerals include chromium, gold, gypsum and oil. Manufacturing industries process foods, and produce such things as cement, fertilizers and textiles. The main exports are cotton, gum arabic and sesame seeds.

Geography and Climate

The Republic of Sudan is the largest country in Africa. From north to south, it spans a vast area extending from the arid Sahara in the north to the wet equatorial region in the south. The land is mostly flat, with the highest mountains in the far south.

Northern Sudan is hot and arid. The centre has an average annual rainfall of 100 mm to 510 mm [4–32 in], while the tropical south has between 810 mm and 1,400 mm [32–55 in] of rain per year.

SUDAN (KHARTOUM)

Sudan extends from the Sahara Desert almost to the Equator, and the climate changes from desert to equatorial as the influence of the intertropical rainbelt increases southwards. At Khartoum, rain falls during the summer months when the rainbelt is at its most northerly extent. The rain may be squally and accompanied by dust storms called 'haboobs'. There is a large daily range of temperature and summer days are very hot.

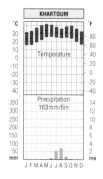

AREA	Nuba 8%, Beja 6%,
2,505,810 sq km [967,493 sq mi]	Nuer 5%, Azande 3%
POPULATION	**LANGUAGES**
36,080,000	Arabic (official), Nubian, Dinka
CAPITAL (POPULATION)	**RELIGIONS**
Khartoum (El Khartûm, 925,000)	Islam (mainly Sunni) 70%,
GOVERNMENT	traditional beliefs 25%,
Military regime	Christianity 5%
ETHNIC GROUPS	**CURRENCY**
Sudanese Arab 49%, Dinka 12%,	Dinar = 10 Sudanese pounds

SURINAM – SEE GUYANA, PAGE 115;
SWAZILAND – SEE SOUTH AFRICA, PAGES 203–205

SWEDEN

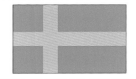

Sweden's flag was adopted in 1906, though it had been in use since the time of King Gustavus Vasa (reigned 1523–60). This king won many victories for Sweden and laid the foundations of the modern nation. The colours on the flag come from a coat of arms dating from 1364.

Geography

The Kingdom of Sweden is the largest of the countries of Scandinavia in both area and population. It shares the Scandinavian Peninsula with Norway. The western part of the country, along the border with Norway, is mountainous. The highest point is Kebnekaise, which reaches 2,117 m [6,946 ft] in the north-west.

Sweden's share of the Scandinavian Peninsula is less mountainous than that of Norway. The northern half of the country forms part of the Baltic, or Fenno-Scandian Shield, a stable block of ancient granites and gneisses which extends around the head of the Gulf of Bothnia into Finland. The shield land is an area of low plateaux which rise gradually to the west. This part of Sweden contains most of the country's rich mineral wealth.

South of the plateaux is a belt of lowlands between the capital city, Stockholm, and the second city, Göteborg (Gothenburg). These lowlands contain several large lakes, the chief of which are Mälaren, near Stockholm, and the larger Vättern and Vänern. The lakes are all that is left of a strait, which during the last Ice Age connected the Baltic with the Kattegat. Now linked by canals, the lakes form an important waterway across Sweden. South of the lakes is a low plateau, sloping gently down to the small lowland area of Skåne (Scania). The scenery has been greatly shaped by ice action and some of the most fertile soils were formed from material deposited on the beds of glacial lakes.

Climate

The two main factors that influence the climate are the northerly latitude and high mountains and plateaux of Norway that cut Sweden off from the mild influences of the Atlantic in the west. However, the Gulf Stream warms the southern coastlands, but continental influences take over in the north. The February temperature in the central lowlands is just below freezing, but in the north it is −15°C [5°F].

Precipitation is low throughout Sweden, but lies as snow for more than six months in the north. The Baltic Sea is usually frozen for at least five months, but ice is rare on the western coast. In summer there is little difference between the north and south. Most areas have an average temperature range between 15°C and 20°C [59–68°F].

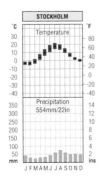

SWEDEN (STOCKHOLM)

Stockholm, in the central lowlands, has cold winters though they are not as long as those in the north. The precipitation is light and the wettest seasons are the summer and autumn. During winter, snow falls on an average of 60 days. Summers are relatively warm, with plenty of sunshine.

Vegetation

Extensive coniferous forests cover much of northern Sweden. In the south, the original cover of mixed deciduous woodland has been cleared for agriculture from areas with better soils. Sweden has much opportunity for agriculture and the typical landscape in the south is farmland interspersed with forest. Trees include beech, pine and spruce, often with birch, the national tree. Sweden is a leading exporter of wood pulp, paper and board.

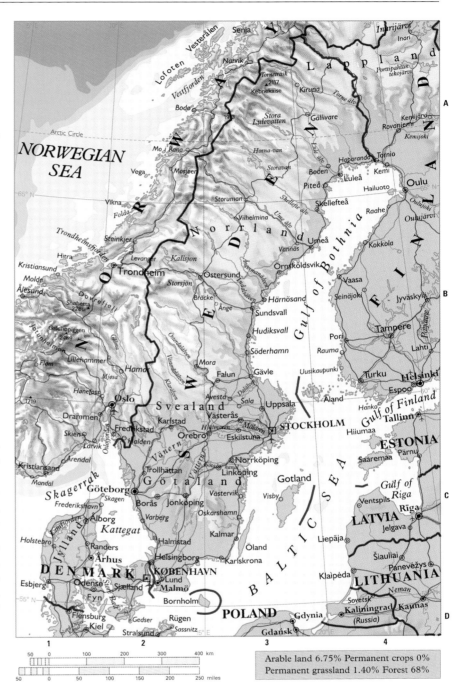

Arable land 6.75% Permanent crops 0%
Permanent grassland 1.40% Forest 68%

History

People began to settle in Sweden around 8,000 years ago, as the ice sheets which blanketed the land during the last Ice Age gradually melted and retreated northwards. The Romans began to trade with people in Sweden around 50 BC and accounts of the people were recorded by the Roman historian Tacitus in about AD 100.

By the seventh century, Teutonic peoples had occupied much of central Sweden. Between the 9th and 11th centuries, Vikings from Scandinavia spread far and wide, conquering, plundering and trading. While the Danish and Norwegian Vikings went west, the Swedish Vikings sailed to the east, across Russia and down to the Black and Caspian seas. Christianity was introduced into Sweden in 869, but it took another 200 years before Christianity triumphed over ancient pagan beliefs.

In the 11th century, Sweden, Norway and Denmark were separate kingdoms. However, in 1388, Sweden, fearing the growing influence of

Germany on Sweden's affairs, turned to Queen Margaret of Denmark and Norway for help. The Germans were defeated in 1389 and, in 1397, Sweden, Denmark and Norway were united by a treaty called the Union of Kalmar. However, in 1523, Sweden defeated the Danes and, under Gustavus Vasa, a Swedish noble, Sweden broke away from the union and Gustavus Vasa was crowned as Gustavus I. Gustavus encouraged followers of Martin Luther to spread their ideas, and, by 1540, Lutheranism became the official religion and it remains so to this day.

From the late 16th century, Sweden became involved in a series of wars, during which it gained territory around the Baltic Ocean. King Gustavus Adolf (Gustav II Adolf) won victories for Sweden and the Protestant cause in the Thirty Years' War (1618–48), and, in 1658, Sweden forced Denmark to give up its provinces on the Swedish mainland. By the early 18th century, Sweden was a major European power. But, in 1709, following defeat at the hands of Tsar Peter the Great at the battle of Poltava in the Ukraine, east-south-east of Kiev, a coalition of Russia, Poland and Denmark forced Sweden to give up most of its European possessions.

More wars in the early 19th century, when Swedes fought against the armies of Napoleon, led to Sweden losing Finland to Russia in 1809, though it gained Norway from Denmark in 1814. The 19th century saw great social and economic changes. A fast-increasing population caused emigration, especially to the United States, but the exodus of people was halted by industrialization. By the late 19th century, Sweden was a major industrial nation. With industrialization came demands for political and social reform, and the Social Democratic Party was set up in 1889 to improve the conditions of workers. In June 1905, Norway's parliament voted for independence from Sweden. Sweden almost went to war, but finally acceded to Norway's secession in September 1905. Sweden was neutral in both World Wars.

Politics

The Swedes, who have avoided war or occupation for nearly two centuries, have achieved a high standard of living that is the envy of most other European countries. It has the highest percentage figure for public spending in the OECD (Organization for Economic Co-operation and Development), with more than 70% of the national budget going on one of the widest ranging welfare programmes in the world. In turn, the tax burden is the world's highest, and some Swedes believe that the 'soft' yet paternalistic approach has led to over-government, depersonalization and uniformity. They also argued that the maintenance of the welfare state had practically halted economic growth and was making Sweden less competitive in world markets.

The elections of September 1991 saw the end of the Social Democratic government, which had been in power for six years since 1932, with voters swinging towards parties advocating lower taxes. Other attractive policies appeared to include curbs on immigration and diversion of Third World aid (Sweden spends well above the OECD per capita average each year) to the Baltic states newly independent from the Soviet Union. Though the conservative-led government's austerity measures helped the Social Democrats return to power in 1994, they, too, were advocating economic stringency. The Social Democrats also emerged as the largest single party in the 1998 elections, though their support was at its lowest for 70 years and the prime minister, Göran Persson, was forced to form a minority government.

Other changes were also in the wind. A founder member of EFTA (European Free Trade Association), Sweden nevertheless applied for membership of the European Economic Community in 1991, finally joining the European Union in 1985 following a referendum. However, along with Denmark, Greece and the United Kingdom, it did not adopt the euro, the EU's single currency, on 1 January 2001.

Sweden remains a key nation in Scandinavia. With its long experience and stability, its wide industrial base built on efficiency and quality, together with its strategically central position and relatively large population, it can claim to be the most important power among the Nordic nations. While maintaining its reputation for neutrality, it has played an important part in world affairs and has acted as a negotiator in international disputes.

While some believe that Sweden's biggest problems are of its own

Åland

Swedish settlers colonized various coastal tracts of Finland from the 12th century onwards, and the 6.5% of the Finnish population who are Swedish-speaking include the 25,102 people of Åland. This group of more than 6,500 islands is situated between the two countries at the entrance to the Gulf of Bothnia, about 40 km [25 mi] off the coast of Sweden. Most of the islands are empty of people, but more than 100 of the islands are inhabited. The largest island in the group, which is also called Åland, contains the capital and chief port of Mariehamn (Maarianhamina) as well as the highest point, Orrdalsklint, which reaches 129 m [423 ft]. The south-eastern part of this island is a rich agricultural region, while the north contains rugged granite scenery.

Although the inhabitants voted to secede to Sweden in a 1917 referendum, the result was annulled in 1921 by the League of Nations for strategic reasons, and Åland (as Ahvenanmaa) remained a Finnish province. However, the islands were granted considerable autonomy and still enjoy a large degree of 'home rule' with their own flag, postage stamps and representation at the annual assembly of the Nordic Council.

Boasting many important relics of the Stone, Iron and Bronze Ages, together with Viking graveyards and many medieval churches, the province's income derives mainly from fishing, farming and, increasingly, tourism.

making, it is possible that it will be vulnerable to forces beyond its control. Like its neighbours, Sweden suffers from acid rain generated by Germany and United Kingdom that kills its forests. Also, after the 1986 disaster at Chernobyl (Chornobyl) in the Ukraine, Sweden was forced to reconsider its electricity-generating programme, which, at that time, was more than 40% dependent on nuclear power stations.

Economy

Sweden is a highly developed country, with a per capita gross national product of US $26,750 in 1999. In 1995, farming accounted for 2.4% of the gross domestic product, as compared with 24% from manufacturing. Cereal crops, potatoes, sugar beet and vegetables are grown for human consumption in Skåne and in central Sweden, but the greatest area of cultivated land is given over to the production of fodder crops for cattle and sheep. Dairy farming is important. Many farmers have left the land, attracted by the higher wages and lifestyles in the towns.

The country has created a high standard of living based on industry. Despite that, apart from its large iron ore deposits, it has to import many essential fuels and minerals. Most iron ore obtained from mines at Kiruna and Gällivare in Arctic Sweden is exported via Narvik in Norway or from Luleå to Germany. Development of hydroelectricity has made up for the lack of oil and coal. Sweden is famous for high-quality engineering products, such as ball bearings, agricultural machines, motor vehicles, ships and aircraft. Sweden also has a major forestry industry. In 1997, the government began its programme of denuclearization when it designated one of its ten reactors for decommissioning. This policy was one of the boldest and most expensive environmental pledges ever made by a government.

Sweden's chief exports are machinery and transport equipment, paper products, chemicals and iron and steel products. The country's main trading partners are Germany, the United Kingdom, Norway, the United States and Denmark.

AREA	ETHNIC GROUPS
449,960 sq km	Swedish 91%, Finnish 3%
[173,730 sq mi]	**LANGUAGES**
POPULATION	Swedish (official), Finnish
8,875,000	**RELIGIONS**
CAPITAL (POPULATION)	Lutheran 89%,
Stockholm (727,000)	Roman Catholic 2%
GOVERNMENT	**CURRENCY**
Constitutional monarchy	Swedish krona = 100 öre

SWITZERLAND

Switzerland has used this square flag since 1848, though the white cross on the red shield has been Switzerland's emblem since the 14th century. The flag of the International Red Cross, which is based in Geneva, was derived from this flag.

Geography

The Swiss Confederation is a landlocked country in Western Europe. Much of the land is mountainous. The Jura Mountains lie along Switzerland's western border with France, while the Swiss Alps make up about 60% of the country in the south and east. Four-fifths of the people of Switzerland live on the fertile Swiss Plateau, which contains most of Switzerland's large cities.

Climate

The climate of Switzerland varies greatly according to the height of the land. The plateau region has a central European climate with warm summers, but cold and snowy winters. Rain occurs all through the year. The rainiest months are in summer.

Switzerland: Arable land 10.4% Permanent crops 0.61% Permanent grassland 29% Forest 31.7%

History and Politics

In 1291, three small cantons (states) united to defend their freedom against the Habsburg rulers of the Holy Roman Empire. They were Schwyz, Uri and Unterwalden, and they called the confederation 'Switzerland'. In the 14th century, Switzerland defeated Austria in three wars of independence. But after a defeat by the French in 1515, the Swiss adopted a policy of neutrality.

In 1815, the Congress of Vienna expanded Switzerland to 22 cantons and guaranteed its neutrality. Switzerland's 23rd canton, Jura, was created in 1979 from part of Bern. Neutrality combined with the vigour of its people have made Switzerland prosperous. In 1993, the Swiss voted against joining the European Union. However, in 2002, the Swiss voted by a narrow majority to end its centuries-old political isolationism and join the United Nations.

Economy

Although lacking in natural resources, Switzerland is a wealthy, industrialized country. Many workers are highly skilled. Major products include chemicals, electrical equipment, machinery and machine tools, precision instruments, processed food, watches and textiles. Farmers produce about three-fifths of the country's food – the rest is imported. Livestock raising, especially dairy farming, is the chief agricultural activity. Crops include fruits, potatoes and wheat. Tourism and banking are also important. Swiss banks attract investors from all over the world.

AREA	Italian 10%, Yugoslav 3%,
41,290 sq km [15,942 sq mi]	Spanish 2%, Romansch 1%
POPULATION	**LANGUAGES**
7,283,000	French, German, Italian and
CAPITAL (POPULATION)	Romansch (all official)
Bern (942,000)	**RELIGIONS**
GOVERNMENT	Roman Catholic 46%,
Federal republic	Protestant 40%
ETHNIC GROUPS	**CURRENCY**
German 64%, French 19%,	Swiss franc = 100 centimes

LIECHTENSTEIN

The Principality of Liechtenstein is sandwiched between Switzerland and Austria, where the Rhine cuts its way out of the Alpine chains. The capital, Vaduz, is situated on the Oberland Plateau above the fields and meadows of the Rhine Valley. The climate is relatively mild and the average annual precipitation is about 890 mm [35 in].

Liechtenstein, whose people speak a German dialect, became independent within the Holy Roman Empire in 1719. Since then, it has escaped incorporation into any of Europe's larger nations. It has a tradition of neutrality and has not been involved in a war since 1866. In 1919, Liechtenstein severed its contacts with Austria. Since 1923, it has been in customs and currency union with Switzerland, which also provides overseas representation. Although many Swiss regard it as their 27th canton, it retains full sovereignty in other spheres.

While Liechtenstein is best known abroad for its postage stamps – an important source of income – it is a haven for international companies, attracted by the low taxation and the strictest (most secretive) banking codes in the world. Since World War II, there has been an impressive growth in specialized manufacturing – the product of a mixture of Swiss engineers, Austrian technicians, Italian workers and international capital investment. Another source of income comes from tourists who are intrigued by this miniature state and its royal castle.

AREA	**CAPITAL**
157 sq km [61 sq mi]	Vaduz
POPULATION	**CURRENCY**
33,000	Swiss franc = 100 centimes

SYRIA

Syria has used this flag since 1980. The colours are those used by the Pan-Arab movement. This flag is the one that was used by the United Arab Republic between 1958 and 1961, when Syria was linked with Egypt and North Yemen.

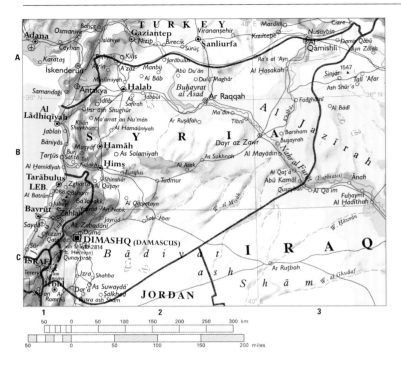

Geography

The Syrian Arab Republic is a country in south-western Asia. The narrow coastal plain is overlooked by a low mountain range which runs north–south. Another range, the Jabal ash Sharqi, runs along the border with Lebanon. South of this range is a region called the Golan Heights. Israel has occupied this region since 1967. East of the mountains, the bulk of Syria consists of fertile valleys, grassy plains and large sandy deserts. This region contains the valley of the River Euphrates (Nahr al Furat).

Climate

The coast has a Mediterranean climate, with dry, warm summers and wet, mild winters. The low mountains cut off Damascus from the sea. It has less rainfall than the coastal areas and becomes drier to the east.

SYRIA (DAMASCUS)

Damascus is isolated from the maritime influence of the Mediterranean by the Lebanon Mountains. Rainfall is lighter here than on the coast. Winter becomes colder further to the east, and frost and snow are common. Frosts can occur at Damascus between November and March. On the higher mountains, patches of snow lie all year. Summers are hot and dry with a large diurnal range of temperature of up to 20°C [36°F].

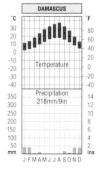

History

In early times, Syria lay at the crossroads of Asia, Africa and Europe. As a result, it is rich in historic sites from a wide range of periods. The earliest known settlers were Semites who arrived around 3,500 years ago. They set up city-states, such as Ebla, which existed between about 2700 and 2200 BC. The people of Ebla used clay tablets inscribed in cuneiform, an ancient system of writing developed by the Sumer people of Mesopotamia. Later conquerors of the area included the Akkadians, Canaanites, Phoenicians, Amorites, Aramaeans and the Hebrews, who introduced monotheism. The Assyrians occupied the area from 732 BC until 612 BC, when the Babylonians took over. The ancient Persians conquered the Babylonians in 539 BC, but

the armies of Alexander the Great swept into the region in 331 BC, introducing Greek culture in their wake. The Romans took over in 64 BC, and Syria remained under Roman law for nearly 700 years.

Christianity became the state religion of Syria in the 4th century AD, but, in 636, Muslims from Arabia invaded the region. Islam gradually replaced Christianity as the main religion, and Arabic became the chief language. From 661, Damascus became the capital of a vast Muslim empire which was ruled by the Ummayad Dynasty. But the Abbasid Dynasty took over in 750 and the centre of power passed to Baghdad. From the late 11th century, Crusaders sought to win the Holy Land from the Muslims. But the Crusaders were unsuccessful in their aim because Saladin, a Muslim ruler of Egypt, defeated the Crusaders and ruled most of the area by the end of the 12th century.

The Mameluke Dynasty of Egypt ruled Syria from 1260–1516, when the region became part of the huge Turkish Ottoman Empire. During World War I, Syrians and other Arabs fought alongside British forces and overthrew the Turks.

Politics

Following World War I, Greater Syria was divided into Syria, which was later divided into Syria and Lebanon, and Palestine, which later became Palestine and Transjordan. France was mandated by the League of Nations to govern Syria and Lebanon. France developed the region's economy, but nationalist Syrians yearned for independence.

Syria became fully independent from France in 1946 and many Syrians wanted to re-create Greater Syria. But the partition of Palestine and the creation of Israel in 1947 led to the first Arab-Israeli war, when Syria and other Arab nations failed to defeat Israeli forces. In 1949, a military coup established a military regime, starting a long period of revolts and changes of government. In 1967, in the third Arab-Israeli war (known as the Six-Day War), Syria lost the strategically important Golan Heights.

In 1970, Lieutenant-General Hafez al Assad led a military revolt, becoming Syria's president in 1971. His repressive but stable regime attracted much Western criticism and was heavily reliant on Arab aid. But, Syria's anti-Iraq stance in the 1991 Gulf War, and the involvement of about 20,000 Syrian troops in the conflict, greatly improved its standing in the West. In the mid-1990s, Syria had talks with Israel over the future of the Golan Heights. Negotiations were suspended after the election of Binyamin Netanyahu's right-wing government in Israel in 1996. Assad died in 2000 and was succeeded by his son, Bashar al Assad, raising hopes of a more pliable policy on the Golan Heights.

Economy

The World Bank classifies Syria as a 'lower-middle-income' developing country. But it has great potential for development. Its main resources are oil, hydroelectricity from the dam at Lake Assad (Buburut al Asad), and fertile land. Agriculture employs about 26% of the population and accounts for around 27% of the total economic production. Crops include barley, cotton, fruits, sugar beet, tobacco and wheat. Sheep are the most important livestock, followed by goats and cattle. Oil is the chief mineral product, and phosphates are mined to make fertilizers. Manufacturing is increasing, especially the production of textiles and processed farm products. Syria's leading export is oil, followed by vegetables and fruits.

AREA	ETHNIC GROUPS
185,180 sq km [71,498 sq mi]	Arab 90%, Kurdish, Armenian
POPULATION	**LANGUAGES**
16,729,000	Arabic (official)
CAPITAL (POPULATION)	**RELIGIONS**
Damascus (Dimashq, 1,394,000)	Islam 90%, Christianity 9%
GOVERNMENT	**CURRENCY**
Multiparty republic	Syrian pound = 100 piastres

TAIWAN

In 1928, the Chinese Nationalists adopted this design as China's national flag and used it in the long struggle against Mao Zedong's Communist army. When the nationalists were forced to retreat to Taiwan in 1949, their flag went with them.

Geography

Taiwan, formerly known as Formosa, is an island about 140 km [87 mi] off the south coast of mainland China. The country also administers a number of islands close to the mainland. They include Quemoy (Jinmen) and Matsu (Mazu). High mountain ranges, extending the length of the island, occupy the central and eastern regions, and only a quarter of the island's surface is used for agriculture. The highest peak is Yü Shan (Morrison Mountain), reaching 3,997 m [13,113 ft] above sea level. Several peaks in the central ranges rise to more than 3,000 m [10,000 ft], and carry dense forests of broadleaved evergreen trees, such as camphor and Chinese cork oak. Above 1,500 m [5,000 ft], conifers, such as pine, larch and cedar, dominate. In the east, where the mountains often drop steeply down to the sea, the short rivers have cut deep gorges. The western slopes are more gentle.

Climate

Taiwan has a tropical monsoon climate. The average annual rainfall almost everywhere exceeds 2,000 mm [79 in]. From July to September, the island is often hit by typhoons. Humidity is high in summer, when the heat may become oppressive.

TAIWAN (TAIPEI)

Taiwan lies on the tropic line, but as the central island range reaches over 3,000 m [10,000 ft] at many points, it bears snow during winter. In Taipei night temperatures fall below 20°C [68°F] from October to March, but may reach over 30°C [86°F] in the day from June to September. Rainfall is heavy, falling mainly in the summer. Sunshine levels in the north are low – under 3 hours per day from December to March and only over 7 hours in July and August. The summer heat, when temperatures soar to 38°C [100°F], may be oppressive due to the high humidity.

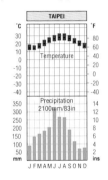

History

Chinese settlers arrived in Taiwan from the 7th century AD, displacing the Aboriginal people, but large settlements were not established until the 17th century. The Portuguese first reached the island in 1590. They named the island Formosa (meaning 'beautiful island'), but did not settle there. The Dutch occupied a trading port in 1624, but they were driven out in 1661 by refugees from the deposed Ming Dynasty on the mainland. A Ming official tried to use the island as a base for attacking the Manchu Dynasty, but the Manchus took the island in 1683 and incorporated it into what is now Fujian province.

The Manchus settled the island in the late 18th century and, by the mid-19th century, the population had increased to about 2,500,000. The island had become a major producer of sugar and rice, which were exported to the mainland. In 1886, the island became a Chinese province and Taipei became its capital in 1894. However, in 1895, Taiwan was ceded to Japan following the Chinese-Japanese War. Japan used the island as a source of food crops and, from the 1930s, they developed manufacturing industries based on hydroelectricity.

Politics

In 1945, the Japanese army surrendered Taiwan to General Chiang Kai-shek's Nationalist Chinese government. Following victories by Mao Zedong's Communists, about 2 million Nationalists, together with their leader, fled the mainland to Taiwan in the two years before 1949, when the People's Republic of China was proclaimed. The influx was met with hostility by the 8 million Taiwanese, and the new regime, the 'Republic of China', was imposed with force. Boosted by help from the United States, Chiang's government set about ambitious programmes for land reform and industrial expansion and, by 1980, Taiwan had become one of the top 20 industrial nations. Economic development was accompanied by a marked rise in living standards.

Nevertheless, Taiwan remained politically isolated and it lost its seat in the United Nations to Communist China in 1971. It was then abandoned diplomatically by the United States in 1979, when the US switched its recognition to mainland China. However, as economic progress continued, the authoritarian regime in Taiwan lifted martial law in 1987. In 1988, a native Taiwanese became president and in 1991 the country's first general election was held.

However, China continued to regard Taiwan as a Chinese province and, in 1999, tension developed when the Taiwanese President Lee Teng-hui stated that relations between China and Taiwan should be on a 'special state-by-state' basis. This angered the Chinese President Jiang Zemin, whose 'one-nation' policy was based on the concept that China and Taiwan should be regarded as one country with two equal governments. Tension mounted in March 2000, when Taiwan's opposition leader, Chen Shui-bian, was elected president, because Chen had adopted a pro-independence stance. However, after the elections, Chen adopted a more conciliatory approach to mainland China.

Economy

The economy depends on manufacturing and trade. Manufactures include electronic goods, footwear and clothing, ships and television sets. The western coastal plains produce large rice crops. Other products include bananas, pineapples, sugar cane, sweet potatoes and tea. The growth of the economy has been a huge success story, and, despite the regional recession in 1997–8, the economy continues to grow.

AREA	mainland Chinese 14%
36,000 sq km [13,900 sq mi]	**LANGUAGES**
POPULATION	Mandarin (official),
22,370,000	Min, Hakka
CAPITAL (POPULATION)	**RELIGIONS**
Taipei (T'aipei, 2,596,000)	Buddhist 43%,
GOVERNMENT	Taoism and Confucianism 49%
Unitary multiparty republic	**CURRENCY**
ETHNIC GROUPS	New Taiwan dollar
Taiwanese (Han Chinese) 84%,	= 100 cents

TAJIKISTAN

Tajikistan's flag was adopted in 1993. It replaced the flag used during the Communist period which showed a hammer and sickle. The new flag shows an unusual gold crown under an arc of seven stars on the central white band.

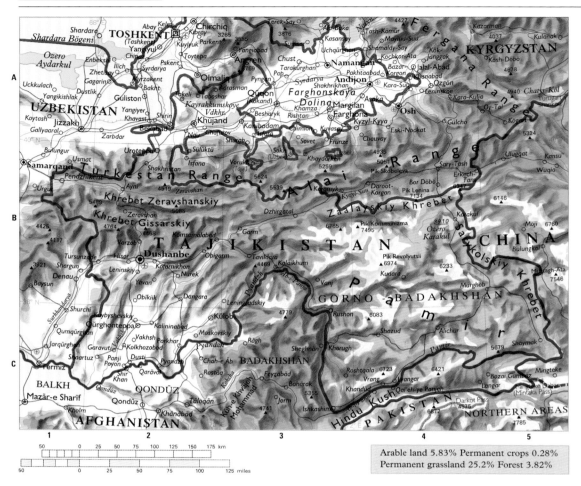

Arable land 5.83% Permanent crops 0.28%
Permanent grassland 25.2% Forest 3.82%

Arab armies conquered the area in the mid-7th century and introduced Islam, which remains the chief religion today. The region was later ruled by various Turkic tribes and later by the Mongols, led by Genghis Khan. Turkic peoples, called Uzbeks, ruled the area from the 16th to the 19th centuries.

Russia conquered parts of Tajikistan in the late 19th century and, by 1920, Russia took complete control. In 1924, Tajikistan became part of the Uzbek Soviet Socialist Republic. However, in 1929, it was expanded, taking in some areas that were populated by Uzbeks, becoming the Tajik Soviet Socialist Republic.

While the Soviet Union began to introduce reforms in the 1980s, many Tajiks demanded freedom. In 1989, the Tajik government made Tajik the official language instead of Russian and, in 1990, it stated that its local laws overruled Soviet laws. Tajikistan became fully independent in 1991, following the break-up of the Soviet Union. As the poorest of the ex-Soviet republics, Tajikistan faced many

Geography and Climate

The Republic of Tajikistan is one of the five central Asian republics that formed part of the former Soviet Union. Only 7% of the land is below 1,000 m [3,280 ft], while almost all of eastern Tajikistan is above 3,000 m [9,840 ft]. The highest point is Communism Peak (Pik Kommunizma), which reaches 7,495 m [24,590 ft]. The main ranges are the westwards extension of the Tian Shan Range in the north and the snow-capped Pamirs (Pamir) in the south-east. Earthquakes are common throughout the country.

Tajikistan has an extreme continental climate. Summers are hot and dry in the lower valleys, and winters are long and bitterly cold in the mountains.

TAJIKISTAN (DUSHANBE)

Dushanbe lies in a cotton-growing valley at the foot of the Gissar Range (Khrebet Gissarskiy). The city's sheltered position moderates temperatures during winter, while the summer heat is mitigated by cool breezes from the mountains to the north-east. The average annual rainfall is low, giving Dushanbe a desert climate. The majority of the scant rainfall occurs during the winter and spring.

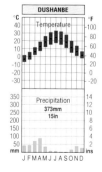

History and Politics

The ancestors of the people of Tajikistan were Persians who had settled in the area about 2,500 years ago. The area was conquered many times. Early invaders were the Persians in the 6th century BC and the Macedonian Greeks led by Alexander the Great in 331 BC. From 323 BC, the area was split into several independent states.

problems in trying to introduce a free-market system.

In 1992, civil war broke out between the government, which was run by former Communists, and an alliance of democrats and Islamic forces. The government maintained control, but it relied heavily on aid from the Commonwealth of Independent States, the organization through which most of the former Soviet republics kept in touch. Presidential elections in 1994 resulted in victory for Imomali Rakhmonov, though the Islamic opposition did not recognize the result. A cease-fire was signed in December 1996. Further agreements in 1997 provided for the opposition to have 30% of the ministerial posts in the government. But many small groups excluded from the agreement continued to undermine the peace process through a series of killings and military actions. In 1999, Rakhmonov was re-elected president.

Economy

The World Bank classifies Tajikistan as a 'low-income' developing country. Agriculture is the main activity and cotton is the chief product. Other crops include fruits, grains and vegetables. The country has large hydroelectric power resources and it produces aluminium.

AREA
143,100 sq km [55,520 sq mi]
POPULATION
6,579,000
CAPITAL (POPULATION)
Dushanbe (524,000)
GOVERNMENT
Transitional democracy
ETHNIC GROUPS
Tajik 65%, Uzbek 25%,
Russian 3%, Tatar,
Kyrgyz, Ukrainian,
German
LANGUAGES
Tajik (official), Uzbek,
Russian
RELIGIONS
Islam (mainly Sunni) 80%
CURRENCY
Somoni = 100 dirams

TANZANIA

Tanzania's flag was adopted in 1964 when mainland Tanganyika joined with the island nation of Zanzibar to form the United Republic of Tanzania. The green represents agriculture and the yellow minerals. The black represents the people, while the blue symbolizes Zanzibar.

Geography

The United Republic of Tanzania consists of the former mainland country of Tanganyika and the island nation of Zanzibar, which also includes the island of Pemba. Behind a narrow coastal plain, the majority of Tanzania is a plateau lying between 900 m and 1,500 m [2,950–4,920 ft] above sea level. The plateau is broken by arms of the Great African Rift Valley. The western arm contains lakes Nyasa (also called Malawi) and Tanganyika, while the eastern arm contains the strongly alkaline Lake Natron, together with lakes Eyasi and Manyara. Lake Victoria occupies a shallow depression in the plateau and it is not situated within the Rift Valley. Kilimanjaro, the highest peak, is an extinct volcano. At 5,895 m [19,340 ft], it is also Africa's highest mountain. Zanzibar and Pemba are coral islands.

Climate

The coast has a hot and humid climate, with the greatest rainfall in April and May. The inland plateaux and mountains are cooler and less humid. The Rift Valley is hot, but Mount Kilimanjaro is permanently covered by snow and ice.

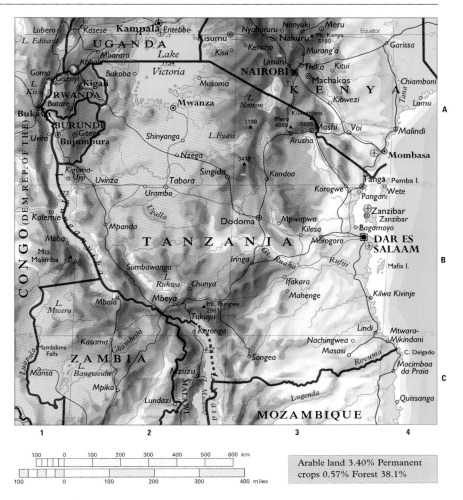

Arable land 3.40% Permanent crops 0.57% Forest 38.1%

TANZANIA (DAR ES SALAAM)

In East Africa the winds blow mainly parallel to the coast and rainfall is lower than in many equatorial regions. The heaviest rain falls in April and May, when the intertropical rainbelt moves north. It is followed by the south-east trades which have lost much moisture over the mountains of Madagascar before reaching East Africa.

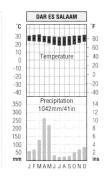

History

Around 2,000 years ago, Arabs, Persians and even Chinese probably traded along the Tanzanian coast, and the old cities and ruins testify to its importance. Arab traders often intermarried with local people and the Arab-African people produced the distinctive Arab-Swahili culture. The Portuguese took control of coastal trade in the early 16th century, but the Arabs regained control in the 17th century. In 1698, Arabs from Oman took control of Zanzibar. From this base, they developed inland trade, bringing gold, ivory and slaves from the interior. During the 19th century, European explorers and missionaries were active, mapping the country and striving to stop the slave trade.

Politics

Mainland Tanganyika became a German territory in the 1880s, while Zanzibar (including Pemba) became a British protectorate in 1890. The Germans introduced a system of forced labour to develop plantations. This led to a major rebellion in 1905, which was put down with great brutality. Britain gained control of Tanganyika in World War I and was granted a mandate to rule it by the League of Nations. Tanganyika won its independence in 1961, followed by Zanzibar in 1963. In 1964, Tanganyika and Zanzibar united to form the United Republic of Tanzania. The country's first president, Julius Nyerere, pursued socialist policies of self-help (called *ujamaa* in Swahili). While many of its social reforms were successful, the country failed to make economic progress. Nyerere resigned as president in 1985, though he remained influential until his death in 1999. His successors, Ali Hassan Mwinyi, who served from 1985 until 1995, and Benjamin Mkapa, who was re-elected in 2000, pursued more liberal economic policies.

Economy

Tanzania is one of the world's poorest countries. Although crops are grown on only 5% of the land, agriculture employs 85% of the people. Most farmers grow only enough to feed their families. Food crops include bananas, cassava, maize, millet, rice and vegetables. Export crops include coffee, cotton, cashew nuts, tea and tobacco. Other crops grown for export include cloves, coconuts and sisal. Some farmers raise animals, but sleeping sickness and drought restrict the areas for livestock farming. Diamonds and other gems are mined, together with some coal and gold. Industry is mostly small-scale. Manufactures include processed food, fertilizers, petroleum products and textiles.

Tourism is increasing. Tanzania has beautiful beaches, but its main attractions are its magnificent national parks and reserves, including the celebrated Serengeti and the Ngorongoro Crater. These are renowned for their wildlife and are among the world's finest. Tanzania also contains a major archaeological site, Olduvai Gorge, west of the Serengeti. Here, in 1964, the British archaeologist and anthropologist, Louis Leakey, discovered the remains of ancient human-like creatures.

AREA
945,090 sq km [364,899 sq mi]
POPULATION
36,232,000
CAPITAL (POPULATION)
Dodoma (204,000)
GOVERNMENT
Multiparty republic
ETHNIC GROUPS
Nyamwezi and Sukuma 21%,
Swahili 9%,
Hehet and Bena 7%,
Makonde 6%, Haya 6%
LANGUAGES
Swahili and English (both official)
RELIGIONS
Christianity (mostly Roman Catholic) 45%, Islam 35% (99% in Zanzibar), traditional beliefs and others 20%
CURRENCY
Tanzanian shilling = 100 cents

Thailand's flag was adopted in 1917. In the late 19th century, it featured a white elephant on a plain red flag. In 1916, white stripes were introduced above and below the elephant, but in 1917 the elephant was dropped and a central blue band was added.

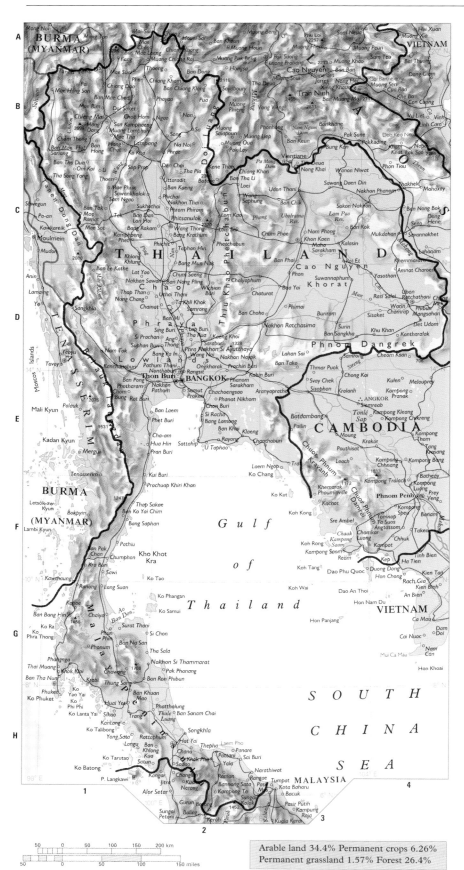

Arable land 34.4% Permanent crops 6.26%
Permanent grassland 1.57% Forest 26.4%

Geography and Climate

The Kingdom of Thailand is one of the ten countries in South-east Asia. The highest land occurs in the north, where Doi Inthanon, the highest peak, reaches 2,595 m [8,514 ft]. The Khorat Plateau, in the north-east, makes up about 30% of the country and is the most heavily populated part of Thailand. In the south, Thailand shares the finger-like Malay Peninsula with Burma and Malaysia.

Thailand has a tropical climate. Monsoon winds from the south-west bring heavy rains between May and October. However, Bangkok is drier than many parts of South-east Asia because mountains shelter the central plains from the rain-bearing winds.

History and Politics

The first Thai state was set up in the 13th century. By 1350, it included most of what is now Thailand. European contact began in the early 16th century. But, in the late 17th century, the Thais, fearing interference in their affairs, forced all Europeans to leave. This policy continued for 150 years. In 1782, a Thai General, Chao Phraya Chakkri, became king, founding a dynasty which continues today. The country became known as Siam, and Bangkok became its capital. From the mid-19th century, contacts with the West were restored.

In World War I, Siam supported the Allies against Germany and Austria-Hungary. But in 1941, the country was conquered by Japan and became its ally. After World War II, Thailand suffered periods of military rule alternating with democratic elected governments. A military group seized power in 1991, but elections were held in 1992, 1995 and 2001.

Economy

Since 1967, when Thailand became a member of ASEAN (Association of South-east Asian Nations), its economy has grown, especially its manufacturing and service industries. However, in 1997, it suffered recession along with other eastern Asian countries.

Despite its rapid progress, the World Bank classifies the country as a 'lower-middle-income' developing country. Manufactures, including food products, machinery, timber products and textiles, are exported, but agriculture still employs two-thirds of the people. Rice is the main food, while other major crops include cassava, cotton, maize, pineapples, rubber, sugar cane and tobacco. Thailand also mines tin and other minerals, and tourism is a major source of income.

AREA	Malay 4%,
513,120 sq km	Khmer 3%
[198,116 sq mi]	**LANGUAGES**
POPULATION	Thai (official), Chinese,
61,798,000	Malay, English
CAPITAL (POPULATION)	**RELIGIONS**
Bangkok (7,507,000)	Buddhism 94%,
GOVERNMENT	Islam 4%,
Constitutional monarchy	Christianity 1%
ETHNIC GROUPS	**CURRENCY**
Thai 75%, Chinese 14%,	Thai baht = 100 satang

TOGO — SEE BENIN, PAGE 54; TONGA — SEE PACIFIC OCEAN, PAGES 174–178; TRINIDAD AND TOBAGO — SEE CARIBBEAN SEA, PAGES 71–76; TRISTAN DA CUNHA — SEE ATLANTIC OCEAN, PAGES 41–43

TUNISIA

Tunisia's flag originated in about 1835 when the country was officially under Turkish rule. It became the national flag in 1956, when Tunisia became independent from France. The flag contains two traditional symbols of Islam, the crescent and the star.

Geography and Climate

The Republic of Tunisia is the smallest country in North Africa. The mountains in the north are an eastwards and comparatively low extension of the Atlas Mountains.

To the north and east of the mountains lie fertile plains, especially between Sfax, Tunis and Bizerte. South of the mountains lie broad plateaux which descend towards the south. This low-lying region contains a large salt pan, called the Chott Djerid, and part of the Sahara.

Northern Tunisia has a Mediterranean climate, with dry summers, and mild winters with a moderate rainfall. The average yearly rainfall decreases towards the south, which forms part of the Sahara.

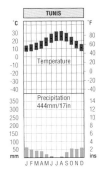

TUNISIA (TUNIS)

Although most rain in Tunisia falls during winter when the region is affected by low pressure, prevailing north-easterly winds from the sea in summer result in a shorter dry season than is found in many parts of the Mediterranean basin. Rain falls on a few days during summer. The influence of the sea also helps to moderate extremes of temperature, and though mostly sunny, summer days are seldom oppressive, humidity being low.

History and Politics

Tunisia has come under the influence of a succession of cultures, each of which has left its mark on the country, giving Tunisia a distinct identity and a long tradition of urban life. The Phoenicians began the Carthaginian Empire in Tunisia around 1100 BC and, according to legend, the colony of Carthage was established in 814 BC on a site near present-day Tunis. At its peak, Carthage controlled large areas in the eastern Mediterranean but, following the three Punic Wars with Rome, Carthage was destroyed in 146 BC. The Romans ruled the area for 600 years until the Vandals defeated the Romans in AD 439. The Vandals were finally conquered by the Byzantines. Arabs reached the area in the mid-7th century, introducing Islam and the Arabic language. In 1547, Tunisia came under the rule of the Turkish Ottoman Empire.

In 1881, France established a protectorate over Tunisia and ruled the country until 1956. Tunisian aspirations were felt before World War I, but it was not until 1934 that Habib Bourguiba founded the first effective opposition group, the Neo-Destour (New Constitution) Party, which was renamed the Socialist Destour Party in 1964, and is now known as the Constitutional Assembly. Tunisia supported the Allies during World War II and it was the scene of much fierce fighting. Following independence, the new parliament abolished the monarchy and declared Tunisia to be a republic in 1957. The nationalist leader, Habib Bourguiba, became president.

In 1975, Bourguiba was elected president for life. His government introduced many reforms, including votes for women. But problems arose from the government's successes. For example, the establishment of a national school system led to a very rapid increase in the number of educated people who were unable to find jobs that measured up to their qualifications. The growth of tourism, which provided a valuable source of foreign currency, also led to fears that Western influences might undermine traditional Muslim values. Finally, the prime minister, Zine el Abidine Ben Ali, removed Bourguiba from office in 1987 and succeeded him as president. He was elected president in 1989, 1994 and 1999, and his party dominated the Chamber of Deputies, though some seats were reserved for opposition parties whatever their proportion of the popular vote. But he faced opposition from Islamic fundamentalists. Occasional violence and suppression of human rights, including the banning of al-Nahda, the main Islamic party, marred his presidency. However, Islamic fundamentalism in Tunisia did not prove to be anything like as effective as in Algeria.

Economy

The World Bank classifies Tunisia as a 'middle-income' developing country. Its main natural resources are oil and phosphates. Agriculture employs 22% of the people. Chief crops are barley, citrus fruits, dates, grapes, olives, sugar beet, tomatoes and wheat. Sheep are the most important livestock, but goats and cattle are also raised. Tourism has grown considerably. The number of tourists in 1996 approached 4 million, most of whom came from Europe.

Since independence, new industries and tourism have transformed a number of coastal towns, though the interior, by comparison, has been neglected. Major manufactures include cement, flour, phosphoric acid, processed food and steel. Exports include clothing and accessories, machinery and electrical products, oil and phosphates. An important stimulus to the economy was the signing of a free-trade agreement with the European Union in 1995. Tunisia became the first Arab country on the Mediterranean to sign such an agreement.

AREA	ETHNIC GROUPS
163,610 sq km [63,170 sq mi]	Arab 98%, Berber 1%, French
POPULATION	**LANGUAGES**
9,705,000	Arabic (official), French
CAPITAL (POPULATION)	**RELIGIONS**
Tunis (1,827,000)	Islam 99%
GOVERNMENT	**CURRENCY**
Multiparty republic	Dinar = 1,000 millimes

Turkey's flag was adopted when the Republic of Turkey was established in 1923. The crescent moon and the five-pointed star are traditional symbols of Islam. They were used on earlier Turkish flags used by the Turkish Ottoman Empire.

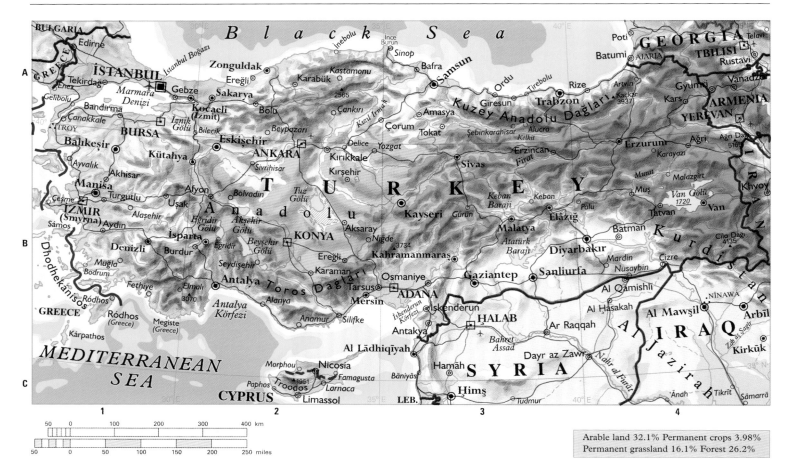

Arable land 32.1% Permanent crops 3.98%
Permanent grassland 16.1% Forest 26.2%

Geography and Climate

The Republic of Turkey lies in two continents. The European section lies west of a waterway between the Black and Mediterranean seas. This waterway consists of the Bosporus, on which the city of Istanbul stands, the Sea of Marmara (Marmara Denizi) and a narrow strait called the Dardanelles. European Turkey, also called Thrace, is a fertile, hilly region. Most of the Asian part of Turkey consists of plateaux and mountains, which rise to 5,165 m [16,945 ft] at Mount Ararat (Agri Dagi) near the border with Armenia.

Central Turkey has a dry climate, with hot, sunny summers and cold winters. The driest part of the central plateau lies south of the city of Ankara, around Lake Tuz. Western Turkey has a Mediterranean climate, while the Black Sea coast has cooler summers.

History and Politics

In AD 330, the Roman Empire moved its capital to Byzantium, which it renamed Constantinople. Constantinople became the capital of the East Roman (or Byzantine) Empire in 395. Muslim Seljuk Turks from central Asia invaded Anatolia in the 11th century. In the 14th century, another group of Turks, the Ottomans, conquered the area. In 1435, the Ottoman Turks took Constantinople, which they called Istanbul. The Ottoman Turks built up a large empire which finally collapsed during World War I (1914–18). In 1923, Turkey became a republic. Its leader Mustafa Kemal, or Atatürk ('father of the Turks'), launched policies to modernize and secularize the country.

Since the 1940s, Turkey has sought to strengthen its ties with Western powers. It joined NATO (North Atlantic Treaty Organization) in 1951 and applied to join the European Economic Community in 1987. But Turkey's conflict with Greece, together with its invasion of northern Cyprus in 1974, have led many Europeans to treat Turkey's aspirations with caution. Political instability, military coups, conflict with Kurdish nationalists in eastern Turkey and concern about the country's record on human rights are other problems. Turkey has enjoyed democracy since 1983, though, in 1998, the government banned the Islamist Welfare Party, accusing it of violating secular principles. In 1999, the Muslim Virtue Party (successor to Islamist Welfare Party) lost ground. The largest numbers of parliamentary seats were won by the ruling Democratic Left Party and the far-right Nationalist Action Party. In 2001, the Turkish parliament adopted reforms to ease the country's entry into the European Union. One reform formally recognized men and women as equals – the former code designated the man as the head of the family.

Economy

The World Bank classifies Turkey as a 'lower-middle-income' developing country. Agriculture employs 47% of the people, and barley, cotton, fruits, maize, tobacco and wheat are major crops. Livestock farming is important and wool is a leading product.

Turkey produces chromium, but manufacturing is the chief activity. Manufactures include processed farm products and textiles, cars, fertilizers, iron and steel, machinery, metal products and paper products. More than 9 million tourists visited Turkey in 1998.

AREA	**ETHNIC GROUPS**
779,450 sq km	Turkish 80%,
[300,946 sq mi]	Kurdish 20%
POPULATION	**LANGUAGES**
66,494,000	Turkish (official),
CAPITAL (POPULATION)	Kurdish
Ankara	**RELIGIONS**
(3,294,000)	Islam 99%
GOVERNMENT	**CURRENCY**
Multiparty republic	Turkish lira = 100 kurus

TURKMENISTAN

Turkmenistan's flag was adopted in 1992. It incorporates a typical Turkmen carpet design. The crescent is a symbol of Islam, while the five stars and the five elements in the carpet represent the traditional tribal groups of Turkmenistan.

Geography

The Republic of Turkmenistan is one of five central Asian republics which once formed part of the Soviet Union. Most of the land is low-lying, with mountains on the southern and south-western borders.

In the west lies the salty Caspian Sea. A depression called the Kara Bogaz Gol (Garabo-gazköl) Bay contains the country's lowest point. Most of the country is arid and Asia's largest sand desert, the Garagum, covers 80% of the country.

Climate

Turkmenistan has a continental climate, with average annual rainfall varying from 80 mm [3 in] in the desert to 300 mm [12 in] in the mountains. Summers are very hot, but temperatures during winter drop below freezing.

Arable land 2.98%
Forest 8.51%

History and Politics

Russia took over the region during the 1870s and 1880s. After the Russian Revolution of 1917, the area came under Communist rule and, in 1924, it became the Turkmen Soviet Socialist Republic. The Communists strictly controlled all aspects of life and, in particular, they discouraged religious worship. But they also improved many services.

During the 1980s, the Soviet Union introduced reforms, and the Turkmen demanded more freedom. In 1990, the Turkmen government stated that its laws overruled Soviet laws. In 1991, Turkmenistan became independent after the break-up of the Soviet Union, but kept ties with Russia through the Commonwealth of Independent States (CIS).

In 1992, Turkmenistan adopted a new constitution, allowing for political parties, providing that they were not ethnic or religious in character. However, Turkmenistan remained a one-party state and, in 1992, Saparmurad Niyazov, the former Communist and now Democratic leader, was the only candidate. In 1999, parliament declared that Niyazov would be president for life, but he later said that he would retire by 2010.

Economy

Faced with numerous economic problems, Turkmenistan joined the Economic Co-operation Organization which was set up in 1985 by Iran, Pakistan and Turkey. The World Bank classifies Turkmenistan as a 'lower-middle-income' country. The chief resources are oil and natural gas, but agriculture is important. The chief crop, which is grown on irrigated land, is cotton. Grains and vegetables are also important.

AREA	ETHNIC GROUPS
488,100 sq km	Turkmen 77%, Russian 17%,
[188,450 sq mi]	Uzbek 9%, Kazak 2%, Tatar
POPULATION	**LANGUAGES**
4,603,000	Turkmen (official), Russian,
CAPITAL (POPULATION)	Uzbek, Kazak
Ashkhabad	**RELIGIONS**
(Ashgabat, 536,000)	Islam
GOVERNMENT	**CURRENCY**
Single-party republic	Manat = 100 tenesi

UZBEKISTAN

The Republic of Uzbekistan is one of five republics in Central Asia which were once part of the Soviet Union. Plains cover most of western Uzbekistan, with highlands in the east. The main rivers drain into the Aral Sea. Most of the country is desert.

Uzbekistan has a continental climate. Winters are cold, but temperatures soar in the summer. The west is extremely arid.

After the Russian Revolution of 1917, Communists took over, setting up the Uzbek Soviet Socialist Republic in 1924. In the late 1980s, people demanded more freedom and, in 1990, the government stated that its laws overruled those of the Soviet Union. Uzbekistan became independent in 1991, but retained links with Russia through the Commonwealth of Independent States. Islam Karimov, leader of the People's Democratic Party (formerly the Communist Party), was elected president in December 1991. In 1992–3, many opposition leaders were arrested because the government said that they threatened national stability. In 2001, Karimov declared Uzbekistan's support for the United States in its campaign against the terrorist al Qaida bases in Afghanistan.

The World Bank classifies Uzbekistan as a 'lower-middle-income' developing country. Uzbekistan produces coal, copper, gold and oil.

AREA	CAPITAL (POPULATION)
447,400 sq km [172,740 sq mi]	Tashkent (Toshkent, 2,118,000)
POPULATION	**CURRENCY**
25,155,000	Som = 100 tiyin

TURKS AND CAICOS ISLANDS – SEE CARIBBEAN SEA, PAGES 71–76;
TUVALU – SEE PACIFIC OCEAN, PAGES 174–178

The flag used by the party that won the first national election was adopted as the national flag when Uganda became independent from Britain in 1962. The black represents the people, the yellow the sun, and the red brotherhood. The crested crane is the country's emblem.

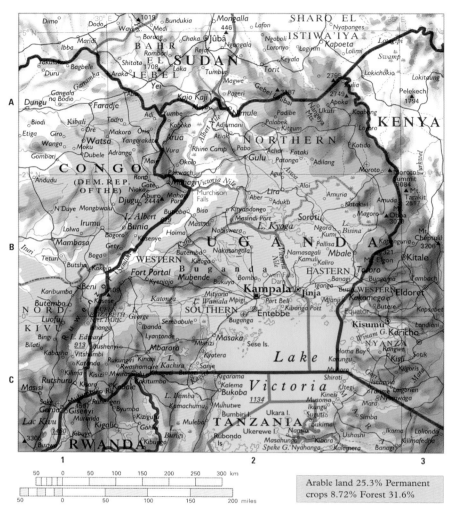

50 0 50 100 150 200 250 300 km

50 0 50 100 150 200 miles

Arable land 25.3% Permanent crops 8.72% Forest 31.6%

Geography

The Republic of Uganda is a landlocked country on the East African Plateau. It contains part of Lake Victoria, Africa's largest lake and a source of the River Nile, which occupies a shallow depression in the plateau. The plateau varies in height from about 1,500 m [4,921 ft] in the south to 900 m [2,953 ft] in the north. The highest mountain is Margherita Peak, which reaches 5,109 m [16,762 ft] in the Ruwenzori Range in the south-west. Other mountains, including Mount Elgon at 4,321 m [14,177 ft], rise along Uganda's eastern border. Part of the Great African Rift Valley, which contains lakes Edward and Albert, lie in western Uganda. The landscapes range from rainforests in the south, through savanna in the centre, to semi-desert in the north.

Climate

The Equator runs through Uganda and the country is warm throughout the year, though the high altitude moderates the temperature. The wettest regions are the lands to the north of Lake Victoria, and the western mountains, especially the high Ruwenzori Range. Much of Uganda has two rainy seasons, but these merge into one, with a distinctive dry season, in the centre and north.

History and Politics

Little is known of the early history of Uganda. When Europeans first reached the area in the 19th century, many of the people were organized in kingdoms, the most powerful of which was Buganda, the home of the Baganda people. Britain took over the country between 1894 and 1914, and ruled it until independence in 1962.

In 1967, Uganda became a republic and Buganda's Kabaka (king), Sir Edward Mutesa II, was made president. Tensions between the Kabaka and the prime minister, Apollo Milton Obote, led to the dismissal of Kabaka in 1966. Obote also abolished the traditional kingdoms, including Buganda. Obote was overthrown in 1971 by an army group led by General Idi Amin Dada. Amin ruled as a dictator. He forced most of the Asians living in Uganda to leave the country and had many of his opponents killed.

In 1978, a border dispute between Uganda and Tanzania led Tanzanian troops to enter Uganda. With help from Ugandan opponents of Amin, they overthrew Amin's government. In 1980, Obote led his party to victory in the national elections. But after charges of fraud, Obote's opponents began guerrilla warfare. A military group overthrew Obote in 1985, but strife continued until 1986, when Yoweri Museveni's National Resistance Movement seized power. In 1993, Museveni restored the traditional kingdoms, including Buganda where a new Kabaka was crowned. Museveni also held national elections in 1994 but political parties were not permitted. Museveni was elected president in 1996 and again in 2001.

In the late 1990s, Uganda faced a huge drain on its economy in containing rebels in the north and west. Another factor was Uganda's support for the rebel forces which overthrew President Mobutu of Zaïre and, later, for the rebels who battled to remove Mobutu's successor, Laurent Kabila.

Economy

By 1991 Uganda was among the world's five poorest countries. Stability was restored under President Museveni and the economy expanded. But, confidence in the country's development was shaken in 1998, when Uganda sent troops into the Democratic Republic of the Congo to oppose Museveni's erstwhile protégé, Laurent Kabila.

Agriculture dominates the economy, employing 80% of the people. Food crops include bananas, cassava, maize, millet, sorghum and sweet potatoes, while the chief cash crops are coffee, cotton, sugar cane and tea. The only important metal is copper. The Owen Falls Dam at Jinja, on the outlet of Lake Victoria, produces cheap electricity.

UGANDA (KAMPALA)

The northern shores of Lake Victoria are the rainiest tracts of East Africa due to the moisture they receive. Temperatures are uniform throughout the year, but are moderated by altitude. There is a double maximum of rainfall, the heaviest rains occurring after the midday sun is at its hottest around the equinoxes. Much of the rain falls in thunderstorms which move northwards from the lake by day.

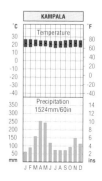

AREA
235,880 sq km [91,073 sq mi]
POPULATION
23,986,000
CAPITAL (POPULATION)
Kampala (954,000)
GOVERNMENT
Republic in transition
ETHNIC GROUPS
Baganda 17%, Karamojong 12%, Basogo 8%, Iteso 8%, Langi 6%, Rwanda 6%, Bagisu 5%, Acholi 4%, Lugbara 4%
LANGUAGES
English and Swahili (both official), Ganda
RELIGIONS
Roman Catholic 33%, Protestant 33%, traditional beliefs 18%, Islam 16%
CURRENCY
Uganda shilling = 100 cents

UKRAINE

Ukraine's flag was first used between 1918 and 1922. It was readopted in September 1991. The colours were first used in 1848. They are heraldic in origin and were first used on the coat of arms of one of the Ukrainian kingdoms in the Middle Ages.

Geography

Ukraine is the second largest country in Europe after Russia. It was formerly part of the Soviet Union, which split apart in 1991. This mostly flat country faces the Black Sea in the south. The Crimean Peninsula includes a highland region overlooking Yalta. The highest point of the country is in the eastern Carpathian Mountains which extend into the Slovak Republic and Romania. The most extensive land region is the central plateau which descends to the north to the Dnipro (Dnieper)-Pripet Lowlands. A low plateau occupies the north-east.

Climate

Ukraine has warm summers, but the winters are cold, becoming more severe from west to east. In the summer, the east of the country is often warmer than the west. The heaviest rainfall occurs in the summer.

Vegetation

Woodland with such trees as ash, oak and pine grows in the north, while pine forests swathe the slopes of the Carpathians and Crimean mountains. Grassy steppe once covered central Ukraine, but much of the steppe is now farmed.

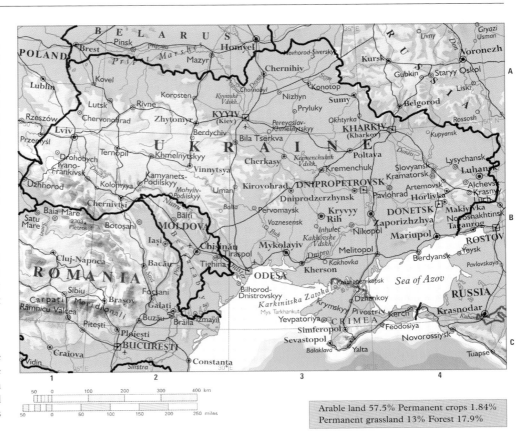

Arable land 57.5% Permanent crops 1.84%
Permanent grassland 13% Forest 17.9%

History

In the 9th century AD, a group of people, called the East Slavs, founded a civilization called Kievan Rus, with its capital at Kiev (Kyyiv). Russians took over the area in 980 and the region became prosperous. In the 13th century, Mongol armies ravaged the area. Later, the region was split into small kingdoms and large areas fell under foreign rule. In the 17th and 18th centuries, parts of Ukraine came under Polish and Russian rule. But Russia gained most of Ukraine in the late 18th century, although Austria held an area in the west, called Galicia. In 1917, following the Bolshevik Revolution, the Ukrainians set up an independent, non-Communist republic.

Austrian Ukraine declared itself a republic in 1918 and the two parts joined together. In 1919, however, Ukrainian Communists set up a second government and proclaimed the country a Soviet Socialist Republic. The Communists ultimately triumphed and, during 1922, Ukraine became one of the four original republics that formed the Soviet Union.

Millions of people died in the 1930s as the result of Soviet policies. Millions more died during the Nazi occupation between 1941 and 1944. In 1945, the Soviet Union added to Ukraine areas that were formerly in Czechoslovakia, Poland and Romania.

Politics

In the 1980s, Ukrainian people demanded more say over their affairs. The country finally became independent when the Soviet Union broke up in 1991. Ukraine continued to work with Russia through the Commonwealth of Independent States. But Ukraine differed with Russia on some issues, including control over Crimea. In 1999, a treaty ratifying Ukraine's present boundaries failed to get the approval of Russia's upper house.

A former Communist, Leonid Kravchuk was elected president in 1991. He was defeated in 1994 by Leonid Kuchma, the prime minister. A new constitution was adopted in 1996, declaring Ukraine to be a democratic, unitary state and guaranteeing civil rights, including

the right to private ownership. Kuchma was re-elected in 1999, defeating the Communist Party candidate. In parliamentary elections in 2002, the Communist Party fared badly while no party emerged with a clear majority.

Economy

The World Bank classifies Ukraine as a 'lower-middle-income' economy. Agriculture is important. Crops include wheat and sugar beet, which are the major exports, together with barley, maize, potatoes, sunflowers and tobacco. Livestock rearing and fishing are also important industries.

Manufacturing is the chief economic activity. Major manufactures include iron and steel, machinery and vehicles. The country has large coalfields. The country imports oil and natural gas, though it has hydroelectric and nuclear power stations. In 1986, an accident at the Chernobyl (Chornobyl) nuclear power plant caused widespread nuclear radiation. The plant was finally closed in 2000.

AREA	Russian 22%, Jewish 1%,
603,700 sq km	Belarussian 1%,
[233,100 sq mi]	Moldovan, Bulgarian,
POPULATION	Polish
48,760,000	**LANGUAGES**
CAPITAL (POPULATION)	Ukrainian (official),
Kiev	Russian
(Kyyiv, 2,621,000)	**RELIGIONS**
GOVERNMENT	Mostly Ukrainian
Multiparty republic	Orthodox
ETHNIC GROUPS	**CURRENCY**
Ukrainian 73%,	Hryvnia = 100 kopiykas

UNITED ARAB EMIRATES – SEE GULF STATES, PAGES 113–114

The flag of the United Kingdom was officially adopted in 1801. The first Union flag, combining the cross of St George (England) and St Andrew (Scotland), dates back from 1603. In 1801, the cross of St Patrick, Ireland's emblem, was added to form the present flag.

Geography

The United Kingdom is a union of four countries: England, Northern Ireland, Scotland and Wales. The islands are confusingly named. Great Britain, the largest island in Europe, was named to distinguish it from Little Britain (Brittany, in France), and includes England, Scotland and Wales. Ireland was once a kingdom, but is currently divided into the Province of Northern Ireland, under the British Crown, and the Republic of Ireland. Great Britain, Northern Ireland and many island groups from the Scillies to the Shetlands, together make up the United Kingdom of Great Britain and Northern Ireland, commonly known as the UK. Even isolated Rockall, far out in the Atlantic Ocean, is part of the UK, but the Isle of Man (see page 228) and the Channel Islands (see page 227) are separate if direct dependencies of the Crown, with a degree of political autonomy and their own taxation systems.

Visitors to England are often amazed at the variety of the landscape. Complex folding, volcanic upheavals and eruptions, glacial planing and changes of sea level have all left their marks on the present landscape. Upland regions include the Pennines which extend southwards from Northumberland to the Trent. The Pennines is a region of rolling hills, plateaux and beautiful valleys known as 'dales'. Two outliers of the Pennines are the Forest of Rossendale, north of Manchester, and the Forest of Bowland in northern Lancashire. Lowlands border the uplands to the east and west. The Eden Valley separates the northern Pennines from Cumbria, which includes the Lake District. This scenic mountain region contains England's highest peak, Scafell Pike, which reaches 978 m [3,210 ft]. Exmoor in the south-west is a sandstone upland, while Dartmoor is a mainly granite area with many prominent tors. Elsewhere are isolated hills, small by world standards, but dramatic against the small-scale background of Britain, as shown by the Malvern Hills of Worcester and the Wrekin, near Shrewsbury.

The English lowland contains chalk downlands, familiar to visitors who enter England through Dover or Folkestone as the white cliffs. These are the exposed edges of the North and South Downs. The North Downs extend westwards to the Hampshire Downs. There is also a northwards extension through the Berkshire and Marlborough Downs to the Chilterns, and then north again into East Anglia to disappear under the edge of the fens near Cambridge. Chalk appears again in the wolds of Lincolnshire and Yorkshire, emerging at Flamborough Head.

Older limestones form the Cotswold Hills and the rolling hills of Leicestershire, the Lincoln and, finally, the North York Moors. England's main rivers are the Thames, Severn, the fenland Ouse, the Trent and the Great Yorkshire Ouse.

Wales is mainly hilly and mountainous. The best known of its highland areas is Snowdonia, a national park which contains Snowdon, the highest mountain in Wales at 1,085 m [3,560 ft]. There are also fine upland areas in central Wales, with the Brecon Beacons in the south. However, most of the people live in the industrialized area of South Wales, which includes the mining villages of Glamorgan.

More than half of Scotland's area lies in the Highlands and Islands which are bounded by a line drawn from Stonehaven, south of Aberdeen, to the mouth of the Clyde. This region is divided into two by the Great Glen, which extends from Fort William to Inverness and includes three lochs – Lochy, Oich and Ness – linked by the Caledonian Canal. The north-western part of the Highlands has fine scenery, as also do the Inner and Outer Hebrides. East of the Great Glen is a richer country, flanked on the east by the lowlands around Aberdeen. Ben Nevis, at 1,342 m [4,401 ft], dominating the town of Fort William in the Great Glen, is the highest peak in the British Isles. In the far north lie the Orkneys and the Shetlands. South of the Highlands and Islands is Scotland's Central Valley, which contains several rolling uplands, Clydeside, the country's greatest industrial area, and Edinburgh, which stands on splendid volcanic ridges. Though less spectacular than the Highlands, the Southern Uplands contain beautiful hills, rolling moorlands and rich valleys. The Tweed, with its numerous tributaries, provides sheltered valleys for farming.

Northern Ireland is a land of rolling plains and low mountains. Its highest mountain is Slieve Donard, which reaches 852 m [2,796 ft] in the Mourne Mountains in the south-east. Other scenic features include Lough Neagh, the largest lake in the British Isles which has an area of 396 sq km [153 sq mi], and Giant's Causeway, a spectacular area of basalt columns formed from an ancient lava flow, north of Coleraine.

Climate

The UK has a mild climate, influenced by the warm Gulf Stream which flows across the Atlantic from the Gulf of Mexico, then past the British Isles. Moist winds from the south-west bring rain, which diminishes from west to east. Winds from the east and north bring cold conditions in winter. The weather is markedly changeable, because of the common occurrence of depressions with their associated fronts.

UNITED KINGDOM – LONDON

South-east England, sheltered from the ocean to the west, is one of the driest parts of the UK. Although rainfall varies little all year, greater evaporation creates a deficit between May and August. London has a small annual temperature range. Its record low is –10°C [14°F] and record high 34°C [93°F]. London creates its own local climate and nights are warmer than those in surrounding regions.

CARDIFF

Winter temperatures are not too cold: averages for December to February are 5°C [41°F]. The averages of the lowest in these months is –4°C to –2°C [25–28°F]. Averages from May to October are over 10°C [50°F], and from June to August 15°C [59°F] plus. Frost and snow-days are among the lowest in the country. Rainfall at 1,000 mm [39 in] is average, falling in all months, with a winter peak.

GLASGOW

Glasgow experiences a maritime climate with mild winters, cool summers, and well-distributed rainfall with an autumn maximum. The Clyde Valley is more sheltered than the estuary, where Greenock receives in excess of 1,500 mm [590 in] of rain annually. At Glasgow rain falls on about 200 days per year. It averages about 3–5 hours of sunshine per day compared to 4–5 hours in the south.

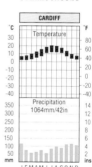

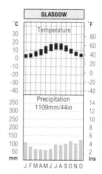

Vegetation

Human activity has greatly modified the landscape and only small patches of the original woodland have survived. The ancient forests, dominated by oak, were cleared to make way for farmland, but forest clearance in marginal areas for grazing has led to the development of moorland and heathland. Moorlands and heathlands now cover about a third of the UK. In lowland Britain, the dominant plant of the heathland is the common heather, whose purple colour adorns the autumn countryside. Most of the former larger mammals which lived in the forests have become extinct.

UNITED KINGDOM

ATLANTIC OCEAN

Shetland Is.
Yell
Unst
Fetlar
Foula
Mainland
Lerwick
Fair Isle

1224

316

530

Orkney Is.
Westray
Sanday
Stronsay
Mainland
Kirkwall
Hoy
South Ronaldsay

Outer Hebrides
Lewis
Stornoway
North Minch
C. Wrath
Thurso
Pentland Firth
Wick
Harris
789
Helmsdale
North Uist
Benbecula
Ullapool
Lairg
Golspie
Moray Firth
St. Kilda
South Uist
Portree
Dingwall
Invergordon
Tain
Nairn
Elgin
Buckie
Banff
Fraserburgh
Skye
North West Highlands
Inverness
1182
L. Ness
Aviemore
Don
Huntly
Peterhead
Inverurie
Inner Hebrides
Rhum
Eigg
Mallaig
Fort William
311
Dee
Aberdeen
Barra
Ben Nevis
1342
SCOTLAND
Grampian Mts.
Ballater
Stonehaven
Coll
Tobermory
Oban
1214
Forfar
Arbroath
Montrose
Tiree
Mull
L. Lomond
Perth
St. Andrews
Dundee
Colonsay
973
Stirling
Glenrothes
Kirkcaldy
238
Jura
Greenock
Dunfermline
Dunbar
Islay
Paisley
Glasgow
Edinburgh
Clyde
East Kilbride
Hamilton
Berwick-upon-Tweed
Arran
Irvine
Kilmarnock
Southern Uplands
Galashiels
Campbeltown
840
Jedburgh
Hawick
816
Cheviot Hills
Alnwick
Ayr
Girvan
Dumfries
Annan
Hexham
Newcastle-upon-Tyne
South Shields
Stranraer
Kirkcudbright
Carlisle
893
Gateshead
Sunderland
Durham
Hartlepool
Redcar
NORTH SEA
Malin Hd.
Buncrana
Coleraine
Workington
Whitehaven
Cumbrian Mts.
978
Darlington
Stockton-on-Tees
Middlesbrough
Scarborough
16

Aran I.
Letterkenny
Lifford
NORTHERN IRELAND
Ballymena
Larne
Antrim
Bangor
Mull of Galloway
Barrow-in-Furness
Lancaster
Bridlington
Donegal
Ulster
Omagh
Lough Neagh
Lisburn
Belfast
Douglas
I. of Man
Harrogate
York
Kingston upon Hull
Bundoran
Lower L. Erne
Enniskillen
Portadown
Lurgan
Armagh
Newry
852
Dundalk
Ballina
Sligo
Clones
UNITED
Blackpool
Keighley
Leeds
Beverley
Achill I.
L. Conn
Castlebar
Leitrim
Cavan
KINGDOM
Preston
Burnley
Bradford
Halifax
Huddersfield
Barnsley
Doncaster
Grimsby
Humber
Lough Mask
Roscommon
Ceanannus Mor
IRISH
Blackburn
636
Rotherham
Scunthorpe
Lincoln
Louth
Connemara
Lough Carrib
Longford
Boyne
Drogheda
Manchester
Bolton
Oldham
Stockport
Sheffield
Skegness
Galway B.
Dublin
SEA
Liverpool
Warrington
Chesterfield
Mansfield
The Wash
Galway
Ballinasloe
Athlone
Mullingar
Lough Ree
Dun Laoghaire
Anglesey
Colwyn Bay
Chester
Crewe
Derby
Nottingham
Cromer
Aran Is.
Tullamore
Bray
Holyhead
Wrexham
Stoke-on-Trent
Stafford
Trent
Grantham
King's Lynn
Ennis
Port Laoise
Athy
Carlow
1085
Snowdon
Cambrian Mts.
Shrewsbury
Telford
ENGLAND
Great
Norwich
Great Yarmouth
Nenagh
Kilkenny
926
Bangor
Pwllheli
Welshpool
BIRMINGHAM
Nuneaton
Leicester
Peterborough
Thetford
Lowestoft
Limerick
Thurles
Clonmel
Carrick-on-Suir
Wexford
Cardigan Bay
Aberystwyth
Wolverhampton
Redditch
Coventry
Rugby
Corby
Ely
Bury St. Edmunds
953
Tralee
Listowel
Tipperary
Waterford
Rosslare
Worcester
Royal Leamington Spa
Northampton
Cambridge
Ipswich
Shannon
Mallow
Dungarvan
Youghal
St. George's Channel
Fishguard
Carmarthen
Brecon
886
Hereford
Cheltenham
Gloucester
Milton Keynes
Stevenage
Colchester
Felixstowe
Dingle
1041
Carrauntoohill
Blackwater
Haverfordwest
Merthyr Tydfil
Cotswold Hills
Oxford
Hemel Hempstead
Luton
Harlow
Harwich
Macgillycuddy's Reeks
Cork
Bandon
Kinsale
Milford Haven
Pembroke
Llanelli
Neath
Rhondda
Cwmbran
Newport
High Wycombe
Slough
Watford
Chelmsford
Valencia I.
Cóbh
99
WALES
Swansea
Port Talbot
Barry
Cardiff
Bristol
Bath
Swindon
Newbury
Reading
LONDON
Thames
Chatham
Southend-on-Sea
Zeebrugge
Oostende
Bantry
Bristol Channel
Weston-super-Mare
Basingstoke
Guildford
Reigate
Maidstone
Canterbury
Dover
Dunkerque
BELGIUM
Brugge
C. Clear
618
Barnstaple
Exmoor
Taunton
Salisbury
Winchester
Crawley
Ashford
Folkestone
Calais
Gris-Nez
St-Omer
Lille
CELTIC
Bude
Yeovil
Fareham
Hastings
Boulogne-sur-Mer
Béthune
Bruay-la-Buissière
Newquay
Truro
Exeter
Dartmoor
Bournemouth
Poole
Weymouth
Southampton
Portsmouth
Brighton
Eastbourne
Worthing
Le Touquet-Paris-Plage
33
36
SEA
Torbay
Exmouth
Newport
Isle of Wight
English Channel
Le Tréport
Abbeville
St. Austell
Plymouth
Dieppe
Amiens
Land's End
Penzance
Falmouth
FRANCE
Isles of Scilly
C. de la Hague
Pte. de Barfleur
Fécamp
Alderney
Noyon

50 0 25 50 75 100 125 150 175 km
50 0 25 50 75 100 125 miles

Arable land 24.6% Permanent crops 0.19%
Permanent grassland 45.9% Forest 10.3%

North Sea Oil

The discovery of gas and oil in the North Sea in the 1960s transformed Britain from an oil importer into the world's fifth largest exporter within a decade. Gas from the new fields rapidly replaced coal gas in the British energy system, and by 1981 the country was self-sufficient in oil. In the peak production year of 1986, the British sector of the North Sea produced 141.8 million tonnes of crude oil, accounting for over 20% of UK export earnings. In 2000, the UK was the tenth largest producer of crude oil, with a total average production of 2.7 million barrels (about 359,500 tonnes) a day, or 131 million tonnes a year. There were also important new discoveries west of Shetland in 1994, while the Foinaven and Schiehallion fields could account for 30% of the UK's known reserves. In 2001, a record 223 offshore fields were in operation. Of these fields, 113 were producing oil, 17 condensates (a lighter form of oil) and 93 were producing gas.

Up to the end of 2000, oil fields on the UK continental shelf had produced a cumulative total of 2,448 million tonnes, while the UK continental shelf reserves were estimated at about 1,490 million tonnes. The fields with the largest production totals are Forties, Brent, Ninian and Piper. The largest onshore oil field is at Wytch Farm, Dorset. The search for new reserves continues and, in 2000, 12 new development projects – six offshore oil fields, five offshore gas fields, and one onshore gas field – were approved.

In taxes and royalties, oil and natural gas from the North Sea gave an immense fillip to British government revenues. There was much discussion as to the best use for this windfall money, which is likely to taper away during the early part of the 21st century before vanishing altogether, but it certainly helped to finance substantial cuts in taxation. The sight of North Sea oil wealth flowing south to the government treasury in London also provoked nationalist resentment in Scotland, off whose coast most of the oil rigs (and much of the gas) are situated.

History

The isolation of the United Kingdom from mainland Europe has made a major impact on its history. The narrow seas separating the British Isles from mainland Europe have served the islanders well against casual invasion, while Britons in turn sailed to explore and exploit the rest of the world. Despite insularity, Britons are of mixed stock.

Early immigrants – land-hungry farmers from the mainland – were often refugees from tribal warfare and unrest. Belgic tribesmen escaping from Imperial Rome, the Romans themselves, whose troops included Macedonian, Spanish and North African mercenaries, the Angles, Saxons, Jutes, Danes and Normans all brought genetic variety. So too did the Huguenots, Sephardic and Ashkenazim Jews, and Dutch, French and German businessmen who followed them. Latterly, the waves of immigrants have included Belarussians, Poles, Italians, Ukrainians and Czechs, most of whom, like their predecessors, were fugitives from European wars, overcrowding and intolerance.

During the 19th century, Britain often took in skilled European immigrants through the front door, while steadily losing her own sons and daughters – Scots and Irish peasants in particular – through the back. Most recent arrivals in Britain are immigrants from crowded and impoverished corners of the British Empire, notably the Caribbean, India and Pakistan, while a new wave of immigration in the 1990s led to an influx of refugees from war-torn former Yugoslavia, the Somali Republic, Sri Lanka and elsewhere.

The recorded history of the area that is now the United Kingdom began with the Roman conquest in 55 BC. Yet human habitation goes back to around 250,000 BC, the start of the Palaeolithic Period (Old Stone Age). The Mesolithic Period began around 8000 BC, at the end of the last phase of the Ice Age. In 5000 BC, rising sea levels finally cut the islands off from mainland Europe through the formation of the English Channel and the North Sea.

Shortly before 4000 BC, the Neolithic (New Stone Age) Period began. The Neolithic marked the introduction of a much more sophisticated farming culture. The Neolithic Period was followed by the Bronze Age and the Iron Age. Towards the end of the Bronze Age, when new immigrants introduced metal-working skills, the first of a succession of waves of Celtic immigrants reached the shores of Britain. Their language displaced earlier languages and it is the ancestor of Gaelic, Irish, Cornish, Manx and Welsh. Around 700 BC, more Celtic immigrants arrived who were skilled in the use of iron to make weapons and tools. In the first century BC, the Belgae, the advanced Celtic tribes, reached southern Britain from France. They built large settlements that became the basis for Britain's first towns.

When the Romans arrived in *Britannia* (the Roman name for Britain), they found a society divided into tribal communities ruled by kings or queens. However, after Julius Caesar's conquests in 55 and 54 BC, the Romans withdrew and did not return until AD 43, when Emperor Claudius captured the southern part of Britain and ruled it for more than 350 years. They built towns, roads, country villas and defensive sites, including Hadrian's Wall, the ruins of which today testify to their civilizing influence.

Christianity was introduced by the Romans and, by the 4th century, the Christian church was established in Britain. The withdrawal of the Romans in the early 5th century heralded the start of a period, often called the Dark Ages, which continued until the Norman Conquest in 1066. It was a period when Anglo-Saxon and Jutish raiders established settlements, displacing the Romanized Celts, many of whom moved northwards into Scotland and westwards into Wales. The small Anglo-Saxon kingdoms gradually merged into larger powers and, eventually, Wessex came to be the major force. From the late 8th century, Wessex resisted the Danish Viking warriors who began to raid Britain. However, the Danes also founded towns and developed trade with countries beyond the North Sea. By 1013, the Danes had conquered most of England and, in 1016, Canute, king of Denmark and Norway, also became king of England.

The Norman Duke William of Normandy, who was later crowned William I, defeated Harold II at Hastings in 1066. The Norman victory, the last successful invasion of Britain, marked the start of the Norman Conquest, during which the Normans gradually extended their rule, building great castles and churches. French became the language of the English court and nobles for the following 300 years, and the English kings ruled large areas in France until the mid-15th century.

Wales, a Celtic stronghold, was conquered in 1282, but Welsh nationalism remained powerful, leading to an unsuccessful rebellion at the beginning of the 15th century. It was the Tudor Dynasty (1485–1603), which was of Welsh origin, that was instrumental (during the reign of Henry VIII) in uniting Wales with England through the Acts of Union of 1536 and 1542, so beginning the evolution of the modern UK.

The Romans never conquered Scotland. During the Middle Ages, wars were fought between Scotland and England and, despite some defeats, the victory of Robert the Bruce over Edward II at the battle of Bannockburn in 1314 ensured the survival of the Scottish kings. The two kingdoms were finally united when Elizabeth I of England was succeeded in 1603 by James VI of Scotland, who became James I of England. However, Scotland and England remained separate territories, apart from a short period of enforced unification under Oliver Cromwell, until 1707, when the Act of Union formally united England (and Wales) with Scotland as the United Kingdom of Great Britain. In the 12th century, Ireland came under the influence of Norman nobles, and relations between England and Ireland gradually became closer. The Act of Union of 1801 created the United Kingdom of Great Britain and Ireland. But following the partition of Ireland in 1922 into the mainly Roman Catholic Irish Free State, and the predominantly Protestant Northern Ireland, this became the United Kingdom of Great Britain and Northern Ireland.

The modern history of the United Kingdom began in the 18th century, with the development of the British Empire, including Canada and India. Despite the loss of its 13 North American colonies, which became the core of the United States as the result of the War of Independence (1775–83), it gained new territories, such as Australia. The existence of the British colonies acquired between the early 17th century and the later 18th century stimulated commerce and trade. The slave trade became important, bringing great wealth to the seaport traders of Bristol and Liverpool. The slave trade was finally abolished throughout the British Empire in 1833.

The 18th century also saw another major development that put Britain at the forefront of technology. This was the start of the Industrial Revolution, whose innovations were to change the world. The 19th century saw the Victorian Age, named after Queen Victoria, who reigned from 1837 until 1901. This was a period of huge economic progress, with iron production increasing by six times between 1833 and 1865. Britain became the 'workshop of the world', and the world's top manufacturing nation. Industrial progress was accompanied by rapid population growth. At the time of the Act of Union in 1707, some 6 million English and Welsh joined about 1 million Scots. By 1801, the first national census revealed that there were 8.9 million people in England and Wales and 1.6 million in Scotland. By 1821, the total British population was 21 million. By 1851, it had risen to 31 million, with the populations of the cities and towns growing at a fast rate. The growing economy was accompanied by a second phase of colonization in the 19th and early 20th centuries, when the British Empire reached its height. Britain's colonies provided raw materials, such as cotton, sugar and tobacco, while they were major markets for Britain's manufactured goods, including textiles and clothing.

However, towards the end of the 19th century, Britain began to face growing competition when countries, such as France, Germany and the United States, became major industrial and trading economies. In the early 19th century, Britain could no longer rely on its policy of 'splendid isolation'. Instead, to maintain its defences, it entered into alliances with other major powers. World War I was fought between the Allies, including Britain, France and the United States, and the Central Powers, including Germany, Austria-Hungary, the Ottoman Empire and Bulgaria. By 1918, the Allies were triumphant, but the war had sapped Britain's economy, shaking its position as a world power.

The inter-war world economic recession created further problems and, by 1932, about 3 million people in the United Kingdom were unemployed. World War II proved an even greater drain on the economy of the UK and, at the end of the war, the United States and the Soviet Union had emerged as the world's two great superpowers.

Politics

A landslide for the Labour Party in 1945 led to many social changes that still affect politics in Britain today. Although the government faced many difficulties in seeking to restore the war-shattered economy, it set up a welfare state, with a social security system that provided welfare for people 'from the cradle to the grave'. The government also recognized the high costs of maintaining the British Empire in the face of growing nationalism and, in 1947, British India was partitioned, creating two new independent nations – India and Pakistan. Sri Lanka (then Ceylon) became independent in 1948, as also did Myanmar (then Burma).

In place of the British Empire, Britain retained much influence in the world through the Commonwealth of Nations, whose original members were Australia, Britain, Canada, Ireland, New Zealand, Newfoundland and South Africa. This policy was continued by the Conservative Party, which won office in 1951 and governed until 1964. During that time, Cyprus, Ghana, Kenya, Malaysia, Malta, Nigeria, Sudan, Tanganyika (now Tanzania), Trinidad and Tobago, and Uganda all became independent. Because of the orderly way in which the British Empire broke up, most of the former colonies joined the Commonwealth when they became independent and, by 1999, the membership stood at 54.

While the UK was breaking up the British Empire, several Western European nations were setting up organizations to increase co-operation between them. At first, Britain wanted to stay out of these new organizations, fearing that it might lose some of its independence and reduce the importance of its partnerships with the Commonwealth of Nations and the United States. In the 1950s, it refused to join the ECSC (European Steel and Coal Community), EURATOM (European Atomic Energy Community) and, most significantly, the EEC (European Economic Community). Instead, in 1960, it helped to set up EFTA (European Free Trade Association) with six other

nations. However, EFTA's performance was modest by comparison with the EEC. In 1963, Britain's request to join the EEC was rejected, largely because it was opposed by the French President Charles De Gaulle, who was suspicious about 'Anglo-Saxon' motives.

The United Kingdom finally joined the EEC in 1973, though a strong body of opinion still feared that the development of a federal Europe would jeopardize British sovereignty. Membership was endorsed by a referendum in 1975, but, at the turn of the century, Britons were still debating whether it was advisable for Britain to adopt the euro, the single European currency which 12 of the 15 European Union members had adopted on 1 January 1999.

Another domestic issue of great importance involves the status of Northern Ireland. Since the 1960s, Northern Ireland has been the scene of conflict between the Protestant majority, who favour continuing union with the UK, and the Roman Catholic minority, many of whom are republicans who would like to see Ireland reunified. British troops were sent to the province in 1969 to control violence between the communities and, at various times, Britain has imposed direct rule over Northern Ireland. In 1998, the 'Good Friday' agreement held out hope for the future, when unionists and nationalists agreed that Northern Ireland would remain part of the United Kingdom, until a majority of its people voted in favour of a change. The agreement also allowed Ireland to play a part in the affairs of the north, while the republic amended its constitution to remove all claims to Northern Ireland. A Northern Ireland Assembly was set up to handle local affairs. Hopes of success were raised in 2001 and 2002 when the IRA (Irish Republican Army) disposed of some of its weapons.

Other problems have arisen in Scotland and Wales, where many nationalists, concerned about maintaining their own cultures, favoured self-government or even, in Scotland, independence. Before 1999, Scotland and Wales were directly ruled by the British parliament in London. But, in 1997, following the landslide victory of the Labour Party under Tony Blair, 74% of the people of Scotland and 50.3% of the people of Wales voted in favour of setting up local assemblies.

The Scottish parliament, which is responsible for local affairs and

---

The Channel Islands

Lying 16 km to 48 km [10–30 mi] from the Cotentin Peninsula on the French mainland, the Channel Islands, known in French as Les Îles Normandes, or Les Îles Anglo-Normandes, are a British dependency and not officially part of the United Kingdom, covering an area of only 200 sq km [78 sq mi] (see map on page 100).

The largest island is Jersey, whose chief town is St Helier. Jersey covers an area of 115 sq km [45 sq mi] and has 85,100 inhabitants. The second largest island is Guernsey, whose chief town is St Peter Port. Guernsey covers an area of 78 sq km [30 sq mi] and has 58,600 people. The other islands, including Alderney, Brechou, Great Sark, Little Sark, Herm, Jethou and Lihou, are dependencies of Guernsey. Together they have a population of less than 3,000. The islands have a mild climate, which, together with fine scenery and beautiful vegetation, attracts tourists. Average temperatures in January and February, the coldest months, are 6°C [43°F].

The only part of the Duchy of Normandy retained by the English Crown after 1204, and the only part of Britain occupied by the Germans in World War II, the islands have their own legal system and government, with lower taxation than that of Britain. This, combined with a favourable climate and fine coastal scenery, has attracted a considerable number of wealthy residents, notably retired people, and established Jersey and Guernsey as offshore financial centres.

The main produce is agricultural, especially early potatoes, tomatoes and flowers for export to Britain, and the countryside has a vast number of glasshouses. Jersey and Guernsey cattle are famous breeds, introduced to several countries. Holiday-makers visit the islands in large numbers during the summer months, travelling by air or by various passenger boats, particularly from Weymouth. English is the official language, but French is widely spoken.

has limited powers to raise or reduce taxes, and the Welsh Assembly, which has no powers over taxation, met for the first time in 1999. Devolution has caused concern among those who fear that it might lead to the break-up of the United Kingdom. Devolution has also focused attention on the question of nationality, especially in England, where there has been discussion about what it means to be English.

Other political issues in Britain involve the future of the welfare state. While most people favour top-quality and free welfare services, they tend to vote for parties which advocate low taxation. The high cost of welfare services is a matter of political controversy that seems likely to continue well into the 21st century. There is also concern about the changing economy, with a decline in traditional manufacturing and the growth of service industries, both of which affect employment. Another issue is immigration and the fear that economic migrants entering the UK will lessen the job opportunities of the indigenous workforce.

Other issues are concerned with Britain's status in the world. Though no longer a top world power, the UK continues to play a major role in world affairs, both diplomatically and militarily. For example, after the terrorist attacks on the United States on 11 September 2001, Britain was prominent in its support for the United States, helping to create the broad alliance that launched the attack on the Taliban government of Afghanistan. However, others are concerned at the cost and morality of British military operations.

Economy

The United Kingdom has the world's fifth largest economy, after the United States, Japan, Germany and France. In 1998, agriculture contributed 1.3% of the gross domestic product, as compared with 21.4% from manufacturing and mining. Of the service industries, tourism is a long-term growth sector. The number of tourists reached more than 25 million in 2000, while tourism and related activities employed 2,100,000 people. London and its historic buildings and cultural institutions is the UK's most popular tourist centre, while the City of London's financial and insurance businesses have made the capital one of the world's leading financial cities.

The United Kingdom has to import about a third of the food it needs, but its farming techniques are modern and scientific, and yields are high. Between 1973 and 1998, agricultural productivity increased by more than 40%, which was largely the result of the declining number of people working on farms, now barely 1% of the country's workforce. The declining proportion of people employed on farms is an inevitable result of agricultural rationalization and improvements in farming methods. Those who deplore this trend might reflect that, though farming formerly employed many more people, it supported them at little more than subsistence level. About two-thirds of all farmland is owner-occupied; the rest is tenanted or rented.

Soils vary from the rich soils of lowland England, such as the fenlands of eastern England, to the poor ones of highland Britain, where grazing is the chief activity. Dairy farms or beef and sheep farms are found mainly in the upland and moorland parts of Northern Ireland, Scotland, Wales and south-western England. Cattle and sheep farming

make up about 35% of the value of Britain's total agricultural output. Pigs and poultry are also important, particularly in East Anglia, north-eastern Scotland and Yorkshire.

Arable farming is important in eastern and central-southern England, and also in eastern Scotland. Major crops include barley, oats, oilseed rape, potatoes, sugar beet and, most important of all, wheat. Eastern England produces most of the country's barley, sugar beet and wheat, while large-scale potato and vegetable production occurs in all areas where the soils are fertile. Mixed farming is common, but its character varies, with an emphasis on livestock in the wetter highlands, and an emphasis on crops in the lowlands. Local products include the hops of Kent and Hereford, the apples of Worcester, and the fine wools that are major products on the chalk downlands. Market gardening and small-scale dairy farming have also developed around almost every major settlement, taking advantage of the ready market close at hand.

Fishing is a major industry and the UK is one of the largest fishing countries in the European Union. Important catches include cod, haddock, mackerel, plaice, pollock, eel and whiting. In 2000, the fishing fleet included more than 7,800 registered vessels, while professional fishermen numbered about 15,000. Though the UK imports most of its timber and wood products, forestry remains an important activity, especially in Scotland, where woodland covers nearly 17% of the land, and Wales, where 9% of the land is forested.

The UK is a leading producer of petroleum, natural gas and coal, together with such non-energy minerals as china clay, potash and salt. The oil and gas come mainly from wells in the North Sea. Although coal still supplies a considerable proportion of the country's primary energy needs, the coal industry has declined in the last 50 years, because of competition with other energy sources. However, in early 2001, the UK had 33 underground mines and 45 opencast mines. Coal and iron-ore reserves were the basis of the Industrial Revolution of the 18th century and the industrial growth of the 19th century, which together resulted in major changes in the landscapes of northern and central England, southern Wales and west-central Scotland.

Like coal, the steel industry has encountered stiff competition from the Far East and elsewhere, but steel production remains important, especially in southern Wales and northern England. The car industry, which depends on steel, has declined since the 1970s and, today, the country imports more cars than it exports. The UK also imports much steel, because its plentiful iron ore reserves are mostly low quality.

Competition from overseas had led the UK to diversify its manufacturing sector so that, today, it produces a wide variety of products. The UK is a major producer of heavy machinery for use in agriculture, manufacturing and mining, together with aircraft, space satellites and armaments. Another important group of products are made by the electronics industries, including television equipment, fibre-optic communications and radar devices. Other major industrial sectors include the chemical industry, producing pharmaceuticals, industrial chemicals and plastics, and the textile industry.

The economy of the UK is dependent on trade and the country ranks fifth in the world in the total value of its overseas trade. The country's leading exports are machinery and transport equipment, vehicles, chemicals, petroleum and petroleum products, textiles, and paper and paper board. The country's top trading partners are the United States, Germany, France and the Netherlands. Also important are other fellow members of the European Union, namely Belgium-Luxembourg, Italy, Ireland and Spain. Japan is another major source of imports for the United Kingdom.

Isle of Man

Covering 590 sq km [227 sq mi], the Isle of Man sits in the Irish Sea almost equidistant from County Down and Cumbria, but nearer Galloway in Scotland. The uplands, pierced by the corridor valley from Douglas to Peel, extend from Ramsey to Port Erin. The population is about 71,700. The climate is temperate.

The first inhabitants of the island were Celts and the almost extinct Manx language is Celtic. English control began in 1406 and the island became a British Crown Possession in 1828. Mainly agricultural, the island is now largely dependent on tourism, especially during the TT (Tourist Trophy) motorcycle races each summer. Douglas, the capital, contains over a third of the population. The Isle of Man remains a dependency and is not part of the United Kingdom. It has its own legislative assembly (Court of Tynwald), legal system and tax controls.

AREA	LANGUAGES
243,368 sq km [94,202 sq mi]	English (official), Welsh, Gaelic
POPULATION	**RELIGIONS**
59,648,000	Anglican 57%,
CAPITAL (POPULATION)	Roman Catholic 13%,
London (8,089,000)	Presbyterian 7%,
GOVERNMENT	Methodist 4%, Baptist 1%,
Constitutional monarchy	Islam 1%, Judaism,
ETHNIC GROUPS	Hinduism, Sikhism
White 94%, Asian Indian 1%,	**CURRENCY**
Pakistani 1%, West Indian 1%	Pound sterling = 100 pence

UNITED STATES OF AMERICA

This flag, known as the 'Stars and Stripes', has had the same basic design since 1777, during the War of Independence. The 13 stripes represent the 13 original colonies in the eastern United States. The 50 stars represent the 50 states of the Union.

Geography

The United States of America is the world's fourth largest country in area and the third largest in population. It contains 50 states, 48 of which lie between Canada and Mexico, plus Alaska in north-western North America and Hawaii, a group of volcanic islands in the North Pacific Ocean. Geographically, the main part (of the 48 states) can be divided into three main regions: the east, including the Appalachian Mountains and the eastern coastal plains; the centre, including the Mississippi Basin and the broad prairie plains; and the west, including the Rocky Mountains and the Pacific coastlands.

Eastern United States is crossed by a band of low, folded mountains which long formed a barrier to settlers. In the north are the Adirondacks, a southern extension of the ancient granite shield of Canada. The Appalachian Mountains, which extend from Maine to Alabama, are younger than the Adirondacks, but much older than the Rockies. They separate the Atlantic coastlands from the Great Lakes and the low plateaux of Ohio, Kentucky and Tennessee. In the north-east, the fertile, wooded six New England states made early settlers feel at home. To the south, the coastal plain widens, to be split by the drowned estuaries of the Susquehanna and Potomac Rivers draining into Chesapeake Bay. From Virginia to Florida, smaller rivers drain eastwards, across a broader plain, many of them entering coastal sounds with offshore bars and islands. In New York State, a major spillway cuts through the mountains between the Adirondacks and the Appalachians, linking the Great Lakes with the Hudson River Valley and the Atlantic Ocean. This is the line of the famous Erie Canal route, the most used of several that gave early settlers access to the Ohio country beyond the mountains. Other routes led to Pittsburgh and, through the southern Appalachians, into Tennessee. Central Ohio, Indiana and Illinois are rolling uplands and plains, smoothed by glaciation in the north, but more rugged in the south, and drained by the Ohio River.

The central states extend from the Dakotas to Texas. Within 1,400 km [875 mi] from the Mississippi to the foothills of the Rockies, the land rises almost 3,000 m [9,850 ft], though the slope is often imperceptible. From the Gulf of Mexico to Minnesota and the Dakotas, the rise is even less noticeable, but the landscape is occasionally relieved by uplands, such as the Ozarks of northern Arkansas. Westwards from the Mississippi, it grows progressively drier. The plains are crossed by a series of long, wide rivers that drain off the Rockies. They include the Missouri, the Platte, the Arkansas, the Canadian and the Red. In contrast to the Ohio, the rivers of the central United States provided little help to settlers moving westwards, due to seasonal variations in flow and the effort required to move upstream when floods gave them depth.

The western United States, for so long the final frontier of a youthful, expanding nation, is still the goal of thousands of immigrants each year and the holiday dream of many more. Topographically, the west is a land of high ranges divided by high plateaux and deep valleys. The highest mountains – the Rockies – form a spectacular eastern flank. The southern Rockies of Colorado and New Mexico, remnants of an ancient granite plateau, are carved by weathering into ranges of impressive peaks. Colorado alone has more than 1,000 peaks of 3,000 m [10,000 ft]. The central Rocky Mountains, towering over western Wyoming, Idaho and Montana, include a number of snow-capped peaks of more than 4,000 m [13,000 ft]. West of the Rockies, beyond the dry plateau scrublands of Arizona, Utah and Nevada, a double chain of mountains runs parallel to the coast from Mexico to Canada. In the south, they form the desert landscape on either side of the Gulf of California. At Los Angeles, they merge, parting again to form the Sierra Nevada and the Coastal Ranges that face each other across the Great Valley of central California. They rejoin in the Klamath Mountains, then continue north on either side of a broad valley – to the west as a lowly coastal chain, to the east as the imposing volcanic Cascade Range.

Climate

The climates of the United States vary greatly, ranging from the Arctic conditions in northern Alaska, where average temperatures plummet to –13°C [9°F], to the intense heat of Death Valley. Death Valley holds the record for the highest shade temperature ever recorded in the United States, namely 57°C [134°F].

New England, the Middle Atlantic States and the Midwest have cold winters and warm summers. By contrast, the southern states have long, hot summers and mild, wet winters. In the central United States, a lack of topographical features bars the northwards movement of hot, moist air from the Gulf of Mexico, and in winter the southwards movement of dry, cold air from the Arctic. These air masses produce contrasts of climate, exacerbated by storms, blizzards and tornadoes.

Parts of California have a pleasant Mediterranean-type climate, but the mountains of the west are much cooler and wetter. The central plains are arid, while deserts occur in parts of the west and south-west.

USA – NEW YORK CITY

New York City's average winter temperature is just above freezing. Temperatures lower than –20°C [–4°F] have been recorded from December to February, while the daily high from May to August is above 20°C [68°F], with temperatures of 35°C to 40°C [95–104°F] having been recorded. Rain and snow are uniform all year, with rain falling on a third of the days. Sunshine totals average 6–9 hours daily from March to October.

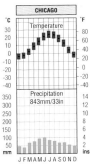

CHICAGO

To the east of the Rockies, the US is isolated from the influence of the Pacific. Here, it experiences very similar extremes to central Eurasia, but the edges of the Great Lakes are warmer in winter and cooler in summer than elsewhere. Temperatures of –20°C [–4°F] have been recorded between the months of December and February. Rainfall is uniform, with a summer maximum. Winter snowfall averages 1,000 mm [40 in].

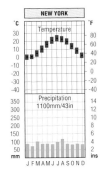

MIAMI

The Florida peninsula experiences the warmest winters of the US mainland, with a winter rainfall minimum. The lowest-ever recorded temperature is 1°C [34°F]. The summer is very hot and humid with prevailing southerly winds and thundery rain. Hurricanes may occur during late summer and they partially account for the high rainfall levels in September and October. Daily sunshine amounts average 7.5–9 hours.

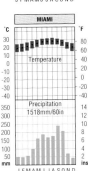

HOUSTON

Southern Texas experiences high rainfall levels throughout the year. During summer, the prevailing winds are from the south-east, and during winter from the north-east. In winter, very cold air from Canada may penetrate as far south as the Gulf, causing a sharp fall in temperature, and in the autumn the region may be affected by hurricanes. Many degrees of frost can be recorded between the months of November and March.

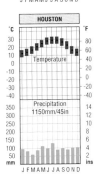

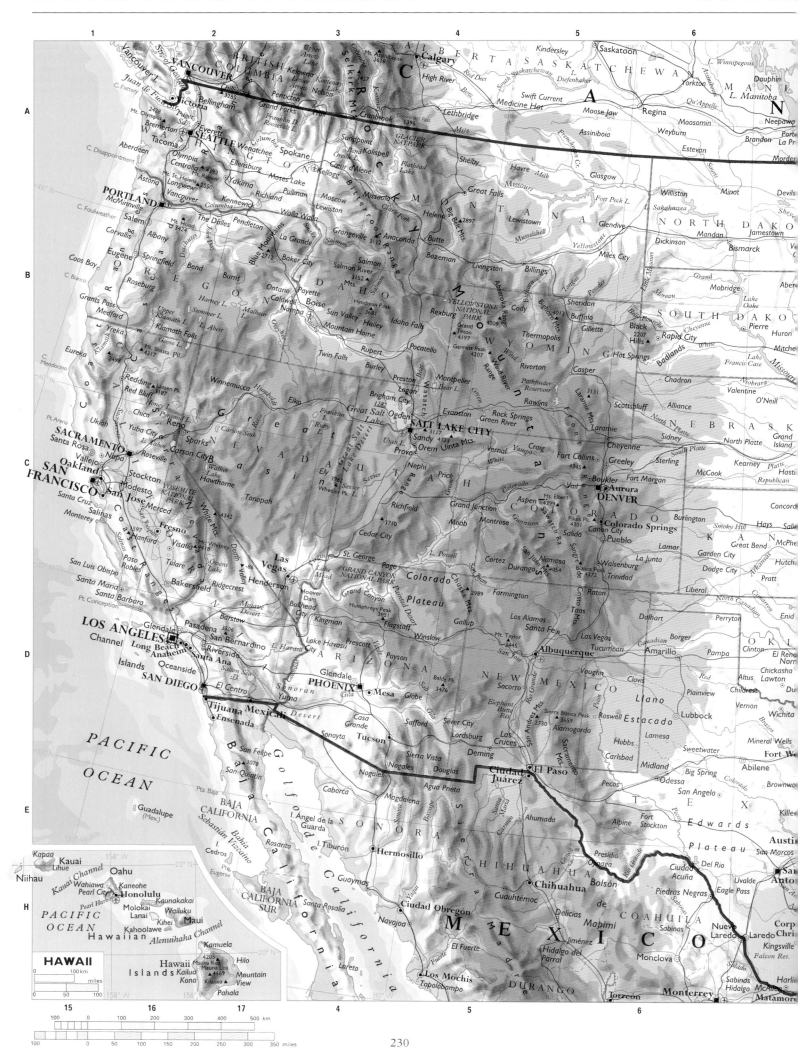

UNITED STATES OF AMERICA

DENVER

Denver is situated at an altitude of over 1,500 m [5,000 ft]. Winters are very chilly but summers are pleasantly warm. The daily temperature range is high: January experiences an average temperature of 6°C [43°F], with a night-time average of −10°C [14°F]. Rainfall is low, with a maximum in April and May, rain falling on ten days in any month. Sunshine levels are high with an average of over 6 hours a day in all months, with over 9 hours in the summer months.

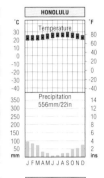

HONOLULU

Hawaii is cooled by the moisture-laden, north-east trade winds. Temperatures remain high throughout the year, ranging from 22°C to 26°C [72–79°F]. Rainfall varies greatly throughout the islands. Mt Waialeale on Kauai experiences a rainfall of 12,000 mm [472 in], while Puako on the leeward side of Hawaii receives less than 250 mm [10 in]. The lofty volcanoes, Mauna Kea and Mauna Loa, are frequently snow-covered.

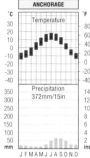

ANCHORAGE

The climate of southern Alaska is drier and more extreme than is expected from its maritime position. From November to May, winds are mainly easterly and winters are very cold, although ports remain ice-free. During the summer months, south-westerly winds increase in frequency, giving a late summer rainfall maximum. Northwards, beyond the Alaskan Range, it is drier and bitterly cold during the winter months.

Vegetation

The original vegetation in the eastern United States was broadleaf deciduous forest of oak, ash, beech and maple, merging northwards into yellow birch, hemlock and pine. In the drier Midwest, woodlands turned to open country. Patchy grasslands covered northern Indiana and southern Illinois. In central Illinois, forests grew along most watercourses, with prairie bluestem grasses on the drier land between. Mixed oak, pine and tulip trees dominated in the southern Appalachians. Pines covered the coastal plains to the south and east, with bald cypress in northern Florida. Spruce blanketed the highlands from northern Maine to the Adirondacks, while spruce, tamarack and balsam fir covered the high Appalachians. Most of the original forest is now gone, but enough is left to leave the mountains a blaze of colour each autumn.

West of the margins of the Mississippi, tall bluestem prairie grasses once extended from the Canadian border to southern Texas. Trees grow only along watercourses – cottonwood and willow in the north, merging into oak and hickory further south. Westwards, the prairie grasslands thinned to the bunch grass and needle grass of the Great Plains in a belt from central North Dakota to western Oklahoma. West of about 100°W meridian, a variety of short grasses stretched from Montana and the Dakotas southwards to north-west Texas. In the far south, low xerophytic shrubs indicated increasing aridity.

Vegetation types in the west range from deserts in the south-west to the rain-soaked forests of Washington State in the north-west. Rising from cactus-and-sagebrush desert in the south-west, the lower slopes of the southern Rockies carry grey piñon pines and juniper scrub, with spruce, firs and pines above. Gnarled bristlecone pines, some 3,000 or more years old, grow at the timberline. Between the ranges, 'parks' of mixed forest and grassland support deer and other game in summer grazing. To the north lies the Wyoming Basin, where herds of bison once grazed. The Rockies are ecologically fascinating, with their forests, grasslands, alpine tundras and marshes. Here tourists may see bison, wapiti, mule, black and brown bears, and beavers.

History

The first people in North America, the ancestors of the Native Americans (or American Indians) arrived from Asia around 15,000 or, according to some scholars, as much as 40,000 years ago. Gradually, they migrated south through North, Central and South America. Another group of migrants from Asia, the Inuit (also called Eskimos), crossed over into northern North America around 6,000 years ago, but they stayed in the far north, around the Arctic Circle. The Vikings were probably the first Europeans to reach North America, probably Newfoundland in Canada, around 1,000 years ago. However, European exploration proper did not begin until Christopher Columbus, an Italian navigator sailing for Spain, reached the Caribbean in 1492.

Spain was active in taking over Mexico, Central and much of South America, but in the north it was Britain and France that supplied the earliest explorers and fur traders. Spain founded the first permanent English settlement in what is now the United States – St Augustine, Florida. Spain also established missions in parts of the west and south. But of much greater significance was the first permanent settlement established in 1607 in Jamestown in what became the colony of Virginia. This was followed in 1620 by the arrival of the Pilgrims at Plymouth Colony, the second permanent English settlement in North America. These and subsequent settlements eventually developed into a string of colonies which, by the mid-18th century, stretched down the eastern seaboard from Maine to Georgia. Most of the settlers came from Britain. However, the colonies attracted other people from western Europe, while African slaves made up about 20% of the total population.

The mid-18th century saw a breakdown in relations with Britain and, on 19 April 1775, the Revolutionary War began. During the war, on 4 July 1776, the colonists declared their independence by adopting the Declaration of Independence and creating a new nation, the United States of America. The last major battle in the Revolutionary War took place in 1781, when the Americans defeated the British at Yorktown, Virginia. The war officially ended in 1783 with the signing of the Treaty of Paris. Washington, D.C., became the national capital in 1800 and the nation almost doubled in size with the acquisition of the Louisiana Purchase in 1803. The early 19th century also saw a westwards expansion, as settlers crossed the mountains in the east and moved into the interior. In 1848, victory in the Mexican War gave the United States vast new territories in the west, extending from Texas to the Pacific. In the mid-19th century, disputes between the North and South (the Confederacy) came to a head over the issue of slavery in the new territories and states. This led to the Civil War (1861–5) during which, on 1 January 1863, President Abraham Lincoln signed the Emancipation Proclamation, proclaiming the freedom of all slaves in all parts of the Confederacy that were still in rebellion against the Union.

The 19th century saw a flood of immigrants into the country through the ports of Boston, New York City, Philadelphia and Baltimore. Many stayed to swell the cities while others moved into the interior to set up farms to feed the city masses. Railways spread over the booming farmlands, linking producer and consumer. Huge manufacturing cities, vast markets in their own right, developed along the Great Lakes as people continued to arrive – first from abroad, but latterly from the countryside – when mechanization threw people off the land into the cities and their factories. Between the late 18th and 19th centuries, the Ohio country passed from Native American-occupied forests and plains into mechanized farmlands of unparalleled efficiency. It became the granary of the Western world and it also spawned some of its greatest and wealthiest industrial cities. However, while the north boomed, the south-eastern states became over-dependent on cotton and they remained outside the mainstream of American prosperity. Today, although prosperity has spread through the east, the densest populations are still in the north-east, while the south-east remains comparatively rural. However, this pattern has been changing recently as the 'Sun Belt' in the southern United States, especially Florida, has attracted people looking for retirement homes.

The central states were formerly occupied by more than 30 major groups of Native Americans. Some, including the Mandan, Omaha and Kansa along the Missouri River, were settled farmers. Others, including the Blackfoot, Crow, Arapaho, Kiowa and Comanche, were nomads who lived on the drier western plains, hunting buffalo. European influence revolutionized their lives. By 1800, the horse, introduced from the south by the Spaniards, made the Indian population mobile as never before. The trappers and traders from the east brought firearms and this made the mounted Native Americans over-efficient at hunting, rapidly depleting their food supply. Behind the traders came the settlers, who killed off the buffalo and crowded in other Native peoples whom they had driven from their homelands in the south-east. As railways, cattle trails and the fences of ranchers crossed the old hunting grounds, the Native American farmers and hunters lost their traditional lands. By the late 19th century, the plains settlement was virtually complete.

The coming of railways after the Civil War not only doomed the remnant Native American societies, but it also introduced long and often bitter competition between different types of European farming. The dry prairies and steppe, which once supported the buffalo, could just as well support herds of cattle, raised to feed the eastern cities. The range lands also often became crop farms. But over-grazing and cultivation made the soil vulnerable to soil deterioration and erosion. With their markets in the East and in Europe, the plains farmers were caught in a vice between the dessication of their farms and the boom and slump of their markets. By the 1930s, agricultural depression led to massive foreclosing on mortgaged lands. When the dust storms of eroded topsoil came, the people were driven away – the 'Okies' of Woody Guthrie and John Steinbeck who fled to California. Much farmed land subsequently reverted to ranching. Farming prospects improved in the 1930s when the New Deal brought better price structures. New approaches to farming practices and widespread irrigation transformed the plains. Nevertheless, these areas are marginal to semi-desert and remain susceptible to periodic changes in precipitation over a wide area. Coupled with worldwide fluctuations in the cereals market, on which Midwestern farmers depend heavily, farming on the plains remains risky.

The Native American cultures of the western United States included hunting, fishing, seed gathering and primitive irrigation farming. Some groups were nomadic, while others lived in mostly small, scattered communities. The first European settlers, who spread northwards from New Spain (Mexico) in the 1760s, made little impact on their ways of life. But their forts and missions, including San Diego, Los Angeles and San Francisco, attracted later settlers who were more exploitative. From the 1840s, pressures increased with the arrival of land-hungry Americans, both by sea and along wagon trails from the east. Some of the immigrants were adventurers attracted by gold rushes. The Oregon coast, though visited by Spanish, British and Russian mariners in search of furs from the 16th century onwards, was first settled by American fur traders in 1811. Immigration began during the 1830s – the famous Oregon Trail across Wyoming and Idaho from the Mississippi coming into full use during the 1840s. After the establishment of the 49th parallel as the boundary with Canada, Oregon Territory (including Washington, Idaho and part of Montana) became part of the United States. Here, in the north-west, many battles were fought before the Native Americans were subdued and confined to reserves. Today, the wagon trails are major highways, the staging posts, mission stations and isolated forts transformed into cities. Gold mining, once the only kind of mining that mattered, has given way to the exploitation of a dozen lesser metals, from copper to molybdenum. Fish canning, food processing, electronics and aerospace are major sources of employment. The movie industry is based in Los Angeles, but this vast urban cluster now has a broad economy based on high-technology industries. The mountain states – once far behind in economic development – have caught up with the rest of the country. But the enduring beauty of the western mountains remains.

Politics

The United States has long played a leading role in industrial, economic, social and technological innovation, creating problems through sheer ebullience, and solving them – more or less – through inventiveness, enterprise, and with huge, wealth-bringing resources of energy and raw materials. The majority of Americans continue to enjoy one of the world's highest material standards of living and the country continues to produce a highly skilled, literate and imaginative population. Yet at the same time, the country faces many problems. One concerns the maintenance of social cohesion as the composition of American society changes. Another is the issue of poverty and the low standards of living of a sizeable underclass of poor and inadequately educated people, many of whom are members of ethnic minorities. Other associated problems include crime, drug addiction and racial conflict.

The United States has one of the most diverse populations of any country in the world. Until about 1860, the population, with the exception of the Native Americans and the southern African Americans, was made up largely of immigrants of British and Irish origin, with small numbers of Spaniards and French. However, after the Civil War, increasing numbers of immigrants arrived from the countries of central and south-eastern Europe, including Italy, the Balkans, Poland, Scandinavia and Russia. This vast influx of Europeans, numbering about 30 million between 1860 and 1920, was vastly different in culture and language from the established population. More recently, the country has received lesser influxes of Japanese, Chinese, Filipinos, Cubans, Puerto Ricans, and large numbers of Mexicans, many of them illegal immigrants. Although strong influences and pressures towards Americanization still exist, members of these groups have tended to maintain their own culture, establishing social and cultural enclaves within American society.

Although the nation has never adopted an official language, English was readily adopted by most immigrants in the late 19th and early 20th century, because they sought acceptance in the 'melting pot' that makes up the United States. However, many of the recent Hispanic immigrants persist in speaking Spanish, which has become the country's second language. Many Americans are concerned about this trend towards 'cultural pluralism' rather than integration through the 'melting pot'. For example, they argue that Hispanics who do not speak English are at a disadvantage in American society and believe that everyone should speak English, either as a first or second language. According to some population forecasts, today's white majority will be outnumbered by other ethnic groups in 2050. With a total projected population of 380 million, Hispanics are expected to number around 80 million by 2050, while African Americans will account for another

Alaska

Alaska became the 49th state of the United States in 1959, becoming the first new state for 47 years. It is the nation's largest state and more than twice the size of Texas, which ranks second in area. The Brooks Range and northern coastal plains lie above the Arctic Circle. South of the Brooks Range lie the Central Uplands and Lowlands which are drained by the Yukon River, while the Alaska Range, including Mount McKinley, the highest peak in North America, is in the south. In the south-west lie the Alaska Peninsula and the volcanic Aleutian Islands – southern Alaska forms part of the 'Pacific ring of fire'. The south-eastern 'panhandle', where the capital Juneau is situated, is a drowned fjordland backed by ice-capped mountains. Forests cover about a third of the state, while the interior tablelands are tundra-covered and rich in migrant birds and mammals.

Southern Alaska, where temperatures are moderated by winds blowing eastwards across the Japan Current, has a relatively mild climate, with heavy precipitation in the south-east. Central and northern Alaska are dry with cold winters.

The United States purchased Alaska from the Tsarist government of Russia in 1867 for US $7 million. It remained a territory for over 90 years. A gold rush during the 1880s stimulated later development of other mineral resources, including copper and oil. Today, Alaska has become a test of the nation's resolve to balance economic development and conservation – the country's six largest national parks are in Alaska. Tourism is a growing industry and more than a million visitors arrive every year. Food-processing, fish and petroleum products are the chief manufactured goods.

62 million. Such a rapid growth of these communities is seen by some as a threat to the majority.

From the 1890s, the United States developed into a world power, and it played a leading role in international affairs throughout the 20th century. It played a key role in World Wars I and II, after which it was one of the world's two superpowers – the other being the Soviet Union. After World War II, it assumed the leadership of the West during the Cold War. Since the end of the Cold War, the United States has faced new threats from terrorists and rogue states. Its vulnerability was demonstrated by the terrorist attacks on New York City and Washington, D.C., on 11 September 2001. The United States responded vigorously, creating an international alliance to combat terrorism and the nations which shelter or aid terrorists.

Economy

Stimulated by education, research and sophisticated machinery following the Civil War, agriculture developed into a highly mechanized industry. Only a generation after the pioneering days, farmers found themselves integrated into a complex economic system with such factors as mortgages, freight prices and world markets as crucial to their success as climate and soil.

To the east of the western mountains, farming was established in a zonal pattern which remains intact today, though much modified. This pattern reflects both the possibilities offered by the climate and the soils, and the inclinations and national origins of the farmers who first farmed the lands. In the north, from Minnesota to New England, lies a broad belt where dairy farming predominates, providing butter, cheese and milk for the industrial cities. Spring wheat is grown further west, where the climate is drier. The eastern and central states, from

Hawaii

Hawaii, the 50th and youngest state of the United States, joined the Union on 21 August 1959. Situated in the mid-North Pacific Ocean, it consists of eight large islands and over 100 others which were formed as the Pacific plate moved across a 'hot spot', or source of heat, in the Earth's mantle. Currently, the hot spot is under the biggest island in the group, which is also called Hawaii. This island contains the extinct Mauna Kea, a huge volcano which measures 10,203 m [33,437 ft] from its base on the sea floor, though only 4,205 m [13,796 ft] is above sea level. Also on Hawaii is the intermittently active Mauna Loa and Kilauea, which provides spectacular displays when it erupts. The climate is warm throughout the year, with heaviest precipitation on the north-eastern sides of the islands. Dense rainforests grow in the fertile volcanic soils on the rainy parts of the islands.

The archipelago, which is part of Polynesia, was visited by the British Captain James Cook in 1778. Following his discovery, the islands became a port-of-call for trans-Pacific shipping and a wintering station for New England whalers. It retained its independence until it was annexed by the United States in 1898. The naval base of Pearl Harbor was of great strategic importance and the Japanese attack on the base on 7 December 1941 brought the United States into World War II. Today, only 2% of its people are full-blooded Polynesians, though another 13% are mainly of Hawaiian descent. The rest are of European, Chinese, Japanese, Korean and Filipino origin. About 75% live on Oahu, with 33% of the state's population living in Honolulu.

Agriculture, fishing and food processing are the main industries, but defence and tourism are important. Sugar cane and pineapples are the leading commercial crops. The island of Hawaii has large cattle ranches, while dairy products and eggs are important on Oahu, Maui and Kauai. Tourism contributes more than US $11 billion to the economy. Tourist attractions include two national parks, the Haleakala National Park on Maui and the Hawaii Volcanoes National Park on Hawaii. The National Memorial marks the spot where the USS *Arizona* was sunk by the Japanese in 1941.

Nebraska to Ohio, form the famous Corn Belt – immensely productive land, formerly prairie and forest, where corn (maize) is the main crop. Now much extended by the development of new, more tolerant strains, maize production has spread into belts on either side. No longer principally a human food, except in the poorer areas of the south-east, maize is grown mainly for feeding to cattle and pigs. Soya beans, oats and other food and fodder crops grow in the Corn Belt, with wheat and dairy farming prominent on the northern border. The cities of the central United States are great trading centres, dependent on agriculture for their prosperity. But some cities, such as Chicago, have diversified to become major manufacturing centres. For example, Chicago is the main Midwestern focus of the iron and steel industry.

Southwards again, stretching from Oklahoma and Kansas to Virginia, is a belt of mixed farming where winter wheat and maize alternate as dominant cereals. In the warmer southern states lies the former Cotton Belt, where cotton and tobacco were once the chief products. Both crops are now concentrated into small, highly productive areas where mechanical handling is possible, while the bulk of the land is used for a wide variety of other crops from vegetables to fruit.

In the west, the long, bone-dry summers once made farming – even ranching – difficult in the central valley of California. But the peaks of the Sierra Nevada, with their thick snow cover in winter, now provide water for summer irrigation. Damming and water channelling have made the semi-deserts and dry rangelands bloom all over southern California, which now produces temperate and tropical fruits, vegetables, cotton and other thirsty crops in abundance, despite severe droughts from the late 1980s.

Agriculture now employs only 2.4% of the labour force. The western plains are the main centres of production. Much of the land farmed by the Pilgrim Fathers and other settlers is now built over, or has reverted to forest. By concentrating effort in this way, the United States has become a leading producer of meat, dairy products, soya beans, maize, oats, wheat, barley, cotton, sugar and many other crops.

The spread of prosperity generated new consumer industries to satisfy demands of a large middle class for ever-increasing standards of comfort. The United States became a pioneer of large-scale industrial production of everything from thumbtacks to motor vehicles. With almost every raw material available within its own boundaries, or readily gained through trading, its mining and extractive industries have been heavily exploited. For several generations, coal formed the main source of power. Anthracite from eastern Pennsylvania, good bituminous and coking coals from the Appalachians, Indiana, Illinois, Colorado and Utah are still in demand, and vast reserves remain.

Oil, first drilled in Pennsylvania in 1859, was subsequently found in several major fields underlying the Midwest, the eastern and central mountain states, the Gulf of Mexico, California and Alaska. Home consumption of petroleum products has grown steadily. Although the United States is a major producer, it is also by far the world's greatest consumer and has long been a net importer of oil. In the Gulf Coast states, the exploitation of oil in Oklahoma, Texas and Louisiana has shifted the former dependence on agriculture to the refining and petrochemical industries. Oil has transformed Dallas-Fort Worth into a major conurbation, while Denver has changed from a small railhead town into a wealthy state capital. Natural gas is also found in abundance, usually associated with oil. It is moved to the consumer areas through a network of pipes.

AREA	African American 12%,
9,372,610 sq km	Asian 3%, other races 2%
[3,618,765 sq mi]	**LANGUAGES**
POPULATION	English (official), Spanish,
278,059,000	more than 30 others
CAPITAL (POPULATION)	**RELIGIONS**
Washington, D.C.	Protestant 56%,
(4,466,000)	Roman Catholic 28%,
GOVERNMENT	Islam 2%,
Federal republic	Judaism 2%
ETHNIC GROUPS	**CURRENCY**
White 83%,	US dollar = 100 cents

URUGUAY

Uruguay has used this flag since 1830. The nine stripes represent the nine provinces which formed the country when it became an independent republic in 1828. The colours and the May Sun had originally been used by Argentina during its struggle against Spanish rule.

Geography

The Eastern Republic of Uruguay, as Uruguay is officially known, is South America's second smallest independent nation after Surinam. The River Uruguay, which forms the country's western border, flows into the Rio de la Plata (River Plate), a large estuary fringed with lagoons and sand dunes, which leads into the South Atlantic Ocean.

The land consists of low-lying plains and hills. The highest point lies south of Minas and is only 501 m [1,644 ft] above sea level. The main river in the interior is the Rio Negro.

Climate

Uruguay has a mild climate, with rain in every month, though droughts sometimes occur. Summers are pleasantly warm, especially near the coast. The weather remains relatively mild throughout the winter.

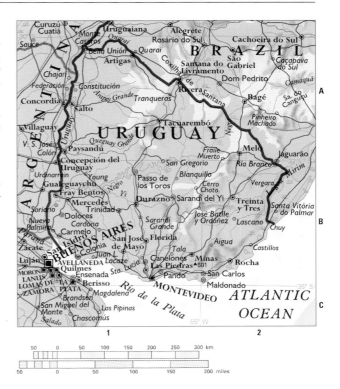

URUGUAY (MONTEVIDEO)

The plains around the estuary of the River Plate have an extremely uniform distribution of rainfall throughout the year. Much of this rain is associated with the advance of the cold air from the Southern Ocean, which may be accompanied by a *Pampero Sucio*. A Pampero Sucio is a violent squall with rain and thunder which is followed by cooler, sunny weather. Near to the ocean, the summers are pleasantly warm and the winters are not as cold as those at similar latitudes in the northern hemisphere.

History

The first people of Uruguay were Amerindians. But the Amerindian population has largely disappeared. Many were killed by Europeans, some died of European diseases, while others fled into the interior. The majority of Uruguayans today are of European origin, though there are some mestizos (of mixed European and Amerindian descent).

The first European to arrive in Uruguay was a Spanish navigator, Juan Diaz de Solis, in 1516. But he and part of his crew were killed by the local Charrúa Amerindians when they went ashore. Few Europeans settled in the area until the late 17th century. In 1726, Spanish settlers founded Montevideo in order to prevent the Portuguese from gaining influence in the area. Uruguay was then little more than a buffer zone between the Portuguese territory to the north and Spanish territories to the west. By the late 18th century, Spaniards had settled on most of the country. Uruguay became part of a colony called the Viceroyalty of La Plata, which also included Argentina, Paraguay and parts of Bolivia, Brazil and Chile.

In 1820, Brazil annexed Uruguay, ending Spanish rule. In 1825, Uruguayans, supported by Argentina, began a struggle for independence. In 1828, Brazil and Argentina recognized Uruguay as an independent republic. Social and economic developments were slow in the 19th century, but, from 1903, governments made Uruguay a democratic and stable country. Since 1828, two political parties have dominated Uruguay. They are the Colorados (Liberals) and the Blancos (Conservatives).

Politics

During World War II, Uruguay prospered because of its export trade, especially in meat and wool. However, from the 1950s, economic problems caused unrest. Terrorist groups, notably the Tupumaros (Marxist urban guerrillas), carried out murders and kidnappings in the 1960s and early 1970s. In 1972, President Juan Maria Bordaberry declared war on the Tupumaros and the army crushed them. However, in 1973, the military seized power, suspended the constitution and ruled with great severity, committing major human rights abuses.

Military rule continued until 1984, when elections were held. General Gregorio Alvarez, who had been president since 1981, resigned and Julio Maria Sanguinetti, leader of the Colorado Party, became president in February 1985, leading a government of National Unity. He ordered the release of all political prisoners. In the 1990s, Uruguay faced problems in trying to rebuild its weakened economy and shoring up its democratic traditions. In 1991, Uruguay joined with Argentina, Brazil and Paraguay to form Mercosur, which aimed to create a common market. Mercosur's secretariat is in Montevideo.

Economy

Meat processing, pioneered at Fray Bentos in the 1860s, started a meat-and-hide export industry that established the nation's fortunes. Today, Uruguay is classed by the World Bank as an 'upper-middle-income' developing country. Although 90% of the population live in urban areas and agriculture employs 4% of the population, the economy depends on the exports of hides and leather goods, beef and wool. Main crops include maize, potatoes, rice, sugar beet and wheat.

The manufacturing sector concentrates on food processing and packing, though with a small domestic market, the economy has diversified into cement, chemicals, leather goods, textiles and steel. With inadequate supplies of fossil fuels, Uruguay depends largely on hydroelectric power for energy and it exports electricity to Argentina.

AREA	Mulatto or Black 4%
177,410 sq km [68,498 sq mi]	**LANGUAGES**
POPULATION	Spanish (official)
3,360,000	**RELIGIONS**
CAPITAL (POPULATION)	Roman Catholic 66%,
Montevideo (1,379,000)	Protestant 2%,
GOVERNMENT	Judaism 1%
Multiparty republic	**CURRENCY**
ETHNIC GROUPS	Uruguay peso =
White 88%, Mestizo 8%,	100 centésimos

UZBEKISTAN – SEE TURKMENISTAN, PAGE 221;
VANUATU – SEE PACIFIC OCEAN, PAGES 174–178;
VATICAN CITY – SEE ITALY, PAGES 131–133

VENEZUELA

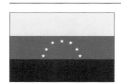

Venezuela's flag, adopted in 1954, has the same basic tricolour as the flags of Colombia and Ecuador. The colours were used by the Venezuelan patriot Francisco de Miranda. The seven stars represent the provinces in the Venezuelan Federation in 1811.

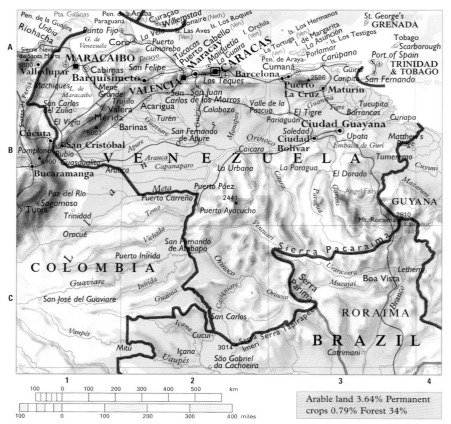

Arable land 3.64% Permanent crops 0.79% Forest 34%

Geography

The Republic of Venezuela, in northern South America, contains the Maracaibo Lowlands in the west. The lowlands surround the oil-rich Lake Maracaibo (L. de Maracaibo). Arms of the Andes Mountains enclose the lowlands and extend across most of northern Venezuela. Between the northern mountains and the scenic Guiana Highlands in the south-east, where the Angel Falls are found, lie the *llanos* (tropical grasslands), a low-lying region drained by the River Orinoco and its tributaries. The Orinoco is Venezuela's longest river.

Climate

Venezuela has a tropical climate. Temperatures are high throughout the year on the lowlands, though the mountains are much cooler. The rainfall is heaviest in the mountains. But much of the country has a marked dry season between December and April.

VENEZUELA (CARACAS)

Venezuela experiences little variation in temperature from month to month, but there are marked wet and dry seasons, the rain falling from May to November. The north-east trade winds leave little rain in the coastal lowlands, but the total increases when they hit the mountains. The monthly temperature of Caracas is between 19°C and 22°C [66–72°F], but this is much lower on the higher land. Some northern Andean peaks have permanent snow.

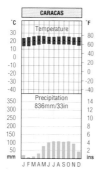

History

The Arawak and Carib Amerindians were the main inhabitants of Venezuela before the arrival of Europeans. The first European to arrive was Christopher Columbus, who sighted the area in 1498. Spaniards began to settle in the early 16th century, but economic development was slow.

In the early 19th century, Spain's colonies in South America began their struggle for independence. The Venezuelan patriots Simón Bolívar and Francisco Miranda were prominent in the struggle. Venezuela was the first South American country to demand freedom and, in July 1811, it declared its independence, though Spaniards still held most of the country. The country did not become fully independent until 1821, after the Venezuelans had defeated the Spanish in a battle at Carabobo, near Valencia. In 1819, Venezuela became part of Gran Colombia, a republic led by Simón Bolívar that also included Colombia, Ecuador and Panama. Venezuela broke away from Gran Colombia in 1829 and a new constitution was drafted in 1830. The country's first president was General José Antonio Páez, one of the leaders of Venezuela's independence movement.

Politics

The development of Venezuela in the 19th century and the first half of the 20th century was marred by instability, violence and periods of harsh dictatorial rule. However, the country has had elected governments since 1958. Venezuela has greatly benefited from its oil resources, which were first exploited in 1917. In 1960, Venezuela helped to form OPEC (the Organization of Petroleum Exporting Countries) and, in 1976, the government of Venezuela took control of the entire oil industry. Money from oil exports has helped Venezuela to raise living standards and diversify the economy.

Financial problems in the late 1990s led to the election of Hugo Chávez as president. Chávez, leader of the Patriotic Pole, a left-wing coalition, who had led an abortive military uprising in 1992, became president in February 1999. He announced that the country's official name would be changed to the Bolivarian Republic of Venezuela and held a referendum on a new constitution. This gave the president increased power over military and civilian institutions. Chávez argued that these powers were needed to counter corruption. In 2002, Chávez survived a coup.

Economy

The World Bank classifies Venezuela as an 'upper-middle-income' developing country. Oil accounts for 70% of the exports. Other exports include bauxite and aluminium, iron ore and farm products. Agriculture employs 8% of the people. Cattle ranching is important and dairy cattle and poultry are also raised. Major crops include bananas, cassava, citrus fruits, coffee, maize, plantains, rice and sorghum. Most commercial crops are grown on large farms, but many people in remote areas farm small plots and produce barely enough to feed their families.

Manufacturing has increased greatly since the 1960s and industry now employs 21% of the population. The leading industry is petroleum refining, which is centred on Maracaibo. Other manufactures include aluminium, cement, processed food, steel and textiles.

AREA
912,050 sq km
[352,143 sq mi]
POPULATION
23,917,000
CAPITAL (POPULATION)
Caracas
(1,975,000)
GOVERNMENT
Federal republic

ETHNIC GROUPS
Mestizo 67%, White 21%,
Black 10%, Amerindian 2%
LANGUAGES
Spanish (official),
Goajiro
RELIGIONS
Roman Catholic 96%
CURRENCY
Bolívar = 100 céntimos

Vietnam's flag was first used by forces led by the Communist Ho Chi Minh during the liberation struggle against Japan in World War II (1939–45). It became the flag of North Vietnam in 1945 and it was retained when North and South Vietnam were reunited in 1975.

Geography and Climate

The Socialist Republic of Vietnam occupies an S-shaped strip of land facing the South China Sea in South-east Asia. The coastal plains include two densely populated, fertile river delta areas. The Red (Hong) Delta faces the Gulf of Tonkin in the north, while the Mekong Delta is in the south. Inland are thinly populated highland regions, including the Annam Cordillera (Chaîne Annamitique), which forms much of the boundary with Cambodia. The highlands in the north-west extend into Laos and China.

Vietnam has a tropical climate, though the drier months of January to March are cooler than the wet, hot summer months, when monsoon winds blow from the south-west. Typhoons sometimes hit the coast, causing much damage.

History and Politics

China dominated Vietnam for a thousand years before AD 939, when a Vietnamese state was founded. The French took over the area between the 1850s and 1880s. They ruled Vietnam as part of French Indo-China, which also included Cambodia and Laos.

Japan conquered Vietnam during World War II (1939–45). In 1946, war broke out between a nationalist group, the Vietminh, and the French colonial government. France withdrew in 1954 and Vietnam was divided into a Communist North Vietnam, led by the Vietminh leader Ho Chi Minh, and a non-Communist South.

A force called the Viet Cong rebelled against South Vietnam's government in 1957 and a war began, which gradually increased in intensity. The United States aided the South, but after it withdrew in 1975, South Vietnam surrendered. In 1976, the united Vietnam became a Socialist Republic.

Vietnamese troops intervened in Cambodia in 1978 to defeat the Communist Khmer Rouge government, but it withdrew its troops in 1989. In the 1990s, Vietnam began to introduce reforms. In 2000, Vietnam and the United States signed a historic trade pact.

Economy

The World Bank classifies Vietnam as a 'low-income' developing country. Agriculture employs 67% of the population and the main food crop is rice. Other products include maize and sweet potatoes, while commercial crops include bananas, coffee, groundnuts, rubber, soya beans and tea. Fishing is also important. Northern Vietnam has most of the country's natural resources, including coal. The country also produces chromium, oil (which was discovered off the south coast in 1986), phosphates and tin. Manufactures include cement, fertilizers, processed food, machinery, steel and textiles. The main exports are farm products and handicrafts, coal, minerals, oil and seafood.

AREA	Tho (Tay), Chinese (Hoa),
331,689 sq km	Tai, Khmer, Muong,
[128,065 sq mi]	Nung
POPULATION	**LANGUAGES**
79,939,000	Vietnamese (official),
CAPITAL (POPULATION)	Chinese
Hanoi (3,056,000)	**RELIGIONS**
GOVERNMENT	Buddhism 55%,
Socialist republic	Roman Catholic 7%
ETHNIC GROUPS	**CURRENCY**
Vietnamese 87%,	Dong = 10 hao = 100 xu

Arable land 18.1% Permanent crops 3.33%
Permanent grassland 1.01% Forest 29.6%

VIRGIN ISLANDS, BRITISH AND US – SEE CARIBBEAN SEA, PAGES 71–76;
WALLIS AND FUTUNA ISLANDS – SEE PACIFIC OCEAN, PAGES 174–178;
WESTERN SAHARA – SEE MOROCCO, PAGE 161

Yemen's flag was adopted in 1990 when the Yemen Arab Republic (or North Yemen) united with the People's Democratic Republic of Yemen (or South Yemen). This simple flag is a tricolour of red, white and black – colours associated with the Pan-Arab movement.

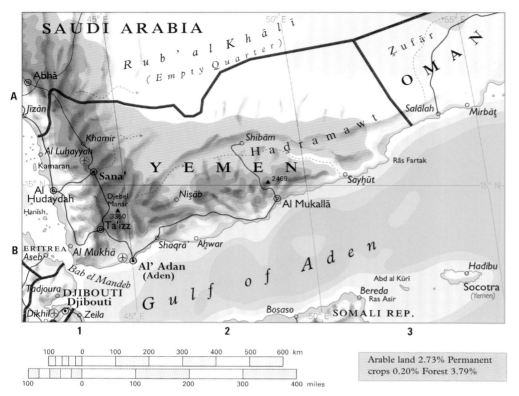

Arable land 2.73% Permanent crops 0.20% Forest 3.79%

Vegetation

Palm trees grow on the coastline, while such plants as euphorbias, acacias and eucalyptus flourish in the interior. Thorn shrubs and mountain pasture are found in mountain areas. Inland lies barren desert.

History

From around 1400 BC, Yemen lay on an important trading route, with frankincense, pearls and spices being the major commodities. But its prosperity declined in the 4th century AD, when it became divided between warring groups.

Islam was introduced during the 7th century by the son-in-law of the Prophet Muhammad. From 897, the country was ruled by a Muslim leader. In 1517, the area was taken over by the Turkish Ottoman Empire and remained under Turkish rule for the next 400 years.

Politics

After World War I, northern Yemen, which had been ruled by Turkey, began to evolve into a separate state from the south, where Britain was in control. Britain withdrew in 1967 and a left-wing regime took power in the south. In 1962, the monarchy was abolished in North Yemen, which became a republic.

Clashes occurred between the traditionalist Yemen Arab Republic in the north and the formerly British Marxist People's Democratic Republic of Yemen. But, in 1990, the two Yemens merged to form one country. The marrying of the needs of the two parts of Yemen has proved difficult. In May 1994, civil war erupted, with President Saleh, a northerner, attempting to remove the vice-president (a southerner). The war ended in July 1994, following the capture of Aden by government forces. In 1995, Yemen resolved border disputes with Oman and Saudi Arabia, but clashed with Eritrea over uninhabited islands in the Red Sea. In 1998–9, militants in the Aden-Abyan Islamic Army sought to destabilize the country. In 2000, suicide bombers, thought to be part of the terrorist al Qaida network, steered their craft into a US destroyer in Aden harbour, killing 17 sailors.

Geography and Climate

The Republic of Yemen faces the Red Sea and the Gulf of Aden in the south-western corner of the Arabian Peninsula. Behind the narrow coastal plain along the Red Sea, the land rises to a mountain region called High Yemen. Beyond the mountains, the land slopes down towards the Rub' al Khali Desert. Other mountains rise behind the coastal plain along the Gulf of Aden. To the east lies a fertile valley called the Hadramaut.

The climate in San'a is moderated by its altitude. Temperatures are much lower than in Aden (Al' Adan), which is at sea level. In summer, south-west monsoon winds bring thunderstorms. But most of Yemen is arid. The south coasts are particularly hot and humid, especially from June to September.

Economy

The World Bank classifies Yemen as a 'low-income' developing country. Agriculture employs up to 63% of the people. Herders raise sheep and other animals, while farmers grow such crops as barley, fruits, wheat and vegetables in highland valleys and around oases. Cash crops include coffee and cotton.

Imported oil is refined at Aden and petroleum extraction began in the north-west in the 1980s. Handicrafts, leather goods and textiles are manufactured. Remittances from Yemenis abroad are a major source of revenue.

YEMEN – SAN'A

San'a lies at over 2,000 m [6,500 ft], on the eastern side of the Yemen highlands. Temperatures are much lower than at sea level and the diurnal range is very large (over 20°C [36°F] in winter), frost occurring in winter. In August, the south-west monsoon brings heavy thunderstorms. As in Ethiopia, across the Red Sea, minor rains fall in spring. The western side of the mountains, famous for coffee plantations, is wetter and cloudier.

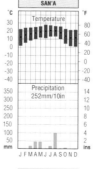

ADEN

Aden (Al' Adan) is situated on the southern coast of Yemen. Temperatures here are uniformly high through the year, and are higher than the temperatures elsewhere in the country. During January, an average of 24°C [75°F] is experienced. In July, this figure rises to 32°C [90°F]. Average annual rainfall in the north of Yemen is 508 mm [20 in]. In coastal areas, rainfall is very low with an annual average of just 46 mm [1.8 in].

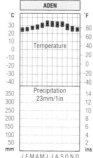

AREA	ETHNIC GROUPS
527,970 sq km	Arab 96%,
[203,849 sq mi]	Somali 1%
POPULATION	**LANGUAGES**
18,078,000	Arabic
CAPITAL (POPULATION)	(official)
San'a	**RELIGIONS**
(Sana', 972,000)	Islam
GOVERNMENT	**CURRENCY**
Multiparty republic	Rial = 100 fils

YUGOSLAVIA

Yugoslavia's flag was adopted in 1992. Yugoslavia now consists of two republics (Serbia and Montenegro) which were formerly part of the socialist Federal People's Republic of Yugoslavia, which also included Bosnia-Herzegovina, Croatia, Macedonia and Slovenia.

Geography and Climate

The Federal Republic of Yugoslavia consists of Serbia and Montenegro, two of the republics which formed part of the former country of Yugoslavia, which broke up in the early 1990s. In 2002, the government announced plans to rename the country the Union of Serbia and Montenegro.

The country has a short coastline along the Adriatic Sea. Inland is a mountainous region including the Dinaric Alps and part of the Balkan Mountains. In the north lie the Pannonian Plains.

The coast has a mild, Mediterranean climate, but the inland upland areas have a more continental climate. The highlands have cold, snowy winters, while the Pannonian Plains have hot, arid summers, with heavy rains in the spring and autumn.

History

People who became known as the South Slavs began to move into the region around 1,500 years ago. Each group, including the Serbs and Croats, founded its own state. But, by the 15th century, foreign countries controlled the region. Serbia and Montenegro were under the Turkish Ottoman Empire.

During the 19th century, many Slavs worked for independence and Slavic unity. In 1914, Austria-Hungary declared war on Serbia, blaming it for the assassination of Archduke Francis Ferdinand of Austria-Hungary. This led to World War I and the defeat of Austria-Hungary. In 1918, the South Slavs united in the Kingdom of the Serbs, Croats and Slovenes, which consisted of Bosnia-Herzegovina, Croatia, Dalmatia, Montenegro, Serbia and Slovenia. In 1929, King Alexander abolished the constitution and renamed the country Yugoslavia. Ruling as a dictator until he was assassinated in 1934, he sought to enforce the use of one language, Serbo-Croatian, and he created new political divisions that failed to acknowledge the historic boundaries determined by the ethnic groups. Hence, the unity of the new state was under constant threat from nationalist and ethnic tensions. The country's troubled history had so stirred the peoples of the region that there was no area that did not contain at least one aggrieved or distrusted minority. In the inter-war period, Yugoslavia was virtually a 'Greater Serbia' and, after the Germans invaded in 1941, Yugoslavs fought the Germans and themselves. The Communist-led partisans of Josip Broz Tito (a Croat) emerged victorious in 1945.

Politics

From 1945, the Communists controlled the country, which was called the Federal People's Republic of Yugoslavia. But after Tito's death in 1980, the country faced many problems. In 1990, non-Communist parties were permitted and non-Communists won majorities in elections in all but Serbia and Montenegro, where Socialists (former (Communists) won control. Yugoslavia split apart in 1991–2 with Bosnia-Herzegovina, Croatia, Macedonia and Slovenia proclaiming their independence. The two remaining republics of Serbia and Montenegro became the new Yugoslavia.

Fighting broke out in Croatia and Bosnia-Herzegovina as rival groups struggled for power. In 1992, the United Nations withdrew recognition of Yugoslavia because of its failure to halt atrocities committed by Serbs living in Croatia and Bosnia-Herzegovina. In 1995, Yugoslavia took part in talks that led to the Dayton Peace Accord, but it had problems of its own as international sanctions struck the war-ravaged economy. In 1998, the fragility of the region was again highlighted, in Kosovo, a former autonomous region in southern Serbia where most people are Albanian-speaking Muslims. In 1998, Serbians forced Muslim Albanians to leave their homes, but they were opposed by the Kosovo Liberation Army (KLA), which took over large areas. The Serbs hit back and thousands of civilians fled for their lives.

In March 1999, after attempts to find an agreement had failed, NATO forces intervened by launching aerial attacks on administrative

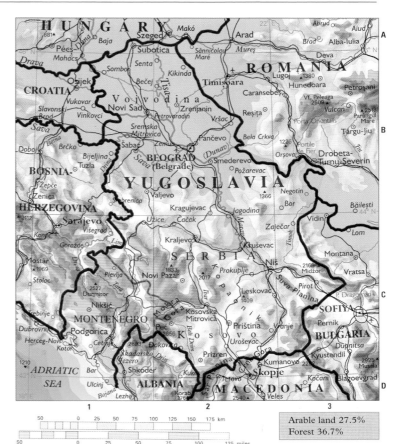

Arable land 27.5%
Forest 36.7%

and industrial targets in Kosovo and Serbia. While the bombings continued, Serbian forces stepped up attacks on Albanian-speaking villages, forcibly expelling the people, who fled into Albania and Macedonia. The NATO offensive ended when Serbian forces withdrew from Kosovo and the KLA was disbanded in September. In 2000, the Yugoslav leader Slobodan Milosevic was defeated in presidential elections and, in February 2002, he faced charges, including crimes against humanity, at the UN War Crimes Tribunal in The Hague.

Many people in Montenegro have long favoured secession from Yugoslavia, but demands for independence were put on hold when Serbia and Montenegro signed an agreement in 2002. Under the agreement, the country will be renamed the Union of Serbia and Montenegro, making both states semi-independent.

Economy

Under Communist rule, manufacturing became important in Yugoslavia. But in the early 1990s, the World Bank classified the country as a 'lower-middle-income' economy. Its resources include bauxite, coal, copper and other metals, together with oil and natural gas. Manufactures include aluminium, machinery, plastics, steel, textiles and vehicles. Chief exports are manufactures, but agriculture remains important. Crops include fruits, maize, potatoes, tobacco and wheat.

AREA	Montenegrin 5%, Hungarian,
102,170 sq km [39,449 sq mi]	Muslim, Croat
POPULATION	**LANGUAGES**
10,677,000	Serbo-Croat (official),
CAPITAL (POPULATION)	Albanian
Belgrade (Beograd, 1,598,000)	**RELIGIONS**
GOVERNMENT	Christianity (mainly
Federal republic	Serbian Orthodox), Islam
ETHNIC GROUPS	**CURRENCY**
Serb 62%, Albanian 17%,	Yugoslav new dinar = 100 paras

Zambia's flag was adopted when the country became independent from Britain in 1964. The colours are those of the United Nationalist Independence Party, which led the struggle against Britain and ruled until 1991. The flying eagle represents freedom.

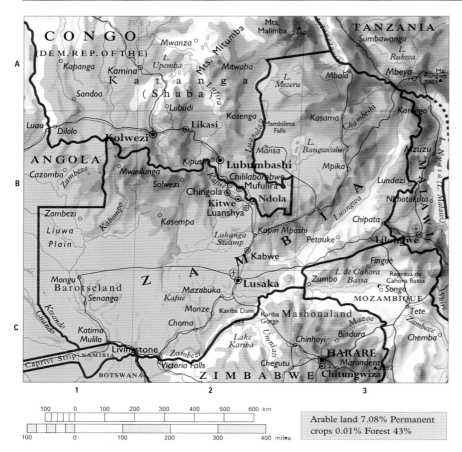

Arable land 7.08% Permanent crops 0.01% Forest 43%

Geography

The Republic of Zambia is a landlocked country in southern Africa. The country lies on the plateau that makes up most of southern Africa. Much of the land is between 900 m and 1,500 m [2,950–4,920 ft] above sea level. The Muchinga Mountains in the north-east rise above this flat land.

Lakes include Bangweulu, which is entirely within Zambia, together with parts of lakes Mweru and Tanganyika in the north. Most of the land is drained by the Zambezi and its two main tributaries, the Kafue and Luangwa. Lake Kariba, dammed in 1961, and the second largest artificial lake in Africa, occupies part of the Zambezi Valley. Zambia shares Lake Kariba and the Victoria Falls with Zimbabwe.

Climate

Zambia lies in the tropics, although temperatures are moderated by the altitude. The rainy season runs from between November and March, when the rivers sometimes flood. Northern Zambia is the wettest region of the country. The average annual rainfall ranges from about 1,300 mm [51 in] in the north down to between 510 mm and 760 mm [20–30 in] in the south.

History

European contact with Zambia began in the 19th century, when the explorer David Livingstone crossed the River Zambezi. In the 1890s, the British South Africa Company, set up by Cecil Rhodes (1853–1902), the British financier and statesman, made treaties with local chiefs and gradually took over the area. In 1911, the Company named the area Northern Rhodesia. In 1924, Britain took over the government of the country and the discovery of copper led to a large influx of Europeans in the late 1920s.

Following World War II, the majority of Europeans living in Zambia wanted greater control of their government and some favoured a merger with their southern neighbour, Southern Rhodesia (now Zimbabwe). In 1953, Britain set up a federation of Northern Rhodesia, Southern Rhodesia and Nyasaland (now Malawi). Local Africans opposed the setting up of the federation. They argued that it concentrated power in the hands of the white minority in Southern Rhodesia. Their opposition proved effective and the federation was dissolved in 1963. In 1964, Northern Rhodesia became an independent nation called Zambia.

Politics

The leading opponent of British rule, Kenneth Kaunda, became president of Zambia in 1964. His government enjoyed reasonable income until copper prices crashed in the mid-1970s, but his collectivist policies failed to diversify the economy and neglected agriculture. In 1972, he declared the United Nationalist Independence Party (UNIP) the only legal party, and it was nearly 20 years before the country returned to democracy. Under a new constitution, adopted in 1990, elections were held in 1991 in which Kaunda was trounced by Frederick Chiluba of the Movement for Multiparty Democracy (MMD) – Kaunda's first challenger in the post-colonial period. Chiluba was re-elected in 1996, but he stood down in 2001 after an MMD proposal to amend the constitution to allow Chiluba to stand for a third term met with substantial popular and parliamentary opposition. In the 2001 elections, the MMD candidate, Levy Mwanawasa, was elected president.

Economy

Copper is the leading export, accounting for 49% of Zambia's total exports in 1998. Zambia also produces cobalt, lead, zinc and various gemstones, but the country's dependence on minerals has created problems, especially when prices fluctuate. Agriculture employs 69% of the people, as compared with 4% in mining and manufacturing. Major food crops include cassava, fruits and vegetables, maize, millet and sorghum, while cash crops include coffee, sugar cane and tobacco. The Copperbelt, centred on Kitwe, is the main urban region, while Lusaka, provides the other major growth pole. Rural-urban migration has increased since 1964, but work is scarce. The production of copper products is the leading industrial activity. Other manufactures include beverages, processed food, iron and steel, textiles and tobacco.

ZAMBIA (LUSAKA)

Lusaka is situated in the south-east of the country near to Lake Kariba. Temperatures are generally uniformly hot throughout the year. The average temperature in January reaches 21°C [70°F], while an average temperature of 16°C [61°F] has been recorded in July. There is a marked maximum of rainfall between November and March. The annual average amount of rainfall at Lusaka is 836 mm [33 in].

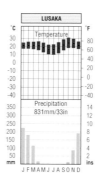

LUSAKA
Temperature
Precipitation
831mm/33in
J F M A M J J A S O N D

AREA	Maravi (Nyanja) 18%,
752,614 sq km [290,586 sq mi]	Tonga 15%
POPULATION	**LANGUAGES**
9,770,000	English (official), Bemba,
CAPITAL (POPULATION)	Nyanja, and about 70 others
Lusaka (982,000)	**RELIGIONS**
GOVERNMENT	Christianity 68%,
Multiparty republic	Islam, Hinduism
ETHNIC GROUPS	**CURRENCY**
Bemba 36%,	Kwacha = 100 ngwee

ZIMBABWE

Zimbabwe's flag, adopted in 1980, is based on the colours used by the ruling Zimbabwe African National Union Patriotic Front. Within the white triangle is the Great Zimbabwe soapstone bird, the national emblem. The red star symbolizes the party's socialist policies.

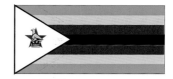

Geography

The Republic of Zimbabwe is a landlocked country in southern Africa. Most of the country lies on a high plateau between the Zambezi and Limpopo Rivers between 900 m and 1,500 m [2,950–4,920 ft] above sea level. The main land feature is the High Veld, a ridge that crosses Zimbabwe from north-east to south-west. Bordering the High Veld is the Middle Veld, the country's largest region. Below 900 m [2,950 ft] is the Low Veld. The country's highest point is Mount Inyangani, which reaches 2,593 m [8,507 ft] near the Mozambique border. Zimbabwe's best-known physical feature, Victoria Falls, is in the north-east. The Falls are shared with Zambia, as too is the artificial Lake Kariba which is also on the River Zambezi.

Climate

During the summer the weather is hot and wet. But in the winter, daily temperatures can vary greatly. Frosts have been recorded between June and August. The climate varies according to the altitude. The Low Veld is much warmer and drier than the High Veld.

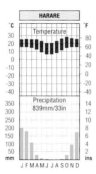

ZIMBABWE (HARARE)

Harare has a large diurnal range of temperature, particularly in the winter, and is cooler than lowlands at the same latitude. The summer rains are brought by south-easterly winds from the Indian Ocean, usually preceded by isolated thundery outbreaks which extend the rainy season from October to March.

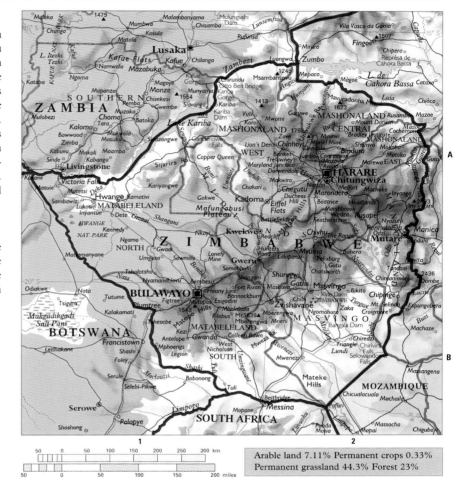

Arable land 7.11% Permanent crops 0.33%
Permanent grassland 44.3% Forest 23%

History

The Shona people were dominant in the region about 1,000 years ago. They built the Great Zimbabwe, a city of stone buildings. Under the statesman Cecil Rhodes (1853–1902), the British South Africa Company occupied the area in the 1890s, after obtaining mineral rights from local chiefs. The area was named Rhodesia and later Southern Rhodesia. It became a self-governing British colony in 1923. Between 1953 and 1963, Southern and Northern Rhodesia (now Zambia) were joined to Nyasaland (Malawi) in the Central African Federation.

Politics

In 1965, the European government of Southern Rhodesia (then known as Rhodesia) declared their country independent. However, Britain refused to accept this declaration. Finally, after a civil war, the country became legally independent in 1980. After independence, rivalries between the Shona and Ndebele people threatened its stability. But order was restored when the Shona prime minister, Robert Mugabe, brought his Ndebele rivals into his government. In 1987, Mugabe became the country's executive president and, in 1991, the government renounced its Marxist ideology. In 1990, the state of emergency that had lasted since 1965 was allowed to lapse – three months after Mugabe had secured a landslide election victory. Mugabe was re-elected in 1996. In the late 1990s, Mugabe threatened to seize white-owned farms without paying compensation to owners. His announcement caused much disquiet among white farmers. The situation worsened in the early 2000s, when landless 'war veterans' began to occupy white-owned farms, resulting in violence and deaths. In 2002, amid accusations of electoral irregularities, Mugabe was re-elected president. Mounting criticism of Mugabe led the Commonwealth to suspend Zimbabwe's membership for 12 months.

Economy

The World Bank classifies Zimbabwe as a 'low-income' economy. However, its economy has become significantly more diverse since the 1960s, having evolved to virtual self-sufficiency during the days of international sanctions between 1965 and 1980. After independence, the economy underwent a surge in most sectors, with successful agrarian policies and the exploitation of the country's mineral resources. However, a fast-growing population continues to exert pressure both on land and resources of all kinds.

Agriculture employs approximately 30% of the people. Maize is the chief food crop, while cash crops include cotton, sugar and tobacco. Cattle ranching is another important activity. Gold, asbestos, chromium and nickel are mined and the country also has some coal and iron ore. Manufactures include beverages, chemicals, iron and steel, metal products, processed food, textiles and tobacco. The principal exports include tobacco, gold, other metals, cotton and asbestos.

AREA	Ndebele 16%,
390,579 sq km	other Bantu-speaking
[150,873 sq mi]	Africans 11%, White 2%,
POPULATION	Asian 1%
11,365,000	**LANGUAGES**
CAPITAL (POPULATION)	English (official),
Harare	Shona, Ndebele
(1,189,000)	**RELIGIONS**
GOVERNMENT	Christianity 45%,
Multiparty republic	traditional beliefs 40%
ETHNIC GROUPS	**CURRENCY**
Shona 71%,	Zimbabwe dollar = 100 cents

INDEX TO
COUNTRY MAPS

How to use the index

The index contains the names of all the principal places and features shown on the country maps. Each name is followed by an additional entry in italics giving the country or region within which it is located. The alphabetical order of names composed of two or more words is governed primarily by the first word and then by the second. This is an example of the rule:

Bac Quang, *Vietnam*	**237**	**A2**
Bacan, Kepuluan, *Indonesia*	**125**	**C7**
Bacarra, *Phil.*	**184**	**B4**
Bacău, *Romania*	**188**	**B4**
Bach Long Vi, Dao, *Vietnam*	**237**	**B3**

Physical features composed of a proper name (Erie) and a description (Lake) are positioned alphabetically by the proper name. The description is positioned after the proper name and is usually abbreviated:

Erie, L., *N. Amer.*	**14**	**E11**

Where a description forms part of a settlement or administrative name however, it is always written in full and put in its true alphabetic position:

Mount Isa, *Australia*	**45**	**D6**

Names beginning with M' and Mc are indexed as if they were spelled Mac. Names beginning St. are alphabetised under Saint, but Sankt, Sint, Sant', Santa and San are all spelt in full and are alphabetised accordingly. If the same place name occurs two or more times in the index and all are in the same country, each is followed by the name of the administrative subdivision in which it is located.

The number in bold type which follows each name in the index refers to the number of the page where the map showing that feature or place will be found.

The letter and figure which are in bold type immediately after the page number give the grid square on the map page, within which the feature is situated. The letter represents the latitude and the figure the longitude.

In some cases the feature itself may fall within the specified square, while the name is outside. This is usually the case only with features which are larger than a grid square.

Rivers are indexed to their mouths or confluences, and carry the symbol ﹍ after their names. A solid square ■ follows the name of a country, while an open square □ refers to a first order administrative area.

The maps and index use the local spellings for most place names, that is the name by which a place or feature is known within the country in which it occurs:

> Roma
> 's-Gravenhage

In the index the English form used in the text is cross-referenced to the local spelling:

> Rome = Roma
> Hague, The = 's-Gravenhage

Spellings of names generally agree with the rules of the U.S. Board on Geographic Names and the Permanent Committee on Geographical Names. Where languages do not use Roman alphabets certain rules are used to transcribe them into the Roman alphabet. These rules are based largely on pronunciation.

How to pronounce place names

English-speaking people usually have no difficulty in reading and pronouncing correctly English place names. However, foreign place name pronunciations may present many problems. Such problems can be minimised by following some simple rules. However, these rules cannot be applied to all situations, and there will be many exceptions.

1. In general, stress each syllable equally, unless your experience suggests otherwise.
2. Pronounce the letter 'a' as a broad 'a' as in 'arm'.
3. Pronounce the letter 'e' as a short 'e' as in 'elm'.
4. Pronounce the letter 'i' as a cross between a short 'i' and long 'e', as the two 'i's in 'California'.
5. Pronounce the letter 'o' as an intermediate 'o' as in 'soft'.
6. Pronounce the letter 'u' as an intermediate 'u' as in 'sure'.
7. Pronounce consonants hard, except in the Romance-language areas where 'g's are likely to be pronounced softly like 'j' in 'jam'; 'j' itself may be pronounced as 'y'; and 'x's may be pronounced as 'h'.
8. For names in mainland China, pronounce 'q' like the 'ch' in 'chin', 'x' like the 'sh' in 'she', 'zh' like the 'j' in 'jam', and 'z' as if it were spelled 'dz'. In general pronounce 'a' as in 'father', 'e' as in 'but', 'i' as in 'keep', 'o' as in 'or', and 'u' as in 'rule'.

Moreover, English has no diacritical marks (accent and pronunciation signs), although some languages do. The following is a brief and general guide to the pronunciation of those most frequently used in the principal Western European languages.

		Pronunciation as in
French	é	day and shows that the e is to be pronounced; e.g. Orléans.
	è	mare
	î	used over any vowel and does not affect pronunciation; shows contraction of the name, usually omission of 's' following a vowel.
	ç	's' before 'a', 'o' and 'u'.
	ë, ï, ü	over 'e', 'i' and 'u' when they are used with another vowel and shows that each is to be pronounced.
German	ä	fate
	ö	fur
	ü	no English equivalent; like French 'tu'
Italian	à, é	over vowels and indicates stress.
Portuguese	ã, õ	vowels pronounced nasally.
	ç	boss
	á	shows stress
	ô	shows that a vowel has an 'i' or 'u' sound combined with it.
Spanish	ñ	canyon
	ü	pronounced as w and separately from adjoining vowels.
	á	usually indicates that this is a stressed vowel.

Abbreviations

A.C.T. – Australian Capital Territory
A.R. – Autonomous Region
Afghan. – Afghanistan
Ala. – Alabama
Alta. – Alberta
Amer. – America(n)
Arch. – Archipelago
Ariz. – Arizona
Ark. – Arkansas
Atl. Oc. – Atlantic Ocean
B. – Baie, Bahía, Bay, Bucht, Bugt
B.C. – British Columbia
Bangla. – Bangladesh
Barr. – Barrage
Bos.-H. – Bosnia-Herzegovina
C. – Cabo, Cap, Cape, Coast
C.A.R. – Central African Republic
C. Prov. – Cape Province
Calif. – California
Cat. – Catarata
Cent. – Central
Chan. – Channel
Colo. – Colorado
Conn. – Connecticut
Cord. – Cordillera
Cr. – Creek
Czech. – Czech Republic
D.C. – District of Columbia
Del. – Delaware
Dem. – Democratic
Dep. – Dependency
Des. – Desert
Dét. – Détroit
Dist. – District
Dj. – Djebel
Domin. – Dominica
Dom. Rep. – Dominican Republic
E. – East

E. Salv. – El Salvador
Eq. Guin. – Equatorial Guinea
Est. – Estrecho
Falk. Is. – Falkland Is.
Fd. – Fjord
Fla. – Florida
Fr. – French
G. – Golfe, Golfo, Gulf, Guba, Gebel
Ga. – Georgia
Gt. – Great, Greater
Guinea-Biss. – Guinea-Bissau
H.K. – Hong Kong
H.P. – Himachal Pradesh
Hants. – Hampshire
Harb. – Harbor, Harbour
Hd. – Head
Hts. – Heights
I.(s). – Île, Ilha, Insel, Isla, Island, Isle
Ill. – Illinois
Ind. – Indiana
Ind. Oc. – Indian Ocean
Ivory C. – Ivory Coast
J. – Jabal, Jebel
Jaz. – Jazīrah
Junc. – Junction
K. – Kap, Kapp
Kans. – Kansas
Kep. – Kepulauan
Ky. – Kentucky
L. – Lac, Lacul, Lago, Lagoa, Lake, Limni, Loch, Lough
La. – Louisiana
Ld. – Land
Liech. – Liechtenstein
Lux. – Luxembourg
Mad. P. – Madhya Pradesh

Madag. – Madagascar
Man. – Manitoba
Mass. – Massachusetts
Md. – Maryland
Me. – Maine
Medit. S. – Mediterranean Sea
Mich. – Michigan
Minn. – Minnesota
Miss. – Mississippi
Mo. – Missouri
Mont. – Montana
Mozam. – Mozambique
Mt.(s) – Mont, Montaña, Mountain
Mte. – Monte
Mti. – Monti
N. – Nord, Norte, North, Northern, Nouveau
N.B. – New Brunswick
N.C. – North Carolina
N. Cal. – New Caledonia
N. Dak. – North Dakota
N.H. – New Hampshire
N.I. – North Island
N.J. – New Jersey
N. Mex. – New Mexico
N.S. – Nova Scotia
N.S.W. – New South Wales
N.W.T. – North West Territory
N.Y. – New York
N.Z. – New Zealand
Nat. – National
Nebr. – Nebraska
Neths. – Netherlands
Nev. – Nevada
Nfld. – Newfoundland
Nic. – Nicaragua
O. – Oued, Ouadi
Occ. – Occidentale

Okla. – Oklahoma
Ont. – Ontario
Or. – Orientale
Oreg. – Oregon
Os. – Ostrov
Oz. – Ozero
P. – Pass, Passo, Pasul, Pulau
P.E.I. – Prince Edward Island
Pa. – Pennsylvania
Pac. Oc. – Pacific Ocean
Papua N.G. – Papua New Guinea
Pass. – Passage
Pen. – Peninsula, Péninsule
Phil. – Philippines
Pk. – Peak
Plat. – Plateau
Prov. – Province, Provincial
Pt. – Point
Pta. – Ponta, Punta
Pte. – Pointe
Qué. – Québec
Queens. – Queensland
R. – Rio, River
R.I. – Rhode Island
Ra. – Range
Raj. – Rajasthan
Récr. – Récréatif
Reg. – Region
Rep. – Republic
Res. – Reserve, Reservoir
Rhld-Pfz. – Rheinland-Pfalz
S. – South, Southern, Sur
Si. Arabia – Saudi Arabia
S.C. – South Carolina
S. Dak. – South Dakota
S.I. – South Island
S. Leone – Sierra Leone
Sa. – Serra, Sierra

Sask. – Saskatchewan
Scot. – Scotland
Sd. – Sound
Sev. – Severnaya
Sib. – Siberia
Sprs. – Springs
St. – Saint
Sta. – Santa
Ste. – Sainte
Sto. – Santo
Str. – Strait, Stretto
Switz. – Switzerland
Tas. – Tasmania
Tenn. – Tennessee
Terr. – Territory, Territoire
Tex. – Texas
Tg. – Tanjung
Trin. & Tob. – Trinidad & Tobago
U.A.E. – United Arab Emirates
U.K. – United Kingdom
U.S.A. – United States of America
Ut. P. – Uttar Pradesh
Va. – Virginia
Vdkhr. – Vodokhranilishche
Vdskh. – Vodoskhovyshche
Vf. – Vírful
Vic. – Victoria
Vol. – Volcano
Vt. – Vermont
W. – Wadi, West
W. Va. – West Virginia
Wall. & F. Is. – Wallis and Futuna Is.
Wash. – Washington
Wis. – Wisconsin
Wlkp. – Wielkopolski
Wyo. – Wyoming
Yorks. – Yorkshire
Yug. – Yugoslavia

Amanab

A

A Coruña, *Spain* 206 A1
A Estrada, *Spain* 206 A1
A Fonsagrada, *Spain* 206 A2
Aachen, *Germany* 106 C1
Aalborg = Ålborg, *Denmark* 93 A2
Aalen, *Germany* 106 D3
Aalst, *Belgium* 52 B3
Aalten, *Neths.* 165 C4
Aalter, *Belgium* 52 A2
Aarau, *Switz.* 213 A3
Aarberg, *Switz.* 213 A2
Aare →, *Switz.* 213 A3
Aargau □, *Switz.* 213 A3
Aarhus = Århus, *Denmark* 93 A3
Aarschot, *Belgium* 52 B3
Aba, *Nigeria* 170 B2
Ābādān, *Iran* 126 C4
Ābādeh, *Iran* 127 C5
Abadla, *Algeria* 36 B2
Abaiang, *Kiribati* 176 A2
Abak, *Nigeria* 170 C2
Abakaliki, *Nigeria* 170 B2
Abakan, *Russia* 191 D9
Abancay, *Peru* 183 C3
Abanga →, *Gabon* 103 B2
Abariringa, *Kiribati* 176 B3
Abarqū, *Iran* 127 C5
Abashiri, *Japan* 136 A9
Abashiri-Wan, *Japan* 136 B9
Abau, *Papua N. G.* 181 F5
Ābay = Nîl el Azraq →, *Sudan* 210 B3
Abay, *Kazakhstan* 140 B4
Abaya, L., *Ethiopia* 98 C2
Abaza, *Russia* 190 D8
Abba, *C.A.R.* 77 B2
Abbay = Nîl el Azraq →, *Sudan* 210 B3
Abbé, L., *Ethiopia* 98 B3
Abbeville, *France* 101 A4
Abéché, *Chad* 78 C3
Abemama, *Kiribati* 176 A2
Abengourou, *Ivory C.* 134 B2
Åbenrå, *Denmark* 93 B2
Abeokuta, *Nigeria* 170 B1
Aber, *Uganda* 222 B2
Abercorn = Mbala, *Zambia* 240 A3
Aberdare Ra., *Kenya* 141 B2
Aberdeen, *S. Africa* 204 C2
Aberdeen, *U.K.* 224 C5
Aberdeen, *S. Dak., U.S.A.* 230 A7
Aberdeen, *Wash., U.S.A.* 230 A2
Abert, L., *U.S.A.* 230 B2
Aberystwyth, *U.K.* 224 E4
Abhā, *Si. Arabia* 196 D3
Abia □, *Nigeria* 170 B2
Abidjan, *Ivory C.* 134 B2
Abilene, *U.S.A.* 230 D7
Abitibi, L., *Canada* 67 E9
Abkhaz Republic = Abkhazia □, *Georgia* 104 A2
Abkhazia □, *Georgia* 104 A2
Abnûb, *Egypt* 95 B2
Åbo = Turku, *Finland* 99 B2
Abo, Massif d', *Chad* 78 A2
Abocho, *Nigeria* 170 B2
Aboisso, *Ivory C.* 134 B2
Abomey, *Benin* 54 D3
Abong-Mbang, *Cameroon* 65 C2
Abonnema, *Nigeria* 170 C2
Aboso, *Ghana* 108 B2
Abou-Deïa, *Chad* 78 C2
Abou-Goulem, *Chad* 78 C3
Abraham's Bay, *Bahamas* 71 B2
Abrolhos, Banka, *Brazil* 20 E7
Abrud, *Romania* 188 B2
Absaroka Range, *U.S.A.* 230 B5
Abū 'Alī →, *Lebanon* 147 A1
Abu Ballas, *Egypt* 95 C1
Abu Dhabi = Abū Ẓāby, *U.A.E.* 113 B2
Abū Du'ān, *Syria* 214 A2
Abu Hamed, *Sudan* 210 B3
Abū Kamāl, *Syria* 214 B3
Abu Qireiya, *Egypt* 95 C3
Abu Qurqâs, *Egypt* 95 B2
Abu Simbel, *Egypt* 95 C2
Abu Sultân, *Egypt* 95 A2
Abu Tig, *Egypt* 95 B2
Abu Zabad, *Sudan* 210 C2
Abū Ẓāby, *U.A.E.* 113 B2
Abuja, *Nigeria* 170 B2
Abukuma-Gawa →, *Japan* 136 D7
Abukuma-Sammyaku, *Japan* 136 E7
Abunã, *Brazil* 58 B2
Abunã →, *Brazil* 58 B2
Abut Hd., *N.Z.* 167 E3
Aby, Lagune, *Ivory C.* 134 B2
Acaponeta, *Mexico* 158 C3
Acapulco, *Mexico* 158 D5
Acarai, Serra, *Brazil* 58 A3
Acarigua, *Venezuela* 236 B2
Accra, *Ghana* 108 B2
Aceh □, *Indonesia* 124 B1
Achill Hd., *Ireland* 128 C1
Achill I., *Ireland* 128 C1
Achinsk, *Russia* 191 D9
Achouka, *Gabon* 103 B1
Acireale, *Italy* 133 F5
Acklins I., *Bahamas* 71 B2
Aconcagua, Cerro, *Argentina* 38 B2
Açores, Is. dos = Azores, *Atl. Oc.* 42
Acornhoek, *S. Africa* 205 A4
Acre = 'Akko, *Israel* 130 B2
Acre □, *Brazil* 58 B1
Acre →, *Brazil* 58 B2
Ad Dāmūr, *Lebanon* 147 B1
Ad Dawḥah, *Qatar* 113 A2
Ad Dīwānīyah, *Iraq* 126 C3
Ada, *Ghana* 108 B3
Adair, C., *Canada* 67 B9
Adaja →, *Spain* 206 B3
Adam, Mt., *Falk. Is.* 43 A2
Adamaoua, Massif de l', *Cameroon* 65 B2
Adamawa □, *Nigeria* 170 B3
Adamawa Highlands = Adamaoua, Massif de l', *Cameroon* 65 B2
Adamello, Mte., *Italy* 132 A3
Adam's Bridge, *Sri Lanka* 209 B1
Adam's Peak, *Sri Lanka* 209 C2
Adana, *Turkey* 220 B3
Adapazarı = Sakarya, *Turkey* 220 A2
Adarama, *Sudan* 210 B3
Adaut, *Indonesia* 125 D8
Adavale, *Australia* 45 E7
Adda →, *Italy* 132 B2
Addis Ababa = Addis Abeba, *Ethiopia* 98 C2
Addis Abeba, *Ethiopia* 98 C2
Addo, *S. Africa* 205 C3
Adelaide, *Australia* 45 F6
Adelaide, *S. Africa* 205 C3
Adelaide Pen., *Canada* 66 C7
Adelaye, *C.A.R.* 77 B3
Aden = Al 'Adan, *Yemen* 238 B2
Aden, G. of, *Asia* 4 E8
Adendorp, *S. Africa* 204 C2
Adi, *Indonesia* 125 C8
Adieu, C., *Australia* 44 F5
Adige →, *Italy* 132 B4
Adigrat, *Ethiopia* 98 B2
Adirondack Mts., *U.S.A.* 231 B12
Adjim, *Tunisia* 219 B2
Adjohon, *Benin* 54 D3
Adjumani, *Uganda* 222 A2
Admiralty G., *Australia* 44 B4
Admiralty Is., *Papua N. G.* 181 B4
Ado, *Nigeria* 170 B1
Ado-Ekiti, *Nigeria* 170 B2
Adonara, *Indonesia* 125 D6
Adoni, *India* 118 C2
Adour →, *France* 100 E3
Adra, *Spain* 206 D4
Adrano, *Italy* 133 F5
Adrar, *Mauritania* 157 B2
Adrar des Iforas, *Algeria* 4 D4
Adrasman, *Tajikistan* 216 A2
Adré, *Chad* 78 C3
Adriatic Sea, *Medit. S.* 28 G8
Adua, *Indonesia* 125 C7
Adwa, *Ethiopia* 98 B2
Adygea □, *Russia* 190 E3
Adzhar Republic = Ajaria □, *Georgia* 104 B3
Adzopé, *Ivory C.* 134 B2
Ægean Sea, *Medit. S.* 28 H10
Aerhtai Shan, *Mongolia* 160 B2
Afghanistan ■, *Asia* 34
Afikpo, *Nigeria* 170 B2
Aflou, *Algeria* 36 B3
Afore, *Papua N. G.* 181 E5
Afram →, *Ghana* 108 B2
Africa 4 E6
'Afrīn, *Syria* 214 A2
'Afula, *Israel* 130 B2
Afyon, *Turkey* 220 B2
Afyonkarahisar = Afyon, *Turkey* 220 B2
Agadès = Agadez, *Niger* 169 B2
Agadez, *Niger* 169 B2
Agadir, *Morocco* 161 B4
Agaie, *Nigeria* 170 B2
Agats, *Indonesia* 125 D9
Agbélouvé, *Togo* 54 D2
Agboville, *Ivory C.* 134 B2
Ağcabädi, *Azerbaijan* 40 A3
Ağdam, *Azerbaijan* 40 A3
Ağdaş, *Azerbaijan* 40 A3
Agde, *France* 101 E5
Agdzhabedi = Ağcabädi, *Azerbaijan* 40 A3
Agen, *France* 100 D4
Ager Tay, *Chad* 78 B2
Aginskoye, *Russia* 191 D11
Agnibilékrou, *Ivory C.* 134 B2
Agofie, *Ghana* 108 B3
Agouna, *Benin* 54 D2
Agra, *India* 118 B2
Ağri, *Turkey* 220 B4
Agri →, *Italy* 133 D6
Ağri Daği, *Turkey* 220 B4
Ağri Karakose = Ağri, *Turkey* 220 B4
Agrigento, *Italy* 133 F4
Agrínion, *Greece* 109 B2
Ağstafa, *Azerbaijan* 40 A2
Agua Prieta, *Mexico* 158 A3
Aguadilla, *Puerto Rico* 75 A1
Aguadulce, *Panama* 88 B2
Aguarico →, *Ecuador* 94 B3
Aguascalientes, *Mexico* 158 C4
Aguila, Punta, *Puerto Rico* 75 B1
Aguilas, *Spain* 207 D5
Aguja, C. de la, *Colombia* 20 B3
Agujereada, Pta., *Puerto Rico* 75 A1
Agulhas, C., *S. Africa* 204 C2
Agung, *Indonesia* 124 D5
Agur, *Uganda* 222 B2
Agusan →, *Phil.* 184 G6
Aha Mts., *Botswana* 57 A1
Ahaggar, *Algeria* 36 D4
Ahamansu, *Ghana* 108 B3
Ahar, *Iran* 126 A3
Ahioma, *Papua N. G.* 181 F6
Ahipara B., *N.Z.* 167 A4
Ahmadabad, *India* 118 B2
Ahmadnagar, *India* 118 C2
Ahmadpur, *Pakistan* 179 E6
Ahmedabad = Ahmadabad, *India* 118 B2
Ahmednagar = Ahmadnagar, *India* 118 C2
Ahoada, *Nigeria* 170 B2
Ahrax Pt., *Malta* 91 B1
Ahvāz, *Iran* 126 C4
Ahvenanmaa = Åland, *Finland* 99 B2
Aḥwar, *Yemen* 238 B2
Aigle, *Switz.* 213 B1
Aigrettes, Pte. des, *Réunion* 123 B1
Aigua, *Uruguay* 235 B2
Aigues-Mortes, *France* 101 E6
Aihui, *China* 81 A6
Aija, *Peru* 183 B2
Aikawa, *Japan* 136 D6
Ailuluai, *Papua N. G.* 181 E6
Aim, *Russia* 191 D13
Aimere, *Indonesia* 125 D6
Aïn Ben Tili, *Mauritania* 157 A3
Ain Dalla, *Egypt* 95 B1
Ain el Mafki, *Egypt* 95 B1
Ain Girba, *Egypt* 95 B1
Ain Qeiqab, *Egypt* 95 B0
Aïn-Sefra, *Algeria* 36 B2
Ain Sheikh Murzûk, *Egypt* 95 B1
Ain Sukhna, *Egypt* 95 B2
Ain Zeitûn, *Egypt* 95 B1
Ainaži, *Latvia* 146 B3
Aiome, *Papua N. G.* 181 C3
Aiquile, *Bolivia* 55 B1
Aïr, *Niger* 169 B2
Air Force I., *Canada* 67 C9
Airdrie, *Canada* 66 D5
Aisne →, *France* 101 B5
Aitape, *Papua N. G.* 181 B2
Aiud, *Romania* 188 B2
Aix-en-Provence, *France* 101 E6
Aix-la-Chapelle = Aachen, *Germany* 106 C1
Aix-les-Bains, *France* 101 D6
Aiyang, Mt., *Papua N. G.* 181 C1
Aíyion, *Greece* 109 B3
Aizkraukle, *Latvia* 146 B3
Aizpute, *Latvia* 146 B1
Aizuwakamatsu, *Japan* 136 E6
Ajaccio, *France* 101 F8
Ajari Rep. = Ajaria □, *Georgia* 104 B3
Ajaria □, *Georgia* 104 B3
Ajdābiyā, *Libya* 149 A4
Ajka, *Hungary* 116 B1
Ajmer, *India* 118 B2
Ajo, C. de, *Spain* 206 A4
Ajuy, *Phil.* 184 F5
Ak-Muz, *Kyrgyzstan* 144 B5
Ak-Tüz, *Kyrgyzstan* 144 A5
Akaba, *Togo* 54 C2
Akabira, *Japan* 136 B8
Akamas □, *Cyprus* 91 A1
Akanthou, *Cyprus* 91 A2
Akaroa, *N.Z.* 167 E4
Akashi, *Japan* 136 F4
Akelamo, *Indonesia* 125 B7
Aketi, *Dem. Rep. of the Congo* 86 B3
Akhalkalaki, *Georgia* 104 B3
Akhaltsikhe, *Georgia* 104 B3
Akharnaí, *Greece* 109 B3
Akhelóös →, *Greece* 109 B2
Akhisar, *Turkey* 220 B1
Akhmîm, *Egypt* 95 B2
Akhtyrka = Okhtyrka, *Ukraine* 223 A3
Aki, *Japan* 136 G3
Akiéni, *Gabon* 103 B3
Akimiski I., *Canada* 67 D8
Akita, *Japan* 136 D7
Akjoujt, *Mauritania* 157 C2
Akkaraipattu, *Sri Lanka* 209 C2
Akkeshi, *Japan* 136 B9
'Akko, *Israel* 130 B2
Aklampa, *Benin* 54 C3
Aklavik, *Canada* 66 C3
Akmolinsk = Astana, *Kazakhstan* 140 A4
Akō, *Japan* 136 F4
Ako, *Nigeria* 170 A3
Akola, *India* 118 B2
Akonolinga, *Cameroon* 65 C2
Akordat, *Eritrea* 98 A2
Akosombo Dam, *Ghana* 108 B3
Akoupé, *Ivory C.* 134 B2
Akourousoulba, *C.A.R.* 77 B3
Akpatok I., *Canada* 67 C10
Akranes, *Iceland* 117 B2
Akron, *U.S.A.* 231 B10
Akrotiri, *Cyprus* 91 B1
Akrotiri Bay, *Cyprus* 91 B1
Aksaray, *Turkey* 220 B2
Aksay, *Kazakhstan* 140 A2
Akşehir Gölü, *Turkey* 220 B2
Akstafa = Ağstafa, *Azerbaijan* 40 A2
Aksu, *China* 80 B2
Aksum, *Ethiopia* 98 B2
Aktogay, *Kazakhstan* 140 B4
Aktsyabrski, *Belarus* 51 C4
Aktyubinsk = Aqtöbe, *Kazakhstan* 140 A2
Aktyuz = Ak-Tüz, *Kyrgyzstan* 144 A5
Aku, *Nigeria* 170 B2
Akure, *Nigeria* 170 B2
Akurenan, *Eq. Guin.* 103 A2
Akuressa, *Sri Lanka* 209 C2
Akureyri, *Iceland* 117 B4
Akwa-Ibom □, *Nigeria* 170 C2
Akyab = Sittwe, *Burma* 63 E2
Al 'Adan, *Yemen* 238 B2
Al Amādīyah, *Iraq* 126 A2
Al 'Amārah, *Iraq* 126 C3
Al 'Aqabah, *Jordan* 139 B1
Al Arak, *Syria* 214 B2
Al Bāb, *Syria* 214 A2
Al Baḥral Mayyit = Dead Sea, *Asia* 10 F7
Al Bārūk, J., *Lebanon* 147 B1
Al Baṣrah, *Iraq* 126 C3
Al Batrūn, *Lebanon* 147 A1
Al Bayḍā, *Libya* 149 A4
Al Biqā, *Lebanon* 147 A2
Al Fallūjah, *Iraq* 126 B2
Al Fāw, *Iraq* 126 C4
Al Ḥadīthah, *Iraq* 126 B2
Al Hamdāniyah, *Syria* 214 B2
Al Ḥamīdīyah, *Syria* 214 B1
Al Ḥasakah, *Syria* 214 A3
Al Ḥayy, *Iraq* 126 B3
Al Ḥillah, *Iraq* 126 B3
Al Ḥillah, *Si. Arabia* 196 B4
Al Hirmil, *Lebanon* 147 A2
Al Hoceïma, *Morocco* 161 A5
Al Ḥudaydah, *Yemen* 238 B1
Al Hufūf, *Si. Arabia* 196 B4
Al Jaghbūb, *Libya* 149 B4
Al Janūb □, *Lebanon* 147 B1
Al Jawf, *Libya* 149 C4
Al Jazirah, *Iraq* 126 B2
Al Junaynah, *Sudan* 210 C1
Al Khiyām, *Lebanon* 147 B1
Al Kufrah, *Libya* 149 C4
Al Kūt, *Iraq* 126 B3
Al Kuwayt, *Kuwait* 113 A1
Al Labwah, *Lebanon* 147 A2
Al Lādhiqīyah, *Syria* 214 B1
Al Līth, *Si. Arabia* 196 C3
Al Luḥayyah, *Yemen* 238 A1
Al Madīnah, *Si. Arabia* 196 C2
Al Manāmah, *Bahrain* 113 A2
Al Marj, *Libya* 149 A4
Al Mawṣil, *Iraq* 126 A2
Al Mayādin, *Syria* 214 B3
Al Minā', *Lebanon* 147 A1
Al Miqdādīyah, *Iraq* 126 B3
Al Mukallā, *Yemen* 238 B2
Al Mukhā, *Yemen* 238 B1
Al Musayyib, *Iraq* 126 B3
Al Owuho = Otukpa, *Nigeria* 170 B2
Al Qāmishlī, *Syria* 214 A3
Al Qaryatayn, *Syria* 214 B2
Al Qaṭ'ā, *Syria* 214 B3
Al Qaṭrūn, *Libya* 149 C3
Al Quds = Jerusalem, *Israel* 130 C2
Al Qunayṭirah, *Syria* 214 C1
Al Qurnah, *Iraq* 126 C3
Al Quṣayr, *Syria* 214 B2
Al 'Ubaylah, *Si. Arabia* 196 C5
Ala-Buka, *Kyrgyzstan* 144 B2
Alabama □, *U.S.A.* 231 D9
Alabama →, *U.S.A.* 231 D9
Alabule →, *Papua N. G.* 181 E4
Alagoas □, *Brazil* 58 B5
Alagoinhas, *Brazil* 58 C5
Alajuela, *Costa Rica* 88 A2
Alakamisy, *Madag.* 152 C2
Alaminos, *Phil.* 184 C3
Alamogordo, *U.S.A.* 230 D5
Alamosa, *U.S.A.* 230 C5
Åland, *Finland* 99 B2
Alania = North Ossetia □, *Russia* 190 E4
Alanya, *Turkey* 220 B2
Alaotra, Farihin', *Madag.* 152 B2
Alapayevsk, *Russia* 190 D6
Alarobia-Vohiposa, *Madag.* 152 C2
Alaşehir, *Turkey* 220 B1
Alaska □, *U.S.A.* 15 C4
Alaska, G. of, *Pac. Oc.* 14 D5
Alaska Peninsula, *U.S.A.* 14 D4
Alaska Range, *U.S.A.* 14 C4
Älät, *Azerbaijan* 40 B4
Alatyr, *Russia* 190 D4
Alausi, *Ecuador* 94 B2
Alaverdi, *Armenia* 40 A2
'Alayh, *Lebanon* 147 B1
Alaykuu = Kögart, *Kyrgyzstan* 144 B4
Alazani →, *Azerbaijan* 40 A3
Alba, *Italy* 132 B2
Alba-Iulia, *Romania* 188 B2
Albacete, *Spain* 207 C5
Albanel, L., *Canada* 67 D9
Albania ■, *Europe* 35
Albany, *Australia* 44 G2
Albany, *Ga., U.S.A.* 231 D10
Albany, *N.Y., U.S.A.* 231 B12
Albany, *Oreg., U.S.A.* 230 B2
Albany →, *Canada* 67 D8
Albatross B., *Australia* 45 B7
Albemarle Sd., *U.S.A.* 231 C11
Alberche →, *Spain* 206 C3
Albert Edward, Mt., *Papua N. G.* 181 E4
Albert L., *Africa* 4 F7
Albert Lea, *U.S.A.* 231 B8
Albert Nile →, *Uganda* 222 A2
Albert Town, *Bahamas* 71 B2
Alberta □, *Canada* 66 D5
Albertinia, *S. Africa* 204 C2
Albertville = Kalemie, *Dem. Rep. of the Congo* 86 D4
Albertville, *France* 101 D7
Albi, *France* 101 E5
Albina, *Suriname* 115 A3
Ålborg, *Denmark* 93 A2
Alborz, Reshteh-ye Kūhhā-ye, *Iran* 127 A5
Albula →, *Switz.* 213 B4
Albuquerque, *U.S.A.* 230 C5
Albury-Wodonga, *Australia* 45 G8
Alcalá de Henares, *Spain* 206 B4
Alcalá la Real, *Spain* 206 D4
Álcamo, *Italy* 133 F4
Alcañiz, *Spain* 207 B5
Alcántara, Embalse de, *Spain* 206 C2
Alcantarilla, *Spain* 207 D5
Alcaraz, Sierra de, *Spain* 207 C4
Alcaudete, *Spain* 206 D3
Alcázar de San Juan, *Spain* 206 C4
Alchevsk, *Ukraine* 223 B4
Alcira = Alzira, *Spain* 207 C5
Alcoy, *Spain* 207 C5
Aldabra Is., *Seychelles* 4 G8
Aldan, *Russia* 191 D12
Aldan →, *Russia* 191 C12
Alderney, *U.K.* 100 B2
Aleg, *Mauritania* 157 C2
Alegrete, *Brazil* 58 D3
Aleisk, *Russia* 190 D8
Aleksandrovsk-Sakhalinskiy, *Russia* 191 D14
Alen, *Eq. Guin.* 103 A2
Alençon, *France* 100 B4
Alépé, *Ivory C.* 134 B2
Aleppo = Ḥalab, *Syria* 214 A2
Alert, *Canada* 67 A10
Alès, *France* 101 D6
Alessándria, *Italy* 132 B2
Ålesund, *Norway* 172 C2
Aletschhorn, *Switz.* 213 B3
Aleutian Is., *Pac. Oc.* 10 D21
Alexander Arch., *U.S.A.* 14 D6
Alexander Bay, *S. Africa* 204 B1
Alexandra, *N.Z.* 167 F2
Alexandria = El Iskandarîya, *Egypt* 95 A2
Alexandria, *Romania* 188 D3
Alexandria, *S. Africa* 205 C3
Alexandria, *U.S.A.* 231 D8
Alexandrina, L., *Australia* 45 G6
Alexandroúpolis, *Greece* 109 A4
Alga, *Kazakhstan* 140 B2
Algarve, *Portugal* 187 D1
Algeciras, *Spain* 206 D3
Algemesí, *Spain* 207 C5
Alger, *Algeria* 36 A3
Algeria ■, *Africa* 36
Alghero, *Italy* 132 D2
Algiers = Alger, *Algeria* 36 A3
Algoa B., *S. Africa* 205 C3
Alhucemas = Al Hoceïma, *Morocco* 161 A5
'Alī al Gharbī, *Iraq* 126 B3
Äli Bayramlı, *Azerbaijan* 40 B4
Aliákmon →, *Greece* 109 A3
Alibori →, *Benin* 54 B3
Alicante, *Spain* 207 C5
Alice, *S. Africa* 205 C3
Alice →, *Papua N. G.* 181 D1
Alice Springs, *Australia* 44 D5
Alicedale, *S. Africa* 205 C3
Alichur, *Tajikistan* 216 C4
Aligarh, *India* 118 B2
Alīgūdarz, *Iran* 126 B4
Alindao, *C.A.R.* 77 B3
Alipur, *Pakistan* 179 E6
Alishan, *Taiwan* 215 C2
Alitus = Alytus, *Lithuania* 150 B3
Aliwal North, *S. Africa* 205 C3
Aljustrel, *Portugal* 187 D1
Alkmaar, *Neths.* 165 B2
Allada, *Benin* 54 D3
Allahabad, *India* 118 B3
Allanridge, *S. Africa* 205 B3
Allaqi, Wadi →, *Egypt* 95 C2
Allegheny Mts., *U.S.A.* 231 C11
Allen, Bog of, *Ireland* 128 C5
Allen, L., *Ireland* 128 B3
Allentown, *U.S.A.* 231 B11
Aller →, *Germany* 106 B2
Alleynes B., *Barbados* 72 B1
Alliance, *U.S.A.* 230 B6
Allier →, *France* 101 C5
Alligator Pond, *Jamaica* 74 B2
Alma Ata = Almaty, *Kazakhstan* 140 B4
Almada, *Portugal* 187 C1
Almadén, *Spain* 206 C3
Almansa, *Spain* 207 C5
Almanzor, Pico, *Spain* 206 B3
Almanzora →, *Spain* 207 D5
Almaty, *Kazakhstan* 140 B4
Almazán, *Spain* 207 B4
Almelo, *Neths.* 165 B4
Almendralejo, *Spain* 206 C2
Almere-Stad, *Neths.* 165 B3
Almería, *Spain* 207 D4
Almirante, *Panama* 88 B2
Alnwick, *U.K.* 224 D6
Aloi, *Uganda* 222 B2
Alon, *Burma* 63 D3
Alor, *Indonesia* 125 D6
Alor Setar, *Malaysia* 154 A2
Alotau, *Papua N. G.* 181 F6
Aloum, *Cameroon* 65 C2
Alpha, *Australia* 45 D8
Alphen aan den Rijn, *Neths.* 165 B2
Alpine, *U.S.A.* 230 D6
Alps, *Europe* 28 F7
Alsace, *France* 101 B7
Alsask, *Canada* 66 D6
Alsasua, *Spain* 207 A4
Altagracia, *Dom. Rep.* 72 B2
Altai = Aerhtai Shan, *Mongolia* 160 B2
Altamura, *Italy* 133 D6
Altanbulag, *Mongolia* 160 A3
Altay, *China* 80 B2
Altdorf, *Switz.* 213 B3
Altea, *Spain* 207 C5
Altiplano = Bolivian Plateau, *S. Amer.* 20 E3
Alto Molocue, *Mozam.* 162 B2
Alton, *U.S.A.* 231 C8
Altoona, *U.S.A.* 231 B11
Altstätten, *Switz.* 213 A4
Altun Shan, *China* 80 C2
Altus, *U.S.A.* 230 D7
Alubijid, *Phil.* 184 G6
Alucra, *Turkey* 220 A3
Alūksne, *Latvia* 146 B4
Alusi, *Indonesia* 125 D8
Alutgama, *Sri Lanka* 209 C1
Alutnuwara, *Sri Lanka* 209 C2
Alxa Zuoqi, *China* 80 C4
Alyata = Älät, *Azerbaijan* 40 B4
Alytus, *Lithuania* 150 B3
Alzira, *Spain* 207 C5
Am Dam, *Chad* 78 C3
Am Géréda, *Chad* 78 C3
Am Loubia, *Chad* 78 C3
Am Timan, *Chad* 78 C3
Amada Gaza, *C.A.R.* 77 C2
Amadeus, L., *Australia* 44 D5
Amâdi, *Sudan* 210 D3
Amadjuak L., *Canada* 67 C9
Amagasaki, *Japan* 136 F4
Amagunze, *Nigeria* 170 B2
Amahai, *Indonesia* 125 C7
Amaile, *Samoa* 177 A2
Amaimon, *Papua N. G.* 181 C3
Amakusa-Shotō, *Japan* 136 G2
Amaliás, *Greece* 109 C2
Amamapare, *Indonesia* 125 C9
Amanab, *Papua N. G.* 181 B1

Chirchiq

Capesterre, *Guadeloupe* 73 **C2**
Capesterre-Belle-Eau, *Guadeloupe* 73 **B1**
Capraia, *Italy* 132 **C2**
Capri, *Italy* 133 **D5**
Caprivi Strip, *Namibia* 163 **A3**
Caquetá →, *Colombia* 85 **D3**
Caracal, *Romania* 188 **C3**
Caracas, *Venezuela* 236 **A2**
Caransebeş, *Romania* 188 **C2**
Caras, *Peru* 183 **B2**
Caratasca, L., *Honduras* 111 **B3**
Caratinga, *Brazil* 58 **C4**
Caravaca = Caravaca de la Cruz, *Spain* 207 **C5**
Caravaca de la Cruz, *Spain* 207 **C5**
Caravela, *Guinea-Biss.* 112 **A1**
Caravelas, *Brazil* 58 **C5**
Caraveli, *Peru* 183 **D3**
Caravelle, Presqu'île de la, *Martinique* 74 **A2**
Carballo, *Spain* 206 **A1**
Carbonara, C., *Italy* 132 **E2**
Carbonear, *Canada* 67 **E11**
Carbónia, *Italy* 132 **E2**
Carcar, *Phil.* 184 **F5**
Carcasse, C., *Haiti* 73 **B1**
Carcassonne, *France* 101 **E5**
Carchi □, *Ecuador* 94 **A2**
Carcross, *Canada* 66 **C3**
Cárdenas, *Cuba* 90 **A1**
Cardiff, *U.K.* 224 **F5**
Cardigan B., *U.K.* 224 **E4**
Cardona, *Uruguay* 235 **B1**
Cardston, *Canada* 66 **E5**
Carei, *Romania* 188 **B2**
Carey, L., *Australia* 44 **E3**
Careysburg, *Liberia* 148 **B1**
Cariacica, *Brazil* 58 **D4**
Caribbean Sea, *W. Indies* 71
Cariboo Mts., *Canada* 66 **D4**
Caribou, *U.S.A.* 231 **A13**
Caribou Mts., *Canada* 66 **D5**
Carigara, *Phil.* 184 **F6**
Carinthia = Kärnten □, *Austria* 49 **B4**
Caripito, *Venezuela* 236 **A3**
Carletonville, *S. Africa* 205 **B3**
Carlisle, *U.K.* 224 **D5**
Carlisle Bay, *Barbados* 72 **B1**
Carlow, *Ireland* 128 **D5**
Carlow □, *Ireland* 128 **D5**
Carlsbad, *U.S.A.* 230 **D6**
Carmacks, *Canada* 66 **C3**
Carmarthen, *U.K.* 224 **F4**
Carmaux, *France* 101 **D5**
Carmelo, *Uruguay* 235 **B1**
Carmen, *Colombia* 85 **B1**
Carmona, *Costa Rica* 88 **B1**
Carmona, *Spain* 206 **D3**
Carnac, *France* 100 **C2**
Carnarvon, *Australia* 44 **D1**
Carnarvon, *S. Africa* 204 **C2**
Carndonagh, *Ireland* 128 **A4**
Carnegie, L., *Australia* 44 **E3**
Carnot, *C.A.R.* 77 **C2**
Carnot B., *Australia* 44 **C3**
Carnsore Pt., *Ireland* 128 **D5**
Carolina, *Puerto Rico* 75 **A3**
Carolina, *S. Africa* 205 **B4**
Caroline I., *Kiribati* 176 **B5**
Caroline Is., *Micronesia* 3 **D17**
Carondelet, *Kiribati* 176 **B3**
Caroni, *Trin. & Tob.* 76 **C2**
Caroni →, *Venezuela* 236 **B3**
Caroni Swamp, *Trin. & Tob.* 76 **C2**
Caronie = Nébrodi, Monti, *Italy* 133 **F5**
Carpathians, *Europe* 28 **F10**
Carpaţii Meridionali, *Romania* 188 **C3**
Carpentaria, G. of, *Australia* 45 **B6**
Carpentras, *France* 101 **D6**
Carpi, *Italy* 132 **B3**
Carrara, *Italy* 132 **B3**
Carrascal, *Phil.* 184 **G6**
Carrauntoohill, *Ireland* 128 **D2**
Carrick-on-Shannon, *Ireland* 128 **C3**
Carrick-on-Suir, *Ireland* 128 **D4**
Carrickmacross, *Ireland* 128 **C5**
Carson City, *U.S.A.* 230 **C3**
Carson Sink, *U.S.A.* 230 **C3**
Cartagena, *Colombia* 85 **A1**
Cartagena, *Spain* 207 **D5**
Cartago, *Colombia* 85 **C1**
Cartago, *Costa Rica* 88 **B2**
Carterton, *N.Z.* 167 **D5**
Carthage, *U.S.A.* 231 **C8**
Cartier I., *Australia* 44 **B3**
Cartwright, *Canada* 67 **D11**
Carúpano, *Venezuela* 236 **A3**
Carvoeiro, C., *Portugal* 187 **C1**
Casa Grande, *U.S.A.* 230 **D4**
Casablanca, *Morocco* 161 **B4**
Casamance →, *Senegal* 198 **B1**
Cascade Ra., *U.S.A.* 230 **A2**
Cascades, Pte. des, *Réunion* 123 **B2**
Cascais, *Portugal* 187 **C1**
Cascavel, *Brazil* 58 **D3**
Cáscina, *Italy* 132 **C3**
Caserta, *Italy* 133 **D5**
Cashel, *Ireland* 128 **D4**
Casiguran, *Phil.* 184 **C5**
Casino, *Australia* 45 **E9**
Casiquiare →, *Venezuela* 236 **C2**
Casma, *Peru* 183 **B2**
Caspe, *Spain* 207 **B5**
Casper, *U.S.A.* 230 **B5**
Caspian Sea, *Eurasia* 10 **E8**
Cassiar Mts., *Canada* 66 **D3**
Cassino, *Italy* 133 **D4**
Castara, *Trin. & Tob.* 76 **A5**
Castellammare di Stábia, *Italy* 133 **D5**
Castelló de la Plana, *Spain* 207 **C5**
Castelo Branco, *Portugal* 187 **C2**
Castelsarrasin, *France* 100 **E4**
Castelvetrano, *Italy* 132 **F4**
Castilla-La Mancha □, *Spain* 206 **C4**
Castilla y Leon □, *Spain* 206 **B3**
Castillos, *Uruguay* 235 **B2**
Castle Bruce, *Domin.* 73 **B2**
Castlebar, *Ireland* 128 **C2**
Castleblaney, *Ireland* 128 **B5**
Castlemaine, *Australia* 45 **G7**
Castlepollard, *Ireland* 128 **C4**
Castlerea, *Ireland* 128 **C3**
Castlereagh →, *Australia* 45 **F8**
Castlereagh B., *Australia* 44 **B5**
Castletown Bearhaven, *Ireland* 128 **E2**
Castres, *France* 101 **E5**
Castricum, *Neths.* 165 **B2**
Castries, *St. Lucia* 75 **A2**
Castro, *Chile* 79 **D1**
Castuera, *Spain* 206 **C3**
Cat Ba, Dao, *Vietnam* 237 **B3**
Cat I., *Bahamas* 71 **A2**
Catalão, *Brazil* 58 **C4**
Catalonia = Cataluña □, *Spain* 207 **B6**
Cataluña □, *Spain* 207 **B6**
Catamarca, *Argentina* 38 **A2**
Catanauan, *Phil.* 184 **E5**
Catanduanes □, *Phil.* 184 **E6**
Catánia, *Italy* 133 **F5**
Catanzaro, *Italy* 133 **E6**
Catarman, *Phil.* 184 **E6**
Catbalogan, *Phil.* 184 **F6**
Cateel, *Phil.* 184 **H7**
Cathcart, *S. Africa* 205 **C3**
Catio, *Guinea-Biss.* 112 **A1**
Cato I., *Australia* 45 **D10**
Catoche, C., *Mexico* 158 **C7**
Catskill Mts., *U.S.A.* 231 **B12**
Catwick Is., *Vietnam* 237 **H4**
Cauca →, *Colombia* 85 **B2**
Caucasus Mountains, *Eurasia* 28 **G14**
Caungula, *Angola* 37 **A2**
Caura →, *Venezuela* 236 **B3**
Caux, Pays de, *France* 100 **B4**
Cavan, *Ireland* 128 **B4**
Cavan □, *Ireland* 128 **C4**
Caviana, I., *Brazil* 58 **A3**
Cavite, *Phil.* 184 **D4**
Cawnpore = Kanpur, *India* 118 **B3**
Caxias, *Brazil* 58 **B4**
Caxias do Sul, *Brazil* 58 **D3**
Cay Sal Bank, *Bahamas* 71 **B1**
Cayambe, *Napo, Ecuador* 94 **A2**
Cayambe, *Quito, Ecuador* 94 **A2**
Cayenne, *Fr. Guiana* 115 **A3**
Cayes, B. des, *Haiti* 73 **B2**
Cayey, *Puerto Rico* 75 **A2**
Cayman Brac, *Cayman Is.* 72 **B2**
Cayman Is. ■, *W. Indies* 72
Cayo Romano, *Cuba* 90 **B2**
Cayon, *St. Kitts & Nevis* 75 **A2**
Cazombo, *Angola* 37 **B3**
Ceanannus Mor, *Ireland* 128 **C5**
Ceará = Fortaleza, *Brazil* 58 **B5**
Ceará □, *Brazil* 58 **B5**
Cebaco, I. de, *Panama* 88 **B2**
Cebu, *Phil.* 184 **F5**
Cechi, *Ivory C.* 134 **B2**
Cedar City, *U.S.A.* 230 **C4**
Cedar L., *Canada* 66 **D7**
Cedar Rapids, *U.S.A.* 231 **B8**
Cedarville, *S. Africa* 205 **C3**
Cedros Bay, *Trin. & Tob.* 76 **D1**
Ceduna, *Australia* 44 **F5**
Cefalù, *Italy* 133 **E5**
Cegléd, *Hungary* 116 **B2**
Celaya, *Mexico* 158 **C4**
Celebes = Sulawesi □, *Indonesia* 125 **C6**
Celebes Sea, *Indonesia* 125 **B6**
Celica, *Ecuador* 94 **C2**
Celje, *Slovenia* 201 **A2**
Celle, *Germany* 106 **B3**
Cenderwasih, Teluk, *Indonesia* 125 **C9**
Central □, *Ghana* 108 **B2**
Central □, *Kenya* 141 **B2**
Central □, *Malawi* 153 **B1**
Central, Cordillera, *Colombia* 85 **C2**
Central, Cordillera, *Costa Rica* 88 **A2**
Central, Cordillera, *Dom. Rep.* 72 **B2**
Central, Cordillera, *Phil.* 184 **C4**
Central, Cordillera, *Puerto Rico* 75 **A2**
Central African Rep. ■, *Africa* 77
Central America, *America* 14 **H11**
Central I., *Kenya* 141 **A2**
Central Makran Range, *Pakistan* 179 **F3**
Central Ra., *Papua N. G.* 181 **C2**
Central Range, *Trin. & Tob.* 76 **D2**
Central Russian Uplands, *Europe* 28 **D12**
Central Siberian Plateau, *Russia* 10 **C14**
Centralia, *U.S.A.* 230 **A2**
Centre de Flacq, *Mauritius* 123 **B2**
Cephalonia = Kefallinía, *Greece* 109 **B2**
Ceram = Seram, *Indonesia* 125 **C7**
Ceram Sea = Seram Sea, *Indonesia* 125 **C7**
Ceres, *S. Africa* 204 **C1**
Cerf, *Seychelles* 123 **B2**
Cerignola, *Italy* 133 **D5**
Cerigo = Kíthira, *Greece* 109 **C3**
Cërrik, *Albania* 35 **B1**
Cerro Chato, *Uruguay* 235 **B1**
Cerro de Punta, Mt., *Puerto Rico* 75 **A2**
Cervera, *Spain* 207 **B6**
Cesena, *Italy* 132 **B4**
Cēsis, *Latvia* 146 **B3**
České Budějovice, *Czech Rep.* 92 **B2**
Českomoravská Vrchovina, *Czech Rep.* 92 **B2**
Çeşme, *Turkey* 220 **B1**
Cessnock, *Australia* 45 **F9**
Cestos →, *Liberia* 148 **B2**
Cetinje, *Montenegro, Yug.* 239 **C1**
Cetraro, *Italy* 133 **E5**
Cévennes, *France* 101 **D5**
Ceylon = Sri Lanka ■, *Asia* 209
Cha-am, *Thailand* 218 **E1**
Cha Pa, *Vietnam* 237 **A1**
Chacachacare I., *Trin. & Tob.* 76 **C1**
Chachapoyas, *Peru* 183 **B2**
Chachoengsao, *Thailand* 218 **E2**
Chachran, *Pakistan* 179 **E6**
Chad ■, *Africa* 78
Chad, L. = Tchad, L., *Chad* 78 **C1**
Chadan, *Russia* 191 **D9**
Chadron, *U.S.A.* 230 **B6**
Chadyr-Lunga = Ciadâr-Lunga, *Moldova* 188 **B5**
Chae Hom, *Thailand* 218 **B1**
Chaek, *Kyrgyzstan* 144 **B4**
Chaem →, *Thailand* 218 **B1**
Chaeryŏng, *N. Korea* 142 **C1**
Chagai Hills = Chāh Gay, *Afghan.* 34 **C1**
Chagda, *Russia* 191 **D13**
Chagos Arch., *Ind. Oc.* 10 **K11**
Chaguanas, *Trin. & Tob.* 76 **C2**
Chāh Bahar, *Iran* 127 **D7**
Chāh Gay, *Afghan.* 34 **C1**
Chahār Mahāll va Bakhtīarī □, *Iran* 126 **B4**
Chainat, *Thailand* 218 **D2**
Chaiya, *Thailand* 218 **G1**
Chakari, *Zimbabwe* 241 **A1**
Chakarnaba, *Chad* 78 **C3**
Chakhānsūr, *Afghan.* 34 **C1**
Chakwal, *Pakistan* 179 **C7**
Chala, *Peru* 183 **D3**
Chalcis = Khalkís, *Greece* 109 **B3**
Chalhuanca, *Peru* 183 **C3**
Chalky Inlet, *N.Z.* 167 **G1**
Challapata, *Bolivia* 55 **B1**
Chalon-sur-Saône, *France* 101 **C6**
Châlons-en-Champagne, *France* 101 **B6**
Chalyaphum, *Thailand* 218 **D3**
Cham, Cu Lao, *Vietnam* 237 **E4**
Chaman, *Pakistan* 179 **D4**
Chambal →, *India* 118 **B2**
Chambéry, *France* 101 **D6**
Chambeshi →, *Zambia* 240 **B3**
Chambri L., *Papua N. G.* 181 **C2**
Chamkar Luong, *Cambodia* 64 **C1**
Chamonix-Mont Blanc, *France* 101 **D7**
Champagne, *France* 101 **B6**
Champaign, *U.S.A.* 231 **B9**
Champassak, *Laos* 145 **E3**
Champlain, L., *U.S.A.* 231 **B12**
Chana, *Thailand* 218 **H2**
Chañaral, *Chile* 79 **B1**
Chandigarh, *India* 118 **A2**
Chandpur, *Bangla.* 50 **C3**
Chang, Ko, *Thailand* 218 **F3**
Ch'ang Chiang = Chang Jiang →, *China* 81 **C6**
Chang Jiang →, *China* 81 **C6**
Changane →, *Mozam.* 162 **C1**
Changchiak'ou = Zhangjiakou, *China* 81 **B5**
Ch'angchou = Changzhou, *China* 81 **C5**
Changchun, *China* 81 **B6**
Changde, *China* 81 **D5**
Changdo-ri, *N. Korea* 142 **C2**
Changhai = Shanghai, *China* 81 **C6**
Changhua, *Taiwan* 215 **B2**
Changhŭng, *S. Korea* 142 **E2**
Changhŭngni, *N. Korea* 142 **B3**
Changi, *Singapore* 199 **A3**
Changjin, *N. Korea* 142 **B2**
Changjin-chŏsuji, *N. Korea* 142 **B2**
Changsha, *China* 81 **D5**
Changyŏn, *N. Korea* 142 **C1**
Changzhi, *China* 81 **C5**
Changzhou, *China* 81 **C5**
Chanlar = Xanlar, *Azerbaijan* 40 **A3**
Channel Is., *U.K.* 100 **B2**
Channel Is., *U.S.A.* 230 **D2**
Channel-Port aux Basques, *Canada* 67 **E11**
Chantada, *Spain* 206 **A2**
Chanthaburi, *Thailand* 218 **E3**
Chantrey Inlet, *Canada* 66 **C7**
Chao Phraya →, *Thailand* 218 **E2**
Chao Phraya Lowlands, *Thailand* 218 **D2**
Chaozhou, *China* 81 **D5**
Chapala, L. de, *Mexico* 158 **C4**
Chapayev, *Kazakhstan* 140 **A2**
Chapayevsk, *Russia* 190 **D4**
Chapleau, *Canada* 67 **E8**
Chapra = Chhapra, *India* 118 **B3**
Chara, *Russia* 191 **D11**
Charagua, *Bolivia* 55 **B2**
Charambirá, Punta, *Colombia* 85 **C1**
Charaña, *Bolivia* 55 **B1**
Charantsavan, *Armenia* 40 **A2**
Chardzhou = Chärjew, *Turkmenistan* 221 **C3**
Charente →, *France* 100 **D3**
Chari →, *Chad* 78 **C1**
Chārīkār, *Afghan.* 34 **B3**
Chärjew, *Turkmenistan* 221 **C3**
Charleroi, *Belgium* 52 **B3**
Charles, C., *U.S.A.* 231 **C11**
Charles City, *U.S.A.* 231 **B8**
Charleston, *U.S.A.* 231 **D11**
Charlestown, *Ireland* 128 **C3**
Charlestown, *St. Kitts & Nevis* 75 **B2**
Charlestown, *S. Africa* 205 **B3**
Charleville = Rath Luirc, *Ireland* 128 **D3**
Charleville, *Australia* 45 **E8**
Charleville-Mézières, *France* 101 **B6**
Charlotte, *U.S.A.* 231 **C10**
Charlotte Amalie, *U.S. Virgin Is.* 76 **B2**
Charlotte Harbor, *U.S.A.* 231 **E10**
Charlotte Waters, *Australia* 44 **E5**
Charlottesville, *U.S.A.* 231 **C11**
Charlottetown, *Canada* 67 **E10**
Charlotteville, *Trin. & Tob.* 76 **A5**
Charlton I., *Canada* 67 **D9**
Charolles, *France* 101 **C6**
Charters Towers, *Australia* 45 **D8**
Chartres, *France* 101 **B4**
Charuma, *Trin. & Tob.* 76 **D2**
Chascomús, *Argentina* 38 **B3**
Chateaubelair, *St. Vincent* 75 **A1**
Châteaubriant, *France* 100 **C3**
Châteaulin, *France* 100 **B1**
Châteauroux, *France* 101 **C4**
Châteaux, Pte. des, *Guadeloupe* 73 **B2**
Châtellerault, *France* 100 **C4**
Chatham = Miramichi, *Canada* 67 **E10**
Chatham, *U.K.* 224 **F7**
Chatkal Kyrka Tooloru, *Kyrgyzstan* 144 **B2**
Chatsworth, *Zimbabwe* 241 **A2**
Chattanooga, *U.S.A.* 231 **C9**
Chaturat, *Thailand* 218 **D2**
Chatyr-Köl, *Kyrgyzstan* 144 **B4**
Chatyr-Tash, *Kyrgyzstan* 144 **B5**
Chau Doc, *Vietnam* 237 **G2**
Chaukan Pass, *Burma* 63 **B4**
Chaumont, *France* 101 **B6**
Chauvay, *Kyrgyzstan* 144 **B3**
Chavakachcheri, *Sri Lanka* 209 **B2**
Chaves, *Portugal* 187 **B2**
Chawang, *Thailand* 218 **G1**
Cheb, *Czech Rep.* 92 **A1**
Cheboksary, *Russia* 190 **D4**
Chechenia □, *Russia* 190 **E4**
Checheno-Ingush Republic = Chechenia □, *Russia* 190 **E4**
Chechnya = Chechenia □, *Russia* 190 **E4**
Chech'ŏn, *S. Korea* 142 **D3**
Cheduba I., *Burma* 63 **F2**
Chegdomyn, *Russia* 191 **D13**
Chegga, *Mauritania* 157 **A3**
Chegutu, *Zimbabwe* 241 **A2**
Cheju do, *S. Korea* 142 **F2**
Chekiang = Zhejiang □, *China* 81 **D6**
Chelkar = Shalqar, *Kazakhstan* 140 **B2**
Chelkar Tengiz, Solonchak, *Kazakhstan* 140 **B3**
Chełm, *Poland* 186 **C5**
Chełmno, *Poland* 186 **B3**
Chelmsford, *U.K.* 224 **F7**
Cheltenham, *U.K.* 224 **F5**
Chelyabinsk, *Russia* 190 **D6**
Chelyuskin, C., *Russia* 10 **B14**
Chemba, *Mozam.* 162 **B1**
Chemin Grenier, *Mauritius* 123 **B1**
Chemnitz, *Germany* 106 **C4**
Chen, Gora, *Russia* 191 **C14**
Chenab →, *Pakistan* 179 **D6**
Chengchou = Zhengzhou, *China* 81 **C5**
Chengde, *China* 81 **B5**
Chengdu, *China* 80 **C4**
Chengjiang, *China* 80 **D4**
Ch'engtu = Chengdu, *China* 80 **C4**
Chenkaladi, *Sri Lanka* 209 **C2**
Chennai, *India* 118 **C3**
Cheom Ksan, *Cambodia* 64 **A2**
Chepén, *Peru* 183 **B2**
Chepo, *Panama* 88 **B3**
Cheptulil, Mt., *Kenya* 141 **A2**
Cher →, *France* 100 **C4**
Cherbourg, *France* 100 **B3**
Cherdyn, *Russia* 190 **C5**
Cheremkhovo, *Russia* 191 **D10**
Cherepanovo, *Russia* 190 **D8**
Cherepovets, *Russia* 190 **D3**
Chergui, Chott ech, *Algeria* 36 **B3**
Cherikov = Cherykaw, *Belarus* 51 **C5**
Cherkasy, *Ukraine* 223 **B3**
Cherlak, *Russia* 190 **D7**
Chernaya, *Russia* 191 **B8**
Chernigov = Chernihiv, *Ukraine* 223 **A3**
Chernihiv, *Ukraine* 223 **A3**
Chernivtsi, *Ukraine* 223 **B2**
Chernobyl = Chornobyl, *Ukraine* 223 **A3**
Chernogorsk, *Russia* 191 **D9**
Chernovtsy = Chernivtsi, *Ukraine* 223 **B2**
Chernysheyskiy, *Russia* 191 **C11**
Cherokee, *U.S.A.* 231 **B7**
Cherskiy, *Russia* 191 **C16**
Cherskogo Khrebet, *Russia* 191 **C14**
Cherven, *Belarus* 51 **C4**
Chervonohrad, *Ukraine* 223 **A1**
Cherykaw, *Belarus* 51 **C5**
Chesapeake B., *U.S.A.* 231 **C11**
Cheshskaya Guba, *Russia* 190 **C4**
Chester, *U.K.* 224 **E5**
Chesterfield, *U.K.* 224 **E6**
Chesterfield Inlet, *Canada* 66 **C7**
Chetumal, *Mexico* 158 **D7**
Chetwynd, *Canada* 66 **D4**
Cheviot Hills, *U.K.* 224 **D5**
Chew Bahir, *Ethiopia* 98 **D2**
Cheyenne, *U.S.A.* 230 **B6**
Cheyenne →, *U.S.A.* 230 **B6**
Chhapra, *India* 118 **B3**
Chhattisgarh □, *India* 118 **C3**
Chhep, *Cambodia* 64 **B2**
Chhlong, *Cambodia* 64 **B2**
Chhuk, *Cambodia* 64 **C2**
Chi →, *Thailand* 218 **D4**
Chia Keng, *Singapore* 199 **A3**
Chiai, *Taiwan* 215 **C2**
Chiali, *Taiwan* 215 **C2**
Chiamussu = Jiamusi, *China* 81 **B7**
Chiang Dao, *Thailand* 218 **B1**
Chiang Kham, *Thailand* 218 **B2**
Chiang Khan, *Thailand* 218 **C2**
Chiang Khong, *Thailand* 218 **A2**
Chiang Mai, *Thailand* 218 **B1**
Chiang Rai, *Thailand* 218 **B1**
Chiang Saen, *Thailand* 218 **A2**
Chiatura, *Georgia* 104 **A3**
Chiávari, *Italy* 132 **B2**
Chiavenna, *Italy* 132 **A2**
Chiba, *Japan* 136 **F7**
Chibemba, *Angola* 37 **C1**
Chibi, *Zimbabwe* 241 **B2**
Chibia, *Angola* 37 **C1**
Chibougamau, *Canada* 67 **E9**
Chibuk, *Nigeria* 170 **A3**
Chicago, *U.S.A.* 231 **B9**
Chicha, *Chad* 78 **B2**
Chichibu, *Japan* 136 **E6**
Ch'ich'ihaerh = Qiqihar, *China* 81 **B6**
Chickasha, *U.S.A.* 230 **C7**
Chiclana de la Frontera, *Spain* 206 **D2**
Chiclayo, *Peru* 183 **B2**
Chico, *U.S.A.* 230 **C2**
Chico →, *Chubut, Argentina* 38 **C2**
Chico →, *Santa Cruz, Argentina* 38 **D2**
Chicoutimi, *Canada* 67 **E9**
Chidley, C., *Canada* 67 **C10**
Chiem Hoa, *Vietnam* 237 **A2**
Chiemsee, *Germany* 106 **E4**
Chiengmai = Chiang Mai, *Thailand* 218 **B1**
Chiese →, *Italy* 132 **B3**
Chieti, *Italy* 133 **C5**
Chiguana, *Bolivia* 55 **C1**
Chiha-ri, *N. Korea* 142 **C2**
Chihli, G. of = Bo Hai, *China* 81 **C5**
Chihuahua, *Mexico* 158 **B3**
Chiili = Shīeli, *Kazakhstan* 140 **B3**
Chikwawa, *Malawi* 153 **C1**
Chilapa, *Mexico* 158 **D5**
Chilas, *Pakistan* 179 **B8**
Childers, *Australia* 45 **E9**
Childress, *U.S.A.* 230 **D6**
Chile ■, *S. Amer.* 79
Chilete, *Peru* 183 **B2**
Chililabombwe, *Zambia* 240 **B2**
Chilin = Jilin, *China* 81 **B6**
Chillagoe, *Australia* 45 **C7**
Chillán, *Chile* 79 **C1**
Chilliwack, *Canada* 66 **E4**
Chiloé, I. de, *Chile* 79 **D1**
Chilumba, *Malawi* 153 **B1**
Chilung, *Taiwan* 215 **B2**
Chilwa, L., *Malawi* 153 **C2**
Chimán, *Panama* 88 **B3**
Chimanimani, *Zimbabwe* 241 **A2**
Chimay, *Belgium* 52 **B3**
Chimbay, *Uzbekistan* 221 **B2**
Chimborazo, *Ecuador* 94 **B2**
Chimborazo □, *Ecuador* 94 **B2**
Chimbote, *Peru* 183 **B2**
Chimkent = Shymkent, *Kazakhstan* 140 **B3**
Chimoio, *Mozam.* 162 **B1**
Chin □, *Burma* 63 **E2**
China ■, *Asia* 80
Chinan = Jinan, *China* 81 **C5**
Chinandega, *Nic.* 111 **C2**
Chincha Alta, *Peru* 183 **C2**
Chinchou = Jinzhou, *China* 81 **B6**
Chinchoua, *Gabon* 103 **A1**
Chinde, *Mozam.* 162 **B2**
Chindo, *S. Korea* 142 **E2**
Chindwin →, *Burma* 63 **E3**
Chingola, *Zambia* 240 **B2**
Chingole, *Malawi* 153 **B1**
Ch'ingtao = Qingdao, *China* 81 **C6**
Chinguetti, *Mauritania* 157 **B2**
Chinhae, *S. Korea* 142 **E3**
Chinhoyi, *Zimbabwe* 241 **A2**
Chiniot, *Pakistan* 179 **D7**
Chinju, *S. Korea* 142 **E3**
Chinko →, *C.A.R.* 77 **C3**
Chinmen, *Taiwan* 215 **B2**
Chinmen Tao, *Taiwan* 215 **B1**
Chinnampo = Namp'o, *N. Korea* 142 **C1**
Chino, *Japan* 136 **F6**
Chinon, *France* 100 **C4**
Chióggia, *Italy* 132 **B4**
Chíos = Khíos, *Greece* 109 **B5**
Chipata, *Zambia* 240 **B3**
Chipinge, *Zimbabwe* 241 **B2**
Chipoka, *Malawi* 153 **B1**
Chiquián, *Peru* 183 **C2**
Chiquinquira, *Colombia* 85 **B2**
Chirchiq, *Uzbekistan* 221 **B5**

F

Knud Rasmussen Land

Knud Rasmussen Land, *Greenland* 43 A4
Knysna, *S. Africa* 204 C2
Ko Kha, *Thailand* 218 B1
Koartac = Quaqtaq, *Canada* 67 C10
Koba, *Indonesia* 125 D8
Kobarid, *Slovenia* 201 A1
Kobayashi, *Japan* 136 H2
Kobdo = Hovd, *Mongolia* 160 B2
Kōbe, *Japan* 136 F4
København, *Denmark* 93 B4
Koblenz, *Germany* 106 C1
Kobryn, *Belarus* 51 C2
Kobuleti, *Georgia* 104 B2
Kocaeli, *Turkey* 220 A1
Kočani, *Macedonia* 151 B3
Kochang, *S. Korea* 142 E2
Kōchi, *Japan* 136 G3
Kochiu = Gejiu, *China* 80 D4
Kochkor, *Kyrgyzstan* 144 A4
Kochkor-Ata, *Kyrgyzstan* 144 B3
Koddiyar B., *Sri Lanka* 209 B2
Kodiak I., *U.S.A.* 14 D4
Kodori →, *Georgia* 104 A2
Koedoesberge, *S. Africa* 204 C2
Kofarnikhon, *Tajikistan* 216 B2
Koffiefontein, *S. Africa* 205 B3
Kofiau, *Indonesia* 125 C7
Koforidua, *Ghana* 108 B2
Kōfu, *Japan* 136 F6
Koga, *Japan* 136 E6
Kögart, *Kyrgyzstan* 144 B4
Køge, *Denmark* 93 B4
Kogi □, *Nigeria* 170 B2
Kogin Baba, *Nigeria* 170 B3
Kogo, *Eq. Guin.* 103 A1
Kohat, *Pakistan* 179 C6
Kohkīlūyeh va Būyer Aḩmadi □, *Iran* 126 C4
Kohtla-Järve, *Estonia* 97 A4
Koin-dong, *N. Korea* 142 B2
Koindu, *S. Leone* 148 A1
Kojō, *N. Korea* 142 C2
Kök-Aygyr, *Kyrgyzstan* 144 B4
Kök-Janggak, *Kyrgyzstan* 144 B3
Kokand = Qŭqon, *Uzbekistan* 221 B5
Kokas, *Indonesia* 125 C8
Kokchetav = Kökshetaū, *Kazakhstan* 140 A3
Koki, *Senegal* 198 A1
Kokkilai, *Sri Lanka* 209 B2
Kokkola, *Finland* 99 B2
Koko, *Nigeria* 170 A1
Koko Kyunzu, *Burma* 63 H2
Kokoda, *Papua N. G.* 181 E4
Kokolopozo, *Ivory C.* 134 B1
Kokomo, *U.S.A.* 231 B9
Kokopo, *Papua N. G.* 181 C7
Koksan, *N. Korea* 142 C2
Kökshetaū, *Kazakhstan* 140 A3
Koksoak →, *Canada* 67 D10
Kokstad, *S. Africa* 205 C3
Kokubu, *Japan* 136 H2
Kola, *Indonesia* 125 D8
Kola Pen. = Kolskiy Poluostrov, *Russia* 190 C3
Kolahun, *Liberia* 148 A1
Kolaka, *Indonesia* 125 C6
Kolar, *India* 118 C2
Kolchugino = Leninsk-Kuznetskiy, *Russia* 190 D8
Kolda, *Senegal* 198 B2
Kolding, *Denmark* 93 B2
Kolepom = Dolak, Pulau, *Indonesia* 125 D9
Kolguyev, Ostrov, *Russia* 190 C4
Kolhapur, *India* 118 C2
Kolia, *Ivory C.* 134 B1
Kolín, *Czech Rep.* 92 A2
Kolkas rags, *Latvia* 146 B2
Kolkata, *India* 118 B3
Kolkhozobod, *Tajikistan* 216 C2
Kollum, *Neths.* 165 A4
Köln, *Germany* 106 C1
Koło, *Poland* 186 B3
Kołobrzeg, *Poland* 186 A1
Koloko, *Burkina Faso* 62 C1
Kolomna, *Russia* 190 D3
Kolomyya, *Ukraine* 223 B2
Kolonodale, *Indonesia* 125 C6
Kolpashevo, *Russia* 190 D8
Kolskiy Poluostrov, *Russia* 190 C3
Kolwezi, *Dem. Rep. of the Congo* 86 E4
Kolyma →, *Russia* 191 C16
Kolymskoye Nagorye, *Russia* 191 C15
Kôm Ombo, *Egypt* 95 C2
Komadugu Gana →, *Nigeria* 170 A3
Komandorskiye Is. = Komandorskiye Ostrova, *Russia* 191 D16
Komandorskiye Ostrova, *Russia* 191 D16
Komárno, *Slovak Rep.* 200 B2
Komatipoort, *S. Africa* 205 B4
Komatou Yialou, *Cyprus* 91 A3
Komatsu, *Japan* 136 E5
Komatsushima, *Japan* 136 G4
Kombissiri, *Burkina Faso* 62 B2
Kombo, *Gabon* 103 B3
Kombori, *Burkina Faso* 62 B2
Komenda, *Ghana* 108 B2
Komi □, *Russia* 190 C5
Kommunarsk = Alchevsk, *Ukraine* 223 B4
Kommunizma, Pik, *Tajikistan* 216 B4
Komodo, *Indonesia* 125 D5
Komoé →, *Ivory C.* 134 B2
Komoran, Pulau, *Indonesia* 125 D9
Komoro, *Japan* 136 E6
Komotini, *Greece* 109 A4
Kompasberg, *S. Africa* 204 C2
Kompong Bang, *Cambodia* 64 B2
Kompong Cham, *Cambodia* 64 C2
Kompong Chhnang = Kampang Chhnang, *Cambodia* 64 B2
Kompong Chikreng, *Cambodia* 64 B2
Kompong Kleang, *Cambodia* 64 B2
Kompong Luong, *Cambodia* 64 C2
Kompong Pranak, *Cambodia* 64 B2
Kompong Som = Kampong Saom, *Cambodia* 64 C1
Kompong Som, Chhung = Kampong Saom, Chaak, *Cambodia* 64 C1
Kompong Speu, *Cambodia* 64 C2
Kompong Sralao, *Cambodia* 64 A2
Kompong Thom, *Cambodia* 64 B2
Kompong Trabeck, *Cambodia* 64 C2
Kompong Trabeck, *Cambodia* 64 B2
Kompong Trach, *Cambodia* 64 C2
Kompong Tralach, *Cambodia* 64 C2
Komrat = Comrat, *Moldova* 188 B5
Komsberg, *S. Africa* 204 C2
Komsomolabad, *Tajikistan* 216 B2
Komsomolets, Ostrov, *Russia* 191 A9
Komsomolsk, *Russia* 191 D13
Kon Tum, *Vietnam* 237 E4
Kon Tum, Plateau du, *Vietnam* 237 E4
Konarhā □, *Afghan.* 34 B3
Kondoa, *Tanzania* 217 A3
Kondratyevo, *Russia* 191 D9
Konduga, *Nigeria* 170 A3
Koné, *Cameroon* 65 B2
Koné, *N. Cal.* 176 A2
Kong = Khong →, *Cambodia* 64 B2
Kong, *Ivory C.* 134 B2
Kong, Koh, *Cambodia* 64 C1
Kong Christian IX Land, *Greenland* 43 C5
Kong Christian X Land, *Greenland* 43 B5
Kong Frederik IX Land, *Greenland* 43 C4
Kong Frederik VI Kyst, *Greenland* 43 C4
Kong Frederik VIII Land, *Greenland* 43 A5
Kong Oscar Fjord, *Greenland* 43 B5
Kongbo, *C.A.R.* 77 C3
Kongju, *S. Korea* 142 D2
Konglu, *Burma* 63 B4
Kongolo, *Dem. Rep. of the Congo* 86 D4
Kongoulou, *Cameroon* 65 C2
Kongoussi, *Burkina Faso* 62 B2
Königsberg = Kaliningrad, *Russia* 190 D2
Konin, *Poland* 186 B3
Konispol, *Albania* 35 D2
Konjic, *Bos.-H.* 56 B2
Konkouré →, *Guinea* 112 B2
Kono, *S. Leone* 148 A1
Konogogo, *Papua N. G.* 181 B7
Konongo, *Ghana* 108 B2
Konos, *Papua N. G.* 181 B6
Konosha, *Russia* 190 C4
Kōnosu, *Japan* 136 E6
Konotop, *Ukraine* 223 A3
Konsankoro, *Guinea* 112 B3
Końskie, *Poland* 186 C4
Konstanz, *Germany* 106 E2
Kontagora, *Nigeria* 170 A2
Kontcha, *Cameroon* 65 B2
Konya, *Turkey* 220 B2
Konza, *Kenya* 141 B2
Kootenay L., *Canada* 66 E5
Kootjieskolk, *S. Africa* 204 C2
Kopaonik, *Yugoslavia* 239 C2
Kópavogur, *Iceland* 117 B3
Koper, *Slovenia* 201 B1
Koplik, *Albania* 35 A1
Koppies, *S. Africa* 205 B3
Koprivnica, *Croatia* 89 A3
Korab, *Macedonia* 151 B1
Korce = Korçë, *Albania* 35 C2
Korçë, *Albania* 35 C2
Korčula, *Croatia* 89 C3
Kordestān □, *Iran* 126 B3
Kordofân, *Sudan* 210 C2
Korea, North ■, *Asia* 142
Korea, South ■, *Asia* 142
Korea Strait, *Asia* 10 F16
Korhogo, *Ivory C.* 134 B1
Koribundu, *S. Leone* 148 A1
Korinthiakós Kólpos, *Greece* 109 B3
Kórinthos, *Greece* 109 C3
Kōriyama, *Japan* 136 E7
Kormakiti, C., *Cyprus* 91 A1
Korneshty = Corneşti, *Moldova* 188 B5
Koro, *Fiji* 175 A2
Koro, *Ivory C.* 134 B1
Koro Sea, *Fiji* 175 A3
Koro Toro, *Chad* 78 B2
Koroba, *Papua N. G.* 181 C2
Korogwe, *Tanzania* 217 B3
Koronadal, *Phil.* 184 H6
Koropelé, *C.A.R.* 77 C2
Körös →, *Hungary* 116 B3
Korosten, *Ukraine* 223 A2
Korraraika, Helodranon' i, *Madag.* 152 B1
Korsakov, *Russia* 191 E14
Korshunovo, *Russia* 191 D11
Korsør, *Denmark* 93 B3
Kortrijk, *Belgium* 52 B2
Koryakskoye Nagorye, *Russia* 191 C17
Koryŏng, *S. Korea* 142 E3
Kos, *Greece* 109 C5
Kościan, *Poland* 186 B2
Kosciuszko, Mt., *Australia* 45 G8
Kosh-Döbö, *Kyrgyzstan* 144 B4
Kosha, *Sudan* 210 A3
K'oshih = Kashi, *China* 80 C1
Koshiki-Rettō, *Japan* 136 H1
Košice, *Slovak Rep.* 200 A3
Koslan, *Russia* 190 C4
Kosŏng, *N. Korea* 142 C3
Kosovo □, *Yugoslavia* 239 C2
Kosovska Mitrovica, *Kosovo, Yug.* 239 C2
Kossou, L. de, *Ivory C.* 134 B1
Koster, *S. Africa* 205 B3
Kôstî, *Sudan* 210 C3
Kostroma, *Russia* 190 D4
Kostrzyn, *Poland* 186 B1
Kostyukovichi = Kastsyukovichy, *Belarus* 51 C6
Koszalin, *Poland* 186 A2
Kota, *India* 118 B2
Kota Baharu, *Malaysia* 154 A2
Kota Belud, *Malaysia* 154 A5
Kota Kinabalu, *Malaysia* 154 A5
Kota Kubu Baharu, *Malaysia* 154 B2
Kota Tinggi, *Malaysia* 154 B2
Kotaagung, *Indonesia* 124 D2
Kotabaru, *Indonesia* 124 C5
Kotabumi, *Indonesia* 124 C2
Kotamobagu, *Indonesia* 125 B6
Kotelnich, *Russia* 190 D4
Kotelnikovo, *Russia* 190 E4
Kotelnyy, Ostrov, *Russia* 191 B13
Kotka, *Finland* 99 B3
Kotlas, *Russia* 190 C4
Koton-Karifi, *Nigeria* 170 B2
Kotonkoro, *Nigeria* 170 A2
Kotor, *Montenegro, Yug.* 239 C1
Kotri, *Pakistan* 179 G5
Kotto →, *C.A.R.* 77 C3
Kotuy →, *Russia* 191 B10
Kouango, *C.A.R.* 77 C3
Koudougou, *Burkina Faso* 62 B2
Kougaberge, *S. Africa* 204 C2
Kouibli, *Ivory C.* 134 B1
Kouilou →, *Congo* 86 C1
Kouki, *C.A.R.* 77 B2
Koula Moutou, *Gabon* 103 B3
Koulen = Kulen, *Cambodia* 64 B2
Koumac, *N. Cal.* 176 A2
Koumameyeng, *Gabon* 103 A2
Koumbia, *Burkina Faso* 62 C2
Koumbia, *Guinea* 112 A2
Koumboum, *Guinea* 112 A2
Koumpenntoum, *Senegal* 198 B2
Koumra, *Chad* 78 D2
Koun-Fao, *Ivory C.* 134 B2
Koundara, *Guinea* 112 A2
Koundé, *C.A.R.* 77 B1
Koundian, *Guinea* 112 A3
Koungheul, *Senegal* 198 B2
Kounradskiy, *Kazakhstan* 140 B4
Koupéla, *Burkina Faso* 62 B2
Kouris →, *Cyprus* 91 B1
Kourizo, Passe de, *Chad* 78 A2
Kourou, *Fr. Guiana* 115 A3
Kourouma, *Burkina Faso* 62 C2
Kouroussa, *Guinea* 112 A3
Koussanar, *Senegal* 198 B2
Koussane, *Senegal* 198 B2
Kousseri, *Cameroon* 65 A2
Kouto, *Ivory C.* 134 B1
Kouvé, *Togo* 54 D2
Kouvola, *Finland* 99 B3
Kowŏn, *N. Korea* 142 C2
Kozáni, *Greece* 109 A2
Kozhikode = Calicut, *India* 118 C2
Kpabia, *Ghana* 108 B2
Kpalimé, *Togo* 54 D2
Kpandae, *Ghana* 108 B2
Kpessi, *Togo* 54 C2
Kra, Isthmus of = Kra, Kho Khot, *Thailand* 218 F1
Kra, Kho Khot, *Thailand* 218 F1
Kra Buri, *Thailand* 218 F1
Kraai →, *S. Africa* 205 C3
Krabi, *Thailand* 218 G1
Kracheh, *Cambodia* 64 B3
Kragujevac, *Serbia, Yug.* 239 B2
Krajina, *Bos.-H.* 56 A2
Krakatau = Rakata, Pulau, *Indonesia* 124 D3
Krakatoa = Rakata, Pulau, *Indonesia* 124 D3
Krakor, *Cambodia* 64 B2
Kraków, *Poland* 186 C3
Kralanh, *Cambodia* 64 B1
Kraljevo, *Serbia, Yug.* 239 C2
Kramatorsk, *Ukraine* 223 B4
Kranj, *Slovenia* 201 A2
Krankskop, *S. Africa* 205 B4
Kraskino, *Russia* 191 E13
Krāslava, *Latvia* 146 C4
Kraśnik, *Poland* 186 C5
Krasnoarmeysk, *Russia* 190 D4
Krasnodar, *Russia* 190 E3
Krasnoperekopsk, *Ukraine* 223 B3
Krasnoselkup, *Russia* 190 C8
Krasnoturinsk, *Russia* 190 D6
Krasnovodsk = Türkmenbashi, *Turkmenistan* 221 B1
Krasnoyarsk, *Russia* 191 D9
Krasnyy Kut, *Russia* 190 D4
Krasnÿy Luch, *Ukraine* 223 B4
Kratie = Kracheh, *Cambodia* 64 B3
Kratke Ra., *Papua N. G.* 181 D4
Kratovo, *Macedonia* 151 A3
Krau, *Indonesia* 125 C10
Kravanh, Chuor Phnum, *Cambodia* 64 C1
Krefeld, *Germany* 106 C1
Kremen, *Croatia* 89 B2
Kremenchug = Kremenchuk, *Ukraine* 223 B3
Kremenchuk, *Ukraine* 223 B3
Kremenchuksk Vdskh., *Ukraine* 223 B3
Krems, *Austria* 49 A4
Kretinga, *Lithuania* 150 B1
Kribi, *Cameroon* 65 C1
Krichev = Krychaw, *Belarus* 51 C5
Krim-Krim, *Chad* 78 D2
Krishna →, *India* 118 C3
Kristiansand, *Norway* 172 D2
Kristiansund, *Norway* 172 C2
Kríti, *Greece* 109 D4
Kriva →, *Macedonia* 151 A2
Kriva Palanka, *Macedonia* 151 A3
Krivoy Rog = Kryvyy Rih, *Ukraine* 223 B3
Krk, *Croatia* 89 B2
Kroonstad, *S. Africa* 205 B3
Krosno, *Poland* 186 D4
Krotoszyn, *Poland* 186 C2
Krrabë, *Albania* 35 B1
Kruger Nat. Park, *S. Africa* 205 A4
Krugersdorp, *S. Africa* 205 B3
Kruisfontein, *S. Africa* 204 C2
Krujë, *Albania* 35 B1
Krulevshchina = Krulyewshchyna, *Belarus* 51 B3
Krulyewshchyna, *Belarus* 51 B3
Krumë, *Albania* 35 A2
Krung Thep = Bangkok, *Thailand* 218 E2
Krupki, *Belarus* 51 B4
Kruševac, *Serbia, Yug.* 239 C2
Kruševo, *Macedonia* 151 B2
Krychaw, *Belarus* 51 C5
Krymskiy Poluostrov = Krymskyy Pivostriv, *Ukraine* 223 C3
Krymskyy Pivostriv, *Ukraine* 223 C3
Kryvyy Rih, *Ukraine* 223 B3
Ksar el Kebir, *Morocco* 161 B4
Ksar es Souk = Er Rachidia, *Morocco* 161 B5
Ksar Rhilane, *Tunisia* 219 B1
Kuala Belait, *Malaysia* 154 B4
Kuala Lipis, *Malaysia* 154 B2
Kuala Lumpur, *Malaysia* 154 B2
Kuala Sepetang, *Malaysia* 154 B2
Kuala Terengganu, *Malaysia* 154 A2
Kualajelai, *Indonesia* 124 C4
Kualakapuas, *Indonesia* 124 C4
Kualakurun, *Indonesia* 124 C4
Kualapembuang, *Indonesia* 124 C4
Kualasimpang, *Indonesia* 124 B1
Kuandang, *Indonesia* 125 B6
Kuangchou = Guangzhou, *China* 81 D5
Kuanshan, *Taiwan* 215 C2
Kuantan, *Malaysia* 154 B2
Kuba = Quba, *Azerbaijan* 40 A4
Kuban →, *Russia* 28 F13
Kubokawa, *Japan* 136 G3
Kubor, Mt., *Papua N. G.* 181 D3
Kuchchaveli, *Sri Lanka* 209 B2
Kuching, *Malaysia* 154 B4
Kuchinotsu, *Japan* 136 G2
Kucing = Kuching, *Malaysia* 154 B4
Kuçovë, *Albania* 35 C1
Kudara, *Tajikistan* 216 B4
Kudat, *Malaysia* 154 A5
Kudymkar, *Russia* 190 D5
Kueiyang = Guiyang, *China* 81 D4
Kufra Oasis = Al Kufrah, *Libya* 149 C4
Kufstein, *Austria* 49 B3
Kugluktuk, *Canada* 66 C5
Kūh-e-Jebāl Bārez, *Iran* 127 C6
Kūhak, *Iran* 127 D7
Kūhhā-ye-Bashākerd, *Iran* 127 D6
Kūhpāyeh, *Iran* 127 B5
Kui Buri, *Thailand* 218 E1
Kuito, *Angola* 37 B2
Kujang, *N. Korea* 142 C2
Kuji, *Japan* 136 C7
Kujū-San, *Japan* 136 G2
Kukawa, *Nigeria* 170 A3
Kukës, *Albania* 35 A2
Kukipi, *Papua N. G.* 181 E4
Kulal, Mt., *Kenya* 141 A2
Kulanak, *Kyrgyzstan* 144 B4
Kuldīga, *Latvia* 146 B1
Kuldja = Yining, *China* 80 B2
Kulen, *Cambodia* 64 B2
Kŭlob, *Tajikistan* 216 C2
Kulpawn →, *Ghana* 108 A2
Kulsary, *Kazakhstan* 140 B2
Kulumadau, *Papua N. G.* 181 E7
Kulunda, *Russia* 190 D7
Kulyab = Kŭlob, *Tajikistan* 216 C2
Kuma →, *Russia* 190 E4
Kumaganum, *Nigeria* 170 A3
Kumagaya, *Japan* 136 E6
Kumai, *Indonesia* 124 C4
Kumamba, Kepulauan, *Indonesia* 125 C9
Kumamoto, *Japan* 136 G2
Kumanovo, *Macedonia* 151 A2
Kumara, *N.Z.* 167 E3
Kumasi, *Ghana* 108 B2
Kumayri = Gyumri, *Armenia* 40 A1
Kumba, *Cameroon* 65 C1
Kumbakonam, *India* 118 C2
Kumbo, *Cameroon* 65 B2
Kumbukkan Oya →, *Sri Lanka* 209 C2
Kŭmch'ŏn, *N. Korea* 142 C2
Kŭmhwa, *S. Korea* 142 C2
Kumi, *Uganda* 222 B2
Kumo, *Nigeria* 170 A3
Kumon Bum, *Burma* 63 B4
Kumusi →, *Papua N. G.* 181 E5
Kunashir, Ostrov, *Russia* 191 E14
Kunda, *Estonia* 97 A4
Kundiawa, *Papua N. G.* 181 D3
Kungrad = Qŭnghirot, *Uzbekistan* 221 B2
Kungur, *Russia* 190 D5
Kunlong, *Burma* 63 D5
Kunlun Shan, *Asia* 10 F12
Kunming, *China* 80 D4
Kunsan, *S. Korea* 142 E2
Kuntaur, *Senegal* 198 B2
Kunua, *Papua N. G.* 181 C8
Kununurra, *Australia* 44 C4
Kuopio, *Finland* 99 B3
Kupa →, *Croatia* 89 B3
Kupang, *Indonesia* 125 D6
Kupiano, *Papua N. G.* 181 F5
Kupyansk-Uzlovoi, *Ukraine* 223 B4
Kuqa, *China* 80 B2
Kür →, *Azerbaijan* 40 B4
Kür Dili, *Azerbaijan* 40 B4
Kura = Kür →, *Azerbaijan* 40 B4
Kurashiki, *Japan* 136 F3
Kurayoshi, *Japan* 136 F3
Kürdämir, *Azerbaijan* 40 A4
Kŭrdzhali, *Bulgaria* 61 C2
Kure, *Japan* 136 F3
Kuressaare, *Estonia* 97 B2
Kurgan, *Russia* 190 D6
Kurgan-Tyube = Qŭrghonteppa, *Tajikistan* 216 C2
Kuria Maria Is. = Khurīyā Murīyā, Jazā 'ir, *Oman* 113 C3
Kurigram, *Bangla.* 50 B2
Kuril Is. = Kurilskiye Ostrova, *Russia* 191 E15
Kuril Trench, *Pac. Oc.* 10 E19
Kurilsk, *Russia* 191 E14
Kurilskiye Ostrova, *Russia* 191 E15
Kurino, *Japan* 136 H2
Kurinskaya Kosa = Kür Dili, *Azerbaijan* 40 B4
Kurkur, *Egypt* 95 C2
Kurnool, *India* 118 C2
Kurow, *N.Z.* 167 F3
Kursk, *Russia* 190 D3
Kuruktag, *China* 80 B2
Kuruman, *S. Africa* 204 B2
Kuruman →, *S. Africa* 204 B2
Kurume, *Japan* 136 G2
Kurunegala, *Sri Lanka* 209 C2
Kurya, *Russia* 190 C5
Kusatsu, *Japan* 136 E6
Kushaka, *Nigeria* 170 A2
Kusheriki, *Nigeria* 170 A2
Kushikino, *Japan* 136 H2
Kushima, *Japan* 136 H2
Kushimoto, *Japan* 136 G4
Kushiro, *Japan* 136 B9
Kushiro-Gawa →, *Japan* 136 B9
Kushka = Gushgy, *Turkmenistan* 221 D3
Kushtia, *Bangla.* 50 C2
Kussharo-Ko, *Japan* 136 B9
Kustanay = Qostanay, *Kazakhstan* 140 A3
Kut, Ko, *Thailand* 218 F3
Kütahya, *Turkey* 220 B2
Kutaisi, *Georgia* 104 A3
Kutaraja = Banda Aceh, *Indonesia* 124 A1
Kutch, Gulf of = Kachchh, Gulf of, *India* 118 B1
Kutkashen, *Azerbaijan* 40 A3
Kutno, *Poland* 186 B3
Kutse, *Botswana* 57 B1
Kutu, *Dem. Rep. of the Congo* 86 C2
Kutum, *Sudan* 210 C1
Kuujjuaq, *Canada* 67 D10
Kuujjuarapik, *Canada* 67 D9
Kuŭp-tong, *N. Korea* 142 B2
Kuusamo, *Finland* 99 A3
Kuwait = Al Kuwayt, *Kuwait* 113 A1
Kuwait ■, *Asia* 113
Kuwana, *Japan* 136 F5
Kuybyshev = Samara, *Russia* 190 D5
Kuybyshev, *Russia* 190 D7
Kuybyshevskiy, *Tajikistan* 216 C2
Kuyumba, *Russia* 191 C9
Kuzey Anadolu Dağları, *Turkey* 220 A3
Kuzomen, *Russia* 190 C3
Kvareli = Qvareli, *Georgia* 104 B4
Kvarner, *Croatia* 89 B2
Kvarnerič, *Croatia* 89 B2
Kwabhaca, *S. Africa* 205 C3
Kwakhanai, *Botswana* 57 B1
Kwakoegron, *Suriname* 115 A2
Kwale, *Kenya* 141 B2
Kwale, *Nigeria* 170 B2
KwaMashu, *S. Africa* 205 B4
Kwangdaeri, *N. Korea* 142 B2
Kwangju, *S. Korea* 142 E2
Kwangsi-Chuang = Guangxi Zhuangzu Zizhiqu □, *China* 81 D4
Kwangtung = Guangdong □, *China* 81 D5
Kwara □, *Nigeria* 170 B2
Kwatisore, *Indonesia* 125 C8
KwaZulu Natal □, *S. Africa* 205 B4

Limburg

263

Ōmuta

Ōmuta, *Japan* 136 G2
Onang, *Indonesia* 125 C5
Onangue, L., *Gabon* 103 B2
Onda, *Spain* 207 C5
Ondaejin, *N. Korea* 142 B3
Ondangua, *Namibia* 163 A2
Ondo, *Nigeria* 170 B1
Ondo □, *Nigeria* 170 B2
Öndverðarnes, *Iceland* 117 B1
Onega, *Russia* 190 C3
Onega →, *Russia* 28 C13
Onega, L. = Onezhskoye Ozero, *Russia* 190 C3
O'Neill, *U.S.A.* 230 B7
Onekotan, Ostrov, *Russia* 191 E15
Oneşti, *Romania* 188 B4
Onezhskoye Ozero, *Russia* 190 C3
Ongarue, *N.Z.* 167 C5
Ongers →, *S. Africa* 204 C2
Ongjin, *N. Korea* 142 D1
Ongkharak, *Thailand* 218 D2
Ongouendjo, *Gabon* 103 B1
Oni, *Georgia* 104 A3
Onilahy →, *Madag.* 152 C1
Onitsha, *Nigeria* 170 B2
Onoda, *Japan* 136 F2
Onpyŏng-ni, *S. Korea* 142 F2
Onslow, *Australia* 44 D2
Onslow B., *U.S.A.* 231 D11
Ontake-San, *Japan* 136 F5
Ontario, *U.S.A.* 230 B3
Ontario □, *Canada* 67 E8
Ontario, L., *N. Amer.* 14 E12
Oodnadatta, *Australia* 45 E6
Ooldea, *Australia* 44 F5
Oost-Vlaanderen □, *Belgium* 52 A2
Oostende, *Belgium* 52 A1
Oosterhout, *Neths.* 165 C2
Oosterschelde →, *Neths.* 165 C2
Oosterwolde, *Neths.* 165 B4
Opala, *Dem. Rep. of the Congo* 86 C3
Opanake, *Sri Lanka* 209 C2
Opava, *Czech Rep.* 92 B3
Ophthalmia Ra., *Australia* 44 D2
Opi, *Nigeria* 170 B2
Opobo, *Nigeria* 170 C2
Opol, *Phil.* 184 G6
Opole, *Poland* 186 C2
Oporto = Porto, *Portugal* 187 B1
Opotiki, *N.Z.* 167 C6
Opua, *N.Z.* 167 A5
Opunake, *N.Z.* 167 C4
Ora, *Cyprus* 91 B2
Oradea, *Romania* 188 B1
Öræfajökull, *Iceland* 117 B5
Oral = Zhayyq →, *Kazakhstan* 140 B2
Oral, *Kazakhstan* 140 A2
Oran, *Algeria* 36 A2
Orange, *Australia* 45 F8
Orange, *France* 101 D6
Orange →, *S. Africa* 204 B1
Orange, C., *Brazil* 58 A3
Orange Free State = Free State □, *S. Africa* 205 B3
Orangeburg, *U.S.A.* 231 D10
Orango, *Guinea-Biss.* 112 A1
Orani, *Phil.* 184 D4
Oranienburg, *Germany* 106 B4
Oranje = Orange →, *S. Africa* 204 B1
Oranje Vrystaat = Free State □, *S. Africa* 205 B3
Oranjerivier, *S. Africa* 204 B2
Oranjestad, *Aruba* 74 A1
Oras, *Phil.* 184 E6
Oraşul Stalin = Braşov, *Romania* 188 C3
Orbe, *Switz.* 213 B1
Orbetello, *Italy* 132 C3
Orbost, *Australia* 45 G8
Orchila, I., *Venezuela* 236 A2
Ord →, *Australia* 44 C4
Ord, Mt., *Australia* 44 C4
Ordos = Mu Us Shamo, *China* 81 C4
Ordu, *Turkey* 220 A3
Ordubad, *Azerbaijan* 40 B3
Ordzhonikidze = Vladikavkaz, *Russia* 190 E4
Ordzhonikidzeabad = Kofarnikhon, *Tajikistan* 216 B2
Ore Mts. = Erzgebirge, *Germany* 106 C4
Örebro, *Sweden* 211 C3
Oregon □, *U.S.A.* 230 B2
Orel, *Russia* 190 D3
Orem, *U.S.A.* 230 B4
Orenburg, *Russia* 190 D5
Orense = Ourense, *Spain* 206 A2
Orepuki, *N.Z.* 167 G1
Orestiás, *Greece* 109 A5
Orgaz, *Spain* 206 C4
Orgeyev = Orhei, *Moldova* 188 B5
Orhei, *Moldova* 188 B5
Orhon Gol →, *Mongolia* 160 A3
Oriental, Cordillera, *Colombia* 85 B2
Oriental, Cordillera, *Dom. Rep.* 72 B3
Orihuela, *Spain* 207 C5
Orikum, *Albania* 35 C1
Orinoco →, *Venezuela* 236 B3
Orissa □, *India* 118 C3
Orissaare, *Estonia* 97 B2
Oristano, *Italy* 132 E2
Oristano, G. di, *Italy* 132 E2
Orizaba, *Mexico* 158 D5
Orizaba, Pico de, *Mexico* 158 D5
Orkney, *S. Africa* 205 B3
Orkney Is., *U.K.* 224 B5
Orlando, *U.S.A.* 231 E10
Orléanais, *France* 101 C5
Orléans, *France* 101 C4
Orlovka, *Kyrgyzstan* 144 A4
Ormara, *Pakistan* 179 G3
Ormoc, *Phil.* 184 F6
Ormond, *N.Z.* 167 C6
Örnsköldsvik, *Sweden* 211 B3
Oro, *N. Korea* 142 B2
Orocué, *Colombia* 85 C2
Orodara, *Burkina Faso* 62 C2
Orodo, *Nigeria* 170 B2
Orol Dengizi = Aral Sea, *Asia* 10 E9
Oron, *Nigeria* 170 C2
Oroquieta, *Phil.* 184 G5
Orosháza, *Hungary* 116 B3
Orotukan, *Russia* 191 C15
Orsha, *Belarus* 51 B5
Orsk, *Russia* 190 D5
Orşova, *Romania* 188 C2
Ortegal, C., *Spain* 206 A2
Orthez, *France* 100 E3
Ortigueira, *Spain* 206 A2
Ortles, *Italy* 132 A3
Orto-Tokoy, *Kyrgyzstan* 144 A5
Ortoire →, *Trin. & Tob.* 76 D2
Ortón →, *Bolivia* 55 A1
Orūmīyeh, *Iran* 126 A3
Orūmīyeh, Daryācheh-ye, *Iran* 126 A3
Oruro, *Bolivia* 55 B1
Oruzgān □, *Afghan.* 34 B2
Orvieto, *Italy* 132 C4
Oryakhovo, *Bulgaria* 61 B1
Osa, Pen. de, *Costa Rica* 88 B2
Ōsaka, *Japan* 136 F4
Osan, *S. Korea* 142 D2
Ösel = Saaremaa, *Estonia* 97 B2
Osh, *Kyrgyzstan* 144 B3
Oshakati, *Namibia* 163 A2
Oshawa, *Canada* 67 E9
Oshmyany = Ashmyany, *Belarus* 51 B2
Oshogbo, *Nigeria* 170 B1
Oshwe, *Dem. Rep. of the Congo* 86 C2
Osi, *Nigeria* 170 B2
Osijek, *Croatia* 89 B4
Osintorf, *Belarus* 51 B5
Osipenko = Berdyansk, *Ukraine* 223 B4
Osipovichi = Asipovichy, *Belarus* 51 C4
Osizweni, *S. Africa* 205 B4
Oskaloosa, *U.S.A.* 231 B8
Oskarshamn, *Sweden* 211 C3
Öskemen, *Kazakhstan* 140 B5
Oslo, *Norway* 172 D3
Oslob, *Phil.* 184 G5
Oslofjorden, *Norway* 172 D3
Osmaniye, *Turkey* 220 B3
Osnabrück, *Germany* 106 B2
Osogovska Planina, *Macedonia* 151 A3
Osorno, *Chile* 79 D1
Osprey Reef, *Australia* 45 B8
Oss, *Neths.* 165 C3
Ossa, Mt., *Australia* 45 H8
Óssa, Óros, *Greece* 109 B3
Osse →, *Nigeria* 170 B2
Ossora, *Russia* 191 D16
Ostend = Oostende, *Belgium* 52 A1
Österdalälven, *Sweden* 211 B2
Östersund, *Sweden* 211 B2
Ostfriesische Inseln, *Germany* 106 B1
Ostrava, *Czech Rep.* 92 B4
Ostróda, *Poland* 186 B3
Ostrołęka, *Poland* 186 B4
Ostrów Mazowiecka, *Poland* 186 B4
Ostrów Wielkopolski, *Poland* 186 C2
Ostrowiec-Świętokrzyski, *Poland* 186 C4
Ostuni, *Italy* 133 D6
Osum →, *Albania* 35 C2
Osun □, *Nigeria* 170 B1
Osuna, *Spain* 206 D3
Oswego, *U.S.A.* 231 B11
Oświęcim, *Poland* 186 C3
Otago □, *N.Z.* 167 F2
Otago Harbour, *N.Z.* 167 F3
Otaheite B., *Trin. & Tob.* 76 D1
Ōtake, *Japan* 136 F3
Otaki, *N.Z.* 167 D5
Otaru, *Japan* 136 B7
Otaru-Wan = Ishikari-Wan, *Japan* 136 B7
Otavalo, *Ecuador* 94 A2
Otjiwarongo, *Namibia* 163 B2
Ötmök, *Kyrgyzstan* 144 A3
Otoineppu, *Japan* 136 A8
Otorohanga, *N.Z.* 167 C5
Otranto, *Italy* 133 D7
Otranto, C. d', *Italy* 133 D7
Otranto, Str. of, *Italy* 133 D7
Otse, *S. Africa* 205 B3
Ōtsu, *Japan* 136 F4
Ōtsuki, *Japan* 136 F6
Ottawa = Outaouais →, *Canada* 67 E9
Ottawa, *Canada* 67 E9
Ottawa Is., *Canada* 67 D8
Ottélé, *Cameroon* 65 C2
Ottilien Reef, *Papua N. G.* 181 C5
Otto Beit Bridge, *Zimbabwe* 241 A1
Ottosdal, *S. Africa* 205 B3
Ottumwa, *U.S.A.* 231 B8
Otu, *Nigeria* 170 B1
Otukpa, *Nigeria* 170 B2
Oturkpo, *Nigeria* 170 B2
Otway, C., *Australia* 45 G7
Otwock, *Poland* 186 B4
Ou →, *Laos* 145 B2
Ou Neua, *Laos* 145 A1
Ou-Sammyaku, *Japan* 136 D7
Ouachita →, *U.S.A.* 231 D8
Ouachita Mts., *U.S.A.* 231 D8
Ouadda, *C.A.R.* 77 B3
Ouagadougou, *Burkina Faso* 62 B2
Ouagam, *Chad* 78 C1
Ouaham →, *C.A.R.* 77 B2
Ouahigouya, *Burkina Faso* 62 B2
Ouahran = Oran, *Algeria* 36 A2
Ouallene, *Algeria* 36 D3
Ouanda Djallé, *C.A.R.* 77 B3
Ouandago, *C.A.R.* 77 B2
Ouandjia, Bahr →, *C.A.R.* 77 B3
Ouango, *C.A.R.* 77 C3
Ouantonou, *C.A.R.* 77 B2
Ouargaye, *Burkina Faso* 62 C3
Ouargla, *Algeria* 36 B4
Ouarkoye, *Burkina Faso* 62 B2
Ouarra →, *C.A.R.* 77 B3
Ouarzazate, *Morocco* 161 B4
Ouatere, *C.A.R.* 77 B2
Oubangi →, *Dem. Rep. of the Congo* 86 C2
Ouddorp, *Neths.* 165 C1
Oude Rijn →, *Neths.* 165 B2
Oudenaarde, *Belgium* 52 B2
Oudtshoorn, *S. Africa* 204 C2
Ouégoa, *N. Cal.* 176 A2
Oueita, *Chad* 78 B3
Ouellé, *Ivory C.* 134 B2
Ouéme →, *Benin* 54 D3
Ouessa, *Burkina Faso* 62 C2
Ouessant, Î. d', *France* 100 B1
Ouesso, *Congo* 86 B2
Ouezzane, *Morocco* 161 B4
Ougarou, *Burkina Faso* 62 B3
Oughterard, *Ireland* 128 C2
Ouham →, *Chad* 78 D2
Ouidah, *Benin* 54 D3
Oujda, *Morocco* 161 B5
Ouli, *Cameroon* 65 B2
Oulou, Bahr →, *C.A.R.* 77 B3
Oulu, *Finland* 99 A3
Oulujärvi, *Finland* 99 B3
Oulujoki →, *Finland* 99 A3
Oum Chalouba, *Chad* 78 B3
Oum Hadjer, *Chad* 78 C2
Oum Hadjer, O. →, *Chad* 78 B3
Oumé, *Ivory C.* 134 B1
Ounianga Kébir, *Chad* 78 B3
Ounianga Sérir, *Chad* 78 B3
Our →, *Lux.* 52 C5
Ourense, *Spain* 206 A2
Ouro Prêto, *Brazil* 58 D4
Ouro Sogui, *Senegal* 198 A2
Oursi, *Burkina Faso* 62 A2
Ourthe →, *Belgium* 52 B4
Outaouais →, *Canada* 67 E9
Outer Hebrides, *U.K.* 224 C3
Outjo, *Namibia* 163 B2
Ouvéa, I., *N. Cal.* 176 A3
Ouyen, *Australia* 45 G7
Ovalle, *Chile* 79 C1
Ovamboland, *Namibia* 163 A2
Overflakkee, *Neths.* 165 C2
Overijssel □, *Neths.* 165 B4
Oviedo, *Spain* 206 A3
Oviši, *Latvia* 146 B1
Ovoro, *Nigeria* 170 B2
Owaka, *N.Z.* 167 G2
Owambo = Ovamboland, *Namibia* 163 A2
Owase, *Japan* 136 F5
Owatonna, *U.S.A.* 231 B8
Owbeh, *Afghan.* 34 B1
Owen Falls Dam, *Uganda* 222 B2
Owen Sound, *Canada* 67 E8
Owen Stanley Ra., *Papua N. G.* 181 E4
Owendo, *Gabon* 103 A1
Owens L., *U.S.A.* 230 C3
Owensboro, *U.S.A.* 231 C9
Owerri, *Nigeria* 170 B2
Owo, *Nigeria* 170 B2
Owyhee →, *U.S.A.* 230 B3
Ox Mts. = Slieve Gamph, *Ireland* 128 B3
Öxarfjörður, *Iceland* 117 A5
Oxford, *N.Z.* 167 E4
Oxford, *U.K.* 224 F6
Oxus = Amudarya →, *Uzbekistan* 221 B2
Oy-Tal, *Kyrgyzstan* 144 B4
Oya, *Malaysia* 154 B4
Oyama, *Japan* 136 E6
Oyem, *Gabon* 103 A2
Oymyakon, *Russia* 191 C14
Oyo, *Nigeria* 170 B1
Oyo □, *Nigeria* 170 B1
Oyūbari, *Japan* 136 B8
Ozamiz, *Phil.* 184 G5
Ozark Plateau, *U.S.A.* 231 C8
Ozarks, L. of the, *U.S.A.* 231 C8
Ózd, *Hungary* 116 A3
Özgön, *Kyrgyzstan* 144 B3
Ozurgeti, *Georgia* 104 B2

P

Pa, *Burkina Faso* 62 C2
Pa-an, *Burma* 63 G4
Pa Mong Dam, *Thailand* 218 C3
Paamiut, *Greenland* 43 C4
Paarl, *S. Africa* 204 C1
Pab Hills, *Pakistan* 179 F4
Pabianice, *Poland* 186 C3
Pabna, *Bangla.* 50 B2
Pabo, *Uganda* 222 A2
Pacaraima, Sa., *S. Amer.* 20 C4
Pacasmayo, *Peru* 183 B2
Pachitea →, *Peru* 183 B3
Pachuca, *Mexico* 158 C5
Pacific Ocean, *Pac. Oc.* 174
Padaido, Kepulauan, *Indonesia* 125 C9
Padang, *Indonesia* 124 C2
Padangpanjang, *Indonesia* 124 C2
Padangsidempuan, *Indonesia* 124 B1
Paderborn, *Germany* 106 C2
Pádova, *Italy* 132 B3
Padre I., *U.S.A.* 231 E7
Padre Las Casas, *Dom. Rep.* 72 B2
Padua = Pádova, *Italy* 132 B3
Paducah, *U.S.A.* 231 C9
Padukka, *Sri Lanka* 209 C2
Paengnyŏng-do, *S. Korea* 142 D1
Paeroa, *N.Z.* 167 B5
Pag, *Croatia* 89 B2
Paga, *Gabon* 103 B2
Paga, *Ghana* 108 A2
Pagadian, *Phil.* 184 H5
Pagai Selatan, Pulau, *Indonesia* 124 C2
Pagai Utara, Pulau, *Indonesia* 124 C2
Pagalu = Annobón, *Atl. Oc.* 4 G4
Pagastikós Kólpos, *Greece* 109 B3
Pagatan, *Indonesia* 124 C5
Page, *U.S.A.* 230 C4
Pagei, *Papua N. G.* 181 B1
Pago Pago, *Amer. Samoa* 177 B2
Pagua B., *Domin.* 73 A2
Pagwi, *Papua N. G.* 181 C2
Pahiatua, *N.Z.* 167 D5
Pai, *Thailand* 218 B1
Paide, *Estonia* 97 B3
Paiho, *Taiwan* 215 C2
Päijänne, *Finland* 99 B3
Pailin, *Cambodia* 64 B1
Painan, *Indonesia* 124 C2
Paint Hills = Wemindji, *Canada* 67 D9
Painted Desert, *U.S.A.* 230 C4
País Vasco □, *Spain* 207 A4
Paisley, *U.K.* 224 D4
Paita, *Peru* 183 B1
Pajares, Puerto de, *Spain* 206 A3
Pak Lay, *Laos* 145 C1
Pak Phanang, *Thailand* 218 G2
Pak Sane, *Laos* 145 C2
Pak Song, *Laos* 145 E4
Pak Suong, *Laos* 145 C2
Pakaraima Mts., *Guyana* 115 A1
Pakhuis, *S. Africa* 204 C1
Pakistan ■, *Asia* 179
Pakkading, *Laos* 145 C2
Pakokku, *Burma* 63 E3
Paktīā □, *Afghan.* 34 B3
Pakwach, *Uganda* 222 B2
Pakxe, *Laos* 145 E3
Pala, *Chad* 78 D2
Palabek, *Uganda* 222 A2
Palagruža, *Croatia* 89 C3
Palana, *Russia* 191 D15
Palanan, *Phil.* 184 C5
Palanan Pt., *Phil.* 184 C5
Palanga, *Lithuania* 150 B1
Palangkaraya, *Indonesia* 124 C4
Palanpur, *India* 118 B2
Palapye, *Botswana* 57 B2
Palatka, *Russia* 191 C15
Palau ■, *Pac. Oc.* 3 D16
Palauk, *Burma* 63 J5
Palawan, *Phil.* 184 G3
Paldiski, *Estonia* 97 A3
Paleleh, *Indonesia* 125 B6
Palembang, *Indonesia* 124 C2
Palencia, *Spain* 206 A3
Paleometokho, *Cyprus* 91 A2
Palermo, *Italy* 133 E4
Palestine, *U.S.A.* 231 D7
Paletwa, *Burma* 63 E2
Palghat, *India* 118 C2
Palioúrion, Ákra, *Greece* 109 B3
Paliseul, *Belgium* 52 C4
Palk Strait, *Asia* 10 H12
Palla Road = Dinokwe, *Botswana* 57 B2
Pallanza = Verbánia, *Italy* 132 B2
Pallës, Bishti i, *Albania* 35 B1
Pallisa, *Uganda* 222 B2
Palm Is., *Australia* 45 C8
Palma, B. de, *Spain* 207 C7
Palma de Mallorca, *Spain* 207 C7
Palma Soriano, *Cuba* 90 B2
Palmas, C., *Liberia* 148 C2
Pálmas, G. di, *Italy* 132 E2
Palmer →, *Australia* 44 D5
Palmerston, *N.Z.* 167 F3
Palmerston, C., *Australia* 45 D8
Palmerston North, *N.Z.* 167 D5
Palmi, *Italy* 133 E5
Palmira, *Colombia* 85 C1
Palmyra = Tudmur, *Syria* 214 B2
Palmyra Is., *Pac. Oc.* 176 A4
Palo Seco, *Trin. & Tob.* 76 D1
Palompon, *Phil.* 184 F6
Palopo, *Indonesia* 125 C6
Palos, C. de, *Spain* 207 D5
Palu, *Indonesia* 125 C5
Palu, *Turkey* 220 B4
Paluke, *Liberia* 148 B2
Pama, *Burkina Faso* 62 C3
Pama →, *C.A.R.* 77 C2
Pamiers, *France* 101 E4
Pamir, *Tajikistan* 216 C4
Pamir →, *Tajikistan* 216 C4
Pamlico Sd., *U.S.A.* 231 C11
Pampa, *U.S.A.* 230 C6
Pampanua, *Indonesia* 125 C6
Pampas, *Argentina* 38 B2
Pampas, *Peru* 183 C3
Pamplona, *Colombia* 85 B2
Pamplona, *Spain* 207 A5
Pampoenpoort, *S. Africa* 204 C2
Panabo, *Phil.* 184 H6
Panaitan, *Indonesia* 124 D3
Panaji, *India* 118 C2
Panamá, *Panama* 88 B3
Panamá, *Sri Lanka* 209 C2
Panama ■, *Cent. Amer.* 88
Panamá, G. de, *Panama* 88 B3
Panama Canal, *Panama* 88 B3
Panama City, *U.S.A.* 231 D9
Panão, *Peru* 183 B2
Panaon I., *Phil.* 184 F6
Panare, *Thailand* 218 H2
Panay, *Phil.* 184 F5
Pančevo, *Serbia, Yug.* 239 B2
Panch'iao, *Taiwan* 215 B2
Pandan, *Antique, Phil.* 184 F5
Pandan, *Catanduanes, Phil.* 184 D6
Pando, *Uruguay* 235 B1
Pandora, *Costa Rica* 88 B2
Panevėžys, *Lithuania* 150 B3
Panfilov, *Kazakhstan* 140 B5
Pang-Long, *Burma* 63 D5
Pang-Yang, *Burma* 63 D5
Pangalanes, Canal des = Ampangalana, Lakandranon', *Madag.* 152 C2
Pangani, *Tanzania* 217 B3
Pangfou = Bengbu, *China* 81 C5
Pangkajene, *Indonesia* 125 C5
Pangkalanbrandan, *Indonesia* 124 B1
Pangkalanbuun, *Indonesia* 124 C4
Pangkalpinang, *Indonesia* 124 C3
Pangnirtung, *Canada* 67 C10
Panguna, *Papua N. G.* 181 D8
Pangutaran Group, *Phil.* 184 H4
Panié, Mt., *N. Cal.* 176 A2
Panj = Pyandzh, *Tajikistan* 216 C2
Panjakent = Pendzhikent, *Tajikistan* 216 B1
Panjang, Hon, *Vietnam* 237 H1
Panjgur, *Pakistan* 179 F3
Panji Poyon, *Tajikistan* 216 C2
Panjim = Panaji, *India* 118 C2
Panjinad Barrage, *Pakistan* 179 E6
Pankshin, *Nigeria* 170 B2
Panmunjŏm, *N. Korea* 142 D2
Pannirtuuq = Pangnirtung, *Canada* 67 C10
Pano Lefkara, *Cyprus* 91 B2
Pano Panayia, *Cyprus* 91 B1
Pantar, *Indonesia* 125 D6
Pante Macassar, *E. Timor* 125 D6
Pantelleria, *Italy* 132 F3
Panyam, *Nigeria* 170 B2
Paola, *Malta* 91 B2
Paoting = Baoding, *China* 81 C5
Paot'ou = Baotou, *China* 81 B5
Paoua, *C.A.R.* 77 B2
Pápa, *Hungary* 116 B1
Papagayo, G. de, *Costa Rica* 88 A1
Papakura, *N.Z.* 167 B5
Papantla, *Mexico* 158 C5
Papar, *Malaysia* 154 A5
Paphos, *Cyprus* 91 B1
Papien Chiang = Da →, *Vietnam* 237 B2
Papoutsa, *Cyprus* 91 B2
Papua, G. of, *Papua N. G.* 181 E3
Papua New Guinea ■, *Oceania* 181
Papun, *Burma* 63 F4
Pará = Belém, *Brazil* 58 B4
Pará □, *Brazil* 58 B3
Paraburdoo, *Australia* 44 D2
Paracale, *Phil.* 184 D5
Parado, *Indonesia* 125 D5
Paragould, *U.S.A.* 231 C8
Paragua →, *Venezuela* 236 B3
Paraguaçu →, *Brazil* 58 C5
Paraguaná, Pen. de, *Venezuela* 236 A2
Paraguarí, *Paraguay* 182 C2
Paraguay ■, *S. Amer.* 182
Paraguay →, *Paraguay* 182 C2
Paraíba = João Pessoa, *Brazil* 58 B5
Paraíba □, *Brazil* 58 B5
Parakou, *Benin* 54 C3
Paralimni, *Cyprus* 91 A2
Parama I., *Papua N. G.* 181 E2
Paramaribo, *Suriname* 115 A2
Paramushir, Ostrov, *Russia* 191 D15
Paran →, *Israel* 130 D2
Paraná, *Argentina* 38 B2
Paraná □, *Brazil* 58 D3
Paraná →, *Argentina* 38 B3
Paranaguá, *Brazil* 58 D4
Paranaíba →, *Brazil* 58 D3
Paranapanema →, *Brazil* 58 D3
Paranas, *Phil.* 184 F6
Parang, *Phil.* 184 J4
Parângul Mare, Vf., *Romania* 188 C2
Paranthan, *Sri Lanka* 209 B2
Paraparaumu, *N.Z.* 167 D5
Parchim, *Germany* 106 B3
Pardes Hanna-Karkur, *Israel* 130 B1
Pardubice, *Czech Rep.* 92 A2
Parecis, Serra dos, *Brazil* 58 C3
Paren, *Russia* 191 C16
Parepare, *Indonesia* 125 C5
Párga, *Greece* 109 B2
Paria, Gulf of, *Trin. & Tob.* 76 D1
Pariaguán, *Venezuela* 236 B3
Parigi, *Indonesia* 125 C6
Parika, *Guyana* 115 A2
Parima, Serra, *Brazil* 58 A2
Parinari, *Peru* 183 A3
Pariñas, Pta., *S. Amer.* 20 D2
Parintins, *Brazil* 58 B3
Pariparit Kyun, *Burma* 63 H2
Paris, *France* 101 B5
Paris, *U.S.A.* 231 D7
Park Rynie, *S. Africa* 205 C4
Parkersburg, *U.S.A.* 231 C10
Parkes, *Australia* 45 F8
Parkhar, *Tajikistan* 216 C2
Parla, *Spain* 206 B4
Parma, *Italy* 132 B3
Parnaíba, *Brazil* 58 B4
Parnaíba →, *Brazil* 58 B4

Ubolratna Res.

Tîrgu-Jiu = Târgu-Jiu, *Romania* 188 C2
Tîrgu Mureş = Târgu Mureş, *Romania* 188 B3
Tirich Mir, *Pakistan* 179 A6
Tiriro, *Guinea* 112 A3
Tírnavos, *Greece* 109 B3
Tirol □, *Austria* 49 B2
Tirrukkovil, *Sri Lanka* 209 C2
Tirso →, *Italy* 132 E2
Tiruchchirappalli, *India* 118 C2
Tirunelveli, *India* 118 D2
Tisa →, *Serbia, Yug.* 239 B2
Tisdale, *Canada* 66 D6
Tissamaharama, *Sri Lanka* 209 C2
Tisza = Tisa →, *Serbia, Yug.* 239 B2
Tit-Ary, *Russia* 191 B12
Titao, *Burkina Faso* 62 B2
Titicaca, L., *S. Amer.* 20 E4
Titiwa, *Nigeria* 170 A3
Titograd = Podgorica, *Montenegro, Yug.* 239 C1
Titule, *Dem. Rep. of the Congo* 86 B4
Tivaouane, *Senegal* 198 B1
Tivoli, *Grenada* 73 A2
Tívoli, *Italy* 132 D4
Tizi-Ouzou, *Algeria* 36 A3
Tjirebon = Cirebon, *Indonesia* 124 D3
Tkibuli = Tqibuli, *Georgia* 104 A3
Tkvarcheli = Tqvarcheli, *Georgia* 104 A2
Tlaxiaco, *Mexico* 158 D5
Tlemcen, *Algeria* 36 B2
To Bong, *Vietnam* 237 F4
Toa Payoh, *Singapore* 199 A3
Toamasina, *Madag.* 152 B2
Toamasina □, *Madag.* 152 B2
Toba, *Japan* 136 F5
Toba, Danau, *Indonesia* 124 B1
Toba Kakar, *Pakistan* 179 D5
Tobago, *Trin. & Tob.* 76 A5
Tobelo, *Indonesia* 125 B7
Tobermory, *U.K.* 224 C3
Toboali, *Indonesia* 124 C3
Tobol →, *Russia* 190 D6
Toboli, *Indonesia* 125 C6
Tobolsk, *Russia* 190 D6
Tobor, *Senegal* 198 B1
Tobruk = Tubruq, *Libya* 149 A4
Tobyl = Tobol →, *Russia* 190 D6
Tocantins →, *Brazil* 58 B4
Tochigi, *Japan* 136 E6
Toco, *Trin. & Tob.* 76 C3
Tocuyo →, *Venezuela* 236 A2
Todeli, *Indonesia* 125 C6
Todenyang, *Kenya* 141 A2
Todos os Santos, B. de, *Brazil* 58 C5
Toecé, *Burkina Faso* 62 C2
Tōgane, *Japan* 136 F7
Togbo, *C.A.R.* 77 B2
Togian, Kepulauan, *Indonesia* 125 C6
Togliatti, *Russia* 190 D4
Togo ■, *W. Afr.* 54
Toinya, *Sudan* 210 D2
Tojikiston = Tajikistan ■, *Asia* 216
Tojo, *Indonesia* 125 C6
Tōjō, *Japan* 136 F3
Tok-do, *Japan* 136 E2
Tokachi-Dake, *Japan* 136 B8
Tokachi-Gawa →, *Japan* 136 B8
Tokala, *Indonesia* 125 C6
Tōkamachi, *Japan* 136 E6
Tokanui, *N.Z.* 167 G2
Tokarahi, *N.Z.* 167 F3
Tokat □, *Turkey* 220 A3
Tŏkch'ŏn, *N. Korea* 142 C2
Tokelau Is., *Pac. Oc.* 176 B3
Tokmak, *Kyrgyzstan* 144 A4
Tokoro-Gawa →, *Japan* 136 A9
Toktogul, *Kyrgyzstan* 144 B3
Toktogul Suu Saktagychy, *Kyrgyzstan* 144 B3
Tokushima, *Japan* 136 F4
Tokuyama, *Japan* 136 F2
Tōkyō, *Japan* 136 F6
Tolaga Bay, *N.Z.* 167 C7
Tolbukhin = Dobrich, *Bulgaria* 61 B3
Tolé, *C.A.R.* 77 B2
Toledo, *Spain* 206 C3
Toledo, *U.S.A.* 231 B10
Toledo, Montes de, *Spain* 206 C3
Toliara, *Madag.* 152 C1
Toliara □, *Madag.* 152 C1
Tolima, *Colombia* 85 C1
Tolitoli, *Indonesia* 125 B6
Tolo, Teluk, *Indonesia* 125 C6
Tolochin = Talachyn, *Belarus* 51 B4
Tolokiwa I., *Papua N. G.* 181 C4
Toluca, *Mexico* 158 D5
Tom Burke, *S. Africa* 205 A3
Tom Price, *Australia* 44 D2
Toma, *Burkina Faso* 62 B2
Tomakomai, *Japan* 136 B7
Tomanivi, *Fiji* 175 A2
Tomar, *Portugal* 187 C1
Tomaszów Mazowiecki, *Poland* 186 C3
Tombadonkéa, *Guinea* 112 A2
Tombador, Serra do, *Brazil* 58 C3
Tombel, *Cameroon* 65 C1
Tombigbee →, *U.S.A.* 231 D9
Tombouctou, *Mali* 156 B3
Tombua, *Angola* 37 C1
Tomelloso, *Spain* 206 C4
Tomini, *Indonesia* 125 B6
Tomini, Teluk, *Indonesia* 125 C6
Tommot, *Russia* 191 D12
Tomnop Ta Suos, *Cambodia* 64 C2
Tomo →, *Colombia* 85 B3
Tomsk, *Russia* 190 D8
Tonda, *Papua N. G.* 181 E1
Tondano, *Indonesia* 125 B6
Tone-Gawa →, *Japan* 136 E6
Tonekābon, *Iran* 126 A4
Tong I., *Papua N. G.* 181 B4
Tonga ■, *Pac. Oc.* 178
Tonga Trench, *Pac. Oc.* 178 B2
Tongaat, *S. Africa* 205 B4
Tongatapu Group, *Tonga* 178 B1
Tongchŏn-ni, *N. Korea* 142 C2
Tongchuan, *China* 81 C4
Tongeren, *Belgium* 52 B4
Tonghua, *China* 81 B6
Tongjosŏn Man, *N. Korea* 142 C3
Tongking, G. of = Tonkin, G. of, *Asia* 20 G14
Tongnae, *S. Korea* 142 E3
Tongobory, *Madag.* 152 C1
Tongres = Tongeren, *Belgium* 52 B4
Tongsa Dzong, *Bhutan* 164 C7
Tongue →, *U.S.A.* 230 A5
Tongyang, *N. Korea* 142 C2
Tonj, *Sudan* 210 D2
Tonkin = Bac Phan, *Vietnam* 237 B2
Tonkin, G. of, *Asia* 20 G14
Tonle Sap, *Cambodia* 64 B2
Tono, *Japan* 136 D7
Tonopah, *U.S.A.* 230 C3
Tonosí, *Panama* 88 B2
Toora-Khem, *Russia* 191 D9
Toowoomba, *Australia* 45 E9
Topeka, *U.S.A.* 231 C7
Topolčani, *Macedonia* 151 B2
Topol'čany, *Slovak Rep.* 200 A2
Topolobampo, *Mexico* 158 B3
Toraka Vestale, *Madag.* 152 B1
Torata, *Peru* 183 D3
Torbat-e Heydārīyeh, *Iran* 127 B6
Torbat-e Jām, *Iran* 127 B7
Torbay □, *U.K.* 224 F5
Tordesillas, *Spain* 206 B3
Torgau, *Germany* 106 C4
Torhout, *Belgium* 52 A2
Torino, *Italy* 132 B1
Torit, *Sudan* 210 E3
Tormes →, *Spain* 206 B2
Torne älv →, *Sweden* 211 A4
Torneå = Tornio, *Finland* 99 A2
Torneträsk, *Sweden* 211 A3
Tornio, *Finland* 99 A2
Toro, Cerro del, *Chile* 79 B2
Torokina, *Papua N. G.* 181 D8
Toronîos Kólpos, *Greece* 109 A3
Toronto, *Canada* 67 E9
Toropets, *Russia* 190 D3
Tororo, *Uganda* 222 B2
Toros Dağları, *Turkey* 220 B2
Torre de Moncorvo, *Portugal* 187 B2
Torre del Greco, *Italy* 133 D5
Torrejón de Ardoz, *Spain* 206 B4
Torrelavega, *Spain* 206 A3
Torremolinos, *Spain* 206 D3
Torrens, L., *Australia* 45 F6
Torrent, *Spain* 207 C5
Torreón, *Mexico* 158 B4
Torres Vedras, *Portugal* 187 C1
Torrevieja, *Spain* 207 D5
Torricelli Mts., *Papua N. G.* 181 B2
Tortola, *Br. Virgin Is.* 76 B2
Tortosa, *Spain* 207 B6
Tortosa, C., *Spain* 207 B6
Tortue, I. de la, *Haiti* 73 A2
Toru-Aygyr, *Kyrgyzstan* 144 A5
Ţorūd, *Iran* 127 B5
Toruń, *Poland* 186 B3
Tory I., *Ireland* 128 A3
Tosa, *Japan* 136 G3
Tosa-Shimizu, *Japan* 136 G3
Tosa-Wan, *Japan* 136 G3
Toscana □, *Italy* 132 C3
Toshkent, *Uzbekistan* 221 B5
Tosu, *Japan* 136 G2
Toteng, *Botswana* 57 B1
Totma, *Russia* 190 D4
Totness, *Suriname* 115 A2
Toto, *Nigeria* 170 B2
Tottori, *Japan* 136 F4
Touba, *Ivory C.* 134 B1
Touba, *Senegal* 198 B1
Toubkal, Djebel, *Morocco* 161 B4
Tougan, *Burkina Faso* 62 B2
Touggourt, *Algeria* 36 B4
Tougouri, *Burkina Faso* 62 B2
Tougué, *Guinea* 112 A2
Toul, *France* 101 B6
Toulepleu, *Ivory C.* 134 B1
Toulon, *France* 101 E6
Toulouse, *France* 100 E4
Toummo, *Niger* 169 A3
Toumodi, *Ivory C.* 134 B1
Tounan, *Taiwan* 215 C2
Toungo, *Nigeria* 170 B3
Toungoo, *Burma* 63 F4
Touraine, *France* 100 C4
Tourane = Da Nang, *Vietnam* 237 D4
Tourcoing, *France* 101 A5
Touriñán, C., *Spain* 206 A1
Tournai, *Belgium* 52 B2
Tournon-sur-Rhône, *France* 101 D6
Tours, *France* 100 C4
Touside, Pic, *Chad* 78 A2
Touws →, *S. Africa* 204 C2
Touwsrivier, *S. Africa* 204 C2
Tovuz, *Azerbaijan* 40 A2
Towada, *Japan* 136 C7
Towada-Ko, *Japan* 136 C7
Townshend I., *Australia* 45 D9
Townsville, *Australia* 45 C8
Towuti, Danau, *Indonesia* 125 C6
Toya-Ko, *Japan* 136 B7
Toyama, *Japan* 136 E5
Toyama-Wan, *Japan* 136 E5
Toyohashi, *Japan* 136 F5
Toyokawa, *Japan* 136 F5
Toyonaka, *Japan* 136 F4
Toyooka, *Japan* 136 F4
Toyota, *Japan* 136 F5
Tozeur, *Tunisia* 219 B1
Tqibuli, *Georgia* 104 A3
Tqvarcheli, *Georgia* 104 A2
Trá Li = Tralee, *Ireland* 128 D2
Tra On, *Vietnam* 237 H2
Trabzon, *Turkey* 220 A3
Trade Town, *Liberia* 148 B2
Trafalgar, C., *Spain* 206 D2
Trail, *Canada* 66 E5
Trákhonas, *Cyprus* 91 A2
Tralee, *Ireland* 128 D2
Tralee B., *Ireland* 128 D2
Tramore, *Ireland* 128 D4
Tramore B., *Ireland* 128 D4
Tran Ninh, Cao Nguyen, *Laos* 145 C2
Trang, *Thailand* 218 H1
Trangahy, *Madag.* 152 B1
Trangan, *Indonesia* 125 D8
Trani, *Italy* 133 D6
Tranoroa, *Madag.* 152 C2
Tranqueras, *Uruguay* 235 A1
Transilvania, *Romania* 188 B2
Transilvanian Alps = Carpaţii Meridionali, *Romania* 188 C3
Transylvania = Transilvania, *Romania* 188 B2
Trants Bay, *Montserrat* 74 A2
Trápani, *Italy* 132 E4
Traralgon, *Australia* 45 G8
Trasimeno, L., *Italy* 132 C4
Trat, *Thailand* 218 E3
Traun, *Austria* 49 A4
Travemünde, *Germany* 106 B3
Travers, Mt., *N.Z.* 167 E4
Traverse City, *U.S.A.* 231 B9
Travnik, *Bos.-H.* 56 A2
Trébbia →, *Italy* 132 B2
Třebíč, *Czech Rep.* 92 B2
Trebinje, *Bos.-H.* 56 B3
Treinta y Tres, *Uruguay* 235 B2
Trelawney, *Zimbabwe* 241 A2
Trelew, *Argentina* 38 C2
Tremp, *Spain* 207 A6
Trenčín, *Slovak Rep.* 200 A2
Trent →, *U.K.* 224 E6
Trento, *Italy* 132 A3
Trenton, *U.S.A.* 231 B12
Tres Arroyos, *Argentina* 38 B2
Três Lagoas, *Brazil* 58 D3
Tres Puntas, C., *Argentina* 38 C2
Treska →, *Macedonia* 151 B2
Treviso, *Italy* 132 B4
Triangle, *Zimbabwe* 241 B2
Tribulation, C., *Australia* 45 C8
Trichinopoly = Tiruchchirappalli, *India* 118 C2
Trier, *Germany* 106 D1
Trieste, *Italy* 133 B4
Triglav, *Slovenia* 201 A1
Tríkkala, *Greece* 109 B2
Trikomo, *Cyprus* 91 A2
Trikora, Puncak, *Indonesia* 125 C9
Trim, *Ireland* 128 C5
Trincomalee, *Sri Lanka* 209 B2
Trindade, I., *Atl. Oc.* 2 F8
Trinidad, *Bolivia* 55 A2
Trinidad, *Cuba* 90 B2
Trinidad, *Trin. & Tob.* 76 D2
Trinidad, *Uruguay* 235 B1
Trinidad, *U.S.A.* 230 C6
Trinidad & Tobago ■, *W. Indies* 76
Trinity →, *U.S.A.* 231 E8
Trinity B., *Canada* 67 E11
Trinity Hills, *Trin. & Tob.* 76 D2
Trinkitat, *Sudan* 210 B4
Tripoli = Tarābulus, *Lebanon* 147 A1
Tripoli = Tarābulus, *Libya* 149 A2
Trípolis, *Greece* 109 C3
Tripolitania, *Libya* 4 C5
Tripolitania, *N. Afr.* 4 C5
Tripura □, *India* 118 B4
Tripylos, *Cyprus* 91 B1
Tristan da Cunha, *Atl. Oc.* 2 F9
Trivandrum, *India* 118 D2
Trnava, *Slovak Rep.* 200 A1
Trobriand Is., *Papua N. G.* 181 E6
Troglav, *Croatia* 89 C3
Trois-Rivières, *Canada* 67 E9
Trois-Rivières, *Guadeloupe* 73 C1
Troitsk, *Russia* 190 D6
Troitsko Pechorsk, *Russia* 190 C5
Trölladyngja, *Iceland* 117 B5
Trollhättan, *Sweden* 211 C2
Trombetas →, *Brazil* 58 B3
Tromsø, *Norway* 172 B4
Tronador, Mte., *Argentina* 38 C1
Trondheim, *Norway* 172 C3
Trondheimsfjorden, *Norway* 172 C3
Troodos, *Cyprus* 91 B1
Tropojë, *Albania* 35 A2
Trout L., *N.W.T., Canada* 66 C4
Trout L., *Ont., Canada* 66 D7
Trouville-sur-Mer, *France* 100 B4
Troy, *Turkey* 220 B1
Troy, *Ala., U.S.A.* 231 D9
Troy, *N.Y., U.S.A.* 231 B12
Troyes, *France* 101 B6
Trucial States = United Arab Emirates ■, *Asia* 113
Trujillo, *Honduras* 111 B2
Trujillo, *Peru* 183 B2
Trujillo, *Spain* 206 C3
Trujillo, *Venezuela* 236 B1
Trung-Phan = Annam, *Vietnam* 237 E4
Truro, *Canada* 67 E10
Truro, *U.K.* 224 F4
Trutnov, *Czech Rep.* 92 A2
Tsaratanana, *Madag.* 152 B2
Tsaratanana, Mt. de, *Madag.* 152 A2
Tsarevo = Michurin, *Bulgaria* 61 B3
Tsau, *Botswana* 57 B1
Tselinograd = Astana, *Kazakhstan* 140 A4
Tsetserleg, *Mongolia* 160 B3
Tsévié, *Togo* 54 D2
Tshabong, *Botswana* 57 C1
Tshane, *Botswana* 57 B1
Tshela, *Dem. Rep. of the Congo* 86 C1
Tshesebe, *Botswana* 57 B2
Tshikapa, *Dem. Rep. of the Congo* 86 D3
Tshwane, *Botswana* 57 B1
Tsigara, *Botswana* 57 B2
Tsihombe, *Madag.* 152 D2
Tsiigehtchic, *Canada* 66 C3
Tsimlyansk Res. = Tsimlyanskoye Vdkhr., *Russia* 190 E4
Tsimlyanskoye Vdkhr., *Russia* 190 E4
Tsinan = Jinan, *China* 81 C5
Tsineng, *S. Africa* 204 B2
Tsinghai = Qinghai □, *China* 80 C3
Tsingtao = Qingdao, *China* 81 C6
Tsinjoarivo, *Madag.* 152 B2
Tsinjomitondraka, *Madag.* 152 B2
Tsiroanomandidy, *Madag.* 152 B2
Tsiteli-Tsqaro, *Georgia* 104 B5
Tsitondroina, *Madag.* 152 C2
Tsivory, *Madag.* 152 C2
Tskhinvali, *Georgia* 104 A4
Tsnori, *Georgia* 104 B4
Tsodilo Hill, *Botswana* 57 A1
Tsogni, *Gabon* 103 B2
Tsolo, *S. Africa* 205 C3
Tsomo, *S. Africa* 205 C3
Tsu, *Japan* 136 F5
Tsuchiura, *Japan* 136 E7
Tsugaru-Kaikyō, *Japan* 136 C7
Tsumeb, *Namibia* 163 A2
Tsuruga, *Japan* 136 F5
Tsurugi-San, *Japan* 136 G4
Tsuruoka, *Japan* 136 D6
Tsushima, *Gifu, Japan* 136 F5
Tsushima, *Nagasaki, Japan* 136 F1
Tsuyama, *Japan* 136 F4
Tsyelyakhany, *Belarus* 51 C2
Tua →, *Papua N. G.* 181 D3
Tual, *Indonesia* 125 D8
Tuam, *Ireland* 128 C3
Tuamotu Arch. = Tuamotu Is., *Pac. Oc.* 2 E2
Tuamotu Is., *Pac. Oc.* 2 E2
Tuao, *Phil.* 184 C4
Tuapse, *Russia* 190 E3
Tuatapere, *N.Z.* 167 G1
Tuban, *Indonesia* 124 D4
Tubani, *Botswana* 57 B1
Tubarão, *Brazil* 58 D4
Tübingen, *Germany* 106 D2
Tubruq, *Libya* 149 A4
Tuc Trung, *Vietnam* 237 G3
Tucacas, *Venezuela* 236 A2
T'uch'ang, *Taiwan* 215 B2
Tuckers Town, *Bermuda* 42 A2
Tucson, *U.S.A.* 230 D4
Tucumcari, *U.S.A.* 230 C6
Tucupita, *Venezuela* 236 B3
Tucuruí, *Brazil* 58 B4
Tudela, *Spain* 207 A5
Tudmur, *Syria* 214 B2
Tufi, *Papua N. G.* 181 E5
Tugela →, *S. Africa* 205 B4
Tuguegarao, *Phil.* 184 C4
Tugur, *Russia* 191 D13
Tui, *Spain* 206 A1
Tukangbesi, Kepulauan, *Indonesia* 125 D6
Tukobo, *Ghana* 108 B1
Tuktoyaktuk, *Canada* 66 C3
Tukums, *Latvia* 146 B2
Tukuyu, *Tanzania* 217 B2
Tula, *Nigeria* 170 B3
Tula, *Russia* 190 D3
Tūlak, *Afghan.* 34 B1
Tulare, *U.S.A.* 230 C3
Tulbagh, *S. Africa* 204 C1
Tulcán, *Ecuador* 94 A2
Tulcea, *Romania* 188 C5
Tuli, *Zimbabwe* 241 B1
Tulita, *Canada* 66 C4
Tulla, *Ireland* 128 D3
Tullamore, *Ireland* 128 C4
Tulle, *France* 101 D4
Tullow, *Ireland* 128 D5
Tulsa, *U.S.A.* 231 C7
Tulua, *Colombia* 85 C1
Tulun, *Russia* 191 D10
Tulungagung, *Indonesia* 124 D4
Tumaco, *Colombia* 85 C1
Tumatumari, *Guyana* 115 A2
Tumba, L., *Dem. Rep. of the Congo* 86 C2
Tumbes, *Peru* 183 A1
Tumeremo, *Venezuela* 236 B3
Tump, *Pakistan* 179 F2
Tumpat, *Malaysia* 154 A2
Tumu, *Ghana* 108 A2
Tumucumaque, Serra, *Brazil* 58 A3
Tumut, *Australia* 45 G8
Tunapuna, *Trin. & Tob.* 76 C2
Tunas de Zaza, *Cuba* 90 B2
Tundzha →, *Bulgaria* 61 B2
Tungshih, *Taiwan* 215 B2
Tungurahua □, *Ecuador* 94 B2
Tunguska, Nizhnyaya →, *Russia* 191 C8
Tunguska, Podkamennaya →, *Russia* 191 C9
Tunis, *Tunisia* 219 A2
Tunis, Golfe de, *Tunisia* 219 A2
Tunisia ■, *Africa* 219
Tunja, *Colombia* 85 B2
Tununirusiq = Arctic Bay, *Canada* 67 B8
Tüp, *Kyrgyzstan* 144 A6
Tupelo, *U.S.A.* 231 D9
Tupiza, *Bolivia* 55 C1
Túquerres, *Colombia* 85 C1
Tura, *Russia* 191 C10
Turabah, *Si. Arabia* 196 C3
Turama →, *Papua N. G.* 181 D2
Tūrān, *Iran* 127 B6
Turan, *Russia* 191 D9
Turda, *Romania* 188 B2
Turek, *Poland* 186 B3
Turen, *Venezuela* 236 B2
Turfan = Turpan, *China* 80 B2
Turfan Depression = Turpan Hami, *China* 10 E12
Tŭrgovishte, *Bulgaria* 61 B3
Turgutlu, *Turkey* 220 B1
Turgwe →, *Zimbabwe* 241 B2
Turia →, *Spain* 207 C5
Turin = Torino, *Italy* 132 B1
Turkana, L., *Africa* 4 F7
Turkestan = Türkistan, *Kazakhstan* 140 B3
Turkey ■, *Eurasia* 220
Türkistan, *Kazakhstan* 140 B3
Türkmenbashi, *Turkmenistan* 221 B1
Turkmenistan ■, *Asia* 221
Turks & Caicos Is. ■, *W. Indies* 76
Turks Is., *Turks & Caicos* 76 B2
Turku, *Finland* 99 B2
Turkwel →, *Kenya* 141 A2
Turnagain, C., *N.Z.* 167 D6
Turneffe Is., *Belize* 111 B2
Turnhout, *Belgium* 52 A3
Tŭrnovo = Veliko Tŭrnovo, *Bulgaria* 61 B2
Turnu Măgurele, *Romania* 188 D3
Turnu Roşu, P., *Romania* 188 C3
Turpan, *China* 80 B2
Turpan Hami, *China* 10 E12
Turrës, Kala e, *Albania* 35 B1
Tursunzade, *Tajikistan* 216 B2
Turtle Is., *S. Leone* 148 A1
Turugart Shankou, *Kyrgyzstan* 144 B6
Turugart Shantou, *Kyrgyzstan* 144 B4
Turukhansk, *Russia* 191 C8
Tuscaloosa, *U.S.A.* 231 D9
Tuscany = Toscana □, *Italy* 132 C3
Tuticorin, *India* 118 D2
Tutong, *Brunei* 154 B4
Tutrakan, *Bulgaria* 61 A3
Tuttlingen, *Germany* 106 E2
Tutuala, *E. Timor* 125 D7
Tutubeia, *Papua N. G.* 181 E6
Tutuila, *Amer. Samoa* 177 B2
Tuva □, *Russia* 191 D9
Tuvalu ■, *Pac. Oc.* 178
Tuxpan, *Mexico* 158 C5
Tuxtla Gutiérrez, *Mexico* 158 D6
Tuy = Tui, *Spain* 206 A1
Tuy An, *Vietnam* 237 F4
Tuy Duc, *Vietnam* 237 F3
Tuy Hoa, *Vietnam* 237 F4
Tuy Phong, *Vietnam* 237 G4
Tuyen Hoa, *Vietnam* 237 D3
Tuyen Quang, *Vietnam* 237 B2
Tuz Gölü, *Turkey* 220 B2
Ţūz Khurmātū, *Iraq* 126 B3
Tuzla, *Bos.-H.* 56 A3
Tver, *Russia* 190 D3
Tweed Heads, *Australia* 45 E9
Twin Falls, *U.S.A.* 230 B4
Two Harbors, *U.S.A.* 231 A8
Twofold B., *Australia* 45 G8
Tychy, *Poland* 186 C3
Tyler, *U.S.A.* 231 D7
Tynda, *Russia* 191 D12
Tyre = Sūr, *Lebanon* 147 B1
Tyrol = Tirol □, *Austria* 49 B2
Tyrrhenian Sea, *Medit. S.* 28 G8
Tyuleniy, Mys, *Azerbaijan* 40 A5
Tyumen, *Russia* 190 D6
Tyup = Tüp, *Kyrgyzstan* 144 A6
Tzaneen, *S. Africa* 205 A4
Tzukong = Zigong, *China* 80 D4

U

U Taphao, *Thailand* 218 E2
U.S.A. = United States of America ■, *N. Amer.* 230
Uaupés →, *Brazil* 58 A2
Uba, *Nigeria* 170 A3
Ubai, *Papua N. G.* 181 C6
Ubangi = Oubangi →, *Dem. Rep. of the Congo* 86 C2
Ubauro, *Pakistan* 179 E5
Ube, *Japan* 136 G2
Úbeda, *Spain* 206 C4
Uberaba, *Brazil* 58 C4
Uberlândia, *Brazil* 58 C4
Ubiaja, *Nigeria* 170 B2
Ubin, Pulau, *Singapore* 199 A3
Ubolratna Res., *Thailand* 218 C3

World Map: Physical

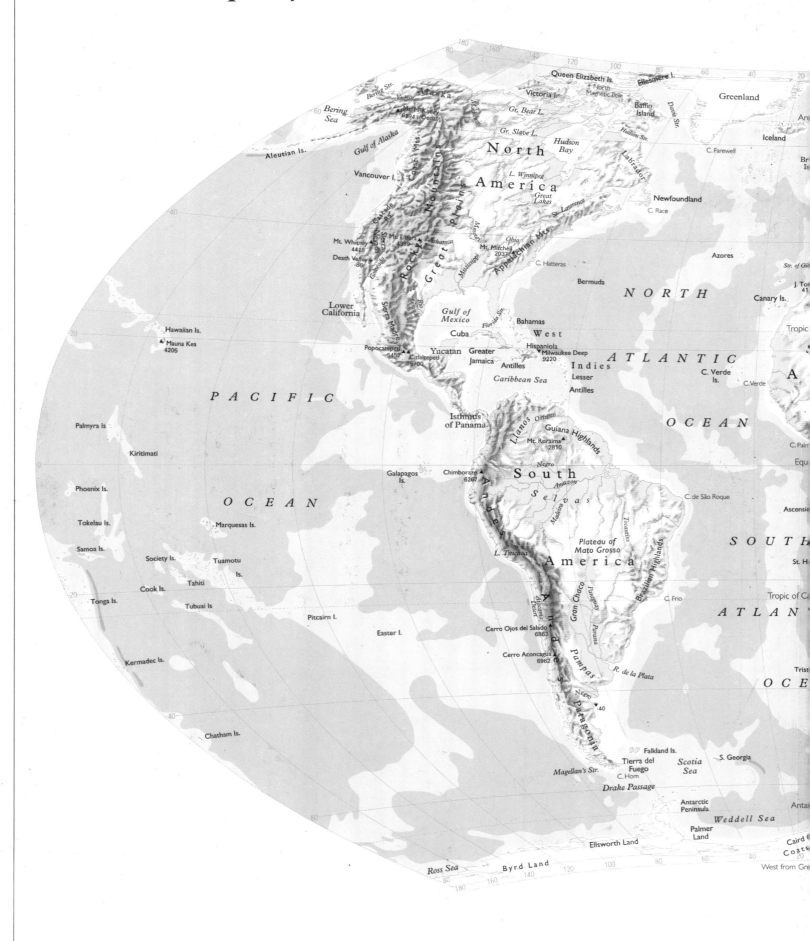

Queen Elizabeth Is.
+ North Magnetic Pole
Ellesmere I.
Greenland
Victoria I.
Bering Str.
Alaska
Mt. McKinley
6194 (Denali)
Baffin Island
Gr. Bear L.
Iceland
C. Farewell
Bering Sea
Gr. Slave L.
Gulf of Alaska
North America
Hudson Bay
L. Winnipeg
Newfoundland
Aleutian Is.
Vancouver I.
Great Lakes
St. Lawrence
C. Race
Azores
Coast Mts.
Cascade Rd.
Rocky Mountains
Great Plains
Mississippi
Missouri
Ohio
Mt. Mitchell
2037
Appalachian Mts.
C. Hatteras
NORTH
Mt. Elbert
4399
Arkansas
Mt. Whitney
4418
Bermuda
Canary Is.
Tropic
Death Valley
-86
Sierra Nevada
Colorado
Rio Grande
Lower California
Gulf of Mexico
Florida Str.
Bahamas
West
ATLANTIC
C. Verde Is.
C. Verde
Popocatepetl
5452
Sierra Madre
Citlaltepetl
5700
Yucatan
Cuba
Greater
Jamaica
Antilles
Hispaniola
Milwaukee Deep
9220
Indies
Lesser
Antilles
OCEAN
PACIFIC
Hawaiian Is.
Mauna Kea
4205
Caribbean Sea
Isthmus of Panama
Orinoco
Llanos
Guiana Highlands
Mt. Roraima
2810
Equ
Palmyra Is
OCEAN
Kiritimati
Galapagos Is.
Chimborazo
6267
South
Negro
Amazon
Selvas
C. de São Roque
Ascensio
Phoenix Is.
OCEAN
Madeira
Tokelau Is.
Marquesas Is.
America
Plateau of Mato Grosso
Tocantins
Brazilian Highlands
SOUTH
Samoa Is.
St. H
Society Is.
Tuamotu Is.
Tahiti
L. Titicaca
Gran Chaco
Paraguay
Panama
Andes
Cook Is.
Tropic of Ca
Tonga Is.
Tubuai Is
Atacama Desert
Pampas
R. de la Plata
C. Frio
ATLAN
Pitcairn I.
Cerro Ojos del Salado
6863
Kermadec Is.
Easter I.
Cerro Aconcagua
6962
Negro
40
OCE
Patagonia
Chatham Is.
Falkland Is.
Tierra del Fuego
Magellan's Str.
C. Horn
Scotia Sea
S. Georgia
Trist
Drake Passage
Antarctic Peninsula
Palmer Land
Weddell Sea
Anta
Ross Sea
Byrd Land
Ellsworth Land
Caird C
Coats
West from Gre